The Cambridge
Literary C

MW00770195

VOLUME 6

# The Nineteenth Century, c. 1830–1914

In the nineteenth century, literary criticism first developed into an autonomous, professional discipline in the universities. This volume provides a comprehensive and authoritative study of the vast field of literary criticism between 1830 and 1914. In over thirty chapters written from a broad range of perspectives, international scholars examine the growth of literary criticism as an institution, the major critical developments in diverse national traditions and in different genres, as well as the major movements of Realism, Naturalism, Symbolism and Decadence. This volume offers a detailed focus on some of the era's great critical figures such as Sainte-Beuve, Hippolyte Taine and Matthew Arnold; and it includes chapters devoted to the connections of literary criticism with other disciplines in science, the arts and biblical studies. The publication of this volume marks the completion of the monumental *Cambridge History of Literary Criticism* from Antiquity to the present day.

M. A. R. HABIB is Professor of English at Rutgers University, Camden. He is the author of seven books, including *A History of Literary Criticism: From Plato to the Present* (2005), *Modern Literary Criticism and Theory: A History* (2008) and *An Anthology of Modern Urdu Poetry in English Translation*.

# The Cambridge History of
## Literary Criticism

FOUNDING EDITORS

Professor H. B. Nisbet
*University of Cambridge*
Professor Claude Rawson
*Yale University*

*The Cambridge History of Literary Criticism* provides a comprehensive historical account of Western literary criticism from classical Antiquity to the present day, dealing with both literary theory and critical practice. The *History* is intended as an authoritative work of reference and exposition, but more than a mere chronicle of facts. While remaining broadly non-partisan it will, where appropriate, address controversial issues of current critical debate without evasion or false pretences of neutrality. Each volume is a self-contained unit designed to be used independently as well as in conjunction with the others in the series. Substantial bibliographical material in each volume provides a foundation for further study of the subjects in question.

VOLUMES PUBLISHED

Volume 1: *Classical Criticism*, edited by George A. Kennedy
Volume 2: *The Middle Ages*, edited by Alastair Minnis and Ian Johnson
Volume 3: *The Renaissance*, edited by Glyn P. Norton
Volume 4: *The Eighteenth Century*, edited by H. B. Nisbet and Claude Rawson
Volume 5: *Romanticism*, edited by Marshall Brown
Volume 6: *The Nineteenth Century*, edited by M. A. R. Habib
Volume 7: *Modernism and the New Criticism*, edited by A. Walton Litz, Louis Menand and Lawrence Rainey
Volume 8: *From Formalism to Poststructuralism*, edited by Raman Selden
Volume 9: *Twentieth-Century Historical, Philosophical and Psychological Perspectives*, edited by Christa Knellwolf and Christopher Norris

# The Cambridge History of
# Literary Criticism

VOLUME 6

## The Nineteenth Century,
## c. 1830–1914

Edited by

M. A. R. HABIB

CAMBRIDGE
UNIVERSITY PRESS

# CAMBRIDGE
## UNIVERSITY PRESS

University Printing House, Cambridge CB2 8BS, United Kingdom

One Liberty Plaza, 20th Floor, New York, NY 10006, USA

477 Williamstown Road, Port Melbourne, VIC 3207, Australia

314-321, 3rd Floor, Plot 3, Splendor Forum, Jasola District Centre, New Delhi - 110025, India

103 Penang Road, #05-06/07, Visioncrest Commercial, Singapore 238467

Cambridge University Press is part of the University of Cambridge.

It furthers the University's mission by disseminating knowledge in the pursuit of education, learning and research at the highest international levels of excellence.

www.cambridge.org
Information on this title: www.cambridge.org/9781316606100

© Cambridge University Press 2013

First published 2013
Reprinted 2014
Paperback edition first published 2016

A catalogue record for this publication is available from the British Library

ISBN 978-0-521-30011-7 Hardback
ISBN 978-1-316-60610-0 Paperback

Cambridge University Press has no responsibility for the persistence or accuracy of URLs for external or third-party internet websites referred to in this publication, and does not guarantee that any content on such websites is, or will remain, accurate or appropriate.

# Contents

# Notes on contributors

**Kimberly VanEsveld Adams** is Associate Professor of English at Elizabethtown College, Pennsylvania. Her publications include *Our Lady of Victorian Feminism: The Madonna in the Work of Anna Jameson, Margaret Fuller, and George Eliot* (2001) and articles on Harriet Beecher Stowe.

**Roger Cardinal's** publications include the books *Surrealism: Permanent Revelation* (with R. S. Short, 1970), *Expressionism* (1984), *The Landscape Vision of Paul Nash* (1989) and *Henry Moore: In the Light of Greece* (2000). His essays have dealt with the writers André Breton, Joë Bousquet, Jacques Dupin, Tristan Tzara and Victor Hugo, and the artists Hans Bellmer, Alberto Giacometti, André Masson, Kurt Schwitters, Wols and Unica Zürn. He is also an international authority on Art Brut, which he introduced to an English audience with *Outsider Art* (1972). He is Emeritus Professor of Literary and Visual Studies at the University of Kent.

**Edith W. Clowes** is Professor of Slavic Languages and Literatures and Director of the US/ED-Title-VI-funded Center for Russian, East European, and Eurasian Studies at the University of Kansas in Lawrence. Among her recent publications are a discursive history of Russian philosophy, *Fiction's Overcoat: Russian Literary Culture and the Question of Philosophy* (2004), and an editorial collaboration, *Sbornik 'Vekhi' v kontekste russkoi kul'tury* (2007). She has also co-edited *Kupecheskaia Moskva: Obrazy ushedshei rossiiskoi burzhuazii* (2007). Her latest book, *Russia on Edge: Imagined Geography and Post-Soviet Russian Identity*, appeared in 2011.

**Macdonald Daly** is Associate Professor in the Department of Cultural Studies at the University of Nottingham. He has published widely on nineteenth- and twentieth-century English literature, cultural theory, Marxist aesthetics and mass media. He is currently writing an analysis of BBC radio and co-editing a volume on the genre of post-conflict testimonies. Most recently, he edited and introduced *Dead Iraqis: Selected Short Stories of Ellis Sharp* (2009).

x                         Notes on contributors

**Nicholas Dames** is Theodore Kahan Professor of the Humanities at Columbia University. He is the author of *Amnesiac Selves: Nostalgia, Forgetting, and British Fiction, 1810–1870* (2001) and *The Physiology of the Novel: Reading, Neural Science, and the Form of Victorian Fiction* (2007).

**Elaine Freedgood** is Professor at New York University and the author of *Victorian Writing about Risk: Imagining a Safe England in a Dangerous World* (2000) and *The Ideas in Things: Fugitive Meaning in the Victorian Novel* (2006).

**Ray Furness** is Professor Emeritus of St Andrews University. He has written widely on modern German literature, Nietzsche, Wagner, Expressionism and Decadence. He is a frequent visitor to Bayreuth and is currently engaged in a further study of Wagner

**Willi Goetschel** is a Professor of German and Philosophy at the University of Toronto. He is the author of *Constituting Critique: Kant's Writing as Critical Praxis* (1994), *Spinoza's Modernity: Mendelssohn, Lessing, and Heine* (2004) and *The Discipline of Philosophy and the Invention of Modern Jewish Thought* (2012). He is also the editor of the collected works of Hermann Levin Goldschmidt and has published widely on topics in modern German literature and critical theory.

**David Goldie** is Senior Lecturer in the Department of English Studies at the University of Strathclyde in Glasgow. He is the author of *A Critical Difference: T. S. Eliot and John Middleton Murry in English Literary Criticism, 1919–1928* (1998) and is the editor, with Gerard Carruthers and Alastair Renfrew, of *Beyond Scotland: New Contexts for Twentieth-Century Scottish Literature* (2004) and the forthcoming *Scotland in the Nineteenth-Century World*.

**M. A. R. Habib** is Professor of English at Rutgers University, Camden. He is the author of seven books, including *The Early T. S. Eliot and Western Philosophy* (1999), *A History of Literary Criticism: From Plato to the Present* (2005) and *Modern Literary Criticism and Theory* (2008).

**Renate Holub** directs the Program in Interdisciplinary Studies at the University of California at Berkeley. She is the author of *Antonio Gramsci: Beyond Marxism and Postmodernism* (1992), and is completing a book entitled *Human Rights Before the State: On Vico's Theory of Global Justice*.

**Poul Houe** is Professor in the Department of German, Scandinavian and Dutch, University of Minnesota, Twin Cities. Since 2000, he has authored or edited the following books: *August Strindberg and the Other: New Critical Approaches*, ed. Poul Houe, Göran Stockenström and Sven

H. Rossel (2002), *Søren Kierkegaard and the Word(s): Essays on Hermeneutics and Communication*, ed. Poul Houe and Gordon D. Marino (2003) and *En anden Andersen – og andres: Artikler og foredrag 1969–2005* (2006).

**David Lyle Jeffrey** (PhD Princeton; Fellow of the Royal Society of Canada) is Distinguished Professor of Literature and Humanities at Baylor University. He is best known as a scholar of biblical tradition in Western literature and art. His books include *A Dictionary of Biblical Tradition in English Literature* (1992), *English Spirituality in the Age of Wesley* (1987, 1994, 2000), *People of the Book: Christian Identity and Literary Culture* (1996), *Houses of the Interpreter: Reading Scripture, Reading Culture* (2003) and a co-authored book on *The Bible and the University* (2007).

**John D. Kerkering** is Associate Professor of English at Loyola University Chicago. He is the author of *The Poetics of National and Racial Identity in Nineteenth-Century American Literature* (2003).

**Wolf Lepenies** is Permanent Fellow Emeritus at the Wissenschaftskolleg (Institute for Advanced Study) Berlin and was Rector of the Institute from 1986 to 2001. Formerly a Long-Term Member of the Institute for Advanced Study, Princeton, NJ, and Chair Européenne at the Collège de France, Paris, he is *doctor honoris causa*, Sorbonne, and Officer of the French Légion d'honneur.

**Rosemary Lloyd** is Rudy Professor Emerita, Indiana University; Fellow Emerita, Murray Edwards College, Cambridge; Adjunct Professor of French, University of Adelaide; and a Fellow of the Australian Academy of the Humanities. Her publications include *Baudelaire's World* (2002) and *Mallarmé: The Poet and His Circle* (1999), republished as a paperback in 2005.

**Clinton Machann** is Professor of English at Texas A&M University. Among his publications are *The Essential Matthew Arnold: An Annotated Bibliography of Major Modern Sources* (1993) and *Matthew Arnold: A Literary Life* (1998). He has edited a special issue of *Nineteenth-Century Prose* devoted to Matthew Arnold (2007), and his book *Masculinity in Four Victorian Epics: A Darwinist Reading* appeared in 2010.

**Steven Monte** is Associate Professor at the College of Staten Island (CUNY). He has published *Invisible Fences: Prose Poetry as a Genre in French and American Literature* (2000) and a collection of translations, *The Selected Poetry of Victor Hugo* (2002). One of his more recent publications is 'Difficulty and Modern Poetry' (2007).

**Gregory Moore** is Assistant Professor of History at Georgia State University. He is the author of *Nietzsche, Biology and Metaphor* (2002) and the translator of *Johann Gottfried Herder: Selected Writings on Aesthetics* (2006).

**James Najarian** is Associate Professor of English at Boston College, where he edits the journal *Religion and the Arts*. He is the author of *Victorian Keats: Manliness, Sexuality, and Desire* (2002), and he is working on a book on the conception of the 'minor poet' in nineteenth-century Britain.

**Hilary S. Nias** studied at the universities of Cambridge, Kiel (Germany) and Reading, where she wrote her doctoral thesis on Hippolyte Taine. This was later published as *The Artificial Self: The Psychology of Hippolyte Taine* (1999). She has also contributed a chapter on Taine to *Key Writers on Art: From Antiquity to the Nineteenth Century*, ed. Chris Murray (2003).

**John Osborne** is Emeritus Professor of German at the University of Warwick. He has published widely on German literature and theatre of the eighteenth and nineteenth centuries. His books include *The Naturalist Drama in Germany* (1971), *J. M. R. Lenz: The Renunciation of Heroism* (1975), *The Meiningen Court Theatre* (1988), *Vom Nutzen der Geschichte: Studien zum Werk Conrad Ferdinand Meyers* (1994) and *Theodor Fontane: Vor den Romanen* (1999). He contributed the chapter 'Drama, after 1740' to Volume 4 of *The Cambridge History of Literary Criticism*.

**Allan H. Pasco** is the Hall Professor of Nineteenth-Century Literature at the University of Kansas. His recent *Revolutionary Love* (2009) traces attitudes towards love in the eighteenth century, while his previous *Sick Heroes* (1997) argues that dysfunctional families led to the French Romantic hero.

**Stephen Prickett** is Regius Professor Emeritus of English at Glasgow University, and Honorary Professor at the University of Kent at Canterbury. His publications include *Coleridge and Wordsworth: The Poetry of Growth* (1970), *Romanticism and Religion: The Tradition of Coleridge and Wordsworth in the Victorian Church* (1976), *Victorian Fantasy* (1978), *The Romantics* (ed.) (1981), *Words and the Word: Language, Poetics and Biblical Interpretation* (1986), *Reading the Text: Biblical Criticism and Literary Theory* (ed.) (1991), *Origins of Narrative: The Romantic Appropriation of the Bible* (1996), *Narrative, Science and Religion: Fundamentalism versus Irony 1700–1999* (2002) and *Modernity and the Reinvention of Tradition: Backing into the Future* (2009).

**Harold Schweizer** is John P. Crozer Professor of English Literature at Bucknell University. His publications include *Suffering and the Remedy of Art* (1997). His most recent book, *On Waiting*, appeared in 2008.

**Joanne Shattock** is Emeritus Professor of Victorian Literature at the University of Leicester. She is editor of *The Cambridge Companion to English Literature 1830–1914* (2010), *Women and Literature in Britain* (2001) and *The Cambridge Bibliography of English Literature 1800–1900* (1999). She is General Editor of *The Works of Elizabeth Gaskell* (2005–6), and of *Selected Works of Margaret Oliphant*, with Elisabeth Jay (2011– ).

**Carol J. Singley** is Professor of English, Director of Graduate Studies and Director of Undergraduate Liberal Studies at Rutgers University, Camden. She is the author of *Edith Wharton: Matters of Mind and Spirit* (1995); the editor or co-editor of six volumes, including three on Wharton and *The American Child: A Cultural Studies Reader* (2003); and the author of *Adopting America: Childhood, Kinship, and National Identity in Literature* (2011).

**Donald Stone** is Professor Emeritus of Queens College and the Graduate Center, City University of New York, and Senior Professor in the Department of English at Peking University. His major publications include *Novelists in a Changing World: Meredith, James, and the Transformation of English Fiction in the 1880s* (1972), *The Romantic Impulse in Victorian Fiction* (1980) and *Communications with the Future: Matthew Arnold in Dialogue* (1997).

**Martin Swales** is Emeritus Professor of German at University College London. He has taught German at the Universities of Birmingham and Toronto and at King's College London and University College London. He has published widely on German literature from the eighteenth century on, including monographs on Goethe, Stifter, Schnitzler, Thomas Mann and German prose writing (the *Novelle*, the *Bildungsroman*, and German Realism).

**David Van Leer** is Professor of English at the University of California, Davis. He has written widely on American culture for the *New Republic* and the *Times Literary Supplement*. He is the author of *Emerson's Epistemology: The Argument of the Essays* (2009) and *The Queening of America: Gay Culture in Straight Society* (1995). He is the editor of *Edgar Allan Poe: Selected Tales* (1998) and book review editor of the *Journal of Bisexuality*.

**Beth S. Wright** is Professor of Art History at the University of Texas at Arlington, and Dean of the College of Liberal Arts. She is the author of

*Painting and History During the French Restoration: Abandoned by the Past* (1997), and the editor of *The Cambridge Companion to Delacroix* (2001). Her publications have appeared in *Art Bulletin, Bulletin de la Société de l'histoire de l'art français, Word & Image, Nineteenth-Century French Studies* and elsewhere.

**Julia M. Wright** is Associate Professor in English at Dalhousie University. She is the author of *Blake, Nationalism, and the Politics of Alienation* (2004) and *Ireland, India, and Nationalism in Nineteenth-Century Literature* (2007); she co-edited *Reading the Nation in English Literature: A Critical Reader* (2009) and edited *Irish Literature, 1750–1900: An Anthology* (2008) and a number of other volumes.

# Acknowledgements

I should like to thank, above all, the contributors to this volume, with whom it has been a pleasure to work. I am humbled by the depth and range of their scholarship, as well as their good will, encouragement and patience over a period of several years. I have also benefited greatly from the expertise of such renowned scholars as the late Sir Frank Kermode and Ron Bush. I should like to thank Tim Laquintano and Evan James Roskos for their valuable help with research, and I am grateful to the editors at Cambridge University Press, Kevin Taylor, Linda Bree and Maartje Scheltens, as well as to the general editors of this series, for their assistance.

M. A. R. Habib

# Introduction

## M. A. R. Habib

The nineteenth century is as rich and remarkable as any century in historical memory. Whether we broach it in terms of diverse intellectual and ideological currents, or of vast political and social upheavals, it yields a dazzling and often frantic display of movement, conflict and cataclysmic change. This single century housed the bourgeois revolutions and the rise to hegemony of the middle classes; the philosophical movements stemming from Hegel, and the counter-movements stemming from Schopenhauer; the blossoming of Romanticism; the German Higher Criticism; Darwin; the rise of nationalism; the dawn of the social sciences; the explosive development of the natural sciences and technology; the era of literary positivism, Realism, Naturalism, Symbolism and Decadence; the climax and catastrophes of imperialism; the articulation of socialism and the imminence of welfare states; the widening of the franchise and the demand for women's rights; the development of ideals of literary autonomy; and, not least in pertinence to this study, the beginnings of literary criticism as an autonomous, professional discipline in the academy.

## Aims of this volume

In bringing together over thirty essays written by experts in their respective fields, this book aims to provide the reader with a clear sense of the development of literary criticism as an institution during the period 1830–1914, as well as the range of themes and concerns which preoccupied literary critics in this era. The chapters attempt to display not only the main lines of literary-critical development within various national traditions, but also the interconnections between major critical movements, and the development of specific genres. This volume attempts, additionally, to highlight the contributions of certain influential critics of the period, such as Charles-Augustin Sainte-Beuve, Hippolyte Taine and Matthew Arnold. It also aims to give due attention to the predominant intellectual contexts of literary criticism, including developments in science, the arts and religious thought, as well as the various tensions between literary scientism or determinism and humanistic visions of artistic autonomy. These broader contexts of criticism are in turn sometimes underlain by important political events and patterns, such as the continuing legacy of the French Revolution, the revolutions of 1830 and 1848, the Franco-Prussian War, the various struggles for national unification, populist insurgency and conflicts between liberal and conservative ideologies. The chapters that follow examine not only the range and richness of literary criticism in this period but also the ways in which it was shaped internally by these larger movements.

## Outline of this volume, its scope and significance

### 1 Literary criticism as an institution

The first three chapters offer various perspectives on the social conditions, ideological conflicts, intellectual contexts and literary debates that shaped the institutional growth of literary criticism. In the opening chapter, on the contexts and conditions of criticism, Joanne Shattock traces the changing nature of periodical literature and the impact of this on criticism as a discipline. By the 1830s, a number of important quarterly reviews had been established, including the *Edinburgh Review*, the *Quarterly* and the *Westminster Review*. Their articles spanned a broad spectrum of disciplines and were heavily political in their orientation. The quarterlies were powerful instruments in creating a middle-class audience. The monthly and later weekly journals that arose addressed a narrower range of subjects, and were more focused on literary topics, largely excluding politics and theology. Periodicals such as *Macmillan's Magazine* and the *Cornhill* had a revolutionary role, generating a culture of serious literary reviewing, as opposed to belletrism. A journal entitled the *Academy*, started in 1869, promoted scholarly standards of criticism and cultivated a readership in the universities. These developments were symptomatic of a growing tension between academic specialists and general reviewers which, arguably, has persisted to this day. Literary criticism was increasingly becoming a professional activity, with its status and function being fiercely debated from 1850 onward. These changes, in turn, were an index of the development of English literature as a discipline.

Indeed, the institution of English literature had tortuous and tangled beginnings, as David Goldie explains in his chapter on 'Literary studies and the academy'. Goldie recounts how within half a century 'academic English literary criticism moved from being a peripheral subject with little establishment recognition to one of the key disciplines, in which the nation could index its every mood and characteristic'. It was only at the beginning of the twentieth century that the ancient universities established Chairs of English Literature and implemented English as a legitimate discipline. It seems that the founding causes of this rise of English to eventual institutional recognition were largely ideological: at the beginning of the nineteenth century, the classics were viewed as the heart of liberal education. But as industrial society developed, there arose a pressing need to educate the urban population, to combine training in literacy with the fostering of national values. Moreover, professional exams, such as those required for the Indian Civil Service, demanded proficiency in English literature – an institutional acknowledgement of a widespread tendency to see English as an index of broader nationalistic patterns and impulses. The first university teachers of English, many of whom came from journalism, were anxious to make it a more scholarly and rigorous discipline in the service of an aesthetic and moral vision. On the other hand, distinguished figures such as A. C. Bradley, Arther Quiller-Couch and Walter Raleigh attempted to resist what they saw as stifling scholarship and theory, urging instead that the role of criticism should be sympathetic and imaginative.

While literature contributed in varying ways to ideological and nationalist struggles in the nineteenth century, it was also obliged to confront the notion of gender. The chapter on 'Women and literary criticism' is intended not to maroon or ghettoize the endeavours of female critics – who are dealt with in many of the chapters here – but to highlight their achievement and their peculiar circumstances. Kimberly Adams's chapter focuses on the most prominent of these critics, Harriet Martineau, Anna Jameson, Margaret Fuller and George Eliot. She stresses that the performance of these women as literary critics, marked by a consciousness of gender, was necessarily politicized. She shows that an important achievement of female literary critics was that they variously helped to define Victorian Realism. They also made a compelling case for the novel as the genre of the age; and they detached 'the discussion of morality from both doctrine and didacticism... All addressed and defended their positions as public intellectuals... They made gender itself a critical concept, theorizing about masculinity, femininity'.

## II National developments in literary criticism

The next series of chapters traces various national movements in criticism. Julia M. Wright's chapter 'Nationalism and literature' introduces this part. Wright traces the ways in which literature became an index of national ideas, inasmuch as a nation's literature was held to reflect its character, its merits, and indeed its political legitimacy and sovereignty. She stresses that what is distinctive of modern nationalism is its emphasis not on a ruling elite but on a common public culture; it was in this, rather than in geographical boundaries, that a nation was understood to reside. Tracing analyses of 'nation' from Locke and Hume through modern theorists on nationalism, she builds on Anthony D. Smith's point that modern nationalism emerges from two schools of thought: Enlightenment philosophy, which emphasized empire, universality and progress, and Romanticism, which stressed the importance of nativism, regionalism and a return to roots. Indeed, the critical concept of national literature emerges out of these polarized eighteenth-century theories. But both sides saw their nation's literature as evidence of a core national identity and a shared national inheritance. Even as universality became prominent as a literary aim, writers in many countries, including the United States, Ireland and Canada, all argued for their own national literatures.

In Germany, as Willi Goetschel explains, modern criticism developed through a struggle to understand the legacy of Romanticism. The situation here was further complicated by the Carlsbad Decrees of 1819, which enforced surveillance of the press, universities and books. Literary criticism became a covert medium for political critique. Many critics reacted against Romantic ideals in insisting that criticism must connect literature and life, some espousing a literary nationalism. The influential poet Heinrich Heine saw Goethe's death in 1832 as the end of the 'period of art', and himself as Goethe's successor. In his enduringly influential work *The Romantic School* (1835), Heine broke new ground for literary criticism, seeing the literary voice as distinctive in its interplay of political, aesthetic and ethical dimensions. The prominent groups in modern German criticism, whether liberal in outlook like Young Germany or more moderate like the Young Hegelians, made the German national idea a central part of their agendas.

Allan H. Pasco notes that French Classicism, after its resurgence early in the century, never again rose to power as a dominant school after 1830. Even when writers like Nisard and Moréas proclaimed the virtues of their Classicism, it had few similarities to the movements of either the seventeenth century or classical Antiquity. Critics continued to emphasize the importance of formal perfection, beauty and objectivity. Many of the traits of Classicism were adopted by those praising modernity. No longer attached either to a particular author or group of authors, or even to a period, Classicism became a complex of traits that could be ascribed to almost any author from Baudelaire to Leconte de Lisle, or to Brunetière, Valéry and Gide. Desmarais observed that pure Classicism was no longer possible.

As Stephen Prickett explains in his chapter on the Romantic legacy in England, Victorian literary criticism was wider in scope and more popular than criticism would ever be in the twentieth century. Journals of the period saw literary criticism as integrally related to philosophy, theology and even science. Nearly all of the notable figures of this period – including Arnold, Carlyle, Thomas De Quincey, E. S. Dallas, the Brownings, Tennyson and George Eliot – ventured into one or more of these areas in their creative and critical endeavours. In this breadth, they were conserving and extending a Romantic heritage, and they addressed many of the issues that had centrally concerned their Romantic forebears: breaking with artificial poetic diction, dissolving barriers between genres, defending the status of literature against a rising tide of bourgeois philistinism and even crafting new theories of poetic imagination. But what distinguished the Victorians' focus on these issues was a new sense of history. Carlyle, Ruskin and Trollope saw not only literature but their own critical endeavours as informed by historical context.

In his chapter on later Victorian literature and culture, James Najarian also stresses the broad concerns of the Victorian 'prophets' such as Carlyle and Arnold. Like Arnold (who is dealt with in a separate chapter), Carlyle was concerned to revitalize what he saw as failing social and ethical norms, viewing literature as assuming some of the functions of religion. John Ruskin saw art as a medium of truth, with a didactic role, and he addressed the creation and dissemination of art in industrial society. Socialists such as William Morris and George Bernard Shaw also developed secular aesthetics, respectively impugning the modes of industrial manufacture and some of the idealistic systems that had replaced Christian belief. This tension between Aestheticism and overt social commitment continued to inform literary criticism through the twentieth century.

By the first decades of the nineteenth century, the United States had established a firm sense of its political identity; it now needed, as David Van Leer argues, a 'theory on the Americanness of its literature to parallel its declarations on the nature of individual liberty'. The most eloquent spokesman of a national literary identity was Emerson, whose famous exhortation to abandon the 'courtly muses' of Europe and to embrace the 'common' was complicated by a poetic theory that he borrowed from Kant. An equal ambivalence is found in Washington Irving, whose Eurocentrism was counterbalanced by a rhetoric of literary nationalism. Poe reacted against European Romanticism, and rebelled against the 'heresy of the didactic' that he attributed to the Transcendentalists, arguing that the poem should be written for its own sake, and that its primary concern should be to produce a unity of effect. The Romanticism of Melville and Hawthorne was infused with scepticism or realism. Common to all American Romanticism was a celebration of nature and the unique expansiveness of the American landscape. By the 1850s, political concerns eventually overturned the philosophical and aesthetic impetus of American Transcendentalism, as seen in the work of both Thoreau, who influenced twentieth-century political resistance movements, and Frederick Douglass. After the Civil War, American literature took a more pragmatic orientation. Thinkers such as C. S. Peirce and William James distrusted metaphysics. With further industrial growth, the 'nature' underlying Romanticism was redefined and eventually dissolved.

If censorship in parts of Europe was harsh, it was perhaps worse in Russia. In the face of the censor, as Edith W. Clowes explains, Russian literary criticism became a seedbed of multiple discourses: political, economic, theological and philosophical. Aesthetic perspectives were integrally tied to political, social and moral agendas. There emerged in the 1830s a debate about Russian national identity, history and society, between Westernizers and Slavophiles. The first professional Russian critic, Vissarion Belinsky, made these issues 'the very foundation of the Russian critical enterprise'. Another notable development was the insistence on artistic autonomy expressed by Vasily Botkin, Aleksandr Druzhinin and Pavel Annenkov. Over the next several years, Aestheticist critics debated with socially engaged critics. The final decades of the century witnessed the first academic Russian critics: Aleksandr Potebnya, who examined language as a sign-system, and Aleksandr Veselovsky, who drew on scientific positivism. Both had a substantial impact on Formalists such as Viktor Shklovsky and Boris Zhirmunsky. In the Modernist era, the greatest Russian poet, Aleksandr Blok, entertained an apocalyptic vision of high culture, while a socialistic current of criticism – treated in more detail elsewhere in this series – was devoted to social transformation. Overall, Russian criticism made major contributions in Realism, Modernism and investigation of the cognitive role of literature.

### III Critical movements and patterns of influence

The focus in this part is on the increasing importance through the nineteenth century of the notion of literary autonomy, as well as the various streams of aesthetics, often conflicting but also intersecting, which stemmed respectively from Hegel and Marx.

The rising emphasis on literary autonomy is traced in its various moral and cultural registers by Harold Schweizer. In modern times it was Alexander Baumgarten and Johann Georg Hamann who first attempted to justify the aesthetic as an independent domain, in opposition to eighteenth-century rationalism and the centuries-old ascription of a mimetic and didactic function to literature. The doctrine of aesthetic autonomy arose as theology declined; it provided a refuge against the rising quantification and commodification of value. Literary autonomy arose through 'productive misappropriations' of Kant's aesthetic theory, which had seen the realm of the aesthetic, of beauty, as autonomous and distinct from the realms of both morality and usefulness.

In the nineteenth century, ideas of autonomy were taken up in various modes, as in Coleridge's concept of organic form, or Matthew Arnold's concept of critical 'disinterestedness', or Baudelaire's flâneur, who is a paradoxical passionate spectator. Radical autonomists such as Flaubert, Mallarmé, Pater and Wilde saw art as a refuge from the world's vulgarity and mediocrity. The contradictions and tensions inherent in autonomy are reflected in its range of ideological significance. The Young Germans saw it as an obstacle to political emancipation, whereas French writers used it to oppose the reactionary dogmatism of writers such as Désiré Nisard and Gustave Planche.

Ironically, while much nineteenth-century literary thought was engaged in extricating art from the pressure to educate or to moralize or to imitate the world of reality, another series of movements, deriving largely from Hegel, aimed precisely to restore our understanding of art as an historical phenomenon, as integrally rooted in the historical process. The chapter on Hegel describes the central features of Hegel's aesthetic theory and his historical account of the development of art through three stages. The first stage, that of symbolic art, is characterized by a relative formlessness and indefiniteness of spiritual and intellectual content. In the next stage, of classical art, the spiritual content achieves individuality in anthropomorphic forms. The highest stage is Romantic art, which embodies a more advanced and self-conscious subjectivity, manifested at its zenith in the art of poetry. This chapter examines Hegel's analysis of the genres of poetry, including his celebrated account of tragedy, and the vast influence of his philosophy and aesthetics.

If Hegelian criticism insisted on situating art within the movement of history, Marxism deepened and problematized this contextualization. Macdonald Daly points out that Marx's own attempts to characterize the connections between a society's economic infrastructure and its superstructure are inconsistent and inconclusive. Marx did, however, implicitly urge his followers to seek the 'inner core' of his thought, which can be broadly identified: 'art...is a "secondary" phenomenon which bears the ineradicable traces or marks of its economic dependency...but...it also creates new needs'. Daly stresses Engels's neglected contributions to Marxist criticism. It was Engels who articulated the notion of Realism – taken up by later writers such as Lukács – as a truthful reproduction of typical characters under typical circumstances. It was Engels who laid the groundwork for discussion of issues such as authorial class allegiance,

ideological tendency and unconscious motivation. Engels undermined
vulgar Marxist notions of art, and he effectively reconceived Marx's
notions in the face of new political circumstances. His most profound
innovation was the notion of mediation, whereby ideological consciousness – acknowledged to have a relative independence – exerts some influence on material interests and historical development. By the end of the
century, Marxism had spread far beyond Germany. Daly traces the development of early Marxist aesthetic theory from Franz Mehring to Herbert
Marcuse and Georg Lukács.

## IV Realism, Naturalism, Symbolism and Decadence

Perhaps the most predominant literary tendencies in the second half of the
nineteenth century were Realism and Naturalism, which in turn provoked
reactions in the form of Symbolism, Aestheticism and what has been
labelled as 'Decadence'. The next part of this volume examines these
movements as they occurred in various countries, with due regard for
patterns of influence and exchange between them.

In her chapter on French criticism, Rosemary Lloyd contextualizes the
rise of Realism. The initial figures of the so-called Realist school were
the painter Gustave Courbet and the writers Champfleury and Edmond
Duranty. Courbet insisted that writers must avoid basing their art on
stereotypes. Champfleury saw Realism as the representation of contemporary life without recourse to social or aesthetic hierarchies. Gustave
Flaubert claimed that the greatest writers 'reproduce the Universe', setting
aside their personalities. Duranty, influenced deeply by the development
of photography, was an outspoken proponent of Realism, relishing the
eternal variety of reality. Hippolyte Taine's ambition to make criticism
less arbitrary and personal had a profound influence on many subsequent
critics and writers, especially Emile Zola. Emile Hennequin aimed to
found 'aesthopsychology', which he defined as 'the science of the work of
art as sign'. Realism was moulded by writers such as Guy de Maupassant,
J.-K. Huysmans and Zola into a Naturalism which embodied a greater
emphasis upon science and causality. There were, however, sustained
reactions against so-called 'scientific' criticism, which drew attention to
its limits and mechanistic nature, as expressed in the views of Ferdinand
Brunetière, Ernest Renan and Edmond Scherer. Scherer points to the subjective and impressionistic criticism that would dominate the work of
Anatole France and others at the end of the century. A further powerful reaction against Realism and scientism came from French Symbolism, whose aesthetics were rooted in Baudelaire, and were further developed by Paul Verlaine, Stéphane Mallarmé, Jean Moréas and Remy de
Gourmont.

In his chapter on the later nineteenth century in Germany, Martin Swales argues that, notwithstanding the provincialism of German literature, grounded as it was in the regionalism of the Holy Roman Empire rather than in a unified nation state, it explores in a sophisticated manner the aesthetics of modern prose. Goethe's death in 1832 effectively marked the end of high art and the onset of a more prosaic cultural condition. Indeed, Hegel viewed the protagonist of the modern novel as mired within the 'prose' of reality: a recurrent conflict in the novel is between 'the poetry of the heart and the countervailing prose of circumstances'. Swales traces this conflict in the *Bildungsroman* through German theorizing on the novel from Friedrich Theodor Vischer, Wolfgang Menzel and Robert Prutz to Lukács, who variously saw the novel as reconciling the claims of poetry and prose. The key theorists Julian Schmidt and Gustav Freytag advocated a style that combined poetry and prose, Idealism and Realism. By the end of the nineteenth century, the Naturalism of figures such as Friedrich Spielhagen and Wilhelm Bölsche had taken root. German Realism, though infused with the poetic, achieves a Realist mentality in the works and critical reflections of Gottfried Keller, Theodor Fontane and especially Thomas Mann. In general, this irresolution or ambivalence between the registers of prose and poetry – deriving from Hegel's enduring insight – lay at the core of Germany's contribution to the literary expression of modernity.

In her chapter on nineteenth-century British views of Realism, Elaine Freedgood examines how the Realistic novelist was obliged to break from literary convention in portraying characters recognizable as members of actual social groups. George Eliot urged the novelist to represent social and individual experience through the most mundane, material means, enlisting the most basic details of everyday life. There was a formidable link between the aesthetic and ethical imperatives of Realism. Many so-called Realist writers were well aware that they were shaping reality as much as reflecting it. Dickens portrayed the urban poor so as to arouse pity. Thackeray distorted social life to evince condemnation. All of the other Realist writers, including Gaskell, Margaret Oliphant, Anthony Trollope, George Eliot, Kipling and Hardy, engineered their own perspectives to create insights into subjects ranging from the status of women through empire to sexuality. G. H. Lewes, Eliot and others were well aware that their representational techniques needed to be selective in choice of material, that they were guiding the reader's interpretative processes, and that reality was a complex concept.

American Realism was influenced by a range of European writers which included Balzac, Flaubert, Turgenev, Tolstoy and Dostoevsky. As Carol J. Singley explains, the most salient European influence was Zola's Naturalism, which, in America, became more distinguished from Realism than its European counterpart. 'Realism' is often used to describe the work of William Dean Howells and Henry James, while 'Naturalism' is applied to writers such as Theodore Dreiser and Frank Norris; a further group including Stephen Crane, Edith Wharton and Kate Chopin display elements of both tendencies. As with their European predecessors, American Realists such as Howells and Hamlin Garland employed Realism as social critique. A darker Realism, in the vein of Zola's Naturalism, was developed by Norris, Crane and Jack London. The sweeping social changes of the century impelled some writers – including Mark Twain, Chopin and Louisa May Alcott – to seek stability in the depiction of regional traditions and customs, a tendency some critics associated with an elementary nationalism. The African American Charles Chesnutt presented the Old South through the eyes of an ex-slave. The literary forms of American Realism were profoundly influenced by James, who pioneered the investigation into inner consciousness and narrative point of view.

It is ironic that an age which laid heavy emphasis on the imitation of science should also spawn a rich range of reactions against such positivism. Ray Furness points out that by the 1890s the term 'Decadence' had come to signify anti-Naturalism, deliberate artifice and amorality; its practitioners were seen as dandies and aesthetes, devoted to the cultivation of beauty. A pioneer of decadence was Théophile Gautier, whose work, rejecting the Christian doctrine of sinfulness, exhibits an infatuation not with spiritual or ethical values but with the visible world. He insisted that art was useless, with no moral purpose, and he anticipated Baudelaire's characterization of the 'dandy' as emblem of a new aristocracy which resists rising bourgeois mediocrity, practicality and philistinism. In England, Aestheticism was inspired largely by Walter Pater, for whom life could only have meaning in perpetual ecstasy and rapt awareness of beauty. This lesson was well learned and even surpassed by Oscar Wilde. Arthur Symons, the first to define 'Decadence' in England, saw it as a preliminary stage of Symbolism. A more powerful voice emerged in Germany, where Nietzsche proclaimed himself the 'highest authority' on Decadence. It is art, he claimed, which provides an antidote to the life-denying decadence of religion and morality. In general, as Furness points out, Decadent writers expanded the boundaries of what was acceptable, and had the courage to be spiritually 'corrupt' and to dream strange dreams.

As Roger Cardinal shows, the twentieth-century avant-garde's fixation upon novelty and surprise was a virulent continuation of the iconoclastic movements of previous decades, inspired by figures such as Baudelaire, Rimbaud, Wilde, Wagner and Schopenhauer. The avant-gardists, ranging from the Futurists and Dadaists to the Expressionists and Surrealists, also rejected materialism and the orthodoxies of Realism and

Naturalism. It was the Polish Italian poet Guillaume Apollinaire who expressed the aspirations of a new generation. In 1911 the Czech version of Cubism staged exhibitions by Picasso, Braque and others. In Germany and Austria, an entire young generation saw the need to sever connections with its cultural inheritance, a rebellious mood reinforced by the experience of the First World War. This mood spawned the widespread movement of Expressionism. Marinetti issued the founding manifesto in 1919 for Italian Futurism, which displayed a fascination with the machine age, technology, speed and surprise. Futurism emerged at a similar period in Russia, while in England, Vorticism arose as an offshoot of Italian Futurism. As Cardinal points out, the most pervasive political disposition of the avant-garde was an anarchic rebelliousness, directed against what was seen as an inflexible education system, conformist art, the contemporary social system and a complacent bourgeoisie.

## v Some major critics of the period

There are a few towering critical figures in the nineteenth century whose voices resonated through subsequent decades, often well into the twentieth century. These figures merit a more detailed assessment, which is undertaken in the ensuing part of this volume. Among them was Charles-Augustin Sainte-Beuve, who, as Wolf Lepenies explains, saw his era as one of impending chaos and fragmenting value systems, intoxicated with the idea of progress at the expense of moral soundness. He saw literature and criticism as the sole intellectual province which could preserve order; literature was effectively a series of acts of 'retributive' poetic justice. Sainte-Beuve highlighted the function of the 'grand diocese' – comprising intellectuals of various persuasions – that shaped the intellectual life of France, and he defended academic freedom: 'the most important thing is to free oneself from absolute authority and blind submission'. As Lepenies states, these words express the mood of European intellectuals who had lost religious faith yet thereby yearned all the more for community and a foundation for morality.

Sainte-Beuve's Italian contemporary Francesco De Sanctis formulated a criticism which attempted to integrate aesthetic and political imperatives, imbued with zeal for the 'risorgimento' or the struggle for Italian national unification and constitutional liberty. As Renate Holub explains, cultural and political resistance in Italy was often spearheaded by reformist intellectuals. De Sanctis's theoretical programme linked aesthetics with Italian language and literature, viewing literary criticism as part of a broader programme for humanist intellectuals to engage in the cultural education of an enlightened citizenry. His renowned *History of Italian Literature* (1870–1) recounts Italy's path to liberty and constitutionalism as expressed by its major literary, cultural and philosophical figures. The work of De Sanctis has been pressed into diverse ideological uses by a spectrum of thinkers ranging from the Marxists Labriola and Gramsci to the Hegelian Benedetto Croce and the fascist philosopher Giovanni Gentile. Overall, De Sanctis's legacy is one of political commitment, which involved him in various public positions, persecution, imprisonment and exile.

An equally influential figure was Hippolyte Taine, whose critical method, as Hilary S. Nias explains, was essentially to analyse literature as defined by its historical moment, its cultural setting and the nationality of its author. This method, enshrined in the famous phrase 'race, milieu et moment', would become one of the hallmarks of Taine's approach, along with his notion of the 'master faculty' or essential character of an author, period or work. Taine's approach is famously expounded in the Preface to his Histoire de la littérature anglaise (1863). He stresses here the causal importance of physical and historical context for the creation of a people's moral disposition. While Taine's work was generally well received by Sainte-Beuve, it also elicited opposition on account of its mechanism and determinism, which were seen as precluding individual personality, as well as its liability to promote atheism. Bergson urged that Taine's formulations lose sight of the deeper, ineffable self whose core is duration (durée). Taine has been viewed as a founder of comparative criticism and a contributor to modern hermeneutics; his stress on historical context is now taken for granted; and he accorded a central importance to psychological analysis before the arrival of Freud.

Another pioneer of comparative criticism, examined here by Clinton Machann, was Matthew Arnold, the most influential English critic of the Victorian period. Arnold, who achieved an early reputation as a poet, saw poetry as a 'criticism of life'. In his seminal essay 'The Function of Criticism at the Present Time' Arnold formulated his definition of criticism as 'a disinterested endeavour to learn and propagate the best that is known and thought in the world'. With his emphasis on the ideal of knowledge for its own sake, he helped prepare the ground for later developments ranging from Pater's Aestheticism to early twentieth-century liberal humanism. Nonetheless, Arnold's own stress was upon the place of literature within a larger social context, in its relation to knowledge and religion. In 1865, Arnold moved from literary criticism per se to larger issues such as culture, which he defined as 'inward' and opposed to a 'mechanical and material civilisation'. He later identified it with 'sweetness' (beauty of character) and 'light' (intelligence). Arnold became viewed, controversially, as the 'apostle of culture'. In his writings on religion, Arnold urged that it is essential to preserve the Bible as poetry, and that scripture, whose language is metaphorical, must remain open to renewed interpretation. In general, he defended the function of the humanities and liberal arts in education, as against those such as Huxley who were advocating a more scientific curriculum. The battles that Arnold was waging continue to rage today, and he stands as the archetypal defender of the role and importance of letters.

It could be said that what Arnold expected from culture, Henry James expected from the novel. In several classic essays, as Donald Stone elaborates, James argued that the novel was a genre that defied codes and restrictions. He examined novelistic form, the use of point of view, the morality of fiction and artistic freedom. Inspired by Arnold's strictures against provincialism, James looked to France for critical guidance. He also adapted Taine's view of the importance of historical conditioning, and was profoundly influenced by Sainte-Beuve's injunction to see life as 'clearly and fully as possible'. James regarded the novelist as the supreme truth-teller, being obliged to view reality unconstrained by aesthetic limitations or moral concerns. The novel must be 'perfectly free'. In 'The Art of Fiction', James made a plea for the treatment of the novel as a major art form. James influenced the theory and practice of many writers, ranging from Conrad and Ford Madox Ford through Edith Wharton and Virginia Woolf to Kazuo Ishiguro and Ian McEwan. He was also original in his stress on the reader's active role in the reading process.

The virtue of cosmopolitanism unites many of the great critical voices of this period. The controversial Danish critic Georg Brandes attempted, albeit only with partial success, to bring his nation into accord with his vision of European modernity. As Poul Houe explains, Brandes urged contemporary writers not to rephrase either the classics or Romantics but rather to grasp the 'poetry and novelty of real-life experience' centred on societal debates. In general, he espoused an objective Aestheticism, seeing the critic as a philosopher rather than a moralist. The impact of Taine was pivotal in orientating Brandes towards Naturalism, positivism, utilitarianism and pluralism. Yet Brandes had reservations about Taine's historical determinism, and he learned from Sainte-Beuve to produce individualized portraits of writers, attending to specific works and genres. He ruggedly espoused independence of thought. Like Arnold, he opposed biblical dogma and evoked the virtues of ancient Greece. A staunch supporter of the rights of workers, minorities and women, he left a controversial legacy of cultural radicalism and internationalism.

## vi *Genre criticism*

The notion of genre was fiercely disputed in the nineteenth century. The chapters in this part demonstrate amply that theories of the novel, poetry and drama proliferated through this period. As a preface to this section, Steven Monte's chapter examines the concept of genre itself, showing how it had widespread implications, ideological, economic, political and literary. The groundwork for nineteenth-century theories was laid by the triadic schemes of German thinkers such as Hegel, which displaced the larger groupings inherited from the Renaissance, typically including epic, tragedy, satire, epigram, ode, elegy and pastoral.

The influence of Hegel's emphasis on generic progression and decline was seen in Thomas Love Peacock's 'The Four Ages of Poetry' and Victor Hugo's historical sequencing of genres as determined by art's connections with society and religion. Like many in this century, Hugo advocated mixed forms and blurred generic distinctions. In Russia, Italy and France, genre theory was advanced by Belinsky, De Sanctis and Brunetière, all of whom fundamentally modified German theories in a broader historicism. Biological and evolutionary metaphors are a staple of nineteenth-century genre theory. The Anglophone critic most thoroughly engaged in genre theory was E. S. Dallas, whose triad of drama, narrative and lyric was grounded in psychology. Wilhelm Dilthey and Benedetto Croce also produced psychological theories of genre. The renowned Georg Gottfried Gervinus believed that poetic and national evolution are concurrent. The twentieth century saw a resurgence of historicist approaches, as in the work of Ortega y Gasset, Georg Lukács and Mikhail Bakhtin. The enduring triadic scheme of narrative–lyric–dramatic seemed suited to the new needs of the century while preserving some continuity with tradition.

The next three chapters analyse theories of specific genres. In his essay on theories of the novel, Nicholas Dames argues that the nineteenth century was a period of innovative attempts to define the novel. These theories acknowledged the incoherence of the novel form as essential to the genre. They also tended to examine the consumption of novels by the public, the affective workings of novels on readers. This focus on cultural reception indicated a disciplinary breadth that effectively vanished after James. The emphasis upon psychology also indicated a retreat from historical and developmental analysis (which had marked late eighteenth-century accounts) towards a more scientific and taxonomic orientation, as in Masson, Walter Bagehot, Brunetière and Balzac, who all classified various kinds of novel. Where psychological and physiological criticism looked to plot, the criticism based on natural history looked to character as determining novelistic meaning and truth-value. This dialectic engendered later notions of the place of the author within narrative, as in the work of Friedrich Spielhagen and Flaubert, who famously asserted that the author must be a godlike presence, 'present everywhere and visible nowhere'. This idea of objectification through character becomes in James the idea of 'point of view'. In general, novelistic theory had shifted from a focus on the audience to one on the author.

Theories of poetry during the nineteenth century, as John D. Kerkering argues, were variously positioned between the two poles of beauty and sublimity as foci of discussion. The French philosopher Victor Cousin saw poetry as the type of artistic perfection, judged by its ability to arouse in readers the sentiments of beauty and the infinite. Cousin's views were echoed by Baudelaire, whose contemporaries in Britain, such as John Keble, John Ruskin and Elizabeth Barrett Browning, also saw poetry as not creating but interpreting already existing correspondences. Taine and Sainte-Beuve, as seen above, viewed a writer's work in his or her national, historical and biographical contexts. John Stuart Mill attributed to poetry a practical role in the conduct of life, viewing it as therapeutic. Such utilitarian notions of poetry came under attack in Arnold's famous view that we should judge poetry by the essential trait of 'high seriousness'. New genres of poetry included the dramatic monologue, associated with Browning, the prose poem, associated with Mallarmé, and the free-verse line of Whitman's poetry. Important efforts to codify poetic forms were made by Poe, Coventry Patmore, Sidney Lanier and George Saintsbury. In the early twentieth century A. C. Bradley, following Pater, saw poetry as autonomous, and anticipated Cleanth Brooks's views of the 'heresy' of paraphrase.

The central question posed by theorists of drama in this period, as John Osborne explains, was whether to invest characters and action with universal import or to represent the peculiar details of their historical and social contexts. Hegel's view of drama as a characteristically modern form paved the way for the rejection of neo-classical drama by nineteenth-century Realists, and indeed a more general Romantic reaction against the Aristotelian model. In Russia, Belinsky called for a socially responsible drama and Gogol saw the stage as a moral institution. The German Friedrich Hebbel viewed the function of drama as unearthing the struggle of individual versus universal.

Social and Realist tendencies came into French criticism through Taine, Sainte-Beuve and the dramatists Emile Augier and Alexandre Dumas *fils*. The Realist and naturalistic conceptions of drama required a new anti-theatrical style of acting, and the plays of Zola, Ibsen, Hauptmann and Chekhov demanded new theatres, a demand met by the Free Theatre movement, led by Antoine, and followed by Brahm and Stanislavsky. Strindberg urged the need to do away with 'theatrical' characters in favour of more complex human beings. Later, Brunetière declared the bankruptcy of naturalism, calling for a drama engaged in metaphysical questions of human will. George Bernard Shaw fostered the drama of ideas, while the theories of Hofmannsthal and Wilde were highly eclectic.

Much of the debate of this period occurred between those who stressed the political function of drama and those, like Francisque Sarcey, Nietzsche and Wagner, who attempted to develop its symbolist and mythological potential.

## VII *Literature and other disciplines*

This volume concludes with a series of chapters examining the connection of literary criticism with science, other arts and religion. Gregory Moore notes that critics of this period attempted to raise their standards beyond seemingly arbitrary individual responses; for some, this meant adopting more 'scientific' models which effectively eliminated the judicial and evaluative components of criticism and promoted the factual investigation of history, psychology and other disciplines. G. H. Lewes espoused a scientific method of criticism based on psychological laws. E. S. Dallas saw criticism as a science of the laws governing the unconscious and the production of pleasure. It was Wilhelm Scherer who became the spokesperson for a new literary positivism which abandoned Hegelianism and Romanticism in favour of an empirical approach to literary history. Dilthey also stressed the need for observation and comparative analysis, though he saw the humanities as distinct from the natural sciences inasmuch as they were characterized by imagination and empathy. Brunetière attempted to apply evolutionary insights to literary study, viewing literary history as an increasing differentiation of genres. Other models, such as Emile Hennequin's 'aesthopsychology', were grounded in sociology.

Literature's connections with the arts have proven equally fertile. Beth S. Wright explains that these connections took many forms: avant-garde artists wrote manifestos and sought literary analogues and advocates; many figures, such as Delacroix, Rossetti, Gautier and Thackeray, were authors and painters; a newly literate mass audience craved increasingly visual texts such as illustrated periodicals. Salient in these developments were the numerous interactions between authors and artists; theories of correspondences and analogies between colour and music recurred, as in Baudelaire's vision of synaesthesia; in turn, Shakespeare, Goethe, Walter Scott and Byron afforded inspiration for composers such as Mendelssohn, Liszt, Tchaikovsky and Berlioz. The 'seeking of a more complete union of aural and narrative emotional expression stimulated opera's development into the pre-eminent musical form of the later nineteenth century', as embodied in the work of Verdi and Wagner. Technological innovations, ranging from the panorama and diorama through the motion picture to medical inventions such as the X-ray, and above all the daguerreotype photographic process, significantly broadened the field of interaction between the arts. Ruskin wished to harness the arts to inspire and educate a mass audience.

Among the most important sources of nineteenth-century literary criticism, as David Lyle Jeffrey points out in the final chapter, were the Bible and biblical criticism. Religious questions were 'at the heart of all reflection on culture and meaning'. In European universities, the connection of the arts curriculum to the discipline of theology at its heart was assumed to be organic. But by the early nineteenth century the status of the Bible as an epistemological norm for other disciplines was in decline. In 1809 the University of Berlin separated theology from the humanities, this model thereafter influencing English and American universities. A number of thinkers, including the German Higher Critics, as well as Voltaire and Locke, urged the study of the Bible as a literary text. But, as in the work of Siegmund Jacob Baumgarten, the 'literal' sense of scripture became increasingly correlated with its factual authenticity.

Another legacy, however, shifted focus away from narrow debates concerning verifiability. In the mid-eighteenth century, Oxford Professor of Poetry Robert Lowth's revolutionary lectures argued that figural writing was the essential mode of the Bible, thereby linking the authority of prophecy with the language of poetry. A further important influence dated back to Hegel's view of the gospel as both history and myth, and Feuerbach's thesis of the projective character of religious knowledge. Any substantial place for the Bible had by this point dissolved. As George Eliot, translator of Feuerbach and David Strauss, said, theology had become anthropology. In the hands of George Eliot and especially Matthew Arnold, 'culture' became imbued with an almost religious authority. By the end of the century criticism of religion had taken root as the quest for a new authority, to be identified neither with state religion nor with literary criticism.

## Concluding remarks

It may be salutary to conclude by highlighting the ways in which the literary criticism of this period anticipates so many of our own critical concerns. To begin with, the debates on the institutional status of literary criticism, and the ideological function of English as a discipline, are still raging. Today, some are calling for a revival of the public intellectual, so germane to nineteenth-century letters. We now take for granted the need to invoke the historical and broader intellectual contexts of literature, as well as the imperative towards cosmopolitanism; the virtues of universality or regionalism are still hotly contested in a now widened context of 'world' literature. The idea of literary autonomy has enjoyed a recent resurgence.

The notions of culture and genre persist in their importance, and gender has been increasingly refined as an object of study; Classicism and Romanticism continue to exert fascination and allegiance. Indeed, our most popular (some would say fashionable) analytic foci, such as class, gender and race, were formulated in very precise terms by thinkers across a wide ideological spectrum from Taine through Arnold to Marx. Our main literary modes still range between variants of Realism and Symbolism, and we now realize that Decadence is here to stay. We also know that the importance of literary analysis to religion (not just Judaeo-Christian but Islamic traditions) cannot be overestimated. We have inherited the positivism as well as the historicism of our forebears; we too struggle with the implications of science and technology, and the connection of literature with other art forms and the media. We are living in a time when literary critics – for a complex of reasons – are largely deprived of a voice in the public sphere. In all of the concerns enumerated above, we have much to learn from our nineteenth-century ancestors, who were often more articulate than we are, more precise, more widely read, more historically aware, and more alert to the important and often urgent issues of the day.

# *Literary criticism as an institution*

# I

# Contexts and conditions
# of criticism 1830–1914

## JOANNE SHATTOCK

Reviewing spreads with strange vigour; that such a man as Byron reckons the Reviewer and the Poet equal... at the last Leipzig Fair, there was advertised a Review of Reviews. By and by it will be found that all Literature has become one boundless self-devouring Review... thus does Literature, also, like a sick thing, superabundantly 'listen to itself'.[1]

Carlyle's undoubtedly jaundiced comment in his essay 'Characteristics', first published in the *Edinburgh Review* in 1831, reflected his irritation with contemporary literary life, in which reviewing paid so well that no man (or woman) of letters could afford to ignore it. Sixteen years later, George Henry Lewes, a prototype of the mid-Victorian reviewer, was to argue that the healthy state of the newly established 'profession' of literature was owing to 'the excellence and abundance of periodical literature'.[2] Both observations were shrewd. By the 1830s there was a significant number of quarterly reviews, together with monthly magazines and weekly papers, that offered a range of criticism on 'literature' in its broadest sense, from history, philosophy, political economy, theology and science to the more popular forms of poetry, art, drama and the novel. Few would have agreed with Carlyle's view that reviewing was a form of self-devouring. On the other hand, most would have acknowledged that the product of the reviews constituted a corpus of 'criticism', though not all of it recognizably 'literary' criticism.

Lewes's article pointed to a related and comparatively recent phenomenon, the possibility of earning one's living from journalism, with accompanying status and respectability, much of it owing to the opportunities provided by weekly, monthly and quarterly reviews. From the 1850s, the so-called 'higher journalism', a term used to describe a number of heavyweight monthlies and weeklies, became an adjunct career for university men who combined it with politics, the bar, the church or the

---

[1] Thomas Carlyle, 'Characteristics' in *Essays*, 4 vols. (London: Chapman & Hall, 1857), vol. III, p. 19.
[2] [G. H. Lewes], 'The Condition of Authors in England, Germany and France', *Fraser's Magazine*, 35 (1847), p. 288.

civil service.[3] The role of 'the critic', as distinct from that of the reviewer or the journalist, began to prompt self-conscious scrutiny by mid-century. Criticism, in the eyes of its practitioners, was becoming a specialized and a more professional activity.

Looking back at the end of century, the historian and critic George Saintsbury commented that there was perhaps 'no single feature of the English literary history of the nineteenth century, not even the enormous popularisation and multiplication of the novel, which is so distinctive and characteristic as the development in it of periodical literature'. Noting the number of important books, non-fiction as well as novels, which were first published serially, he reflected that had reprints not taken place 'more than half the most valuable books of the age . . . would never have appeared as books at all'.[4] The fashion for collecting and reprinting essays and reviews was one which began in the late 1830s and soon became de rigueur for a generation of critics who regarded themselves as professionals. The resulting collections were unlikely to have been among the 'valuable books of the age' that Saintsbury had in mind. But the first generation of *Edinburgh* and *Quarterly* reviewers, Francis Jeffrey, Sydney Smith, Macaulay and Robert Southey, followed by mid-Victorian critics like Richard Holt Hutton, Walter Bagehot, John Morley and Leslie Stephen, and later by Arnold, Pater and Wilde, solidified their reputations as critics by the publication of their collected reviews. What Saintsbury's observation indirectly highlights is the large and variable body of criticism which was *not* collected or republished under its authors' names, and which remains anonymously embedded in its original place of publication.

The task of writing authoritatively about literary criticism in the period 1830 to 1914 is complicated by the scale of the primary materials and the difficulty of getting to grips with it. There is a risk of focusing on a small number of identifiable critics, and excluding a large amount of excellent as well as typical criticism by anonymous authors in a vast array of weeklies, monthlies and quarterlies. There is also the danger, which periodical historians like Laurel Brake emphasize, of divorcing nineteenth-century criticism from its original periodical context, a context that reveals much about the nature of the criticism, and indeed did much to shape it.[5]

The fact that writing for the periodical press in the nineteenth century was respectable and that reviewing was well paid was almost entirely

---

[3] See Christopher Kent, 'Higher Journalism and the Mid-Victorian Clerisy', *Victorian Studies* 13 (1969), 181–98.

[4] George Saintsbury, *History of Nineteenth Century Literature* (London: Macmillan, 1896), p. 166.

[5] See Laurel Brake, *Subjugated Knowledges* (Basingstoke: Macmillan, 1994), esp. ch. 1, 'Criticism and the Victorian Periodical Press'.

owing to the *Edinburgh Review*, which in Walter Bagehot's words 'began the system' in 1802. It was, as Margaret Oliphant later acknowledged, 'the first-born of modern periodicals'.[6] Its founding editor, Francis Jeffrey, had initially determined that the review would be 'all gentlemen and no pay', but was persuaded to change his mind. The high rates of pay, ten guineas a sheet (of sixteen pages), which soon rose to sixteen guineas, set a standard which successive reviews struggled to match. But a marker had been put down which was crucial to the future development of criticism. Jeffrey's reviewers regarded themselves as gentlemen, and therefore amateurs, and the generous scale of payment made reviewing worthwhile. The policy of anonymity, which was practised by all the quarterly reviews, offered protection, so it was argued, to public and professional men who could voice their opinions on a range of subjects without fear of exposure or reprisal. They spoke with a collective voice, employing the corporate 'we', to which all in theory subscribed. Anonymity in turn afforded considerable powers to editors, whose task it was to establish the cultural authority of their reviews, and who could alter the work of their contributors with impunity. It was the collective voice of the periodical rather than the individual voice of the reviewer which exuded authority.

The quarterlies were serious, general reviews which included a broad spectrum of subjects in their remit. Their approach to knowledge, as Marilyn Butler has observed, was non-hierarchical and non-specialized.[7] Reviews of contemporary poetry, fiction and drama occupied a relatively small proportion of their contents. Jeffrey's famous comment that the *Edinburgh* stood on two legs, 'literature no doubt is one of them, but its Right leg is politics',[8] was applicable to the 'great triumvirate' of early quarterlies, the Whig-affiliated *Edinburgh*, the Tory *Quarterly*, founded in response to the *Edinburgh* in 1809, and the Radical *Westminster*, established in 1824. The quarterlies established later also had specific, though not always political agendas, among them the *Foreign Quarterly* (1827), devoted to European literature and thought; the *Dublin Review* (1836), the organ of the Catholic revival; the short-lived, Oxford-supported *London Review* (1829); its namesake the *London Review* (1835), which amalgamated with the *Westminster* in 1836; and the *British and Foreign Review* (1835), with its focus on contemporary European politics.

6  Walter Bagehot, 'The First Edinburgh Reviewers' in *Literary Studies*, ed. R. H. Hutton, 2 vols. (London: Longmans, Green, 1884), vol. I, p. 6; [Margaret Oliphant], 'New Books', *Blackwood's Magazine*, 126 (1879), p. 92.
7  Marilyn Butler, 'Culture's Medium: The Role of the Reviews' in *The Cambridge Companion to British Romanticism*, ed. Stuart Curran (Cambridge University Press, 1993), pp. 120–47.
8  Francis Jeffrey, *Contributions to the Edinburgh Review*, 4 vols. (London: Longman, 1844), vol. I, pp. xiv–xv.

Other mainly sectarian quarterlies were founded at mid-century: the
*North British* (1844), initially the organ of the Free Church of Scotland;
the nonconformist *British Quarterly* (1845); the High Church *Christian
Remembrancer* (1845); the Methodist *London Quarterly* (1853); and
the liberal Catholic *Home and Foreign* (1862). These were among the
reviews whose sectarian affiliations Arnold was to deplore in his essay
'The Function of Criticism at the Present Time', published in 1864. The
quarterlies founded from the 1840s onward were swimming against the
tide. The bulky reviews dominated the first four decades of the nineteenth
century in terms of critical and political influence. But their heyday was
over by the end of the 1830s, as the emergence of a responsible newspaper
press began to erode their political power, and the length of their articles
proved unattractive to a growing middle-class readership.

The quarterlies' expansiveness and with it their selectivity had been
developed in response to their predecessors, the *Monthly* (1756), the
*Critical* (1757) and later the *Analytical* (1788) reviews, which provided
summaries or abstracts of a wide range of publications, with a minimum
of critical commentary. But Derek Roper has shown that contrary to
popular perception the older monthlies actually contained substantial
critical assessments. Nevertheless the quarterlies prided themselves on
being selective in the books they reviewed, and robust and opinionated
in their critical judgements, in contrast to the encyclopedic model of the
monthlies, whose purpose was to keep readers abreast of the state of
knowledge in all fields.[9] Each quarterly number was approximately 250
octavo pages in length, containing between eight and ten articles.

A book was deemed to be important by virtue of its selection for
review, according to the *Edinburgh*'s prospectus. What was described
as its 'slashing' or 'damnatory'[10] style of criticism, directed by Jeffrey
and his colleagues at contemporary poetry and fiction, was notorious in
its day, and roundly condemned later. The *Quarterly*'s equivalent was
scarcely more temperate. By the 1830s the tone of the literary reviews
in the quarterlies had become more measured. The quarterlies founded
at mid-century eclipsed the original three in the quality and quantity of
their reviews of contemporary literature, particularly their response to
new fiction. But the length of their articles and their frequency ultimately
proved their undoing. More than one observer termed their articles 'dis-
sertations', and warned that their length and the inability to respond
quickly would become a disadvantage.[11]

[9] Derek Roper, *Reviewing before the Edinburgh 1788–1802* (Newark: University of
   Delaware Press, 1978), p. 19. See also ch. 1, pp. 19–48.
[10] The phrase was Coleridge's in *Biographia Literaria*, ch. 21.
[11] See James Mill's attack on the *Edinburgh* and the *Quarterly*, 'Periodical Literature: The
   Edinburgh Review', *Westminster Review*, 1 (1824), 206–49.

Their price of between four and six shillings was an indication of their readership. Jon Klancher has argued that reviews like the *Edinburgh* were powerful instruments for creating a middle-class reading audience in the nineteenth century, one based not on rank or social order, as had been the case with eighteenth-century reviews, but whose determinants were essentially economic.[12] Jeffrey himself estimated the *Edinburgh*'s readers as 'some twenty thousand' among 'fashionable or public life', by which he meant civil servants, the clergy, upwardly mobile merchants and manufacturers, the gentry and professionals, all earning more than eight hundred a year. In 1812 he gave an estimate of a further 200,000 of the so-called 'middling classes' who might be attracted to the review. By middling classes, he explained, 'we mean almost all those who are below the sphere of what is called fashionable or public life, and who do not aim at distinctions or notoriety beyond the circle of their equals in fortune and situation'.[13] The circulation figures which exist suggest that his first estimate, some 20,000, was the more likely readership of the *Edinburgh* and also the *Quarterly*, at the height of their influence. But the sense of a potential audience comprised of the expanding 'middling classes' was astute, and proleptic.[14]

It was just such an audience that a group of recently established magazines sought to capture with a new style of reviewing and some innovative features in the 1830s. The ambitious and commercially minded publisher Henry Colburn had launched his *New Monthly Magazine* in 1814, aimed at middle-class readers, and with both a political and a literary agenda. He began a new series in 1821, under the editorship of the poet Thomas Campbell, this time with a more pointedly literary focus. Campbell was succeeded in turn as editor in 1831 by the novelist Bulwer-Lytton. *Blackwood's Edinburgh Magazine* was established by the Edinburgh publisher William Blackwood in 1817 as another Tory challenge to the *Edinburgh*. The *London Magazine* under the charismatic John Scott was founded in 1820, also in response to *Blackwood's*, attracting De Quincey, Lamb and Hazlitt as contributors. Its title indicated its position within a metropolitan literary culture, as distinct from the implied and unashamed provincialism of its rival. In 1830 *Fraser's Magazine for Town and Country* was launched by the publisher William Fraser, with a Tory agenda and sharing many of Blackwood's contributors. In 1832, the radical publisher William Tait challenged Blackwood on his home territory by founding

12   Jon Klancher, *The Making of English Reading Audiences 1790–1832* (Madison: University of Wisconsin Press, 1987), pp. 50–2.
13   John Clive, *Scotch Reviewers: The Edinburgh Review 1802–1815* (London: Faber, 1957), pp. 143–4.
14   See Joanne Shattock, *Politics and Reviewers: The Edinburgh and the Quarterly in the Early Victorian Age* (Leicester University Press, 1989), pp. 97–100.

*Tait's Edinburgh Magazine*, which soon claimed, with reason, to outsell its rival in Scotland.

The magazines deliberately targeted a large and growing readership, one which was closer to Jeffrey's 'middling classes' than that of the quarterlies. It was a readership, too, which included women, one of the acknowledged 'blind spots' of the quarterlies.[15] The personality-dominated and often scurrilous literary reviewing of the Regency was evolving into a more polite and scholarly mode in the magazines of the thirties. The practice of 'puffing', the term used to describe the blatant promotion of a publisher's list by reviewers in his employment, had died down by the 1830s, although Thomas Hood alleged that it was still going on in Colburn's *New Monthly* as late as 1843.[16] Literary reviews were unsigned, but some contributors were identifiable by an initial or a pseudonym. The acquisition of well-known contributors was often an open secret, leading to an early version of the celebrity or 'star system' which became a feature of late nineteenth-century journalism. The *London Magazine*'s meteoric reputation, and also those of *Fraser's* and the *New Monthly*, owed much to their illustrious contributors.

The magazines had a number of stratagems for involving readers. *Blackwood's* 'Noctes Ambrosianae', a series of dialogues or conversations in an Edinburgh tavern (Ambrose's), which ran between 1822 and 1835, sought to engage its readers by inviting a response to its high-spirited and sometimes outrageous criticism and comment. The *London Magazine*'s equivalent 'Lion's Head' series was a kind of literary gossip column.[17] Literary reviews in the magazines, like all of their features, were shorter and more informal in tone than those in the quarterlies. The emphasis on the literary was a deliberate antidote to the magazines' political agendas. Leigh Hunt advised William Tait to profit from Henry Colburn's experience: 'Politics are undoubtedly the great thing just now... but a magazine, I am sure, is the better for having a good deal of its ground broken up into smaller and more flowery beds; and the people in London have been complaining of the excess of politics in the New Monthly.'[18]

With their octavo format, the magazines resembled the quarterlies in appearance, but individual numbers were shorter, from 100 to 120

---

[15] See Stuart Curran, 'Women and the *Edinburgh Review*' in *British Romanticism and the Edinburgh Review*, eds. M. Demata and Duncan Wu (London: Palgrave, 2002), pp. 195–208.

[16] See Brake, *Subjugated Knowledges*, p. 20.

[17] On both features, see Mark Parker, *Literary Magazines and British Romanticism* (Cambridge University Press, 2000).

[18] Quoted in L. A. Brewer, *My Hunt Library* (Iowa City: Iowa University Press, 1938), p. 198.

pages. Articles averaged ten to fifteen pages. Many magazines used double columns, a signal that they were not to be regarded as multiple parts of a book, which was the image projected by the quarterlies, with their good-quality paper, generous margins and clear type. The range of subjects for review was narrower, the magazines again deliberately eschewing theology, ancient literatures and other scholarly subjects in favour of poetry, drama, history, art and the novel in acknowledgement of the tastes of their readers. With their now more polite emphasis on personalities, which extended even to the editor (*Blackwood's* 'Ebony' and *Fraser's* mythical 'Oliver Yorke'), and their willingness to experiment, as in the 'Noctes' or *Fraser's* illustrated 'Gallery of Illustrious Literary Characters', the magazines of the 1830s – *Tait's, Fraser's, Blackwood's,* the *New Monthly* and the *Metropolitan* – were effectively literary miscellanies, rather than literary magazines. Selling at between two shillings and sixpence and three shillings and sixpence, they successfully courted a new and expanding middle-class readership, and paved the way for the shilling monthlies of the 1850s and 1860s, which even more successfully blended publishers' interests and readers' demands.

*Macmillan's Magazine*, established in November 1859 by the Cambridge publishing house of Macmillan, and the *Cornhill Magazine*, founded in January 1860 by George Smith, of Smith, Elder and Co., revolutionized the role of the monthly magazine. Fiction featured prominently as entire novels by eminent contemporaries were serialized in successive issues. This was combined with criticism of current publications, avoiding politics, and in the case of the *Cornhill*, religion, in tacit recognition of the family and in particular the female readership of the new-style magazines. The *Cornhill's* first editor was Thackeray, a further endorsement of its literary focus. *Macmillan's* was edited by David Masson, a prominent critic and a professor of literature. The most significant feature of the new magazines was their price of a shilling.[19] *Macmillan's* took another important step in allowing a large proportion of articles to be signed. The unprecedented sales of the first number of the *Cornhill*, in the region of 100,000, soon stabilized at 20,000. The sales of *Macmillan's* were half that number, because the authors of its serialized fiction were less well known. Its reviewing, on the other hand, was undertaken by authoritative specialists, among them Arnold and Walter Pater. Under the editorship of Leslie Stephen (1871–82) the *Cornhill's* critics included Arnold, R. L. Stevenson, Edmund Gosse, J. A. Symonds and Stephen himself. With the emergence of *Macmillan's* and the *Cornhill* it became possible to

[19] *Tait's Edinburgh Magazine* became the first of the so-called shilling monthlies when it dropped its price from two shillings and sixpence to a shilling in 1834.

identify a culture of serious 'literary' reviewing in the magazines, as distinct from the more wide-ranging, mandarin cultural criticism offered by the quarterlies, and the free-wheeling, personality-driven experiments of the magazines of the 1830s.

Frequency had become an increasingly relevant factor in reviewing. The emergence of two new monthly reviews in the 1860s reinforced the general impatience with the leisurely rhythm of the quarterlies. The *Fortnightly Review*, established in 1865, was intended 'to be for England what the *Revue des Deux Mondes* was for France'.[20] It was published twice monthly. Emulating its continental forebear, the *Fortnightly* promised that its contributors would be free to express their own views, independent of an editor or of a party.[21] Its policy of signed articles and an 'open platform' for discussion was to have a profound impact on the reviews which followed.

Although several publications experimented with it, fortnightly publication did not catch on, and after eighteen months the *Fortnightly* became a monthly. Its first editor, G. H. Lewes, attracted a strong corps of reviewers, including his partner the novelist George Eliot, Walter Bagehot, the positivist Frederic Harrison and the scientist J. F. W. Herschel. Trollope's *The Belton Estate* was serialized in the first number.

The *Contemporary Review*, which was founded the following year, in 1866, copied the *Fortnightly*'s policy of signature and an open platform. Under its second editor, James Knowles, its core contributors were closely linked to the newly established Metaphysical Society, a group of prominent intellectuals brought together to debate the religious and philosophical issues of the day. It was this group that Knowles took with him when he founded another new monthly, the magisterially titled *The Nineteenth Century*, in 1877. Knowles's success in attracting eminent reviewers whose names or initials were appended to their articles led to charges of lion-hunting, and with it an acknowledgement that a 'star system' had emerged in the world of reviewing.

The *Fortnightly*, the *Contemporary* and the *Nineteenth Century* shaped public opinion on a wide range of issues, philosophical, political and religious as well as literary from the 1860s onwards. In their range of influence they resembled the quarterlies in the first two decades of the century. As the scholar and critic Mark Pattison commented in 1877, 'those venerable old wooden three-deckers, the *Edinburgh Review* and the *Quarterly Review*, still put out to sea under the command, I believe,

---

[20]  T. H. S. Escott, *Anthony Trollope* (London, 1913), p. 173, as quoted in the *Wellesley Index to Victorian Periodicals*, ed. W. E. Houghton, 5 vols. (London: Routledge, 1972), vol. II, p. 173.
[21]  As stated in the *Saturday Review* for 25 March 1865. See *Wellesley*, vol. II, p. 173.

of the Ancient Mariner, but the active warfare of opinion is conducted by the three new iron monitors, the *Fortnightly*, the *Contemporary*, and the *Nineteenth Century*'.[22]

The *Nineteenth Century*'s and the *Contemporary*'s price of two shillings and sixpence, and the *Fortnightly*'s two shillings, compared favourably with the six shillings now universally charged by the quarterlies. Price, frequency and the size of audience were inextricably linked. 'Men at the present date live too fast for the slow-going quarterlies... The great daily newspaper is the kind of journalism', an American weekly, soon to become a daily, observed after the demise of the *North British Review* in 1871.[23] The length of review articles was also relevant. 'Long-winded literary articles are going out of date; and a good thing too. They never fell properly within the province of the "dailies"', the journalist Innes Shand grumbled in *Blackwood's* in 1878.[24] Both comments signalled the growing impact of newspapers, but apart from *The Times*, the daily press was slow to institute regular features on contemporary literature until the 1890s.

Weekly papers, on the other hand, had made a point of reviewing poetry, fiction and the arts generally, beginning with Colburn's *Literary Gazette* in 1817. As a format the weekly maintained its appeal throughout the century, priced between four and six pence, and covering a wide range of subjects, including politics. The *Athenaeum*, founded in 1828, sustained a reputation for responsible reviewing into the twentieth century. The *Spectator* (1828) and the *Examiner* (1808), two equally long-lived general weeklies, reviewed literature, the proportion dependent on the preferences of the editor of the day. The *Critic of Literature, Art, Science, and the Drama* (1843), originally a department of the *Law Times*, had a strong literary focus, much of its reviewing done by George Gilfillan and Francis Espinasse. Its frequency fluctuated between monthly, weekly and fortnightly over its twenty-year history. The *Leader*, founded jointly in 1850 by G. H. Lewes and Thornton Hunt, was a radical publication aimed at an artisan as well as a middle-class readership. Lewes was responsible for the literary reviewing, much of which he did himself. In consequence the *Leader*'s criticism of both the novel and contemporary drama in the 1850s was some of the most distinctive and distinguished of the period.

The abolition of the stamp duty on newspapers in 1855 had an impact on the numbers of weeklies as well as dailies. J. D. Cook's *Saturday*

---

[22]  Mark Pattison, 'Books and Critics', *Fortnightly Review*, 22 (1877), p. 663.
[23]  Quoted by F. L. Mott, *American Magazines 1865–1880* (Iowa City: Midland Press, 1928), p. 11.
[24]  Innes Shand, 'Contemporary Literature I: Journalists', *Blackwood's Magazine*, 124 (1878), p. 661.

*Review*, established in 1855, offered its own brand of opinionated criticism with a Tory slant, and revitalized the role of the general weekly at mid-century. Following the success of their magazine, Macmillan's established the *Reader: A Review of Current Literature* in 1863. Like the magazine, the weekly *Reader* drew on the firm's authors and supporters. It also had a specific brief to review scientific and religious subjects in the wake of the controversy surrounding the publication of Darwin's *Origin of Species* in 1859. A range of sectarian weeklies, among them the Roman Catholic *Tablet* and the Church of England *Guardian*, reviewed contemporary literature in the middle decades of the century.

The foundation of the aptly titled *Academy* in 1869 was a sign of things to come. Established by Charles Appleton, an Oxford don, and published by John Murray, the *Academy* modelled itself on the German *Litterarisches Centralblatt* and the French *Revue critique*. Its object was to promote scholarly standards of criticism across a spectrum of disciplines, with the universities both its target audience and initially the main source of its contributors. Gradually, as it moved from monthly to fortnightly and then to weekly publication, its tone lightened, and it expanded the ranks of its reviewers to admit men of letters like Andrew Lang, Edmund Gosse and George Saintsbury. But the tensions within the *Academy* between academic specialists and general reviewers, the scholars versus the 'belletrists', were symptomatic of larger tensions within criticism generally. The *Academy*'s attractions for specialist reviewers would influence the development of academic journals in individual disciplines, including English literature, once they began to be taught in the universities.

The founding of a number of cheaper reviews, both weekly and monthly, from the mid-1880s onward testified to the popularity of shorter articles and to the demand for serious reviewing at popular prices. W. Robertson Nicoll's *British Weekly* (1886) and later the monthly *Bookman* (1891), and W. E. Henley's weekly *Scots Observer*, later the *National Observer* (1888), attracted eminent reviewers and also published contemporary poetry and fiction. The *New Review* (1889), its title designed to capture the vogue for all things 'new' at the *fin de siècle*, attracted a group of young and energetic writers, particularly under Henley's editorship from 1895. These included Gosse, James, Hardy, Olive Schreiner, Shaw, Stevenson, Kipling and Yeats.

The alacrity with which publishers wooed the public with new journals coupled with the vogue for shorter articles in the 1880s was, like the establishment of the *Academy* a decade earlier, an indication of future trends. Literary criticism was beginning to channel itself into two competing streams, one the preserve of scholars and specialists and the other of mainly metropolitan men and women of letters, professional in their reviewing, but determinedly non-academic and non-specialist in their approach.

Female reviewers were in a minority in the world of the quarterlies and the monthly magazines from the 1830s through to the 1850s. Notable exceptions like Harriet Martineau, single, independent and earning her living by her pen, as she proudly professed, presented themselves as operating within a man's world and abiding by its rules. Christian Isobel Johnstone was ahead of her time when in 1832 she began a fourteen-year-long association with *Tait's Edinburgh Magazine*. Johnstone had, with her husband, conducted two earlier Scottish publications, and in 1834 become the de facto editor of *Tait's* as well as contributing the major portion of the literary reviews.[25] Anonymity protected Marian Evans at the *Westminster* where she too effectively performed the function of associate editor, and wrote a substantial number of full-length as well as shorter reviews. Eliza Lynn Linton moved from Keswick to London in the 1840s to further a writing career. She was taken on by J. D. Cook at the *Saturday Review* and later boasted that she was the first female journalist to be paid a regular salary. Anna Jameson, Anne Mozley, Hannah Lawrance, Maria Jane and Geraldine Jewsbury were among a small band of women reviewers who gradually made inroads into the predominantly masculine world of literary criticism up to the mid-century.

Margaret Oliphant's forty-year-long association with *Blackwood's Magazine* began in the 1850s. As well as serializing her fiction in the magazine she became one of its most prolific reviewers. At the end of her career she was to lament that the ultimate accolade in the world of letters, the editorship of a serious journal, was denied her.[26] Successful popular novelists, notably Mary Elizabeth Braddon and Ellen Wood, became editors of *Belgravia* and the *Argosy* in the 1860s on the strength of their reputations, but these were not journals of opinion. Christian Johnstone and Marian Evans exercised editorial power, but without public acknowledgement. In general, female reviewers before the 1890s, however able, could not participate in the public world of letters, the gatherings round editorial tables at *Blackwood's* and *Fraser's*, the clubs or the networks which emanated from the universities. In consequence the larger prizes – editorships, the publication of collected essays and public recognition – eluded them.

---

[25]  See Joanne Shattock, 'Reviews and Monthlies' in *The Edinburgh History of the Book in Scotland*, 4 vols. (Edinburgh University Press, 2007), vol. III, pp. 355–6, and Alexis Easley, *First Person Anonymous: Women Writers and Victorian Print Media, 1830–1870* (Aldershot: Ashgate, 2004), pp. 61–79.

[26]  See Elisabeth Jay, *Mrs Oliphant: 'A Fiction to Herself'* (Oxford University Press, 1995), esp. ch. 7.

By the 1870s there were more opportunities for women. The *Athenaeum* opened its poetry columns to a number of women poets, among them Mathilde Blind, Edith Nesbit, Mary Robinson, Rosamond Marriott Watson and Augusta Webster.[27] Newer publications like the *National Observer*, the *New Review*, and the *Woman's World* under the editorship of Oscar Wilde in the 1890s gave encouragement to women contributors. The conspicuous absence of women as reviewers as well as reviewing subjects in the early decades of the nineteenth century had by its end been at least partially remedied.

Christopher Kent has termed the 'higher journalism', represented by reviews like the *Fortnightly*, the *Contemporary*, the *Nineteenth Century*, the *Saturday* and the *Academy*, as 'one of the most characteristic cultural manifestations of nineteenth-century Britain', and has linked its emergence with the reforms and expansion of the ancient universities at mid-century.[28] Increasing numbers of self-confident graduates looking for opportunities beyond the bar, the church and the universities, or in combination with them, flocked to the new journals. The fact that it was now possible to earn one's living by writing for the periodical press meant that the same 'profession-consciousness', as Kent termed it, attached itself to the world of reviewing as to other professional occupations. Literary critics – and the term was used self-consciously in preference to 'reviewers' – now saw themselves as professionals, and the production of literary criticism as a professional rather than amateur occupation.

Consequently the status and function of criticism, together with the role of the critic, were under constant debate from the 1850s onward. The first signal for reflection and retrospection was prompted by the publication of the collected essays and later the memoirs and correspondence of the first generation of *Edinburgh* reviewers. These were reviewed by Walter Bagehot, David Masson, Leslie Stephen and John Morley, a new generation of reviewers, professional in outlook, holding or poised to inherit editorships of influential journals, and full of self-confidence:

Let us speak the plain truth at once. Everyone who turns from the periodical literature of the present day to the original 'Edinburgh Review' will be amazed at its inferiority. It is generally dull, and when not dull flimsy . . . One may most easily characterise the contents by saying that few of the articles would have a chance of acceptance by the editor of a first-rate periodical today.

Leslie Stephen's assertion, written as editor of the *Cornhill* in 1878, echoed the sentiments of his colleagues. The difference between then and

---

[27]  See Marysa Demoor, *Their Fair Share: Women, Power and Criticism in the Athenaeum, from Millicent Garrett Fawcett to Katherine Mansfield 1870–1920* (Aldershot: Ashgate, 2000).
[28]  Kent, 'Higher Journalism', p. 181.

now, according to Stephen, was that the earlier reviewers had not been sufficiently professional: 'The chief contributors were in no sense men who looked upon literature as a principal occupation.'[29] For David Masson, reviewing Cockburn's *Life* of Jeffrey in 1852 'the sketchy "beauty and blemish" species of criticism in which Jeffrey excelled... has been succeeded, at least in all our higher periodicals, by a kind of criticism intrinsically deeper and more laborious'.[30] John Morley, with an exaggerated flourish, declared that: 'Of literary ability of a good and serviceable kind, there is a hundred or five hundred times more in the country than there was when Jeffrey, Smith, Brougham and Horner devised their Review in a ninth story in Edinburgh seventy-six years ago.'[31]

The confidence of the new generation of critics was palpable. But there were also anxieties. Writing in the *Fortnightly* in 1882, prompted by a recent article in the *Revue des deux mondes* about the 'decay' of French criticism, the novelist and critic Grant Allen pronounced English criticism as coming into its own: 'Just at the moment when the critical impulse is dying out in France, it has begun to live in England.' English critics owed much to their French colleagues: 'they have learnt much from the Villemains and the Sainte-Beuves on the one hand, from the Taines, the Renans, and even the Gautiers on the other'. But the current demand for shorter articles, and the limitations imposed by the daily and weekly press, were posing a serious threat to the authority and the integrity of criticism:

the state of the periodical press makes serious criticism an absolute impossibility. Journalism no longer demands either special aptitude, special training, or special function. Nowadays, any man can write, because there are papers enough to give employment to everybody. No reflection, no deliberation, no care: all is haste, fatal facility, stock phrases, commonplace ideas, and a ready pen that can turn itself to any task with equal ease because supremely ignorant of all alike.

There were far too many publications producing reviews, far too many books being published. As a result 'critics' were becoming 'reviewers', forced to provide summaries of books and snap judgements:

Look at the space placed at the disposal of each reviewer... does not the mere word 'reviewer' call up a wonderfully different mental concept from the word 'critic'? Well, the reviewer has to say what he has got to say in some two or

29  Leslie Stephen, 'The First Edinburgh Reviewers', *Cornhill Magazine*, 38 (1878); rpt in *Hours in a Library*, new edn, 3 vols. (London: Smith, Elder, 1899), vol. III, pp. 243–4, 248.
30  [David Masson], 'Lord Cockburn's *Life* of Jeffrey', *North British Review*, 17 (1852), p. 322.
31  John Morley, 'Memorials of a Man of Letters', *Fortnightly Review*, 23 (1878); rpt in *Nineteenth-Century Essays*, ed. Peter Stansky (University of Chicago Press, 1970), p. 269.

three short columns at the outside. How absurdly inadequate for anything like real criticism![32]

The distinction between 'reviewer' and 'critic' was one that could only have been made in the second half of the century. The first generation of quarterly reviewers saw themselves as writing what Walter Bagehot dubbed 'the review-like essay and the essay-like review'.[33] The typical review essay was earnest, discursive, sometimes rich in information, often prodigal of quotation. Some reviewers used the book under review as a 'peg', in the jargon of the day, on which to hang a much broader discussion. To Frederick Oakley, writing anonymously in the *Dublin Review* in 1853, the essay was *the* genre of present times. The age preferred it to books and treatises. The essay was a form which shared 'the character of earnest conversation', and one which more than any other literary form could be regarded as 'a simple transcript of the writer's mind'.[34]

But the discursive essay, like the expansive quarterlies which nurtured and developed it, was no longer what the modern, less well-educated reader wanted. Allen's argument, however, was not with the demise of the essay, but rather with the conditions of criticism at the present time. The authoritative and intellectual role which he envisaged for literary criticism could not, in his view, be delivered by the shorter review articles now in fashion, and the timescale in which the critic was required to write. But the alternative, a more specialized, scholarly criticism based in the universities, whose end product was the lengthy monograph, was equally detrimental to the health of criticism. Specialism was rampant in the universities, he argued, and it was a 'second-hand German specialism'. There was a danger that English critics were 'a little over-anxious to convert ourselves forthwith into the image of the fashionable Teutonic monographist'.[35]

In *Conditions for Criticism* Ian Small argues that there were profound changes in the nature of intellectual authority in all disciplines at the end of the nineteenth century.[36] The changes in literary criticism between 1865 and 1900, he suggests, paralleled the development of English literature as an academic discipline. By the turn of the century literary criticism, like the study of history, philosophy, theology and the sciences, was on its way to becoming the preserve of university departments. The authority and prestige of the general critic, the man of letters, was under threat from the professor and the don.

---

[32]  Grant Allen, 'The Decay of Criticism', *Fortnightly Review*, 31 (1882), pp. 342, 344, 347.
[33]  Bagehot, 'The First Edinburgh Reviewers', p. 6.
[34]  [Frederick Oakley], 'Periodical Literature', *Dublin Review*, 34 (1853), p. 544.
[35]  Allen, 'Decay of Criticism', pp. 350–1.
[36]  Ian Small, *Conditions for Criticism: Authority, Knowledge, and Literature in the Late Nineteenth Century* (Oxford: Clarendon Press, 1991).

The conflict was symbolized by a famous attack in the *Quarterly Review* in 1886 by John Churton Collins, an Oxford-educated classicist, on the scholarly standards of Edmund Gosse, the quintessential late Victorian 'man of letters'. The attack focused on Gosse's recent Clark lectures, given in Cambridge and published in his book *From Shakespeare to Pope* in 1885. Valentine Cunningham has suggested that the Gosse–Collins feud is an allegory for what he sees as the 'false dichotomy' between 'literary scholarship', as practised in universities, and the work of the critic or reviewer 'on the street', the journalist, the belletrist; a dichotomy which, he argues, still exists.[37] At the time, the furore touched a raw nerve. Collins's charge was that Gosse's slovenly scholarship and hasty judgements were symptomatic of current reviewing practices, the work of so-called 'professional' critics in the periodical press, who were reviewing too quickly and superficially. The urbane and metropolitan Gosse had eloquent and eminent defenders, Henry James, Browning and Tennyson among them. The provincial Collins (he became the first Professor of English Literature at the University of Birmingham in 1905) was an uninspiring representative of the new breed of literary scholar. But in his espousal of specialist scholarship based in the academy he was a symbol of the future of literary criticism. The process was a gradual one, but Allen's concern about the current malaise of criticism in the press, and his dismay at the possibility of criticism in the form of turgid monographs, were, in 1882, far-sighted.

The gradual abandonment of anonymity in favour of signed articles in the 1860s was linked to new attitudes to criticism and to the role of the critic. Few reviews before the 1860s carried the name of the author. Anonymity was absolute in the quarterlies, and for the most part in the magazines and weeklies, although, as has been noted, some contributions carried an initial or occasionally a pseudonym. The well-rehearsed defences of the old system – that it enabled editors to establish a unified, corporate voice for their journals; that it provided opportunities to little-known reviewers, whereas signature demanded established names; that it offered protection and freedom to eminent public figures – no longer stood up in the new reviewing climate. The discussion had been ongoing for more than a decade and still the arguments were finely balanced.[38] Some converts to signature found themselves arguing, paradoxically, that signature would force critics to produce what was expected of them, whereas

---

37  Valentine Cunningham, 'Darke Conceits: Churton Collins, Edmund Gosse, and the Professions of Criticism' in *Grub Street and the Ivory Tower*, eds. Jeremy Treglown and Bridget Bennett (Oxford: Clarendon Press, 1998), p. 75.

38  See Oscar Maurer, 'Anonymity vs Signature in Victorian Reviewing', *Texas Studies in English*, 27 (1948), 1–28, and Dallas Liddle, 'Salesmen, Sportsmen, Mentors: Anonymity and Mid-Victorian Theories of Journalism', *Victorian Studies*, 41 (1997), 31–68, for the arguments on each side.

anonymity would provide the truest freedom of expression. Experienced editors like John Morley when taking over the *Fortnightly* found himself genuinely divided on the issue, even though the *Fortnightly* had made signature one of its most important innovations.[39]

In practice authorship had always been a badly kept secret, and gossip in literary and political circles was full of revelations of who was responsible for the latest articles and reviews. The anonymous system was also open to abuse. It was not unusual for reviewers to review the same book more than once, making minor adjustments, or adroitly cutting and pasting to produce a 'new' article in a different journal. De Quincey was adept at making the most of his material in order to accommodate the several periodicals to which he was committed. Coventry Patmore, who undertook extensive reviewing of modern poetry for the *Edinburgh*, the *North British* and *Macmillan's* in the 1850s, cynically plagiarized one of his own articles. Stories of such practices were legion in the lore of nineteenth-century (and twentieth-century) reviewing, but it would have been much more difficult to pull off had contributions been signed.[40]

The growth in professionalism amongst critics was followed by a call for responsible reviewing. Journals like the *Fortnightly* and the *Contemporary* were no longer willing to cede ultimate authority to the editor, but relied on the attraction of named contributors. The influence of French journals on English practice in this respect, and the *Revue des deux mondes* in particular, was considerable. Later in the century, in 1893, the novelist Emile Zola, an experienced reviewer, extolled the virtues of signature in literary criticism by emphasizing its individualism:

In criticism, as we understand it, there is a creative function which distinguishes it from a mere summary or report. It calls for personal penetration, for logical power, not to mention a very wide erudition. All this constitutes a very distinct individuality, capable of producing a work of its own. Here, then, it is desirable that the articles should be signed, because the writer stands out from the ranks.[41]

By this time he was speaking to the converted. Even the daily press had begun to introduce signed articles by the 1890s. The quarterlies were among the last to relinquish anonymity. The *Edinburgh's* contributions remained anonymous until 1912. The *Athenaeum's* and *Spectator's* reviews were unsigned until the end of the century. But by the 1880s a large proportion of literary reviews bore the signature of their authors.

In his article on 'The Condition of Authors in England, Germany and France' in *Fraser's Magazine* for 1847 G. H. Lewes asserted that

---

[39]  See Kent, 'Higher Journalism', pp. 195–6.
[40]  See Joanne Shattock, 'Spreading it Thinly: Some Victorian Reviewers at Work', *Victorian Periodicals Newsletter*, 9 (1976), 84–7.
[41]  See Maurer, 'Anonymity vs Signature', p. 23.

'Literature has become a profession. It is a means of subsistence, almost as certain as the bar or the church.'[42] An average journalist in England would be unlucky if he did not earn between £200 and £1,000 a year, according to Lewes. The same was not true for his counterparts in Germany and France, where it was impossible to live by one's pen, where payments for newspaper and periodical articles were much less, and where the range of weekly, monthly and quarterly publications open to the English journalist did not exist. The highest rate currently offered by the *Revue des deux mondes*, whose contributors included Victor Cousin, Rémusat, Sainte-Beuve and Alfred de Musset, was £10 (250 francs) a sheet, less than the rate established by Jeffrey at the *Edinburgh* in 1802.

With his interests in European literature – he was soon to embark upon his life of Goethe – and his personal contacts among literary figures on the continent, Lewes was well placed to comment on the literary profession in Europe. In his insistence that writing for the press should not be regarded as a trade, he was entering a long-running debate about the status of journalism, in which careful lines were drawn between writing for the newspaper press, which had tradesman-like connotations, and writing for quarterly reviews, which was deemed the role of gentlemen. The distinction was no longer a live issue by the 1840s, but Lewes's point about criticism as a profession was ahead of its time. It was to surface, as we have seen, in the retrospective reflections on the first generation of *Edinburgh* reviewers. In nineteenth-century Scotland, as Grevel Lindop has pointed out, there was a 'fluid' frontier between academic and journalistic worlds, and authors, editors, publishers and professors exchanged roles with ease, thus making it difficult to separate critics into a specific social group. And as Frederick Oakley suggested in 1853, the press had 'furnished the ladder by which so many remarkable men have risen to distinction'.[43]

The conduct of a professional literary life, the process of establishing oneself as a reviewer and earning a living by it, evolved over the period. Up to the 1850s, reviewers were usually recommended to editors through personal contacts. Payment was the only form of contract and writers moved freely between journals. The *Edinburgh* and the *Foreign Quarterly* regularly shared reviewers. The same was true of *Blackwood's* and *Fraser's*. De Quincey began with *Blackwood's*, whose conservative politics were closest to his own, moved to the radical *Tait's* in 1833 when Blackwood rejected one of his articles, and kept both in play over a period of nearly

---

[42] Lewes, 'Condition of Authors', p. 285.
[43] Grevel Lindop, 'DeQuincey and the Edinburgh and Glasgow University Circles' in Treglown and Bennett, *Grub Street*, p. 45; [Oakley], 'Periodical Literature', p. 549.

twenty years, while also writing for *Hogg's Instructor* and *Titan* in the 1850s. When writing his 1847 article for *Fraser's* Lewes had first-hand experience of *Bentley's Miscellany*, *Blackwood's*, the *British and Foreign*, *Fraser's*, the *British Quarterly*, the *Edinburgh*, the *Foreign Quarterly*, the *Monthly Chronicle* and the *Westminster*. He was soon to add the *Leader*, the *Cornhill*, the *Fortnightly* and the *Pall Mall Gazette*.

The agreements between reviewer and editor were in principle only, with reviewers suggesting broad areas in which they would like to review, and often specifying subjects they would not undertake. The proposal to review a particular book often came from the reviewer, not the editor. In the gentlemanly world of the quarterlies most reviewers positively disliked being asked to review a specific book. The historian Henry Hallam bridled when Macvey Napier, as editor of the *Edinburgh*, suggested two new works he might review. Dionysius Lardner similarly claimed he could not bring himself to write reviews 'to order'. Later in the century, as Laurel Brake has shown, the process of assigning reviews varied.[44]

Free review copies were unknown. It was assumed that reviewers were responsible for acquiring copies of the books they needed. When John Chapman, as editor of the *Westminster*, wrote to Lewes and Marian Evans, then in Weimar, suggesting that one of them might like to review Victor Cousin's recent book on Madame de Sablé, Marian Evans immediately set off to order it, along with several others she proposed to include in her review. For another *Westminster* article, also commissioned while they were in Germany, she managed to borrow the books from their acquaintances.[45] Carlyle was at a disadvantage when working from Craigenputtoch, 'like an old Hebrew doomed to make Bricks and no straw allowed him', as he told Macvey Napier. When Napier loaned him the three volumes of Taylor's *Historic Survey of German Poetry* for his March 1831 article he impulsively sent them to Goethe at Weimar, and then had to ask that the cost be deducted from his next fee.[46] Reviewers routinely applied to the publisher of the journal for a loan of books for review. John Murray, as editor of the *Quarterly*, belonged to a circulating library for this purpose. C. W. Dilke when editor of the *Athenaeum* bought review copies from bookshops rather than soliciting them from publishers. E. S. Dallas, on the other hand, described a table of review copies at the offices of *The Times*, but this seems not to have been usual practice with the publishers of magazines and reviews.[47]

[44] See Shattock, *Politics and Reviewers*, p. 88; Brake, *Subjugated Knowledges*, p. 11.
[45] See *The George Eliot Letters*, ed. Gordon S. Haight, 9 vols. (New Haven, CT: Yale University Press, 1954–78), vol. I, p. xxx.
[46] Shattock, *Politics and Reviewers*, pp. 120–2.
[47] See Brake, *Subjugated Knowledges*, p. 11.

In general the perks of reviewing were confined to the fee. Only occasionally were books used as payment, as in the case of Macaulay's six-year posting to India, in the mid-1830s, when he arranged to have a selection of recent books in lieu of a fee for his reviews in the *Edinburgh*, as a means of keeping up to date while out of the country.

Few journalists confined themselves to a single subject area, particularly where contemporary writing was concerned. None of the major reviews had literary editors in the modern fashion, nor were there exclusively 'literary' reviewers. 'Popular literature', as contemporary poetry and fiction were often termed before the 1840s, was regarded as a subject on which anyone might have a view, and one to which most reviewers felt able to turn their hands. It mattered little that their main areas of interest or expertise might be politics, science or theology.

Editors could insist on revisions, and in theory at least could radically revise contributions to suit the policy of the journal. Most of the evidence of editorial high-handedness comes from the 1830s and 1840s, as in Carlyle's memorable description of Jeffrey's 'light Editorial hacking and hewing to right and left' with his *Edinburgh* articles, and Harriet Martineau's allegations of interpolation of material into her articles by J. W. Croker and J. G. Lockhart in the *Quarterly*.[48] Henry Reeve, a later editor of the *Edinburgh*, had a reputation for 'revising' articles submitted to him, but in general, with the advent of signature, editorial power over individual reviewers dwindled, and reviewers accepted responsibility for their own articles.

Lewes's 1847 article on 'The Condition of Authors in England, Germany and France' was no doubt accurate in its assessment of the earning potential of his European counterparts. But it signalled too the amount of criticism that was being published across the channel, and the range of journals that sustained it. Half a century later George Saintsbury, in his *A History of Criticism and Literary Taste in Europe* (1904), was to make the same point. Periodicals, he wrote, had 'multiplied criticism and ha[d] multiplied good criticism. It is very difficult to conceive of any other system under which a man like Sainte-Beuve – not of means, and not well adapted to any profession – could have given his life practically to the service of our Muse as he actually did.'[49]

Sainte-Beuve's total output, when collected, ran to between fifty and sixty volumes of essays, almost all of which were first published in newspapers and periodicals. His first reviews were published in the newly

48  Shattock, *Politics and Reviewers*, pp. 64–6, 76–80.
49  George Saintsbury, *A History of Criticism and Literary Taste in Europe, from the Earliest Texts to the Present Day. Vol. 3: Modern Criticism* (Edinburgh and London: Blackwood, 1904), p. 420.

established but short-lived *Globe*, a liberal paper founded in 1824 by Pierre Leroux and P. F. Dubois, which began as a thrice-weekly publication and later became a daily. *Le Globe*'s contributors included the politician and historian Thiers, the social historian A. F. Villemain, J. J. Ampère, a professor of literature and close friend of Sainte-Beuve, Charles de Rémusat, the politician and dramatist, the historian Augustin Thierry, and Théodore Jouffroy, a philosopher and professor at the Ecole Normale Supérieure. Sainte-Beuve contributed more than thirty short pieces to the paper over a six-year period.

He was at the same time writing for the *Journal des débats*, the *Mercure de France* and the London-based *Foreign Quarterly Review*. With the closure of *Le Globe* in 1832 he welcomed an invitation from Louis Véron to write for his newly established *Revue de Paris*. In 1849, again at Véron's invitation, he began to write his famous *Causeries du lundi*, for another of Véron's papers, *Le Constitutionnel*, like *Le Globe* a daily, and the organ of the upper middle-class conservative Bonapartists. Following that, he wrote for *Le Moniteur*, a much older broadsheet which reported foreign and domestic news and had strong government support. At the very end of his life he was to write for *Le Temps*, founded in 1861, as the paper of the governing elite during the Third Republic.

But it was *La Revue des deux mondes*, a bimonthly founded in 1829 by Mauroy and Ségur-Dupeyron, and managed by two generations of the Buloz family, that established itself as the most celebrated of all French reviews in the nineteenth century. Politically liberal, its articles covered politics and economics as well as a wide range of contemporary art and culture, and it included fiction. Its editor from 1831 to 1874 was François Buloz, one of the most influential figures in the French literary world. He was succeeded by his son Charles. Buloz later controlled the *Revue de Paris*, where he published material that he considered below the standard of the *Revue des deux mondes*. Early contributors to the *Revue des deux mondes* included De Musset, Balzac and George Sand as well as Sainte-Beuve, the vast majority of whose critical writing appeared in the journal, beginning in 1831. The number of the *Revue*'s subscribers rose from 1,000 in 1834 to 2,000 in 1843 and 5,000 in 1851. When Buloz retired in 1874 the *Revue* had 18,000 subscribers. Their number increased to 26,000 in 1885 and to 40,000 in 1914.

The *Revue* soon outstripped the daily newspapers as a vehicle for literary criticism. Its articles, lengthy in comparison with those in the newspapers, suited critics like Sainte-Beuve who preferred to write more expansive and reflective pieces. By the 1860s it had become the most widely read of all European reviews. The founders of *Macmillan's Magazine* as well as the *Fortnightly* regarded it as a possible model. Its policy of signature, the norm for all French journals of opinion following a ruling of the French Assembly in 1850, was of crucial importance in the arguments against anonymity in the 1850s and 1860s.

Criticism continued to be published in French newspapers, most writers distinguishing in their own minds between the short, opinionated and popularizing articles required by the newspapers, and the more considered and thoughtful essays demanded by the reviews. Zola was an example of a younger generation whose entry on to the literary scene was sustained by regular reviewing for both the provincial and the Parisian press. The future novelist's motives were mainly financial, but he used his journalism, not all of which was literary reviewing, as an opportunity to bring his name, and his views, before the public. The papers which carried his articles in the period 1865–70 included *Le Petit journal*, *L'Evénement*, *Le Figaro*, *L'Evénement illustré*, *La Tribune*, *Le Gaulois* and *Le Rappel*.[50]

As the nineteenth century progressed, new, more specialized periodicals emerged, established in support of literary movements. *La Revue blanche*, an organ of the Symbolist movement, was founded in 1889. Its contributors included Mallarmé, Henri de Régnier, Debussy, who wrote the music criticism, and the socialist leader Léon Blum, who wrote most of its literary and drama criticism. Academic journals too gradually emerged, some of which were concerned with literary history and with particular periods: *Romania* (1872–), a journal of medieval studies, the *Revue des langues romanes* (1870–) and the *Revue d'histoire littéraire de la France* (1894–). They were soon matched by specialized academic publications in Britain.

German literary criticism in the post-Romantic period was equally prolific, although initially it had less impact on the English reading public. The introduction of the term *Literaturwissenschaft* to denote a distinctive literary scholarship, including literary theory and literary history, in contrast to *Literaturkritik*, or literary journalism, in the 1830s, was to have ramifications across the channel later in the century. As Valentine Cunningham has observed, the distinction between 'the professor [and] the feuilletoniste', as it was commonly labelled in German circles, was replicated in the row between Collins and Gosse, in the tensions between the scholar and the man of letters, and in Grant Allen's anxieties about the 'decay' of criticism.[51]

In the period from 1830 to 1848 the German press played a major role in shaping public opinion, despite the censorship applied to journals, pamphlets and all publications shorter than twenty pages. Critics like Ludwig Börne, Wolfgang Menzel and Heinrich Heine became adept at utilizing

---

50  See F. W. J. Hemmings, 'Zola's Apprenticeship to Journalism 1865–70', *PMLA*, 71 (1956), 340–55.
51  Cunningham, 'Darke Conceits', p. 75.

newspaper articles to debate political questions, often under the guise
of literary or cultural criticism. The 'feuilleton' or cultural supplement
was adopted from the French press. Annual or bi-annual subscriptions
to newspapers became increasingly popular with the public. Writers and
critics belonging to the liberal 'Young German' movement maintained
themselves financially by writing for the press in the 1830s and 1840s.
Journalists were mobile, often moving from place to place in the absence
of a national press. Some, like Heine, moved to Paris, just as later in the
century the novelist Theodor Fontane lived in London for a while and
wrote for *The Times*.

According to one authority, by the early nineteenth century there were
so many magazines and literary periodicals that it was impossible to read
every review or commentary on a particular work.[52] As new publishing
houses were founded, and the production of books increased, the role of
newspaper critics in promoting new works, and of selecting and sorting
new publications for bemused readers, intensified. In 1827 Menzel commented that 'Several hundred journals circulate daily in Germany, covering all literary subjects, being read daily by millions of readers; and the
majority of German readers read more journals than independent works.'
His colleague Börne, more cynically, claimed that 'German reviews can be
concisely compared to nothing so well as to the blotting-paper on which
they are printed.'[53]

Between 1815 and 1850 it was estimated that there were more than
2,000 magazines in circulation. Many were short-lived, but some became
important organs of opinion, like the *Blätter für literarische Unterhal-
tung*, the *Literaturblatt* (literary supplement) of the *Morgenblatt für
gebildete Stände*, and the well-known newspaper the *Allgemeine Zeitung*.
Many journals were associated with particular interest groups, so much
so that Heine argued that they had become 'fortresses from which one
can carry on the struggle against rival parties'.[54] The followers of Hegel,
known as the 'Young Hegelians', were associated with two in particular,
the *Hallische Jahrbücher* and the *Deutsche Jahrbücher*.

The readership of the journals was confined to an educated elite –
academics, professionals and secondary-school teachers. It was estimated
that the readership for serious literary reviews was little more than 10
or 15 per cent of the reading public as a whole, and despite the vast
increase in the reading public after 1848, this figure did not change.
In the decades following the revolutions of 1848, the defeat of which

---

[52] Peter Uwe Hohendahl, 'Literary Criticism in the Epoch of Liberalism 1820–1870' in *A
History of German Literary Criticism 1730–1980*, ed Peter Uwe Hohendahl (Lincoln:
University of Nebraska Press, 1988), pp. 179–276.
[53] Quoted by Hohendahl, p. 182.    [54] Quoted by Hohendahl, p. 187.

ushered in a new conservatism in Germany, several influential literary magazines were established. These included the *Deutsches Museum*, the *Grenzboten* (edited by Gustav Freytag and Julian Schmidt) and *Westermanns Monatshefte* (edited by Wilhelm Dilthey). These new publications were influential, but they too had print runs of between 1,000 and 1,500, catering for the same privileged segment of the reading public as their predecessors. The emergence of family-oriented magazines in the 1850s and 1860s acknowledged the needs of a rapidly growing reading public and mirrored the shilling monthly magazines in Britain. But unlike their British counterparts the new magazines did not contain serious literary reviews, although some had special supplements.

By 1870 a clear division had emerged between the reviews published in newspapers – the work of the 'feuilletonistes', subjective, full of literary gossip, and unrigorous – and university-led academic criticism, the product of newly established academic departments and specialist journals. The language of the new literary criticism became more and more inaccessible to the general reading public, and the separation was set to widen.

Transatlantic relations, in terms of literary reviews and reviewing, were more fraught than relations with Europe. Until the international copyright act of 1891 British books were unprotected from both unscrupulous and more responsible American publishers. Entire issues of quarterly reviews were pirated or, as they termed it, 'reprinted' by New York, Boston and Philadelphia firms, their illegitimate status recognizable from their double columns in contrast to the full pages of the originals.[55] But even while piracy was at its peak, an indigenous North American periodical press was taking shape, closely modelled on British lines.

The quarterly *North American Review* was established in 1815 by the Boston firm of Wells and Lilly. Modelled on the *Edinburgh Review*, it became and remained the most important American review for most of its 125-year history. The *Edinburgh* flatteringly pronounced it 'the best and most promising production'[56] of American publishers in 1820. Its influence was extended in the 1880s when its place of publication moved to New York. Next to the *North American*, the *Atlantic Monthly*, founded in 1857 as an organ of the New England literary establishment, was the most influential of American reviews. Published by Phillips Sampson and Company, and from 1868 by Ticknor and Fields, its editors included James Russell Lowell, William Dean Howells, Thomas Bailey Aldrich and Horace Scudder. Its contributors matched the editors in literary eminence.

55 See Shattock, *Politics and Reviewers*, appendix, pp. 160–1, for details of imprints.
56 Quoted in Edward Chielens (ed.), *American Literary Magazines: The Eighteenth and Nineteenth Centuries* (New York: Greenwood Press, 1986), p. 290.

Mid-century publishers, most notably Harper Brothers, Putnam's and Scribner's, established magazines along the lines of their British counterparts, mindful of the commercial advantages of combining fiction with other features of a literary magazine. Of these the most aggressive was *Harper's Monthly Magazine*, founded in 1850 by the firm of Harper Brothers. The magazine published mainly British fiction in its early years, using the 'advance sheet' system for which it paid a fee to the publishers, but it incurred the wrath of British authors, who received no compensation. Its features, including reviews, were written by American critics, among them Howells, who contributed the column 'The Editor's Study' between 1886 and 1892. *Putnam's Monthly Magazine*, established in 1853, in contrast, was designed to showcase American authors. In its reviewing it covered both British and American publications, and contained a variety of feature articles, prompting Thackeray to pronounce it 'much the best Mag. in the world... better than Blackwood is or ever was'.[57] *Putnam's* merged with *Scribner's Monthly*, which was established in 1870 as a direct challenge to *Harper's*. *Scribner's*, which became the *Century Illustrated* in 1881, was at its peak in the 1890s, with a circulation of over 200,000. Under the editorship of Richard Watson Gilder it published fiction by eminent American writers, and articles and reviews by distinguished American and English critics. The American publications were notable for their longevity, the *Atlantic Monthly*, *Harper's* and the *Century Illustrated* as well as the *North American Review* surviving into the twentieth century.

Grant Allen's impassioned attack on the state of current criticism ended with a cry from the heart. English criticism had been greatly influenced by the French in the past, and was now in danger of falling prey to influence from 'the lecture-rooms of Berlin':

Are we not too apt to forget that England also has by native inheritance her great and invaluable mental qualities, above all the grand quality of grasp?... Even in pure *belles lettres*, our literature has been marked by a certain kindred noble expansiveness that is wholly alien to the microscopic pettiness of modern specialism... Surely our own English traits are well worth preserving, and we would be ill-advised indeed if we were lightly to exchange them for a base imitation of German ponderousness, or even for a futile endeavour after French lucidity, grace, and brilliance. Let us be English before all things, and then we need scarcely fear that the higher criticism in its best and widest aspect will ever really be lacking in professors among us.[58]

Inward-looking it might have seemed, but it also expressed a heart-felt belief in a future for English criticism at the end of a period of unprecedented expansion and development – from the encyclopedic monthly

---

[57] Chielens, p. 328.    [58] Allen, 'Decay of Criticism', p. 351.

reviews at the end of the eighteenth century, through the quarterlies of the first four decades of the nineteenth, two generations of monthly magazines, those of the thirties and of the sixties, the 'higher journalism' of the mid-century, followed by the cheaper weeklies and monthlies of the seventies and eighties, and the emerging literary scholarship of the universities. By the end of the nineteenth century, and even more certainly by 1914, the conditions and the contexts of literary criticism had been completely transformed.

# 2

# Literary studies and the academy

## DAVID GOLDIE

In 1885 the University of Oxford invited applications for the newly created Merton Professorship of English Language and Literature. The holder of the chair was, according to the statutes, to 'lecture and give instruction on the broad history and criticism of English Language and Literature, and on the works of approved English authors'. This was not in itself a particularly innovatory move, as the study of English vernacular literature had played some part in higher education in Britain for over a century. Oxford University had put English as a subject into its pass degree in 1873, had been participating since 1878 in extension teaching, of which literary study formed a significant part, and had since 1881 been setting special examinations in the subject for its non-graduating women students. What was new was the fact that this ancient university appeared to be on the verge of granting the solid academic legitimacy of an established chair to an institutionally marginal and often contentious intellectual pursuit, acknowledging the study of literary texts in English to be a fit subject not just for women and the educationally disadvantaged but also for university men. English studies had earned some respectability through the work of various educational establishments in the years leading up to this, but now, it seemed, it was about to be embraced by the academy – an impression recently confirmed by England's other ancient university, Cambridge, which had incorporated English as a subject in its Board for Medieval and Modern Languages in 1878. Several well-qualified literary scholars recognized the significance and prestige attached to this development by putting themselves forward for the Oxford chair, among them A. C. Bradley, John Churton Collins, Edward Dowden, Edmund Gosse and George Saintsbury. It was even rumoured that Matthew Arnold might find himself appointed to the position.

In the end, though, Oxford chose not to appoint a literary scholar after all. In a gesture that betrayed a common anxiety about the academic validity of English literary studies the university chose instead a Teutonic philologist, A. S. Napier – a rather perverse decision, perhaps, given that Napier had very little taste for any literature after Chaucer and that the university already had a number of chairs devoted to linguistic and philological subjects, among them Celtic, comparative philology, and Anglo-Saxon. Though the literary study of English had been set back, it could not, in the longer term, be denied. The Oxford decision actually prompted a public controversy in which the subject's advocates were able to state and develop their case. This was the first time that a sustained and systematic argument had been made for a subject that had hitherto developed in an often rather piecemeal fashion. The appearance of John Churton Collins's *The Study of English Literature: A Plea for Its Recognition and Organization at the Universities* (1891) and A. C. Bradley's *The Teaching of English Literature* (1891) marked the beginning of a new, self-conscious debate about pedagogy and English literature that was joined by, among others, Walter Raleigh's *The Study of English Literature* (1900) and the pamphlet publications of the English Association (founded in 1907), and whose first phase culminated in the report of the Newbolt Commission, *The Teaching of English in England* (1921). This developing case for English proved persuasive, even in the fastnesses of the ancient universities. By 1894 Oxford had established a School of English and had, in the following year, begun its renowned B.Litt. in English. In 1904 it converted the Merton Professorship into a Chair of English Literature. Cambridge took a little longer to come round, setting up its first literature chair in 1911 and eventually establishing its English Tripos in 1917.

It would be wrong to see all of these developments as comprising the foundational moment in the history of English studies; Brian Doyle, for one, has rightly warned against taking too Oxbridge-centred an approach to this history.[1] But they were potentially a defining factor. The arguments of the 1880s and 1890s, and the subsequent work of the early practitioners of English studies, began the process of moulding a fluid and often unstable subject into the shape it would hold for much of the following century. The fact that academic English was granted its seal of approval at this particular moment is significant too. For this was a time in which English culture was undergoing a 'nationalization', with the formation of diverse national cultural institutions such as the *Dictionary of National Biography*, the National Trust and the *Oxford English Dictionary*. The new academic discipline of English literature, emerging from the shadows of continental models, suited well this nationalizing mood. One of the most influential nineteenth-century historians of English literature, the Frenchman Hippolyte Taine, had made the connection between literature and national character the central argument of his four-volume *History of English Literature* (1863–4), describing his research into English literary

---

[1] Brian Doyle, 'The Hidden History of English Studies' in *Re-Reading English*, ed. Peter Widdowson (London: Methuen, 1982), p. 18.

history as the 'search for the psychology of a people'.[2] And this prompt
would be followed by many of the first practitioners of academic English
literature, among them Henry Morley, who believed that 'the full mind of
a nation is its literature' and that 'to a true history of the literature of any
country must belong a distinct recognition of the national character that
underlies it'.[3] The general effect, as Stefan Collini has noted, amounted
to a 'Whig reinterpretation of English literature' in which the national
literature swiftly acquired a continuous, discrete history and a place very
near the centre of the national consciousness.[4]

   This literary-critical Whiggism would increasingly marginalize a somewhat inconvenient truth, namely that much of its inspiration derived from
continental Europe. English literary critics had long sought models from
classical and modern continental literatures, and in the nineteenth century
Thomas Carlyle and Matthew Arnold were only the two most prominent
of many contemporary examples. Carlyle's stylistic and substantive debt
to the philosophy of Kant and Fichte and the writing of Goethe, Schiller
and Novalis was apparent in a number of his early works, from the
*Life of Friedrich Schiller* (1823–4) to *Sartor Resartus* (1836). These writings indicted the perceived intellectual and moral slackness of English
empiricism, and to Carlyle, at least, European thought seemed an ideal
stick with which to beat it. Elements of this attitude were also to be
found, albeit expressed more felicitously, in Arnold's writing. Arnold's
later *Essays in Criticism* (1865) was one of the most significant works
of nineteenth-century English criticism, but it rarely lingered long on
English literary subjects. The book covered a range of topics from Marcus Aurelius and Spinoza to Heinrich Heine, Maurice and Eugénie de
Guérin; where it discussed English writers at all, however, it tended to
place them in unflattering comparison to their continental counterparts.
In education, as in literature and criticism, it was to the east of the English
Channel that Arnold looked for his lead, seeing both a superior pedagogy
and a more enabling structure of academies, through which the British
might be educated out of their inveterate philistinism.

   Through the work of critics like Carlyle and Arnold, continental philosophy, literature and criticism were still widely influential and in some
ways actually constituted the models for, and the basis of, much modern
English criticism. Though the German Romantic influences associated

[2] 'J'entreprends ici d'écrire l'histoire d'une littérature et d'y chercher la psychologie d'un
    peuple': Hippolyte Taine, *Histoire de la littérature anglaise*, 4 vols. (Paris: Librairie de L.
    Hachette, 1863), vol. I, p. xlvi.
[3] Henry Morley, *English Writers: An Attempt Towards a History of English Literature*,
    11 vols. (London: Cassell, 1887), vol. I, p. 1.
[4] Stefan Collini, *Public Moralists: Political Thought and Intellectual Life in Britain 1850–
    1930* (Oxford: Clarendon Press, 1991), p. 47.

with Carlyle waned as the century progressed, Arnold ensured that the ideas of critics and philosophers such as Sainte-Beuve and Renan had a wider dissemination in the English-speaking world and would continue to resonate within both criticism and the academy. In criticism, the legacy was a continued engagement with European, particularly French, literature that would animate both Symbolism and Modernism and which was immediately apparent in the work of extramural critics such as Arthur Symons, T. S. Eliot, John Middleton Murry and Ezra Pound. Similar engagement was also to be found within the walls of the developing English academy, giving the new 'nationalized' discipline an occasional cosmopolitan flavour. In between writing copiously on English writers, for example, George Saintsbury would find time to publish, among several other works on French subjects, *A Short History of French Literature* (1882) and *Essays on French Novelists* (1891); and Edward Dowden, Professor of English Literature at Trinity College Dublin produced *A History of French Literature* (1897). Even an academic critic as bluff in his Englishness as Sir Arthur Quiller-Couch could still draw on an Arnoldian worldliness to ask his Cambridge students rhetorically why they shouldn't 'treat our noble inheritance of literature and language as scrupulously, and with as high a sense of their appertaining to our national honour, as a Frenchman cherishes *his* language, *his* literature?'[5]

Notwithstanding these examples, the trend of English academic criticism was inexorably towards a more insular reading of the national tradition – a trend that would be accelerated by the literary chauvinism engendered by the First World War and reinforced by the Newbolt Commission.[6] It was as a decisively 'national' subject that academic English literary criticism moved from being a peripheral activity with little establishment recognition to one of the key disciplines, in which the nation could index its every mood and characteristic.

Before the controversy surrounding the Merton chair is examined, however, it is worth taking stock of the way academic English had developed up to this point, not only in the realm of the university but in the often much more dynamic branches of education that lay beneath it. To understand the doubts of Oxford, as well as other centres of education, that English studies was not quite a proper subject for its undergraduates, it is necessary first to examine the subject's tangled beginnings and uneven development.

---

5  Sir Arthur Quiller-Couch, 'On a School of English' in *On the Art of Reading: Lectures Delivered in the University of Cambridge 1916–17* (Cambridge University Press, 1920), p. 113.
6  See, for example, Quiller-Couch's two essays 'Patriotism in English Literature' in *Studies in Literature* (Cambridge University Press, 1918), pp. 290–322.

## Literacy and elementary education

The academic discipline of English studies can, as D. J. Palmer had
shown, be traced back a century and more before this point.[7] While
the English grammar school and university traditions continued, in the
spirit of the Renaissance, to construe Greek and Latin as the exclusive,
authentic discourses of linguistic and humanistic learning, English had
in the eighteenth century begun, albeit very slowly, to exert its own
claims to academic legitimacy. Dissenting academies, with their emphasis on practicality and useful learning, recognized the English language
as a proper medium of academic discourse and approached English texts
as worthwhile subjects of study. An exemplar of such an approach was
Philip Doddridge, founder of the Northampton Academy in 1729, who –
unusually for the time – lectured in English, and who encouraged the
stylistic and literary study of English texts. The Scottish universities, similarly committed to a largely practical pedagogy, had likewise made the
study of English texts a central part of their humanities curricula. Frances
Hutcheson, who became Professor of Moral Philosophy at Glasgow University in 1730, began the trend by delivering his lectures in English. He
was followed by, among others, Hugh Blair at Edinburgh. Blair's *Lectures
on Rhetoric and Belles Lettres* (1783), a series of talks delivered originally
at Edinburgh University, marked this emphasis in its willingness to draw
exemplary materials from both ancient and modern vernacular literatures. The book became one of the best-known early works of academic
literary criticism, and would be used as a textbook in literary education
for over a hundred years.

While such innovation was unimaginable in England's grammar
schools and two ancient universities, English studies – largely in the form
of elementary literacy teaching – began, in the early nineteenth century,
to become a matter of increasing concern. For educators like Doddridge
and Blair, English was not so much a replacement for classical humanities
as a more direct route to the same end – an effective means of promoting the cultured, discriminating individualism on which classical liberal
humanism was predicated. The emphasis for elementary educationalists
in the early nineteenth century was, however, necessarily different. The
pressing need to educate a growing, and sometimes restive, urban population – to develop the literacy skills and basic education required of a
dynamic, industrial society – tended to shift pedagogical emphasis away

7  D. J. Palmer, *The Rise of English Studies: An Account of the Study of English Language
and Literature from its Origins to the Making of the Oxford English School* (London:
University of Hull, 1965), pp. 1–14.

from disinterested notions of individual development to more pragmatic ones related to social organization and economic planning. And as the state took hold of what would become a national elementary education system in the first half of the nineteenth century, it found in English a subject that was not only more accessible and immediately relevant than classics but which might also combine instruction in basic literacy with an education in national values. For the utilitarian educational reformer Henry Brougham, 'the function of reform was to strengthen the English social structure, not to enrich people's intellectual or emotional lives'.[8] To foster literacy, according to this view, was to dissipate the potential for mobbing and rebellion among the working classes and to turn them instead into responsible subjects.

Similar debates were taking place across the Channel. In France education had, during the revolutions and restorations of the first half of the nineteenth century, been a battleground between the claims of church and state. The state took increasing control through a number of measures. It had gained an effective monopoly on all levels of education with Napoleon's foundation of the Imperial University in 1806 (partially undone as a consequence of the Falloux laws of 1850–1); and it had attempted to establish compulsory attendance at primary schools in 1816 (achieved under the Ferry laws of 1881–2, which made attendance at primary schools both compulsory and free). It thereby ensured that the ends served by elementary national education were those of what Rousseau had termed the *volonté générale*, the general will, over individual personal development, with an emphasis on the creation of national linguistic uniformity and social and economic utility.[9] While English education remained essentially voluntary and sporadic in its provision before 1870, French education had become, in intention at least, a rationalized arm of national policy. The nation's elementary education was notionally, and then during the Second Republic actually, compulsory for all, while secondary schooling remained the preserve of the bourgeoisie, espousing a liberal ethos but being largely dedicated to the vocational training of professionals, teachers and administrators who might serve the state and the national economy. At these higher levels there was some scope for literary study, especially after 1852 when senior pupils in *lycées*, following four years of a general humanities and sciences education, were given the opportunity to study for either a science or a literary *baccalauréat* that

---

8  Richard D. Altick, *The English Common Reader: A Social History of the Mass Reading Public 1800–1900* (University of Chicago Press, 1957), p. 143.
9  Michalina Vaughan and Margaret Scotford Archer, *Social Conflict and Educational Change in England and France 1789–1848* (Cambridge University Press, 1971), pp. 117–30.

contained elements of French and foreign literatures alongside history, geography and a little Latin.[10]

Though the French were well ahead of the English in terms of providing education and vernacular literary study, they were behind the Germans, particularly the pre-unification states of Prussia and Bavaria. Though these states generally promoted a more liberal education than that found in England and France, especially before 1871, that education was, at an elementary level, less dedicated to enabling social mobility or individual realization than developing the strength of the state, largely through its appropriation of Herder's ideas of the *Volk*. Both attendance and literacy rates in German schools were conspicuously higher than those in French and English schools, with Prussia having an adult literacy rate of 80 per cent by 1850.[11] While the principal aim of the extensive and well-funded network of elementary *Volksschulen* was to engender basic literacy and the applied skills crucial to a developing local rural economy and increasingly to the wider industrial economy, German elementary education would also play an important part in creating a national consciousness that was crucial to the process of unification in 1871 and which was expressed with full force in 1914. As such, a limited amount of literary and cultural education, especially where it served the ends of nation-building, was embedded at lower levels of German education.

Nineteenth-century German educational culture was pervaded, however, by a countervailing burden of *Bildung*, a notion of self-realization and self-perfection that is commonly associated with the theorist and administrator who founded the Prussian education system, Wilhelm von Humboldt. Schooled in German Idealism, and influenced by the ideas of self-formation articulated by the third earl of Shaftesbury and by Rousseau, Humboldt was intimate with Goethe and Schiller and with the philosophy and literary culture of Weimar. His resulting educational philosophy, one that emphasized the development of a Kantian *Selbstbewußtsein* or self-assurance, played down vocationalism and the immediate economic needs of the state. These traits were most evident in the creation of the modern Prussian *Gymnasium*, a secondary school that placed a strong emphasis on the learning of modern languages and German language and culture alongside classical and mathematical studies. At tertiary level the Humboldtian legacy was expressed most forcefully in the new university of Berlin (1810), particularly in the application by Friedrich Schleiermacher – appointed by Humboldt to the university's

---

[10]  Joseph N. Moody, *French Education since Napoleon* (Syracuse University Press, 1978), p. 62.
[11]  Karl A. Schleunes, *Schooling and Society: The Politics of Education in Prussia and Bavaria 1750–1900* (Oxford: Berg, 1989), p. 109.

foundation committee – of hermeneutics to a more general understanding of self in society, and in the articulation by the university's first *Rektor*, Johann Gottlieb Fichte, of a *Nationalerziehungsplan* – a national plan of education based on a concept of *Selbständigkeit* or true personal independence.

German education would change its character significantly in the latter part of the nineteenth century as a consequence of unification, moving away from its promulgation of a disinterested idealism towards a more focused vocational and scientific technical education. For much of the century, though, it was divided between a disinterested and often socially insulated secondary and tertiary system embracing philology, history and the general propagation of *Kultur* through the working of *Bildung*, and an elementary education that promoted above all the development of basic literacy and practical skills and which had, until its focus shifted towards the cultural knowledge needed for *Volksbildung*, little place for the development of literary skills.

Though as the century progressed, English education travelled somewhat in the opposite direction – from the vocational and controlling to the cultural and emancipatory – what it had in common with France and Germany at its elementary levels was the aim of increasing literacy without necessarily building the independent literary and critical thinking that might create articulate dissent. State-sponsored academic English, then, was largely restricted in its nineteenth-century beginnings to functional, linguistic study. Earlier notions of the subject as a humanizing, literary discipline were relegated to a secondary status. The consequence of this was that schoolchildren in all but the best of private schools were exposed to a very limited range of reading material. Often one book, the English Bible, encompassed the beginning and end of their literary and linguistic education. After the 1840s, some voluntary schools supplemented the Bible with a school reader, but the quality of such readers left much to be desired – especially to school inspectors such as Matthew Arnold, who had close knowledge of educational developments on the continent. Arnold wrote angrily in his report for 1860 that these books, filled with either 'dry scientific disquisitions' or 'literary compositions of an inferior order', promoted a 'grave and discouraging deficiency in anything like literary taste and feeling'. The result, he wrote, was that the average school student 'has, except his Bible, no literature, no *humanizing* instruction at all'.[12] Other educationalists however, were more tentative in their endeavours towards the teaching of vernacular literature. In his

---

[12] Peter Smith and Geoffrey Summerfield (eds.), *Matthew Arnold and the Education of the New Order: A Selection of Arnold's Writings on Education* (Cambridge University Press, 1969), pp. 214–15.

contribution on 'The Teaching of English' to the influential *Essays on a Liberal Education* (1867), J. W. Hales was plainly not able to go as far as Arnold.[13] Hales was perhaps as liberal as Arnold in spirit (he was the Professor of English at Bedford College for Women) but in practice his principal concern was to establish the English language at the centre of liberal education in place of the classics. Like many other university academics of the time, his first aim was to foster systematic study and inculcate confident usage of the vernacular language, which meant that the study of literature, for all its liberalizing possibilities, was reduced to an ancillary role.

Some steps were taken towards a more Arnoldian position, among them the introduction to schools in 1871 of the new subject of 'English literature', which seemed explicitly to shift emphasis away from straightforward linguistic instruction towards a more complex, culturally freighted literary education. Within ten years this became the most popular school subject, prompting a spate of literary histories, primers and other critical books designed to help students pass its examinations. But in practice, the subject that had promised humane, liberal learning was – partly as a consequence of the regime of examination and payment by results introduced by the Revised Code of 1862 – threatening to become just another educational grinding mill. Some efforts were made to alter this; for example, the Mundella code of 1883, which attempted to enlarge the scope of literary education, empowering inspectors to test the more able senior pupils on standard authors such as Shakespeare, Milton, Goldsmith, Lamb, Cowper, Scott, Wordsworth, Byron and Macaulay. But the battle for a distinct literary, as opposed to a straightforward linguistic, education was still nowhere near a satisfactory conclusion.[14]

The higher reaches of secondary education before the 1870s were similarly restricted in their study of English literature. The teaching of humanities in the public schools, as the Clarendon Commission Report of 1864 showed, retained its emphasis on the study of the classics. English literature, it was felt, was a leisure activity better suited to private perusal than classroom analysis. The Taunton Commission into endowed grammar schools of 1865–7 similarly found little evidence in those schools of formal teaching in English literature, but, in contrast to the complacencies of the Clarendon Commission, concluded that this was a state of affairs that ought to be changed. The commissioners noted the decline of Latin and Greek in the grammar schools and proposed that England follow the examples of continental Europe in basing a national literature

[13] J. W. Hales, 'The Teaching of English' in *Essays on a Liberal Education*, ed. F. W. Farrar (London: Macmillan, 1867), pp. 293–312.
[14] Altick, *English Common Reader*, pp. 160–1.

on the study of vernacular writing. This teaching, in addition, should not be restricted to rhetoric or philology: according to the commission's summary report, 'the true purpose of teaching English literature' was not 'to find material with which to teach English grammar, but to kindle a living interest in the learner's mind, to make him feel the force and beauty of which the language is capable, to refine and elevate his taste'.[15] This recommendation was very high-minded and recognized the need for the development of critical as well as practical literary skills, but it is a moot point whether such educational reform came near to developing the intended critical responsiveness in many school pupils. Into the early twentieth century most Elementary pupils and trainee teachers continued to learn their literature by rote, making the study of literature as much a test of memory as of critical responsiveness.

## Further and higher education

The growing educational endorsement of English studies, with a slow but rising emphasis on the humanizing potential of literary education rather than the discipline of linguistic study, was progressive and undoubtedly contributed to the subject's increasing popularity. The subject might be derided from time to time as a lower-status substitute for the classics, but this in fact proved to be its great strength. For the rising lower middle and upper working classes created by the century's economic development and attendant political reform, literary study offered a legitimizing and confidence-building means of access to culture: it was, in a sense, a rational democratic equivalent to the hierarchical classical model. This may have escaped the attention of the ancient universities, but it had been recognized by the higher education institutions that had sought, from earlier in the century, to widen educational participation. The Mechanics' Institutes which had sprung up from the 1820s, and which numbered well over 500 by 1850, had been established to bring practical education to aspiring members of the working class. These institutions had at first been suspicious of literary studies, just as the Public Libraries movement, which effectively began in 1849, had been wary of stocking library shelves with literature rather than more practical and ostensibly improving books.[16] But, in practice, these institutions and the Working Men's Colleges that followed quickly found the benefit of placing literary teaching nearer the

---

15  *Taunton Commission* I, pp. 25–6, quoted in Altick, *English Common Reader*, p. 183.
16  J. M. Golby and A. W. Purdue, *The Civilisation of the Crowd: Popular Culture in England 1750–1900* (Stroud: Sutton, 1999); Altick, *English Common Reader*, pp. 126–7.

centre of their curricula, especially when literature was construed, as it increasingly was in schools, as an accessible repository of both moral and national values and a humanizing complement to technical subjects. Figures such as F. D. Maurice, Professor of English Literature and History at King's College (1840–53) and from 1854 principal of the London Working Men's College, brought an evangelical zeal to this task, emphasizing the inspirational qualities of vernacular literature and broadening the academic constituency to working-class men and middle-class women. This constituency, especially that of women, assumed an increasing role in the development of English literary study. Maurice had been one of the founders of Queen's College for Women in 1848, which was followed by Bedford College in the following year, and then later, starting with Girton in 1869, by the women's colleges of London, Oxford and Cambridge in the 1870s and 1880s. These later developments were the product of a noticeable surge of interest in middle-class female education in the late 1860s, which had prompted the establishing, especially in the north of England, of a number of women's educational associations.[17]

These, in turn, directly inspired the University Extension movement, which after 1873 quickly spread across England, encouraging the founding of the new university colleges in regional cities such as Birmingham, Sheffield, Leeds, Liverpool and Manchester. Women students tended to predominate in extension lectures – one contemporary account estimated that they formed two-thirds of extension classes at Oxford in 1888–9 – and although they were less well represented in the university colleges their influence was felt strongly.[18] That influence, as it pertained to the study of English literature, was both practical and moral: English was both an easier alternative to the classics, needing little preliminary linguistic schooling, and a suitable subject for the female's supposedly less rational, more instinctive faculties. Such, at least, were the arguments put forward by Charles Kingsley in his introductory lecture to his female students as Professor of English at Queen's College. 'God' he told his students, 'intended woman to look instinctively at the world', and as a consequence a literary education might not only 'quicken women's inborn *personal interest*' but also develop 'that woman's heart' that would 'help to deliver man from bondage to his own tyrannous and all-too-exclusive brain'.[19] The study of English literature in such a context almost

[17]  See John Dixon, *A Schooling in 'English': Critical Episodes in the Struggle to Shape Literary and Cultural Studies* (Milton Keynes: Open University Press, 1991), pp. 14–17; and Stuart Marriott, *University Extension Lecturers: The Organisation of Extramural Employment in England, 1873–1914* (University of Leeds, 1985), pp. 2–4.
[18]  June Purvis, *A History of Women's Education in England* (Milton Keynes: Open University Press, 1991); Altick, *English Common Reader*, p. 110.
[19]  Charles Kingsley, 'On English Literature' in *Introductory Lectures, Delivered at Queen's College, London* (London: John W. Parker, 1849), pp. 58–9.

inevitably tended to stress empathetic response over critical analysis. As one of the most influential extension lecturers Richard Moulton put it, 'sympathy is the grand interpreter'.[20]

The belief that English literature was, to use Chris Baldick's phrase, 'a civilizing subject' that might help bring a measure of classical sweetness and light to the previously educationally disadvantaged, and perhaps instil in them a sense of social responsibility and political moderation, made it a powerful presence in adult education (as well as in the programmes of the more practical 'provincial' universities of London, Scotland, Ireland and Wales).[21] But it was plainly not to its advantage in the ancient universities, where the subject's accessibility and lack of formal rigour made it suspect. From this point of view English literature might be suitable as a recreation but not as a discipline: 'To mix up the study of a subject which was enthusiastically argued around undergraduate study fires with subjects suitable to be set for examinations, to make Work-matter out of a fascinating spare-time hobby, was', as Stephen Potter would later put it, 'against academic nature.'[22]

The first generation of full-time university English teachers, then, were the inheritors of a subject that had a clear social and educational purpose, but a less well-defined set of critical and scholarly objectives. In order to make the subject grow (and often to secure their salaries) these teachers had to enthral the imaginations of substantial numbers of students, but in order to make 'academic nature' more amenable to their subject they had to ensure that the subject conformed to conventional notions of scholarship and pedagogy. Such pressures were bound to have an impact on the work of the early academic specialists in English literature, many of whom brought the additional complication of having come to the academy through careers in literary journalism. Negotiating between the demands of establishing and popularizing a new discipline, producing literary criticism, and engaging in original literary scholarship was one of the main challenges they faced.

Two of the early figures faced with these differing roles, David Masson and Henry Morley, were successive Professors of English Language and Literature at University College, London. As a critic, Masson wrote penetratingly about contemporary authors, among them Dickens and Thackeray, as well as producing scholarly disquisitions on Milton; as an editor he published and helped establish the reputations of Thomas Hughes, Charles Kingsley and others. During this time he had been appointed to

[20]  Quoted in Dixon, *Schooling in 'English'*, p. 38.
[21]  See Chris Baldick, *The Social Mission of English Criticism 1848–1932* (Oxford: Clarendon Press, 1987), pp. 59–85.
[22]  Stephen Potter, *The Muse in Chains: A Study in Education* (London: Jonathan Cape, 1937), p. 169.

the Chair of English Language and Literature at University College, a position he held from 1852. He was the first wholly successful holder of this chair, and during his tenure the study of English language and literature became established in 1859 as an integral part of the syllabus. Masson left in 1865 to take up the Chair in Rhetoric and Belles Lettres at Edinburgh University, the position originally held by Hugh Blair and which was renamed on Masson's appointment as the Chair of Rhetoric and English Literature. He was effectively the first person to build a full-time career as a university teacher of English literature, spending forty-three years publishing academic and critical works, lecturing, and designing curricula for the new subject. In the year that Oxford was making its first tentative steps towards establishing an honours school Masson was a veteran, confidently putting Edinburgh students (who were required to show this knowledge in order to graduate with their general MA Arts degrees) through their paces in an impressive range of literary texts from Chaucer to Tennyson.[23]

Much of Masson's criticism is, like that of the other early professionals in academic English studies, broadly historical and evaluative, involving the marking out of the main lines in the development of English literature and making tentative classifications. On the one hand his work involves the skills of the critic and biographer, seen for example in the lectures collected posthumously as *Shakespeare Personally* (1914) and in *Carlyle: Personally and in His Writings* (1885), in which he follows that writer in locating literary style as much in individual sensibility as in historical circumstance, typically, for example, noting the '*moral* element in Carlyle's constitution' that gave his work 'its special character of originality'.[24] On the other hand he exhibits the more academic impulse to historicize and categorize, evident in *British Novelists and their Styles* (1859), in which Masson constructs a developmental history of the genre and then sifts contemporary novels to identify thirteen distinct modes, an early attempt to fix the flux of contemporary artistic practice into a communicable, teachable system.[25] In much of his writing Masson can be seen to be balancing the competing demands of criticism and scholarship, satisfying the academic reader with a cumulus of fact while remaining sensitive to the individual human element – the 'Imagination', as Masson figures it – that evades systemic determination and finds fugitive expression

[23] See Jo McMurtry, *English Language, English Literature: The Creation of an Academic Discipline* (London: Mansell, 1985), pp. 128–31, for a detailed description of this curriculum for 1883.
[24] David Masson, *Carlyle: Personally and in His Writings* (London: Macmillan, 1885), p. 66.
[25] See David Masson, *British Novelists and their Styles: Being a Critical Sketch of the History of British Prose Fiction* (Cambridge: Macmillan, 1859), pp. 214–27.

in the singular work of literary art. This combination is visible in the work on Milton for which he is probably best known, his three-volume *The Poetical Works of John Milton* (1890), with its massive apparatus of introductions, memoirs, notes and essays; and his six-volume *The Life of John Milton: Narrated in Connexion with the Political, Ecclesiastical, and Literary History of His Time* (1859–80). This latter (with vol. 1 revised and enlarged in 1881, and its seventh-volume index added in 1894) amounted to over 4,500 pages of unprecedentedly detailed examination of Milton's historical contexts. It was a work, as Masson put it in his preface, that might stand as a 'History of his Time'; but it was also firmly the story of an atypical individual and the development of his distinctive genius.[26]

Henry Morley followed Masson at University College, taking up the Professorship of English Language and Literature in 1865, having previously been a lecturer at King's College. Morley was one of the most active and visible evangelists of English literature in the second half of the nineteenth century, travelling the country lecturing to women's educational associations (of which he was, like Masson, a staunch supporter), extension classes and diverse philosophical and debating societies. His written criticism had an even greater impact than his charismatic performances at the lectern. His *First Sketch of English Literature*, published in 1873, was widely read, selling between 30,000 and 40,000 copies in its first twenty-five years of publication.[27] The main aim of the book was to construct a history of English literature from its earliest days to the nineteenth century. The tone was brisk and the evaluations of writers breezy, offering a reliable, readable guide for the growing numbers of academic readers. Morley followed this up with a much more ambitious, and more scholarly work, *English Writers: An Attempt Towards a History of English Literature*. This was conceived as a twenty-volume history that reflected, as he recognized, the significance of his role as an academic rather than simply as a critic: he noted in his preface that as a consequence of his work as teacher he had been admitted 'to a new field of labour, in which study of Literature, until then the chief pleasure, became also the chief duty of his working life'.[28] The first volume of *English Writers* appeared in 1864 but it was not until the 1880s that he resumed the project, producing ten of the projected twenty volumes before his death in 1894 – although only managing to take the story of English writing as far as Shakespeare in its 4,000 pages. A more important contribution, certainly

26  David Masson, *The Life of John Milton: Narrated in Connexion with the Political, Ecclesiastical, and Literary History of His Time*, 7 vols. (London: Macmillan, 1859–94), vol. 1, p. xi.

27  Altick, *English Common Reader*, p. 185.     28  Morley, *English Writers*, p. v.

to education in the wider sense, was Morley's lifetime commitment to
the publication and dissemination of cheap editions of classic texts. He
edited in the course of his professional life some 300 volumes of English
and foreign classics in his own Morley's Universal Library, published by
G. Routledge and Sons and selling for a shilling a volume, and in other
series including Cassell's National Library, which retailed at threepence in
paper covers and sixpence in cloth. These were among the most popular
in the English-speaking world, with each volume of the Cassell's library
selling somewhere between 50,000 and 100,000 copies.[29]

As the careers of Morley and Masson show, early full-time literary
academics were subject to the competing demands of popularization and
scholarship. Their role as men of letters was to shape public debate about
literary value, which they effected in lectures, literary journalism and
popular literary histories. The other, more strictly academic role was that
of literary scholar and analyst, subjecting texts and contexts to exacting
technical scrutiny. If English literature was to become established in a
university environment such rigour had to be emphasized in order to
convince sceptical scholars in other disciplines, but if it was to become a
truly popular subject expressing a social and national mission it needed to
highlight its credentials as a cornerstone of a humane general education.
Thus it was, for example, that an academic like Edward Dowden, who
had been appointed to the Chair at Trinity College Dublin in 1867,
catered for an academic audience with his *Shakspere: A Critical Study of
his Mind and Art* (1876) and pioneering two-volume biography of Shelley
(1886), but also provided books for the popular literary audience, such
as his biography of Southey in the English Men of Letters series.

Many others in this first generation of professionals similarly sought
to bridge the gulf between publishing and scholarly research. At one end
of the spectrum was F. J. Furnivall, the scholar, editor and lecturer at F.
D. Maurice's Working Men's College in London, who had an important
role in founding the Early English Text Society in 1864: a body which
had by the end of the century produced over 100 volumes of previously
unavailable manuscripts and early printed books. At the other end of
this spectrum was Edward Arber, who had been a student of Morley's
at King's College, and who subsequently became a lecturer at University
College under Morley before becoming in 1881 Professor of English at
Mason Science College (later to become the University of Birmingham).
Much of Arber's career was dedicated to the editing of popular editions,
including *Arber's English Reprints* in thirty volumes (1868–71), the eight-
volume *An English Garner: Ingatherings from our History and Literature*

---

[29]  Henry Shaen Solly, *The Life of Henry Morley, LL.D.* (London: Edward Arnold, 1898),
       p. 357.

(1877–96) and *The Scholar's Library of Old and Modern Works* in six-teen volumes (1880–4).

This popularization of primary texts was matched by a growth in various types of primers and literary histories, often designed for the new examinations in the subject of English literature that proliferated in the second half of the nineteenth century. One of the first academics in this field was George Lillie Craik, a Scotsman who was Professor of English Literature and History at Queen's College Belfast from 1849 to 1866. Craik had published his six-volume *Sketches of the History of Literature and Learning in England from the Norman Conquest to the Present Day* between 1844 and 1845, and he followed it up with a dense, 1,000-page, two-volume *A Compendious History of English Literature and the English Language from the Norman Conquest* in 1861, which he boiled down to a more manageable one volume in his *A Manual of English Literature* in the following year: a work that continued in print well into the twentieth century, appearing as a part of the Everyman Library in 1909. Craik was an examiner for the Indian Civil Service in 1859 and 1862, so was well aware of the potential market for this kind of literary history.

Thomas B. Shaw, who had had to look a little further afield for an academic position, holding the posts of Professor of English Literature at the Imperial Alexander Lyceum in St Petersburg and Lector of English Literature at the University of St Petersburg, similarly recognized the market opened up by the new emphasis on proficiency in English literature demanded by professional examinations, such as those for the Indian Civil Service (instituted in 1855), as well as those in the academic environment, such as the Oxford and Cambridge Local Examinations, which had begun in 1858. His *A History of English Literature* (1864) was a self-conscious attempt to address this market. Published in John Murray's Student's Manuals series, it was, according to its editor, intended to be as 'useful as possible to Students preparing for the examination of the India Civil Service, the University of London, and the like'.[30]

A similar, early work was William Spalding's *A History of English Literature: With an Outline of the Origin and Growth of the English Language* (1853). Spalding was Professor of Logic, Rhetoric, and Meta-physics at the University of St Andrews and had designed his book specif-ically for 'the instruction of young persons'. It was both a historical primer and an attempt to inculcate the appropriate critical spirit: its modern sections in particular making attempts 'to arouse reflection, both by occasional remarks on the relations between intellectual culture and

---

[30]  William Smith, Preface to Thomas B. Shaw, *A History of English Literature* (London: John Murray, 1864), pp. iii–iv.

the other elements of society, and by hints as to the theoretical laws on which criticism should be founded'.[31] The book has a strong philosophical and linguistic content, which perhaps gives some substance to Spalding's claim that it was more than merely chronology. And the mix seems to have had appeal, with the book going through fourteen editions by 1877.

Thomas Arnold, brother of Matthew Arnold and father of Mrs Humphry Ward, who was Professor of English Literature at the Catholic University of Ireland (later University College Dublin), made a similar attempt to get beyond straightforward history in his *A Manual of English Literature: Historical and Critical* (1862) by dividing the book into a Historical Section and a Critical Section, dealing separately with the individual works and their generic, rhetorical and philosophical qualities. Arnold professed himself indebted to Craik and Spalding as well as to the popularizing work of Robert Chambers (while decrying their overindulgent attitudes towards Scottish writers), and styled his book as an 'educational manual' that reflected the views of 'an ordinary Englishman'.[32] Like the others mentioned, this was a work that covered the whole history of literature in England from its earliest beginning to the present, and like them it went through steady republication for the rest of the nineteenth century and the early parts of the next.

Equally wide in scope, but with a slightly narrower critical framework, was the work of another academic in Ireland, William Francis Collier of Trinity College Dublin. Collier's *A History of English Literature* (1862) was, as its subtitle *In a Series of Biographical Sketches* suggested, a book which was based on the premise that 'true criticism cannot separate the author from his book' and which offered a quick sprint (if some 550 pages can be so described) through lives and books from 'nine eras', stretching from an Anglo-Saxon 'pre-era' to the contemporary ninth era inaugurated by the death of Sir Walter Scott.[33]

By the time Morley was publishing his *First Sketch of English Literature* in 1873 the popular, and cheap, histories and student editions were appearing in significant numbers, and literary academics were finding themselves competing in a crowded market with schoolmasters, ministers and professional writers. Morley's book sold well but was put in the shade by the Rev. Stopford A. Brooke's primer *English Literature*

[31] William Spalding, *A History of English Literature: With an Outline of the Origin and Growth of the English Language: Illustrated by Extracts: For the Use of Schools and Private Students*, 14th edn (Edinburgh: Oliver & Boyd, 1877), pp. 1–2.

[32] Thomas Arnold, *A Manual of English Literature: Historical and Critical* (London: Longman, Green, Longman, Roberts, & Green, 1862), p. v.

[33] William Francis Collier, *A History of English Literature: In a Series of Biographical Sketches* (London: T. Nelson & Sons, 1882), p. iii.

*from* AD *670 to* AD *1832* (1876), which sold 25,000 copies in its first
ten months and had, by 1916, gone through thirty-six reprintings in four
editions and sold nearly half a million copies.[34] Men of letters like Austin
Dobson, with his *Civil Service Handbook of English Literature* (1874),
Edmund Gosse in *A Short History of Modern English Literature* (1897),
and Stephen Gwynn in *The Masters of English Literature* (1904) all
aimed directly at the reader formed by the teaching of English literature
at school, college or university. Others sought ever more schematic ways
to render this history, among them Frederick Ryland's *Chronological
Outlines of English Literature* (1890), which was almost wholly taken
up with extensive information in tabular form, and William Renton's
*Outlines of English Literature* (1893), a work aimed squarely at extension students (being part of John Murray's series of University Extension
Manuals) and which featured a number of innovative diagrammatic aids,
among them a Venn diagram to illustrate intersections in the American
literary tradition.[35]

## Oxford and academic respectability

Literary academics competed in this market, but were by the end of
the century attempting to find ways to emphasize the seriousness and
the distinctiveness of their work: to impose critical principles on what
seemed a sprawl of mere chronology. George Saintsbury, another who
had arrived in academe from a career in periodical journalism, and who
took over from Masson as Professor of Rhetoric and English Literature
at Edinburgh University in 1895, prefaced his 818-page *A Short History
of English Literature* (1898) with the unusual remark that no part of the
book was based on his lectures, and the announcement, perhaps in a dig
at the quality of popular literary history, that 'the substitution of bird's-
eye views and sweeping generalizations for positive knowledge has been
very sedulously avoided'. The book might contain his own critical opinions, wrote Saintsbury; however, the object has not 'been to make these
opinions prominent, but rather to supply something approaching that
solid platform, or at least framework, of critical learning without which
all critical opinion is worthless'.[36] Saintsbury's criticism signals an intention to put the historical study of literature back on a firm empirical and

34 See Collini, *Public Moralists*, p. 354.
35 See William Renton, *Outlines of English Literature* (London: John Murray, 1893),
    p. 233.
36 George Saintsbury, *A Short History of English Literature* (London: Macmillan, 1898),
    pp. v–vi.

systematic basis, witnessed, among many other works, in his three-volume *A History of Criticism and Literary Taste in Europe from the Earliest Texts to the Present Day* (1900–4) and in his contribution of twenty-one chapters to the *Cambridge History of English Literature* (1907–16). In this he is perhaps typical of the generation of academic literary scholars which followed Masson and Morley: a generation which still often had roots in the world of literary journalism but which was struggling to reconcile its critical facility and fluency with a more explicitly methodical scholarly and pedagogical earnestness.

Nowhere was this struggle more apparent than in the ancient universities. The broadly liberal and democratic impulse which had made English literature an increasingly suitable subject for national secondary education and the extension movement was recognized and to some extent welcomed in these universities, but it also offered a threat to the assumptions of its professoriate, many of whom were convinced, especially in the wake of Mark Pattison's *Suggestions on Academical Organisation, with Especial Reference to Oxford* (1868), that the university should define itself more along the lines of the contemporary German university as a place of advanced scholarship rather than general education. At Oxford there was, as D. J. Palmer has put it, a distinct and unresolved 'conflict of interests between the party of research and the party of liberal education'.[37]

The pressure that led to the establishing of the Merton chair, and the controversy that followed the appointment of its first holder, brought such arguments under a wider public spotlight and exposed literary English to a rigorous examination. The main protagonist in this controversy was John Churton Collins, a literary journalist and energetic lecturer for the London and Oxford extension societies – and a disappointed contender for the chair. In the wake of this failure he made it his business to establish English literature as the subject of a separate honours school in the university – a task he took up with characteristic vigour and polemical relish. From the outset, Collins was conscious of the need for English literature to be seen to be placed on a rigorous, systematic footing: this was the consistent theme of a series of articles that would form the core of his *The Study of English Literature: A Plea for its Recognition and Organization at the Universities* (1891). Faced with scholarly scepticism about the subject's credentials – the most notorious expression of which was the comment of the Regius Professor of History, E. A. Freeman, that literary study might amount to little more than 'mere chatter about

---

[37]  D. J. Palmer, 'English' in *The History of the University of Oxford. Vol. 7: Nineteenth-Century Oxford, Part 2*, ed. M. G. Brock and M. C. Curthoys (Oxford: Clarendon Press, 2000), p. 398.

Shelley' – Collins sought to establish it not just as a liberal art, but as a defensible academic discipline.

This was not simply opportunism. Like Saintsbury he was conscious of the need to establish professional standards of criticism, and was aware that some forms of academic discussion were slipping into impressionism and slipshod scholarship. Before the Merton controversy, in three articles published in 1880–1, Collins had acquired notoriety for his detailed analysis of what might now be described as the intertextuality of Tennyson's poetry. Collins believed he was engaging in valuable scholarship in pointing to the many antecedent texts woven into Tennyson's work, but to those unused to such critical rigour this looked like an accusation of plagiarism. Tennyson certainly felt this way and famously dubbed Collins 'the louse on the locks of literature'.[38] Collins carried this attention to literary detail, along with a rather characteristic tactlessness, into his discussions of other critics: most famously in his astringent reviews of John Addington Symonds's *Shakspere's Predecessors in the English Drama* (1884) and Edmund Gosse's Clark Lectures at Cambridge, *From Shakespeare to Pope* (1885). In the view of Collins, who was in the process of formulating his first interventions in the Oxford debate, both books exemplified the kinds of dilettantism commonly found not just in the contemporary Aesthetic movement but also in the burgeoning literary-critical and academic marketplace.

The complaint about standards was one that Collins carried into *The Study of English Literature*, where he criticized the university presses for 'authorizing works to circulate with the *imprimatur* of the University, the flimsiness and shallowness of which are only exceeded by the incredible blunders with which they absolutely swarm'.[39] But while he was critical of such lapses from high scholarly standards, Collins was insistent that English literature should not be reduced merely to the dry business of remembering literary dates accurately or paying dogged attention to the historical development of literary language. For Collins, the reading of literature as a mere repository of linguistic and historical knowledge was the desiccating vice of philology – the dry demi-science that stifled the imaginative engagement on which literary study was predicated. What he was calling for instead was a systematizing study of English literature that would put rhetorical, philosophical and critical skills in the service of a predominating aesthetic and moral vision. He was particular about what such a system might involve, outlining an overambitious programme for

---

38  Anthony Kearney, *John Churton Collins: The Louse on the Locks of Literature* (Edinburgh: Scottish Academic Press, 1986), pp. 88–92.
39  John Churton Collins, *The Study of English Literature: A Plea for its Recognition and Organization at the Universities* (London: Macmillan, 1891), p. 61.

teaching English literary texts in tandem with classical and with modern
European literatures, but was still perhaps a little vague about defining
the principles on which such a critical pedagogy would actually be built.
There is, arguably, something both typical and unsatisfying in attempts
like the following to define exactly what it is that lies at the heart of good
teaching and criticism:

> It is the interpretation of power and beauty as they reveal themselves in
> language, not simply by resolving them into their constituent elements, but by
> considering them in their relation to principles. While an incompetent teacher
> traces no connection between phenomena and laws, and confounds accidents
> with essences, blundering among 'categorical enumerations' and vague
> generalities, he who knows will show us how to discern harmony in apparent
> discord, and discord in apparent harmony.[40]

Such talk of aesthetic harmony and critical principles is the warrant
of a worthy set of aims, but it exposes in its inexactness the problem
Collins and his successors would have in attempting to work a liberal
arts philosophy into an academic system. In order to refute the jibes that
it was merely 'chatter' or a subject that 'is very pleasant to ramble in, but
one that is exceedingly difficult to reduce to a definite and teach-worthy
system', Collins made promises about the rigour of the discipline that the
discipline would quickly have doubts about the wisdom of delivering.[41]

## Modern languages and literatures in the university

The late acceptance of the literary study of English by the ancient universities was matched by their tentativeness in embracing the teaching of
modern European literature. As with English literary study, the study of
European literatures was taken up first by the new universities and was
then further advanced by the need to cater for the particular interests
of women students. The first half of the nineteenth century saw some
significant English-language scholarship of European literature, the most
notable being Henry Hallam's monumental *Introduction to the Literature of Europe during the Fifteenth, Sixteenth, and Seventeenth Centuries*
(1837–9), but within the academy there was little evidence of such scholarly endeavour. The only notable academic posts in modern European
languages up to this point were four professorships established at University College London in 1828. In 1847 the University of Oxford had,

---

[40] *Ibid.*, p. 51.
[41] The first jibe is E. A. Freeman's; the second was made by John Earle, Professor of
Anglo-Saxon at Oxford, in *The Times*, 8 June 1887, p. 16; cited in Kearney, *Louse on
the Locks of Literature*, p. 77.

through the bequest of Sir Robert Taylor, established the Taylor Institution, with an associated new chair in modern European languages as well as a post of librarian and two language teachers. Like the academic posts in London, the main work of these academics was in practical language teaching and research rather than literary study. The first holder of the Oxford chair, the charismatic Friedrich Max Müller, lectured on German civilization and literature, most notably on Goethe and Schiller, but his research was directed specifically towards philology. When he took up a new chair in comparative philology at Oxford in 1868 the university abolished the chair in modern languages.[42] Modern European languages, specifically French and German, were made options on the pass degree in 1873, and an honours school of modern languages was finally instituted in 1903. In many senses modern languages had been much less well served at Oxford than oriental languages, to which the university had granted a separate faculty board in 1882 and an honours school in 1886.[43]

Other universities had been quicker to develop academic capacity in modern languages, with Belfast, Dublin and Manchester establishing chairs in the 1860s, and Birmingham, Leeds, Liverpool, Nottingham and Sheffield following suit in the years between 1890 and 1904. That a large part of this was driven by the demands of women students was illustrated by developments at Cambridge, the first university to establish a complete curriculum for modern language and literature. Cambridge's tripos in Medieval and Modern Literatures was established in 1886, and in its early years women students outnumbered men. The tripos itself leaned significantly more to the medieval than to the modern, and while the medieval had a strong literary element, which included early English authors, the modern language examination was largely practical: the literary, cultural and historical study that would later form an important part of the degree was barely present at its beginning. The influence of the German academy could be felt in the emphasis placed on philology, and it was perhaps significant that the leading light of medieval and modern literatures in its early years at Cambridge was the philologist and luminary of the Early English Text Society, Walter William Skeat, Bosworth Professor of Anglo-Saxon from 1878 to 1912.[44] Though there were some notable advances in scholarship in the field in the late years of the century, particularly through the efforts of the Modern Language Association of Great

[42] Giles Barber, 'The Taylor Institution' in *The History of the University of Oxford. Vol. 6: Nineteenth-Century Oxford, Part 1*, ed. M. G. Brock and M. C. Curthoys (Oxford: Clarendon Press, 1997), pp. 631–40.
[43] Rebecca Posner, 'Modern Languages and Linguistics' in Brock and Curthoys, *History of the University of Oxford. Vol. 7*, pp. 413–27.
[44] Christopher N. L. Brooke, *A History of the University of Cambridge. Vol. 4: 1870–1990* (Cambridge University Press, 1993), pp. 431–6.

Britain and its journal, the *Modern Language Quarterly*, begun in 1897, which contained a diversity of articles on issues of English and European language and literature, the academic study of modern languages was often a matter of language learning and teaching and philological study before it was a literary-critical activity. It was also significantly under-represented in the academy until a prime-ministerial committee during the First World War took matters in hand, and proposed increases in the number of university posts in modern languages alongside a greater synthesis of linguistic, literary, historical and philosophical approaches to European cultures.[45]

## Critical dissatisfactions

In the two decades between the establishing of the Oxford English School and the beginning of the First World War, scholarly criticism in English was in a healthy position in universities, as was shown by Saintsbury's *Short History*, by A. C. Bradley's work on Shakespeare and Walter Raleigh's work on Milton, as well as the *Cambridge History of English Literature*. Textual scholarship, too, was being taken to new levels by luminaries such as R. B. McKerrow and W. W. Greg (an early editor of the *Modern Language Quarterly*) in their work on the Elizabethan drama, and by H. J. C. Grierson's editing of Donne. But there was a definite ambivalence about literary study more generally, and particularly about the ways in which teaching might encourage the singular imaginative engagement with the text without burying it under superfluous scholarly detail and overly schematic pedagogy.

A fifty-year period had seen the introduction of English literature as a subject in schools, as a key component in the exams for the Indian Civil Service and Oxford and Cambridge Local Examinations, as the dominant subject in the rapidly growing area of women's education and the extension movement, and it now seemed ready to topple classics as the cornerstone of a liberal arts education in the university. Yet several university teachers of English now seemed to step back and reflect on whether the unique quality of sympathetic engagement with texts which their subject cultivated was being enhanced or stifled by the whole academic apparatus that now surrounded it. Many remained sceptical of examinations, for example. Oxford critics like E. A. Freeman had worried that the subject was unexaminable, and therefore unfit for university status, to which Collins had responded by indicating the types of

---

[45] *Modern Studies: Being the Report of the Position of the Committee on Modern Languages in the Educational System of Great Britain* (London: HMSO, 1918).

questions that might suitably be asked. While this showed the possibility of examining English, it did not establish its desirability or its propriety as a method. Many who followed Collins were much less sanguine about examinations, among them Walter Raleigh, who in his inaugural lecture as Professor of English Language and Literature at Glasgow University characterized the examiner as 'a snail that crawls over the fairest flowers', adding that 'it would do no irreparable harm to anyone if English Literature were never examined on from now to the crack of doom'.[46] The man whom he succeeded in this post, A. C. Bradley, had been little more impressed, talking of 'the valley of dry bones where bad examiners walk'.[47] George Birkbeck Hill similarly told a meeting of the Teachers University Association at Oxford that 'Examiners and school inspectors like cows are always trying to break in where by their clumsy trampling they can only do mischief', and cautioned his audience to 'resist, as far as we can, their invasion of that part of the mind where they can only work havoc'.[48]

The common ground for complaint here was the familiar one that the systematic learning being practised in schools and universities was threatening to kill the literary spirit it was charged with nurturing. Hill argued that imaginative engagement with narrative and the fostering of 'an ardent and noble curiosity' were a fundamental of all good teaching, and especially that of English literature. To bring students to literature, or as Hill put it to 'keep our children in the company of great writers', needed therefore to be done with the lightest of touches so as not to rub the bloom from that first almost magical encounter.[49] Bradley similarly sought to preserve and enhance the quality of this first engagement with the literary text. He emphasized in his pamphlet *The Teaching of English Literature* (1891) that texts had to be appreciated first as experiences before the tools of factual, historical and grammatical analysis might usefully be brought to bear: the primary role of both criticism and teaching was the sympathetic 're-creation of a work in the imagination'.[50]

Sir Arthur Quiller-Couch, who was effectively Cambridge's first Professor of English Literature, similarly emphasized the need for a kind of wilfully naïve reading of literary texts, warning in his inaugural lecture of the need to eschew 'all general definitions and theories, through the

46  Walter Raleigh, *The Study of English Literature: Being the Inaugural Lecture Delivered at the University of Glasgow on Thursday, October 18th, 1900* (Glasgow: James MacLehose & Sons, 1900), p. 6.
47  A. C. Bradley, *The Teaching of English Literature* (Glasgow: James Maclehose & Sons, 1891), p. 8.
48  George Birkbeck Hill, *Writers and Readers* (London: T. Fisher Unwin, 1892), p. 177.
49  Birkbeck Hill, *Writers and Readers*, pp. 177, 182.
50  Bradley, *The Teaching of English Literature*, p. 10.

sieve of which the particular achievement of genius is so apt to slip'.[51]
For Quiller-Couch, there was little need for academic definitions of terms
like 'the Grand Style' when these could be grasped by any competent,
initiated reader: what need for definitions, as he put it, when 'I recognise
and feel the *thing*?'[52]

The scepticism of Oxford's own first Professor of English Literature,
Sir Walter Raleigh, was if anything even greater. He had already, in *Style*
(1897), talked of 'the palsy of definition' and signalled his preference for
a vital Romantic attitude to a Classicism whose adherents are 'lovers of
generalisation, cherishers of the dry bones of life' and whose 'art is transformed into a science, their expression into an academic terminology'.[53]
His inaugural address at the University of Glasgow continued this theme.
In a manner that might seem rather incompatible with the occasion,
Raleigh expressed the opinion that he could not 'see that lectures can do
so much good as reading the books from which the lectures are taken'.
This was part of a wider problem that he expressed in the following way:

Literature is the expression in words of all the best that man has thought and
felt: how are we to catch it and subdue it to the purposes of the class-room?
Other studies there certainly are that find their natural home in a University;
some indeed that are cherished and furthered nowhere else. But the spirit of
literature is a shy, difficult, vagrant spirit; it will not submit to imprisonment nor
to the rules of an academy.[54]

Raleigh's definition of literature here is no doubt intended to recall
Matthew Arnold's description of culture as 'the best that has been thought
and said in the world'.[55] As such, it is perhaps designed to emphasize just
how far Raleigh's view of the academy as a confining, constraining institution is from Arnold's opinion of thirty-five years before, that the academy
might offer the best hope of broadening the intelligence and refining the
tone of what Arnold saw as the narrow British 'provinciality' of critics as
diverse as Addison and Ruskin.[56]

Having worked so hard to get into the academy, it seemed that English
studies was now attempting to squeeze back out of it, or at any rate rene-
gotiate itself into a more accommodating position. Raleigh did institute

[51] The first King Edward VII Professor of English Literature, the Classicist A. W. Verrall,
died shortly after being appointed to the post.
[52] Arthur Quiller-Couch, *On the Art of Writing*, new edn (Cambridge University Press,
1923), pp. 13–14.
[53] Walter Raleigh, *Style* (London: Edward Arnold, 1897), p. 40.
[54] Raleigh, *Study of English Literature*, p. 4.
[55] Matthew Arnold, *The Complete Prose Works of Matthew Arnold. Vol. 5: Culture and
Anarchy*, ed. R. H. Super (Ann Arbor: University of Michigan Press, 1965), p. 233.
[56] Matthew Arnold, 'The Literary Influence of Academies' in *The Complete Prose Works
of Matthew Arnold. Vol. 3: Lectures and Essays in Criticism*, ed. R. H. Super (Ann
Arbor: University of Michigan Press, 1962), pp. 232–57.

pedagogic change at Oxford, introducing a curriculum that enacted a clear separation between literary and linguistic approaches. But this was not based on any clear sense of literary-critical principles. If anything, after his arrival at Oxford, Raleigh was becoming even less sure that rigorous critical principles were either possible or desirable. By 1911, he was welcoming what he saw as a 'new freedom and antinomianism' in criticism, heralded by Saintsbury's *History of Criticism* and Joel Spingarn's lecture 'The New Criticism'. For Raleigh, this deepening 'scepticism which refuses standards and axioms and laws' was a happy release from the dogmas and systems that were threatening to stultify literary criticism in the academic environment: the problem Quiller-Couch identified when he described a pedagogy 'obtruding lesser things upon [the student's] vision until what is really important, the poem or the play itself, is seen in distorted glimpses, if not quite blocked out of view'.[57] Raleigh posited instead a drawing back of critical aims, a refusal of the role of literary judge, believing it to be 'a good sign, and a vital sign, when humility is recognised as the first essential for this task, and when the conclusions attained are modest, and dubious, and few'.[58]

Literary studies had come a long way in the academy since Masson and Morley, but on the eve of the First World War some of its practitioners had started to wonder whether it had not come a little too far a little too quickly. Literary and textual scholarship had established themselves strongly and were plainly thriving in the academic environment. But literary criticism was much less easy in its academic role – its uneasiness would continue after the First World War, manifesting itself in the hesitant nationalistic platitudes of the Newbolt Report.[59] It was, then, perhaps a little disappointing that after years of struggle for recognition of the subject, the Professors of English Literature at England's two most august institutions could find themselves concluding, as Raleigh did, that 'when a real book finds a real reader half the questions of criticism vanish. Appetite justifies itself.'[60]

---

57  Walter Raleigh, 'A Note on Criticism' in *On Writing and Writers*, ed. George Gordon (London: Edward Arnold, 1926), p. 216; Quiller-Couch, *On the Art of Writing*, p. 11.
58  Raleigh, 'Note on Criticism', pp. 216–17.
59  *The Teaching of English in England: Being the Report of the Departmental Committee Appointed by the President of the Board of Education to Inquire into the Position of English in the Educational System of England* (London: HMSO, 1921).
60  Raleigh, 'Note on Criticism', p. 215.

# 3

# Women and literary criticism

KIMBERLY VANESVELD ADAMS

A discussion of female literary criticism in the nineteenth century could begin with Corinne. This fictional character – 'poet, writer, *improvatrice*, and one of the most beautiful women in Rome' – gives a British lord a course in literary and artistic analysis as she leads him on a tour of the city.[1] Corinne, for instance, contrasts the graceful lightness of the Pantheon with the detailed massiveness of St Peter's, and then suggests an analogy to literature: 'In like fashion, classic poetry sketched in the overall picture alone, leaving it to the listener's thoughts to fill in the gaps; in every genre, we moderns say too much.'[2] Corinne's creator, the French aristocrat Germaine Necker de Staël (1766–1817), was similarly a writer of international glamour, honoured in Italy for her accomplishments, and hated and exiled by an emperor, Napoleon. De Staël grew up among Enlightenment thinkers at her mother Suzanne's salon, and her major works *On Literature* (1800) and *On Germany* (1813) were a product of the Enlightenment in their encyclopedic scope. In *On Literature*, for example, she explored the impact of landscape, government, religion and customs on European literature, and developed a contrast between Southern and Northern literary productions.[3] But de Staël was educated according to the precepts of Rousseau. In works such as 'Essay on Fictions' (1795), she helped to shape early Romanticism with her emphasis on individual judgement and the feelings, the historically conditioned nature of taste, and medieval and national literatures.[4] De Staël's literary criticism also adumbrated the concerns of the Victorians. In 'Essay on Fictions', she defended the modern genre of the novel, claiming that it appeals to the imagination, the most important human quality, and to the emotions; hence it can teach morality more effectively than philosophy and history can. She moreover contended that Realism – defined as attention to ordinary existence and the interior life – was the most

[1] Germaine de Staël, *Corinne, or Italy* (1807), intro. and trans. Avriel Goldberger (New Brunswick, NJ: Rutgers University Press, 1991), p. 19.
[2] *Ibid.*, p. 39.
[3] Germaine de Staël, *Germany*, trans. W. Wight, 2 vols. (Boston: Houghton Mifflin, 1859).
[4] Germaine de Staël, 'Essay on Fictions' in *Major Writings of Germaine de Staël*, trans. Vivian Folkenflik (New York: Columbia University Press, 1987), pp. 60–78.

effective narrative mode. Like later critics (e.g., Martineau and Eliot), she found the plethora of love stories tiresome and called for an expanded repertoire of plots to encompass the range of human experience.[5] In *On Literature Considered in its Relation to Social Institutions* (1800), de Staël addressed the struggles of women writers to be educated and to achieve literary fame: 'In monarchies, women have ridicule to fear; in republics, hatred.'[6]

After de Staël came the notorious George Sand (Aurore Lucile Dupin Dudevant, 1804–76), whose most famous literary criticism is found in her correspondence with fellow novelist Gustave Flaubert, first published in the 1880s.[7] Against Flaubert and his creed of impersonal and elitist art, Sand argued for literature that was passionate, progressive and engaged with the largest possible audience:

> You want to write for all time . . . What I've tried to do is rather to act upon my contemporaries, even if I influence only a few, and make them share my idea of goodness and poetry . . . The eternal struggle of barbarism against civilization is a subject of much grief to those who have cast off the element of barbarity and are in advance of their time. But even in that great pain and in its secret angers there is a great stimulus, which gives us new heart by inspiring us with the need to act.[8]

She and Flaubert disagreed on the same issues for years.[9] Sand published literary essays and reviews in the *Revue des deux mondes* and other periodicals. Her fictional practice, notably her commitment to both Realism and Idealism, shaped contemporaneous criticism, as George Eliot showed: 'George Sand is the unapproached artist who, to Jean-Jacques' eloquence and deep sense of external nature, united the clear delineation of character and the tragic depth of passion.'[10]

A discussion of female literary critics could, however, begin elsewhere: with the German *salonistes* of the Romantic era: figures such as Rahel Levin Varnhagen (1771–1833), Caroline Schlegel-Schelling (1763–1809) and Bettina von Arnim (1785–1859), who had French role models, including de Staël. They practised a form of literary commentary considered appropriate for women; their striking insights into writers such as Goethe and Schiller were shared with salon guests or developed in letters notable for their self-expression and innovative language. Their work shows once

---

5  *Ibid.*
6  de Staël, *On Literature Considered in its Relation to Social Institutions* in *Major Writings*, pp. 201–8.
7  Gustave Flaubert and George Sand, *Flaubert–Sand: The Correspondence*, trans. Francis Steegmuller and Barbara Bray (New York: Knopf, 1993), p. 404.
8  *Ibid.*, p. 296.    9  *Ibid.*, pp. 3, 87–8, 248–9, 379–94.
10 George Eliot, 'Woman in France' in *Selected Essays, Poems, and Other Writings*, eds. A. S. Byatt and Nichols Warren (London: Penguin, 1990), p. 10. Hereafter cited as *WF*.

again how gender opens up questions of genre. Can literary criticism be conversational (even oral) in style, epistolary in genre, usually intended for a private audience, and available to modern readers in embedded form (within letters or editions of letters)? Or should literary criticism continue to be defined by the work of professional (and mostly male) writers – as occurring in the form of reviews, extended essays or sometimes personal narratives, and written with the intent of publication?[11]

This account will focus on a group of women writers who saw themselves as professionals, and while cognizant of the *salonistes*, sought to distance themselves from such traditionally feminine achievements. Harriet Martineau, Anna Jameson, Margaret Fuller and George Eliot were the most prominent female literary critics in mid-century Britain and America. They were generally aware of each other's work, competed with each other, and acknowledged the impact of one or both of the French giants, de Staël and Sand.[12]

What did these mid-century critics, and their French predecessors, achieve? Did they make a significant contribution to literary analysis, or were they notable mainly because they were the first women to make a mark in two professions – criticism and journalism – dominated by men? Second, how did they attain their position? The second question proves easier to answer than the first, because the lives of female critics in this period had some striking similarities.

The critical performances of Martineau, Jameson, Fuller and Eliot, like those of de Staël and Sand, were inevitably marked by gender consciousness, because of nineteenth-century preconceptions about women as writers and intellectuals. The female critic might be considered a freak of nature. She was often characterized as masculine – sometimes as a sincere or grudging tribute to an intellect unusually powerful for a woman, sometimes in recognition of her literary or actual cross-dressing, and sometimes in intrusive analyses revealing more about the gender anxieties of the viewer than the woman herself. George Sand, for example (Flaubert's '*chère maître*'), was known for her trousers, cigars and socialist views. Unsurprisingly, the female literary critic was criticized as fallen, for in her pursuit of a career she did not conform to nineteenth-century feminine ideals. She might take lovers (so de Staël, Sand, Fuller and Eliot). Or she might sully her reputation simply out of professional necessity,

[11]  Heidi Tewarson, *Rahel Levin Varnhagen: The Life and Work of a German Jewish Intellectual* (Lincoln: University of Nebraska Press, 1998), pp. 29–30, 45–6; Margaretmary Daley, *Women of Letters: A Study of Self and Genre in the Personal Writing of Caroline Schlegel-Schelling, Rahel Levin Varnhagen, and Bettina von Arnim* (Columbia, SC: Camden House, 1998), pp. x, 5–7, 23.
[12]  The exception was Eliot; her work was not known to Fuller, because she did not begin her London career as a reviewer and novelist until after the American's death in 1850.

losing her gentility, as Martineau said, in order to support herself publicly by writing.[13]

The mid-century literary critic had an understandably complex relationship with the category of 'lady writer', which carried with it the expectation of difference and the assumption of inferiority. She knew that the achievements of women might not always equal those of men, and sometimes said so (WF, p. 8). But her own experience made her acutely aware of the obstacles her male peers did not face. She developed strategies to define and justify her public role. And she was often a democratizing force in belles-lettres, devising criteria for assessing the work of those who, like her, were not considered part of the literary elite. Given the era in which she lived and worked, her performance as a literary critic was necessarily politicized.

In their work Martineau, Jameson, Fuller and Eliot explored issues that de Staël and Sand had first defined. They considered national character in literature (with the nascent literature of the United States central to the discussion). There were also the imaginative possibilities of the novel, a relatively new genre, and the limitations – psychological, socio-political, stylistic – of current performances. Finally, there was the nature of Realism, a commodious term that the four British and American critics would fill with meaning, reacting to the Romanticism of de Staël's era as she did to Napoleonic neo-Classicism. They would consider the interrelations among Idealism, Realism and morality. And they would evaluate the descriptive energies that the Victorians directed towards both interior and exterior worlds.

Harriet Martineau (1802–76) first came to the notice of contemporaries as 'the little deaf woman at Norwich' who published *Illustrations of Political Economy* (1832–4). She was best known as a writer on social, economic, political and religious issues, but she contributed lengthy literary essays to the *Westminster Review* and other leading periodicals. And as the chief editorial writer for the *London Daily News* from 1852 to 1866, she regularly reviewed books and summed up the careers of writers in memorial notices, later collected as *Biographical Sketches*. She published one novel, *Deerbrook* (1839), and there was considerable commentary on other authors and the writer's craft in her *Autobiography* and works such as *Society in America* (1837), the product of her travels in the United States. The best way to sum up Martineau as a critic is to call her the anti-Corinne of the early Victorian period. She offered astute and consistent, if somewhat limited, principles for the evaluation of literature, which were often echoed in the work of her successors. She was wary of

---

13  Harriet Martineau, *Autobiography* (1877), ed. Gaby Weiner, 2 vols. (London: Virago Press, 1983), vol. I, p. 142.

the 'morbid' and subjective elements she associated with Romanticism, and voiced an early preference for the objective and panoramic Realism that became a mark of Victorianism. She was a role model for subsequent women writers seeking to make their way as public intellectuals. And she was both a sharp-tongued critic and a champion of American literature, upholding its democratic principles over against the 'aristocratic' ones of the Old World.

Martineau stopped short of calling fiction the queen of literary genres, but she early identified her dynamic era as the age of the novel. Fiction, she said, was the form best suited to expressing the national mind and representing all classes, views and ways of life.[14] Martineau identified three levels of fiction: the merely imitative; the descriptive; and that reached by the great artist or genius (exemplified by Sir Walter Scott and Charlotte Brontë). Ever practical-minded, she did not consider genius a mysterious, ineluctable quality (as Carlyle did), but was always interested in the conditions that fostered it. In an astute analysis of a temperament quite unlike her own, she suggested that Scott's boyhood love of romance novels and nature, and neglect of his studies, should be considered a 'wild kind of discipline', a kind of instinctive training for his future career.[15]

Martineau discussed the other two levels of fiction, the descriptive and the imitative, in a long essay on Catharine Sedgwick and American fiction. Washington Irving was her main example of the lowest kind of writer, the imitative. Fiction such as his only added a few New World characters, such as the Indian and the Pilgrim father, to century-old English plots. Descriptive literature such as Sedgwick's, in contrast, was 'a transcript of real life'.[16] Martineau intended no insult in placing Sedgwick in the second tier of writers. Her British counterpart there was Jane Austen, and each writer was called an exemplar, and in Sedgwick's case a creator, of her nation's literature.[17]

A question often debated by nineteenth-century critics was whether America had produced a literature of its own. Martineau was sometimes dubious. American legislation, she said, implied the greatness of the national mind and morals. But if America were judged by its extant literature, 'it may be pronounced to have no mind at all'. At least the Americans appreciated British writers such as Maria Edgeworth, Wordsworth and Carlyle. More importantly, they had produced a Bryant (the poet), a

---

[14] Harriet Martineau, 'Miss Sedgwick's Works', *Westminster Review*, 27–8 (1837), p. 22.
[15] Harriet Martineau, 'Characteristics of the Genius of Scott', *Miscellanies* (1836), 2 vols. (rpt New York: AMS Press, 1975), vol. I, p. 10.
[16] Martineau, 'Miss Sedgwick's Works', p. 24.    [17] *Ibid.*, pp. 23, 31, 34.

Bancroft (the historian) and a Sedgwick.[18] Martineau's American notes clearly reveal her literary politics. She upheld democratic values over against the aristocratic ones of Britain (and Scott). The argument that talent and worth should alone determine rank, and genius knows no class, could prove as empowering to a middle-class Englishwoman as to the aspiring authors of the New World.[19]

Martineau's general antipathy towards Romanticism can be seen in her treatment of Charlotte Brontë. She praised the novelist's originality and power, but criticized her work as morbidly painful and (like Sand's) too love-obsessed.[20] Ann Radcliffe, the author of Gothic romances, was condemned for 'slovenly indefiniteness', especially in contrast to the Realist novelist Austen. The critic's dislike of Romantic self-consciousness, found in her comments on Wordsworth and Byron, proved a double bind for feminists such as Mary Wollstonecraft and Anna Jameson. Martineau said: '[Such women's] advocacy... becomes mere detriment, precisely in proportion to their personal reasons for unhappiness... The best friends of the cause are the happy wives and the busy, cheerful, satisfied single women, who have no injuries of their own to avenge.'[21] But such contented women would not be likely to complain of oppression, and Martineau's comments occurred, oddly enough, in a personal narrative, her autobiography.

Martineau's *Autobiography* and *Biographical Sketches* are notable for their often sharp and self-serving comments on fellow writers – snapshots in a daguerreotyped age. Her comments on Dickens, for example, highlighted what she considered his inaccuracies and lack of principles.[22] She never felt obliged to speak well of the dead (e.g., of John Croker, the Tory reviewer).[23] But she also used her memorial notices to praise women writers she admired, such as the Brontë sisters, or to draw attention to those who might otherwise be forgotten: her neighbour Mrs Wordsworth, for example, whose emotional strength and household skills made the poetry possible.[24]

Anna Brownell Murphy Jameson (1794–1860) was an Anglo-Irish professional writer with a wide range. She published a popular analysis of

---

18  Harriet Martineau, *Society in America* (1837), 3 vols. (New York: AMS Press, 1966), vol. III, pp. 205–6, 213–21.
19  Martineau, *Miscellanies*, vol. I, p. 10; 'Miss Sedgwick's Works', pp. 31–4.
20  Harriet Martineau, 'Review of *Villette* by Currer Bell', *London Daily News*, 3 February 1853, in *Critical Essays on Charlotte Brontë*, ed. Barbara Gates (Boston: G. K. Hall, 1990), pp. 253–6.
21  Martineau, *Autobiography*, vol. I, pp. 387, 400–1, 418–19; 'Mrs. Jameson' in *Biographical Sketches, 1852–1868*, 3rd edn (London: Macmillan, 1870), pp. 429–36.
22  Martineau, *Autobiography*, vol. II, pp. 418–19.
23  Martineau, *Biographical Sketches*, pp. 376–85.
24  Martineau, 'Charlotte Brontë' in *Biographical Sketches*, pp. 360–6.

Shakespeare and later became known as an art critic and historian. Her earliest books included popular biographical sketches, of a sort considered appropriate for a lady writer: *The Loves of the Poets* (1829) and *Celebrated Female Sovereigns* (1831). She also produced accounts of her European travels, the fictionalized *Diary of an Ennuyée* (1826) and *Visits and Sketches at Home and Abroad* (1834), which continued Carlyle's work of introducing the British to German culture and society, though with particular attention to women writers and artists. These two works were influenced by de Staël.[25] Jameson's *Winter Studies and Summer Rambles in Canada* (1838) was a more significant piece of travel writing, a narrative of a generally miserable year spent at first in Toronto, to which the author had travelled in an attempt to save her marriage to Robert Jameson, the lieutenant-governor of Upper Canada. Jameson's 'winter studies', which preceded her wilderness 'rambles', contained considerable literary commentary. Frequently ill and depressed, she found 'a file for the serpent'[26] in analysing the books she had brought with her by Coleridge, Schiller and Goethe (whose daughter-in-law Ottilie had become a close friend in Germany). She took issue with these authors, for example, criticizing Goethe's 'sultanish, Byronic' view of women and later noting ordinary Canadian men's similar, and inappropriate, expectations for a wife on the frontier.[27] Of the four critics of this chapter, Jameson was the one who wrote most consistently about her own sex. Such a decision was partly market-driven. But as *Winter Studies* suggests, Jameson's voice, always personal, became increasingly feminist. She interwove her assessments of literature with statements about women's need for improved status and more rights. And she used her own activity as a writer to argue for female self-reliance – intellectual, economic and emotional.

Jameson's primary work of literary criticism was *Shakespeare's Heroines* (1832), an often-reprinted book immensely popular in both Britain and the United States. The liberal humanist design of the work was indicated by the original title, *Characteristics of Women*. Jameson claimed that since Shakespeare had a genius's insight into human nature, his plays revealed the true character of woman and therefore elucidated current debates. Using a thematic rather than generic or chronological approach to the plays, Jameson discussed the heroines under four headings: Characters of Intellect (e.g., Portia, Beatrice); Characters of Passion

[25] Judith Johnston, *Anna Jameson: Victorian, Feminist, Woman of Letters* (Aldershot: Scolar Press, 1997), p. 101; Anna Jameson, *Visits and Sketches at Home and Abroad* 2 vols. (New York: Harper & Brothers, 1834), vol. I, pp. 36–7.

[26] Anna Jameson, *Winter Studies and Summer Rambles in Canada* (1838), 2 vols. (New York: Wiley & Putnam, 1839), p. 103.

[27] *Ibid.*, pp. 76–9, 246–8, 256–9.

and Imagination (e.g., Juliet, Ophelia); Characters of the Affections (e.g., Desdemona, Cordelia); and Historical Characters (e.g., Cleopatra, Lady Macbeth). Martineau, who seems to have been rather jealous, complained that the book was 'superficial' and all the heroines eventually sounded alike.[28] *Shakespeare's Heroines* in fact has perceptive analyses of character and style and displays considerable knowledge of European literature, criticism and art.[29] Martineau's second criticism was more valid, because Jameson's reluctance to criticize the bard, and her essentialist belief in a female nature more gentle and affectionate than the male, led her at this time to praise blind love and passive virtue (cf. the later *Winter Studies and Summer Rambles*). But she did anticipate Virginia Woolf's *A Room of One's Own* in her preference for Shakespeare's fictional women over the limited and distorted portraits in Renaissance histories (*SH*, pp. 54–5).

Shakespeare was the figure who, after contemporary authors, attracted the most critical attention during the Victorian period. His plays were, like novels, read aloud in domestic circles. Jameson's approach to the dramatist had similarities to the narrative criticism of writers such as Martineau and George Eliot. Her assessments were character-driven, and also showed her concern to establish the kind of context and 'back story' more possible in diachronic than synchronic forms of literature. For example, the critic presented Juliet as an example of teenage self-absorption: 'Romeo and Juliet . . . see only themselves in the universe' (*SH*, p. 133). While they chose to '[quaff] off the cup of life . . . in one intoxicating draught', the heroine's parents were given a share in the tragedy:

Then Lady Capulet comes sweeping by with her train of velvet, her black hood, her fan, and her rosary – the very *beau-idéal* of a proud Italian matron of the fifteenth century, whose offer to poison Romeo in revenge for the death of Tybalt, stamps her with one very characteristic trait of the age and country. Yet she loves her daughter.                                    (*SH*, pp. 137–8, 147)

Similarly vivid writing, and psychological insights relevant for Victorian families, figured in the discussion of Ophelia. Polonius taught his son about the world while shielding his daughter, Jameson said. Yet he then brought her to court – where she served a guilty queen, whose love for the young woman (one of her few positive traits) was the kind of complex touch found only in Shakespeare. Had Ophelia understood Hamlet, Jameson continued, she could not have loved him: 'Such a woman as Portia would have studied him; Juliet would have pitied him; Rosalind

---

[28]  Martineau, *Biographical Sketches*, pp. 431–3.
[29]  E.g., Anna Jameson, *Shakespeare's Heroines* (1832), ed. and intro. Cheri Hoeckley (Peterborough, Ontario: Broadview Editions, 2005), pp. 73, 79, 147–8. Hereafter cited as *SH*.

would have turned him over with a smile to the melancholy Jaques; Beatrice would have laughed at him outright.' But the credulous Ophelia loved him for what he only appeared to be, a gentle, able prince (*SH*, pp. 177–8, 181–2).

In her most compelling discussion, of Lady Macbeth, Jameson's attention to the blind spots of male readers not only justified her own enterprise but also anticipated the academic gender criticism of the twentieth century. She observed that writers such as Schlegel, Hazlitt and Dr Johnson analysed this figure in reference to her husband or the plot, not as a fully realized character, and dismissed her as a depraved monster. But Lady Macbeth's crime was tied to her strengths, Jameson contended; she was a devoted wife who had her husband's full confidence, and her intellectual gifts, determination and courage far exceeded his. She was, however, ambitious only for him. This character terrifies us, Jameson said, in proportion as we see our best selves in her (*SH*, pp. 360–2, 368).

More than the other writers of this study, Jameson was slow to claim authority as a critic. In *Shakespeare's Heroines*, for example, she used the playwright's status as a 'genius' to justify her own interpretations (*SH*, pp. 47–74). She more assertively defined her role in her series *Sacred and Legendary Art* (1848–64). This introduction to European religious art, which went through numerous editions, was designed for British and American Protestants making the Grand Tour. As in her earlier criticism, Jameson followed the precedent of Romantics (such as de Staël) in including personal impressions, but now her mastery of art, religion and history supported large, confident arguments. *Sacred and Legendary Art* involved some degree of literary criticism, as Jameson interpreted the biblical stories and saints' lives represented in art and sometimes deftly used them to address the position of modern women. For example, she said that Mary Magdalene typified the repentant and forgiven sinner – a category including women of the streets, known as 'Magdalenes' in Victorian times, whose fall was usually thought to be irrevocable.[30] The journey of the Magi to see the Mother and Son prompted comments on the victimization of women, especially as slaves in America.[31] The author's favourite representations of the Madonna were as the Virgin without the Child (a colossal figure of 'beneficence, purity, and power') and as a heavenly queen shown sharing the throne of Christ rather than kneeling before him.[32] While *Shakespeare's Heroines* made Jameson one

---

[30] Anna Jameson, *Sacred and Legendary Art* (1848), 2 vols. (New York: AMS Press, 1970), vol. I, pp. 343–4, 393–4.

[31] Anna Jameson, *Legends of the Madonna* (1852), 4th edn (London: Longmans, Green, 1867), p. 212.

[32] *Ibid.*, pp. xvii, 4.

of the leading nineteenth-century interpreters of the playwright,[33] her major achievement as a critic was seen in her later works. Like Fuller she produced a distinctive blend of literary insights, art-historical scholarship and feminist politics.

Harriet Martineau considered Margaret Fuller (1810–50) the most pedantic resident of that overbearing city, Boston. Edgar Allan Poe said that none but Fuller could have published *Woman in the Nineteenth Century* – or wanted to.[34] But even such detractors recognized the singularity of her achievements for a woman and an American. In the 1830s, Fuller organized her 'Conversations', a kind of single-sex salon designed to give Boston women some of the opportunities for self-development that she, and their brothers at Harvard, enjoyed – this despite her fears of being seen as a 'paid Corinne'.[35] A free-thinking Unitarian, Fuller became a leading member of the Transcendentalist circle, introducing Emerson to German literature and George Sand, and editing the group's journal, the *Dial*, from 1840 to 1842. She then moved to New York City to become the literary editor for Horace Greeley's reformist *New-York Tribune*. Most of her literary criticism appeared in the *Dial* and the *Tribune* and was collected as *Papers on Literature and Art* (1846). Her work gave readers a 'cosmopolitan education',[36] yet she often felt buried in the American backwoods, where simply obtaining books was a problem.[37] Fuller was critical of her country's literary shortcomings, but she took pride in being an American. Her work stands out as well for her extended meditations on the role of the critic, her expansive if not always consistent standards for literary judgement, and her awareness of the constraints of gender roles on both male and female authorship.

Fuller's book *Summer on the Lakes* (1844) was an account of her journey to the 'West' – to Michigan, Illinois and Wisconsin – just as these regions were being settled. While this work only occasionally contained literary criticism, Fuller's western experience formed a crucial context for her reflections on a national literature. She was impressed with the energy of Chicago and Buffalo: 'They are the two correspondent valves that open and shut all the time, as the life-blood rushes from east to

[33] Tricia Lootens, *Lost Saints: Silence, Gender, and Victorian Literary Canonization* (Charlottesville: University of Virginia Press, 1996), p. 97.
[34] Martineau, *Autobiography*, vol. II, pp. 20, 252–3; Edgar Allan Poe, 'Sarah Margaret Fuller' in *Essays and Reviews*, ed. G. R. Thompson (New York: Library of America, 1984), p. 1172.
[35] Margaret Fuller, *The Letters of Margaret Fuller*, ed. Robert Hudspeth, 6 vols. (Ithaca, NY: Cornell University Press, 1983–94), vol. II, p. 97.
[36] Hudspeth, 'Introduction' in Fuller, *Letters*, vol. IV, p. 6.
[37] E.g., Margaret Fuller, 'Browning's Poems' in *Papers on Literature and Art*, 2 vols. (New York: AMS Press, 1972), vol. II, pp. 31–2.

west, and back again from west to east.'[38] But she feared that the vast expanse of land and sky would not mean open minds. Such themes were developed in Fuller's critical essays on American authors, which dated from the 1830s and early 1840s, a hiatus between the gleaming years of the early republic and the American literary renaissance. In the most significant essay, 'American Literature', she said her title indicated what did not yet exist, for most Americans were too busy building the country to have time for belles-lettres.[39] But while Fuller's assessment thus far resembled Harriet Martineau's in *Society in America*, she found that work hasty and insulting.[40] She may have replied to it in her criticisms of British models:

[T]here is in English literature, as in English character, a reminiscence of walls and ceilings, a tendency to the arbitrary and conventional... What suits Great Britain... does not suit a mixed race... with ample field and verge enough to range in and leave every impulse free, and abundant to develope [sic] a genius, wide and full as our rivers, flowery, luxuriant and impassioned as our vast prairies, rooted in strength as the rocks on which the Puritan fathers landed.[41]

Fuller here called for a literature that was original rather than imitative, and also true to nature, in the sense of reflecting both the emergent national character and the natural landscape. Using these criteria to rank American authors, she gave the first place to her friend Emerson, as a philosopher and a poet, though she noted some limitations of his style.[42] She similarly praised the fiction writers Charles Brockden Brown and Nathaniel Hawthorne for their original voices. Realism was never Fuller's favourite mode, but she recognized the regional novelists Catharine Sedgwick and Caroline Kirkland, while denigrating James Fenimore Cooper for his ungentlemanly character and meagre imaginative power.[43] She was typical of nineteenth-century reviewers in basing literary judgements on character as well as performance.

Although Fuller became a defender of her country's literature, she grew up feeling like a European in exile. When the publisher of *Papers on Literature and Art* forced her to make extensive cuts, most of the reviews she chose for inclusion were of British authors. There is an intriguing and productive tension between her public and private assessments of this literature. In 'British Poets' (the counterpart of her survey of American literature), she offered the usual criticisms of Byron (his 'moral perversion'

---

[38] Margaret Fuller, 'Summer on the Lakes' in *The Essential Margaret Fuller*, ed. Jeffrey Steele (New Brunswick, NJ: Rutgers University Press, 1995), p. 87.
[39] Fuller, 'American Literature' in *Papers on Literature and Art*, vol. II, p. 122.
[40] Fuller, *Letters*, vol. I, pp. 307–10.    [41] Fuller, 'American Literature', pp. 123–4.
[42] *Ibid.*, p. 128; 'Emerson's Essays' in *Essential Margaret Fuller*, pp. 380–2.
[43] Fuller, *Papers on Literature and Art*, vol. II, pp. 143–50, 128–30.

and 'diseased passions'), and she called Shelley's work uneven, though some passages had 'infinite beauty'.[44] Wordsworth was the best of the recent poets, for he expressed 'serenity and hope' and showed what was eternal in human nature. His verses had the philosophical and formal unity that Shelley's lacked. Fuller's praise of Wordsworth, however, seems oddly lacking in energy and affection, and her letters to friends in fact indicated a marked preference for the younger Romantics. 'My whole being is Byronized at this moment[!]' 'Shelley was all eros. – How full! how bright would have been his final conviction.' In contrast, the poet of the Lake District, she observed, was probably not a favourite of the 'young and ardent'.[45] Her treatment of Goethe and Milton was comparable to that of Wordsworth.

What accounts for such differences between Fuller's private and public writings? It seems likely that her literary tastes underwent some change as she grew older; most of her letters praising the Romantics predated her reviews. But her conception of the critic's role is an even more compelling explanation. She objected to the partisan tone of most American periodicals and found the standards for reviewing deplorably subjective. The true critic, she said, needed the power to enter into the writer's work but also the ability to stand above it and judge it by an ideal standard.[46] As a reviewer, then, Fuller appealed to shared – in fact, what might be termed classic – standards of value, such as comprehensiveness, power, unity and mastery. But privately she remained a Romantic: 'Pour moi, a Shelley *stirs* my mind more than a Milton and I'd rather be excited to think than have my tastes gratified.'[47] Fuller, moreover, believed that elite standards were appropriate for educated writers such as Elizabeth Barrett Browning, but should not be imposed on the 'poets of the people' (such as William Thom and John Critchley Prince). Here the critic ought to be a democrat, praising whatever revelation of the soul, whatever natural grace, the work contained.[48] Given the complexity of her responses to literature, Fuller was, unsurprisingly, less consistent in her standards of value than other female literary critics. Originality and integrity were perhaps the only constants. But she made a singular contribution by going beyond Martineau-like rules for text and genre. Building on the Romantic view of the poet's calling, she was equally self-conscious about the role of the critic.

Fuller was at her best in her longer works, which accommodated her learned, personal and often digressive style. Her most important essay,

---

[44] *Ibid.*, vol. I, pp. 69–80.    [45] Fuller, *Letters*, vol. I, p. 164; vol. VI, pp. 194, 197.
[46] Fuller, 'A Short Essay on Critics' in *Papers on Literature and Art*, vol. I, pp. 1–8.
[47] Fuller, *Letters* [17? June 1833], vol. VI, p. 205.
[48] Fuller, 'Miss Barrett's Poems' in *Papers on Literature and Art*, vol. II, pp. 22–30; 'Poets of the People' in vol. II, pp. 1–14.

*Woman in the Nineteenth Century* (1845), was an expanded version of *The Great Lawsuit* (1843), which first appeared in the *New-York Tribune*. *Woman in the Nineteenth Century* contained literary criticism, but of a specialized sort. Fuller surveyed a large number of literary, religious and historical texts and ranked them on the basis of their treatment of women. Her argument was that the two sexes have a complementary relationship: 'they are the two halves of one thought'. But whereas man has always been able to discover his nature and develop his abilities, woman has not; she instead has been defined in terms of man and limited by his needs. It was time for the 'idea of woman' to be realized.[49] Fuller used this phrase to indicate both the potential of the sex and the achievements of remarkable women; she examined classical, biblical, Native American and European literature for evidence of what woman had been or could be (*MF*, pp. 266, 278–9).

In *Woman in the Nineteenth Century*, Fuller saw gender differences as both fixed and fluid. The sexes had to have some essential differences in order for their relationship to be complementary and for all to benefit if the 'idea of woman' were fully brought out. But Fuller noted that 'all men of genius...shared the feminine development', and she saw women as having a masculine side – intellectual and emotional self-sufficiency – which she used the mythological figure of Minerva to represent. She moreover observed that Nature delighted in exceptions, creating warrior women and 'set[ing] Hercules spinning' (*MF*, pp. 308–12). Fuller's notions of gender, particularly her Romantic interest in the androgyny of talent, led to some sly role reversals in her literary criticism. An example is her review of Sir James Mackintosh, a Scottish writer who, in her eyes, failed to realize his potential. He was famous as a conversationalist, whereas his contemporary Madame de Staël was sometimes (like Fuller herself) criticized for her tendency towards monologues. But that simply was testimony to de Staël's powers as a writer, Fuller said. While Mackintosh had the 'feminine refinement of thought' to appreciate some of the French author's insights, he could not soar with her, being merely a 'butterfly' compared to this 'eagle'.[50] Fuller began a review of Milton's prose works with high praise: the author, with his heroic gifts, was possibly the human being who most resembled God. And he was more American than any native-born writer: 'He is the purity of Puritanism.' She then deftly dealt with the misogyny of the divorce tracts not by taking sides, but by saying they reflected the unhappiness of any marriage that was not a union of souls (a theme also of *Woman in the Nineteenth*

---

49 Fuller, *Woman in the Nineteenth Century* in *Essential Margaret Fuller*, pp. 245, 252. Hereafter cited as *MF*.
50 Fuller, 'Life of Sir James Mackintosh' in *Papers on Literature and Art*, vol. 1, pp. 52–4.

*Century*). In such marriages, the man would be inclined to 'mannishness, almost the same with boorishness', whereas the woman would be impoverished, emotionally and mentally.[51] Fuller here put masculinity on the same level as femininity; it was not a norm, but a changing set of behaviours, potentially a problem, and certainly open to investigation. Thus the nineteenth-century Woman Question was shown to encompass a debate about man.

Fuller tended to have a competitive relationship with female intellectuals, such as Jameson, who were not primarily novelists or poets, but wrote in the same genres she did. Though called the 'American Corinna', she did not mind identifying weaknesses in the late de Staël's work.[52] Fuller befriended Harriet Martineau during the latter's visit to the United States, but she considered the Englishwoman an Abolitionist extremist, while Martineau thought Fuller and her Transcendentalist circle useless intellectuals because of their avoidance of political commitments. Fuller and her writing changed, however, as she reported on urban life for the *New-York Tribune* and then travelled to Europe in 1846 as a foreign correspondent for the paper. In Britain and France, she visited some of her literary heroes and realized she had outgrown them. Wordsworth was an old man in a tame garden. Carlyle's ill-temper was singeing when encountered off the page.[53] And while Sand's boldness in love showed her integrity, the novelist's powers were seen as waning.[54] Fuller's arrival in Italy completed her transformation from a literary critic into a commentator primarily on political, social and economic issues. Her last book was to be a history of the Roman revolution, which she saw as reflecting the American struggle for freedom. It was lost when she and her new family – Giovanni Ossoli, an aristocratic supporter of the revolution, and their young son – all died in a shipwreck in 1850, within sight of the New York coast.

George Eliot (1819–80) wrote most of her literary criticism in the 1850s, when she was still Marian Evans, associate editor of the *Westminster Review*, the influential quarterly, and a contributor to the *Leader*, a weekly co-edited by George Henry Lewes. Her reviews, like Fuller's, attest to her intellectual range: British, American, French, German and classical literature, religion, intellectual history, and in Eliot's case the social and natural sciences. She had earlier abandoned evangelical Anglicanism

---

[51] Fuller, 'The Prose Works of Milton' in *Papers on Literature and Art*, vol. I, pp. 35–42.
[52] Fuller, *Letters*, vol. VI, pp. 129, 260.
[53] Margaret Fuller, *'These Sad but Glorious Days': Dispatches from Europe, 1846–1850*, eds. Larry J. Reynolds and Susan Belasco Smith (New Haven, CT: Yale University Press, 1991), pp. 53–8, 100–2.
[54] Margaret Fuller, *Memoirs of Margaret Fuller Ossoli*, 2 vols. (Boston: Phillips, Sampson, 1852), vol. II, pp. 193–9; Fuller, *Letters*, vol. I, p. 46; vol. V, p. 215.

to become a free-thinker, and her first published books were translations of D. F. Strauss (*The Life of Jesus*, 1846) and Ludwig Feuerbach (*The Essence of Christianity*, 1854), which controversially brought German higher biblical criticism and radical Hegelianism to English-speaking readers. Strauss in particular was blamed for many Victorian crises of faith. In 1854 Eliot left London for an extended trip to Germany with G. H. Lewes, who became her life partner (she referred to him as her husband). Their relationship brought her social notoriety but gave her the confidence and happiness to attempt fiction, she said. Her seven novels included *Adam Bede* (1859), *The Mill on the Floss* (1860), *Middlemarch* (1871–2) and *Daniel Deronda* (1876).

John Chapman, a charismatic book publisher and intellectual lightweight (according to his associate editor), purchased the *Westminster Review* in 1851, and Eliot was the primary author of the prospectus they issued.[55] The editors announced that they would take progressive positions on certain political, economic and religious issues, such as the gradual extension of the vote, free trade, national education and the 'fearless examination' of church privilege and dogma. But their review would evidently resemble a modern academic journal in the new field of social science. They would evaluate and try to synthesize competing theories, and ascertain to what extent proposed social reforms '[might] be sustained and promoted by the actual character and culture of the people'.[56] The tensions in the new design are mirrored in Eliot's literary criticism. Eliot was an 'insurgent' (A. S. Byatt's term)[57] when dealing with the world of ideas or the imagined worlds of literature, where her arguments would have an impact only on her peers. But she seemed to have a 'base and superstructure' view of society, with literature and scholarship considered part of the superstructure.[58] She became quite cautious when addressing issues that might be matters of social and public policy and could affect all classes: 'There is a perpetual action and reaction between individuals and institutions; we must try and mend both by little and little.'[59] The radical and conservative sides of Eliot's intellectual character were partly responsible for the richness and complexity of her fiction. But they often proved more problematic for her lengthy literary essays, a genre usually requiring a single line of argument. As a critic she was at her best in the short reviews, most of which fell into the 'insurgent' category.

Eliot's lengthy essay 'Woman in France: Madame de Sablé' (1854) illustrates the tensions between radicalism and conservatism in her thought

---

55  Eliot, *Selected Essays*, pp. 3–7.    56  Eliot, 'Prospectus' in *Selected Essays*, pp. 5–7.
57  A. S. Byatt, 'Introduction to Eliot' in *Selected Essays*, p. xi.
58  E.g., Eliot, 'The Influence of Rationalism' in *Selected Essays*, pp. 392–3.
59  Eliot, 'Margaret Fuller and Mary Wollstonecraft' in *Selected Essays*, p. 337.

(*WF*, pp. 8–37). She described the achievement of seventeenth-century Frenchwomen (among them the title figure) as authors and habituées of salons, and attempted to account for it. The main explanation offered was physiological. '[I]n France alone, woman has had a vital influence on the development of literature; in France alone the mind of woman has passed like an electric current through the language.' The reason was her vivacious temperament and small brain. In contrast, the English or German woman, with her large intellectual capacity but phlegmatic temperament, 'can seldom rise above the absorption of ideas; her physical conditions refuse to support the activity required for spontaneous activity' (*WF*, pp. 9–11). This problematic argument is of interest as one of Eliot's earliest applications of evolutionary theories to literature (something she would do more successfully in her novels). In addition, the portrayal of the aspiring 'Teutonic' author was evocative of Eliot herself, a learned woman with a large cranium (remarked upon by contemporaries), who had not yet done creative work.

'Woman in France' may unexpectedly reveal the influence of Margaret Fuller. For example, Eliot's statement 'We have no faith in feminine conversazioni, where ladies are eloquent on Apollo and Mars' seems a slighting reference to the single-sex 'Conversations' on mythological figures that Fuller had organized in Boston. There are also echoes of *Woman in the Nineteenth Century* (1845). Fuller had claimed that women (and men) have both feminine and masculine elements in their natures. The woman in whom the feminine element predominates is the Muse: 'electrical in movement, intuitive in function, spiritual in tendency. She excels not so easily in clarification, or re-creation, as in an instinctive seizure of causes...More native is to her...to inspire and receive the poem, than to create it.' The more masculine woman is Minerva, whom Fuller associated with 'virginal' self-reliance and cultivation of the intellect but not energy, sex appeal or creativity (*MF*, pp. 309–12). Here, respectively, are Eliot's French and German woman. Eliot was known for her powers of synthesis and unusually retentive memory, and the essay here may be unintentional or uncredited homage to a better-established author.

Eliot's physiological argument fell in the conservative, 'little by little' category, and it was countered by more radical claims in 'Woman in France'. First, there was her discussion of literary cross-dressing. She noted that female authors who imitated men were too swashbuckling, too masculine. This statement might imply that the unnaturalness of their performance was the problem. But the critic then stated that the best representation of a female voice so far was by Samuel Richardson, in *Clarissa*, and Eliot herself frequently cross-dressed in her reviews and novels (*WF*, p. 16). Physiology, then, was not always determinative of authorial style. The interplay here of truth and convention, of nature and illusion, would recur in Eliot's treatment of Realism. The critic's physiological argument for Frenchwomen's literary achievement was, moreover, less convincing than the available class-based explanation would be. As Eliot observed in the essay, the eminent women of the seventeenth century were well-educated aristocrats, and their knowledge of Spanish and Italian literature, notable for chivalric ideals and wit, helped to create a distinctive French style. In addition, these women organized or had access to salons, where the sexes mixed freely. Finally, they benefited from extramarital liaisons, which were based on intellectual and physical attraction, without the domestic responsibilities that impeded a wife's self-development (*WF*, pp. 11–13). But these points about aristocratic adultery were not stressed; it was safer to attribute Frenchwomen's literary success to the smaller Gallic brain.

Eliot's literary criticism, like that of Martineau, set up a hierarchy of authors. First came the geniuses (de Staël among them), and then most of the nineteenth-century poets and Realist novelists. At the bottom were the imitative, the ignorant, the unworthy of publication. Eliot's reviews almost always contained some severe criticism, and her writers of genius were not spared. Carlyle sometimes breathed out 'threats and slaughter'. Ruskin could be contradictory and absurd. Margaret Fuller's mind 'was like some regions of her own American continent, where you are constantly stepping from sunny "clearings" into the mysterious twilight of the tangled forest'.[60] But the faults of these writers were irrelevant when compared with their 'power', 'ample being', 'vigour', 'truth' and 'colossal intellect' (all recurrent terms). Of the English poets, Eliot concurred with Martineau in placing Shakespeare and Scott (with the addition of Barrett Browning) in the first rank, and other Romantics and Victorians (Keats, Byron, even Wordsworth, along with Tennyson and Robert Browning) in the second. She could be scathing about stylistic failings, for example, castigating the third-rate Edward Young for 'furious bombast'.[61] But like Martineau and Fuller, she more highly valued largeness of mind and a kind of Promethean energy. Scott and the novelist Stowe surpassed the self-enclosed 'sentimentalists' like Byron and Tennyson in having the ability to imagine whole worlds, and bring to life minds and emotions quite unlike their own.[62]

One of Eliot's greatest contributions to nineteenth-century literary criticism was her richly developed theory of Realism (soon to inform her fictional practice). Much of this material was presented negatively, in her criticisms of second- and third-tier work. She almost always

---

[60]  Eliot, *Selected Essays*, pp. 299, 368, 333.
[61]  Eliot, 'Worldliness and Other-Worldliness: The Poet Young' in *Selected Essays*, p. 173.
[62]  Eliot, 'John Ruskin's *Modern Painters*' in *Selected Essays*, pp. 375–7.

evaluated a writer's powers of observation and accurate description.[63]
But careful representation was not an end in itself. Rather, it was the only
way to beauty and greatness in art. Moreover, a faithful study of nature,
including human nature, increased knowledge, sympathy and tolerance.[64]
Sympathy was not easily won, however. In one review essay, Eliot contrasted the unlovable actual peasant – slouching like a camel, coarse in his
jests, devoid of family affection – with the rosy-cheeked impostor found
in most fiction.[65]

Eliot's comments sometimes suggested a tension between 'truth' and
genre or narrative convention. In the famous chapter on literary Realism
in *Adam Bede* ('In which the story pauses a little'), the narrator (using a
male voice) told the 'lady readers' he could not make his characters better
than they were for the sake of conveying a clear moral. Rather, they could
only be true to life, with the benefit that readers could recognize similar
types in the workaday world outside the novel. But the narrator then
noted his indebtedness to Dutch paintings of the seventeenth century;
Realism here (as Tvestan Todorov has argued) evidently meant fidelity to
conventions, not to 'life'.[66] *Adam Bede* was a more naïve and problematic
statement of Realism than Eliot's reviews, which described the creative
process as involving imaginative visualization of a scene or character
as well as 'photographic' description. Her aim, as a critic and later a
novelist, was evidently to cover the sharp corners of the genre used, so
that it seemed less of a jerry-built stage set and might evoke a living world.
Moreover, like Martineau, she disliked the plethora of novels that were
'imitations of imitations': the tale of pseudo-antiquity; the 'silver-fork
school'. Praising Stowe for inventing the 'negro novel', she thought British
writers needed to look outside the familiar upper-class house of fiction
and bring other oppressed groups to public attention, such as the working
class. She joined writers such as Gaskell and Dickens in underlining the
political urgency of this agenda: the revolutions of the nineteenth century
had shown the dangers of lower-class violence, which might be overcome
if novels were thrown into the breach – novels properly instructing the
middle class in ways to sympathize and help. In contrast to Martineau,
whose assessments often seemed based, in an eighteenth-century way, on
a list of virtues, Eliot's criticism revealed a complex literary ethic, linking
imagination, vision, representation, sympathy and community. Vision
remained the key, on the part of both author and reader: the ability to see

---

63  E.g., Eliot, 'Charles Kingsley's *Westward Ho!*' in *Selected Essays*, p. 311.
64  Eliot, 'John Ruskin's *Modern Painters*', pp. 369–71.
65  Eliot, 'The *Natural History of German Life*' in *Selected Essays*, p. 109.
66  Tvestan Todorov, 'An Introduction to Verisimilitude' in *The Poetics of Prose*, trans.
    Richard Howard (Ithaca, NY: Cornell University Press, 1977), p. 83.

the world anew, and to transform action into narrative representation, or representation back into social action.

The ameliorative, largely conservative character of Eliot's Realism contrasted with her 'insurgent' reaction to Victorian literary moralizing. She strongly disliked didacticism and one-sided characterization.[67] Eliot would eliminate 'poetic justice', of the sort that threw a villain under a train (Dickens's *Dombey and Son* was the target). Such tactics were not just ineffective but hypocritical: a sharp demarcation between virtuous and vicious characters, 'so far from being a necessary safeguard to morality, is itself an immoral fiction'.[68]

Eliot was well aware of a double standard in Victorian literary criticism – a distinction between 'writing' and 'ladies' writing'.[69] In praising literary genius, she often minimized differences between male and female achievement and, like Fuller suggested some androgyny in talent.[70] But at other times Eliot said that women, because of their sex, had a special literary contribution to make: Barrett Browning was 'all the greater poet because... intensely a poetess'.[71] By arguing sometimes for sexual sameness and sometimes for difference, Eliot compelled recognition of female greatness while also honouring earlier women such as Madame de Sablé, whose very emergence as an author was remarkable, quite apart from her performance.

Eliot could, however, play with the idea of difference, implying that gender in literature, at least, was nothing more than performance. In her most famous essay, she cross-dressed as a male critic and had merciless fun satirizing inferior female novelists, who 'write in elegant boudoirs, with violet-coloured ink and a ruby pen... they must be entirely indifferent to publishers' accounts, and inexperienced in every form of poverty except poverty of brains'.[72] This element of class antagonism was often found in Eliot's literary criticism. She felt that untalented authors had no business writing when they did so only out of vanity.[73] J. S. Mill was confident that the literary marketplace would place the right value on inferior ideas. Eliot, however, thought the aristocratic dilettantes should find another hobby, because they would crowd out the professionals, such as herself and Lewes, who needed to earn a living. Her comments also pointed to a feminist agenda. Eliot critiqued 'silly novels' lest readers think they were the best women could do, and fail to recognize the real

---

[67] E.g., Eliot, 'Charles Kingsley's *Westward Ho!*', pp. 312–13.
[68] Eliot, 'The Morality of *Wilhelm Meister*' in *Selected Essays*, pp. 308, 310.
[69] E.g., Eliot, 'Geraldine Jewsbury's *Constance Herbert*' in *Selected Essays*, p. 320.
[70] Eliot, 'Margaret Fuller and Mary Wollstonecraft' in *Selected Essays*, p. 333.
[71] Eliot, Review of *Aurora Leigh* in *Selected Essays*, p. 168.
[72] Eliot, 'Silly Novels' in *Selected Essays*, p. 142.
[73] E.g., Eliot, 'Lord Brougham's Literature' in *Selected Essays*, p. 303.

talent of a Martineau, a Brontë or a Gaskell.[74] Eliot was reluctant to be a feminist activist; her reasons included her conservatism about social change and her irregular relationship with Lewes. But she had a clear sense of solidarity with other women in her profession.

Eliot's main role models early in her career seem to have been Mary Wollstonecraft and Margaret Fuller because she identified with their struggles to find both happiness and a vocation.[75] As Byatt says, they were 'mirrors for her sense of self'.[76] Fuller's emergence from the forests of America to become a journalist and then a presence on the world stage must have inspired a young woman from the provinces. Eliot's comments on Fuller may be her warmest praise of any writer other than Carlyle:

In conversation she was as copious and oracular as Coleridge, brilliant as Sterling, pungent and paradoxical as Carlyle; gifted with the inspired powers of a Pythoness, she saw into the hearts and over the heads of all who came near her; and, but for a sympathy as boundless as her self-esteem, she would have despised the whole human race! Her frailty, in this respect, was no secret either to herself or her friends. She quizzed them and boasted of herself to such an excess as to turn disgust into laughter – yea, so right royally did she carry herself that her arrogance became a virtue, worshipful as the majesty of the gods.[77]

The tone of exasperated affection registered how Fuller learned to live with her well-founded sense of greatness.

Before the collective and individual achievements of Martineau, Jameson, Fuller and Eliot are summed up specifically in the area of literary criticism, some caveats are necessary. They all were read widely, even transatlantically, by their contemporaries. But the criticism of any period is more ephemeral than the literature. All now have primarily an academic audience, with Eliot and Fuller best known today because of the former's novels and the latter's Transcendentalist connections to Emerson and Thoreau. Moreover, there was generally a hiatus in editions of the four critics' works between the late nineteenth century and the late twentieth century, no doubt attributable to the frequent deprecation of women's writing, and even more to the modern cultural reaction that caused Lytton Strachey to publish *Eminent Victorians* (1918) and Griff House, Eliot's childhood home in Nuneaton, to be made into a tavern rather than a historic site.

74  Eliot, 'Silly Novels' in *Selected Essays*, pp. 161–3.
75  Eliot, 'Margaret Fuller and Mary Wollstonecraft', pp. 332–8.
76  Byatt, 'Introduction to Eliot', p. xv.
77  Eliot, 'Contemporary Literature of America', *Westminster Review*, 57 (1852), pp. 353–4.

What did the four literary critics achieve? Perhaps most importantly, they helped to define Victorian Realism. Martineau's antipathy towards Romantic confessionalism and 'morbidity' helped to differentiate the age of Carlyle from that of Byron. Jameson's attention to the psychological complexities of the heroines and the family dynamics in Shakespeare's plays highlighted what were also characteristic features of Victorian fiction. Eliot's contribution was her awareness (shared especially with Sand) that Realism did not preclude Idealism – that characters and events could carry symbolic value – and that 'mere' description of exterior and interior worlds had the potential of promoting sympathy among readers. While Fuller praised regional fictions, she is the odd person out here, with her enduring preference for Romanticism. (More than the others, she had de Staël as a role model.) Her work does, however, highlight the dialectic between Romantic and Victorian values in nineteenth-century Realism. All four writers praised (to varying degrees) the detailed, even totalizing, descriptions of the rural landscape, the industrial city, and emerging and vanishing ways of life. But all also looked for power and originality in literature – the individual vision, the distinctive voice – with Fuller continuing the Romantic emphasis on self-consciousness in the authorial or critical enterprise. While the four critics were hardly alone in calling the novel the genre of the age, they did make a compelling case for what it could be. In particular, they sought to make it a more democratic genre. It should teach the meritocratic values of America (so Martineau), represent all ranks and ages, and develop plots other than the love story. Most of these comments occurred in assessments of American literature. The critics thus explored connections between national character and literature which were seen earlier in de Staël. And they helped foster respect for New World writing by saying the Yankees sometimes set the standard for innovation and excellence, and British writers would do well to imitate Sedgwick and Stowe.

Martineau, Jameson, Fuller and Eliot published their criticism in an intensely religious age. But they managed to detach the discussion of morality from both doctrine and didacticism. Even Martineau (whom her biographer R. W. Webb called relentlessly didactic) did not always specify which values should be taught. The emphasis thus appropriately moved to literary performance. Rather than proscribing sordid lives, the critics considered how best to represent them. They moreover denigrated extremes in characterization (for too often Victorian fiction was of the Dudley Do-Right/Snidely Whiplash variety).

While Mary Wollstonecraft (with her Kate-Millett-like attack on Milton) and de Staël (with her complaints about the abuse of female writers) were important predecessors in the history of gender criticism, the four Victorian writers did help to introduce this approach to a popular audience.[78] All addressed and defended their positions as public intellectuals. They also promoted the careers of women writers by reviewing their work – Eliot at times ruthlessly, by distinguishing writers of genuine talent from silly lady novelists. Jameson stands out here as a feminist activist who in every literary genre addressed the status of women. *Shakespeare's Heroines* influenced the representations of the playwright's heroines by later artists and critics, both male and female.[79] Jameson moreover anticipated the agenda of feminist literary critics in the late twentieth century by assuming Shakespeare's work reflects the female reader's experience and by contrasting the biases of male critics with her own interpretative competence. The most interesting work on gender was done by Fuller and also Eliot. They made gender itself a critical concept, theorizing about masculinity, femininity and the various forms of creative transgendering (androgyny, literary cross-dressing). They showed that gender was a category analogous to nationality, in that it shaped and constrained the self – the masculine self, the imperial self – as well as the other.

Some of the terms suggested in the opening section of this chapter do apply to the four writers. The female literary critic could indeed be considered a freak of nature, or of society – a woman with an unusual upbringing and intellectual gifts, and an extraordinary drive to do the nearly inconceivable: compete with men, criticize men (both rulers and authors), and raise her voice not in the comparatively private space of the novel but in the public sphere of newspaper and periodical. In her century she was notable not least because of her gender, surmounting barriers not placed before men of the same class. Martineau's achievement as a literary critic was perhaps least of the four, because most of her energies were directed towards social reform. Though her judgements could be acute, she was a woman of limited imaginative power and emotional range, as she herself noted. Jameson's impact on her contemporaries was greatest as an art critic and feminist activist. While her drama criticism and travel writing attract more attention today, her work on Shakespeare, though insightful, is limited by her reluctance to say anything negative about the bard. What Foucault would call Shakespeare's author function was of primary importance, because it legitimized hers. Eliot's relatively brief period as a literary critic and editor was her intellectual training as a novelist. While her longer essays insightfully advanced discussion of key topics, such as Realism, and her shorter reviews were incisive, her rare talent to synthesize, seize and judge was not fully on display until her fiction. Fuller, in contrast, from the start fitted Woolf's definition of a 'born writer', one who would 'plunge and stumble and jump at boughs

---

[78] de Staël, *On Literature*, pp. 172, 201.     [79] Lootens, *Lost Saints*, pp. 97–8.

beyond his grasp'.[80] Her work, always *essais* or 'attempts', is the most
original and engrossing of the four critics'. Yet, as noted before, these
writers' achievement does not simply lie in their publications. Like de
Staël and Sand before them, the four served as role models to each other
and to younger writers.[81] A career in literary criticism – in journalism,
now in the academy – became progressively easier for women because
others had gone before.

---

[80]  Virginia Woolf, *Congenial Spirits: The Selected Letters of Virginia Woolf*, ed. Joanne
      Trautmann Banks (New York: Harvest/HBJ, 1989), p. 282.
[81]  See Ellen Moers, *Literary Women* (New York: Oxford University Press, 1985), p. 43.

# National developments in literary criticism

# 4

# Literature and nationalism

## JULIA M. WRIGHT

> The literature of the Continent during the last few years
> has been essentially political, revolutionary, and war-
> like.... Calm has fled from the minds of writers. Poetry
> is silent, as if frightened by the storm now gathering in
> the hearts of men. Romance becomes rarer every day;
> it would find no readers. Pure art is a myth.... There
> are in Europe two great questions; or, rather, the ques-
> tion of the transformation of authority, that is to say,
> of the Revolution, has assumed two forms; the question
> which all have agreed to call social, and the question of
> nationalities.[1]
>
> Giuseppe Mazzini, 'Europe: Its Condition
> and Prospects' (1852)

In the 1790s, William Blake wrote a nationalist poem that is also arguably his most scatological work, 'When Klopstock England Defied'. Reportedly, the German poet Friedrich Gottlieb Klopstock 'had been declaring to English visitors that their language was incapable of the epic grandeur of hexameters, and he had spoken with scorn of English writers' coarseness of tone traceable to Swift'.[2] This was not the first time that Klopstock had appeared to pose a threat to English poetic supremacy: his *Der Messias* (1748–73; 'The Messiah'), written in German hexameters, was 'Quickly hailed as Germany's answer to Milton'.[3] In Blake's contri-bution to the German–English hexameter wars, 'English Blake' is called to answer Klopstock's challenge, and the poet does so, with characteristic

I am grateful to the Canada Research Chairs Program and the Social Sciences and Human-ities Research Council of Canada for generously supporting this research, and to Jason Haslam for his very helpful comments on an earlier version of this chapter.

[1] Giuseppe Mazzini, 'Europe: Its Condition and Prospects', *Westminster Review*, 112 (1852), pp. 236, 242.
[2] David V. Erdman, 'Textual Notes' in *The Complete Poetry and Prose of William Blake*, rev. edn (New York: Doubleday, 1988), p. 863n.
[3] Ernest Bernhardt-Kabisch, '"When Klopstock England Defied": Coleridge, Southey, and the German/English Hexameter', *Comparative Literature*, 55 (2003), p. 131.

verve, in a patriotic retort on the mock-epic subject of defecation.[4] This is
no mere literary-historical footnote to an eccentric poem by an eccentric
poet, but points to an international competition to excel in hexameters
as a matter of nationalist pride, and more broadly to the nationalist
investment in literature that emerged in the West in the late eighteenth
century. For Blake, Klopstock is refusing English poets access to an elite
literary form, and one that held considerable prestige during Blake's
lifetime, particularly because of the association of epic with national
power and empire-building. In his comprehensive *Elements of Criticism*
(1762), Henry Home (Lord Kames) limits his discussion of 'versification'
to only two metrical forms, 'French and English heroic verse' and 'Latin
or Greek hexameter', even though, he notes, 'Many attempts have been
made to introduce Hexameter verse into the living languages, but without
success.'[5] Because of its difficulty for 'the living languages', the hexameter
form posed a special challenge for modern competitors seeking to claim
the neo-classical laurel for their nation and hence the title of heir to
(imperial) Greece and Rome. Blake's poem makes the national stakes
explicit: 'England' has been 'defied' and 'English Blake' must defend his
nation.

   While patriotism and national identity as concepts existed in European
culture well before the Enlightenment, the origins of modern nationalism
are generally located in the late eighteenth century. Modern nationalism
is distinctive for its emphasis on the people, rather than a ruling elite, as
the basis for both sovereignty and national identity. Anthony D. Smith,
for instance, 'define[s] the concept of nation' on these terms: 'a named
human community occupying a homeland, and having common myths
and a shared history, a common public culture, a single economy and
common rights and duties for all members'.[6] The emphasis on terms
such as 'common', 'shared' and 'public' speaks to the modern requirement of full participation in the nation by its citizens, as distinct from
obedience from its subjects. But more crucial here is the requirement of
a 'common public culture'. As the Klopstock example attests, national
pride invests that public culture with considerable value. It could be used
to sanction imperial claims to superior civility, and legitimize counter-
imperial claims made by oppressed peoples on the basis of a unique

---

[4] William Blake, 'When Klopstock England Defied' in *Complete Poetry and Prose of William Blake*, line 6.
[5] Henry Home (Lord Kames), *Elements of Criticism* (1762), intro. Robert Voitle, 3 vols. (New York: Georg Olms, 1970), vol. II, pp. 359, 446.
[6] Anthony D. Smith, *Nationalism: Theory, Ideology, History* (Cambridge: Polity, 2001), p. 13. See also Elizabeth Sauer and Julia M. Wright (eds.), *Reading the Nation in English Literature: A Critical Reader* (New York: Routledge, 2009).

cultural identity that authorizes their national sovereignty. As American clergyman William Ellery Channing remarks in 1830, 'We are accustomed to estimate nations by their creative energies.'[7] Critical reflection on literature also became a vital part of the 'public culture'. The Russian writer Ivan Kireevsky claims in 1828, 'only our concerted effort can achieve what all well-meaning people have desired for so long and, nevertheless, we still do not have: to wit, public opinion – which is both a result and condition of national culture and therefore of national welfare'.[8] This Habermasian concern with the public sphere reveals the ways in which the nation was understood to reside in 'public culture' rather than territory, shifting the theatre of inter-national battle, at least in part, from muddy fields to readers' critical judgements. Moreover, Kireevsky's remarks address the ways in which that public culture was also subject to improvement through literary labour in ways that could be of national benefit.

   To address some of the ways in which literature became not only a vehicle for the expression and circulation of nationalist ideas but also a measure of the nation and therefore an object of national policy through criticism itself, this chapter pursues three broad areas of inquiry: first, the continuities and distinctions between contemporary nationalism studies and articulations of nationality in the history of ideas in the West, particularly in relation to nationalism's often contradictory agenda of pursuing both progress and continuity with the past; second, the development of national literary history as a synecdoche for the nation's history and hence a measure of its progress; third, the ways in which the failure of national literature was tied to the incomplete development or decline of the nation. National literature is located in criticism of the long nineteenth century at the crux of a contradiction between neo-classical aspirations to empire, universal standards and the progress towards perfection on the one hand, and nativist longing for a specific territory, local cultural traditions and the conservation of the past on the other – a contradiction that troubles nationalism itself. The first is expansive, locating Britain, for instance, in an imperial genealogy that stretches back to Greece and Rome, and authorizing it to shape the world in its image and understand itself as the fullest expression of a universal modernity which others should seek; the other is insular, grounding individuals in the specific landscape, culture and history of the region in which they were born.

---

7  William Ellery Channing, *The Importance and Means of a National Literature* (London: Edward Rainford, 1830), p. 35.
8  Ivan Kireevsky, 'On the Nature of Pushkin's Poetry' (1828) in *Literature and National Identity: Nineteenth-Century Russian Critical Essays*, trans. and ed. Paul Debreczeny and Jesse Zeldin (Lincoln: University of Nebraska Press, 1970), pp. 3, 4.

I

To use the term 'nationalism' is not only to engage a diverse history of political movements, ranging from liberatory anti-imperialism to the worst fascism (as many nationalism scholars have noted), but also to negotiate between two modes for defining it: the history of ideas and nationalism studies. The study of nationalism has largely been shaped by political science, sociology and history, and hence has focused on the conditions under which nationalism emerges, the key features which define it, and the relationship it bears to government structures and policies. Smith argues that 'social constructionists' such as E. J. Hobsbawm have had the ascendancy in recent years, supporting a model in which claims about the nation are fictions which solicit popular support in order to further the agenda of an elite; Smith offers instead an 'ethnosymbolic' approach which pays due attention to 'the pre-existing symbols and cultural ties and sentiments in which nations are embedded'.[9] But both Smith's argument and social constructionism (which cultural critics would recognize as broadly Althusserian or Gramscian) make the people largely innocent of nationalism: it is either a cultural inheritance or foisted upon them by a manipulative elite. I note this similarity to stress the ways in which nationalism, on a theoretical level, runs directly counter to Lockean notions of citizenship in which an individual willingly cedes his personal sovereignty in order to join a 'civil society'.[10] Nationalism fundamentally cannot allow such a personal choice. Italian nationalist leader Giuseppe Mazzini wrote in 1852,

> They speak the same language, they bear about them the impress of consanguinity, they kneel beside the same tombs, they glory in the same tradition, and they demand to associate freely, without obstacles, without foreign domination, in order to elaborate and express their idea, to contribute their stone also to the great pyramid of history.[11]

Mazzini's remarks are typical not only for making language and history central to national identity, in the vein of Johann Gottfried von Herder and others long before 1852, but also for including an unacknowledged conflict between the determinism of nationality and the promise of self-determination: they must 'speak the same language' and 'kneel beside

---

[9]  Anthony D. Smith, *The Nation in History: Historiographical Debates about Ethnicity and Nationalism* (Hanover: University Press of New England, 2000), p. 75. See E. J. Hobsbawm, *Nations and Nationalism since 1780* (Cambridge University Press, 1990).
[10] John Locke, *Two Treatises of Government*, ed. Peter Laslett (Cambridge University Press, 1988), p. 325.
[11] Mazzini, 'Europe', p. 247.

the same tombs', while they 'demand to associate freely... in order to elaborate and express their idea'. Although John Locke makes theoretically possible the transfer of national sovereignty from a monarch to a sovereign people by 'placing popular sovereignty at the core of any account of political legitimacy',[12] nationalism must always stress the will of the *people* rather than individual consent. Individuals cannot choose their nation, their language or the tombs at which they will kneel, and can find their freedom only through the nation into which they were born. Hence the roots of nationalism in European intellectual history lie largely in formulations of 'national character', theorizations which sidestep Locke and the Enlightenment premise of universality in order to rationalize age-old stereotypes, as well as distil a plurality of individuals into a singular people who share a 'character'.

Ernest Gellner grounds this imperative for a uniform population in the standardized education demanded by the Industrial Revolution in order that workers could be moved easily from site to site. He usefully outlines the ways in which nationalism can tip standardization through 'well-defined educationally sanctioned and unified cultures' into a totalizing hegemonic culture:

The cultures now seem to be the natural repositories of political legitimacy. Only *then* does it come to appear that any defiance of their boundaries by political units constitutes a scandal... In these conditions, men will to be politically united with all those, and only those, who share their culture. Polities then will to extend their boundaries to the limits of their cultures, and to protect and impose their culture within the boundaries of their power. The fusion of will, culture, and polity becomes the norm.[13]

Benedict Anderson's claims for print culture are a variation on Gellner's arguments about standardization: 'the convergence of capitalism and print technology on the fatal diversity of human language created the possibility of a new form of imagined community, which in its basic morphology set the stage for the modern nation'.[14] These two influential theorists, then, agree on some broad general principles: nationalism emerges in relation to various pressures which homogenize culture as well as give wide access to that culture, creating a political stake for individuals in a culturally defined community, whether 'imagined' (Anderson) or only apparent (Gellner), and fostering the state's interest in popular support and the legitimacy that it offers.

[12] David Resnick, 'John Locke and Liberal Nationalism', *History of European Ideas*, 15 (1992), p. 512.
[13] Ernest Gellner, *Nations and Nationalism* (Ithaca, NY: Cornell University Press, 1983), p. 55.
[14] Benedict Anderson, *Imagined Communities: Reflections on the Origin and Spread of Nationalism*, rev. edn (New York: Verso, 1991), p. 46.

Although they disagree in many respects, both Gellner and Anderson assert that nationalism was made possible by the Reformation: Anderson suggests that 'The coalition between Protestantism and print-capitalism, exploiting cheap popular editions, quickly created large new reading publics... and simultaneously mobilized them for politico-religious purposes'; Gellner argues that 'The stress of the Reformation on literacy and scripturalism, its onslaught on a monopolistic priesthood... its individualism and links with mobile urban populations, all make it a kind of harbinger of social features and attitudes which... produce the nationalist age.'[15] Gellner's and Anderson's attention to the Reformation is particularly striking because Victorians found in the Reformation not only the seeds of their national identity but also the origin of their recovery of a truly native literature: it was in the Reformation that Anglo-Saxon studies began, in part to legitimate a church independent of Rome through reference to Saxon translations of the Bible and a married clergy.[16] The Reformation in this view was not a critical turning point in the standardization of culture, as Gellner and Anderson would have it, but rather a sloughing off of foreign influences, a return to a nativist sense of self of the sort idealized within Romanticism – marked by 'its greater sincerity and earnestness', as Matthew Arnold puts it in his praise for the Hebraizing impulse of the Reformation.[17] These two views of the Reformation – a casting off of foreign corruption and the consolidation of uniformity within the nation's borders – point to the ways in which nationalism relies on modern mechanisms (such as print, transportation and widespread literacy) even when it is proposing a return to the past.

Arnold is illustrative here for the ways in which his analysis of the Hebraic and Hellenic in *Culture and Anarchy* (1869) echoes nationalism's contradictory investment in both the conservation of the past and the promise of development. Smith frames this ambivalence as an 'interplay' between 'a civic neo-classicism and a "historicist" Romanticism'.[18] Like Gellner and Anderson, Smith suggests that the growing significance of education is instrumental in the development of modern nationalism, but Smith generatively attends to the contradictions between neo-classical ideals of an 'educated public' and Romantic ideals of the natural and the authentic, particularly in the former's 'standardising tendencies' and the

---

[15] *Ibid.*, p. 40; Gellner, *Nations and Nationalism*, pp. 40–1.

[16] John Petheram, *An Historical Sketch of the Progress and Present State of Anglo-Saxon Literature in England* (London: Edward Lumley, 1840).

[17] Matthew Arnold, *Culture and Anarchy* (1869), ed. J. Dover Wilson (Cambridge University Press, 2001), p. 140.

[18] Anthony D. Smith, 'Neo-Classicist and Romantic Elements in the Emergence of Nationalist Conceptions' in *Nationalist Movements*, ed. Anthony D. Smith (London: Macmillan, 1976), p. 74.

latter's privileging of 'a programme of self-purification which drew its inspiration from a visionary image of a pristine past and a transfigured future', or more broadly a 'return to Nature'.[19] Neo-classical, Enlightenment views of an ideal educated citizen and the Romantic desire for a 'return' to a privileged origin, such as pre-Conquest, Anglo-Saxon England, were crucially resolved through a narrative of education as 'a process of self-development':

> It is from the genuine and sacred realms of culture and ethics that neo-classicists draw inspiration for their reform of politics, while Romantics wish to go further and revolutionise politics . . . in the name of Nature. . . . [B]oth movements grope towards a non-political theory of politics, one which draws its categories from the untainted bonds of culture.[20]

These movements' 'elevation of culture as the source of politics', in Smith's phrase, makes culture the basis of both national identity and individual membership in the nation, appearing to resolve the conflict noted above with respect to Mazzini: national culture is the means by which the individual develops, and vice versa.

Cultural development and national character were linked, however, as early as David Hume's 1748 essay 'Of National Characters'. Strenuously rejecting '*physical* causes', including climate and region, for which his French contemporaries continued to argue, Hume suggested that tendencies among national groups arose from '*moral* causes', that is, 'all circumstances which are fitted to work on the mind as motives or reasons, and which render a peculiar set of manners habitual to us'.[21] History is the force which propagates and intensifies the effects of these causes that we would now term 'cultural', and through it one striking individual can change the course of a nation's development: 'If on the first establishment of a republic, a BRUTUS should be placed in authority . . . such an illustrious example will naturally have an effect on the whole society, and kindle the same passion in every bosom. Whatever it be that forms the manners of one generation, the next must imbibe a deeper tincture of the same dye.'[22] Hume extends this principle to his discussion of literature, arguing that 'A few eminent and refined geniuses will communicate their taste and knowledge to a whole people, and produce the greatest improvements.'[23] Hume's ideas were similarly disseminated, widely dispersed beyond the realm of strict philosophy throughout the long

---

[19] *Ibid.*, pp. 78, 80, 81.   [20] *Ibid.*, pp. 83–4.
[21] David A. Bell, *The Cult of the Nation in France: Inventing Nationalism, 1680–1800* (Cambridge, MA: Harvard University Press, 2001), pp. 224n, 144; David Hume, 'Of National Characters' (1748) in *Political Essays*, ed. Knud Haakonssen (Cambridge University Press, 1994), p. 78.
[22] Hume, 'Of National Characters', pp. 82–3.   [23] *Ibid.*, p. 87.

nineteenth century. In 1792, Frodsham Hodson won the Oxford English
Prize for an essay which closely follows Hume's dismissal of 'physical
causes' to contend that 'the prominent features of national character are
formed by Education and Government'.[24] An 1839 review in the British
*Athenaeum* also follows a Humean causation:

> It is also pretty generally known that America is over-dosed with religious
> stimuli; that the descendants of the 'pilgrim fathers' have inherited a fanatical
> temperament, at once gloomy and excitable;... and that education, instead of
> resisting, aids in propagating an epidemic and diseased enthusiasm.[25]

In Ireland, James Byrne traced differences between the Anglo-Saxon and
the Celt in 1863 (shortly before Arnold's infamous *On the Study of Celtic
Literature*) along a broadly Humean model: 'these national differences
arose from the different degrees in which the respective nations were
occupied with industry or with adventure when their national character
was forming'.[26] A century and a half after Hume, French critic Ernest
Renan suggested that the nation is defined not by geography but by its
past and 'the will to preserve worthily the undivided inheritance which
has been handed down', as well as 'constituted by the sentiment of the
sacrifices that its citizens have made' and imbued with 'a living soul,
a spiritual principle'.[27] Renan recalls Edmund Burke's *Reflections on
the Revolution in France* (1790) more than Hume in his emphasis on
conserving the past rather than development – 'the excellence of races
is to be appreciated by the purity of their blood and the inviolability of
their national character'[28] – but he yet demonstrates the ways in which
national character remained firmly yoked to history and culture rather
than essential determinants such as 'race' or region.

For thinkers of the Scottish Enlightenment, social progress was marked
not specifically through literature but more broadly through civility –
taste, the arts, the sciences, economic structures and political improvements. Hume thus suggests that 'The spirit of the age affects all the arts;
and the minds of men, being once roused from their lethargy, and put
into a fermentation, turn themselves on all sides, and carry improvements

[24] Frodsham Hodson, 'The Influence of Education and Government on National Character' in *Oxford English Prize Essays*, 5 vols. (Oxford: D. A. Talboys, 1836), vol. 1,
pp. 277–94.
[25] Review of *A Voice from America*, by an American Gentleman, *Athenaeum*, 598 (1839),
p. 267 (attributed to Lady Morgan by the *Athenaeum Index*, http://athenaeum.soi.city.
ac.uk/reviews/contributors/contributors files/MORGAN, Lady Sydney Owenson.html ).
[26] James Byrne, 'The Influence of National Character on English Literature' in *The Afternoon Lectures on English Literature* (London: Bell and Daldy, 1863), p. 6.
[27] Ernest Renan, 'What Is a Nation?' in *Poetry of the Celtic Races and Other Studies*,
trans. William G. Hutchison (1896; rpt London: Kennikat Press, 1970), pp. 79–81.
[28] Ernest Renan, 'The Poetry of the Celtic Races' in *Poetry of the Celtic Races and Other
Studies*, p. 4.

into every art and science.'[29] Home similarly argues that literature is less
an effect of civility than a contributor to it. In his *Elements of Criticism*,
a crucial work in the history of literary study as a modern discipline, he
follows the fundamental precept that literature trains the social affections
and so contributes to national virtue, which in turn contributes to stable
government: 'Among the many branches of education, that which tends
to make deep impressions of virtue, ought to be a fundamental measure
in a well-regulated government: for depravity of manners will render ineffectual the most salutary laws; and in the midst of opulence, what other
means to prevent such depravity but early and virtuous discipline?'[30]
These virtues are energized by patriotism, which is itself contingent on
the nation's status, so Home argues in *Sketches of the History of Man*
(1778) that the 'national spirit subsides' when a nation's power relative to other nations becomes 'stationary' or 'sunk', while 'Patriotism is
enflamed by a struggle for liberty, by a civil war, by resisting a potent
invader, or by any incident that forcibly draws the members of a state into
strict union for the common interest' – or, as poet William Drennan put
it in 1799, 'common calamity may produce a common country'.[31] Home
further insists, 'patriotism is connected with every social virtue; and when
it vanishes, every virtue vanishes with it', and that the effects of patriotism include public works for the greater good, such as universities and
libraries.[32] The standardization noted by modern theorists is idealized
in these Enlightenment views in which the nation is improved through
the education of its citizens. While Hume, Home and others paved the
way for cultural nationalism by tying national greatness to education and
cultural excellence, as well as entrenching the idea that national character
was a reflection of 'moral causes', it was left to antiquarians and their
nineteenth-century successors to develop the idea of a national literature.

II

If we follow Smith's broad articulation of the concept of nation as 'a
named human community occupying a homeland, and having common
myths and a shared history, a common public culture, a single economy
and common rights and duties for all members',[33] then Hume's essay

---

[29]  Hume, 'Of Refinement in the Arts' (1752) in *Political Essays*, p. 107.
[30]  Home, *Elements of Criticism*, vol. I, p. vi.
[31]  Henry Home, *Sketches of the History of Man* (1774), 4 vols. (Hildesheim: Georg Olms,
      1968), vol. I, p. 295, vol. II, pp. 317–18; William Drennan, *A Letter to the Right
      Honorable William Pitt* (Dublin: James Moore, 1799), p. 27. See also, for instance,
      Renan, 'What Is a Nation?'
[32]  Home, *Sketches*, vol. II, pp. 246, 318.    [33]  Smith, *Nationalism*, p. 13.

'Of National Characters' addresses 'a shared history', 'a common public culture' and 'a single economy', while Home stresses the significance as well of 'common rights and duties for all members'. National literature as a critical concept emerges out of such eighteenth-century theorizations, but critics divided roughly into two camps on the subject that correspond to Smith's distinction between the neo-classical and the Romantic: on the one hand, there is Enlightenment civic progress, in which learning is cumulative and society improves along with its cultural traditions, producing a measurable greatness that can be discerned on the international stage; on the other, there is an origin, a 'spirit' that transcends historical change and to which the nation's citizens must be true, as in the arguments of Mazzini and Renan.

In the nativist 'Romantic' tradition, a seminal text appeared in 1765. Bishop Percy's *Reliques of Ancient English Poetry* linked the national past with the popular form of the ballad, offering 'such specimens of ancient poetry' that 'either shew the gradation of our language, exhibit the progress of popular opinions, display the peculiar manners and customs of former ages, or throw light on our earlier classical poets'.[34] Work on 'ancient English poetry' continued over the next century, so much so that by 1840 John Petheram could publish a substantial history of scholarship on Anglo-Saxon language and literature from the sixteenth to the nineteenth century. Petheram represents 'the revival of this language by the Reformers of the sixteenth century' as 'truly patriotic', finding the origin of England's imperial might in its Anglo-Saxon roots and a history which is valuable for 'elucidating the history of the human mind, and of explaining the reason of the fact, that the inhabitants of an island so small as that on which we live should have spread her name, and language, and power, over the whole earth'.[35] Outside of the English metropole, work in this nativist vein included collections of verse from Sir Walter Scott's *Minstrelsy of the Scottish Border* (1802) to Thomas Moore's *Irish Melodies* (1807–34) and Felicia Hemans's *Welsh Melodies* (1822), as well as 'national tales' which sought to explicate the cultures of the Celtic periphery, from Lady Morgan's *The Wild Irish Girl* (1806) to Scott's *Waverley* (1814). Similar ideas were put forward on the continent. Friedrich Schiller wrote in 1795, 'They [rural and ancient peoples] are what we *were*; they are what we *should become again*. We were natural like them.'[36]

At the neo-classical end of the spectrum, Thomas Warton offered a *History of English Poetry* (1774) that moved out of the antiquarian frame

34  Thomas Percy, *Reliques of Ancient English Poetry* (1765), 3 vols. (London: Routledge/ Thoemmes Press, 1996), vol. I, p. ix.
35  Petheram, *Anglo-Saxon Literature*, pp. 1, 2.
36  Friedrich Schiller, *On the Naive and Sentimental in Literature* (1795), trans. Helen Watanabe-O'Kelly (Manchester: Carcanet New Press, 1981), p. 22.

and into an English modernity defined by elite, rather than popular or antique, culture. Thus, Warton proposes 'to develop the dawnings of genius, and to pursue the progress of our national poetry, from a rude origin and obscure beginnings, to its perfection in a polished age', and organizes his work chronologically in order to trace English progress.[37] Warton, as I have argued elsewhere, helped to spawn a new kind of anthology that was not only chronologically arranged but also polemically pitched towards the celebration of a national literature in the elite form of poetry.[38] Such anthologies include George Ellis's *Specimens of the Early English Poets* (1790; expanded in 1801), Thomas Campbell's *Specimens of the British Poets* (1819), William Hazlitt's *Select Poets of Great Britain* (1825) and Robert Southey's *Select Works of the British Poets* (1831). Warton and later anthologists maintained the Enlightenment connection between taste and virtue, but deployed it for more recognizably nationalist purposes on terms consistent with Hume's representation of the impact of literature in communicating 'taste and knowledge'. For instance, in his much-anthologized essay 'On Some of the Characteristics of Modern Poetry' (1831), Arthur Henry Hallam declares, 'The knowledge and power thus imbibed became a part of national existence; it was ours as Englishmen; and amidst the flux of generations and customs we retain unimpaired this privilege of intercourse with greatness.'[39] Although Hallam draws on Burkean conservatism in the emphasis on 'retain[ing] unimpaired', the fundamental model here is Hume's. Whether focusing on pride in the national past or in the national present that grew out of that past, these anthologists and their successors promulgated a particular view of the nation's literature as evidence of a core national identity as well as a shared national inheritance.

In 1818, the anonymous essay 'Of a National Character in Literature' appeared in an early volume of the conservative periodical *Blackwood's*. The essay opens with the suggestion, 'It would appear, that the pleasure we receive from making ourselves acquainted with the literature of a people, and more especially with their literature of imagination, is intimately connected with an impression, that in their literature we see the picture of their minds.'[40] Language is not only unique to the nation – as the Young

---

37 Thomas Warton, *The History of English Poetry, from the Twelfth to the Close of the Sixteenth Century*, ed. W. Carew Hazlitt, 4 vols. (London: Reeves and Turner, 1871), vol. I, p. 3.

38 Julia M. Wright, '"The Order of Time": Nationalism and Literary Anthologies, 1774–1831', *Papers on Language and Literature* 33 (1997), 339–65.

39 Hume, 'Of National Characters', p. 82; Arthur Henry Hallam, 'On Some of the Characteristics of Modern Poetry' (1831) in *The Broadview Anthology of Victorian Poetry and Poetic Theory*, eds. Thomas J. Collins and Vivienne Rundle (Peterborough: Broadview Press, 2000), p. 544.

40 'Of a National Character in Literature', *Blackwood's Edinburgh Magazine*, 3 (1818), p. 707.

Europe movements spawned by Mazzini in the mid-1800s insisted – but also to the literature, so that 'no access can ever be obtained to the wealth of a people's literature in any language but their own'.[41] The *Blackwood's* author tends to represent the national character as static, so that the literature expresses an identity rather than a moment in the development of that identity, and that identity is only subject to change through cultural contact: 'How are we to estimate the benefit to the literature of a people from the influx upon them of the literature of another, even though that other have far surpassed them in all intellectual cultivation?'[42] Rhapsodies on the novelty of knowing another people thus give way to the pragmatic queries of conquest, as the author segues from the exotic frisson of 'That spell which holds the traveller – by which he walks in high imagination through the paths of common life... To him new scenes are disclosed – a new people arise' to images of possession in which the reader 'owns the power of their spirit – the very voice of their speech is in his ears'.[43] In 1830, Channing draws on similar premises in 'stating what we mean by national literature. We mean the expression of a nation's mind in writing.... We mean the manifestation of a nation's intellect in the only forms by which it can multiply itself at home, and send itself abroad.' But then he turns from national expression to the 'public good': 'We mean that a nation shall take its place, by its authors, among the lights of the world... and it is for the purpose of quickening all to join their labours for the public good, that we offer the present plea in behalf of a national literature.'[44] National literature circulates more widely than the coin of the realm, producing an international space in which nations can be recognized as such – can 'take [their] place... among the lights of the world'.

National literature thus became not merely an expression of the nation's character but also evidence of the nation's merit and even legitimacy. Various nineteenth-century critics thus contended that literature was evidence of the nation at its best. Irish poet Lady Jane Wilde, for instance, claimed in 1887, 'The written word, or literature,' is 'the fullest and highest expression of the intellect and culture, and scientific progress of a nation.'[45] In 1846, English writer William Johnson Fox went further and dismissed most Humean 'moral causes' in favour of only two fields of writing: 'Philosophy and poetry are *the mind of a nation*', 'So that to do justice to any country you must take, not its socially prominent men, not its rank and station, not those robed with the authority of government, and not even religion itself, with all its priests or ministers; but you

[41] *Ibid.*, p. 709.    [42] *Ibid.*    [43] *Ibid.*, p. 708.
[44] Channing, *Importance and Means of a National Literature*, pp. 3–4.
[45] Lady Jane Wilde, *Ancient Legends, Mystic Charms, and Superstitions of Ireland*, 2 vols. (London: Ward and Downey, 1887), vol. I, p. v.

must look to its poets and philosophers.'[46] But not all nationalists were self-congratulatory, and literary failure could be used to register national decline. Hallam laments,

But the age in which we live comes late in our national progress. That first raciness and juvenile vigor of literature . . . is gone, never to return. Since that day we have undergone a period of degradation. . . . With the close of the last century came an era of reaction, an era of painful struggle to bring our over-civilised condition of thought into union with the fresh productive spirit that brightened the morning of our literature.[47]

Hallam consequently praises 'the heroic poems of Old England, the inimitable ballads' of the sort included in Percy's seminal anthology, and deplores 'Modern Ballads' as 'miserable abortions'.[48] Neo-classical progress is represented as 'degradation' for taking the nation further and further from its vital origin. Throughout the nineteenth century, then, critics continued to identify national literature as the register of the nation's success and therefore testimony to its merits, leaving aside the question of how to establish the relative merits of national literatures – and hence nations.

## III

If, as Channing suggests, 'We are accustomed to estimate nations by their creative energies',[49] then the question of how to do so is a particularly urgent one for nations that sought to maintain imperial power through cultural hegemony, and for the national groups which sought to resist empire in the absence of material means. David Lloyd has usefully addressed this problem through an examination of the seemingly neutral identification of literary works as either 'major' or 'minor'. Addressing European critical theory from Schiller to S. T. Coleridge, Lloyd suggests, 'The totalizing drive of culture and its need of central standards demand that the essence of the human be seen as universal and that whatever deviates from that central archetype be seen as incompletely developed historically rather than as radically different.'[50] The distinction between the universal and the particular undergirds the Victorians' separation

46 William Johnson Fox, 'The Genius and Poetry of Campbell' in *Lectures Addressed Chiefly to the Working Classes*, 4 vols. (London: Charles Fox, 1846), vol. III, pp. 51, 52.

47 Hallam, 'On Some of the Characteristics', p. 544.    48 *Ibid.*, p. 549.

49 Channing, *Importance and Means of a National Literature*, p. 35.

50 David Lloyd, *Nationalism and Minor Literature: James Clarence Mangan and the Emergence of Irish Cultural Nationalism* (Berkeley: University of California Press, 1987), p. 17.

of 'major' and 'minor' works, where the former is both universal and 'disinterest[ed]' and so, tacitly, the latter is not – and it is 'precisely from this disinterest or indifference that [the major work] gains its hegemonic force'.[51] Lloyd articulates the mechanisms by which the idea of a national literature could be used to argue for, and against, national sovereignty: the nation that is mature can be self-determining (like a citizen who has attained legal 'majority'), and a nation that exhibits its minority through a literature that fails to achieve an expression of a universal human nature is not yet mature and so capable of political autonomy.

Nineteenth-century critics thus argued for universality as a literary aim. Irish essayist and poet Aubrey Thomas De Vere quotes William Wordsworth, arguably the leading nationalist poet of early Victorian Britain, as saying that young poets should 'study carefully those first-class poets whose name is universal, not local, and learn from them: – learn from them especially how to observe and how to interpret Nature'.[52] De Vere's Russian contemporary Vladimir Solovev calls attention to the stakes involved in raising the national literature to the level of the universal: 'Verity can only be *universal*, and the deed of service to this universal verity is demanded of a people, even, indeed *indispensably*, at the sacrifice of its national egoism.'[53] While Lloyd's emphasis is on the British identification of Irish minority, British letters were also charged with minority when it suited other nationalist ends. Channing, for instance, uses the decline of English literature as the basis for an American break from English literary hegemony, concluding 'we think, that at present [England's] intellect is laboring more for herself than for mankind, and that our scholars, if they would improve our literature, should cultivate an intimacy not only with that of England, but of continental Europe'.[54] English literature is no longer worthy of leading the world, having fallen from universality into the 'national egoism' decried by Solovev, and so, Channing contends, American readers must look to Europe as they build their own, distinctively American literature on a more 'common' (in Lloyd's terms) basis.

Worse than minority was mere dependence, and writers in English-speaking nations beyond Britain's shores actively promoted a national break from English letters in order to establish a national literature of their own. Channing thus argues for an American literature: 'Shall America be only an echo of what is thought and written under the aristocracies

---

[51]  *Ibid.*, p. 20.
[52]  Aubrey [Thomas] De Vere, 'Recollections of Wordsworth' in *Essays, Chiefly on Poetry*, 2 vols. (London: Macmillan, 1887), vol. II, p. 280.
[53]  Vladimir Solovev, 'In Memory of Dostoevsky' (1881) in *Literature and National Identity*, p. 179.
[54]  Channing, *Importance and Means of a National Literature*, pp. 42–3.

beyond the ocean? ... A foreign literature will always, in a measure, be foreign. It has sprung from the soul of another people, which, however like, is still not our own soul. Every people has much in its own character and feelings, which can only be embodied by its own writers, and which, when transfused through literature, makes it touching and true.'[55] Similarly, Byrne makes a plea for an Irish literature in English: 'every day brings us into more intimate union with the English nation, and subjects us more to English influence; and we need to have the independence of our thought maintained by a countervailing Irish influence'.[56] Both Byrne and Channing, moreover, argue for the importance of education in the development of the national culture. Byrne pleads for 'the spread of intellectual cultivation throughout the entire people', a project pursued by the series of lectures of which his essay forms a part, lectures 'delivered in some suitable building of unsectarian or neutral character' in Dublin and at a time when women and working men 'could conveniently attend'.[57] The educational, civic project of the Enlightenment is thus melded with nativist values to argue for a national literature that is distinguishable from the larger mass of English letters and will be the foundation on which to build a form of national 'independence'.

The difficulty of this foundational national literary project is compounded by colonialism and the sharing of what Byrne carefully terms 'the literature which has been given to the world in the English language'.[58] French-born American linguist Peter Du Ponceau remarked in 1834, 'Literature has never flourished *any where* under a colonial system of government',[59] a point echoed by a number of Irish critics in particular. William Carleton contends that Irish literature has remedied anti-Irish depictions in order to generate 'good-will and confidence between' Britain and Ireland, and yet, he suggests, the dominance of British literature in Ireland 'remain[s] as a reproach against our character as a nation'.[60] The problem was not literary genius, but socioeconomic conditions which drove authors to the metropolis: 'Our men and women of genius uniformly carried their talents to the English market, whilst we laboured at home under all the dark privations of a literary famine.... Thus did Ireland stand in the singular anomaly of adding some of her most

---

55  *Ibid.*, pp. 25–6. See also, for instance, Peter S. Du Ponceau, *A Discourse on the Necessity and Means of Making Our National Literature Independent of that of Great Britain* (Philadelphia: E. G. Dorsey, 1834).
56  Byrne, 'Influence of National Character on English Literature', p. 40.
57  *Ibid.*; R. Denny Urlin and R. H. Martley, 'Preface' in *The Afternoon Lectures on English Literature*, p. x.
58  Byrne, 'Influence of National Character on English Literature', p. 3.
59  Du Ponceau, *Discourse on the Necessity and Means*, p. 15.
60  William Carleton, *Traits and Stories of the Irish Peasantry* (1842–3), 2 vols. (Gerrards Cross: Colin Smythe, 1990), vol. I, pp. iv, v.

distinguished names to the literature of Great Britain, whilst she herself remained incapable of presenting anything to the world beyond a school-book or a pamphlet.'[61] Other authors turned entirely from the English language. William O'Brien argued (albeit in English) that 'there [is] a holy well of uncontaminated Gaelic from which any distinctively National literature will have to derive its inspiration. Davis, and Mangan, and Ferguson, are great in proportion as they caught the Gaelic glow, and Moore failed in so far as he was a stranger to it.'[62] O'Brien's remarks are part of the spawning of a nationalism centred on the Irish language at the end of the nineteenth century, in the wake of arguments by Herder, Mazzini and others that language is the fundamental basis of nationhood. Hence, he praises poets who were also translators of Irish-language literature and condemns Moore for not speaking Irish, but he also echoes Hallam's lament and other nativist criticisms of the present state of the nation: whether heralding 'a holy well of uncontaminated Gaelic' (O'Brien) or deploring 'French contagion' (Hallam), both measure the success of the nation's writers on the basis of their proximity to the national past.

Such nativist movements thus ironically remained tied to the neo-classical standardization of nationalist thought: nationalism as a set of principles and values migrates freely across national borders to be recognizable as 'nationalism' around the world. The circulation of ideas of nationhood as well as bodies of regional folk literature and their appropriation by other national movements constantly undercuts attempts to locate them within a particular national trajectory. Partha Chatterjee has fruitfully discussed the East/West divide in the 'implantation' of European nationalist discourse in other regional spheres,[63] but such 'implantation' is part of a larger history of migration in which ideas of nationality and nationhood as well as particular discourses of nationality flowed across borders and over oceans. For instance, Moore's and Morgan's writings were widely translated on the continent, and used to articulate nationalist grievances under the European empires that dominated linguistic groups that did not yet have a nation – Germany, Italy, Poland – and Irish writers in turn often invoked continental conflicts, from Morgan's *Italy* (1821) to Wilde's *Ugo Bassi: A Tale of the Italian Revolution* (1857).[64]

---

61  *Ibid.*, p. v.
62  William O'Brien, *The Influence of the Irish Language on Irish National Literature and Character* (Cork: Guy, 1892), p. 16.
63  Partha Chatterjee, *Nationalist Thought and the Colonial World: A Derivative Discourse* (Minneapolis: University of Minnesota Press, 1986), p. 27.
64  See Julia M. Wright, '"Sons of Song": Irish Literature in the Age of Nationalism' in *Romantic Poetry*, ed. Angela Esterhammer (Amsterdam: John Benjamins, 2002), pp. 333–53.

The national tale, particularly via Scott's wildly popular *Waverley*, was appropriated by nascent movements to define nationality in North American literature, most notably by James Fenimore Cooper, while both Scott and Cooper influenced many Canadian novels of the Victorian period which sought to define Canadian identity around the time of Confederation in 1867.[65] Scott's *Minstrelsy* was similarly influential in North America, and Moore's poetry influenced a number of Victorian-era Canadian poets. European national literatures even played a role in community formation in colonial settings where inter-national jockeying for pre-eminence was played out in multinational settlements. Amidst such tensions in Toronto in 1863, national literature was waved like a flag when an Irish Canadian rowing team competed against an English Canadian one: the English Canadian team was from the 'Shakespeare club' and the Irish Canadians' boat was dubbed the 'Lalla Rookh' after Thomas Moore's 1817 work of that name, in which Irish nationalist concerns are thinly allegorized through colonial conflicts set in Iran and India.[66] The very tension between the nativist and the neo-classical resides in the history of nationalism's migration around the globe: everywhere used in the same way to articulate essential difference. The phantasmatic dimension of nationalism lies not only in the myths it offers about a specific nation – the possibility of perfect agreement in societies divided by class, sex, religion, education and ideas, the promise of an unassailable argument for national autonomy – but also in the elision of its global circulation as an ideology.

Fraught with simultaneous affiliations to both conservatism and liberalism – particularly in the conflicting aims of preserving the cultural past and of progressing towards a more enlightened future through education – nationalism retains its apparent coherence in part by avoiding material specifics. Thus, while thinkers such as Hume and Home tied cultural progress closely to civic progress, the nineteenth-century emphasis on literature as a synecdoche for both national identity and greatness helped to separate nationalism from political reform. National subjects could become full participants in the nation through their reflection of the 'national character', their attachment to its cultural traditions, and their

---

[65] Katie Trumpener, *Bardic Nationalism: The Romantic Novel and the British Empire* (Princeton University Press, 1997); Andrea Cabajsky, 'The National Tale from Ireland to French Canada: Putting Generic Incentive into a New Perspective', *Canadian Journal of Irish Studies*, 31 (2005), 29–37; Andrew Newman, 'Sublime Translation in the Novels of James Fenimore Cooper and Walter Scott', *Nineteenth-Century Literature*, 59 (2004), 1–26.

[66] Dennis Ryan and Kevin Wamsley, 'A Grand Game of Hurling and Football: Sport and Irish Nationalism in Old Toronto', *Canadian Journal of Irish Studies*, 30 (2004), p. 24.

affective response to the nation as an idea. They need not be inspired by their involvement in a democratic form of government, for instance, or participation in territorial claims through ownership of land. National literature thus helps to focus nationalism on cultural identification and so render popular involvement in the nation state peculiarly virtual.

# 5

# Germany

## From restoration to consolidation: Classical and Romantic legacies

WILLI GOETSCHEL

During most of the nineteenth century, German political and cultural life was shaped by the absence of a unified nation state with clearly defined borders. In an endeavour to achieve national cohesion, artists, authors and critics united in the project of articulating a strong and unambiguous German identity. Until Bismarck consolidated Germany into a modern nation state in 1871, culture and politics remained situated on precarious ground as their proponents sought to fill the oversized, worn-out shoes of what had once been the Holy Roman Empire. Dissolved in 1806, the empire's demise in the wake of the revolutionary and counterrevolutionary wars represented a formidable challenge to the sovereigns of German lands. The German sovereigns' response to liberation – or, as many Germans came to see it, French occupation – led to promoting modern nationalism as a defence of their interests in reaction to the 'foreign' French threat. In consequence, not only the political borders, but also the intellectual and cultural ones, were anything but clear. Amused by the situation, Goethe and Schiller, for instance, could not resist poking fun at it when they penned their formally perfected distich: 'Germany? Where is it? I cannot find the country, / Where the intellectual begins, the political ends.'[1]

The fatal separation between the intellectual and political in Germany was to shape literary production in a profound way. As censorship intensified and state control of literary production tightened, writers and critics inhabited a world quite foreign to the benign paternalism that had previously existed in the duchy of Weimar under the minister of cultural affairs, Goethe. A period of transition, the 1820s marked both the end of the classical and Romantic age and an eagerly awaited new beginning: the dawn of modernity. Goethe was the pre-eminent figure who represented to a certain degree both sides of the divide, the old and the new. He became not only the leading literary figure but also the most debated author of his day.

---

[1] Johann Wolfgang Goethe, *Sämtliche Werke*, ed. Ernst Beutler, 24 vols. (Zurich: Artemis, 1953), vol. II, p. 455.

At this juncture, the classical and Romantic legacies not only represented a challenge and a liability, but also provided the opportunity for
legitimacy and freedom to formulate new positions over and against the
conventional aesthetic norms that had become stale and obsolete. Modern
literary criticism developed through the struggle to negotiate the tensions
between these legacies, between the claim to aesthetic autonomy of literary form and the claim that a literary work's content or meaning, that is,
its ethical and political significance, was equally irreducible. But during
this period the struggle played itself out less in the attempts by liberal
literary historians like Gervinus to write a national history of German literature than in the work of literary critics like Börne, Heine and the group
of Young Germans. As the literary criticism of Romantics like Tieck and
Eichendorff defined the scene, Varnhagen van Ense, a loyal admirer of
Goethe and a strong supporter of the emerging voices of a young critical generation, among them Heine, exerted his lasting influence as the
period's most open-minded and perceptive literary critic. While Gervinus
and others safely resigned these legacies to a historical past, Heinrich
Heine distinguished himself by addressing the ongoing cultural war as
one that would define the present and shape the future.

More successfully than any other poet and critic, Heine staged the struggle over the legacy of Classicism and Romanticism in a literary-critical
approach whose paradigmatic significance resonated throughout the century. For Nietzsche, Fontane, Kerr and even Karl Kraus, Heine gained
exemplary significance. For Heine's generation and the generations leading up to the turn of the century, the prescriptive status of Classicism and
Romantic nostalgia became increasingly problematic, as these translated
into political and aesthetic agendas no longer in step with the challenge
of the French and Industrial Revolutions; at this point, the spread of
mechanization and mass production made their impact upon the German
lands. The demise of the Holy Roman Empire of the German Nation,
and in its wake the struggle among progressive, liberal and nationalist
forces, created a public sphere troubled by the protracted transition from
abandoned empire to modern nation state. In public, the struggle turned
into open conflict between the literary critics, who pursued the creation
of a free space for criticism, and the state, whose policy of surveillance
led to control of the press and an unrelenting policing of free thought and
speech.

With the passing of the Carlsbad Decrees in 1819, Metternich introduced a harsh regime of supervision of the universities, pre-publication
censorship for all newspapers, journals and books of fewer than
twenty printed sheets (320 pages), as well as a central surveillance
apparatus for monitoring all revolutionary activities. Unable to contain
criticism entirely, the Prussian–Austrian alliance succeeded, however,

in enforcing these severe restrictions, with lasting impact. The alliance's heavy-handed censorship and prosecution of unfavourable critics defined public discourse wherever the arms of the state reached its subjects; more profoundly and enduringly, literary criticism found itself defined, in subtle and sometimes not-so-subtle ways, by the exigencies of this new political climate. Critics became increasingly wary of the ostensibly apolitical aesthetics of Classicism and Romanticism, which, however, in fact implied consequences of a distinctive political character.

The transition to mass production and distribution created new opportunities for reaching larger segments of the public. The launching of new journals opened a new literary market, casting the literary critic in a key role, as in the case of Karl Gutzkow. But not until the second half of the century did the journals and newspapers with their feuilletons (i.e., the culture pages, which included both literary criticism and serial novels) begin to reach out to the larger masses of the newly emerging, educated middle class (*Bildungsbürger*). Interestingly, in German lands, the emergence of competitive capitalism can first be observed in its distinct features in the literary market. Schiller's *Horen* and the Schlegel brothers' *Athenäum*, the voices of Classicism and Romanticism respectively, already operated as marketing tools.[2] The expansion of the literary market in the first half of the century promised literature and the press new heights of significance. The governments of Prussia, Austria and other nations in Europe were not the last to appreciate the opportunities of an emerging new literary market as they introduced a tight network of literary espionage, going so far as to plant spies as publicists. After cracking down on subversive political publications, the authorities quickly understood that criticism had begun to migrate to the safe haven of literary production and criticism. The Young German critic Theodor Mundt described this development in a fitting image when he noted: 'What the steam machines and railroads do for physical and commercial traffic, the journals have already done for the intellectual sphere.'[3]

## Ludwig Börne

The most eminent figure of the new form of journalism that forged literary criticism into a carefully directed critique of politics and conviction was Ludwig Börne. In the announcement of his own first journal, *Die Waage* ('The Scales') in 1818, he argued that the true task of his and

---

[2] Peter Uwe Hohendahl, 'Literaturkritik in der Epoche des Liberalismus' in *Geschichte der deutschen Literaturkritik*, ed. Peter Uwe Hohendahl (Stuttgart: Metzler, 1985), p. 131.
[3] Theodor Mundt, *Schriften in bunter Reihe* (1834), p. 5, quoted in Hohendahl, 'literaturkritik', p. 136.

other journals must be to sustain the communication between theory and practice.[4] As a diary of the time, a journal must be open to every view, because it is through contradiction that truth grows stronger. For Börne, the task of criticism is, as he explains in a letter to his publisher Cotta, not just to pass judgement on publications but to make the connection 'between literature and life, i.e. to connect the ideas with the real world'. Criticism, in other words, should aim at touching 'the point where science and art speak to all people'.[5] Börne's concern is therefore not merely aesthetics. Beauty must cede to the good, aesthetics to morality, or, to put it in more contemporary terms, the autonomy of art must cede to the criterion of social relevance. In consequence, the moral character of an author and his political convictions become more important than his philosophical and aesthetic views.[6]

If reviewers are judges, as Börne argued, they are also required to disclose the grounds on which they arrive at their decisions. Their task is to elucidate the reader's impression and account for the criteria that lead the reader to assign quality to one text and withhold it from another.[7] This task can be a bloody business, as Börne granted the reviewer permission to wield the proverbial pen in executing the bad author. However, tearing an author to pieces was against the protocol.[8] Also, Börne was sensitive about literary cartels. In a response to the announcement of the publication of the *Berliner Jahrbücher* by an association for scholarly critique in Berlin that did not disclose the names of any of its members, Börne reminded his readers that criticism must follow democratic rather than monarchic rules and procedures.[9] However, this objective did not exclude his occasionally categorical and autocratic verdicts on literature and authors. While Goethe and Schiller are taken to task for their morally questionable stances – Goethe as an open hypocrite and Schiller as a fighter for the good cause on shaky moral grounds – Börne celebrates Jean Paul in a moving address as Germany's sole true champion of freedom of thought and feeling.[10] In Börne's take-no-prisoners counter-attack on Menzel, *Menzel der Franzosenfresser* ('Menzel the French-eater'), he

4  Ludwig Börne, *Sämtliche Schriften*, eds. Inge and Peter Rippmann, 5 vols. (Düsseldorf: Melzer, 1964–8), vol. I, pp. 667–84, 669.
5  Börne, letter to Cotta, 10 March 1821 in *Sämtliche Schriften*, vol. V, p. 666f.
6  Börne, 'Bemerkungen über Sprache und Stil' in *Sämtliche Schriften*, vol. I, p. 591. For an authoritative discussion of Börne and his significance for the Young Germans see Hartmut Steinecke, *Literaturkritik des Jungen Deutschland: Entwicklungen – Tendenzen – Texte* (Berlin: E. Schmidt, 1982), pp.18–20.
7  Börne, 'Über den kritischen Lakonismus' in *Sämtliche Schriften*, vol. I, pp. 771–6.
8  *Ibid.*, p. 774.
9  Börne, 'Einige Worte über die angekündigten Jahrbücher der wissenschaftlichen Kritik' in *Sämtliche Schriften*, vol. I, pp. 622–32.
10 Börne, 'Denkrede auf Jean Paul' in *Sämtliche Schriften*, vol. I, pp. 789–98.

reminds his readers that, unlike the conservative demagogue Menzel, his own intention is not to instruct but simply to inspire his readers to judge for themselves: 'We don't want to change the German people, we want to wake it up for it is asleep. We are its gadflies that hum around its ears and tickle its face; at least as far as I am concerned, I never believed I was more than that.'[11]

While Börne represented a new political style and approach that would become a model for many young German critics, Heine remained more attuned to literary and aesthetic concerns. Börne's literary criticism focuses on the author's political conviction and liberal commitment as standards of judgement, whereas Heine's playful, mercurial strategy seeks to stake out a free discursive space for self-critical reflection that is foreign to Börne's militant criticism. For Börne and those who followed him, literature was to be judged in terms of political and moral concerns rather than its aesthetic qualities. The shift from aesthetic to political standards had a powerfully liberating effect on the generation of 'Young Germany'; it turned literary criticism into a medium of political critique. The new direction helped authorize the politicization of poetry and fiction, which assumed an increasingly sharp political edge despite the ubiquitous censorship. Ironically, however, these new norms undermined the aesthetic autonomy that literature had enjoyed – if often only in name – in the classical and Romantic period and which it now radically revoked in favour of liberalism and progress. Heine's literary criticism addresses this problematic as it proposes an approach that attends to both the profound political, social and cultural implications of literary creation, and its aesthetic dimension. But for Börne, the priorities presented themselves differently. Confronted with a fatally repressive political situation, literary criticism becomes the last resort for an otherwise muted political critique. Assuming the mantle of moral and political infallibility, Börne's critique falls victim to a self-righteous fixation no less problematic than that of his political adversaries.

Börne's unsparing and unforgiving criticism singled out the author's character, attitude and moral convictions while ignoring formal concerns. After an initial friendship with Heine, Börne took him to task in a devastating critique for what he saw as his fatal adoration of art, form and beauty, as well as his refraining from telling the truth.[12] Two years later, in a review of Heine's *On the History of Religion and Philosophy in Germany*, Börne became more directly personal, condemning Heine as a self-absorbed opportunist eager to please his readers with the most

---

[11] Börne, *Menzel der Franzosenfresser* in *Sämtliche Schriften*, vol. III, pp. 871–984, 932–3.
[12] Börne, letter 109 of *Briefe aus Paris* from 25 February 1833 in *Sämtliche Schriften*, vol. III, pp. 809–15.

exquisite forms of expression, and wholly indifferent to substance and content.[13]

However, Börne's uncompromising view of literature as an expression of the author's character, moral convictions and politics did not prevent him from underwriting the classical canon of aesthetics. For him, the canon itself was not in question, but rather the priority accorded to aesthetics. Heine, however, viewed Börne's position as an ultimately fatal affirmation of a retrograde aesthetics whose ideological purpose called for critical examination. In the late 1820s and early 1830s, Börne and Heine consequently emerged as the two models for progressive literary criticism. Whereas many critics followed Börne for his clear moral and political line, they found themselves siding with Heine when it came to the critique of a Classicist aesthetics which Börne's moralist approach did not criticize *per se* but only for its political aberrations. Börne's moralist attitude seemingly endorsed an ultimately dated aesthetics which, for Heine, had become problematic for its very aesthetic limitations. The literary criticism of the time steered an uncomfortable middle course, commending Börne for his moral position and following Heine in his aesthetic sensitivities.

## Wolfgang Menzel

The publication of Wolfgang Menzel's *Die deutsche Literatur* ('German Literature', 1828) caused a controversy with a lasting impact on the literary criticism of the period. Menzel had gained a reputation as the foremost critic of German literature, a claim that his book was to legitimate further. He left no doubt where he stood with regard to Goethe, who had become the particular object of his contempt. Most importantly, his project was to rejuvenate what he had come to consider a dead scene. In his eyes, the times called for a new beginning, far away from both Goethe's world and the frivolous literary exploits of the new generation of 'materialists' and liberals. For Menzel, only a return to a patriotic and self-consciously nationalist agenda would bring about the much-needed advancement of German literature. In 1828, however, Menzel was still moderate; his anti-French feelings were rigid, but his xenophobia and anti-Semitism had not yet reached the vitriolic intensity that they would in the 1830s. In the concluding chapter, Menzel spelled out the task of literary criticism. This was to be a criticism removed from what he pointedly called the factory-like conditions where critics found themselves forced to churn out their pre-assigned work: 'the reviewers here sit just like factory workers and

13  Börne's review of Heine's *De l'Allemagne* in *Réformateur*, 30 May 1835 in *Sämtliche Schriften*, vol. II, pp. 885–903.

perform their task'.[14] Against this modern, economy-driven, piecemeal mode of production, Menzel sought to mobilize a form of literary criticism that would arise from the undivided national spirit, rather than from one or another class:

> In criticism, at least, the spirit of the nation should raise itself above the internal differences and schisms in culture and opinions... The nation should see itself reflected in it as in a great mirror, and should learn to know and value all the workings of its spirit in one clear survey... There should be a higher, – a national criticism, – which should supply neither these notes for the mere scholar, nor this tattle for women and beaux; but which should promote a popular esteem for all the intellectual works which have proceeded from, and are of importance to the nation.[15]

Given the limited platforms of partisan divisions from which literary criticism was practised, Menzel's point seemed well made. But his diagnosis rested on the presupposition of a unified and homogeneous national spirit that had become questionable in the face of a restoration politics whose merciless recourse to 'national interests' was suspect to many. For Menzel, Goethe's vision of a cosmopolitan concept of world literature thriving on a vivid exchange between cultures and nations presented a dangerous and direct assault on *Nationalliteratur*. Against such a view, he mustered the notion of a homogeneous tradition of national literature tightly allied with patriotic interest and honour as well as civic duty.[16] According to Menzel, Goethe typified all the vicissitudes of a past that had to be overcome. He represented an egotism, hedonism and narcissism no longer acceptable in the age of nationalism. But the greater threats came from Börne and Heine; the second edition even goes so far as to castigate the entire Young Germany. By contrast, Menzel's heroes included Schiller ('our most popular poet') because of his ascetic, rigid idealism and what Menzel identified as his national agenda,[17] as well as Tieck, 'this most national' and 'most German of our poets'.[18] With his book, and the steady flow of literary criticism in his *Literaturblatt*, which accompanied the Stuttgart *Morgenblatt für gebildete Stände* from 1826 until 1849 when the *Morgenblatt* ceased publication, and then from 1852 until 1869 when he edited his journal independently, Menzel defined the literary debates of his time in an enduring manner. Radicals like Arnold Ruge and even well-adjusted liberals like Julian Schmidt would later follow him in debunking Romanticism and privileging Schiller over Goethe;

---

[14]  Wolfgang Menzel, *Die deutsche Literatur*, 2nd edn, 4 vols. (Stuttgart: Hallberger, 1836), vol. IV, p. 349f; English translation: *German Literature*, trans. Thomas Gordon, 4 vols. (Oxford: D. A. Talboys, 1840), vol. IV, p. 314.
[15]  *Ibid.*, pp. 314–15.
[16]  *Ibid.*, p. 331. This passage was added in the second edition.
[17]  *Ibid.*, pp. 93–111.    [18]  *Ibid.*, p. 121.

Young Germany's line, however, was to be critical, but more tolerant of Goethe and Romanticism, whose early, progressive impulses deserved a more forgiving reception.


## Heinrich Heine

Whereas Börne and Menzel were concerned with distancing themselves from the classical and Romantic canon, Heine was provocatively less anxious about drawing such lines. This allowed him to acknowledge those aspects of the literary heritage of Goethe and the Romantics that he recognized to be instrumental to the progressive and liberal agenda he envisioned for literature, culture and politics alike. Perceptively strategic, Heine's literary criticism negotiated the conflicting claims of creative-aesthetic and socio-political concerns. For Heine, literature provided the scene for staging this tension creatively. The task of literary criticism was less to adjudicate and deliver judgement than to highlight – even to act out – the problematic that the literary text articulates and to examine the way in which the text reflects, responds to or possibly even challenges aesthetic and political views.[19]

The July revolution of 1830, Hegel's death in 1831 and subsequently Goethe's in 1832 marked a sea change in German letters, which would no longer allow for a return to the aesthetics of perfection and self-perfection. The 'end of the period of art', as Heine had called it,[20] mandated a new form of literary criticism. Heine's literary development in the 1820s had already pointed in this direction, and in the 1830s he began to develop a critical style that would change literary criticism in crucial ways. The historical context of the 1830s yielded a number of developments: the pointedly political positions of the exponents of Young Germany; the counter-movement of the objective Realists in the 1850s, which suggested a quietist return to apolitical literary approaches to reality; and Fontane's literary-critical endeavour to reconcile political and literary elements in a new notion of the social. All of these emerged in response to the reviled – yet influential – approach that Heine had developed, a model that even his most pronounced detractors studiously emulated.

In his review of Menzel's *Die deutsche Literatur*, Heine commended Menzel for his critical approach, which pointed to life and knowledge (*Wissenschaft*) as the new criteria for understanding literature. Yet the

---

[19]  For the best survey of Heine and the context of his period, see Gerhard Höhn, *Heine-Handbuch: Zeit – Person – Werk* (Stuttgart and Weimar: Metzler, 2004).

[20]  Heinrich Heine, *Sämtliche Schriften*, ed. Klaus Briegleb, 6 vols. (Munich: Deutscher Taschenbuchverlag, 1997), *Romantische Schule*, vol. III, p. 361. This edition is hereafter cited as B followed by the volume and page numbers.

tone and diction of the review remain pointedly ambiguous. Heine charts
a strategy for steering away from the doctrinaire rejection of Goethe that
Menzel espouses in his fatigue with the classics. Heine's line of argument
was motivated not only by Varnhagen van Ense's insistent appeal to Heine
to stay loyal to Goethe, but also by Heine's self-perception as successor to
Germany's most eminent poet. His distinction between the Goethe cult
and Goethe's own poetic work, voice and thought (*Denkweise*) – 'this
flower that, amidst the manure of our time, will blossom more and more
beautifully' – argues for a literary criticism sensitive to the progressive
tendency which comprises the distinctively creative feature of literature.
Playful, whimsical, but at the same time critically to the point, Heine's text
signals that an important aim of his literary criticism is to facilitate the
author's reflection and self-clarification. In his review, Heine announces
the end of 'the period of art' (*Kunstperiode*), an expression that would
become canonical for capturing the spirit of the time.[21]

Heine's short essay 'Romanticism' (1820), his inaugural piece of literary criticism, had already expressed a more nuanced view than Menzel's
simple-minded rejection, one that both praised and criticized the Romantics. Wary of the fixation on the past that seemed to drive much of
the Romantic impulse of his contemporaries, Heine proposed a different
notion of Romanticism freed from anachronistic medieval trappings, a
Romanticism whose literary project was just as poetic and contemporary
as that of its opposition, the 'plasticists', and their classical aesthetics.
Moreover, Heine's revision of Romanticism did not exclude these classical aesthetics but productively integrated them, as in the case of Goethe.[22]

In his 'Briefe aus Berlin' ('Letters from Berlin', 1822), Heine developed
his literary-critical approach a step further to test the limits of censorship.
Facing the general prohibition on critique, theatre criticism became the
hiding place for political critique. As a result, Heine signalled to his
readers that the review of concert and stage performances had become the
last free channel of communication.[23] However, he distinguished himself
from Börne by refusing to reduce literature and culture to mere functions
of social and political life. Rather, the 'Letters' indicate a critical sensibility
with regard to the intricate intertwining of the different social spheres.
With a wry smile at the contingency of modern urban experience, the
'Briefe' suggest that, in the absence of a pre-established affinity between
art and politics, literary criticism is not bound by any canon, but can act

---

[21]  Heine, B I, pp. 444–56, esp. pp. 455, 446.
[22]  Heine, 'Die Romantik' in B I, pp. 399–401.
[23]  Jost Hermand, 'Heines "Briefe aus Berlin": Politische Tendenz und feuilletonisti-
      sche Form' in Käte Hamburger and Helmut Kreuzer (eds.), *Gestaltungsgeschichte
      und Gesellschaftsgeschichte: Literatur-, Kunst- und musikwissenschaftliche Studien*
      (Stuttgart: Metzler, 1969), pp. 84–305.

as a pointed yet nevertheless intangible political critique, able to examine literary and cultural production on its own terms. While politics may produce its own art, it can never control the audience, just as creative art enunciates its own response to politics.[24]

Paving the way for a new mode of writing that would have a formative impact on the course of modern German literature, Heine's *Reisebilder* ('Pictures of Travel', 1826–30) also played a signal role in developing a distinctive form of criticism. Interlacing fiction and reality in a narrator's perspective that continually oscillated between reflective detachment and picaresque involvement, Heine's new writing style not only performed the critical pose that it portrayed, but also problematized it through critical exposure. Heine thus gives Romantic irony the political edge that the Schlegels carefully avoided. A unique moment of the *Reisebilder* is its overt and covert play with the forms and conventions of literary criticism, which performs a double operation. By reclaiming the authority of literary criticism, his writing declares its independence; it also highlights the particularly literary dimension that defines literary criticism as a mode of writing. In his critical response to the brothers Schlegel, Heine maintained that not only is literary criticism, as the Schlegels had stressed, a poetic activity, but it also always already informs poetic creativity. For Heine, criticism represents a constitutive moment of literary style and imagination. Heine's new prose style allowed him to articulate some of his most innovative ideas on literary criticism in his literary writing, with a claim to its prosaic truth-value.

In a passage arguing that future generations would be able to discover in Goethe many features that then contemporary readers were incapable of seeing, Heine noted: 'Every age, when it gets new ideas, gets with them new eyes, and sees much that is new in the old efforts of mind which have preceded it.'[25] While Börne took Heine to task for what he saw as his unconditional surrender to the reign of art and beauty, Heine's early confession in 'Journey from Munich to Genoa', his excursus on political liberation and emancipation, left no doubt as to the way he conceived his own mission as 'a brave soldier in the war of freedom of mankind': 'Poetry, dearly as I have loved it, has always been to me only a holy plaything or a consecrated means to attain a heavenly end.'[26] But unlike Börne, Heine cautiously resists any blind privileging of political or other values external to the freedom of literary expression. Rather, the 'Journey from Munich to Genoa' projects a narrative line that challenges the old aesthetic and moral conventions as standards of a world long gone.

---

[24] Heine, 'Briefe aus Berlin' in B II, pp. 29–31.
[25] Heinrich Heine, *Pictures of Travel*, trans. Charles Godfrey Leland (New York: D. Appleton, 1904), p. 102; B II, p. 221.
[26] Heine, *Pictures of Travel*, pp. 259–60; B II, p. 382.

Heine's insistence on the critical need to examine the intricate implications of form and aesthetics was, however, occasionally lost on his audience. Historically, his attack on August von Platen in 'The Baths of Lucca' was widely considered to be a tastelessly misfired polemic. But behind the painfully unforgiving personal note of Heine's assault stands a fundamental criticism, one crucial for his self-positioning in contrast to what he sees as the false pretence of Platen's poetry.[27] Like the Börne book a decade later, Heine's attack on Platen acquired its extreme pointedness because it radically clarified Heine's own stance on literature.

Heine's *Die romantische Schule* ('The Romantic School') was a book-length essay that broke new ground for literary criticism. Extremely popular, the essay had a lasting impact on the public and critics alike. Here Heine not only demonstrates his provocative method, but also describes the prophetic power he ascribes to the critic: 'A critic who dissects a new poet with a sufficiently sharp knife can easily prophesy therefrom how Germany will behave – as from the entrails of an animal sacrificed.'[28] If Heine suggests a deep connection between literary criticism and the political life of a nation, his approach is anything but simple. Literary history, he claims, is not unlike natural history in that phenomena ranging from the insignificant to the magnificent all testify equally to divine power. Heine holds that the great facts and books are not produced accidentally, but are necessary and interconnected with their larger historical contexts: 'Deeds [*Fakta*] are merely the results of ideas', he notes, and suggests that the time may have come to write a 'literary astrology, and in it explain the appearance of certain ideas or of certain books wherein these reveal themselves according to the constellation of starry intellects [*Gestirne*, i.e., stars]'.[29] Never without an ironic twist, Heine aims less at ridiculing literary history as a project than at exposing the flaws of a kind of approach that, in the wake of the Hegelian propensity for systemization, follows a strict determinism. In a suggestive move, Heine introduces 'constellation' as the critical paradigm that renders cultural, literary and intellectual history legible.

*Die Romantische Schule* articulates this point both allegorically and through his literary criticism, which exposes the curious incongruence between literary history and Hegelian historical determinism. Heine's concluding discussion of the Swabian poet Uhland highlights the limits of the categories of literary historiography. Albeit typical and representative

[27]  For a helpful analysis of the significance of Heine's critique of Platen for Heine's literary criticism see Wolfgang Kuttenkeuler, *Heinrich Heine: Theorie und Kritik der Literatur* (Stuttgart: Kohlhammer, 1972), pp. 64–78.

[28]  Heinrich Heine, *Works*, trans. Charles Godfrey Leland (London: Heinemann; New York: D. Appleton, 1892–1906), vol. VI [1906], p. 39; B III, p. 467.

[29]  Heine, *Works*, vol. VI [1906], p. 38; B III, p. 466.

of Romanticism with all its problematics, Uhland's later enthusiasm for democracy and his Protestant conviction defy Romantic conventions. Heine thus points out that an individual's identity and literary production resist complete subjection to the categories of literary history, be they dictated by formal aesthetic or by political affiliation. Uhland's example suggests instead that there always remains an irreducible singularity of the individual as poet and person that defies reduction to purely aesthetic or political criteria; the poet expresses the creative interplay between art and politics, aesthetics and ethics, that produces a distinctive literary voice.

Resonating with Saint-Simonism and increasingly with a post-Hegelian Spinozist impulse, Heine highlights the mutually constitutive link between the cultural and socio-political spheres with a novel use of the allegory of mind and body. His insistence on the mutual complicity of mind and body has therefore larger implications for the conception of history: 'In the world's history not every event is the direct result of another; all events rather exert a mutual influence.'[30] This in turn entails a crucial change in the way literary criticism is conceived. If literature defies both the notion of the eternal validity of aesthetic principles and historical determinism, the traditional distinction between form and content becomes as questionable as the mind/body divide, which Heine exposes as the slapstick comedy that Cervantes's Don Quixote and Sancho Panza are condemned to perform. The Spanish duo's continual struggles highlight their profound complicity and symbiotic relationship. Just as Sancho Panza follows on Don Quixote's heels while always relying on his own more reasonable self, so the materialist side often ends up standing in for the spiritual one that it makes possible: 'Indeed, the body often seems to have more insight than the soul, and man thinks frequently far better with his back and belly than with his head.'[31]

Challenging the opposition between matter and mind, form and content, Heine presents a literary criticism no longer merely designed to engage with literature, politics and society but more as a practice poignantly self-aware of the need to reflect on the assumptions of its own discourse. The dialectic between mind and body, and their mutual interdependence, serve both a theologico-political and an aesthetic agenda. In the same way, literary criticism finds itself sent back and forth between form and content – its mind and body – never able to settle finally on either.

But in *Die Romantische Schule* Heine is not just looking backwards but welcomes the most recent literary movements. Spelling out the new

[30] Heine, *Works*, vol. v [1906], p. 235; B III, p. 370.
[31] Heine, *Works*, vol. v [1906], p. 358; B III, p. 431.

programme of literature as one that no longer separates life from writing, politics from science, art and religion, Heine introduces Young Germany as a movement whose exponents are at once 'artists, tribunes, and apostles'.[32]

In the sequel, *On the History of Religion and Philosophy in Germany*, Heine provided the theoretical background for his literary criticism. Designed as a 'general introduction to German literature', this playful survey of German intellectual history pokes fun at the projects of narrowly conceived nationalist literary histories. Placing the Dutch Jewish philosopher Spinoza squarely at the heart of its genealogy of modern German poetry, the text's pointedly eccentric presentation forces the reader to revisit traditional accounts of the history of philosophy. In declaring Luther the creator of the modern German language and literature, Heine does more than just follow Hegel and a commonplace view of his time.[33] In contrast with Herder, Hegel and their contemporaries, Heine's recognition of Luther's Bible translation as an act of modern cultural affirmation allowed him to delineate a different genealogy of modern literature from the usual ones that affiliated it to Greek and Roman Antiquity. For Heine, Luther's accomplishment was to have animated a language that was not yet alive by translating a dead one. This project of translating a 'dead' past into a future 'not yet alive' created a German whose poetic force Heine saw as less indebted to the aesthetic legacy of ancient Greece and Rome than to the spiritual tradition of the Bible.[34]

Heine's declaration that modern German literature begins with the poetry of Luther's hymns challenges the Romantics' claim to an authentic view of history: 'He who will speak of modern German literature must begin with Luther.'[35] With Luther, spiritualism is replaced by the concern for material well-being, the Third Estate arises, and the revolution announces itself; literature now expresses the feelings, thoughts and needs of the time. Romantic form is replaced by classical form, as ancient literature is now revived: 'The general character of modern literature lies in this, that individuality and skepticism now prevail . . . Poetry is now no longer objective, epic, and naïve, but subjective, lyrical, and reflecting.'[36] More than just an apt self-description, this literary programme encapsulates the agenda of an entire generation: the authors and critics of Young Germany in the 1830s and 1840s.

One of the poetic high points of Heine's literary criticism is his eloquent description of Goethe's lyrics. Whether or not Heine in fact accurately captures the essence of Goethe's poetry as a whole is less significant

---

[32]  Heine, *Works*, vol. V [1906], pp. 6, 41.     [33]  *Ibid.*, pp. 54, 61, 359, 544, 549.
[34]  *Ibid.*, p. 55; B III , pp. 3, 545.     [35]  Heine, *Works*, vol. V, p. 61; B III, p. 549.
[36]  Heine, *Works*, vol. V, p. 66ff.; B III, pp. 551–2.

than the powerful manner in which he gives voice to his own poetic programme, which he understood as standing in legitimate succession to Goethe's. After a brief discussion of *Werther* and *Faust* as the great examples of world literature that signal the formative role of Spinoza's pantheism, Heine turns to Goethe's poetry as the most exquisite expression of Spinozist thought and feeling:

> But it is in the ballads of Goethe that this Pantheism shows itself most charmingly and purely. Here the doctrine of Spinoza has broken from the mathematical chrysalis, and flutters round us as a Goethean song... These Goethean songs have a mocking magic which is indescribable. The harmonious verses wind round the heart like a tender true love; the word embraces while the heart [thought] kisses thee![37]

The notion that the play of form and content creates a poetic space that produces a particular effect on the reader is central to Heine's own poetic project. The image of the embracing word setting the stage for the poetic kiss of the thought does not describe the Spinozist moment as an explicit paraphrase of Spinozist ideas, but rather reminds the reader to recognize Spinoza's presence in the poetic form itself. Just as Spinoza stresses the interdependence of mind and body, Heine treats linguistic form and content as the product of an inseparable unity that the mind might distinguish as form and content but which, in reality, constitute each other.[38] Heine's poetic programme articulates an aesthetics that does not simply reject classical notions of form and beauty, but moves to a dialectical notion of the relationship beyond the conventional opposition between form and content.

Taken to task by Börne, and by both the political right and left for what they considered to be his cowardly resignation from politics, Heine settled his scores with his critics in *Ludwig Börne: Eine Denkschrift* ('Ludwig Börne: A Memorial', 1840), a book written to account for their differences, but which only served to alienate even Heine's more loyal readers. As personal as the book seems, its argument addresses the key distinction that Menzel had introduced, that Börne applied to Heine, and that defined the literary criticism on both sides of the political divide. Conservatives, liberals and especially radicals consented to Menzel's and Börne's emphasis on the distinction between the moral or political preferences of

---

[37] Heine, *Works*, vol. V, p. 176ff.; B III, p. 620.
[38] For Heine's Spinozist bent see Willi Goetschel, 'Heine's Spinoza' in the special issue *Spinoza in Dialogue*, ed. Jeffrey Bernstein, *Idealistic Studies*, 33 (2003), 207–21, and Willi Goetschel, 'Heine's Dis/Enchantment of Hegel's History of Philosophy' in *Spinoza's Modernity: Mendelssohn, Lessing, and Heine* (Madison: University of Wisconsin Press, 2004), pp. 253–65.

an author – that is, his character – and the aesthetic qualities of his work – that is, its style.

Taking the reader in his *Denkschrift* into an artfully labyrinthine web where the status of texts and authorship, intertexts and contexts becomes increasingly precarious, Heine highlights the speciousness of the distinction between character and its opposite, be it talent, art or style. His little genealogy of morals exposes the dogmatism of the kind of morality to which both Menzel and Börne, that is, the right and left, subscribe. In Heine's analysis, the recourse to such morality is vacuous whereas universal ethics are built on the pure sentiment of humanity and reason of the heart. Consequently, aesthetics are inseparable from political and moral 'content' and vice versa. Style and content must be read with, and through, each other; both are different aspects of the same artwork. As the inner consistency between form and content provides the final criterion for the literary work, criticism no longer takes its cue from the outside; instead, it looks at the ways in which prose and poetry respond to the challenge of creating ever-new configurations of the mind/body and form/content problematic.

Some of Heine's most striking literary criticism is found in his lyrical poetry. His critique of the popular *Zeitgedicht* (poetry addressing issues of its time), a poetic genre meant to speak to the present time and its problems, and the *Tendenzgedicht* (politically partisan poetry) was as unforgiving as anything written in prose. For Heine, a formally and stylistically poorly composed poem would always lack political credibility and force. In *Atta Troll* (1843) he lampooned such misguided contemporary attempts to write political poetry. An entirely different note is struck in 'Jehuda ben Halevy', the central poem of the cycle 'Hebrew Melodies', where Heine offers an alternative: here, the poem's message is that poetry produces the tune for the modern time, as it celebrates Yehuda Halevi's engaging tradition and innovation creatively. This alternative poetics inspires literary criticism to move beyond social and political critique towards a notion of redemptive critique.

But it was most of all Heine's journalism that had an enduring impact, assuming formative importance as a model that many rejected, but at the same time could not resist adopting. For succeeding critics like Fontane, Kerr and Kraus, Heine's literary criticism became the model to follow. In its spirited and playful manner, Heine's free associative style, provocatively changing pace and tone, became the critics' paradigm. His followers and critics turned his art of combining the unmasking power of irony, parody and satire into a technique that gained wide popularity – ironically often among the very critics who preferred to distance themselves publicly from him.

## Young Germany

The emergence of Young Germany in the mid-1830s marks a key moment in the history of modern German literary criticism. Criticism took on the role of the leading genre, not only making and breaking literature, but now assuming an important role in moulding the literary imagination itself. While the exponents of Young Germany emerged in response to a relentless suppression of freedom of speech and the press by a powerful state apparatus of censorship and persecution, they succeeded in assuming prominent status.[39] Associated with Heine by Prussian and Austrian authorities, critics like Karl Gutzkow, Ludolf Wienbarg, Heinrich Laube and Theodor Mundt gained notoriety through the indictment and prohibition of their work in German lands. Gutzkow and Wienbarg, the two most important liberal critics of the time, planned the launching of a new journal, the *Deutsche Revue*. This publication was to unite the talents of the literary and political opposition to build a formidable intellectual front. Not to be outdone, the authorities responded with a harsh policy of prohibiting manuscripts before publication or submission.

The prohibition of the *Deutsche Revue* had severe and long-lasting consequences. Not only did the decree declare any existent and even future publications by Heine, Gutzkow, Wienbarg, Mundt and Laube to be illegal – an unheard-of novelty barely in line with legal thought, as Heine dryly observed – but it also lumped them together, which had the effect of levelling out their respective political differences, and consequently polarized the political parties. The consequences of censorship and persecution were palpable and profound. Practically no critic or literary historian of the period evaded imprisonment unless they had wisely exiled themselves, as Börne, Heine, Ruge, Marx and others had done. Gutzkow, Wienbarg, Laube, Mundt and also liberals who had been members of parliament, like the literary historian Gervinus and the critic Robert Prutz, had served time.

If censorship – and, in many cases, self-censorship – shaped literature and criticism at the time, experience with the less subtle instruments of criminal prosecution also left its mark. Until their prosecution, the Young Germany group represented for a couple of years a new and resolutely liberal and emancipatory style of literary criticism and journalism. But in the wake of the 1835 prohibition, the spirit of the movement was broken, the critics' careers were shattered, and they were forced into compromise or even withdrawal and resignation. However, during the

---

[39] For a concise discussion of the aesthetic and political programme of Young Germany see Steinecke, *Literaturkritik des Jungen Deutschland*, pp. 9–57. Cf. also Hohendahl, 'Literaturkritik', pp. 134–49.

short time until censorship caught up with the group, it succeeded in redefining the compass and scope of literary criticism. More importantly, it posed the central issues, concerns and questions that would stay with literary criticism throughout the century and beyond.

The most systematic formulation of the Young German view on aesthetics, Ludolf Wienbarg's *Ästhetische Feldzüge* ('Aesthetic Campaigns', 1834), addressed the functional aspect of literature as key to its critical understanding. According to Wienbarg, beauty is no longer identifiable as an intrinsic quality ('there is no longer any genuine aesthetics possible') but as a function producing an effect. Beauty, in other words, is 'nothing ideal and abstract but something concrete and particular that comes into appearance with a determinate matter, be it a deed, marble, flesh and blood'.[40] Aesthetics is thus always a product of a particular historical moment in time. Identifying *Faust* as Goethe's most significant contribution to world literature, Wienbarg lists the three most significant authors of modernity: Byron as poet, Goethe as dramatist, and Heine as master of prose.[41] Indeed, throughout the book, Heine serves as the single most important source of inspiration. Unafraid of openly signalling his affinity with Heine, Wienbarg concludes his book with a lengthy quotation that casts wit and satire as the only alternative to death when it comes to protection against the lords of the world. Taken from Heine's 1828 review of Menzel, the passage's combative impulse resonates with Wienbarg's 'aesthetic campaign', which the title of his book announces.[42]

The critic with the most distinct profile and the greatest staying power was Gutzkow, a prolific author of literary criticism, fiction, drama and political journalism. A merciless polemics ensued over Gutzkow's novel *Wally die Zweiflerin* ('Wally the Sceptic'), with Menzel, his former mentor, now turned into his worst persecutor. The novel's date of publication in 1835 coincided with the ban on Young Germany. For the indecent content of this novel, Gutzkow was imprisoned and expelled from the state of Baden.[43] A second major controversy occurred two decades later over *Die Ritter vom Geiste* ('The Knights of the Spirit'), another novel by Gutzkow that played a role in the debate on poetic Realism and the historical novel.[44] A restless publicist and skilled navigator in the shallow waters of repressive press restrictions, Gutzkow often oscillates

40  Ludolf Wienbarg, *Ästhetische Feldzüge* (Hamburg: Hoffmann & Campe, 1934), pp. 135, 150ff., 186.
41  *Ibid.*, p. 284.     42  Heine, *Works*, vol. I, pp. 447–8.
43  For a succinct survey of Gutzkow's work and career see, 'Introduction' in Karl Gutzkow, *Liberale Energie: Eine Sammlung seiner kritischen Schriften*, ed. Peter Demetz (Frankfurt, Berlin and Vienna: Ullstein, 1974), pp. 9–33.
44  Peter Uwe Hohendahl, 'Einleitung' in *Literaturkritik: Eine Textdokumentation zur Geschichte einer literarischen Gattung. Vol. IV: 1848–1870*, ed. Peter Uwe Hohendahl, 8 vols. (Vaduz: Topos, 1984), pp. 65–8.

between outspoken directness and carefully coded allusions. His literary
instinct and perspicacity made him a prominent figure from the 1830s
well into the 1860s. For instance, he was one of the first to recognize the
significance of Georg Büchner. His introduction to the literary section of
the *Phönix* (1835) exhibited the conflictual situation of progressive liberal
criticism, caught between compliance and the urge for freedom. Opening
with a bold acknowledgement of the significance of criticism, Gutzkow
hastens to qualify this by urging that the task of criticism, once crucial
for the 'literary revolution', has now become more than just the nemesis
of the past: criticism's new task is to be the mouthpiece for the future and
to serve as its oracle.[45] In a strikingly unusual turn, Gutzkow defines the
new criticism he seeks to introduce as undertaking 'a surgical task' that
is 'supposed to heal, restore, and complement'.[46] Challenging the norms
of the established order, Gutzkow claimed criticism as a literary activity
in its own right. Both a prolific writer of fiction and a staunch critic, he
raised literary criticism to an independent line of production that assumed
equal rather than secondary standing with literature in social and political
importance.

While Gutzkow did not always realize his own vision in practice, he
became an important critical voice as he provided an attractive alternative to the theoretically more advanced, but normatively more problematic, doctrinaire criticism of the *Hallische Jahrbücher für deutsche
Wissenschaft und Kritik* ('Halle Yearbooks for German Scholarship and
Critique'). Published daily, the journal displayed the distinctively academic tone and outlook of the Young Hegelians. Literary criticism, however, was not uniform and different authors could disagree in their judgements. But the editors, Theodor Echtermeyer and Arnold Ruge, saw to
it that the main course of political liberalism was followed. This meant
that the editors' categorical rejection of Romanticism would not exclude
another contributor's more sympathetic assessment of a late Romantic
poet. In their manifesto, 'Der Protestantismus und die Romantik: Zur
Verständigung über die Zeit und ihre Gegensätze' ('Protestantism and
Romanticism: Towards a Greater Understanding of the Present and its
Antagonisms'), Echtermeyer and Ruge leave no doubt as to where their
sympathies lie.[47] Romanticism and admiration of Goethe are things of
the past, whereas Lessing and Schiller assume central importance for a
national canon. But this generation of critics also marks its critical distance from Heine, who, in their eyes, has become a liability like Goethe,

[45] *Phönix Literatur-Blatt* (1835), p. 24; cf. Steinecke, *Literaturkritik des Jungen Deutschland*, p. 82.
[46] *Phönix Literatur-Blatt* (1835), p. 24.
[47] 'Der Protestantismus und die Romantik: Zur Verständigung über die Zeit und ihre
Gegensätze. Ein Manifest', *Hallische Jahrbücher*, 12 October–27 December 1839.

whereas Börne and Schiller are now seen as the champions of liberal steadfastness and moral integrity, though the *Jahrbücher* remain critical of Börne.[48]

While the Young Germans had made moral and political conviction their central concern, the *Jahrbücher* elevated such conviction to the exclusive criterion for literature. Schiller was now clearly to be preferred to Goethe, and Heine's provocatively frivolous prose rejected, while critics agreed on the merits of the aesthetic aspects of his poetry. Critical of Young Germany, the editors and critics of the *Jahrbücher* sought to pursue a more moderate political and aesthetic course. But politics caught up with them, as the journal was closed down by the authorities in 1843. Ruge left for Paris, where he co-edited with Marx the *Deutsch-Französische Jahrbücher*.

As censorship continued to tighten its grip, poets and critics fled into exile, mainly to neighbouring Switzerland and France. Since books of 320 pages or more were exempt from censorship, authors sought to respond with the publication of voluminous books. In consequence, mere aesthetic criteria would no longer suffice: 'content' and the authors' 'conviction' became the unifying criteria. In such a climate, anthologies became a popular way of bypassing censorship. Notorious for its teasing title were the *Einundzwanzig Bogen aus der Schweiz* ('Twenty-One Printed Sheets from Switzerland'), an omnibus of politically radical writings edited by Georg Herwegh.

If literary historians and critics from Menzel to Gervinus and the Young Hegelians made the German national idea a central concern of their agenda, they remained wedded to the classical aesthetics they desired to abandon. The kind of literary criticism that promoted a dialectic between the aesthetic and socio-political dimensions of literature, as the Schlegel brothers had envisioned – an agenda Heine and the Young Germans had followed, thereby broadening the meaning of literature – seemed to have run its course. Following Gutzkow, Herwegh still defines the task of criticism in 1839 as providing a succinct description (i.e., a 'profile' [*Steckbrief*] and 'physiognomic sketch') of the works under review.[49] But the 'positive' and 'productive' criticism of progressive liberals like Gutzkow and Herwegh was soon overtaken by the more assertive and less sympathetic approach of critics whose scholarship determined their views and values. It seemed as if the interregnum of the poet-critic from

---

[48] For a detailed survey of the *Jahrbücher*'s literary criticism see Else von Eck, *Die Literaturkritik in den Hallischen und Deutschen Jahrbüchern (1838–1842): Ein Beitrag zur Geschichte der deutschen Literaturwissenschaft* (1926; rpt Nendeln: Kraus, 1967). Cf. also Hohendahl, 'Literaturkritik', pp. 175–80.

[49] Georg Herwegh, *Frühe Publizistik 1837–1841*, ed. Bruno Kaiser (Glashütten im Taunus: Detlev Auvermann, 1971), p. 168.

Goethe to Heine had ended and the scholar-critic had returned. Lessing, who had always been considered more a scholar than a poet, rose again to paradigmatic significance.

## The aborted revolution of 1848: break or continuity?

If it seemed for a moment that 1848 had brought a change, literary historians tend now to agree that the change was one of degree rather than quality. In the wake of 1848, authors and critics were forced to face the need for reorientation more resolutely. Concluding his reflections at the beginning of the new year in 1849, Gustav Freytag encapsulated the mood of a generation disenchanted by the old idols of literature and politics: 'We no longer want any Goethe, we don't want any Napoleon.'[50] But it was not only the sentiment of disappointment and betrayal, of withdrawal and resignation, that defined the scene; a steady increase of productivity and commercialization of the press and book production had transformed the scene altogether. Forced into literature and criticism, critics nonetheless found unprecedented access to new and larger audiences. New types of literary journals designed to reach larger parts of the reading population, a change in the copyright laws in 1867 that lifted the hold on copyrights of the classics and made it possible to mass produce editions at low costs, and the publication of serial novels in newspapers and literary journals created a new literary market.

In this phase Leipzig, which had always been the centre of German book production, became something of a hub for Realist criticism. While Ruge's and Echtermeyer's *Jahrbücher* had 313 subscribers at the end of 1839 and 500 in the spring of 1842,[51] Gutzkow's *Unterhaltungen am häuslichen Herd* ('Hearthside Conversations', 1852–62) reached 7,000 subscriptions, and Robert Prutz's *Deutsches Museum* ('German Museum', 1851–67) had 600 subscriptions in 1856,[52] while Hermann Marggraff's *Blätter für literarische Unterhaltungen* ('Leaves for Literary Entertainment', 1853–64), Kühne's *Europa* ('Europe', 1846–59) and *Die Grenzboten* ('The Border Messengers'), edited by Julian Schmidt and Gustav Freytag from 1848, reached a maximum of 10,000 subscriptions. But none of them compared to the best-selling *Gartenlaube* ('Bower'), which in 1863 had 160,000 subscriptions, rising, thanks to the

[50] Gustav Freytag, 'Tod und Leben beim Jahreswechsel', *Grenzboten*, 8 (1849), 46–8.
[51] Hans Rosenberg, 'Arnold Ruge und die *Hallischen Jahrbücher*', *Archiv für Kulturgeschichte*, 20 (1930), p. 136 n8.
[52] Ulf Eisele, *Realismus und Ideologie: Zur Kritik der literarischen Theorie nach 1848 am Beispiel des 'Deutschen Museums'* (Stuttgart: Metzler, 1976), p. 12.

Eugenie Marlitt novels, to 400,000 in 1875, with an estimated following of 2 million readers.[53]

With the exhaustion of the combative impetus of the political rhetoric that had informed literary criticism during the period of revolution and restoration, readers and critics were now looking for soothing forms of fiction, poetry and drama. The role of the critic changed from advocate and guarantor of public free speech to that of guide and counsellor. Claiming no less authority as judges and arbitrators than before, critics were, however, forced to address a newly emerging audience whose taste, concerns and needs dictated the success of their media in larger numbers and more palpably than before. Both critics and readers, no longer interested in open politics, sought escape and relief in the literary fiction of true Realism. The line between naïve duplication of the readers' world or worldview and its artful transfiguration into fiction was a fine one, but it became the decisive distinction for literary criticism.

## Poetic Realism

From 1850 to 1880, the literary criticism of poetic Realism was defined by its urge to maintain this fine line of distinction. As a result, form and content were now redesigned to fit the Realists' ideal of the 'true' representation of reality. Realism did not completely break with the conventions of Classicism, but was rather to be seen as its continuation – albeit stripped of its speculative dimension. Despite or because of this, the attitude of critics towards Goethe, the classics and Romantics was mostly negative. In his *Geschichte der Romantik* ('History of Romanticism', 1848), Julian Schmidt leaves no doubt as to what is to blame: Romanticism is the self-alienated spirit that, having absorbed a foreign culture and mistaken it for its own, is haunted by the restlessness of the self that escapes it.[54] But Schmidt was not original in settling his scores, and closely followed Ruge.

Nevertheless, while vacating the political realm, the trajectory of literary criticism did not mark a withdrawal from reality. Instead the search for a more essential, poetic access to reality redefined literature's task. After Hegel, post-speculative sentiment led Realist critics to seek in literature the agency that represented the real poetically. For the Realists, however, literature proceeded in the opposite direction to that of

53  Thomas Nipperdey, *Deutsche Geschichte 1800–1866: Bürgerwelt und starker Staat* (Munich: Beck, 1991), p. 593.
54  Julian Schmidt, 'Preface' in *Geschichte der Romantik in dem Zeitalter der Reformation und der Revolution: Studien zur Philosophie der Geschichte*, 2 vols. (Leipzig: Herbig, 1848), vol. i, pp. xiii–xiv.

idealism. In order to achieve a semblance of reality, Realism was expected to work with a method of representation defined by the ideal reflection (*Widerspiegelung*) of reality in sensuous-concrete fashion. This process of transfiguration was imagined as a sort of sublimation or distillation whereby the essential core of reality crystallized to present the reader with the 'objective truth in things' or 'objects themselves'.[55] Proceeding from the finite to the infinite, from appearance to essence, literature was expected to carve out the core of the real and present its ideal form.[56]

As a result, poetic transfiguration returned the dignity of individuality to things, as well as to characters, whose depiction as real people of 'flesh and blood' earned the highest praise. Responding to the post-metaphysical stalemate between materialism and idealism, Realist criticism casts the literary scene as the stage on which immanence and transcendence are reconciled. This happens through a secularized transfiguration that, in a paradoxically circular exercise, imports the ideal into the real to find it in reality's core. Positing thus a positive reality over and against 'untruth' and 'tastelessness', literary texts were now judged with regard to their 'truth'. 'Normalcy' measures deviance, as the 'insane' and 'unhealthy' are rejected.[57]

Literary criticism responded to the crisis of reality – experienced as ever more intangible, elusive and alienated – by presenting a literary programme that relied on a seemingly secure, yet also precarious, notion of reality. This tension, critically addressed in some of the poetic Realist texts, made the literary critic the central arbiter of perception, a claim soon to be challenged by the Naturalists. As a consequence of the professionalization and bourgeoisification of society and culture, the literary critic assumed the characteristics of the emerging new class of the employee. In the second half of the nineteenth century, literary criticism became the business of salaried newspaper and journal editors.

With Fontane, a new style of literary criticism emerged. Self-conscious, but also self-reflective, Fontane's writing displayed a suave sophistication and cosmopolitan urbaneness that critics of the mid-century lacked because of their parochial and upwardly mobile bourgeois-liberal orientation. His lighthearted conversational style forged the art of criticism into a humane affair that replaced the customary vitriol and rancour with

55 Eisele, *Realismus und Ideologie*, pp. 67, 71.
56 For a critical discussion of the political programme and politics of poetic realism in *Die Grenzboten* see Michael Thormann, 'Der programmatische Realismus der *Grenzboten* im Kontext von liberaler Politik, Philosophie und Geschichtsschreibung', *Internationales Archiv für Sozialgeschichte der deutschen Literatur*, 18 (1993), 37–68, and Michael Thormann, 'Realismus als Intermezzo: Bemerkungen zum Ende eines Literatur- und Kunstprogramms', *Weimarer Beiträge*, 42 (1996), 561–87.
57 Robert Prutz, *Deutsches Museum*, 1 (1855), pp. 20, 728; quoted in Eisele, *Realismus und Ideologie*, p. 94.

serene placidity. This was the criticism of urbane and gentle persuasion. Winning rather than running over the hearts and minds of its readers, his form of criticism saw its task less in self-contained argumentation than in cultivating the audience's sensitivities into a mature and liberal attitude.[58]

In the 1880s, the Naturalist movement redefined the aesthetic canon, foregrounding social questions and anticipating the Modernist movement at the turn of the century. The signal venue of literary criticism, the Hart brothers' journal *Kritische Waffengänge*, announced the critic's new mission as that of the visionary of national renewal. In pronounced opposition to bourgeois aesthetics, the literary critic is no longer a reflective observer whose task is to understand and interpret rather than pass judgement or assign value. Rather, the critic's new role is as educator of the people in order to consolidate the national project, which had assumed a new urgency with the constitution of the German Empire in 1871.[59] Radical in gesture, the literary criticism of the 'Naturalists' was, however, opposed to the emerging Modernist tendencies, a tension that became visible in Otto Brahm, the exponent of the literary criticism of Berlin Modernism.[60] The Expressionists and other critics followed in their steps, adopting the Naturalists' insurgent rhetoric, fashioning their advance into a more cosmopolitan approach to Modernism. In a new manner, authors began to present literary criticism as another form of literary activity, and it became more a venue for broadcasting the literary programme of Modernism than a hermeneutic exercise.

Literary criticism reached its impressionist phase with Alfred Kerr and Karl Kraus, the champions of a new and self-consciously independent approach to literary and aesthetic sensitivity.[61] Attending to the minutiae of linguistic detail and aesthetic form, this new criticism engaged in a pointedly subjective practice that highlighted the profound ethical and political implications of literature, art and culture. When Kraus's journal *Die Fackel* began publication in 1899, he envisioned a literary criticism emphatically opposed to the increasing pressures that had turned it into 'journalistic industrialism', as the opening editorial of *Die Gesellschaft*,

---

58  For Fontane see Russell A. Berman, 'Literaturkritik zwischen Reichsgründung und 1933' in Hohendahl, *Geschichte der deutschen Literaturkritik*, pp. 205–74, and Russell A. Berman, *Between Fontane and Tucholsky: Literary Criticism and the Public Sphere in Imperial Germany* (New York, Bern and Frankfurt: Peter Lang, 1983).

59  Berman, 'Literaturkritik zwischen Reichsgründung und 1933', pp. 219–22.

60  *Ibid.*, pp. 225–7, and Helmut Kreuzer, 'Nachwort: Zur Rezeption der Literatur in der deutschen Kritik zwischen 1870 und 1914' in *Deutschsprachige Literaturkritik 1870– 1914: Eine Dokumentation*, ed. Helmut Kreuzer, 4 vols. (Frankfurt: Peter Lang, 2006), vol. IV, pp. 385–413.

61  For Kerr see Berman, 'Literaturkritik zwischen Reichsgründung und 1933', pp. 227–34, and Berman, *Between Fontane and Tucholsky*.

Munich's voice of Naturalism, had called it.[62] Run and owned by
himself, Kraus's critical initiative, lasting until his death in 1936, signalled both a heroic rebellion against the process of commercialization
and an inevitable surrender to the dictates of the all-consuming capitalist
forms of production. With Franz Mehring, socialist and Marxist literary
criticism began to emerge in the 1890s. But it was not until later in the
twentieth century that a theoretically consistent Marxist literary criticism
would appear.[63]

---

[62]  M. G. Conrad (ed.), *Die Gesellschaft, Realistische Wochenschrift für Litteratur, Kunst
      und öffentliches Leben* (Nendeln: Kraus, 1970), p. 1.
[63]  For the early history of Marxist literary criticism and a concise summary of Mehring's
      approach see Peter Demetz, *Marx, Engels, and the Poets: Origins of Marxist Literary
      Criticism*, trans. Jeffrey L. Sammons (University of Chicago Press, 1967).

# 6

# France: the continuing debate
# over Classicism

ALLAN H. PASCO

After the end of the eighteenth century, Classicism would never again enjoy significant authority as a focused movement, though the values of clarity, precision, order and unity continued to be valued among the most outstanding Romantics, Realists, Parnassians and Symbolists, whether they admitted it or not. Though the terms 'classic' and 'classical' were applied to various nineteenth-century artists and critics like Baudelaire, Brunetière and Gide, it was a Classicism that eighteenth-century practitioners would not have recognized.

The sentiments of Romantics progressively infused French popular audiences, who wept copious tears with the self-pitying, obsessive, dreamy, passionate Romantic heroes of literature.[1] They felt at home meditating at the edge of volcanoes, in gloomy grottoes and in the midst of ruins and cemeteries. They were awe-struck by the lush colours of exotic nature, by howling winds, raging storms, torrential streams, and inaccessible cliffs rising high above tenebrous forests. The relative youth of the Romantics was an item to be exploited in the battle with Classicism. Stendhal, for example, writes: '*Romanticism* is the art of presenting people with literary works that, in the current state of their behaviour and belief, are susceptible of giving them the most possible pleasure. *Classicism* to the contrary presents literature that gave the greatest possible pleasure to their great-grandfathers.'[2]

Romanticism had become increasingly aggressive since the publication of Lamartine's *Méditations* of 1820, and by the early 1830s, the points of contention were clear. In the 'Préface' to the 1828 edition of *Odes et ballades*, Hugo announced: 'A great school is arising.' Then, at the performance of *Hernani* two years later, his violent young friends shouted down the doddering Classicists, and Romanticism was renewed, if not exactly born, given the remarkably successful pre-Romanticism of the last third of the eighteenth century and its subsequent popularity under the radar

---

[1] Allan H. Pasco, *Sick Heroes: French Society and Literature in the Romantic Age, 1750–1850* (University of Exeter Press, 1997), pp. 31–52.

[2] Stendhal, *Racine et Shakspeare* in *Œuvres complètes*, eds. Victor del Litto and Ernest Abravanel, 50 vols. (Geneva and Paris: Slatkine, 1986), vol. XXXVII, p. 39.

of officialdom. In 1832, young radical Romantics like Gautier and the *Jeunes France* angrily went up against the entire 'senescent' art establishment. Perhaps the most frenetic of them was the republican Pétrus Borel, the self-styled Lycanthrope who identified himself with Icarus and tried to use the short-lived newspaper, *La Liberté, journal des arts* to provide leadership for the ardent second generation of 'little' Romantics (1830–40). For the bohemian aesthetes, 'bourgeois' became a curse word synonymous with crass, unrefined greed. 'Death to the Institute! Death to all professors!' exclaims the founder of *La Liberté*. 'Art can suffer neither lock nor chain / It breaks every tie that impedes or hampers it.'[3] When the reactionary Bourbon king Charles X was replaced by the more liberal Louis-Philippe in 1830, censorship was more permissive towards the new literature, and Romanticism emerged from the subterranean depths to which it had been consigned, even though in the end it could not entirely reject the formal qualities of Classicism.

François-René de Chateaubriand (1768–1848) had a certain amount of acclaim shortly after the turn of the century, but he was increasingly preoccupied with his religion and posthumously published autobiography. His real impact came after 1820, when young people rediscovered *René* (1802), and continued throughout the century. Although his persistent melancholy (*le mal de René*), his love of exotic nature and the extremes of sentiment mark him as a disciple of Rousseau and Bernardin de Saint-Pierre, one should not ignore the writer's formative, classical education that is so obvious in *Les martyrs* (1809), *Moïse* (1828) and, indeed, in the *Mémoires d'outre-tombe* (1849–50). His admiration for such classical writers as Homer, Tasso and Virgil is everywhere evident in the *Mémoires*, as it is in his much-loved model Racine, whom on one occasion he consciously attempted to rival with his own play. He was furthermore well acquainted with Jean-François de La Harpe, the Chevalier de Parny, Nicolas Chamfort, Louis de Fontanes and Louis Ginguené, all fine Classicists. In fact, Chateaubriand serves as an important lesson. Despite his flights of melodic, image-laden prose occasioned by love, depression and mysticism, one should never ignore the close relationship between his Romantic, lyrical excesses and his classical form, logic, clarity, symmetry and periodicity. Like all nineteenth-century Classicists, he was very aware of old traditions, forms, monuments and generic limitations. Likewise, Lamartine was for a time felt to be a good classical poet, despite his weak rhymes, lyricism and self-centred focus.

---

[3] I quote Borel's convulsions, the first from *La Liberté*, the second from his poem 'Sur l'art', from L. Cassandra Hamrick, 'Borel, Gautier et Baudelaire: de la "périphérie" du romantique au centre du "moderne"' in *Poésie et poétique en France, 1830–1890: hommage à Eileen Souffrin-Le Breton*, ed. Peter J. Edwards (New York: Peter Lang, 2001), pp. 94, 91.

Well-educated readers and theatregoers, journalists working for a controlled press, academics, critics and even the clergy, almost all of whom learned to appreciate literature under Louis XV and XVI, agreed that France's glory was in Classicism, whether that of France or of Antiquity. The dramatist and academician Alexandre Duval, for example, extolled Classicism in 1836, while reserving thunderbolts for Romantics and innovators.[4] He and his classical colleagues considered novels feminine and overly sentimental. Because the subject matter was almost always love, romances were certainly not suitable for young people. Comedies and melodramas were moreover frivolous entertainments intended for the hoi polloi. Despite official prizes and censorship, however, the changing social mood prompted the public to flood the theatres and buy cartloads of novels, the purveyors of Romantic ideas. The critical elite had lost some of its influence. The enormously important salons that bloomed during the seventeenth- and eighteenth-century classical period were replaced in the early nineteenth century first by male-dominated *cénacles* or literary coteries and later by a predominantly middle-class, male, café society that was more interested in business than literature. There are, in addition, indications that the prevailing bourgeois patriarchy severely curtailed female education during and after the Revolution, limiting it to what a woman needed to run a household or to pursue such gender-dominated activities as flower painting, handiwork and music. Consequently, the beneficent influence of women on letters had decreased, for they were less well grounded.[5]

The French Academy's position as guardian of the glorious past was clear when the noun 'Romanticism' was not included in the sixth edition of its dictionary (1835), and the adjective *'romantique'* was defined as referring to those who 'affect freeing themselves of the rules of composition and style established by classical authors'. Others preferred making appropriate distinctions by considering the source: whether, on the one hand, in a classical or neo-classical past and, on the other, in the Christian tradition. In most classical writers of the nineteenth century, lip-service was paid to moral values, if only in terms such as 'moderation' and 'modesty'. Desmarais also noted that the other predominant tendency among critics was to select a trait or two that became the

---

4  Charles Simond, *Paris de 1800 à 1900 d'après les estampes et les mémoires du temps. Tome 2 (1830–1870): la Monarchie de Juillet, la seconde République – le second empire* (Paris: Plon, 1900), p. 115.
5  Guy Richard, *Histoire de l'amour en France: du moyen âge à la belle époque* (Paris: J. C. Lattès, 1985), p. 181; Olwen H. Hufton, *Women and the Limits of Citizenship in the French Revolution* (University of Toronto Press, 1992), pp. 3–50; Nicolas-Edme Restif de La Bretonne, *Les gynographes*, 2 vols. (The Hague: Gosse & Ruet, 1777), vol. 1, pp. 65–6; and Germaine de Staël, *Œuvres complètes*, 3 vols. (Paris: Firmin Didot frères, 1836), vol. 1, p. 302.

keystone to understanding. Writers who had good taste were Classicists; the vulgar were Romantics. Clarity was another favoured acid test, especially in considering Romantic texts, which were pronounced incomprehensible. Indeed, classical writers seldom thought of Classicism's connections to seventeenth-century France and classical Antiquity, except for passing references to Racine, though they continued to emphasize formal perfection, beauty and objectivity. Of course, Classicists refrained from rugged scenes in nature, while Romantics sought extraordinary and sublime scenes imbued with emotion.[6]

Victor Hugo, like de Staël, wanted a national drama that would be inspired by Christianity. More than anything else, he proclaimed the revolutionary nature of the new art, while Baudelaire summarized its war cry in the *Salon de 1846*: 'He who says Romanticism says modern art – that is, intimacy, spirituality, colour, and aspiration for the infinite expressed by all possible aesthetic means.'[7] Conversely, the Minister of the Interior, L.-A. Thiers, vowed to hunt down and crush all remaining survivors of Romanticism.[8] The publication of Hugo's 'Preface' to *Cromwell* had served as a manifesto to put the classical coterie on notice that drama mixing sublime and grotesque was the genre of preference for the modern world. It would be formed not of some abstract 'nature' removed from reality, but with the force, substance and colour of real life.

For the drama's style, we would like a verse that is free, open, honest, daring to say anything without prudishness, expressing everything without effort, passing from the natural allure of comedy to tragedy, from the sublime to the grotesque; alternately concrete and poetic, both artistic and inspired, profound and unexpected, sweeping and true; knowing how to break and displace the caesura appropriately, so as to disguise the alexandrine's monotony.[9]

The essay was, to the Romantics' intense satisfaction, roundly condemned. Théophile Gautier, not to be outdone, took a walk in the Tuileries Gardens in 1836 and was disgusted by rows of mediocre statues all cut out of the same pseudo-classical mould. 'Who', he asked in mock despair, 'will deliver us from these Greeks and Romans?'[10] Later, in

---

[6]  Cyprien Desmarais, *Essai sur les classiques et les romantiques* (1824; rpt Geneva: Slatkine, 1973), pp. 2–5, 62.

[7]  Charles Baudelaire, 'Salon de 1846' in *Œuvres complètes*, ed. Claude Pichois, 2 vols. (Paris: Gallimard, 1974–5), vol. II, p. 421.

[8]  Quoted from L. Cassandra Hamrick, 'Artistic Production and the Art Critic in a Bourgeois Era: The Case of Théophile Gautier', *Il confronto letterario: quaderni del Dipartimento di Lingue et Letterature Straniere Moderne dell'Universita di Pavia*, 17 (2000), p. 246.

[9]  Victor Hugo, 'Preface' to *Cromwell* in *Œuvres complètes: édition chronologique*, ed. Jean Massin, 18 vols. (Paris: Club Français du Livre, 1967), vol. III, pp. 74–5.

[10] Hamrick, 'Artistic Production', p. 250. Baudelaire will repeat the apothegm in 'L'école païenne' in *Œuvres complètes*, vol. II, p. 625.

1854, Hugo would remember his early proclivities and proudly proclaim his responsibility for the literary Revolution: 'I trampled good taste and old French verse / Beneath my feet' and 'created havoc as much in the subject matter as in the form'. He even put a 'red [revolutionary] cap on the old dictionary'.[11]

Though Madame de Staël died in 1817, her influence long continued and was particularly evident in the 1830s and early 1840s. She insisted on the importance of the unfettered individual, which had not sat well with Emperor Bonaparte, the royalists or, in general, the Classicists. But as Henri Peyre said, she was never really comfortable with Spanish drama or Shakespeare, both of enormous importance to French Romantics.[12] She recognized rather the genius of Racine and the magnificence of his poetry, but she was quite sure that as a model for subsequent literature Racine lacked the philosophical framework that eighteenth-century *philosophes* could provide in order to touch modern man. 'Historical subjects must not be rejected . . . human nature must be ennobled . . . everyday circumstances must be dignified and grand events must be painted with simplicity.'[13] Though such 'renewal' was, of course, not what the emperor and other classical promoters had in mind, her ideas eventually triumphed in 'Modernism', a term that for the most part by mid-century excluded overt imitation of classical authors but otherwise included the traditional traits of Antiquity and the French seventeenth century. Classicism was no longer attached either to a particular author, or group of authors, or even to a period. It was a complex of traits.

Like those of the best nineteenth-century writers, Chateaubriand's innovations are in no way limited to creations that can be termed classical or Modernist or Romantic. Despite the exciting experimentation that followed in Alfred de Musset, Charles Baudelaire, Aloysius Bertrand, Lautréamont and others, France's Romanticism generally maintained such classic tendencies as order, clarity and reason. Even the young genius Rimbaud was well versed in Latin poetry and maintained a certain logic and unity in the best of his unrestrained verses. Indeed, given that standard rules failed utterly to describe good taste, some have maintained that any distinction between Classicism and Romanticism was futile. All too often 'Romantic' meant extravagant, and 'classical' a work that was measured and well written.

What made the issue more difficult was that both terms had changed their meaning since appearing in the work of Chateaubriand and Madame

[11] Victor Hugo, 'Réponse à un acte d'accusation' in *Œuvres complètes*, vol. IX, pp. 74, 75.
[12] Henri Peyre, *Le Classicisme français* (New York: Maison française, 1942), p. 207.
[13] Germaine de Staël, *De la littérature considérée dans ses rapports avec les institutions sociales* (1800) in *Œuvres complètes*, vol. I, p. 310.

de Staël. Desmarais thought it was better to recognize simply that all writers of the period were knowingly or unknowingly inspired by a new literature that was a direct result of the 'misfortunes of the Revolution and the philosophical errors of the eighteenth century'. He believed that this inspiration might explain literature's apparently desperate need for religion, and went so far as to suggest that all Romantic literature grew from Christianity, while Classicism was inspired by pagan gods. Similarly, although classical doctrines and feelings were unquestionably tied to the monarchy, he felt that some might term the results a manifestation of classical immobility. Perhaps critics should recognize simply that there was a new literature in the air, though Desmarais puts it this way: 'It is no longer possible to have anything but *classical-Romantic*; pure Classicism has become impossible.'[14] Classicism had shifted its ground. Though proponents like Julien-Louis Geoffroy might well respect Antiquity, they were in no way bound by it. When Baudelaire and others in this period term a work 'classic', they mean disciplined, restrained, ordered, true and logical. For them, it reflects '[t]his inner taste of form and formal perfection' that is eternal. In 1861, Baudelaire leaves no doubt as to where he places Gautier in his pantheon of beauty: 'One day, people will cite Théophile Gautier in the way they cite La Bruyère, Buffon, Chateaubriand, that is to say, as one of the surest and rarest masters of language and style.'[15]

Curiously, Romanticism showed signs of fading almost immediately after *Hernani*'s triumphant debut in 1830, making way for early manifestations of Realism. Only two decades after the publication of Desmarais's *Essai sur les classiques*, Hugo's *Les Burgraves* (1843) failed to find an audience and, for most scholars, marked the end of Romanticism. Within a few weeks, *Lucrèce* by the dramatist François Ponsard (1814–67) was a hit. Although the play was universally praised as a salutary return to the summits of classical theatre, Ponsard's aspirations were far more modest. He wished simply to find a dramatic golden mean, a theatrical world where Shakespeare and Racine could cohabit the same, eclectic stage. The possibilities of some sort of mixture had been broached in the 1820s by Victor Cousin and Claude Fauriel, but, in truth, the success of *Lucrèce* probably had more to do with Rachel's brilliant performance and the public's fatigue with Romanticism than with a new Classicism: people had become as tired of feudal settings and other Romantic extremes, whether Hugo's sublime and grotesque or twenty-four-carat villains and angelic prostitutes, as they were of stodgy unities and jaded alexandrines.

---

[14] Desmarais, *Essai sur les classiques*, pp. 46, 32–3, 110, 54–5.
[15] Charles Baudelaire, 'Théophile Gautier' (1859) in *Œuvres complètes*, vol. II, pp. 694, 724.

Ponsard struggled to establish a new 'school of good sense' and high morality, attempting in everything to avoid extremes like adulterous, depraved or, even, divorced female characters. He was anti-clerical, as was much of the upper class, but, however much he abhorred excessive religious influence on government, he avoided attacking either the church or religion. Like the good liberal republican he was, he sought to reconcile royalists with democrats, and the *ancien régime* with the Revolution, while protecting a republican, nationalistic ideal from the ravages of the far right and, conversely, from socialism. He wished to be a conciliator. He found good in both Romanticism and Classicism, though he attempted to avoid either label, for both had been reduced to reified lists of canonical traits rather than fine works of art growing from the concerns of contemporary society.

While today Ponsard garners no more than a rare footnote, he is emphasized here because he provides a good example of what happens during the birth, life and death of literary movements and what indeed happened to the rivalry between Classicism and Romanticism. They coalesce, they rise, they ebb, they join the recent flow of creations reflecting current circumstances and new philosophies, and they occasionally find a brilliant artist who can bring them back to life. By 1883, some fifty years after the clamorous declarations elevating Romanticism over Classicism, Emile Deschanel could publish a book entitled *Le Romantisme des classiques* ('The Romanticism of the Classicists'). Emile Faguet introduced his essay on the criticism of the second half of the nineteenth century by saying that the period had, 'if not stopped being militant, at least ... no longer split critics into two hostile camps. Otherwise, it tried to become scientific, to constitute itself as a science and to become what might appropriately be called *literary science* [that is, literary theory].'[16] The two major schools of the early part of the century made use of recognizable concepts as they reappeared in a devitalized Romanticism, Parnassianism, positivism, Realism, Symbolism and Naturalism. Reason and science were often mentioned, by which critics meant solid, thorough, impersonal research that produced true, objective explanations and descriptions.

Despite the classicist Désiré Nisard's vigorous campaign against Romanticism, the movement did not disappear with the failure of *Les Burgraves* in 1843. It bobbed up repeatedly in the sea of competing '-isms' during the remainder of the century. In 1851, for example, Théophile Gautier cried out for an aesthetic 'anarchy', by which he meant much the same as he had twenty years earlier when he called for Romantic

---

[16] Emile Faguet, 'La critique' in *Histoire de la langue et de la littérature française des origines à 1900. Vol. 8: Dix-neuvième siècle: période contemporaine (1850–1900)*, ed. L. Petit de Julleville (Paris: Armand Colin, 1903), p. 358.

revitalization. This time, however, the quest for modernity had already led to Realism, 'art for art's sake', and the positivistic reflection of the scientific age in objective, seemingly impersonal Parnassian poetry.[17] Parnassians like José Maria de Heredia and Leconte de Lisle took the demand for formal beauty from Classicism, while exploiting difficult verse forms that portrayed 'scientifically' accurate history and exotic lands honestly and objectively. Art had no obligation but to create art, refined, highly polished art. Parnassians split early into two discernible groups: those who preferred themes of recent events and intimacy and those who made much of their allegiance to Hellenism, philosophy and science. A neo-Romanticism shortly became an important part of Naturalism's renewal of mythology and the extremes of passion in numerous critical works by Emile Zola, Joris-Karl Huysmans and others.

Leconte de Lisle (1818–94) declared in his 1852 preface to *Poèmes antiques* that there had been no great poetic movements since the Greece of Homer, Aeschylus and Sophocles, an opinion he repeated in 1886 when he was elected to the French Academy. Shakespeare, Dante and Milton were merely brilliant exceptions to a feckless reality.[18] There is no question about the appropriateness of the classical epithet applied to Leconte de Lisle, for he not only chose his poetic models from Antiquity, but also proclaimed the necessity of objectivity. His poems, despite their exoticism and realism, expertly exploit classical prosody in a noble style and reveal what some term frigid impersonality. He admirably translated a number of Greek and Roman poets, and he never changed in his desire both to crush the last remnants of Romanticism and to replace them with poems modelled on the great poets of Antiquity.

All the while, Désiré Nisard (1806–88), a member of the French Academy and a widely respected classical writer, used his influence to continue his attacks on the Romantic movement that on the whole had lost its power. Brunetière, who often had an appropriate word, said that Nisard 'wanted to take criticism backward'.[19] Nisard consequently was marginalized, soon forgotten. Nonetheless, one of Nisard's most telling critiques of Romantic writing was that it was a '[f]acile literature', as he titled one of his articles, and great writers of the Parnassians, the Realists and the Modernists insisted on the importance of craftsmanship and

---

[17]  M. A. R. Habib, *A History of Literary Criticism from Plato to the Present* (Oxford: Blackwell, 2005), p. 424; L. Cassandra Hamrick, 'Gautier et l'anarchie de l'art' in *Relire Théophile Gautier: le plaisir du texte*, ed. Freeman G. Henry (Amsterdam and Atlanta: Rodopi, 1998), pp. 91–117.

[18]  Charles Marie René Leconte de Lisle, 'Préface' in *Poèmes antiques*, ed. Claudine Gothot-Mersch (Paris: Gallimard, 1994), pp. 311–12. See also the Gothot-Mersch preface, pp. 10–11.

[19]  Ferdinand Brunetière, *L'évolution des genres dans l'histoire de la littérature. Vol. 1: L'évolution de la critique* (Paris: Hachette, 1906), p. 213.

formal perfection. Even Verlaine took a position against facile verse. In a frequently reprinted poem of 1882, he demanded poetry that resembled marble statuary, lacking technical flaws, whether weak rimes or faulty metrics, and, thus, capable of lasting for an eternity. Of course, he recanted this theoretical position in 1890, claiming that his 'Art poétique' was nothing but a song.

Charles-Augustin Sainte-Beuve (1804–69) started as a full-blown Romantic with few allegiances to Classicism. He published a volume of sentimental poems, *Joseph Delorme*, in 1829 and a novel, *Volupté*, in 1834. If nothing else, the two works established his bona fides for the Romantic circles that were gathering. Contemptuous of the new school's negligent conventions, formulas and rules, however, he slowly gravitated towards a classical style of simplicity and clarity, unity and coherence, since, he came to realize, great writers are neither barbarians nor madmen. In *Chateaubriand et son groupe* (1861) he explicitly turned away from Romanticism and its excesses. Throughout his career, however, he never deviated from a thoroughly Romantic lack of interest in the generalized humanity that the classical age called *nature*. In the hundreds of weekly essays he wrote, published first in newspapers then in collected volumes (especially *Les causeries du lundi*, collected 1851–62, and *Nouveaux lundis, collected* 1863–70), he usually offered portraits of single authors. In works like *Port-Royal* (1840–59), however, he was able to rise above particular individuals and details to portray groups. He always sought the essential characteristic of an individual author's mind (*génie*) and those traits that derive from it, as well as the traits that brought him into relationship with a particular group or movement. By 1850, his definition of a 'classic' had become

an author who has enriched the human spirit . . . who has discovered some unequivocal moral truth or who has reformulated some eternal passion in a core where everything seemed known and explored, who has rendered his thought, his observation, or his invention in some form . . . who has spoken to everyone in his own style . . . without neologisms . . . easily contemporaneous to every age. [T]his definition . . . especially includes the requirements of regularity, wisdom, moderation, and reason that dominate and contain all others.[20]

Sainte-Beuve, whose knowledge of Greek and Roman authors was exemplary, developed his thoughts about classical Antiquity in his subsequent 'De la tradition en literature' (1858). He argued that most important characteristics of the great writers of the past become an integral part of civilization. Classicism was apparent in our laws, institutions, education, behaviour, and without question in the concise, elegant diction of

[20]  Charles Augustin Sainte-Beuve, 'Qu'est-ce qu'un classique?' in *Causeries du lundi*, 15 vols. (Paris: Garnier, 1852), vol. III, pp. 42–3.

all great literature, though it was a general, rather than a particular, orientation. He made a great deal of the 'science' behind his own creativity (as did Heredia and Gustave Flaubert), for his objective comprehension of individuals and groups could be attained only through extensive research. His psychological insight produced admirable descriptions of many authors, though he was curiously unable to appreciate his truly outstanding contemporaries like Honoré de Balzac, Stendhal, Charles Baudelaire and Victor Hugo. The personal acquaintance he had with these writers, not to mention Flaubert and Gerard de Nerval, left him incapable of evaluating their works objectively. What Proust called Sainte-Beuve's 'cecity'[21] led him to his satirical portrait of Mme de Villeparisis, who makes her absurd aesthetic judgements on the basis of biography.

The language of criticism became more and more imprecise. Modernity took many of the traits of Classicism. The terms depended on the critics who were using them. There were numerous attributes that suggested traditional Classicism: restraint, simplicity, gravity, order, unity, reason, clarity, harmony, polish and precision... other qualities could be added. Late eighteenth-century classical critics disagreed on whether contemporary texts should be modelled on the great writers of Louis XIV's France of 1661–82 (the position of early eighteenth-century Moderns) or on Greek and Roman masterworks (and thus the Ancients). Was harmony important? The defining traits functioned rather like a Jungian archetype. Each period, indeed each critic, defined Classicism in their own way, as certain qualities were included or excluded to reflect the interests of the period and the critic or artist. There was little agreement about the dominant traits of Classicism. Baudelaire believed that only with inspiration from his own age could he possibly achieve greatness. Still, Sainte-Beuve graced him with the term 'classic', to Baudelaire's obvious delight.[22] While praising Modernism, a term trailing clouds of the classical quarrel of the Ancients and Moderns, Baudelaire despised Realism, because its proponents were willing to stop with perfect copies of reality, whereas he wished to go beyond to formal, aesthetic and spiritual beauty. Mid-century critics thought Romanticism was little more than egotistic sentimentalism, while Classicism was virtually synonymous with formalism and precision. Realism raised a new set of demands, insisting on objective description of reality and scientific truth. A work's attempt to achieve formal perfection justified suggestions that it was classical. Using

[21]  Marcel Proust, *Pastiches et mélanges*, Bibliothèque de la Pléiade (1919; rpt Paris: Gallimard, 1971), p. 190.
[22]  Charles Baudelaire, 'Une réforme à l'Académie' in *Œuvres complètes*, vol. II, p. 190 and n. 7.

such explanations that insisted on science, philosophy, exact truth and concrete reality, Sainte-Beuve claimed to be a Classicist.[23]

For Baudelaire's own poetry, it seemed that none of the contemporary terminology was adequate. His individualistic inspiration, lexicon, images and conventions were all held strictly subordinate to the needs of the poem. As Charles A. Porter said in another context, 'classical' means the 'belief that there are rules and principles to be sought out, developed, and followed'.[24] Gide later noted the general, terminological imprecision, as well: 'It would not take very much for people to call all great and beautiful works classical.'[25]

The Classicism of Brunetière (1849–1906) late in the nineteenth century had to do with language more than with particular models. He sought the linguistic core, devoid of idiosyncratic dialects, idioms, foreign words, provincialisms and pedantic neologisms; in short, he looked for a common language that could not exist until it was fixed in a national literature, but which continued to live across time and to remain intelligible to all native participants of the linguistic community in question. The language was, in addition, a unifying force. In the case of France, he held up the French language canonized during the age of Louis XIV. He did not believe, however, that language remained fixed and thus stagnant; inspired by Darwin, he attempted to grasp the evolution of language and literature. Brunetière felt that Romanticism's mistake was to neglect the classical age and go to the medieval period for inspiration. Romanticism was moreover too 'personal', too eccentric, leaving the language in a state of confusion. As a result, 'however high the Lamartines, the Mussets, the Hugos might rise, they would never be classical'. They had 'moved too far away from the period of the language's perfection'. Furthermore, 'foreign literatures have too deeply influenced them'.[26] Brunetière wanted to establish criticism as a science of literature, with precise methodology, fixed rules and principles, subordinated to an acceptable morality. He was firmly opposed to subjective literature. He wanted a literature which, like traditional Classicism, raised issues that were common to humankind.

Brunetière saw himself as what linguists call a 'native informant'. Thoroughly grounded in the great classical artists, he believed he could on that foundation make critical judgements on the literature of the present. The goal of his work, like that of all great literature in his view, was to direct people towards the sustenance and progress of morality. Consequently he

---

[23] As he told the Senate on 1 May 1868. See Pierre Moreau, 'Le bilan de Sainte-Beuve', *Revue des sciences humaines*, 34 (1969), 353–63.

[24] Charles A. Porter, 'Chateaubriand's Classicism', *Yale French Studies*, 38 (1967), p. 156.

[25] André Gide, 'Billets à Angèle' in *Essais critiques* (Paris: Gallimard, 1999), p. 282.

[26] Quoted from Gilles Boulard, 'Ferdinand Brunetière et le classicisme, ou la conjonction des nationalismes', *Revue d'histoire littéraire de la France*, 100 (2000), p. 227.

was adamantly opposed to 'art for art's sake', which he felt encouraged frivolous, self-centred works that had no real value to the community. Such were the positions behind his *Manuel de l'histoire de la littérature française* (1897), which exerted considerable influence for many years. While in no sense a polemicist, his 'critique des défauts' was frequently memorable. Balzac, for example, was 'one of the worst writers that ever tormented this poor French language'.[27]

Despite Brunetière, however, and the undoubted importance of formalist concerns, Classicism would never again predominate. The minor Symbolists after Rimbaud and Verlaine rode herds of Romantic horses through bejewelled, enchanted forests in search of precious visions, though later proponents of Symbolism, like Stéphane Mallarmé and Paul Valéry, focused on difficult poetics and on internal, ideational realities. They were then frequently linked to Classicism. Even André Gide is known for his technical mastery and is frequently referred to as a classicist.

Jean Moréas (1856–1910), an expatriate Greek, was deeply involved with the Symbolists and their self-proclaimed leader. In the understated opinion of Kenneth Cornell, the pretentious Greek was 'loud in theory, [but] somewhat disappointing in deed. Innovation in technique and conscious literary artistry are offset by an instinct for imitation.'[28] After perhaps justifiably claiming to have originated the Symbolist name in 1891, Moréas abandoned symbolic self-expression and imagination to establish the Roman School (*L'école romane*). He had come north, he proclaimed, to rectify the crudity of his erstwhile colleagues, since the South was the only area capable of producing sweet and harmonious melodies. Charles Maurras wrote a brief news item announcing the foundation of the new group, which was followed up in a letter and several days later in an article by Jean Moréas, all three published in the *Figaro*. Jouanny maintains that the subsequent article, published on 23 September 1891, was the veritable manifesto of the new school. The group proclaimed the necessity of returning to true Classicism, the severest of traditional verses, and pure French, the direct descendant of Greek and Latin. The watchwords were beauty, idealism and the Graeco-Roman tradition. The enemy was, of course, Romanticism, from which most of the other poetic movements of the century had been derived: 'Romanticism corrupted three generations of writers.'[29] It would be easy to exaggerate the importance of

[27] Quoted from Gaëtan Picon, 'Le roman et la prose lyrique au XIXe siècle' in *Histoire des littératures. Vol. 3: Littératures françaises, connexes et marginales*, ed. Raymond Queneau (Paris: Gallimard, 1958), p. 1069.

[28] Kenneth Cornell, *The Symbolist Movement* (New Haven, CT: Yale University Press, 1952), p. 54.

[29] Robert A. Jouanny, *Jean Moréas: écrivain français* (Paris: Lettres Modernes Minard, 1969), pp. 550–3, 554.

this return to Hellenism, but some fine artists were indeed showing a new interest in Classicism. Of course, Francis Vielé-Griffin had never forsaken ancient Greece, Pierre Quillard and Pierre Louÿs were translating from the Greek, Paul Valéry and André Gide had alluded to Narcissus, and Heredia continued to publish his exquisite sonnets.

In that Moréas knew the changing literary movements well, he has some resemblance to Sainte-Beuve, though he started much later. Both began as Romantics and spent important time with the Parnassians. Of course, Sainte-Beuve never had much sympathy for Symbolism, which was an important component of Moréas's intellectual and aesthetic history. But both ended as committed Classicists, feeling themselves to be modern, if not Modernist. It is also true that despite their sympathy for, if not adherence to, several schools, neither was able to free himself completely from Romanticism. As Barrès said, 'If what is called a Romantic sentiment is taken to a superior degree of culture, it takes on characteristics of classicism.'[30] Both Gide and Valéry said that the best of Classicism grows from a Romantic past.[31] Whatever the case, superior artists increasingly valued Classicism as they understood it.

Saint-Marc Girardin's (1801–73) best-known work, *De l'usage des passions dans le drame* (1843–63), grew from a series of lectures at the Sorbonne, where he defended ancient writers against the Moderns and decried the Romantics' inadequacies. He and most of the critics responsible for the rebirth of Classicism at the *fin de siècle* have been forgotten, though at the time the controversies between the still active Symbolists and the Surrealists were significant. Charles Maurras (1868–1952) is remembered because of his considerable impact in conservative political and artistic circles. Previously mentioned for his importance in bringing attention to Jean Moréas's conversion to Classicism, he additionally founded the 'Action Française', and he continued to oppose Romanticism, Naturalism and Symbolism, all in favour of a new Classicism.

Time has dealt much more gently with Paul Valéry (1871–1945). He gained a good reputation among the Symbolists with his early poems, but he was soon struck by depression, perhaps because he perceived that Mallarmé's influence on his work was pernicious. Whatever the cause, he fell silent for sixteen years. On returning to publication, the change was perceptible. He had become a Classicist whose interests were primarily orientated towards subordinating content to form. Some have thought that his love for Huysmans's *A rebours* indicated the lingering influence of the Symbolists, though it seems likely that he was especially struck by the

[30] Quoted from Robert Niklaus, *Jean Moréas: poète lyrique* (Paris: Presses Universitaires de France, 1936), p. 217.
[31] Peyre, *Le Classicisme Français*, p. 49.

subtle structure apparent in the novel.[32] Unquestionably, he understood
the importance of formal rules and conventions, simplicity, perfection,
and appropriate models that might include Dante or Shakespeare. As
Maarten van Buuren argues, the most important of these conventions
concerns formal constraints.[33] It would be wrong to argue that Valéry's
Classicism was limited to the imitation of classical models, for the conventions that he borrowed, primarily from the seventeenth century, were
adapted to his own needs and, he maintained, to those of his period.
Indeed, as he pointed out in 'Introduction à la méthode de Léonard de
Vinci', it was form that 'generated' a given poem. In the rules and conventions, however arbitrary they might be, Valéry saw a means to go beyond
himself. What he wanted to create was an intransitive poetry that communicated nothing but itself, that encouraged the reader's contemplation
of its genesis. It was not a matter of imitating classical poems, but rather
of creating new poems on the foundation of ancient structures.

André Gide (1869–1951) claimed to be a Classicist, at least after 1909.
He began in the Symbolist camp, being one of the young people who con-
gregated in Mallarmé's home in the *rue de Rome*. Indeed, the influence
of the Symbolists continued throughout his life, though he resisted Surrealism and insisted on choice of the right word, constraint, concentration,
harmony, order, sincerity, stylization and suggestion. Furthermore, 'Classicism seems to me . . . a French invention' where 'the French genius was
most fully realized'. Perhaps most importantly, he held that the 'classical
method' requires the renunciation of 'individuality',[34] at least until such
submission is internalized and becomes a part of the artist's creation, as
when Gide's narrator instructs: 'Nathanaël . . . when you have read me,
throw away this book – and leave.'[35]

Gide goes so far as to suggest that all art is particular, but it must allow
generalization: 'Art is painting a particular subject powerfully enough so
that the general on which it depends is included.'[36] 'Classicism', he contended, 'tends without exception toward litotes. It is the art of expressing
the most by saying the least.'[37] He regularly sought understatement, but
as with all effective litotes, he stressed understatement that would expand

---

[32] Allan H. Pasco, '*A rebours* à rebours', *Revue d'histoire littéraire de la France*, 109 (2009), 621–44.

[33] Maarten van Buuren, 'Paul Valéry et le classicisme' in *Histoire, jeu, science dans l'aire de la littérature: mélanges offerts à Evert van der Starre* (Amsterdam: Rodopi, 2000), p. 26.

[34] 'I can tell you now that today I consider myself as the best representative of Classicism': see Gide, 'Billets à Angèle', pp. 281–2.

[35] André Gide, *Les Nourritures terrestres* in *Œuvres complètes*, 13 vols. (Paris: NRF, 1932–9), vol. II, p. 57.

[36] André Gide, *Paludes* in *Œuvres complètes*, vol. I, p. 412.

[37] Gide, '*Billets à Angèle*', p. 283.

with intense, general meaning. From a writer primarily interested in psychology, this kind of generalization much resembles the classical concept of *nature*, that is, the essence of humankind. Although his essays, journals and fictions seem to attain classical simplicity, it is only on the surface. The works themselves are intensely complicated structures that work out conflicts between Realism and Idealism, reason and imagination, egotism and self-sacrifice, harmony and discordance, irony and plain speaking, and, most important, between Gide and his society.

Gide maintains that, with the exception of *Les nourritures terrestres*, all his work is ironic.[38] While it is common for classical writers to choose difficult traditional forms, Gide's structures are indeed so complicated that one critic claims: 'The resultant network of tensions puts extraordinary demands on readers, who must participate actively.'[39] Gide himself said, 'I read the way I would like to be read, that is, very slowly. For me, to read means to go away for two whole weeks with the author.'[40] He can then insist that art depends on reason, while not only presenting characters in the throes of emotional upheaval, but attempting to touch the sentiments of his reader.

In fact, of course, there is no such thing as either pure Classicism or unadulterated Romanticism. Such labels are useful as battle cries, when young artists try to shove their elders off to the side, or when rulers and regimes attempt to enslave literature and turn it into a tool for their own preservation. Labels are in addition useful for analysis and instruction in the classroom. Isolated efforts that imitated the great works of Antiquity or of seventeenth-century France had little real effect in the nineteenth and early twentieth centuries until they were integrated into the predominant aesthetic movements of the period. Classicism's real success grew from its ability to encourage rigour that had the possibility of rising above its sources. Chateaubriand's stunning success was possible only because he could express his subjectivism in highly disciplined ways that some would call classical. Despite the success of a proliferation of schools that occupied the nineteenth century, the best of their artists take significant traits from Classicism. If, as Gide would maintain, Classicism is reason and fine craftsmanship, then great art will always be, to a degree, classical.

---

38 Gide, *Paludes*, in *Œuvres complètes*, vol. I, pp. 439–40.
39 Allan H. Pasco, 'Subversive Structure in Gide's *L'immoraliste*' in *Novel Configurations: A Study of French Fiction* (Birmingham, AL: SUMMA, 1994), p. 99.
40 Gide, *Journal 1889–1939* (Paris: Gallimard, 1951), p. 132.

# 7

# England: Romantic legacies

## Stephen Prickett

Any understanding of the Romantic heritage in Victorian critical writing must start with the overall context – intellectual, cultural, philosophical, religious and economic – not to mention the practical conditions of publishing. For reasons that are clearly connected, criticism in the mid-nineteenth century was both wider in scope and more popular in appeal (if not in absolute numbers of readers) than in the late twentieth or early twenty-first centuries. It was the heyday of the heavyweight intellectual journals. Names like *Blackwood's*, the *British Critic*, the *Cornhill Magazine*, the *Edinburgh Review* and the *Westminster Review* represent only a fraction of the magazines of the period. Most were fiercely partisan. There was a journal for almost every political grouping or religious faction. The *Methodist Magazine*, founded by John Wesley in the eighteenth century for his 'Methodist' followers, was the oldest magazine in the world;[1] the *British Critic* was High Church; the *Westminster*, Benthamite radical; *Household Words*, owned and edited by Dickens, was primarily the chosen vehicle for his own novels – but also encouraged and published other, younger, novelists. Many others, such as *Blackwood's* or the *Cornhill*, carried high-quality fiction in weekly or monthly instalments, and nearly all had long, serious review articles – 5,000 to 10,000 words was not an uncommon length, and some were considerably longer.

Such reviews ranged very widely. Unlike today, at that time literature, and its associated aesthetic criticism, was still seen as having direct philosophical and theological implications. For the leading critics of the period, such as Matthew Arnold (1822–88), Thomas Carlyle (1795–1881), E. S. Dallas (1828–79), Thomas De Quincey (1785–1859), John Keble (1792–1866) or John Ruskin (1819–1900) (to name but a few) the idea that the proper field of criticism was solely literature would have seemed as extraordinary as it would to many of the leading poets and novelists – the Brownings, George Eliot or Tennyson, for instance. Equally significantly,

---

[1] The current society gossip magazine the *Tatler* claims direct descent from the eighteenth-century journal of the same name – and therefore to be the world's oldest (it held a 300th birthday party in 2009). Since Steele's journal ceased publication in 1711, and the modern one, actually founded in 1901, bears almost no relation to the original in clientele or purpose, this claim should be treated with caution.

it was still widely assumed that philosophy, theology – and even science – were suitable and appropriate areas for literature and literary criticism.

Arnold wrote volumes of poetry and criticism (using ethnological and racial scientific theories in the latter),[2] as well as three books of theology. Both Robert and Elizabeth Barrett Browning tackled contemporary theological and social questions in their poetry. Tennyson agonized over both theology and (Lamarckian) evolution in *In Memoriam*. Dallas's *Gay Science* (1866), an attempt to ground criticism not in literary texts but in psychology, is based on a fully fledged theory of the unconscious a generation before Freud or Jung. But it is in the work of someone like George Henry Lewes (1817–78), George Eliot's 'husband' and partner of many years, that one can find expression of the full spread of possibilities in the era.[3] In addition to two novels, and numerous essays on drama and on British and continental writers, he produced *A Biographical History of Philosophy* (1845/6), as well as volumes on *Spanish Drama* (1846), *Comte's Philosophy of the Sciences* (1853), *The Life and Works of Goethe* (1855), *Sea-Side Studies at Ilfracombe, Tenby, the Scilly Isles, and Jersey* (1858), *The Physiology of Common Life* (1859), *Studies in Animal Life* (1862), *Aristotle: A Chapter from the History of Science* (1864) and *Actors and Acting* (1875). Moreover, though by the 1860s scientists had established themselves as a learned profession, and were increasingly successful in distancing their specialist work from what they saw as uninformed lay criticism – or even, as in the case of the Darwin debate, deliberate obscurantism[4] – Lewes's scientific work cannot even so be dismissed as mere journalism. It was the fruit of genuine research, and at least one of his ideas – what is now called the doctrine of the functional indifference of the nerves – has stood the test of time.

It is in the light of this polymathic intermixture of literary and scientific criticism that Ruskin's much-abused *Storm Cloud of the Nineteenth Century* (1884) should also be viewed. For many in the still newly professionalized scientific community Ruskin's observations on the weather – a mixture of aesthetics, meteorology and dire prophecy – represented the very worst kind of amateur dabbling in matters beyond the understanding of the layman. For some it was simply evidence of his madness. But as we have seen, this kind of argument had in fact a long and honourable tradition behind it. Moreover, time has vindicated Ruskin's argument that industrial pollution had ruined the weather. It had indeed.[5]

[2] See, for instance, Frederick E. Faverty, *Matthew Arnold the Ethnologist* (Evanston, IL: Northwestern University Press, 1951).
[3] See Rosemary Ashton, *G. H. Lewes: A Life* (Oxford: Clarendon Press, 1991).
[4] See Adrian Desmond and James Moore, *Darwin* (New York: Warner Books, 1992).
[5] See Tim Hilton, *John Ruskin: The Later Years* (New Haven, CT: Yale University Press, 2000), p. 483.

Perhaps no less significant is that this kind of 'then' and 'now' writing was part of a new sense of history. For a generation that had grown up with the traumas and violent aftermath of the French Revolution, it was no longer possible to assume that things were very much as they always had been. Recent European history had made the irony of Gibbon's Enlightenment epigram that history was little more than the record of the 'crimes, follies, and misfortunes of mankind' begin to look very threadbare. The underlying assumption of Thomas Gray's hugely popular *Elegy in a Country Churchyard* (1750), that the life of a contemporary ploughman in the Buckinghamshire village of Stoke Poges was essentially similar to that of the peasantry in the first-century *campagna* around Rome (as described in Lucretius's *De Rerum Natura*), was no longer even remotely tenable. History could never again be a record of particular events against a background of stasis, but from henceforth had to involve a study of change itself. The translation of Niebuhr's massive *History of Rome* by Julius Hare (1795–1855) and Connop Thirlwall (1797–1825) in 1827 has (in retrospect) sometimes been seen as a watershed in British historiography but, in truth, it would be no less accurate to see it as a 'sign of the times' – itself a phrase taken up as a title by Thomas Carlyle. Though the work was not as thoroughgoing as the principles of so-called 'scientific' history, later to be pioneered by his younger contemporary Leopold von Ranke (1795–1886), Barthold Georg Niebuhr (1776–1831) was the first modern historian to attempt to go beyond the accretions of myth and tradition handed down by the Latin authors themselves, and to search for documentary evidence. Where that was impossible, he looked for explanations in areas not necessarily always obvious to contemporary observers, such as institutions, laws, class, culture and even race. Carlyle's own titles, from his *Signs of the Times* (1829) to *Past and Present* (1843), hammer home the message of historical flux and transformation – a theme central to his monumental history of *The French Revolution* (1837) itself, which explored change not so much as process but as apocalypse.

Not all this new emphasis on historical change was progressive. In many cases what had begun as a Romantic and often wildly unscholarly interest in a largely imaginary Middle Ages became transposed into an idealization of the past in comparison with what was seen as the grime and materialism of the present. *Contrasts* (1836) by Augustus Welby Pugin (1812–52) delivers its message of catastrophic moral and aesthetic decline in a series of prints comparing an idealized Catholic medieval England with the civic decay induced by industrialism and the harshness of the Poor Law. Carlyle's pre-Reformation Abbot Samson in *Past and Present* is a heroic figure, who stands in marked contrast to the degeneracy of modern leaders. What he called 'the condition of England question' was to dominate much of Carlyle's writing on contemporary Britain. Similarly *Sybil* (1845) by Benjamin Disraeli (1804–81) swiftly gives the reader a contrast between the honest communal labour for the common good by the monks of old, and a dissolute modern aristocracy ('a Venetian oligarchy') whose family fortunes were based on the theft of monastic lands at the Reformation. As the century wore on this theme of social and cultural criticism, and the commercial or aesthetic degeneracy of the times, becomes ever stronger. It was a theme that was to dominate much of Ruskin's artistic and social criticism – and is clearly implicit in even the titles of such novels as *The Way We Live Now* (1875) by Anthony Trollope (1815–82). The worship of medievalism was to reach its final apotheosis in the five-volume *Broad Stone of Honour* (1876/7) by Kenelm Digby (1796–1880)

Not surprisingly, therefore, the criticism of the Victorians is distinguished from that of its Romantic precursors as much by its historicist bias as by specifically differing judgements. Whereas Wordsworth, Coleridge or Shelley are content to ground their criticism in general principles that might equally well have pleased Johnson, De Quincey or Dallas are eager to show off – even at the expense of lengthy digressions – their grasp of the history of critical thought, and to show how modern criticism differs from its classical, Elizabethan or Enlightenment forebears. Almost all this next generation of critics seem to be engaged in an ideological battle with their Romantic progenitors – Wordsworth, Shelley and, above all, Coleridge.

Sometimes this is merely a matter of a rhetorical put-down, as when De Quincey adopts the plain-man approach:

Coleridge, as we have often heard, is in the habit of drawing the line with much philosophical beauty between Rhetoric and Eloquence. On this topic we were never so fortunate as to hear him: but, if we are here called upon for a distinction, we shall satisfy our immediate purpose by a very plain and brief one.[6]

Similarly Dallas is not above a quick sneer – as when he dismisses the idea of art as imitation: 'Notwithstanding Richter's, notwithstanding Coleridge's adhesion to it, the theory of imitation is now utterly exploded.'[7] More disturbingly, perhaps, Dallas is also prepared to steal ideas from Coleridge and pass them off as his own even while he is abusing him:

---

6  Thomas De Quincey, 'Rhetoric', Review of Whately's *Elements of Rhetoric* (December 1828) in *Collected Writings of Thomas De Quincey*, ed. David Masson, 14 vols. (London and Edinburgh: A. & C. Black, 1896), vol. X, p. 92.
7  E. S. Dallas, *The Gay Science*, 2 vols. (1866; rpt New York: Garland, 1986), vol. I, p. 84.

The most royal prerogative of imagination is its entireness, its love of wholes, its wonderful power of seeing the whole, of claiming the whole, of making whole, and – shall I add ? – swallowing whole.[8]

But more often there is a dispute of real substance. Attempting to define 'literature', De Quincey is almost immediately compelled to take issue with Wordsworth's Preface to the *Lyrical Ballads*. 'The vulgar antithesis to *knowledge* is *pleasure*', he writes, but

> this wretched antithesis will be of no use to us... The true antithesis to knowledge, in this case, is not *pleasure*, but *power*. All that is literature seeks to communicate power; all that is not literature, to communicate knowledge.[9]

Much of this can be explained by Bloom's theory of the anxiety of influence.[10] Critics, like poets, can feel dominated and even hamstrung ('castrated' would be the more Freudian term) by the perceived hegemony of the outstanding figures of the previous generation, and, like sons with dominant fathers, must engage in a struggle with them before they can establish their own individuality and freedom.

But there is, of course, a more serious side to this challenge to the criticism of the Romantics. These poets (whether we call them the 'Lake Poets' [Wordsworth, Coleridge and Southey], the 'Cockney School' [Keats and Hunt] or simply aristocratic scandal-raisers and satirists [Shelley and Byron]) saw themselves as doing many things: breaking with the artificiality of neo-classical poetic diction (Wordsworth); rescuing and reviving the reputations of older writers too often dismissed as crude and barbaric (Coleridge); reviving older poetic forms, such as folk ballads (Wordsworth and Coleridge); breaking down rigid generic barriers between prose and verse (Shelley); satirizing the follies, corruptions and hypocrisy of the times (Shelley and Byron); not to mention a spirited defence of the status of literature (and poetry in particular) in the face of a growing scientific philistinism and 'plebification of knowledge' (Wordsworth, Coleridge, Shelley and Peacock). All of these concerns are to be found in their Victorian successors, sometimes argued with even greater vehemence and passion. Where they differed from the earlier generation was that the Victorians *historicized* them.

Rather than representing a breakaway return to freedom and nature (perhaps an aesthetic singularity, like the French Revolution), the reaction of these poets and critics was itself increasingly seen as part of a historical process – and even as one of a series of such historical moments. This

---

[8] *Ibid.*, p. 268.

[9] Thomas De Quincey, 'Letters to a Young Man Whose Education Has Been Neglected', Letter III (1823), in *Collected Writings*, vol. X, pp. 47–8.

[10] Harold Bloom, *The Anxiety of Influence: A Theory of Poetry* (Oxford University Press, 1975).

is a point very important for Dallas. 'In so far as a science of human
nature is possible, it lies not in the actions of the individual, but in those
of the race; not in the developments of a lifetime, but in those of ages and
cycles.'[11] The stream of literary history, he argues, though continuous,
has never yet been properly followed with anything like precision and
comprehensiveness:

> It is needless to dwell on the fact that the history of a nation's poetry has seldom
> been written with much reference to the national life from which it springs. It is
> the study of botany apart from geography. What is more remarkable than this,
> however, is that poetry has been studied and its history written in utter
> forgetfulness of the kindred arts – music, architecture, painting, sculpture... the
> intellectual flora of a country must be studied as a whole.[12]

The strategy behind the exposition of his new theory of criticism, which
rests on the power of the unconscious imagination, is twofold: first, to
place criticism within a historical framework, relating it to the philosophy
and theology of its particular age, so that the Romantics can be seen in
perspective; and, following from this, to wrest possession of exclusive
rights to the word 'imagination' away from Coleridge, so that he can use
it in his own peculiar sense as an attribute of the unconscious creative
mind.

In his 1811–12 *Lectures on Shakespeare*, Coleridge had reapplied his
concept of method, elaborated in his earlier and somewhat intermittent
periodical the *Friend*, to Shakespeare, not so much as an individual writer
on his own, but as an example of the flowering of literary tradition.[13]
Here he is, for instance, on Shakespeare:

> few there have been among critics, who have followed with the eye of the
> imagination the imperishable, yet ever-wandering, spirit of poetry through its
> various metempsychoses, and correspondent metamorphoses; – or who have
> rejoiced in the light of clear perception at beholding with each new birth, with
> each rare avatar, the human race frame to itself a new body, by assimilating
> materials of nourishment out of its new circumstances, and work for itself new
> organs of power appropriate to the new sphere of its motion and activity.[14]

This close cross-reference between the inner development of the poet
and the outer framework of the tradition within which he worked is of
tremendous significance – not merely in the development of Coleridge's
own critical theory, but also in the way it shaped the thinking of later
critics. Creativity is the mark not just of the great writer, but of the

[11] Dallas, *Gay Science*, vol. I, p. 19.    [12] *Ibid.*, pp. 22–3.
[13] See Stephen Prickett, *Coleridge and Wordsworth: The Poetry of Growth* (Cambridge
University Press, 1970), pp. 115–17.
[14] Samuel Taylor Coleridge, *Shakespeare Criticism*, ed. T. M. Raysor, 2 vols. (London:
Everyman 1960), vol. I, pp. 174–5.

sustaining literary tradition – here Coleridge resorts to a Goethe-like image of organic and vegetable growth. Moreover, this is not, we notice, here a pluralistic or fragmented line, but the main stream of developing human consciousness: 'the spirit of poetry'. The true critic sees 'with the eye of the imagination' a continuing process of organic growth, in which each new 'avatar' involves a re-creation of all that has gone before in a form appropriate its time and purpose. The word 'avatar' comes from India – describing the descent of a Hindu deity to the earth in a particular incarnation. Though this constant aesthetic re-creation can be interpreted in an idealist, almost Platonic way (and there are times in the *Friend* when Coleridge seems to be implying this), the general trend of this argument is increasingly concrete and historical.

This is even more marked in the criticism of Coleridge's most immediate disciple, Julius Hare. Hare's aphoristic criticism reveals a sense not merely of the enormous range and diversity of his own literary heritage, but also of how far it had developed and changed over the years. This shift in perspective is very clear in a lengthy piece devoted to a comparison between ancient and modern poetry:

Goethe in 1800 does not write just as Shakespeare wrote in 1600: but neither would Shakespeare in 1800 have written just as he wrote in 1600. For the frame and aspect of society are different; the world which would act on him, and on which he would have to act, is another world. True poetical genius lives in communion with the world, in a perpetual reciprocation of influences, imbibing feeling and knowledge, and pouring out what it has imbibed in words of power and gladness and wisdom. It is not, at least when highest it is not, as Wordsworth describes Milton to have been, 'like a star dwelling apart'. Solitude may comfort weakness, it will not be the home of strength... In short, Genius is not an independent and insulated, but a social and continental, or at all events a peninsular power... Now without entering into a comparison of Shakespeare's age with our own, one thing at least is evident, that, considered generally and as a nation, we are more bookish than our ancestors... While the conflict and tug of passions supplied in Shakespeare's days the chief materials for poetry, in our days it is rather the conflict of principles... This appears not only from the works of Goethe and others of his countrymen, but from the course taken by our own greatest poets, by Wordsworth, Coleridge, and Landor. They have been rebuked indeed for not writing otherwise: but they have done rightly; for they have obeyed the impulse of their nature, and the voice of their age has been heard speaking through their lips.[15]

If there was any doubt about Coleridge's, there is no doubt at all about Hare's commitment to a progressive and historical rather than an idealist aesthetic. This strong historical sense is impelled by a thoroughly

---

[15] Augustus Hare and Julius Hare, *Guesses at Truth, by Two Brothers*, 2 vols. (London: Macmillan, 1827), vol. II, pp. 136–40.

English pragmatism. The development of human sensibility is indeed closely enmeshed with the particular conditions of time and place, rather than with any abstract Hegelian outworking of the spirit of the age. Wordsworth, Coleridge and Landor are not just products of the prevailing *Geist*, but of specific and concrete historical and cultural conditions – and none the less great for that. This is not merely a retrospective explanation of why Goethe in 1800 should differ from Shakespeare in 1600; it lays down the principle of why Goethe *had* to differ. The same work written two hundred years later would be, of necessity, a different work simply because of its context – or, in T. S. Eliot's words 'it would not be new, and would therefore not be a work of art'.[16]

Two other characteristics, both immensely important, were to result from this growing critical-historical awareness. The first, which is clearly evident in the passage of Hare just quoted, is a sense of English literature as something inseparable from the wider European scene. The second was the idea that it was possible to construct a specifically literary history. The two ideas are closely interconnected.

Thus the comparison between Shakespeare and Goethe is more than a comparison between two specific periods. For Hare, not merely do Shakespeare and Goethe represent the greatest of their respective ages, but the comparison also reminds us that no country (not even England) is a cultural island in itself. Though Coleridge's *Shakespeare Lectures* are rightly seen as a milestone in the British appreciation of Shakespeare, the fact is, of course, that they follow A. W. Schlegel's in Germany in both time and substance. But just as Schlegel in Germany has learned to appreciate Shakespeare's genius – and, incidentally, taught the British to do so – so Britain must learn to respond to the genius of Goethe. With Carlyle's great translation of *Wilhelm Meister* in 1824, Goethe was to become as much a part of English literature as Shakespeare had in German literature with Schlegel's translations.[17] 'True genius lives in communion with the world' – or, as T. S. Eliot was to say a hundred years later, in relation to that reformulated collective cultural entity, 'the mind of Europe'.[18]

But whereas Coleridge's borrowings from German philosophy and criticism were not something he wished to advertise (giving rise on occasions to charges of plagiarism), Hare, a generation later, when constructing *Guesses at Truth* in 1827 with his brothers, Augustus, Francis and Marcus, has no problems in acknowledging his debts to the fragmentary style

---

16   T. S. Eliot, 'Tradition and the Individual Talent' in *Selected Essays* (London: Faber & Faber, 1951), p. 15.

17   See Rosemary Ashton, *The German Idea: Four English Writers and the Reception of German Thought 1800–1860* (London: Libris, 1994), pp. 76–91.

18   See Eliot, 'Tradition and the Individual Talent', pp. 14–15.

of the Jena Romantics' journal the *Athenaeum* – not to mention that to the epigrammatic terseness of Pascal's *Pensées* or La Bruyère's *Caractères*. But what is an obvious fact for Hare or for Carlyle in the 1820s has become for Arnold, forty years later, itself a critical principle. For him, the literature of the English-speaking peoples, however rich and varied, cannot be understood merely within its own historical terms. It must always be understood in relation to both its classical antecedents and its European context, past and present. It had always been one of Arnold's lifelong ambitions to make insular British readers aware of the great continental writers – in his *Essays in Criticism* discussions of Marcus Aurelius and the English Romantics rub shoulders with those on Amiel, Maurice and Eugénie de Guérin, Heine, Joubert, Spinoza and Tolstoy. No islands – especially the British Isles – are islands unto themselves.

Similarly, no account of the Romantic critical legacy in Britain is complete without some account of continental influences. Though *Le Génie du Christianisme* (1802) by François-René de Chateaubriand (1768–1848) was initially written for a French Catholic audience, it was largely written during his exile in England, and much of its argument, concerning the transformation and internalization of the classical literary tradition under the influence of Christian thought and practice, was derived from his English experience and reading, and was equally applicable to a Protestant context. As we shall see, this was one of the earliest statements of an argument that, in various forms, would recur in English criticism throughout the century. De Quincey, for instance, uses it extensively in his 1823 *Letters to a Young Man*. An English translation of Chateaubriand, with the rather anodyne title of *The Beauties of Christianity*, appeared in 1813 and a fuller, more scholarly translation was made in America in 1856.[19]

Other French exiles were to play an even bigger part in the development of critical thought. *On Germany* by Mme de Staël (1776–1817) was first published in 1810 in both French and English in England, where she had fled from Napoleon.[20] Her projection of the Jena group's self-description of 'Romantic' as a Europe-wide idea whose time had come was more a publicity coup than a critical insight, but it was to have far-reaching repercussions.[21] It was not, however, Germaine de Staël, but another French critic, Hippolyte Taine (1828–93), who, as late as 1863, first used

[19] François–René de Chateaubriand, *The Beauties of Christianity*, trans. Frederic Shoberl, 3 vols. (London: Colburn, 1813); *The Genius of Christianity*, trans. Charles White (Baltimore, MD: J. Murphy, 1856).

[20] Germaine de Staël, *On Germany* in *An Extraordinary Woman: Selected Writings of Germaine de Stael*, trans. and intro. Vivian Folkenflik (New York: Columbia University Press, 1987).

[21] See John Claiborne Isbell, *The Birth of European Romanticism: Truth and Propaganda in Staël's 'De l'Allemagne' 1810–1813* (Cambridge University Press, 1994), p. 4.

the term the 'Romantic School' (by analogy from the French) for the English poets in his *History of English Literature*.[22] It is worth noting that none of those English poets and critics we now describe under that name would have recognized themselves as 'Romantics' – nor would the title of this chapter have been intelligible either to them, or to those critics here described.

Germany was to play an even greater part in the development of nineteenth-century English criticism – but therein lay a paradox. Everything German was immensely fashionable in the early nineteenth century in Britain. The British royal family maintained strong links with its Hanoverian roots. Britain and Prussia had enjoyed not merely close military but ever closer cultural ties since their victory at Waterloo in 1815, and this love of things German was given a royal seal by Queen Victoria's marriage to her beloved Prince Albert of Saxe-Coburg-Gotha in 1840. German bands played in the streets, and trendy families gathered at Christmas around the Christmas tree – newly imported by Prince Albert. Nevertheless much of the popular picture of Germany was based on sheer ignorance. Though things had improved slightly since 1821, when Edward Bouverie Pusey, the future Regius Professor of Divinity at Oxford, on setting out to learn about new developments in German theology, had discovered that only two people in the entire university knew any German at all, German was still not taught in British schools or universities.[23] The revolutionary philosophy of Kant and Hegel, like the no less iconoclastic theology of Strauss and Feuerbach, remained largely untranslated until mid-century, and much of the writings of the German Romantics, including Novalis, the Schlegels and Schleiermacher, remained so until the twentieth century.[24] Those who could read them in the original, like Carlyle, Coleridge, De Quincey, Lewes, MacDonald or George Eliot, and had attempted to create a wider awareness of German culture through translation and articles, appealed only to a narrow section of the reading public.[25] For most people, Germany was not so much the land of advanced thought or literary criticism as one of dark forests, romantic castles and musical boxes.

As we have seen, De Quincey makes extensive reference to German literature – not all of it complimentary. We have also mentioned Lewes's

---

[22]  Not translated into English until the 1880s, the term only took root in England at the end of the century. See David Perkins, *Is Literary History Possible?* (Baltimore, MD: Johns Hopkins University Press, 1992), p. 98.

[23]  The University of Glasgow, for instance, only introduced its first post in German (a lectureship) under pressure from a Royal Commission in the 1850s.

[24]  See Perkins, *Is Literary History Possible?*; also Andrew Bowie, *Aethetics and Subjectivity* (Manchester University Press, 1990), and Andrew Bowie, *From Romanticism to Critical Theory* (London: Routledge, 1997).

[25]  See Ashton, *German Idea*.

biography and Carlyle's translations of Goethe – which were also to form
the bases of a number of critical essays on German literature. Carlyle had
not merely personally corresponded with Goethe, but also knew the published work of Novalis – the pen-name of Friedrich von Hardenberg
(1772–1801), whose works, carefully edited after his death by August
Schlegel and Ludwig Tieck, were to produce an idealized literary construction somewhat remote from their original.[26] Hare, as we have seen,
was fully cognisant of Coleridge's continental mentors – including Kant,
Fichte, Schelling and the Schlegels. He also knew personally and corresponded with Schleiermacher and Tieck and read Jean Paul (Richter), as
well as having read Novalis. George MacDonald was equally widely read
in the German Romantic poets and critics, and makes extensive reference
to them in both his fiction and literary essays.[27]

Perhaps the most unlikely German Romantic influence on critical
thought in the English-speaking world, however, was that of Johann Gottfried Herder (1744–1803). Given the relatively tiny number of British
who knew German at the end of the eighteenth and the beginning of
the nineteenth centuries, Herder's influence was surprisingly pervasive.
Coleridge (of course!) was reading the *Ideen*[28] as early as 1799, and the
collected *Marginalia* reveals an extensive knowledge of Herder by the
early 1830s.[29] Something of Herder's general reputation in the 1820s is
revealed by De Quincey, who compares Herder and Coleridge in an essay
of 1823 with the implication that his readers are likely to know both
at least by reputation.[30] De Quincey's own knowledge of the German
scene is not above question: in an effort to impress readers he throws out
names of many deeply obscure German 'authorities', and at one point he
seems to confuse Friedrich Schlegel with his brother, August.[31] Nevertheless, his reference to Herder, like his references to the Schlegel brothers,
implies some expectation that his readers would be reasonably familiar
at least with Herder's name. Carlyle was reading Herder in the early
1820s at the same time as he was at work on his translation of *Wilhelm
Meister*.[32] Felicia Hemans (1793–1835), one of the most popular poets of

[26]  See William Arctander O'Brien, *Novalis: Signs of Revolution* (Durham, NC: Duke
      University Press, 1995).
[27]  See, for instance, the chapter headings to *Phantastes* (1858) and essays in *A Dish of
      Orts* (London: S. L. Marston, 1882); published in the USA as *The Imagination and
      Other Essays* (Boston: Lothrop, 1883).
[28]  30 September 1799 in *Letters of Samuel Taylor Coleridge*, ed. E. R. Griggs, 4 vols.
      (Oxford: Clarendon Press, 1956), vol. I, p. 535.
[29]  *The Collected Works of Samuel Taylor Coleridge: Marginalia*, ed. George Whalley, 5
      vols. (London and Princeton: Routledge/Princeton University Press, 1984), vol. II, pp.
      1048–88.
[30]  De Quincey, 'Letters to a Young Man', p. 12.      [31]  *Ibid.*, p. 41.
[32]  See Hill Shine, 'Carlyle's Early Writings and Herder's *Ideen*: The Concept of History'
      in *Booker Memorial Studies*, ed. Hill Shine (Chapel Hill: University of North Carolina

the day, was also reading Herder in German at much the same time.[33] For
those outside the relatively elite circle of those who could read German, a
whole chapter of Mme de Staël's best-seller, *On Germany*, was devoted
to a eulogistic introduction to Herder and his ideas. Meanwhile a steady
stream of English translations of Herder's work (some of dubious quality)
had been appearing from 1790 onwards, so that by the early 1830s there
were perhaps a dozen or so available – some complete, some consisting
of selections or extracts, sometimes with obscure titles.[34]

The first full English translation of Herder's most influential work in
England, *The Spirit of Hebrew Poetry*, was not published until 1833, fifty
years after it had appeared in Germany. The translator was James Marsh
(1794–1842), a New England Congregationalist minister, who had been
first Professor of Philosophy and then President of the University of Vermont (1826–33). An Emersonian Transcendentalist, Marsh was a key
figure in the introduction of Coleridge's philosophy to American readers,
producing editions of *Aids to Reflection*, *The Friend* and *The Statesman's
Manual*.[35] Though careful to distance himself from Herder's assumptions
that the Old Testament was symbolic rather than historical, Marsh makes
an effective bridge between Herder and Lowth,[36] bringing the aesthetic
criticism of the Hebrew psalms into the mainstream of English poetic
criticism at the very time when the evangelical revival, which reached its
peak in fervour if not in absolute numbers around the 1850s, meant a
resurgence of interest in the Bible after the all-time low in church attendance and religious practice at the beginning of the century. Because for
many twentieth-century social commentators and historians 'Victorianism' has come to include assumptions of widespread religiosity, it is easy
to forget how unlikely such a revival would have seemed (and did seem)
to many contemporaries in the first half of the century.[37] The cumulative effect of such figures as Coleridge and Hare, and the translations of

Press, 1950), pp. 3–33; and René Wellek, 'Carlyle and the Philosophy of History' in
*Confrontations: Studies in the Intellectual Relations between Germany, England, and
the United States during the Nineteenth Century* (Princeton University Press, 1965),
p. 89.

33 Felicia Hemans, *The Forest Sanctuary and Other Poems* (London: John Murray, 1825),
p. 106.
34 Bayard Quincy Morgan, *A Critical Bibliography of German Literature in Translation
1481–1927* (New York: Scarecrow Press, 1965).
35 See Anthony J. Harding, 'James Marsh as Editor of Coleridge' in *Reading Coleridge:
Approaches and Applications*, ed. Walter B. Crawford (Ithaca, NY: Cornell University
Press, 1979).
36 Robert Lowth, *Lectures on the Sacred Poetry of the Hebrews*, trans. G. Gregory (London: Thomas Tegg, 1839). See also Stephen Prickett, *Words and the Word: Language,
Poetics and Biblical Interpretation* (Cambridge University Press, 1986), pp. 105–14.
37 See Robert Currie, Alan Gilbert and Lee Horsley, *Churches and Churchgoers: Patterns
of Church Growth in the British Isles since 1700* (Oxford: Clarendon Press, 1977).

Herder, prepared the way for the religious debates over 'faith and doubt'
that were to occupy so much critical and novelistic energy, as well as for
Arnold's critico-theological writings: *St Paul and Protestantism* (1870),
*Literature and Dogma* (1873) and *God and the Bible* (1875).

The most original, if not the most popular, piece of religio-poetic theory
of the first half of the century, however, came from the best-selling poet
of the century, John Keble. *The Christian Year*, published in 1827, was
to sell an average of 10,000 copies a year for the next fifty years – a figure
only distantly challenged by Tennyson's *In Memoriam*, and far greater
than anything ever achieved by Wordsworth. Keble was rooted firmly in
the classics and the symbolic theory of the Middle Ages, and owed little
or nothing to contemporary European ideas. Keble, like Robert Lowth
before him and Matthew Arnold after him, was Professor of Poetry at
Oxford. His *Lectures on Poetry*, given between 1832 and 1841, were
published as they had been delivered, in Latin, in 1844 – and were not
translated into English until 1912. In many ways *De Poeticae Vi Medi-
cae* represents the culmination of the English Romantic poetic tradition.
Dedicated to Wordsworth, the lectures take up the Wordsworthian idea
of poetry as the spontaneous overflow of powerful feelings. But whereas,
for Wordsworth, the image behind that phrase seems to be spring, or
natural fountain, for Keble, writing at the height of the railway boom,
the metaphor appears to suggest something more like the safety valve
of a steam boiler. To J. T. Coleridge (nephew of the poet, and later to
be Keble's biographer) in 1832, Keble writes: 'My notion is to consider
poetry as a vent for overcharged feelings, or a full imagination, and so
account for the various classes into which poets naturally fall, by reference to the various objects which are apt to fill and overpower the mind,
so as to require a sort of relief.'[38]

Poetry, for Keble, was the product of tension or repression, issuing in
disguised or ironic utterance. Someone who, under emotional stress, can
find easy expression for their feelings is, by definition, no poet.[39] As early
as 1828 he argued in a review of Lockhart's *Life of Scott* that 'Poetry is
the indirect expression in words, most appropriately in metrical words, of
some overpowering emotion, or ruling taste, or feeling, the direct indulgence whereof is somehow repressed.'[40] Repression or reserve – tension
between what is felt and what finally finds expression – is at the creative
heart of 'the poetic' – a quality, incidentally, not peculiar to poetry. All

---

[38]  J. T. Coleridge, *Memoir of the Rev. John Keble* (Oxford and London: James Parker,
       1869), p. 199.
[39]  John Keble, *Keble's Lectures on Poetry*, trans. E. K. Francis, 2 vols. (Oxford University
       Press, 1912), vol. I, p. 36.
[40]  John Keble, Review of *Life of Scott* (1838) in *Occasional Papers and Reviews* (Oxford
       University Press, 1877), p. 6.

art forms, including not merely literature but music, sculpture, painting and even architecture, had, according to Keble, a 'poetical' (and therefore ironic) element in them. 'What is called the poetry of painting', he says, 'simply consists in the apt expression of the artist's own feeling' – feeling, of course, expressed under tension.[41] Such a radical reshaping of genres would make meaningless the traditional categories that had dominated criticism ever since Aristotle. In this new 'expressionistic' framework 'there will be as many kinds of poems as there are emotions of the human mind'.[42]

For Keble there were two main classes of poets: Primary and Secondary. The Primary are 'those who, spontaneously moved by impulse, resort to composition for relief and solace of a burdened or over-wrought mind'; the Secondary, 'those who, for one reason or another, imitate the ideas, the expression, and the measures of the former'.[43] His list of Primary poets was strictly classical, ending properly with Virgil – though Dante seems to have been added as an afterthought.[44] Keble seems to have had problems with his favourite moderns. Wordsworth, despite having had the published lectures specifically dedicated to him, remains tactfully unlisted by category. As a poet, he obviously belonged to the Primary, but, as a man, he suffered from the grave disadvantage of being neither an ancient Greek nor a Roman. Though Keble toyed with the idea of sub-stituting 'modern examples for the Greek and Latin', mentioning Byron and Shelley as those 'mentally affected' by the intolerable tensions of their art, he never included them in the text of the Lectures.[45]

Keble's theory takes to its logical conclusion Wordsworth's sleight of hand in the Preface to the Lyrical Ballads, whereby the definition of a poem is framed in terms of its author's characteristics ('what is a poem? . . . a poet is . . . '). Keble now classified poetry by the emotions of the writer, who sought his own relief and health by disguised utterance. In other words, irony, the language of disguise, is also necessarily the key to mental health and stability. Poetry is, par excellence, the healing art. For M. H. Abrams, writing on Keble in the mid-years of the twentieth century, this constituted nothing less than a 'radical, proto-Freudian theory, which conceives literature as disguised wish-fulfilment, serving the artist as a way back from incipient neurosis'.[46] How radical we can see from Keble's definition of poetry itself. 'Each several one of the so-called liberal arts', he declares, 'contains a certain poetic quality of its own, and . . . this lies in its power to heal and relieve the human mind when agitated by care,

---

[41]  Keble, Lectures, vol. I, p. 38.    [42]  Ibid., p. 88.
[43]  Ibid., pp. 53–4.    [44]  Ibid., vol. II, p. 471.
[45]  Letter to J. T. Coleridge, 5 July 1844 in Coleridge, Memoir, p. 205.
[46]  M. H. Abrams, The Mirror and the Lamp (1953; rpt New York: Norton, 1958), p. 145.

passion, or ambition.'[47] This is such a bold and unexpected inversion of standard Romantic aesthetics that it is easy to miss what Keble is actually saying here. He does *not* believe that one of the powers of 'the poetic' is that it can heal or give relief to the person under strain; he believes that we must *define* 'the poetic' by this healing power. *Ibi ars medica, ubi poesis.* Where there is healing, there is the poetic.

The mere fact that Keble has problems with what an earlier generation would have called the relation of 'the Ancients and the Moderns' points to the fact that behind this apparently psychological theory of poetry lies a nascent literary history. Such histories become increasingly explicit as the century progresses, and can be seen very clearly in the development of anthologies. Anthologies – named from the Greek word for posies or garlands of flowers – had been around since classical times, often as personal and handwritten collections, but at the end of the eighteenth century they had received a powerful boost not merely from rapidly increasing literacy but also from the Romantic penchant for fragments.[48] At the same time, developmental histories of human society, such as Gotthold Ephraim Lessing's *Education of the Human Race* (1774), Friedrich Schiller's *Aesthetic Education of Man* (1794), Chateaubriand's *Genius of Christianity* or Schlegel's *Lectures on Dramatic Art*, stressed the idea that art and literature could only be properly understood in historical terms. In keeping with this trend, nineteenth-century anthologies tend increasingly to have a historical base.

Thus Dr (John) Aikin's *British Poets* (1820), though it has no accompanying commentary or explanation, advertises itself as offering 'a *chronological* series of the best and purest works of our most eminent poets' (my italics). Going one further, *England's Antiphon* (1868), by George MacDonald (1824–1905), is what one might call a critically annotated anthology: perhaps half text, half exposition and commentary. Devoted to the history of devotional and religious verse in English, it begins with early medieval poetry and concludes with Tennyson's *In Memoriam*. Not by any means the first such critical anthology of devotional verse, it is nevertheless remarkable in its commentary and the space devoted to the metaphysical poets, Donne, Herbert, Marvell, Crashaw and Vaughan, none of whom was well known at the time. Perhaps even more surprising is the inclusion of Charles Wesley, William Blake and, possibly the most surprising of all, the contemporary Elizabeth Barrett Browning. The purpose of this collection, as MacDonald tells us, is not merely to acquaint the reader with works with which they might otherwise be unfamiliar

---

[47] Keble, *Lectures*, vol. I, p. 53.
[48] See foreword by Rodolphe Gasché to Friedrich Schlegel, *Philosophical Fragments*, trans. Peter Firchow (Minneapolis: University of Minnesota Press, 1991).

(this is probably the first critical discussion of *The Pearl*, from the Cotton Nero MS – which, like many medieval texts, had only just been published by the Early English Text Society and would have been very difficult for the ordinary reader to obtain) but also to 'commend [these works] to [the reader's] imagination and judgement'.

In this stress on the historical development of the imagination, we see how MacDonald belongs to the same post-Romantic generation as Dallas, in seeking to explore and understand the imagination as a psychological and cultural force across time. As David Perkins shows in his polemically entitled book *Is Literary History Possible?*, narrative literary histories are very much a product of this period:

[The] fundamental premises of literary history as a discipline come to us from the romantic movement.[49] Among these are the importance attached to the beginnings or origins, the assumption that a development is the subject of literary history, the understanding of development as continual rather than disjunctive, and the creation of suprapersonal entities as the subjects of this development.[50]

Such figures, ranging from Chateaubriand's 'genius' (echoing and parodying the mysterious 'genius' of Volney's *Ruins of Empires*) to MacDonald's 'England', are among many examples of such 'suprapersonal' developmental entities we have seen in the course of this discussion. Perhaps more dubious is Perkins's assumption that behind such developmental narratives is a belief in the possibility of objectivity, and that this in the end invalidates all such attempts at classification.

For approximately the first seventy-five years of the nineteenth century, literary history enjoyed popularity and unquestioned prestige. It was characterized, at this time, by three fundamental assumptions: that literary works are formed by their historical context; that change in literature takes place developmentally; and that this change is the unfolding of an idea, principle, or suprapersonal entity. Viewing literary works in relation to their historical context, we can, it was argued, achieve a juster interpretation and a more complete appreciation than is otherwise possible. We can explain features of texts as products and expressions of the social structures, ways of life, beliefs, literary institutions, and so on, of the communities in which they were created. As a synthesis of history and criticism, literary history seemed more powerful, for some purposes, than either discipline separately.[51]

Though this may be superficially persuasive it fails to describe what we have been looking at. Of the various narratives discussed here, including

---

49  See Clifford Siskin, *The Historicity of Romantic Discourse* (Oxford University Press, 1988).
50  Perkins, *Is Literary History Possible?*, p. 86.      51  *Ibid.*, pp. 1–2.

those of Carlyle, Hare, De Quincey or MacDonald, none stress notions of objectivity, and though it might be possible to interpret Arnold or Dallas in such a manner, most readers would, I suspect, think it against the grain. On the whole, post-Romantic historicism is too alive to subtleties of context for its practitioners to believe over much in critical objectivity. There is no evidence to suggest that those, like De Quincey or MacDonald, who classified or created historical narratives necessarily believed that their particular classification, created for a particular purpose at a particular time (in other words, also coming from a specific historical context), represented absolute 'truth'. Classification normally tells us about context and perspective, not about essence. Nor, on the other hand, is this an argument for total Romantic subjectivity. As E. H. Carr once commented about the study of history, 'the fact that a mountain looks different when seen from different angles does not mean either that it has no shape or an infinity of shapes'.[52] As that suggests, many of the same arguments have been advanced in the older debate among historians about the possibility of 'intellectual history'. In this context, John Burrow, the historian, has drawn an analogy between entering the hermeneutical circle of the past and the process of learning another language:

although we can characterize the method in very general and perhaps unnecessarily pretentious terms as hermeneutic, there are no recipes. We may get guidance, tuition, and above all, example, from those who know the language, and we may learn by rote some of the rules of grammar, but ultimately, to come to inhabit a language, we must learn as we say, to play it by ear.[53]

Just as the Romantics were prone to deny the possibility of translation, before embarking on more translation than ever before, so a claim to understand literary history is not necessarily incompatible with a recognition that there might be many such 'histories'. Romantic historicization was never an absolute process, nor (despite Hegel and Marx) was it commonly a path to single grand-narrative interpretations. It might have delighted at least those Romantics addicted to the Middle Ages to think that it was more like a return to the polysemous narratives of that period. Thus any danger that historicization could be seen as providing some kind of 'explanation' for the past – that Coleridge's criticism, for instance, could simply be placed as 'Romantic', or that Keble's theories of irony merely reflected the religious sensibility of the 1840s – was most evidently avoided by a growing awareness of pluralism throughout the century. If there was self-evidently no single 'Romantic' sensibility in the

[52] E. H. Carr, *What Is History?* (London: Macmillan, 1961), p. 1–2.
[53] John Burrow, 'The Uses of Philology in Victorian England' in *Ideas and Institutions in Victorian Britain*, ed. Robert Robson (London: Bell, 1967), pp. 19–20.

early years of the century, it was even more evident that there were many more and conflicting religious sensibilities in the 1840s. Even among the Tractarians there was no common critical voice. Taine's late-developed idea of English 'Romanticism', if it is a valid label at all, describes not so much a movement as what Wittgenstein was to call a 'family resemblance' – a matter of a common climate of feeling rather than theory. For the Romantics' successors that climate had become increasingly fractured and turbulent.

# 8

# England: literature and culture

## JAMES NAJARIAN

The authors discussed in this chapter were all literary critics only to a limited extent: for all but Walter Pater, literary criticism was a phase or outlier in their careers. Carlyle started as a literary critic and translator, but became a social critic and historian. John Ruskin was an art and aesthetic theorist who examined almost every subject including literature, Bernard Shaw at first a music critic and novelist who became a successful playwright and social commentator. Arnold, who has his own chapter in this volume, moved from poetry to literary to social to, finally, religious criticism. Likewise, the work of George Eliot, who started her career as a critic and editor, developed into a novelist who also wrote criticism and poetry, is analysed elsewhere in this volume. It is a commonplace that these critics, whatever their purview, used their criticism to create or enforce ethical and social norms and attitudes in the context of the fading power of Protestantism. None of them could be called a conventional Christian, though Ruskin and Pater did late in their lives return to private, revised Christianities. In the late nineteenth and early twentieth centuries, these authors were characterized as Victorian sages and their works gathered in anthologies, suggesting that the age needed and had found a source of wisdom to replace the scriptures.

William McKelvy has recently complicated the tidy narrative of the decline of religion and its seemingly inevitable replacement by literature, one that Matthew Arnold and Thomas Carlyle announced in different ways. McKelvy dates the replacement to between 1770 and 1880. He posits two related orthodox accounts: one, the declinist, sponsored by nineteenth-century critics such as Thomas Carlyle and contemporary ones such as David Riede, sees the authority of literature as a substitute for a declining religion; the other sees an aesthetic revival coming out of the crisis of faith.[1] Walter Pater might represent this second tendency.

Yet however one sees the move, as substitution or opportunity, it generated its own ambivalence. Writers were anxious about what the newly

---

[1] William R. McKelvy, *The English Cult of Literature* (Charlottesville: University of Virginia Press, 2006) pp. 9–10. See also David G. Riede, *Oracles and Hierophants: Constructions of Romantic Authority* (Ithaca, NY, and London: Cornell University Press, 1991).

important literature and its criticism might mean in a society where literature, like everything else, had become a mechanized commodity. When
Carlyle, Arnold and Ruskin take on the 'machinery' of nineteenth-century
culture, they themselves are implicated in that machinery. 'Literature,
the printed communication of thought, has its Paternoster-row mechanism... its huge, subterranean, puffing bellows... Books are not only
written, but printed and sold by machinery', Carlyle wrote in 1829.[2]
'Machinery' is both a persistent metaphor for what they see as the difficulties of industrial culture and an actual process; literature and publication
are industrialized, like any other nineteenth-century mode of production:
handmade paper and handmade books are replaced by much less durable
machine-made paper and machine-made books in the 1820s and 1830s.
The long poem, a staple of the 1810s, is replaced by the novel, both
standing alone and serialized in magazines.[3] Sir Walter Scott's journey
from poet to novelist renders in a single life the change in taste and
readership. The reading public grew larger, and unlike in the eighteenth
century, became a mass public, with mass tastes, what William St. Clair
calls a 'reading nation'.[4] To become a sage may be desirable; to become
the sage of a mechanical age perhaps less so. So while Arnold, Ruskin and
Eliot, for example, literally seek to educate the working class – Arnold
in his work as a school inspector and proponent of universal public education, Ruskin in the Working Men's Colleges and in texts meant to
instruct working-class readers, Eliot in 'Felix Holt's Address to Working Men' – they fear what a large reading public might read and prefer:
Arnold's 'populace', Ruskin's 'mob', Eliot's horde of lady novelists. The
task of the literary critic, the 'man of letters', in the nineteenth century
is partly disciplinary. Book reviewing, translating, recommending foreign
authors, commenting on the classics, writing introductions for selections
and anthologies – all this work attempts to sort through, classify, and
correct the taste and purchasing habits of an exploding and potentially
unruly readership.

## Thomas Carlyle (1795–1881)

Carlyle came from the margins of British society, from a poor family in
rural Scotland, his father a stonemason. Carlyle was raised in the small

2  Thomas Carlyle, 'Signs of the Times' in *Thomas Carlyle: Collected Works*, 30 vols.
   (London: Chapman & Hall, 1869), vol. II, pp. 319–20.
3  See Lee Erikson, *The Economy of Literary Form: English Literature and the Industrialization of Publishing 1800–1850* (Baltimore, MD, and London: Johns Hopkins University
   Press, 1996), pp 3–18.
4  See William St. Clair, *The Reading Nation in the Romantic Period* (Cambridge University
   Press, 2004), esp. pp. 446–7.

village of Ecclefechan in Scotland and though he went to university in Edinburgh intending to become a minister, much of his learning was autodidactic. At Edinburgh in his late teens and twenties, he read deeply in geography, history and English literature. This reading determined him to write some great work of his own. Having lost his traditional faith through exposure to Gibbon, he formally gave up a ministerial career in 1817. A short stint as a tutor did not appeal, and the study of mineralogy turned out to be a chore. Most important for his literary and spiritual life, in early 1819 he began to study German. It was this learning of German, a language few English readers knew well, that enabled his initial entrance into publishing.

A life of Schiller and a translation of Goethe's *Wilhelm Meister* were his first significant works. German literature created what were to become Carlyle's ideals for literature: a literature strong in a secular spiritual ethic. Carlyle yearned to contribute to this literature (he tried his hand at and gave up the novel); the first outlets he found for publication were literary-critical. Art is meant, in Carlyle's terms, to reveal truth: 'We cannot but believe that there is an inward and essential Truth in Art; a Truth far deeper than the dictates of mere Mode, and which, could we pierce through these dictates, would be true for all nations and men. To arrive at this Truth, distant from every one at first, approachable by most, attainable by some small number, is the end and aim of all true poetry.'[5] Writers who for him revealed philosophy and morality in their work (Goethe, Schiller, Novalis) were far superior to those who did not (Keats, Scott, Voltaire); the former are secular seers, with vision that comes from a place beyond thought 'underneath the region of argument and conscious discourse...in its quiet mysterious depths'.[6] Carlyle was the age of the second-generation Romantics, not of the high Victorians; his creed is certainly Romantic, but derives from German Idealist sources rather than English ones. His version is somewhat historicized, as the great writers not only speak universal truths, but stand for a whole age: they become, for readers after them, heroes and prophets, fomenters of moral and spiritual reform that rises from within rather than without.

Carlyle's critical method is primarily biographical, historical and moral. He seeks to find the unity of a work with the intellectual and moral life of the author; writing is not a separate art or habit. For him, Goethe's character and writing are one and the same: 'his poetry is the voice of the whole harmonious manhood: nay, it is the very harmony of that rich manhood which forms his poetry'.[7] Carlyle's criticism tends if

[5] Carlyle, 'Goethe' in *Collected Works*, vol. I, p. 269.
[6] Carlyle, 'Characteristics' in *Collected Works*, vol. III, p. 333.
[7] Carlyle, 'Goethe', p. 244.

anything to concentrate on the life of the author, particularly in mythologized moral crises. Also of importance to him was the relationship of the author to his national tradition. Carlyle's sources for these ideas are the German Idealists and Romantics from Kant through Fichte, as well as the English Romantic critics including Coleridge, Wordsworth and Lamb. He opposed the literary tradition of judging by taste and diction, as exemplified by Francis Jeffrey. Because he formulated such a rigorously moral version of Romantic criticism, he became ambivalent about most of the English Romantic poets, especially Byron, whose energy he admired and whose poetry he deplored. He also disdained most Romantic novel production.

As Roe says, Carlyle was 'the first great interpreter of German thought to the English people'.[8] Carlyle famously ordered the reader to 'Close thy Byron: open thy Goethe.' German literature, despite the German roots of the royal family, was little read in England, with the one exception of Goethe's *Werther*. (Coleridge and De Quincey, both of whom were proficient in the German language, did little to introduce its literature to the public.) Primarily for Carlyle German Literature meant Goethe: in his first essay on the writer he praises and describes Goethe's universality and delineates his moral progress in the context of his period. But in Carlyle's second essay, written four years later in 1832, the social criticism is more pronounced. He praises Goethe along with Napoleon as heroes of their era; Carlyle's worship of power and fundamental political conservatism are apparent. His interest in German literature was limited to the interpretative side of German Romanticism, not the speculative. He dismissed German Romantic drama.

On the other hand, English Romanticism came in for severe criticism, chiefly in the personages of Byron and Scott – he found their work lacking in meaning: Byron unhealthily self-conscious and Scott ineffectually nostalgic. Even Scott's novels, which he did admire, were simply entertainments. Carlyle only wrote three essays on British writers – on Burns, Boswell and Johnson, and Scott, though Byron comes in for extensive treatment in *Sartor Resartus*. Carlyle clearly identifies with Burns, the Scottish peasant, and curiously absolves the poet from much responsibility for a failed personal life. Carlyle treats him with considerable national affection. Johnson is less of a problem for the Carlyle who wanted to find the heroic in literature. Carlyle and Johnson had personal similarities too – they both struggled for a place in literature, were 'haters of cant and sham', and were sceptical of schemes of reform and of loud backers of political or social equality. For Carlyle, Johnson is a hero of literature

---

[8]  Frederick William Roe, *Thomas Carlyle as a Critic of Literature* (New York: Columbia University Press, 1910), p. 90.

and of English life, a man who tells the truth, an ethical hero – but his writings are an afterthought. Carlyle praises Boswell, who was regarded by many nineteenth-century critics as a ninny, for his discipleship. Carlyle's view of Scott is and has been more controversial; though initially an enthusiastic reader of Scott's novels, with more exposure to German literature he found Scott lacking any spiritual or moral message, viewing him as merely 'the song-singer and pleasant tale-teller to Britain and to Europe'[9] and as a literary capitalist rather than a writer of note. Some personal animus may have motivated Carlyle's opinion, but it is entirely consistent with his critical development.

Carlyle's faith in literature was vigorous but short-lived. A. Abbot Ikeler has traced the decline of that faith and its eventual violent repudiation, culminating in the political polemics of Carlyle's late career.[10] Soon after his essay on Scott, Carlyle turned to social criticism – the literary notions that we see, for example, in *Sartor Resartus* and 'The Hero as Poet' are subsidiary to a larger cultural argument. He was not a fan of the Victorian novel or the great mass of Romantic and Victorian poetry. What he was looking for – philosophy and morality – he found more particularly in writing history and biography, as evident in the Johnson and Scott essays. But finally, literary criticism did not engage Carlyle in the way social criticism could because, outside of Goethe and Richter, he did not find the heroic, transcendental element in it. Even as Carlyle is writing about Goethe, he seems to be seeking something more from literature, something that led him to biography and history. In his series of lectures *Heroes and Hero Worship*, which deals extensively in two chapters with heroes of literature ('The Hero as Poet' and 'The Hero as Man of Letters'), the actual works of the writers in question come under little scrutiny. It is their lives which interest Carlyle – each of the men he chooses comes into prominence from straitened circumstances and creates a national ethical voice. Dante and Shakespeare are prophets in their own distinct way. Less conspicuous lights, treated in 'The Hero as Man of Letters', can also work in prophetic ways: 'the Man of Letters is sent hither specially that he may discern for himself, and make manifest to us, this same Divine Idea: in every new generation it will manifest itself in a new dialect; and he is there for the purpose of doing that'.[11] What these men share is Carlyle's frequently mentioned 'sincerity': they do not share in the scepticism of the eighteenth century or in the 'dilettantism' Carlyle sees in his own age. He praises these men, and their works, for their prophetic function.

9   Carlyle, 'Sir Walter Scott' in *Collected Works*, vol. V, p. 234.
10  A. Abbot Ikeler, *Puritan Temper and Transcendental Faith: Carlyle's Literary Vision* (Columbus: Ohio State University Press, 1972), pp. 3–38.
11  Carlyle, 'The Hero as Man of Letters', *Heroes and Hero-Worship* in *Collected Works*, vol. VI, p. 186.

# John Ruskin (1819–1900)

Though not now known primarily as a literary critic, John Ruskin commented extensively on literature. At the height of his career he formed a complete aesthetic view that took elements from many disciplines: an aesthetics that took into account the creation and dissemination of artistic production in an industrial society. Ruskin was the most highly theoretical of Victorian critics, as shown in his masterwork, *Modern Painters*, which established a theory of Beauty. Its appeal and influence continued well into the twentieth century.

Ruskin was born into money and opportunity. His father was a successful wine dealer who travelled extensively. The young Ruskin and his mother accompanied the elder Ruskin in his many travels both in the British Isles and on the continent. Ruskin's mother was a devout evangelical Christian, so Ruskin was not permitted toys or light reading, and his mother accompanied him to Oxford, which he entered as a gentleman commoner – that is, as a man not expected to complete his degree but to acquire some finishing from the experience. While at Oxford, Ruskin published a series of papers on architecture and began the first volume of what would be one of his major works, *Modern Painters*. Throughout his life, he wrote extensively. He moved from painting to architecture to social criticism that was part of his aesthetics – premised on the idea that the morality of a society could be deduced from its artistic production – with forays into art instruction, children's literature, mineralogy, political economy, education, natural history and autobiography.

Ruskin wrote three extensive essays on literature from the beginning to the end of his writing career. In these essays, which do not quite agree, we can see the ways in which his moral criticism of society infuses his comments about fiction and poetry. The first, an essay on literature written for his Oxford tutor in 1836, is surprising in the context of the later, mature Ruskin. In 1836, he defends literature from commonplace puritan accusations of moral weakness or falsity: some clergymen attacked fiction as comprising 'lies' or 'falsehoods'. Ruskin argues that a 'moderate' use of fiction is not just harmless, but healthy: 'Now intoxication is detrimental to the health, but a moderate use of wine is beneficial to it; and voracity in works of fiction is detrimental to the mind, but moderation . . . is beneficial to it, and much better than total confinement to the thick water-gruel of sapient, logical and interminable folios.'[12] Ruskin asserts that the mind needs fiction as much as it needs non-fiction, theology, or facts. Though he ranks Scott above Bulwer (not yet Bulwer-Lytton), he praises both for raising the historical sense and the sentiments. He even defends Byron,

---

[12] John Ruskin, *The Works of John Ruskin*, eds. E. T. Cook and Alexander Wedderburn, 39 vols. (London: George Allen, 1903–12), vol. I, p. 365.

largely condemned for moral reasons by clergymen of the nineteenth-century, for the ways in which he induces ethically charged emotion: 'What other moralist ever felt so deeply?'[13]

After this early essay, literature comes into his purview usually as an extension of his cultural criticism. Art is a medium for conveying permanent truths. For Ruskin, as George Landow puts it, painting is 'a form of language and the greatest painting a form of poetry'.[14] Even the phrase 'the pathetic fallacy', which we attribute to Ruskin, comes from a discussion of painting. Ruskin considered how the influence of nature enters into art. The 'pathetic fallacy' is the application of human emotive terms to nature. It takes two forms: one where it is used willfully, without any expectation that it should be believed, which Ruskin condemns as false, and the other where it is caused by an excited state of the feelings. For Ruskin, in the second variety the emotions are at least true.

In his social and cultural criticism Ruskin emphasized the social and personal costs of industrial production – on the labourer or artisan turned into a machine, and also on the middle-class consumer. The purchasing consumer is inherently making choices. This ethical economics has a moral element that is inherently nationalistic, as Ruskin repeatedly points out Britain's singular economic success and moral degradation: '*The beginning of art is in getting our country clean, and our people beautiful*' (his emphasis).[15] His moralistic attitude towards the fine arts goes back to Plato. Ruskin saw his own discussions of the fine arts, including literature, as part of the training of a people who were increasingly consuming but not yet educated in ethical tastes or choices. His life and written work can be seen as interventions in the market on behalf of the new reading public. He tried to intervene practically in his endeavours with the Working Men's Colleges and the ill-fated Guild of St George. He attempted to guide the reading of his readers, to educate them through his own works, and to give them ethical guidelines. Those new readers included the newly literate working classes and especially women. As Linda Austin notes, his difficult style and relatively high prices created a split between the intended working-class audience of a work like *Fors Clavigera* and its actual upper middle-class readership.[16]

In short, Ruskin's criticism of literature emphasizes literature's didactic role in strong terms: it tends to be personalized: 'Great art is the expression of the mind of a great man, and mean art, that of the want of mind of

---

[13] *Ibid.* p. 373.

[14] George Landow, *Elegant Jeremiahs: The Sage from Carlyle to Mailer* (Ithaca, NY: Cornell University Press, 1986), p. 61.

[15] Ruskin, *Works*, vol. XX, p. 107.

[16] Linda M. Austin, *The Practical Ruskin: Economics and Audience in the Late Work* (Baltimore, MD, and London: Johns Hopkins University Press, 1991), p. 2.

a weak man. A foolish person builds foolishly; and a wise one, sensibly; a virtuous one, beautifully; and a vicious one, basely.'[17] Moreover, and perhaps more strikingly, Ruskin is concerned with the ethical influence of the literary as a secular scripture, as exemplary or even performative language:

All pieces of such art are didactic in the purest way, indirectly and occultly, so that, first, you shall only be bettered by them if you are already hard at work in bettering yourself; and when you *are* bettered by them it shall be partly with a general acceptance of their influence, so constant and subtle that you shall be no more conscious of it than of the healthy digestion of food; and partly by a gift of unexpected truth, which you shall only find by slow mining for it.[18]

His 'Of King's Treasures' endorses the construction of public libraries at a time that endorsing wide reading for the working and middle classes was controversial: he praises 'good' reading over other pastimes related to consumption or collecting. But he is also careful to sort this reading out into 'good books for the hour', 'good books for all time', 'bad books for the hour' and 'bad books for all time'. Writing in an era where books are becoming more readily available, Ruskin feels the need to tell the newly reading, if not newly literate, classes which books to take up, and take up permanently: 'The very cheapness of literature is making wise people forget that if a book is worth reading, it is worth buying.'[19]

It should be no be surprise that Ruskin had great doubts about the work of his literary contemporaries, particularly in imaginative literature. *Fors Clavigera* repeatedly lambastes 'cheap literature', which inherently implies a mass-produced literature for a large reading public: 'cheap' is synonymous with 'harmful'. *Fiction, Fair or Foul* takes on Dickens and Eliot for the urban novel, which he relates to dirt and disease:

All healthy and helpful literature sets simple bars between right and wrong; assumes the possibility, in men and women, of having healthy minds in healthy bodies, and loses no time in the diagnosis of fever or dyspepsia in either; least of all in the particular kind of fever which signifies the ungoverned excess of any appetite or passion. The 'dulness' which many modern readers inevitably feel, and some modern blockheads think it creditable to allege, in Scott, consists not a little in his absolute purity from every loathsome element or excitement of the lower passions ... while, in the railway novel, interest is obtained with the vulgar reader for the vilest character, because the author describes carefully to his recognition the blotches, burrs and pimples in which the paltry nature resembles his own. *The Mill on the Floss* is perhaps the most striking instance extant of this study of cutaneous disease.[20]

[17] Ruskin, 'The Queen of the Air' in *Works*, vol. XIX, p. 389.     [18] *Ibid.*, p. 308.
[19] Ruskin, 'Of King's Treasuries' in *Works*, vol. XVIII, p. 85.
[20] Ruskin, *Fiction, Fair or Foul* in *Works*, vol. XXXIV, pp. 376–7.

Ruskin's devaluation of his literary contemporaries shows frustration in his role as prophet. Carlyle abandoned his belief in literature for history and politics. Ruskin found that his belief could not sustain him: or that the world would not sustain his beliefs. The role of the prophet was already written as one crying in the wilderness – abstracted from his potential listeners – and Ruskin eagerly took up this role. In some ways, that abstraction from his public proved to him that he was a prophet.

## Walter Pater (1839–1894)

Ruskin and Carlyle readily took on the role of the prophet, as did Matthew Arnold and George Eliot, though with more ambivalence. The second group of nineteenth-century critics might be seen as a second generation: Pater, Morris and Shaw were all exposed to the earlier writers in their youths. Pater read Ruskin's *Modern Painters* while in his teens. Arnold, Ruskin and Eliot are for them somewhere between contemporaries and predecessors. Carlyle, who was born in the previous century, certainly was a predecessor. Like these, Pater came into literary criticism somewhat obliquely. Originally hired at Brasenose College, Oxford, to teach German philosophy, he used his fellowship to write on other subjects: first publishing on Coleridge, moving to studies of the Renaissance, French literature, classics and contemporary poetry, and to curious prose fictions like *Imaginary Portraits* and *Marius the Epicurean*. It is difficult to read Pater's work in developmental stages, given that his refined style is so consistent. As William Shuter has noted, Pater's later texts 'function to convert the earlier texts into anticipations of themselves and thereby appear to reshape the body of that work'.[21]

Pater's university position and temperament enabled him to be less involved in and concerned about the marketing of his works. One could argue that his primary audience was not the book-buying one but his students, who included Gerard Manley Hopkins and Oscar Wilde. Pater turned away from the grander pronouncements of other Victorian authors: *The Renaissance*, while one of the most influential prose texts of the century, is a collection of essays on a theme rather than a polemic. He opposed himself gently to Coleridge, Ruskin and other English prophets. It should be no surprise that Pater often wrote on 'minor' figures like Charles Lamb and Sir Thomas Browne. Wolfgang Iser identifies this as Pater's 'skeptical' or 'relative' spirit, which receives experience but does

---

[21] William Shuter, *Re-Reading Walter Pater* (Cambridge University Press, 1999), p. x.

not attempt to manipulate it.[22] Pater actually did admit that the literary was taking the role of the religious text, but retreated from the next ideal that Carlyle, Ruskin and Arnold took on so readily: that therefore the writer, especially the literary critic who sorts through the literary production of his time, had to take on a prophetic role. The religious text is for Pater an experience, largely conveyed through style, not a systemization of ethics or ethical choices.

'The Vulgate, the English Bible, the English Prayer Book, the writings of Swedenborg, the Tracts for the Times': these texts engage widely different phases and styles of religious feeling. For Pater, secular texts, written by some of the so-called 'prophets' of the Victorian age, can approach this religious sensibility through their own perfection of personal style. And they are compared favourably to religious documents. But he is sceptical about the cultural-critical and ethical pretensions of his contemporary critics: 'as we say sometimes, "prophets"' – those are his own quotation marks around the word. What makes the best of these writers is not ethical content (what Arnold would call 'conduct') but 'soul' allied to content that comes through as style.[23] While Pater agrees that works of secular criticism can have a religious tone, he is indifferent to their ethical content. Artistic perfection realizes an experience in reading these works akin to reading religious ones: the impression is not that the religious works are replaced or replayed. And the reader does not even have to share the belief system to be moved.

Pater's aesthetic theory has been usually summed up as 'Art for art's sake'. That is, art for him is not didactic, improving or inherently moral. Questions of morality fall away as he emphasizes the individual relationship to and reception of beauty. His theory of art directly responds to Ruskin's moral and ethical economics, one that ends up classifying books into 'helpful' or 'harmful'. As Kenneth Daley points out, Ruskin's difficulty with Romanticism stems from his 'ambivalent theory that regards the modern period as a perversion of the Romantic ideal', while Pater embraces the richness of individual sensory experience and of individual vision.[24] He liberates Romanticism from Ruskin's moral difficulties – which are only a version of the complexities of Carlyle, Arnold and Eliot writ large – and embraces the quality of self-involved post-Romanticism that Arnold condemned in the 'Preface of 1853'. For

22  Wolfgang Iser, *Walter Pater: The Aesthetic Moment*, trans. David Henry Wilson (Cambridge University Press, 1987), pp. 17–18.
23  Walter Pater, *Appreciations, with an Essay on Style* (Evanston: Northwestern University Press, 1987), p. 26.
24  Kenneth Daley, *The Rescue of Romanticism: Walter Pater and John Ruskin* (Athens: Ohio University Press, 2001), p. 2.

Pater, artistic production can only be received as individual experience. Although the following well-known passage begins by agreeing with the initial quotation from Arnold, it quickly undermines Arnoldian ideals:

'To see the object as in itself it really is,' has been justly said to be the aim of all true criticism whatever, and in aesthetic criticism the first step towards seeing one's object as it really is, is to know one's own impression as it really is, to discriminate it, to realise it distinctly. The objects with which aesthetic criticism deals – music, poetry, artistic and accomplished forms of human life – are indeed receptacles of so many powers or forces: they possess, like the products of nature, so many virtues or qualities. What is this song or picture, this engaging personality presented in life or in a book, to *me*? What effect does it really produce on me? Does it give me pleasure? and if so, what sort or degree of pleasure? How is my nature modified by its presence, and under its influence? The answers to these questions are the original facts with which the aesthetic critic has to do; and, as in the study of light, of morals, of number, one must realise such primary data for one's self, or not at all. And he who experiences these impressions strongly, and drives directly at the discrimination and analysis of them, has no need to trouble himself with the abstract question what beauty is in itself, or what its exact relation to truth or experience – metaphysical questions, as unprofitable as metaphysical questions elsewhere. He may pass them all by as being, unanswerable or not, of no interest to him.[25]

This passage seems, and only seems, to confirm Arnold's notion of objective criticism and his ideal of 'disinterestedness'. But very quickly, Pater uses Arnold's formulation to move so far beyond it that he is actually contradicting it. For Pater's scepticism about generalizations and theories turns 'the object itself as it really is' to the object as the individual senses it, implying that no two individuals sense it the same way. Furthermore, the real test of sensation is not a scientific investigation of sight or sound, but the amount and kind of pleasure that it gives the individual receiver, that is, 'me'. There is no attempt to appreciate the pleasure of other people: one can only determine 'the sort or degree of pleasure' for oneself.

This individuality – an individuality that only pleasure can register – finally takes away the pressure that so many critics feel as they attempt to replace a failing Christianity with a prose that can provide at least a secular ethics. Even while praising Mary Arnold Wards's serious, best-selling *Robert Elsmere*, about a clergyman wracked with doubt, Pater gently takes on her philosophical purposefulness:

Robert Elsmere was a type of a large class of minds which cannot be sure that the sacred story is true. It is philosophical, doubtless, and a duty to the intellect

---

[25]  Walter Pater, *The Renaissance: Studies in Art and Poetry: The 1893 Text*, ed. Donald L. Hill (Berkeley and Los Angeles: University of California Press, 1980), pp. xix–x.

to recognize our doubts, to locate them, perhaps to give them practical effect. It may be also a moral duty to do this. But then there is also a large class of minds which cannot be sure it is false – minds of very various degrees of conscientiousness and intellectual power, up to the highest. They will think those who are quite sure it is false unphilosophical through lack of doubt. For their part, they make allowance in their scheme of life for a great possibility, and with some of them that bare concession of possibility (the subject of it being what it is) becomes the most important fact in the world . . . Their particular phase of doubt, of philosophic uncertainty, has been the secret of millions of good Christians, multitudes of worthy priests. They knit themselves to believers, in various degrees, of all ages.[26]

Pater dislikes the positing of definite answers in an age of religious doubt, and wants us to admit these doubts as part of belief. Ward, Arnold, Eliot and Ruskin all in different ways assume that literature has an ethical or philosophical purpose – or else we would not have to close our Byron and open our Goethe. Morris and Bernard Shaw, too, believe that their works have an ethical duty to foster, model or encourage changes in belief or society. Pater deliberately abandons this burden.

Moreover, the praise of pleasure and sensation for the sake of experience – the famous admonition to 'burn always with a hard gem-like flame'[27] – actually calls into question the normative rules of society, particularly around sexuality. If one is to get as many kinds of the sensations of pleasure as are necessary to achieve 'success in life', rules about the nature and manner and kinds of pleasure – and implicitly sexual pleasure – seem barely relevant. Though many late twentieth-century writers have tried to depict Pater primarily as a sexual provocateur, I would agree with Jonathan Loesberg, who writes that 'Pater's concern for building a philosophy . . . upon sensation [was] more homosexual than were his more explicitly homoerotic passages.'[28] Pater's shocking morality is only in quest of sensuous experience, which stems from artistic understanding that puts convention to one side.

In this way Pater partially sidesteps, or corrects, the quandary so many of these authors fell into: the ambivalence about their position as writers in a world of machinery. I say only partially, because Pater did withdraw, correct and reissue these controversial statements when it became apparent that they shocked his readers. But the secular embrace of individual vision, without prophetic pretensions, is what is important here.

26 Walter Pater, *Essays from the Guardian* (1901; rpt New York: Books for Libraries Press, 1968), pp. 67–8.
27 Pater, *The Renaissance*, p. 189.
28 Jonathan Loesberg, *Aestheticism and Deconstruction: Pater, Derrida and De Man* (Princeton University Press, 1991), p. 186.

## William Morris (1834–1896) and George Bernard Shaw (1856–1950)

As a transitional figure between Ruskin and Shaw, it is important to recognize the work of William Morris, one of England's first and most influential socialists. He was not primarily a critic of literature – literary criticism was one of the very few fields he barely tried his hand at. He was a contemporary and friend of Ruskin and the Pre-Raphaelites; he trained as an architect and was one of the original Victorian thinkers. Under the influence of Ruskin, Morris began to develop his aesthetic philosophy of rejecting low-quality mass industrial manufacture. Through his workshops, he led the way in design and production of textiles, decorative arts, stained glass, furniture and books. His own aesthetic was secular, economic and applied, as opposed to the Christian and historical aesthetic of Ruskin. Morris was also a considerable writer, poet, and author of prose fantasies and utopian fictions. While he wrote very little literary criticism, he is an important figure between Ruskin and Shaw: one example of what might happen to Ruskin's ideas upon exposure to Marx. I would argue that Morris's literary productions – his utopian socialist magazine *Commonweal* and his hand-produced Kelmscott Press – editions of his own works and of the classics – are themselves a kind of literary criticism: an attempt to remove literary production from Carlyle's machinery, and to resolve the dilemma of someone like Ruskin, whose anti-laissez-faire polemics were implicated in the economic system they deplored.

George Bernard Shaw began as a critic of art, music and theatre. His five attempts at socialist novels were failures. In turning to the drama, he took advantage of its often-disdained 'popular' appeal. With the possible exception of verse drama, nineteenth-century dramatic production was regarded as a popular, undistinguished genre. Shaw succeeded in re-establishing the drama as both literature and social critique. He wrote polemical prefaces to many of his plays. His dramas often deal with the effects of belief, most notably *Major Barbara* (1905) and *Androcles and the Lion* (1912). These plays and their prefaces challenge the hypocrisy he saw in contemporary Christianity. As he writes in the preface to *Androcles and the Lion*, 'the political, economic and moral opinions of Jesus, as guides to conduct, are interesting and important: the rest is mere psychopathy and superstition'.[29]

Yet Shaw never discounted the role of the spiritual; he simply wanted to redirect its energies. As Charles Berst puts it, 'Habitually his eye moves beyond the social to the spiritual, and at this point he finds that the

---

[29]  George Bernard Shaw, *The Complete Plays with Prefaces*, 6 vols. (New York: Dodd, Mead, 1963), vol. v, p. 407.

spirit, mind, and aesthetics go together.'[30] Shaw understood something of the religious mind and appreciated how necessary it was for the kinds of social transformation he supported. In 1912, speaking to the New Reform Club on the theme of 'Modern Religion', he said:

What I mean by a religious person is one who conceives himself or herself to be the instrument of some purpose in the universe which is a high purpose, and is the motive power of evolution – that is, of a continual ascent in organization and power and life, and extension of life. Any person who realizes that there is such a power, and that his business and joy in life is to do its work and his pride and point of honor is to identify himself with it, is religious... Any man of honor is a religious man.[31]

Shaw supports the dogmatic over the sceptical temperament: in fact, he decrees it necessary. And he is the primary example, as well as exponent, of this new 'religious' temperament.

For his whole career, Shaw eagerly assumed the role as prophet of his own belief system, one that takes over from Christianity. This role is apparent in the prefaces, where he defends his version of every belief system and institution that appears in the plays. His most famous and relevant work in this context is his *Quintessence of Ibsenism*, published in 1891. Throughout his life, Shaw worked for social causes and the Fabian socialist party. He wrote political and social pamphlets and essays, advocated causes (some cranky, like spelling reform and anti-vaccination) and even helped found the London School of Economics. His plays, and writing about them, intervened to advocate certain social changes and policies – creating what he called 'social drama'. By comparison, Ruskin and Carlyle would have been content merely to point the problems out; Arnold very seldom advocates specific policies and then quite late in his career. Pater's aesthetic philosophy deliberately skirts them. But Shaw resolutely recommends beliefs and policies for his society and his art in the *Quintessence*.

The *Quintessence of Ibsenism* descends directly from the vatic aspirations of Shaw's predecessors; Shaw, no less than Carlyle, Eliot or Ruskin, is interested in replacing religious discourse. The book was sponsored by the Fabian Society, though cleverly marketed by Shaw himself. He argues that Ibsen takes on the belief systems that have replaced Protestant Christianity, what he calls 'Idealism'. 'Our ideas, like the gods of old, are constantly demanding human sacrifices.'[32] Those ideas, at least

[30] Charles Berst, 'In the Beginning: The Poetic Genesis of Shaw's God', *Shaw: the Annual of Bernard Shaw studies*, 1 (1981), p. 7.
[31] 'Modern Religion' in *The Religious Speeches of Bernard Shaw*, ed. Warren Sylvester Smith (University Park: Pennsylvania State University Press, 1963), pp. 38–9.
[32] George Bernard Shaw, *Major Critical Essays* (London: Constable, 1932), p. 25.

as he specifies them, are the secular codes of conduct – societal conventions like marriage, family life and femininity, and legal ones like private property – that in many circles only grew stronger as belief in Christianity declined. Furthermore, Shaw argues not only that literature can replace Christian belief systems, but that it already has: 'modern European literature and music now form a Bible far surpassing in importance to us the ancient Hebrew Bible that has served us so long'.[33] The effort to make literature and its criticism a scripture has succeeded. He announces that Ibsen (implicitly with Shaw) 'has his own right to canonical rank as one of the major prophets of the modern Bible'.[34] That modern Bible, at least as Shaw sees it, has to withdraw or negate a false idealistic morality – sometimes called 'duty' – still influenced by a weakened Christian belief.

Literature, then, has to instil these new beliefs in place of old ones: 'We want a frankly doctrinal theatre.'[35] 'Doctrinal' here is a telling word, taken directly from theology. Shaw's writings do not just enjoin policies (as John Galsworthy's contemporary plays did); they enforce a creed. Theatre is interesting as a choice of venue because it was not directly implicated in the publishing machine of the Victorian era, largely due to problems with copyright and censorship. And Shaw had already tried periodical criticism and the novel. Of course, theatre had its own kind of machine. But Shaw, as Katherine Kelly points out, was quite canny in exploiting the late nineteenth-century moment. He created his own celebrity and political identity and took hold of the opportunity for making money by both performance and publication of his work in Great Britain and the United States: 'Shaw improvised a strategy for writing, designing, printing, binding, and marketing his plays that would recognize the value of his labor while fashioning his identity as a literary socialist with high-art appeal.'[36] At the same time Shaw's theatrical efforts and persona enabled him to deal with his audience (of whatever class) in part by exploiting the potential mass reading market for dramatic works.

Whether Shaw's easy assumption of the role of prophet (a role Pater declined) was successful is left open to question. Shaw announced in the preface to the 1922 edition of the *Quintessence* that the First World War might have been prevented, 'had the Gospel of Ibsen been understood and heeded'.[37] This is an astonishing claim to make for a work of literature, and an even more astonishing one to make for Shaw's *Quintessence*, which is solely responsible for reinventing Ibsen as a 'Gospel'. Shaw is actually convinced of his work's ability to change history. One of the

---

[33] *Ibid.*, p. 147.   [34] *Ibid.*, p. 148.   [35] *Ibid.*, p. 149.
[36] Katherine Kelly, 'Imprinting the Stage: Shaw and the Publishing Trade, 1883–1903' in *The Cambridge Companion to George Bernard Shaw*, ed. Christopher Innes (Cambridge University Press, 1998), p. 16.
[37] Shaw, *Essays*, p. 3.

least attractive 'cranky' causes he came to endorse was Stalinism: a visit to the Soviet Union only energized him, and some of his subsequent work can be seen as an apologia for Stalin's terror. In context, one might see this enthusiasm as a natural growth, rather than an aberration.

While it might be tempting to view twentieth-century writers as either Paterians or Shavians, it is more interesting to see literature in the Modernist period as profiting from the tensions between these two poles, even within individual works. At its most debased, Pater's theory could lead to literature as mere private utterance, an idioglossia – and Shaw's to Socialist Realism. Much of the energy of the works of Woolf, Eliot, Joyce or Lawrence comes from their working their way through and around these earlier positions, and by testing the limitations of earlier, strong, conflicting claims for the value of the literary, in different combinations of secular and religious.

## 9

# Literary nationalism and US
# Romantic aesthetics

### DAVID VAN LEER

In US Romantic aesthetics what is theoretical is not American, and what is American is not theoretical. Before 1860, US writers made no broad statements in politics or literature; the United States presented the world with no *Leviathan* or 'Treatises of Government', no *Biographia Literaria* or 'Preface to the *Lyrical Ballads*'. Not only was there no *summa*; the few statements interpreted as overarching manifestos were more nearly attempts to evolve a political identity for American literature than to articulate a set of aesthetic principles. The victory in the War of 1812 gave the United States a sense of its status as an international power. Beating England once in 1783 might have been sheer luck; beating it twice meant that the US was a nation to which the world must attend. The fiftieth anniversary of the Revolution – with the deaths of both John Adams and Thomas Jefferson on 4 July 1826 – was symbolically important to literati. The US had reached its political adulthood. Now it needed a theory on the Americanness of its literature to parallel its declarations on the nature of individual liberty.

Statements about such 'literary nationalism' were mostly parochial. In New York, writers wished to state America's intellectual independence without attacking the apparent Eurocentrism of Yorker celebrities Washington Irving and James Fenimore Cooper. Some, like Charles Fenno Hoffman and Lewis Gaylord Clark, wrote in the *Knickerbocker* about the uniqueness of the American landscape as a way of supporting the conservative politics of Irving and Cooper. Others, like Evert Duyckinck, Cornelius Mathews and the other Young Americans, used virtually identical rhetoric to support their more liberal agendas in the *Literary World* and later the *Democratic Review*. For both groups practical problems, like the need for a copyright law as set forth by Charles Dickens, lay at the centre of their aesthetic claims. The ensuing, acrimonious debates in newspapers and literary journals caught in their webs not only these figures, but also more famous writers like Herman Melville and Edgar Allan Poe.

In New England, literary nationalism grew less out of publishing politics than out of mid-century religious reform. The influence of Irving and Cooper was overshadowed there by that of Bostonian writers Henry

Wadsworth Longfellow, James Russell Lowell and especially William Ellery Channing. Channing rebelled against the severe theology of Calvinism to offer instead the stylistically more poetic interpretation of 'Liberal Christianity', today known as Unitarianism for its discomfort with the doctrine of a tripartite God united in the Trinity. Subsequently W. H. Channing, Orestes Brownson, George Ripley and others substituted the Romantic vocabulary of an idealized nature for the 'corpse-cold' rhetoric of Unitarian sermons. In his first published work, his 1842 review of *Natural History of Massachusetts* in the Transcendentalist journal the *Dial*, Henry David Thoreau combined the realistic natural writing for which he would become famous with the Wordsworthian language of joy and inspiration:

What is any man's discourse to me, if I am not sensible of something in it as steady and cheery as the creak of crickets? In it the woods must be relieved against the sky. Men tire me when I am not constantly greeted and refreshed as by the flux of sparkling streams. Surely joy is the condition of life.[1]

Similarly, women writers, using 'nature' to mean simultaneously 'the natural world' and 'personal character', adapted Romantic rhetoric to the genres most open to women – the sentimental novel, the travel narrative and the political tract. In her *Summer on the Lakes* (1843), Margaret Fuller sees the natural nobility of Native Americans as superior to the imagined glories of Europe.[2]

The leader of such American Romanticism was Ralph Waldo Emerson, and his 1837 Phi Beta Kappa address on the traditional, assigned topic of 'The American Scholar' most eloquently represents America's search for a literature of its own. Emerson's argument is not itself particularly unusual. In 'The Hasty Pudding', his 1793 epic celebrating the American Revolution (and simplicity of diet), Joel Barlow had already deified the everyday aspects of the US: 'I sing the sweets I know, the charms I feel, / My morning incense, and my evening meal – / The sweets of Hasty Pudding.'[3] Emerson's formulations of this familiar association of America with the natural assert the commonplace experience of everyday life: 'I embrace the common, I explore and sit at the feet of the familiar, the low. Give me insight into today, and you may have the antique and future worlds. What would we really know the meaning of . . . The meal in the firkin; the milk in the pan; the ballad in the street; the news of the boat;

[1] *The Transcendentalists: An Anthology*, ed. Perry Miller (Cambridge, MA: Harvard University Press, 1950), pp. 335–6.
[2] Margaret Fuller, *Summer on the Lakes* in *The Essential Margaret Fuller*, ed. Jeffrey Steele (New Brunswick, NJ: Rutgers University Press, 1995), pp. 100–1.
[3] Joel Barlow, 'The Hasty Pudding' in *The Oxford Book of American Poetry* ed. David Lehman, (Oxford University Press, 2006), p. 15.

the glance of the eye; the form and the gait of the body.'[4] Throughout his career, however, Emerson's nationalist statements were accompanied by, and ultimately overshadowed by, a theory of poetic inspiration borrowed from German Idealist philosophy, especially that of Immanuel Kant.

The politically motivated, philosophically haphazard quality of many early statements of US aesthetics, however, did not prevent authors from outlining – in prefaces, reviews, even letters and journals – interesting literary theories almost in spite of themselves. Perhaps the earliest statement of an American aesthetic appears in the most unlikely of places – *The Sketch-Book of Geoffrey Crayon, Gent* (1819) by the politically conservative Washington Irving. No one would think of the cosmopolitan author as a literary nationalist or, for that matter, a Romantic writer. A lifelong Europhile, Irving has been criticized for borrowing from German folklore the plots for his two most famous works, 'Rip Van Winkle' and 'The Legend of Sleepy Hollow'. Yet the adaptation of foreign stories to local settings can be seen as an Americanization of the foreign equally well as a preference for European culture. Similarly ambiguous are his famous statements in 'The Author's Account of Himself'. This anti-American preface to *The Sketch-Book* presents less Irving's view than that of his flawed narrator Geoffrey Crayon. Crayon's fondness for Europe's 'accumulated treasures of age' – the 'charms of storied and poetical association', the 'ruins' of its 'shadowy grandeurs of the past' – is Irving's own. But 'charmed' and 'storied' are not entirely positive adjectives, and the language of 'accumulation' reduces literary excellence to monetary profit. Even as he praises Europe, he unironically reproduces the rhetoric of literary nationalism. Crayon locates that superiority not in the cultural sophistication of England's literature but in the framed copies of imitations he sees while window-shopping in London's print shops. Anticipating later critiques by Walter Benjamin, Marshall McLuhan, Roland Barthes and Susan Sontag, Crayon implies that the content of the frame is less important than its mode of presentation. Mechanically reproduced and packaged within a frame, any landscape picturesque or sublime is equally 'commodified' as part of the process of selling the scenery to middle-class vacationers and tourists.[5]

Irving implies that Romanticisms alter the content but not the character of reference. Edgar Allan Poe's reservations about Romanticism are more direct. Poe's ultimate hostility to Romanticism is odd, given his apparent commitment to it. Few biographies seem more Romantic. His excessive

---

[4] Ralph Waldo Emerson, 'The American Scholar' in *Selections from Ralph Waldo Emerson*, ed. Stephen E. Whicher (Boston, MA: Houghton Mifflin, 1960), p. 78.
[5] Washington Irving, *The Sketch-Book of Geoffrey Crayon, Gent*, ed. Susan Manning (Oxford University Press, 1996), pp. 12–13.

life and alcoholic death have been taken as the model of the *poète maudit*. He swam six miles on the James River in apparent imitation of Byron's famous crossing of the Hellespont. His fictional themes also seem to promote an intensely Romantic project. His frequent use of *doppelgängers*, twins and the transmigration of souls, and his interest in premature burial (with or without a subsequent resurrection), look back to models in E. T. A. Hoffman and Ludwig Tieck. His raven probably owes something to Coleridge's albatross. And his study of the urban wanderer in 'The Man of the Crowd' (1839) anticipates the figure of the flâneur in Charles Baudelaire and later Walter Benjamin. Even his morbid and somewhat misogynistic claim that the most poetic theme is the death of a beautiful woman seems of a piece with the view of feminity in Keats's 'La Belle Dame Sans Merci' and Tennyson's 'The Lady of Shalott'.

Yet these apparent similarities disguise Poe's very un-Romantic approach to supposedly Romantic commonplaces. Take the example of one of his most successful gothic tales, 'Ligeia'. Before displaying its philosophical and psychological depths, Richard Wilbur comically summarizes its plot.[6] A man marries a romantically mysterious first wife only to lose her in an unexplained, inexplicable death. Alienated from his pursuit of spirituality he marries the everyday (Scottian) Rowena. When she too dies, he dreams of the more ethereal Ligeia, who finally arises from Rowena's funeral shrouds. This somewhat silly story seems to celebrate the Keatsian trope of the deadly female. Yet its tone belies its apparently Romantic plot. In describing the eyes of his beloved, the narrator ranges through a series of un-Romantic metaphors, ending by referencing the coldly astronomical 'twin stars of Leda [Castor and Pollux]', inappropriate in tone, gender and sexuality.[7] More obviously, in a direct and explicit attack on Coleridge, he insists that 'the mind of man can imagine nothing which does not really exist; if it could, it would create not only ideally but substantially, as do the thoughts of God'.[8]

Poe's non-fiction aesthetic statements – the first of their kind in US literature – similarly owe less to Romanticism than to the Enlightenment, less to Wordsworth than to Pope. Despite his conservative politics, Poe's aesthetics mean to ally themselves with Democratic progressive liberalism, and were so read by the New York literati. His notorious attacks on the pedantry of Bostonian moralism smack of regional jealousy, and of the desire to curry favour with Evert Duyckinck and other powerful

---

6  Richard Wilbur, 'Edgar Allan Poe: 1809–1849' in *Major Writers of America*, ed. Perry Miller, 2 vols. (New York: Harcourt Brace & World, 1962), vol. I, pp. 369–82.

7  David Van Leer (ed.), *Edgar Allan Poe: Selected Tales* (Oxford University Press, 1980), pp. 28, 327.

8  *The Complete Works of Edgar Allan Poe* ed. James A. Harrison, Virginia edn, 16 vols. (New York: Thomas Y. Crowell, 1902), vol. XV, p. 13n.

New York editors. Similarly, his hostility to Wordsworth and Coleridge
and their deification of experience, intuition and the imagination is only
intermittent, and seems to comprise both Oedipal strife and aesthetic
judgement.

Poe's primary concern is that meaning should not overwhelm the work.
It was such a 'heresy of the Didactic' that he charged the Transcendentalists with: 'the rendering this [excess of meaning] the upper instead of
the under-current of the theme – which turns into prose (and that of the
very flattest kind), the so-called poetry of the so-called transcendentalists'.
Yet his most famous statements – 'The Rationale of Verse' (1848), 'The
Poetic Principle' (1848) and especially 'The Philosophy of Composition'
(1846) – speak of Beauty much as the Romantics do of intuition. His
famous insistence that a poem should be 'written solely for the poem's
sake' may have inspired the *symbolistes* and other Modernist poets. Yet
this 'poem *per se*' does not look forward to Mallarmé so much as it looks
backward to Kant: beauty is autonomous, possessing, in Kant's influential
phrase, 'purposiveness without a purpose'.[9]

Not purely theoretical, Poe's aesthetic theories seek primarily to establish the professionalism of the poet. Poe was sceptical about Coleridge's
claims to 'originality' and indifferent to the notion of a work's organic
growth from a primal seed. Beauty must be autonomous, may even be
original; but the process by which the poet represents the beautiful is a
specific historical and cultural act of work. As the Greek origin of the
word 'poetry' suggests, the poet 'makes' as well as 'means'. Poe's description in 'The Philosophy of Composition' of the writing of 'The Raven'
can seem mechanical, with its explanation of how Poe achieved his tonal
effects, reducing his aesthetic performance to a cheap parlour trick. His
account of the 'unity of effect', however, means to emphasize the first
noun, 'unity', more than the second, 'effect': it is not that every work
must build up to a surprise ending but that in art everything in the work
must belong there, that a work must start doing whatever it intends to
do from its very first sentence. This emphasis does not deny that poetry
might be an experience recollected in tranquillity. It aims only to recast
the process of recollection as an act of cultural work.[10]

Poe's fellow New Yorker Herman Melville, in a similar attempt to
court Evert Duyckinck, was less precise about his aesthetic principles. In
his late novel *Pierre* (1852), he used the rhetoric of the Young Americans
to excoriate New York publishing politics. And his masterpiece *Moby-
Dick* (1851) contains within its encyclopedic account of the universe

[9]  *Poe: Essays and Reviews*, ed. G. R. Thompson (New York: Library of America, 1984),
    pp. 75–6. Kant expresses a similar notion of aesthetics in his *Critique of Judgment*
    (1790).
[10] *Poe: Essays and Reviews*, pp. 14–15.

many theories about ways of knowing. Like Freud, Ahab understands truth as the something (or nothing) hidden behind a mask, which the true seeker must remove. Like Locke, Ishmael understands reality as delusion, the paint which the 'harlot' natural world uses to obscure an unknowable reality. The most famous epistemological theory is that of the Alabama cabin boy Pip. The mysterious doubloon onto which others project their own preoccupations, like Wittgenstein's duckrabbit, represents for Pip only the ambiguities of the act of interpretation: 'I look, you look, he looks; we look, ye look, they look.'[11]

Melville's fullest statements about the Romantic origins of his aesthetics occur in his review of and letters to Nathaniel Hawthorne. The sexual language of the review 'Hawthorne and His Mosses' (1850) – and especially its claim that Hawthorne 'shoots his strong New-England roots into the hot soil of my Southern soul' – can make the essay seem primarily a sexual pass.[12] Yet whatever the homosexual undercurrents, Melville does here articulate some of his underlying literary assumptions in his most memorable prose. The review anticipates Modernist criticism in its longing for a literature of Beauty and genius without authors. Melville takes seriously Hawthorne's historicist critique of Calvinism, to find in the author a Puritan 'gloom' and a belief in 'something like Original Sin'. Yet, unlike Hawthorne, Melville sees this 'power of blackness' as universal: not just the psychological disposition of a certain community of early settlers, but the general condition of post-Enlightenment experience. As the English Romantics celebrated the classical outcasts Cain, Prometheus and Satan, Melville names his *isolatoes* after notorious scapegoats like Ahab and especially Ishmael.

The letters to Hawthorne are even more suggestive. Melville's ambivalence about the existence of absolute truths oscillates between the cynicism of Ishmael and the titanism of Ahab. 'And perhaps, after all, there is no secret. We incline to think that the Problem of the Universe is like the Freemason's mighty secret, so terrible to all children. It turns out, at last, to consist in a triangle, a mallet, and an apron, – nothing more!' Yet as later Nietzsche would locate God's oppressiveness in grammar, so here Melville finds it in vocabulary: 'But it is this Being of the matter; there lies the knot with which we choke ourselves. As soon as you say Me, a God, a Nature, so soon you jump off from your stool and hang from the beam. Yes, that word is the hangman. Take God out of the dictionary, and you would have Him in the street.' Even more representative of Melville's uncertainty (and his desire to court Hawthorne with his intellect) is his

---

11   Herman Melville, *Moby-Dick*, eds. Hershel Parker and Harrison Hayford (New York: Norton, 2002), pp. 144, 179, 362.
12   Reprinted in *ibid.*, p. 529.

letter two months later, with its three postscripts. Accusing Goethe of what he will later charge Emerson with more explicitly, Melville complains of an immense amount of 'flummery' in him. Melville's first postscript has Hawthorne say 'Amen', although it is unclear whether Melville means Hawthorne to assent to Goethe's flummery or Melville's own. In his second postscript, however, Melville celebrates the nature he rejected, as the 'all feeling'.[13] Whether Melville here anticipates Whitman or recalls Goethe's schizophrenic friend Lenz who in Büchner's retelling desired to 'burrow his way into the all', the statement is clearly at odds with both his previous scepticism and Hawthorne's own resistance to pantheism.

Nathaniel Hawthorne's relation to Romantic theory is more explicit and complicated than Melville's. Some works – particularly 'The Birth-Mark' (1843), 'Rappaccini's Daughter' (1844), 'The Artist of the Beautiful' (1844) and *The Marble Faun* (1860) – entertain aesthetic positions that seek to imitate the beauty of nature. These arguments, however, are so specific to the flawed characters who present them that it is dangerous to extrapolate from their pronouncements a clear aesthetic theory. When Hawthorne does address contemporary debates, it is with a desultoriness that suggests less conviction than bemusement. In 'Drowne's Wooden Image' (1844), the cosmopolitan painter John Singleton Copley questions the value of Shem Drowne's more homely woodcarvings, but Hawthorne's lack of rhetorical fervour – to say nothing of his pre-Revolutionary setting – distance the gentle tale from the literary nationalism associated in his own age with the Young Americans or the Phi Beta Kappa lectures.

If Hawthorne does present his aesthetic principles it is in the prefaces to his four famous novels. The most influential of these statements opens *The House of the Seven Gables* (1851):

When a writer calls his work a Romance, it need hardly be observed that he wishes to claim a certain latitude, both as to its fashion and material, which he would not have felt himself entitled to assume had he professed to be writing a Novel.

The passage seems to suggest that there is a categorical difference between a novel and a romance, a distinction that has subsequently been read by Richard Chase and others to differentiate American fiction by Hawthorne, Melville and Fanny Fern from the English Realist tradition of Charles Dickens and George Eliot. Yet the delineation between the genres is not clear. Hawthorne elsewhere aligned himself with that most Realist of novelists Anthony Trollope; he wishes to view America as a

---

[13]  *Ibid.*, pp. 536–41.

kind of 'Faery Land' not because it is one, but because, unlike England, it lacks such storied enchantment. Inverting Irving's preference for the 'shadowy grandeurs of [a European] past', Hawthorne asks simply to be able to explore shadows in the newer world. The romanticization of the US does not import the foreign but discovers romance already present in the country's forgotten past: 'The point of view in which this tale comes under the Romantic definition lies in the attempt to connect a bygone time with the very present that is flitting away from us.' American Romance exists not apart from historical reality but within it, whether in a forgotten past or a repressed present.[14]

A similar conflation informs the most 'Romantic' of prefaces, that to the novel itself called *The Blithedale Romance* (1852). In his disingenuous attempt to distance himself from the utopian experiment of Brook Farm and the Transcendentalists Hawthorne fictionalizes in this *roman-à-clef*, he once again bemoans the absence of an American 'Faery Land' equivalent to that of England.

In the old countries, with which Fiction has long been conversant, a certain conventional privilege seems to be awarded to the romancer . . . and he is allowed a license with regard to every-day Probability . . . Among ourselves, on the contrary, there is as yet no such Faery Land, so like the real world, that, in a suitable remoteness, one cannot well tell the difference, but with an atmosphere of strange enchantment, beheld through which the inhabitants have a propriety of their own. This atmosphere is what the American romancer needs.[15]

The terminology of 'privilege' and 'license' seems fully as legalistic as aesthetic – less a celebration of the imagination than a defence against libel. The imagination plays even less of a role in his application of poetic licence to utopianism. Hawthorne does not claim that in Brook Farm he imagines the possibility of romance but represents an episode that was itself 'romantic'. However much it approached the Faery Land he sought in American history, Brook Farm was decidedly 'yet a fact'. And attributing the dreamlike quality of the experience not to himself but to its participants, Hawthorne includes the word 'romance' in his title not so much because he is writing a romance set at Brook Farm or even romanticizing Brook Farm; instead he accurately represents the romance implicit in the theoretical foundations of Brook Farm from the beginning.

The slipperiness, not to say irrelevance, of the aesthetic claims in the prefaces is most evident in 'The Custom House', Hawthorne's long preface to his most famous work, *The Scarlet Letter* (1850). Told by a

---

14  Nathaniel Hawthorne, *The House of the Seven Gables*, ed. Seymour Gross (New York: Norton, 1967), p. 1.
15  Nathaniel Hawthorne, *The Blithedale Romance*, eds. Seymour Gross and Rosalie Murphy Baum (New York: Norton, 1978), p. 2.

character clearly not Hawthorne and, as a satire of nineteenth-century party politics, in no way introducing the Puritan narrative that follows, 'The Custom House' nevertheless contains some of Hawthorne's most extended and in fact moving aesthetic descriptions. In a wholly fiction-alized passage, the narrator encounters on the second 'storey [*sic*]' of the building the packet left by a former surveyor, Jonathan Pue, con-taining not only a manuscript but an embroidered scarlet letter, which the bureaucrat pointlessly tells us measures $3\frac{1}{4}$ inches. Thoughts of Pue's story awaken the functionary from the 'torpor' of 'intellectual effort' to the 'invigorating charm of Nature'. In this reinvigorated state the narrator sees in his fireplace a vision that has become one of the central statements of the American Romantic imagination:

Moonlight, in a familiar room, falling so white upon the carpet, and showing all its figures so distinctly – making every object so minutely visible, yet so unlike a morning or noontide visibility – is a medium the most suitable for a romance-writer to get acquainted with his illusive guests. There is the little domestic scenery of the well-known apartment... all these details, so completely seen, are so spiritualised by the unusual light, that they seem to lose their actual substance, and become things of intellect. Nothing is too small or too trifling to undergo this change, and acquire dignity thereby. A child's shoe; the doll, seated in her little wicker carriage; the hobby-horse – whatever, in a word, has been used or played with during the day is now invested with a quality of strangeness and remoteness, though still almost as vividly present as by daylight. Thus, therefore, the floor of our familiar room has become a neutral territory, somewhere between the real world and fairy-land, where the Actual and the Imaginary may meet, and each imbue itself with the nature of the other. Ghosts might enter here without affrighting us. It would be too much in keeping with the scene to excite surprise, were we to look about us and discover a form, beloved, but gone hence, now sitting quietly in a streak of this magic moonshine, with an aspect that would make us doubt whether it had returned from afar, or had never once stirred from our fireside.[16]

The set piece is an impressive one, and justly famous. Yet it is unclear exactly what Hawthorne thinks of the functionary's discoveries. The specificity of the child's toys does not seem to require the mystification with which they are endowed, especially not to a Hawthorne who was fascinated most by his daughter's earthly qualities, qualities he would capture in the hard-nosed realism of the imp-child Pearl. The language of the strange and the remote less reproduces traditional Romanticism than anticipates the dehumanizing techniques of Bertolt Brecht and the postmodern project of representational defamiliarization. The language

---

[16] Nathaniel Hawthorne, *The Scarlet Letter*, ed. Brian Harding (Oxford University Press, 1990), pp. 35–6.

of fairy lands and the imaginary here is given a scientific explanation else-where rejected by Hawthorne. The spiritualizing light that robs objects of their substance recalls the failures of Aylmer and Rappaccini in their attempts to purify woman. This disapproval of spiritualizing matter in the tales is continued in *The Scarlet Letter*, whose narrative clearly rejects the Puritans' conflation of a piece of cloth with a spiritual truth, and may even question the parental efficacy of Hester's belief that her illegitimate daughter may be the 'devil's child'. Given the novel's uncertainty about what links matter and spirit, it is at least important to recognize that in 'The Custom House' the narrator's transfiguring moonlight is by the end of the passage a much less positive 'moonshine'.

Hawthorne's own voice may appear more exactly in the epilogue to his little-known tale 'The Hall of Fantasy' (1846). Finding that the Hawthorne figure is unimpressed by the possibility of an ideal world, his friend calls him 'the very spirit of earth, imbued with a scent of freshly turned soil'.[17] Whether or not this nostalgia for the everyday represents Hawthorne's unmediated opinion, it is at least as close as one of his narrators ever gets to an Emersonian embrace of the common.

Although no single position can represent American Romanticism, one characteristic is common: a coupling of the Romantic celebration of nature with a sense of the unique expansiveness of the American land-scape. North America is, of course, much bigger than the British Isles from which many immigrants came; and even though the US did not occupy the whole continent, the mid-century doctrine of Manifest Destiny encour-aged it to do so. The climatic conditions of forests in New England and the Middle States allowed a diverse range of plants to grow together, with the result that the turning of the leaves in the Fall was much more colour-ful than had been known in England. The landscape had always played a role in American literature, although in the seventeenth century most commonly as typology or real estate. At the famous landing scene in *Of Plymouth Plantation* (1630), William Bradford emphasizes God's mirac-ulous protection of the Pilgrims, much as He had protected the Israelites. For Bradford, Cape Cod was 'a hideous and desolate wilderness, full of wild beasts and wild men'. More interested in attracting investors to his new colony, Thomas Morton in his *New English Canaan* (1637) finds in the land 'millions of turtledoves on the green boughs, which sat pecking of the full ripe pleasant grapes that were supported by the lusty trees, whose fruitful load did cause the arms to bend'. And lest anyone miss the halcyon quality of his description, he ends his paragraph with an

---

[17] *Mosses from an Old Manse: The Centenary Edition of the Works of Nathaniel Hawthorne*, eds. William Charvat *et al.*, 23 vols. (Columbus: Ohio State University, 1962–), vol. x, p. 184.

alexandrine couplet: 'For in mine eye t'was Nature's masterpiece, [/] her chiefest magazine of all where lives her store. [/] If this land be not rich, [/] then is the whole world poor.'[18]

By the nineteenth century, however, the landscape was incorporated into the project of national self-advertisement. The systematic identification of sites as quintessentially American was intimately tied to the rise of tourism. Just as Irving's Crayon found nature in London prints, so those visiting famous American landscapes went less to discover new wonders than to recreate experiences they had already had from art and novels. As Fuller says of Niagara in *Summer on the Lakes*, 'When I first came I felt nothing but a quiet satisfaction. I found that drawings, the panorama, &c. had given me a clear notion of the position and proportions of all objects here; I knew where to look for everything, and everything looked as I thought it would.'[19] Despite this artificial framing of the landscape, there was a degree of geographic precision to American Romantic naturalism that was less common in European forms. American naturalists, after all, did not set their works somewhere 'above' Tintern Abbey, but at specific locations – whether Glens Falls, the Hudson River's Ox-Bow, the 'Old Man' of Vermont's Green Mountains or Concord's Walden Pond. Such a preoccupation with specific locales was already beginning to appear at the end of the seventeenth century. Samuel Sewall's *Phaenomena quaedam Apocalyptica* (1697) is like *Of Plymouth Plantation* imbued with American typological references, and its thesis like Bradford's is that God's favour can be measured in the success of the community.[20]

Despite differences in rhetoric and religion, it is not much of a leap from Sewall's Merrimack and pickerel to their reappearance one hundred and fifty years later in the writings of Henry David Thoreau. The influence of Thoreau, the inventor of the venerable American genre of literary nature writing, is very much alive in the work of Rachel Carson, John McPhee, Sally Carrigan and contemporary ecocritics and environmentalists. Thoreau's literariness is far more self-conscious than the personal preoccupations that necessarily shape the account of any explorer or ethnographer. All his works were carefully revised and rewritten, even his supposedly 'private' journals. His more famous early books – *A Week on the Concord and Merrimack Rivers* (1849) and *Walden* (1854) – mix naturalism, politics and sometimes even eroticism. Precise descriptions of

[18] Willliam Bradford, *Of Plymouth Plantation, 1620–1647*, ed. Samuel Eliot Morrison (New York: Knopf, 1964), p. 62; Thomas Morton, *New English Canaan*, ed. Jack Dempsey (Scituate: Digital Scanning, 2000), p. 54.
[19] Fuller, *Summer on the Lakes* in *Essential Margaret Fuller*, p. 72.
[20] Samuel Sewall, *Phaenomena quaedam Apocalyptica* in *The American Puritans: Their Prose and Poetry*, ed. Perry Miller (New York: Columbia University Press, 1956), pp. 214–15.

the rivers and ponds are accompanied by digressions about the massacre of the Indians, the mistreatment of Irish labourers and even Thoreau's homoerotic dalliance with a 'Paphlagonian' woodchopper.

It is this precision of description that most fascinated and then disconcerted Thoreau's mentor Emerson. Emerson's ambivalent eulogy at Thoreau's funeral (1862) betrays both his praise and his reservations. Emerson offers what is probably still the loveliest definition of Thoreau's talent as a naturalist: 'He saw as with microscope, heard as with ear-trumpet, and his memory was a photographic register of all he saw and heard.' Yet although Emerson asserts that each observation 'lay in glory in his mind, a type of the order and beauty of the whole', he is less certain than he suggests about Thoreau's desire to transcend the particular: 'Instead of engineering for all America, he was the captain of a huckle-berry party. Pounding beans is good to the end of pounding empires one of these days; but if, at the end of years, it is still only beans!'[21] Emerson's concern is not, as he implies, with Thoreau's lack of ambition, and certainly not with his political inactivity, since Emerson was by far the less political of the two. Instead the problem lay more fundamentally in their understanding of spirit and the Transcendental movement founded to foster it.

Both Emerson and Thoreau emphasized the distinction between mind and matter – between the Me and the Not-Me. They disagreed, however, on the meaning of mind and its intersection with nature. For Thoreau, mind was personal, a blend of individual honesty and moral conscience. With his philosophical interest in Kantian Idealism, Emerson took mind to mean simply 'consciousness', the fact that we perceive and how that perception links us to a higher spiritual oneness. Emerson could never have approached the dichotomy so lightly as Thoreau did in *Walden* when he wondered, 'Shall I go to heaven or a-fishing?' There was no place for the world or the person in Emersonian Idealism, and no book has less nature in it than Emerson's Transcendental credo *Nature* (1836). Early in his career, consciousness seemed to make him 'part or particle of God'. Later 'Self-Reliance' (1841) seemed more an inescapable fact than a call to prophecy: no man can escape 'his own nature' because 'nature' is the only thing man has. Distanced from the persona of 'Orphic Poet' that he adopted at the end of *Nature*, a considerably chastened Emerson 'would write on the lintels of the door-post, *Whim*', hoping his pronouncement to be 'somewhat better than whim at last', but also knowing that 'we cannot spend the day in explanation'.[22] In later essays like 'Experience' (1844) and 'Fate' (1851), Emerson's diffidence reads like full-blown despair. He

---

[21]  Ralph Waldo Emerson, 'Thoreau' in *Selections from Emerson*, pp. 388–93.
[22]  Emerson, 'Self-Reliance' in *Selections from Emerson*, pp. 24, 150.

cannot even truly feel grief at the death of his young son Waldo. Man's
subjective role in shaping reality is now seen as mere subjectiveness, the
'Fall of Man' that teaches us forever to distrust our perceptions; if subject-
lenses have a creative power, then perhaps there are no objects: 'Once
we lived in what we saw; now, the rapaciousness of this new power
[scepticism about objective reality], which threatens to absorb all things,
engages us. Nature, art, persons, letters, religions, objects, successively
tumble in, and God is but one of its ideas.'[23]

Although less obviously, Emerson's aesthetic pronouncements also
become increasingly reserved. Early, Jeremy Bentham's observation that
our spiritual vocabulary is drawn from our language about the natural
world led Emerson to flirt with the Swedenborgian theory of correspondences: that every natural fact was merely the sign of a spiritual fact.
Although never tempted like the Swedish mystic to write a social history
of angels, Emerson did at the end of *Nature* introduce the bardic voice
of the 'Orphic Poet' to declare man a 'god in ruins'. Once man conforms
his life to the pure godlike 'idea' in his mind, a 'correspondent revolution
in the things' of the world will return him to his original majesty. In his
essay 'The Poet' (1844), perhaps the most famous statement of American
orphism, Emerson excepts the poet from the crippling consciousness of
subjectivity he elsewhere lamented: godlike in his relation to the world,
in his ability to name beauty, he too speaks through fiat: 'The poet is the
sayer, the namer, and represents beauty. He is a sovereign, and stands on
the centre. For the world is not painted, or adorned, but is from the beginning beautiful; and God has not made some beautiful things, but Beauty
is the creator of the universe. Therefore the poet is not any permissive
potentate, but is emperor in his own right.'

Yet despite his creative ability, the poet is himself never quite real: 'I
look in vain for the poet whom I describe.' As poetry was all written
before time, so the poet seems to stand outside it, or at least largely in
the past. And when Emerson reduces 'language-making' to 'metre-making
argument', it is hard not to side more with Poe's denigration of Bostonian
inspiration as mere didacticism.[24] The excessive belief in inspiration in
this opening to Emerson's second series of *Essays* is probably best understood in terms of the irony in 'Nominalist and Realist' (1844), the work
that ends the volume. Here, man is not godlike but only representative,
and the universe retains its autonomy: 'Nick Bottom cannot play all the
parts, work it how he may: there will be somebody else, and the world
will be round.'[25]

[23] Emerson, 'Experience' in *Selections from Emerson*, p. 269.
[24] Emerson, *Nature* and 'The Poet' in *Selections from Emerson*, pp. 56, 224–5, 238.
[25] Emerson, 'Nominalist and Realist' in *Collected Works of Ralph Waldo Emerson*,
   eds. Robert Spiller *et al.*, 16 vols. (Cambridge, MA: Harvard University Press, 1971),
   vol. III, p. 139.

As the reformist 1820s and 1830s turned into the more radical 1840s and 1850s, political concerns informed and finally overturned the more broadly philosophical and aesthetic concerns of American Transcendentalism. Neither Hawthorne nor Emerson acted on his supposedly liberal beliefs. Largely silent on political issues, Hawthorne did write the campaign biography of his Bowdoin classmate, the conservative Franklin Pierce, whose presidential actions might be seen as pro-slavery. Emerson was similarly slow to speak on what other Bostonians considered pressing issues. In refusing to join the Fourierist experiment at Brook Farm, Emerson clearly stated his sense that reform meant individual purification and not group activism; in his journal he snarled, 'Shall I raise the siege of this hencoop, and march away to a pretended siege of Babylon?' Other Transcendentalists – like Orestes Brownson, George Ripley, Theodore Parker, Bronson Alcott and Elizabeth Palmer Peabody – made the reform in education, class inequality and of course abolition their first priority.[26]

The most enduring political achievements were those of Fuller and Thoreau. One of the most learned Transcendentalists, Fuller was also the most cosmopolitan, editing the *Dial* in Boston, writing reviews for Horace Greeley in New York, and fighting for Italian unification under Garibaldi. Her work in women's rights was probably her most important political achievement. Not enjoying group activity, she did not attend the Seneca Falls Convention in 1848 with its 'Declaration of Sentiments' on the rights of women; nor, like Emerson, did she join Brook Farm. She did, however, write some of the most important feminist tracts of the nineteenth century. Her masterpiece – 'The Great Lawsuit. Man versus Men. Woman versus Women', an essay published in the *Dial* in 1843 and expanded two years later into the book *Woman in the Nineteenth Century* – stands as the central feminist tract between Mary Wollstonecraft's *A Vindication of the Rights of Woman* in 1792 and Virginia Woolf's *A Room of One's Own* in 1929. Emphasizing the virtues of an essential feminine character, the book can seem old-fashioned compared to modern arguments for female equality. Yet the argument is actually two-pronged, perhaps inconsistent, but more probably manipulating rhetorically the assumptions of the male readers whose support was necessary if women were to gain power. Whatever its literary merits, the prose strongly affected its readers, with its redefinition of spinsters as oracles, and its ringing insistence that women might 'be sea captains, if you [men] will [permit]'.[27] Its success is measured not merely by the international fame it afforded Fuller, but by the jokes hurled back at her: although praising Fuller in print, in private Poe divided the human race into men, women and Margaret Fuller.

26 Emerson, 'Journal' in *Selections from Emerson*, p. 145. For more political writings by the Transcendentalists, see Miller, *Transcendentalists*.
27 Margaret Fuller, *Woman in the Nineteenth Century* (New York: Greeley & James Brown, 1845), p. 201.

Whatever the literary and political power of the book, however, it is important to understand that its elevation of womanhood was based on a feminization of Transcendental theories of the self. Her model of the unity of man and woman may go as far back as Aristophanes's bisexual spheres in *The Symposium*; the specifics, however, are drawn from Transcendental and especially Emersonian theories of unity:

By Man I mean both man and woman; these are the two halves of one thought. I lay no special stress on the welfare of either. I believe that the development of the one cannot be effected without that of the other.

My highest wish is that this truth should be distinctly and rationally apprehended, and the conditions of life and freedom recognized as the same for the daughters and the sons of time; twin exponents of a divine thought.[28]

Characterizing woman as Muse temporarily masquerading as Minerva, Fuller not only tempers her own apparent essentialism but appropriates for the female half of thought the inspiration and intellect most valued by the Transcendentalists. She found Emerson's poet and he was female.

The full range of Fuller's political legacy is still questioned. Thoreau, however, stands undeniably at the head of twentieth-century political resistance movements. Both Mahatma Gandhi and Dr Martin Luther King acknowledged Thoreau's 1849 essay 'Resistance to Civil Government' (retitled 'Civil Disobedience' after his death) as the formative influence in the development of their own strategies. Such testimonials, however, do not take full account of the implicit radicalism of Thoreau's Transcendentalist individualism. The essay opens with a call for the abolishment of all civil government, and the famous word play about 'the majority of one' begins by dismissing the statistical dimension to voting, and plays with the spiritual difference between a godly One and a demonic Other. It concludes, however, with the elitist, not to say demagogic, claim that 'any man more right than his neighbors constitutes a majority of one already'.[29] It is important to note at least that, however non-violent the programmes of Gandhi and King, there is no such stipulation in Thoreau's essay. He would later, in 'A Plea for John Brown' (1859), defend the moral conscience of an abolitionist whose raids at Pottawatomie and Harper's Ferry had killed more than twelve people before he was himself hanged in 1859.

The most striking expression of political Romanticism, and perhaps the most philosophically sophisticated, is, surprisingly enough, *The Narrative of the life of Frederick Douglass, an American Slave, Written by Himself* (1845). The full title of the *Narrative* is the best clue that

---

[28] Margaret Fuller, 'The Great Lawsuit. Man versus Men. Woman versus Women' in *Essential Margaret Fuller*, p. 245.
[29] Leonard Harris, Scott L. Pratt and Anne S. Waters (eds.), *American Philosophies: An Anthology* (Oxford and Malden, MA: Blackwell, 2002), p. 329.

Douglass is writing something more here than the most powerful Abolitionist tract of the mid-century. He asserts not simply that he is a slave but
an 'American' one: the suggestion is both that slaves are part of American
society, and that whether enslaved or free he in particular is an American. Moreover, his claim that the book is 'written by himself' does not
simply deny that the text's language and structure were improved by a
professional (presumably white) editor; it asserts more importantly that
despite the rhetoric of slavery (and even of some Abolitionists) he has a
'self'. Individual self-reliance is essential in Douglass's *Narrative*, playing
a greater role than in some of the more communal slave narratives like
Harriet Jacobs's *Incidents in the Life of a Slave Girl, Written by Herself*
(1861). Like Emerson, Douglass defines selfhood in terms of knowledge,
whether of his birthday, or of reading, or of the slave community he leaves
behind. His ambivalent relation to the slave songs sung in the South is a
moving account not simply of the problems of slave culture, but of the
epistemological paradox that informs Romantic idealism and especially
Emerson's despairing relation to it. Spirituals were for Douglass the most
revealing account of the 'horrible character' of slavery:

They told a tale of woe which was then altogether beyond my feeble
comprehension; they were tones loud, long, and deep; they breathed the prayer
and complaint of souls boiling over with the bitterest anguish. Every tone was a
testimony against slavery, and a prayer to God for deliverance from chains.

Although the words were 'full of meaning to [the singers] themselves',
however, they were to Douglass only 'unmeaning jargon'. The problem
was not simply that the boy could not fully understand adult meanings,
but that his experience of the songs prevented knowledge about them:
'I did not, when a slave, understand the deep meaning of those rude
and apparently incoherent songs. I was myself within the circle; so that I
neither saw nor heard as those without might see and hear.' Douglass's
dilemma involves more than emotion recollected in tranquillity. It represents the doubleness not only of African American life behind the veil,
but of any Transcendental experience. The consciousness required to
understand sensation calls the reality of that sensation into question. The
passage is as moving as Emerson's mourning of his son in 'Experience'
(1944). And it appals for the same reason.[30]
    Emersonian aesthetics continued strongly to influence American poets,
especially Walt Whitman and Emily Dickinson, whose work spanned the
mid-century and the transition from pre-war Romanticism to turn-of-
the-century Realism. Whitman obviously took his lead from Emerson's

---

[30]  Frederick Donglass, *The Narrative of the Life of Frederick Douglass, an American Slave,
    Written by Himself* (Garden City, NY: Doubleday, 1973), p. 14; Emerson, 'Experience'
    in *Selections from Emerson*, pp. 256–7.

call for an American poet: he saw himself as the 'sayer' whom Emerson sought, and in fact on the second edition of *Leaves of Grass* was embossed in gold Emerson's praise of the first edition, much to the older man's irritation. Some of the influences are quite clear: in 'Song of Myself' Whitman's brief stanza – 'Do I contradict myself? / Very well then I contradict myself, / (I am large, I contain multitudes)' – merely paraphrases Emerson's statements about contradiction and misperception in 'Self-Reliance'. Yet Whitman wholly lacked Emerson's restraint: Whitman's inclusiveness, his pansexuality and his metrical freedom welcomes with open arms the great and crescive self whose advent Emerson saw as the Fall of Man. The particularity of Emily Dickinson's work another ten years later was more temperamentally attuned to Emerson's Transcendentalism: her understanding that 'The soul selects her own society – / Then – shuts the door – ' is far closer to Emerson's exclusionary self than to Whitman's assumptive one. But here too the Transcendentalists had no faith in the precision of observation and diction that defines Dickinson, and of course they were incapable of the fierce intellectualism of her ambiguous diction.

In the broadest sense American aesthetics are still imbued with Romanticism. Critics as different as Hyatt Waggoner, Harold Bloom and Helen Vendler find signs of it not only in the overtly Romantic work of A. R. Ammons and Amy Clampitt but in the more fractured visions of John Ashbery's 'Self-Portrait in a Convex Mirror' or Tony Kushner's *Angels in America*. Nevertheless, the Civil War changed the tone of the country and of its literature. As Louis Menand demonstrates, the great principles of the earlier generation seemed as much the cause of as the solution to the conflict, and subsequent generations resisted the pursuit of Big Ideas.[31] In Cambridge the 'Metaphysical Club' of William James, Charles Sanders Peirce and Oliver Wendell Holmes Jr may have continued the spirit of the earlier 'Transcendental Club', but with the significant difference that these men distrusted metaphysics as much as the Emersonians had embraced Transcendentalism. With industrial growth and technological advances, the nationalism that underwrote Romanticism was redefined, fractured and finally annihilated. And while Romanticism's hope in inspiration and the individual may persist in our postnational global culture, its faith in origins and universals appears only fleetingly in a world today always already decentred and displaced.

---

[31]   Louis Menand, *The Metaphysical Club: A Story of Ideas in America* (New York: Farrar, Straus, & Giroux, 2001).

# 10

# Russia: literature and society

## EDITH W. CLOWES

When in the 1830s literary criticism became an important activity in Russian culture, it rapidly attained a significance and stature that it could not have in European societies relatively unburdened by censorship. Overtly treating current literary and cultural themes, literary criticism became the seedbed in which many other discourses – social-political, economic, theological and philosophical – grew and flowered. Since then, criticism has remained a crucial aspect of Russian intellectual history. Much more than a description and evaluation of works of literary art, Russian criticism is motivated by a particular aesthetic, often prescriptive and often bound up with a pressing social, political or religious agenda. Among the critics most familiar to an English-speaking audience are the civic radicals of the 1850s and 1860s, with their goal of fostering a progressive social and moral consciousness. Before them, the Romantic critics of the 1830s and 1840s saw in literary art a fundamental expression of national identity. After them, Symbolist critics of the 1890s and the first decade of the twentieth century sought in literature the key to metaphysical and mystical truths that would regenerate the modern world.

The practice of literary criticism came to Russia in the eighteenth century as a part of the Westernizing reforms of Emperor Peter the Great and, later, Empress Catherine the Great. Criticism became the chief way of shaping 'correct' literary practice, as well as the mores of the newly Westernized aristocracy. During this time Russia became a major player in European political life, first destroying the kingdom of Poland, then challenging Turkey's footholds in Europe. After breaking the back of Napoleon's Grande Armée, by the end of the Second Napoleonic War (1812–14), Russia had won universal acknowledgement as a premier European power. Many of the young aristocrats who made this victory possible, and who would later become known as the Decembrists, sought for themselves and their countrymen firmer political rights, including a constitutional monarchy. The tragic result was the crushing defeat of the reformers and the cream of the Russian aristocracy after the Decembrist Revolt of 14 December 1825. Repression under Emperor Nicholas I (reigned 1825–55) made political action impossible, thus giving writing culture – and particularly criticism – inordinate importance.

In the 1830s and 1840s, as literary criticism became a profession, literary discussion directed at a newly emerging reading public crucially contributed to a debate about national identity, which became known as the debate between the Westernizers and the Slavophiles. Westernizers such as Ivan Turgenev, the critic Vissarion Belinsky and the reformist thinker Aleksandr Herzen wanted to follow the European trajectory laid out by Peter the Great towards a Europeanized, secular culture. The Slavophiles, who included Nikolai Gogol, the Aksakov family, which produced a number of outstanding memoirists and critics, and the philosopher Aleksei Khomiakov, idealized Russia's deep pre-modern cultural history, rural folk customs and religious traditions. The second half of the century saw more complex critical approaches, springing from the debate between proponents of Westernization and Slavophiles. During this period the first seminal works of academic criticism appeared. At the century's end, the literary criticism of such Symbolists as Dmitry Merezhkovsky, Zinaida Gippius, Andrei Belyi and Viacheslav Ivanov moved beyond purely social and national questions, advancing the search in literary art for a new mystical consciousness. Finally, Symbolists and other Modernists engaged in a literary criticism which generally understood poetic language and form as an avenue towards creating a new life and vibrant culture.

Every generation revisits and reshapes the historical narrative bequeathed to it. The account of Russian literary criticism offered here will differ from Soviet-era accounts in its vocabulary (which is less political and more literary-cultural, following the usage of the critics themselves) and in its greater emphasis on cultural and intellectual networks of people and ideas. In the post-Soviet period, merely tracing the roots of the official Stalinist aesthetic known as 'Socialist Realism' is no longer obligatory or paramount. We are now able to appreciate the full range of Russia's critical heritage and accomplishments in an ideologically unconstrained environment.

Although a public Russian literary-critical idiom started to develop in the early years of the nineteenth century with Ivan Krylov and Nikolai Karamzin, the first real flowering of journals with a regular literary section started in the 1830s. During the preceding hundred years, after Peter the Great had opened the door wide to Western political and cultural influences, literary-critical life was centred on the imperial court. It focused in part on rewriting French neo-classical prescriptions for good literature and, later, under Catherine the Great (reigned 1762–96), on social satire, particularly theatre. The issue of national identity, of contributing to the European family of nations as an independent partner, started with Karamzin's *Pantheon of Russian Authors* (1801–2), but developed fully in the generation of young Russian nobles who fought and won the Second Napoleonic War. Yearning for a constitutional monarchy and an end to serfdom, they staged the Decembrist uprising a decade later, in 1825. In the late 1820s and 1830s, inspired in part by the German Idealist thought of Herder, Schelling and Hegel, Russian intellectuals started to ask what positive aspects of contemporary culture one could call uniquely Russian. Writers explored the pre-Petrine past, Muscovite history, and folk culture in the vast rural districts of the Russian empire. When political action failed, literary criticism was the chief platform for this quest for national identity. At first, literary discussion was conducted *sub rosa*, in literary works themselves, in private letters, and within small groups of trusted friends among university students who gathered in the two capitals, St Petersburg and Moscow. During the mid-1830s, literary criticism emerged as a profession, and, along with articles on history, science and topics of current interest, it became an integral part of that longstanding institution of public Russian writing culture, the 'thick journal'.

By 1830, Russia's great poet Aleksandr Pushkin (1799–1837) started to publish reviews, generally anonymously or under a pseudonym, in Baron Delvig's *Literaturnaia gazeta* ('Literary Gazette') and in *Teleskop* ('Telescope'). He called for a fuller, more sophisticated literary culture in which new works came into the public eye and received public discussion through critical reviews. Concerned to help establish the institution of literary criticism, in 1836 he founded the famous thick journal *Sovremennik* ('The Contemporary'), which later, in the 1850s, would occupy centre stage as the tribunal for the civic critics, starting with Nikolai Nekrasov and Nikolai Chernyshevsky. Although in such articles as 'Does the Public Need to Know?' and 'On Literary Criticism' (1830), Pushkin welcomed the birth of an active literary-critical culture, his own essays exercised only a limited influence. Suppressed by the censor, many saw the light of day only in the second half of the nineteenth century and, in some cases, only in the twentieth century.

By the mid-1830s Nikolai Gogol (1809–52) joined in the discussion about a national Russian literature. In his essay 'A Few Words about Pushkin' (written 1834, published 1835 in his compendium *Arabesques*), he hailed Pushkin as the 'Russian national [*natsional'nyi*] poet' and an ideally cultivated Russian type, 'as he may appear in 200 years'.[1] In his short essay 'On Ukrainian Songs' in *Arabesques*, he discussed Ukrainian, or, as he called it, 'Little Russian', folklore as a topic worthy of his Russian readers' attention. If in the Pushkin essay he wrote of the 'national' high culture or '*natsional'noe*', here Gogol devotes his attention to the roots of Russian poetry among the *narod*, the people. He finds the real source of Russian identity here, with the Slavic-based word *narodnoe*, instead of

---

[1] N. V. Gogol', 'Neskol'ko slov o Pushkine' in *Sobranie sochinenii*, 6 vols. (Moscow: GIKhL, 1953), vol. VI, p. 33.

the Latin-based 'national' or *natsional'noe*, imposed from above through state-sponsored Europeanization. Folk songs, Gogol claims, are a veritable archive of 'popular history', lively and colourful, 'setting forth the whole life of the people'.[2]

Although Pushkin and Gogol were among the first to give voice to crucial social and national issues, Russia's first professional critic, Vissarion Belinsky (1811–48), made these questions the very foundation of the Russian critical enterprise. The first venue for the emerging national debate was Nikolai Nadezhdin's Moscow journal, *Teleskop*. This journal closed in 1836 after the publication of philosopher Petr Chaadaev's provocative 'Philosophical Letter', in which he castigated Russians for their derivative culture, lacking history and substance. The participants in the debate unleashed by Chaadaev's brave act, Westernizers, such as Belinsky, and Slavophiles, such as the critic Konstantin Aksakov and the philosopher Aleksei Khomiakov, also started their careers in *Teleskop*. In his first important article, 'Literary Reveries' (1834), Belinsky presented the generally Romantic view of literature as an expression of higher consciousness and national diversity, and offered a semi-ironic elegy on the possibility of a Russian national literature.[3]

Belinsky's aesthetic theory stemmed from the German Idealist tradition, particularly Herder, Schelling and Hegel. Although, he fundamentally agreed with Kant's separation of aesthetic appeal from practical sensual, moral or political interest, Belinsky built his main critical practice on Schelling's and Hegel's 'organicist' aesthetic philosophy, which would exert a continuing influence on the Russian critical tradition.[4] He saw works of art (and, in particular, literature) as an integral expression of the world-soul, internally linked to other levels of being through inner form and higher vision. In his view, works of art held a higher status than works of nature. Belinsky believed in the strong cognitive and prophetic role of art: because it participates in the higher, hidden, more 'real' substance of the world, that is, thought thinking itself, artistic intuition is able to reveal psychological, historical and social truths before science and reason can.[5] In contrast to Hegel's hierarchy of discourses, in which philosophy occupies the crowning position, Belinsky reasoned that literary art was the more powerful because it possesses this intuitive prophetic

---

[2] N. V. Gogol', 'O malorossiiskikh pesniakh' in *Sobranie sochinenii*, vol. VI, p. 67. See also V. I. Kuleshov, *Istoriia russkoi kritiki: 18.–19. vv.*, 2nd edn (Moscow: Prosveshchenie, 1978), p. 137.

[3] Francis B. Randall, *Vissarion Belinskii* (Newtonville: Oriental Research Partners, 1987), p. 51.

[4] Victor Terras, *Belinskij and Russian Literary Criticism: The Heritage of Organic Aesthetics* (Madison: University of Wisconsin Press, 1974), p. 48.

[5] *Ibid.*, pp. 15–16.

vision.[6] In his major aesthetic statement of 1841, 'The Idea of Art' (1859), Belinsky famously asserted that art is the '*immediate* contemplation of truth', or 'thinking [expressed] in *images*'.[7] Art is always much more than a reflection *of* the world: it is a reflection *on* the world.

Finally, with Herder and Hegel, Belinsky viewed literary art as a crucial expression of nationhood.[8] On this theoretical basis, he conceived what we might call a theory of national type: literary characters gain depth and originality in so far as they embody an essential national idea that informs concrete social, historical and psychological circumstances. For Belinsky in his 1835 article 'Gogol and the Russian Tale', it was Gogol, rather than Pushkin, who epitomized the 'national [*narodnyi*]'.[9] *Narodnost'* Belinsky defined as 'faithfulness in depiction of mores, customs, and character' of a people.

Among his major achievements, Belinsky was the first Russian critic to speak of the 'real' as a literary category. While the French, who popularized literary Realism in the 1850s, related this concept to scientific empiricism, Belinsky related it to the Hegelian concept of the 'real' as higher 'rationality'.[10] By these terms Belinsky meant that literary characters could be considered 'real' if they became 'vessels of the spirit', that is, if they embodied more than just their particular life experience and aimed for that higher self-consciousness towards which, in Hegel's theory, 'world-historical' peoples and nations have striven for centuries.[11] Art, in Belinsky's view, should not imitate mere sensory reality: the 'real' is that which combines exact local, 'present', social observation with higher 'rational' truth.[12] It should be noted that in Russia Aleksandr Herzen was the first to use the term 'Realism' in his 1846 essay 'Letters on the Study of Nature'.[13] In 1849 the critic Pavel Annenkov replaced Belinsky's term 'naturalness' with 'Realism'.[14] Although he never employed the term 'Realism', Belinsky did use the term 'real' [*deistvitel'nyi* or *real'nyi*] from his 1835 article on Gogol onwards, in which he had examined 'real poetry'. He differentiated here between 'ideal' and 'real' poetry, finding

6  Edith W. Clowes, *Fiction's Overcoat: Russian Literary Culture and the Question of Philosophy* (Ithaca, NY: Cornell University Press, 2004), p. 40.

7  V. G. Belinskii, 'Ideia iskusstva' in *Sobranie sochinenii*, 13 vols. (Moscow: Akademiia nauk, 1953–9), vol. IV, p. 585. Italics are in the original.

8  There is some disagreement about the date when the Russian-root word '*narodnost*'' or 'nationality' was first coined by Prince P. A. Viazemsky. Terras claims that it was in 1817 (*Belinskij*, pp. 17–18), while Wayne Dowler suggests 1819 in *Dostoevsky, Grigor'ev, and Native Soil Conservatism* (University of Toronto Press, 1982), p. 25.

9  V. G. Belinskii, 'O russkoi povesti i o povestiakh Gogolia' in *Sobranie sochinenii* (1953–9), vol. I, p. 295.

10  Rene Wellek, *History of Modern Criticism, 1750–1950*, 8 vols. (Cambridge University Press, 1983), vol. III, pp. 244–5.

11  V. G. Belinskii, 'Gore ot uma' in *Sobranie sochinenii* (1953–9), vol. III, p. 436.

12  Terras, *Belinskij*, p. 161.    13  Kuleshov, *Istoriia*, p. 301.    14  *Ibid.*, p. 301.

the latter in prose genres, the tale and the novel, which, in his view, offered a superior expression of a concrete historical moment.

Russian Realism began to be developed in the 1840s by the young writers Fedor Dostoevsky, Ivan Turgenev and Ivan Goncharov, with strong guidance and encouragement from Belinsky. He had nudged Dostoevsky away from the fantastic towards the real, hailing the young writer's burgeoning talent in his first long work, *Poor People*, and castigating him for the fantastic novella *The Double*. Similarly, in his last article, 'Russian Literature in 1847', Belinsky guided Turgenev away from poetry to prose writing.[15] Here he admired the very first of Turgenev's stories and physiological sketches from Russian life, later compiled as *Sketches from a Hunter's Notebook* (1852).

Despite his concern with raising Russian readers' social consciousness and focusing literary art on Russian 'reality', in distinction from later civic critics, Belinsky insisted on art's independence from ideological demands and its unique combination of artifice and naturalness. In the 1830s, he held that, because it expresses a form of spiritual truth, 'artistic truth' does not need to coincide formally with the empirical truth of science and history. Although in the 1840s, after his break with conservative Hegelianism, Belinsky embraced an 'objective' concept of truth and insisted ever more fervently on the social relevance of art, he still held to the view that the real and the true must be a function of higher reason.[16] As he wrote in his 1840 essay on the real in the famous play *Woe from Wit*, by Russia's premier dramatist of the early 1820s, Aleksandr Griboedov: 'A person drinks, eats, and dresses – this is a world of phantoms ... but when a person feels, thinks, and recognizes himself as an organ, a vessel of the spirit, a finite particle of the general and the infinite – this is the world of reality.'[17]

In the mid-1840s, Belinsky started to use the term 'natural' to speak of the materially observable. Earlier, in his Gogol essay of 1835, he had dubbed Gogol the writer of the 'real' (*real'noe*), the 'positive' (*polozhitel'noe*) and the 'actual' (*deistvitel'noe*).[18] Now, ten years later, in 1845, he gave his imprimatur to the Natural School (*Natural'naia shkola*) headed by the poet and editor of *Sovremennik*, Nikolai Nekrasov (1821–78). Belinsky wrote a long article for Nekrasov's 1845 miscellany *The Physiology of Petersburg*. In his review, 'Russian Literature in 1845', Belinsky identified the 'national' increasingly with the life of the masses of ordinary people and, in literature, with Nekrasov's Natural

[15] V. G. Belinskii, 'Vzgliad na russkuiu literaturu 1847 goda' in *Sobranie sochinenii* (1953–9), vol. x, p. 344.
[16] Terras, *Belinskij*, p. 82.
[17] Belinskii, 'Gore ot uma' in *Sobranie sochinenii* (1953–9), vol. III, p. 436.
[18] Belinskii, 'O russkoi povesti' in *Sobranie sochinenii*, (1953–9), vol. I, pp. 270, 291, 302.

School.[19] In his review of Nekrasov's first *Petersburg Miscellany* (1846), he hailed Dostoevsky as the leading light of the 'new' Russian literature and predicted a decisive role for him in Russia's literary future.[20] He wrote a fuller description of the principles of the Natural School in 'A Look at Russian Literature in 1846'. Following the social upheavals of 1848 any signs of progressive thought were firmly suppressed. The term 'Natural School' was outlawed and replaced with the euphemism 'Gogolian movement' (*gogolevskoe napravlenie*), which Chernyshevsky and other civic critics were obliged to use.[21]

Belinsky's view of literature as the bearer of enlightened social consciousness intensified throughout the 1840s, after his break with conservative Hegelianism in 1841. He characterized the role of criticism in his 1842 article 'A Speech about Criticism': criticism expresses the 'spirit of the time [*dukh vremeni*]', which he defined as the 'judgement and analysis of society'.[22] Belinsky's critical essays on the major literary talents of his day, Gogol (1835), Griboedov (1840), Lermontov (1841) and Pushkin (1843–6), always functioned as masked social criticism. In his articles on Pushkin he linked the poet with Realism and described his novel in verse, *Evgeny Onegin*, as the 'encyclopedia of Russian life and a national [*narodnoe*] work in the highest degree'.[23] Probably the most disputed judgement in Belinsky's œuvre is his view of Gogol as a Realist writer with progressive social ideas, though he never used the word 'Realist' to describe Gogol. Although Belinsky was certainly justified in pointing out the social aspects of Gogol's art, he was mistaken in believing that Gogol desired the same reforms as he did. Formidable Modernist critics of the early twentieth century, among them Dmitry Merezhkovsky, Andrei Belyi and Vasily Rozanov, toppled Belinsky's prevalent view, arguing that Gogol was a metaphysical, comic or absurd writer, anything but Realist.

In the 1840s, literary criticism became an important forum for the Slavophile–Westernizer debate about Russia's history and identity. The Westernizers (particularly Belinsky, Herzen and Turgenev) affirmed Peter's Westernizing reforms and believed that Russia should continue on the path to becoming a rational, law-abiding European state. In contrast, the Slavophiles (among them, the Aksakov family and Gogol) castigated Peter for denying Russians their medieval, Orthodox Christian roots.

---

[19]  V. G. Belinskii, 'Russkaia literatura v 1845 godu' in *Sobranie sochinenii* (1953–9), vol. IX, p. 382.

[20]  V. G. Belinskii, 'Peterburgskii sbornik' in *Sobranie sochinenii*, vol. IX, pp. 475–6.

[21]  Hugh McLean, 'Realism' in *Handbook of Russian Literature*, ed. V. Terras (New Haven, CT: Yale University Press, 1986), p. 366.

[22]  V. G. Belinskii, 'Rech' o kritike' in *Sobranie sochinenii* (1953–9), vol. VI, p. 271.

[23]  V. G. Belinskii, 'Sochineniia Aleksandra Pushkina' in *Sobranie sochinenii* (1953–9), vol. VII, p. 503.

They generally affirmed serfdom and the patriarchal agrarian life as being 'natural' and insisted that all Russians, rich and poor, free and enserfed, were joined by the organic bonds of life-giving, spiritual community, or *sobornost*. The Westernizers migrated to the St Petersburg journals, *Otechestvennye zapiski* ('Annals of the Fatherland') and *Sovremennik*, while the Slavophiles were generally located in Moscow, associated with the journals *Moskvitianin* ('The Muscovite') and the relatively short-lived *Moskovskii sbornik* ('Moscow Miscellany').

   Many of the Westernizers and Slavophiles had studied at university together in the 1830s and had been close friends. They shared a broad approach to literature based largely on German Idealist philosophy. Among the most gifted of this group was Ivan Kireevsky (1806–56), who searched for a philosophical grounding for literary criticism and called for Russian intellectuals to go beyond European forms of thought. In his early series of outstanding articles on Pushkin, such as 'On the Character of Pushkin's Poetry' (1828), and surveys of Russian letters for 1829 and 1831, he became the first critic to speak of Pushkin as a 'poet of reality', and to discuss particularly Pushkin's treatment of 'Russian reality' (*russkaia deistvitel'nost'*). Belinsky later adopted this concept from Kireevsky to work out his own influential idea of Realism.[24] The debate between advocates of Westernization and Slavophiles had its roots in a number of different areas, including history and philosophy as well as literary-critical disagreements. In 1842, for example, Belinsky parted ways with his old friend from student days, Konstantin Aksakov (1817–60), over divergent interpretations of Gogol's *Dead Souls*. Aksakov, who later became a leading voice among the most conservative Slavophiles, appreciated Gogol's masterpiece as a 'Homeric' epic, a work that did the Slavs proud. Belinsky, on the other hand, focused on the contemporary social ills that he found reflected in the text.[25]

   An important development in criticism closer to the Westernizer side of the debate was the work of three important critics – Vasily Botkin, Pavel Annenkov and Aleksandr Druzhinin – each of whom argued for the independence of art from ideology. All had been friends or colleagues of Belinsky, and all were against serfdom. The oldest of them was Vasily Botkin (1811–69), a member of the Moscow literary-philosophical circles in the 1830s. During these years he helped his good friend Belinsky, who had no usable knowledge of foreign languages, to understand post-Hegelian German thought. When in the 1850s a new generation of socially committed critics grew more intense and one-sided, he came to the view that political debate and dogma were the 'death of art'.[26] In his

---

[24] Kuleshov, *Istoriia*, p. 204.    [25] *Ibid.*, pp. 209–11.    [26] Quoted in *ibid.*, p. 223.

later essays, for example 'The Poetry of A. A. Fet' (1857), he defended the aesthetic independence of poetry.

In the 1840s, Pavel Annenkov (1813–87) wrote letters from Europe for *Otechestvennye zapiski*. He was the first Russian critic to use the term 'Realism' (*realizm*), in an article of 1849, 'Notes on Russian Literature of 1848', published in *Sovremennik*. His use of the term focused on the faithful depiction of ordinary life.[27] In the 1850s, despite his strong belief in social reform and the end of serfdom, Annenkov became something of a counterweight to the new generation of socially orientated critics as their tone became more strident. He published a volume of critical essays, *On the Meaning of Literature for Society*, in which he argued for the freedom of art from ideological concerns. In addition, Annenkov was active as a scholar and memoirist. In 1855 he published the first critical edition of Pushkin's works, in seven volumes. His famous memoirs, *The Extraordinary Decade*, published in 1880, created a powerful historical image of the 1840s with its portraits of the most famous Slavophiles and Westernizers.

The third aesthetically orientated critic was Aleksandr Druzhinin (1824–64). Although early on Druzhinin supported the important social role of literature, in the 1850s he too grew hostile to the ever more strident socially engaged camp and argued for an aesthetic independent of ideological interests. In one of his noted essays, 'A Critique of the Gogolian Period' (1856), he spoke out against Belinsky's 'Realist', socially progressive reading of Gogol, which the next generation, led by Nikolai Chernyshevsky, had turned into social dogma. In addition, he argued that Belinsky had misjudged the heroine of Pushkin's *Evgeny Onegin*, Tatyana Larina, and criticized his overestimation of George Sand's novels.[28] Druzhinin also criticized Ivan Turgenev for ruining his art by entering into contemporary political debates.[29]

Worried about a resurgence of socially progressive sentiment, the censorship banned mention of Belinsky's name between his death in 1848 and the death in 1855 of the oppressive 'gendarme of Europe', Emperor Nicholas I.[30] In this period of relative stagnation, post-Westernizer and post-Slavophile forces were developing that bloomed in the late 1850s and 1860s, when Russian society sprang to life during the Great Reforms of Emperor Alexander II, which led to major judicial and educational reforms and, finally, in 1861, to the abolition of serfdom. The most famous post-Westernizer critics were the utilitarian, 'civic' critics, led by Nikolai Chernyshevsky (1828–89), who viewed literature as a vehicle for raising social consciousness and spurring increasingly radical demands for social change. As a young critic and journalist,

[27] *Ibid.*, p. 225.   [28] *Ibid.*, p. 219.   [29] *Ibid.*, p. 221.   [30] *Ibid.*, p. 216.

Chernyshevsky admired Belinsky's social commitment, the social determinism he saw in the English utilitarians Jeremy Bentham and John Stuart
Mill, and the philosophical anthropology of the left-Hegelian philosopher
Ludwig Feuerbach. Starting in 1855 as the chief literary critic at *Sovremennik*, Chernyshevsky dictated progressive literary taste in the 1860s,
much as Belinsky had in the 1840s. In 1855, he defended his master's
thesis, 'The Aesthetic Relation of Art to Reality'. Here he argued that
'reality' – by which he meant material actuality – is far superior to art,
which is at best a 'reproduction' of reality and has value not so much for
its reflection of reality as for its rhetorical and didactic depictions.[31] In
brief, art should be a 'living judgement on phenomena'.[32]

In general, Chernyshevsky, a cruder critic than Belinsky, aimed to
replace art with didactic discourses on socioeconomic 'reality'. In his
first major critical study, 'Studies in the Age of Gogol' (1856), he revived
interest in Belinsky, now that it had again become possible to discuss
his ideas openly. Chernyshevsky expounded a utilitarian literary theory,
seeing literature as a mirror in which Russians could view and evaluate themselves and their society.[33] In his major philosophical work *The
Anthropological Principle in Philosophy* (1860), he argued that literary
expression is conditioned by social factors and that writers should serve
ideological purposes. Significantly, as editor of *Sovremennik*, Chernyshevsky alienated the journal's leading young literary stars, Lev Tolstoy
and Ivan Turgenev, even as he won to his side a whole generation of
university students.[34]

In 1857 Chernyshevsky gave up his literary pulpit at *Sovremennik* to
Nikolai Dobrolyubov (1836–61) and turned his attention to what he
viewed as more pressing economic and political issues and to co-editing
the entire journal. The next generation of literary 'activists', known as
'Young Russia' – particularly Dobrolyubov and Dmitry Pisarev – conducted a full frontal attack on the arts and the aesthetic as a category
of human thought and endeavour.[35] Of all the arts, they salvaged literature alone for its social utility. Dobrolyubov was interested in literary
art as a method of diagnosing social ills. His essays retain their historical significance primarily because of their fearlessly critical social views
and because they spurred a debate with the post-Slavophile *pochvenniki*
('men of the native soil'), particularly Fedor Dostoevsky. In his critiques

[31] N. Chernyshevsky, *Sochineniia*, ed. I. K. Pantin, 2 vols. (Moscow: ANSSSR, 1986–7),
vol. I, p. 156.
[32] *Ibid.*, p. 166.       [33] *Ibid.*, vol. I, p. 302.
[34] Leonard Schapiro, *Turgenev: His Life and Times* (Cambridge, MA: Harvard University
Press, 1978), pp. 156–7.
[35] Abbott Gleason, *Young Russia: The Genesis of Russian Radicalism in the 1860s* (New
York: Viking, 1980), pp. 171–2.

of plays by Nikolai Ostrovsky, 'The Kingdom of Darkness' (1859) and 'A Ray of Light in the Kingdom of Darkness' (1860), Dobrolyubov praised Ostrovsky as an offshoot of the Natural School, whose plays exposed the ignorance of Russia's merchant estate. In 'What is Oblomovism?' (1859) Dobrolyubov saw in Goncharov's character Oblomov from the eponymous novel a symbol of the sluggishness of Russian life, which it behove the young generation to correct.

Dmitry Pisarev (1840–68), the one professed nihilist and the most talented among this group, actually tried to destroy the value and credibility of the literary art on which he was commenting. He believed fervently in the power of science and education, and used examples from literature in his articles to popularize science. Pisarev argued that in the age of science one no longer needed literature. In 'The Abolition of Aesthetics' (1865) and 'Pushkin and Belinskii' (1865) he stood against aesthetics as a category of value and in favour of an empirically based concept of 'truth'. In these articles he dismissed Pushkin and Gogol as belonging to the past. Pisarev read literature naïvely for its 'real-life' moral and social-political lessons. Literary terms became euphemisms for political attitudes – for example, 'Realist' meant 'revolutionary', and 'Realism' became shorthand for scientific materialism and political socialism. In his discussion of literature Pisarev emphasized social utility and 'truth content', viewing characters as powerful social types: he respected literary heroes as 'our teachers' and believed that 'we wouldn't be here without them'.[36] In 'The Realists' (1864), for example, he held up such activist characters as Turgenev's Bazarov (*Fathers and Sons*) and Chernyshevsky's Rakhmetov (*What Is To Be Done?*) as role models for young Russians.

While the civic critics dominated the literary scene, other, more talented critics developed different themes and directions. One of the last of the Westernizing generation, Ivan Turgenev, developed a version of typological criticism. His most famous essay, 'Hamlet and Don Quixote' (1860), stemmed from Belinsky's theory of national types. He delivered it as a lecture on 10 January 1860. Here Turgenev's two famous types are more than just the 'superfluous men' of the reign of Emperor Nicholas I, educated but without the will to change an oppressive society, or the revolutionaries, like Mikhail Bakunin, who fought in Paris but could do nothing at home. For Turgenev they represented two tragic moral types, Hamlet the sceptical egoist, the doubter who takes no action but inflicts suffering upon himself, and Don Quixote the dedicated idealist, ready to sacrifice himself for an elusive, even futile purpose.[37]

The most influential post-Slavophile criticism came from *pochvennichestvo* or the 'native soil' movement, a group of nationalist critics,

---

[36] Quoted in Kuleshov, *Istoriia*, p. 291.     [37] Schapiro, *Turgenev*, p. 149.

including the Dostoevsky brothers Mikhail and Fedor, Nikolai Strakhov and Apollon Grigoriev, which formed in the early 1860s around the Dostoevsky brothers' two journals, *Vremia* ('Time', 1861–3) and *Epokha* ('The Epoch', 1863–5). These writers and critics appropriated aspects of both Westernizing and Slavophile views. They recognized the value of the reforms introduced by Peter the Great but believed that Russians should synthesize acquired European, secular culture with their Eastern Orthodox traditions to forge their unique way into the future. The literary beliefs of the *pochvenniki*, or men of the native soil, combined progressive social concerns with a strong sense of pride in Russian history and culture. It left aside the mystic sense of mission of earlier Slavophiles but retained their strongly organicist critical approach to contemporary culture.

The *pochvenniki* moulded their position in debate with the civic critics and their radical social determinism. Among the most famous of these polemics was Fedor Dostoevsky's essay, 'Mr –bov and the Question of Art' (1861), which responded to Dobrolyubov's reviews, 'Features for the Characterization of the Russian Common People' (1860) and 'The Poems of Ivan Nikitich' (1860). These articles provided a snapshot of Dobrolyubov's anti-aesthetic criticism, highlighting his interest in art only in so far as it depicted the dignity of ordinary peasants and the oppressive conditions of their lives.[38] In his essay Dostoevsky struck a path between the critics interested only in aesthetic issues and the social utilitarian Dobrolyubov. He argued, much in Belinsky's vein, that great art functions in a social context, satisfies human needs and treats themes of contemporary interest, while also occupying an aesthetic sphere in which it is free to develop forms and style adequate to its thematic material. While Dostoevsky agreed that literary Realism was essential to contemporary art, he lambasted the utilitarians for their callousness towards the complexities of the human psyche and towards its spiritual and aesthetic dimension, even claiming that their ultimate goal was to eradicate art.[39] This essay was the first foray in a polemic that found classical expression in Part One of *Notes from Underground* (1864), in which the 'underground man' articulates his resentful, seemingly irrational challenge to the utilitarians, as if from the unconscious 'underground' of the human psyche.

Nikolai Strakhov (1828–96) was a crucial voice in formulating the middle position of the *pochvenniki* between the radically Westernizing civic, utilitarian critics and the cultivated but politically

---

[38] James P. Scanlan, *Dostoevsky the Thinker* (Ithaca, NY: Cornell University Press, 2002), pp. 123–4.
[39] *Ibid.*, p. 127; Dowler, *Dostoevsky*, p. 121.

conservative Slavophiles. Far from being an aesthetically orientated critic, like Pavel Annenkov or Aleksandr Druzhinin, or a social utilitarian, Strakhov believed in art's high moral purpose while also assuring art its own aesthetic sphere.[40] He was unique for his close relationship to the two greatest talents of the age, Dostoevsky and Tolstoy. In the 1860s Strakhov became one of Dostoevsky's staunchest promoters, at a time when few people were taking his talent seriously, writing, for example, a sympathetic review of *Crime and Punishment* in *Otechestvennye zapiski* in 1867. In addition, he played a creative role in Dostoevsky's literary career, providing him with the philosophical background for some of the ideas developed in his greatest novels.[41] Strakhov was also acquainted with Tolstoy. In his book *A Critical Analysis of War and Peace* (1871), he was the first to characterize Tolstoy as a 'psychological Realist', able to describe natural surroundings from characters' points of view and to bridge the gap between sensory reality and the ideal.[42] He recognized Tolstoy's metaphysical search as the core of his art. He was among the first critics to view works of Russian literature in the light of Russia's particular history and tradition, seeing, for example, *War and Peace* as a descendant of Pushkin's novel *The Captain's Daughter*. Another aspect of Strakhov's project was to call Russian writers to produce a new Russian hero that could bridge the 'humble' Russian 'little man' and the overbearing, 'predatory' Westerner.[43] In his review of Turgenev's *Fathers and Sons* in the Dostoevskys' journal *Vremia* in 1862, Strakhov admired Bazarov as a true Russian character.[44] Most of all, Strakhov and his fellow *pochvenniki* longed for the emergence of a Russian writer with the stature of Shakespeare.[45]

The seminal thinker among the *pochvennik* critics was Apollon Grigoriev (1822–64), who like Strakhov sought a middle way between the Westernizers and the Slavophiles. An early play, entitled *Two Egoisms* (1845), dealt with the Westernizing head of a socialist circle, Mikhail Petrashevsky, and the Slavophile Konstantin Aksakov. Grigoriev's ideas received further development in the work of both Fedor Dostoevsky and Strakhov. For six years, 1850–6, he worked as the editor of the moderately Slavophile journal *Moskvitianin*, which was committed less to criticizing European currents in contemporary Russia than to affirming Russian culture and history. Grigoriev's criticism lay directly in the organicist

---

40  See, for example, Strakhov's 'Zametki o Belinskom' in *Bor'ba s Zapadom v nashei literature* (St Petersburg: S. Dobrodeev, 1886), vol. III, for a distinctive *pochvennik* view of literature.
41  Clowes, *Fiction's Overcoat*, pp. 84–8.
42  Linda Gerstein, *Nikolai Strakhov* (Cambridge, MA: Harvard University Press, 1972), p. 83.
43  *Ibid.*, p. 87.    44  *Ibid.*, p. 96.    45  *Ibid.*, p. 89.

tradition. He used the term 'organic criticism' for the first time in 1859 in letters and reviews in *Russkoe slovo* ('The Russian Word'). Like Belinsky, he was an intellectual descendant of Herder and Schelling. Literature, for him, is not just the tendentious recapitulation of social actuality as the civic critics would have it. He agreed with Belinsky that art reveals truth through intuition and spontaneity (*neposredstvennost'*).[46] Grigoriev saw literature meshed with mores, social values and cultural habits as the intuitive re-enactment of the spiritual life of a nation. Indeed, he added to what Belinsky and others had achieved by drawing attention to questions of literary history: in his generally Hegelian view, 'the history of a nation's literature was the history of the organic progress of nationality toward self-consciousness'.[47]

Criticism, in Grigoriev's view as expressed in 'On Truth and Sincerity in Art' (1856), provides judgement of genuine art and relates it to the whole body of national literature. Following Belinsky, Grigoriev saw great literature in its best characters, which as 'types' blend individual consciousness with social, national and universal human qualities. The theory of types became central to the *pochvennik* belief in *narodnost'* or national character in cultural and social life. Grigoriev's contribution was to perceive Russian literature in terms of a historical process of development of a national canon: *pochvennik* literary criticism related literary 'recreations' (not reflections) to the national literary canon and to the life of the nation itself.[48] Each age, Grigoriev argued, has its own central personality. If Gogol was the central writer for the 1840s, then, in Grigoriev's view, the prolific Moscow playwright and satirist Nikolai Ostrovsky fulfilled that role in the 1850s. Grigoriev recognized the playwright Ostrovsky for his broad, humorous and optimistic view of Russian society. Finally, art, in Grigoriev's view, has prophetic powers. Grigoriev's specific critical achievements were to recognize the national significance of Pushkin's prose works, particularly *The Tales of Belkin*, and to recognize Gogol as an important religious thinker. In his attention to religious themes Grigoriev was certainly an important forerunner of the metaphysical criticism of the turn of the century.

The 1870s saw a new generation of socially engaged literary critics, particularly the populist journalist and sociologist Nikolai Mikhailovsky (1842–1904). From 1868 to 1884 Mikhailovsky edited Belinsky's journal *Otechestvennye zapiski*. In 1892 he became chief editor of the legal populist journal *Russkoe bogatstvo* ('Russian Wealth'), staying at that post until his death in 1904. Mikhailovsky was a political and cultural moderate among radicals. He moved beyond their social determinism and sought a form of socialism that encouraged each individual's

---

[46] Dowler, *Dostoevsky*, p. 43.    [47] *Ibid.*, pp. 33–4.    [48] *Ibid.*, p. 33.

self-realization. Although he agreed with the civic critics that literary art is first and foremost a vehicle of social commentary, he opposed Pisarev's radically anti-aesthetic nihilism. As a sociologist Mikhailovsky was interested in the social role of literature, but also tended to belittle the contribution of specific works of art. For example, in 'The Left and Right Hands of Count L. N. Tolstoy' (1875), he criticized what he saw as Tolstoy's simplistic and contradictory pedagogical theories. In his article 'A Cruel Talent' (1883), he criticized Dostoevsky as a psychologist scrutinizing human pathologies and as a stylistically uneven writer.

Perhaps surprisingly, Mikhailovsky was a significant early popularizer of the philosophy of Friedrich Nietzsche when the anti-rationalist philosopher was first becoming known in the early 1890s. The influence of civic criticism had gradually waned after the fiery political debates of the 1860s and 1870s. Chernyshevsky had been imprisoned, tried and exiled to Siberia. Dobrolyubov and Pisarev succumbed to untimely deaths. After Dostoevsky died in 1881, Turgenev in 1883, and Lev Tolstoy retreated to a religious, didactic form of writing, literary life experienced a serious decline. Nonetheless, by the early 1890s a generation of young poets led by Dmitry Merezhkovsky and Valery Bryusov engaged in more innovative metaphysical and cultural criticism. Nietzsche's popularity was just one of the signs of the times.

The first original and influential Russian academic critics also emerged at this time. The most prominent was Aleksandr Potebnya (1835–91), a Professor of Philology at Kharkov University. Potebnya's wife and students copied and published his lectures on linguistics and poetics, including *Lectures on the Theory of Writing Culture*.[49] A follower of the German linguist Wilhelm von Humboldt, Potebnya investigated the creative relationship between language and thought, focusing particularly on the semiotic nature of language. As he put it in an early work, *Thought and Language* (1862), 'language is a matter involving agreement' between speaker and listener; it is an 'assemblage of conventional signs'[50] that possess an 'internal form' encoded with a particular vision or valuation, standing '*for* something *to* someone *in* some circumstance'.[51] Potebnya differed from other early semioticians, such as Charles Sanders Peirce, in his view that this internal form of the sign was strongly shaped by ethno-psychology.[52]

49  Aleksandr Potebnia, *Iz lektsii po teorii slovesnosti* (Kharkov: K. Schasni, 1894), pp. 97–100, 123–9.
50  Aleksandr Potebnia, *Mysl' i iazyk* (Moscow: Labirint, 1999), p. 10.
51  John Fizer, *Aleksandr A. Potebnja's Psycholinguistic Theory of Literature: A Metacritical Inquiry* (Cambridge, MA: Harvard Ukrainian Research Institute, 1986), p. 2.
52  *Ibid.*, p. 3.

The other major academic critic of this period was Aleksandr
Veselovsky (1838–1906), a Professor of Comparative Literature and
Folklore at St Petersburg University and a member of the Academy
of Sciences. Among his most significant works were a brief history of
poetics published in 1894, his articles 'History or Theory of the Novel'
(1886) and 'Psychological Parallelism and its Forms in Reflections of
Poetic Style' (1898), and his book *The Poetics of Plot* (1897–1906). He
applied techniques of scientific positivism, leaving aside the Schellingian
and Hegelian assumptions of earlier critics and historians. Both Potebnya
and Veselovsky found an enthusiastic and profound response among the
early Formalists, for example Viktor Shklovsky and Boris Zhirmunsky.

Beginning with a reaction against the dominance of Realism in art and
the civic tradition in criticism, the late 1880s and 1890s saw an increase in
the wealth and complexity of Russia's literary culture. Now, again, literary criticism served as an important seedbed from which other discourses
sprang, this time particularly an innovative speculative philosophy. Following Schopenhauer, Solovyov and Nietzsche, literature, and especially
poetry, was valued as a form of both philosophical inquiry and mystical quest. Literary critics apprehended in literature the seeds of mystical
insight and cultural renewal. Starting with the criticism of Russia's greatest nineteenth-century philosopher, Vladimir Solovyov (1853–1900), one
finds a powerful actualization of Dostoevsky's dictum 'Beauty will save
the world.' In critical essays such as 'Three Talks in Memory of Dostoevsky' (1881–3), 'Beauty in Nature' (1889), 'The General Meaning
of Art' (1890) and 'The Poetry of Fedor Tyutchev' (1895), Solovyov
polemicized against the utilitarian, civic viewpoint and focused on art as
the embodiment of a sublime, mystical beauty. In 'The Poetry of Yakov
Polonsky' (1896), Solovyov framed the goals of the literary critic that
would dominate the early decades of Russian Modernism: to reveal the
roots of creativity in the poet's mind, roots which Solovyov found in
the poet's philosophical intuition.[53] Possibly his most concerted effort to
realize this critical role came with his three articles on Pushkin published
in *Vestnik Evropy* ('Herald of Europe') between 1897 and 1899. Here,
Solovyov attacked both civic and aestheticist interpretations of Pushkin
and devoted himself to understanding Pushkin's creative process.

Literary criticism was an integral part of the creative practice of most
Russian Modernist poets. They typically used criticism to set forth their
aesthetic programme as a manifesto, or to study the craft of a precursor.
Among the most influential critics (both personally and publicly) in the
early, formative years of Russian Symbolism were a husband and wife,

[53] See Heinrich Stammler, 'Vladimir Solov'ev as a Literary Critic', *Wiener Slavistisches Jahrbuch*, 19 (1973), p. 49.

the novelist Dmitry Merezhkovsky (1865–1941) and the poet Zinaida
Gippius (best known as a critic by her pseudonym Anton Krainy, 1869–
1945). Both grew up in the late populist period, reading Mikhailovsky,
Herbert Spencer and Auguste Comte, but became disillusioned with their
utilitarian-positivist view of culture. Each experienced a religious crisis,
which powered their search for a fruitful religious ground of cultural
rebirth. In 1901, to further their quest and to gather like-minded intellectuals, Gippius started the successful St Petersburg Religious-Philosophical
Meetings. They collaborated in various Modernist journals, including the
lavish *Mir iskusstva* ('World of Art'), and they edited their own journals, such as *Novyi put'* ('The New Way') and *Voprosy zhizni* ('Questions of Life') in which they reported the proceedings of the Religious-
Philosophical Meetings and propounded their new life-affirming concept
of religious culture. Zinaida Gippius published criticism of a new kind.
In *Mir iskusstva* and other Modernist journals she conveyed her aesthetic
judgements on prominent contemporary poets and writers as if engaging in an intimate conversation. She gathered these essays and published
them in 1908 under the title *Literary Diary, 1899–1907*. Together they
provide important insight into the nucleus of Russian Modernist culture
at the turn of the century.

Merezhkovsky's and Gippius's combination of seeking a life-affirming
religious belief and shaping a cultural rebirth became known as 'Godseeking' (*bogoiskatel'stvo*). In the 1890s, while the couple was travelling
in Europe, Merezhkovsky discovered ancient Greek and Roman culture.
Inspired by the famous classical historian Jacob Burckhardt and Nietzsche's tragic concept of culture, Merezhkovsky adopted Antiquity and
the Italian Renaissance as models for discerning cultural and religious
rebirth in contemporary Russia. He made effective use of criticism to
diagnose the current impoverished condition of literary culture and to
measure its rich possibilities. Starting in 1893 with his path-breaking
article 'On the Reasons for the Decline and on New Trends in Contemporary Russian Literature', he argued that Russia lacked an organic
literary culture, and laid the groundwork for a Symbolist aesthetic based
on the concept of the poem as the expression of 'primitive force', a 'direct
divine gift', something akin to theophany.[54]

With his ensuing critical essays Merezhkovsky celebrated the crowning achievements of Russia's greatest writers, thereby capturing the large
patterns of Russian literary history and its movement towards a metaphysical as well as aesthetic renaissance. In all his writings, whether novels
or essays, he shaped a myth tracing the failure of Christian asceticism and

---

[54]  D. Merezhkovskii, *O prichinakh upadka i o novykh techeniiakh sovremennoi russkoi
literatury* (St Petersburg: B. M. Vol'f, 1893), p. 3.

heralding the imminent 'Third Testament', the future synthesis of Christian self-discipline and pagan sensuality, a metanarrative to which most major Symbolist poets responded. Merezhkovsky's volume of articles *Eternal Companions* (1897) marshalled major poets and writers from Antiquity (Homer, Aeschylus, Marcus Aurelius, Dante) and modernity (Cervantes, Pushkin, Flaubert) as the 'classical' foundation for cultural rebirth. In *Tolstoy and Dostoevsky* (1901) Merezhkovsky challenged Mikhailovsky's positivist criticisms and probed the religious sensibility of the two great novelists. He discussed in an original way each writer's conception of corporeal being. Most originally, he emphasized the dramatic element in Dostoevsky's works and the particular voice of each of his characters, anticipating Mikhail Bakhtin's concept of 'polyphony'. In his remarks about Tolstoy in *Tolstoy and Dostoevsky* and about Gogol in *Gogol and the Devil* (1906), Merezhkovsky tackled the culture-spurning asceticism and its centuries-long roots in Russian life and religion. In 1911 he published *M. Iu. Lermontov*, in which he sought a life-affirming principle of moral regeneration in Russian culture in the works of Mikhail Lermontov, nineteenth-century Russia's most famous Romantic 'black sheep'.

A belated populist attack on the Modernists' forays into new, esoteric aesthetic territory came from the ageing Lev Tolstoy, who in 1898 published his tract *What is Art?* Here, he rejected Modernist experimentation in the arts – Wagner's opera, Nietzsche's philosophy, French and Russian Symbolist poetry. Tolstoy developed the theory that art is only valid when it is accessible to ordinary people and when it can 'infect' the reader with genuine moral feeling, creating a bond or sense of moral community between author and reader.[55]

The third major poet and critic of the 1890s who articulated a Modernist, 'Symbolist' aesthetic was the Moscow poet Valery Bryusov (1873–1924). His three compendia of experimental poetry, entitled *Russian Symbolists* (1894–1895), enjoyed a *succès de scandale*, which brought no lasting respect but rather the label of 'Decadent'.[56] In an effort to establish himself as the leading theorist of the new movement, Bryusov answered Tolstoy's anti-Modernist criticism in his own essay 'On Art' in 1899. Here, clearly affected by Tolstoy's tirade, he stepped away from his earlier worship of beauty and its pleasures for their own sake and stressed instead that poetry is a form of momentary communication between poet and reader, in which the reader gains insight into the poet's soul.[57] Still,

---

[55] Tolstoy adopted the term 'infect' from Eugène Véron's *L'Esthetique* (1878).
[56] See, for example, Vladimir Solovyov's review, 'O Briusove iz broshiury "Russkie simvolisty"' in *Sobranie sochinenii*, 12 vols. (Brussels: Foyer Oriental Chrétien, 1966), vol. VII, pp. 159–70.
[57] V. Briusov, *O iskusstve* (Moscow: A. I. Mamontov, 1899), pp. 8–12.

despite his Tolstoy-inspired observations about art as communication of higher feeling, the crucial quality of true art, in Bryusov's view, remains its freshness and originality. Bryusov's other notable essay was his introduction to the first issue of the Symbolist journal *Vesy* ('The Scales'), 'The Keys to the Mysteries', published in January 1904.[58] Offering a programmatic statement for the journal, Bryusov rehearsed the usual Symbolist concept of art as higher, intuitive cognition. Although he argued that it is the province of science to describe the phenomena of the world accessible to the senses, art is more exalted because it illuminates and reveals the mysteries of the universe through the artist's intuition. A classicist and poetic craftsman at heart, Bryusov was now sounding some of the mystical themes first expressed by Solovyov, Merezhkovsky and Gippius.

During the 1890s and 1900s, as a diverse critical culture was developing among Modernist poets, politically engaged intellectuals were struggling to combine older civic critical thought with the newest radical political theory, Marxism. Russia was now undergoing broad industrialization, and its cities swelled with peasants seeking work in the factories. The Marxists soon adopted them as their new proletariat, the social force that would bring about revolution and a new, more just society. Marx had offered no clear approach to literary criticism, and Georgy Plekhanov (1856–1918) and other Marxist critics were anxious to delineate a Marxist aesthetic and to make literature relevant to the socioeconomic transformations around them. Plekhanov's aesthetic combined Marxist sociology with aspects of a Kantian aesthetic. His *Letters with No Address* (1899–1900) defined art as part of society's superstructure, which, while dependent on the historical development of social and economic trends, also occupied an aesthetic sphere of its own. In a series of studies on Belinsky (1897), Chernyshevsky (1897) and Dobrolyubov (1911), Plekhanov contrasted his aesthetic view with those of earlier civic critics, who, he argued, did not emphasize the historical development of literature and often ignored its special aesthetic dimension.

The founder of the Soviet state, Vladimir Lenin (1870–1924), envisioned a much narrower role for literature than Plekhanov had. He clearly subjugated art to political interests, and, in the era of revolution, specifically to the revolutionary needs of the Social Democratic Party. In his most influential work, the brief essay 'On Party Organization and Party Literature', written during the first revolution of 1905, Lenin argued for developing a body of literature loyal to the Social Democratic Party that would serve as part of the ideological arm of the political struggle. Following the general view of literature set forth by his greatest literary hero, Chernyshevsky, Lenin urged socially engaged writers to use

[58] V. Briusov, 'Kliuchi tain', *Vesy*, 1 (1904), 3–21.

their art to raise the political consciousness of Russia's nascent working class. He called for the development of new proletarian heroes to inspire ordinary Russians. In his tract he coined the concept of 'party loyalty' (*partiinost'*), the notion that art should take its moral, thematic and ideological guidance from the Social Democratic Party. Along with *narodnost'* and *ideinost'*, or ideologically correct thinking, *partiinost'* would in 1934 become one of the three pillars of Stalinist socialist realism.

Towards the end of the 1890s, before Lenin developed his narrowly utilitarian concept of party literature, a few critics gathered around Russia's most popular writer of the early twentieth century, Maksim Gorky (A. M. Peshkov, 1868–1936), to work out a more creative role for literary criticism within a Marxist worldview. The Nietzschean-Marxist critic Andreevich (pseudonym of Evgeny Solovyov, 1863–1905) was hired by Gorky's publisher to write a critical text with two goals in mind: to sell more books and to raise a more aggressive social-political consciousness. In the resulting book, *Maksim Gorky and A. P. Chekhov* (1900), Andreevich emphasized the new 'Nietzschean' voluntarism that readers of Gorky's stories found so inspiring.[59] In 1905, rocked by workers' strikes and political revolt across the empire, Gorky spearheaded the 'Godbuilding' movement among a few Russian Marxist writers and philosophers. This group borrowed the symbolists' mythopoetic narrative of Godseeking, changing it into a more provocative Godbuilding myth of the transformation of the working masses into a Promethean collective possessed of world-creative genius, will and energy. In 'An Essay in the Philosophy of Russian Literature' (1905), Andreevich discussed the history of the concept of *lichnost'* or personhood in Russian literature and discerned a monumental concept of mass personhood emerging in Russian socially engaged art.

The Marxist critic Anatoly Lunacharsky (1875–1933) wrote two major essays in which he defined the pathos of the Godbuilding movement. In 'Dialogue on Art' (1905) Lunacharsky captured the aggressively cheerful mood of the rebelling collective of workers who welcome 'more light, more struggle, more energy, life'.[60] In his review of Gorky's play *Summerfolk* (1905), he welcomed the notion of a mass hero who would destroy outmoded beliefs and forge new world visions. In 'The Tasks of Social Democratic Art' (1907) Lunacharsky contrasted the new Godbuilding writer with the old, 'pitying' utilitarian. The former spoke for the politically self-aware proletariat, ready to take charge and chart a new historical course.[61]

---

[59] Edith W. Clowes, *The Revolution of Moral Consciousness: Nietzsche in Russian Literature, 1892–1914* (DeKalb: Northern Illinois University Press, 1988), pp. 177–8.
[60] A. Lunacharskii, quoted in *ibid.*, p. 206.     [61] *Ibid.*, p. 204.

One of the vital characteristics of literary criticism in the Modernist period was its philosophical nature. The philosopher and journalist Vasily Rozanov (1856–1919) wrote book-length studies on writers who focused on philosophical issues. Rozanov's first major work of criticism, *The Legend of the Grand Inquisitor* (1894), as the first text to appreciate the philosophical depth of Dostoevsky's moral thought, proved to be a critical milestone. In two articles on Gogol attached to the 1906 edition of *The Legend of the Grand Inquisitor* and later in other essays in *Among the Artists* (1914), Rozanov strongly disagreed with Belinsky's view of Gogol as a Realist, arguing instead that Pushkin was the real founder of Russian Realism. Rozanov began to produce an aphoristic form of philosophy, for example in *Solitaria* (*Uedinennoe*, 1912) and *Fallen Leaves* (*Opavshie list'ia*, 1913–15), that combined trenchant critiques of radical aesthetics, brilliant insights into contemporary literature and culture, and a private, lyrical religious sensibility.

Lev Shestov (Leib Shvartsman, 1866–1938), a lawyer and mathematician by training, started to write literary criticism, which soon merged into philosophical inquiry. For example, he thought of Shakespeare as his 'first philosophy teacher', and his first critical work, *Shakespeare and His Critic Brandes* (1896), offered an interesting critique of Kantian thought in the light of the moral insights of the Bard.[62] Shestov's early classic of philosophical criticism, *L. Tolstoy and Nietzsche* (1899), focused on Tolstoy's moral philosophy against the background of Kantian ethics and Nietzsche's critique thereof. In *Dostoevsky and Nietzsche: The Philosophy of Tragedy* (1902), Shestov presented philosophizing as a tragic, existential process of seeking. In later essays, he experimented with fragments and aphorisms that are overtly orientated towards one writer but explore universal conditions and experiences. His best work in this vein was *The Apotheosis of Groundlessness* (1905), devoted to the ageing Turgenev's experience of death.

The third major critic to bridge the gap between criticism and philosophy was the Christian existentialist Nikolai Berdyaev (1874–1948). His major work of philosophical criticism, *Dostoevsky's Worldview*, came at the end of the Russian civil war in 1921. Here, he claimed Dostoevsky (and not Solovyov, as many contemporaries supposed) as the primary inspiration for the rich development of philosophy in Russia in the two decades before the revolution. Dostoevsky's art opens up new worlds of human potential and transports humankind beyond mere necessity. Instead of providing abstract systems, Dostoevsky shows the dramatic process of ideas developing in the minds of his characters, which Berdyaev took to be the very stuff of his key concept of the 'creative act'.

---

[62]  Quoted in Clowes, *Fiction's Overcoat*, p. 134.

If the first generation of Symbolists – Merezhkovsky, Gippius and Briusov – had reorientated Russian literary life, the second generation produced even more gifted critics. Viacheslav Ivanov (1866–1949) and Andrei Belyi (1880–1934), viewing poetry as a door leading to insight into a higher cosmic order, used original tropic and structural analysis as a way to open that door. They anticipated aspects of formalist, structuralist, archetypal and cultural criticism in the twentieth century. Aleksandr Blok (1880–1921), typically acknowledged as the greatest poet of Russian Modernism, wrote literary and cultural essays that read like stylized extensions of his poetic works. Between 1907 and 1909 he edited the literary-critical section of the modernist journal *Zolotoe runo* ('The Golden Fleece'), where he published a number of his most famous essays. Blok's best-known criticism, for example 'On Lyric Poetry' (1907) and 'On the Contemporary Condition of Russian Symbolism' (1910), was written towards the end of the Symbolist period, when he became disillusioned with his own, Solovyov-inspired concept of the poet as seer and lyric poetry as a means to mystical insight. Of still greater concern to him in other essays, such as 'The People and the Intelligentsia' (1908), devoted to Maksim Gorky, and 'Elemental Force and Culture' (1908), was the widening gap he sensed between the layers of Russian society, the educated elite and ordinary people. Blok expressed apocalyptic forebodings about the future of high culture, which he saw teetering on the edge of the abyss.

Andrei Belyi was perhaps the most erudite and most restless mystical spirit of the Modernist age. He spent his life trying to build a unified philosophy of spiritual and cultural regeneration, a project that met with little success but produced some of the most interesting literary and critical works of the era. Beginning in the early years of the twentieth century he read widely in classical, European and Russian philosophy and Romantic literature, attempting to discern the signs of regeneration. Since he perceived human cognition to be essentially related to language, Belyi used all avenues of verbal expression to pursue his goal of opening the path to cosmic regeneration – poetry, criticism and theoretical articles. He wrote many reviews for Bryusov's Symbolist journal *Vesy*, which were later collected in three volumes, *The Green Meadow* (1910), *Symbolism* (1910) and *Arabesques* (1911). These volumes contain such important Symbolist essays as 'The Art of the Future' (1907), 'Symbolism' (1908), 'Lyrics and Experiment' (1909) and 'The Magic of Words' (1909). Like Bryusov and Merezhkovsky, Belyi was an outstanding philologist and later wrote longer studies of individual writers, most famously *The Mastery of Gogol* (1934).

Viacheslav Ivanov, classicist and poet, was the leading theorist of the younger Symbolists, and arguably the most brilliant critic of the Symbolist age as a whole. He developed the metaphysical critical approach begun by Solovyov, using criticism to theorize the mystical Symbolist concept of art as theophany. Clothed in the discourse of neo-Platonism, Ivanov's articles registered sharp and original insights into mythopoetic structures underlying Russian Romantic and Symbolist poetry. In his essays he drew parallels between Russian poetry and the ancient Greek canon. Following Nietzsche's *The Birth of Tragedy*, Ivanov made a contribution to the study of ancient Greek ritual and its impact upon early Christianity in his series of lectures 'The Hellenic Religion of the Suffering God' (published in *Novyi put'*, 1904) and in his doctoral dissertation, *Dionysos and Pre-Dionysism* (1923). In 1904, he began to contribute critical essays on contemporary cultural issues to *Vesy* and *Voprosy zhizni*, and in 1906 to the new, lavish literary journal, *Zolotoe runo*. He collected his essays in two books, *Following the Stars* (1909) and *Furrows and Landmarks* (1916).

Modernist criticism often focuses on the poet's self-definition and debate with competing literary groups in the form of programmatic statements and manifestos. The Symbolists can be considered Modernists rather than neo-Romantics in this sense, and the complex of literary groups and movements that succeeded them only deepened this approach to the critical enterprise. Symbolism having lost its lustre by 1910, a number of directions emerged in Modernist criticism. As the poet Mikhail Kuzmin suggested with his essay title 'On Beautiful Clarity' (1910), poets were striving for 'clarity' and palpability, exploring existence in historical time and physical, cultural space. A number of different movements revolted against the mystical vagaries of Symbolism, the Acmeists in favour of craft and precision, and the various Futurists in favour of complete liberation of language from thought. Avant-garde poets as diverse as the Cubo-Futurists Vladimir Mayakovsky and Velimir Khlebnikov, the erstwhile Centrifuge poet Boris Pasternak, and other Modernists such as the Acmeists Osip Mandelshtam and Anna Akhmatova, were probing the nature of literary language, its relation to the sensory world and its inherent history and traditions. Since Russian avant-garde criticism is treated elsewhere in this volume, we close with a brief sketch of the Acmeists.

Embracing the older, Decadent poet Innokenty Annensky (1855–1909) as their 'mentor', the Acmeist poets published in *Apollon* ('Apollo', 1909–17). Their leader was Nikolai Gumilyov (1886–1921), who first defined the basic 'Acmeist' ideas of 'craftsmanship' and 'gesture' in an essay of 1910, 'The Life of Verse'.[63] Soon after, other programmatic essays appeared in *Apollon*, such as Gumilev's 'Acmeism and the Precepts of

---

[63] Nikolai Gumilev, 'The Life of Verse' in *Modern Russian Poets on Poetry*, ed. C. R. Proffer, intro. Joseph Brodsky (Ann Arbor: Ardis, 1976), pp. 23–32.

Symbolism' (1913) and Sergei Gorodetsky's 'Some Currents in Contemporary Russian Poetry' (1913). The best of these defining articles was Osip Mandelshtam's classic essay 'The Morning of Acmeism' (written in 1912 and published in 1919), in which the author compared the Acmeist poet with a mathematician or an architect, both of whom build their creations with precision.[64]

During the nineteenth century, both academic and public institutions of literary criticism burgeoned in Russia. Critics made original contributions to a number of literary trends, particularly Realism and various aspects of Modernism. We find three major directions in their criticism. The first was criticism as mediation between literature and society, a vehicle for the education of social consciousness. This form of criticism tended to be prescriptive, laying the groundwork for aspects of Russian sociology of culture, on the one hand, and the stultifying cultural policies of the Stalinist era, on the other. The second trend was the consideration of the literary work as an autonomous aesthetic object, an approach that anticipated the path-breaking insights of Formalism. Finally, Russian criticism was unusual in its focus on the intuitive epistemological function of literature as mediator between the world available to the senses and other philosophical or religious dimensions. This third concern had important implications for the development of a broad-ranging philosophical-cultural criticism, paving the way for the wonderful discoveries of a theorist familiar to English-speaking audiences, Mikhail Bakhtin.

[64]  Osip Mandelstam, *The Complete Critical Prose and Letters*, ed. J. G. Harris, trans. J.
      G. Harris and C. Link (Ann Arbor: Ardis, 1979), p. 62.

# III

## Critical movements and patterns of influence

# Literary autonomy: the growth of a modern concept

## HAROLD SCHWEIZER

Although the concept of the aesthetic is commonly traced back to Alexander Baumgarten's *Aesthetica* (1750 and 1758) and Johann Georg Hamann's *Aesthetica in nuce* ('Aesthetics in a Nutshell', 1762), Aristotle, with his famous stipulation that a tragedy have a beginning, a middle and an end, was the first to emphasize the structural integrity of literary form – a form that the Victorian Walter Pater (1839–94), at the other end of the historical spectrum, considered an 'architectural conception of work, which foresees the end in the beginning'.[1] As in the case of Aristotle, who sought to describe and legitimize tragedy against the moral objections Plato had raised, Baumgarten and Hamann aimed to establish aesthetics as justified on its own terms, apart from and in opposition to the rationalist philosophy of the eighteenth century. The causes for their advocacy of aesthetic autonomy, as Andrew Bowie points out, were not only 'the decline of theology and the disintegration of theologically legitimated social orders', but also the quantification and commodification of values, against which the aesthetic offered resistance.[2] The evolution and ideology of aesthetic autonomy through the nineteenth and twentieth centuries can thus be associated with religious, social and philosophical developments, in which contexts the autonomous aesthetic realm would not only provide a mental or spiritual refuge, but also justify a renunciation of history and culture radically transformed by the Industrial Revolution and expanding economic markets.

I

The notion of literary autonomy – popularized through the 'art for art's sake' movement in the nineteenth century – is the result of what one might call productive misappropriations of Immanuel Kant's

---

[1] Walter Pater, 'Style' in *Walter Pater: Three Major Texts*, ed. William E. Buckler (New York University Press, 1986), pp. 403–4. See also Kai Hammermeister, *The German Aesthetic Tradition* (Cambridge University Press, 2002), p. 15.

[2] Andrew Bowie, *Aesthetics and Subjectivity: From Kant to Nietzsche* (New York: St. Martin's Press, 1990), pp. 3–4.

(1724–1804) immensely influential aesthetic theory in his *Critique of Judgment* (1790). Indebted to Shaftesbury's and Hutcheson's unsystematic distinctions between beauty and utility, Kant conceives of the beautiful as neither a cognitive nor a conceptual category but a liking (*Wohlgefallen*) that is attained – spontaneously, freely and without interest – through the harmonizing of nature and the cognitive faculties. What Kant calls the 'free play' of the imagination is free to the extent that it comprises a harmonious response to 'flowers [that] are free natural beauties': 'we like them freely and on their own account' (§16).[3]

How we can like anything freely and on its own account is of course the crucial question implicit in the idea of aesthetic autonomy. Kant answers it by positing the subjective universality of taste. Because of the absence of interest or desire that would turn the beautiful object into an object of either knowledge or sensual gratification, Kant's concept of taste is not determinative but reflective. While subjective, taste is at the same time devoid of subjective determinants and limitations; it is thus universal. 'A *pure judgment of taste*', Kant insists, 'is one that is not influenced by charm or emotion... and whose determining basis is therefore merely the purposiveness of the form' (§13). Such mere forms, such free beauty (*pulchritudo vaga*) – free from meaning or mimetic obligations and thus from any kind of interest[4] – are, for example, 'designs *à la grecque*, the foliage on borders or on wallpaper' or 'music not set to words' (§16).

Judgements of taste are to be radically individual, autonomous, free from institutional or social constraints, free from empirical proofs or ideological traditions; they are not imitative or coerced, and are confirmed only by what Kant calls a 'deeply hidden basis, common to all human beings, underlying their agreement in judging the forms under which objects are given them' (§17). The same 'agreement', or what Kant also calls *sensus communis*, is still at work – necessarily without conscious effort or articulation – in public gatherings today to hear music or poetry, or to view exhibitions of art. Here, as in the aesthetic experience posited by Kant, we might be called upon to enter into an agreement to suspend private interests or circumstances in favour of exercising a 'free lawfulness of the imagination', so that 'our imagination is playing, as it were, while it contemplates the shape [of the object]' (§16).[5]

In the course of the nineteenth century, these Kantian propositions were taken up by such writers as Friedrich Schiller (1759–1805), Samuel

---

[3] Immanuel Kant, *Critique of Judgment*, trans. Werner S. Pluhar (Indianapolis: Hackett, 1987).

[4] As opposed to accessory beauty (*pulchritudo adhaerens*), which presupposes a concept because it is accessory to an object with a purpose, such as a church; see M. A. R. Habib, *A History of Literary Criticism: From Plato to the Present* (Malden: Blackwell, 2005), p. 373.

[5] See Hammermeister, *German Aesthetic Tradition*, p. 37.

Taylor Coleridge (1772–1834), Edgar Allan Poe (1809–49), Matthew Arnold (1822–88), Théophile Gautier (1811–72), Charles Baudelaire (1821–67), Stéphane Mallarmé (1842–98), Charles Algernon Swinburne (1837–1909), Walter Pater and Oscar Wilde (1854–1900). With varying interests and emphases, these writers derive from Kant's philosophy the concept of organic form, of aesthetic disinterestedness, of aesthetic education, of art as subversive of instrumental knowledge, as independent from conventions of taste and as resistant to institutional and political coercion. Thus, Matthew Arnold advocates a criticism which would exercise a *'disinterestedness ...* [b]y keeping aloof from what is called "the practical view of things"; by resolutely following the law of its own nature, which is to be a free play of the mind on all subjects which it touches. By steadily refusing to lend itself to any of those ulterior, political, practical considerations'.[6] Or thus, Baudelaire's 'perfect *flâneur*' becomes the exemplary artistic genius, the paradoxical 'passionate spectator, absorbed and aloof at once'.[7] Baudelaire differentiates – as does Kant – between the true, the good and the beautiful;[8] and like Kant, who distinguishes the agreeable from the beautiful, Baudelaire distinguishes 'the sensitivity of the heart', which he deems unfavourable to poetic composition, from the 'sensitivity of the imagination', which discerns the 'self-sufficient' qualities of poetic form.[9]

Kant's famous declaration that '*Beauty* is an object's form of *purposiveness* insofar as it is perceived in the object *without the presentation of a purpose*' (§17) will in Coleridge's theories turn into the concept of organic form, whereby the poem is to be seen as a 'harmonious whole': for 'nothing can permanently please, which does not contain in itself the reason why it is so'.[10] In the lectures of Benjamin Constant (1767–1830) and Victor Cousin (1792–1867), both of them popularizers of Kant's aesthetic in France, Kant's famous definition of beauty's purposeful purposelessness would lead to an emphasis on the *form* of purposiveness – as it does in Coleridge – at the expense of the experience of perception that Kant would have foregrounded. What in Kant was merely a 'free

---

6  Matthew Arnold, 'The Function of Criticism at the Present Time' in *Matthew Arnold's Essays in Criticism*, ed. Thomas Marion Hoctor (University of Chicago Press, 1968), p. 18.
7  Charles Baudelaire, 'The Painter of Modern Life' in *The Painter of Modern Life and Other Essays*, trans. and ed. Jonathan Mayne (Greenwich: Phaidon, 1964), p. 9. See also Edgar Allan Poe, 'The Poetic Principle' in *Poe: Essays and Reviews*, ed. G. R. Thompson (New York: Library of America, 1984), p. 76.
8  Charles Baudelaire, 'Further Notes on Edgar Allan Poe' in Mayne, *Painter of Modern Life*, p. 107.
9  Charles Baudelaire, 'Philosophic Art' in *ibid.*, p. 210.
10  *The Collected Works of Samuel Taylor Coleridge*, ed. Kathleen Coburn, 16 vols. (London and Princeton: Routledge & Kegan Paul/Princeton University Press, 1969–2001), vol. VII, p. xxx.

play' of the imagination, merely an act of perception, would be reified, some would say fetishized, in the aesthetic object.[11] Even when Kant, distinguishing between the beautiful and the sublime, talks of beauty as 'the form of the object, which consists in its being bounded' (§23), he is speaking – despite the form's deceptive materiality – not of an object's *being* but of its *form*, its appearance, 'as it is perceived' rather than 'as it is'. For we cannot know it as it is.

The concept of purposiveness, in other words, *presupposes* an aesthetic order in nature which we cannot strictly *know* to exist. The German word *Zweckmässigkeit* renders more overtly the mere appearing of purpose through aesthetic form. Martin Seel draws attention to a subtle terminological difference that clarifies the difference at stake here, that between an object's appearances (*Erscheinungen*) and 'their process of appearing (*Erscheinen*)'.[12] It is this *appearing* that renders the object aesthetic – a 'shape' or 'form' without content, for the content could only be supplied if the object were to be known as an object. Aspiring to such a phenomenological aesthetic, Stéphane Mallarmé will distinguish his aesthetic from that of the Parnassians, who 'treat their subjects as the old philosophers and orators did: that is, they present things directly, whereas I think that they should be presented allusively. Poetry lies in the *contemplation* of things, in the image emanating from the reveries which things arouse in us.'[13] Literature, he writes in his essay 'Music and Literature', is 'our mind's ambition (in the form of language) to define things; to prove to the satisfaction of our soul that a natural phenomenon corresponds to our imaginative understanding of it'.[14] If Mallarmé here echoes Kant's concept of the harmony of the mental faculties in the aesthetic experience, the imaginative understanding elicited through literature also reflects Kant's ideal that art should 'appear to be nature', that it should not display 'the embarrassment (*Peinlichkeit*) of academic form'. A successful work of art, in other words, while heeding the constraints of form must at the same time appear altogether free from constraints; it must correspond to our understanding of it 'as if it were a product of mere nature' (§45).

These epistemological and formal aspects of the Kantian aesthetic have implications for the emergence of literary autonomy and the aspirations inherent in this concept. Kant 'sees human existence as having value

[11] See William Pietz, 'Fetish' in *Critical Terms for Art History*, eds. Robert S. Nelson and Richard Shiff (University of Chicago Press, 1996), p. 199.

[12] Martin Seel, *Aesthetics of Appearing*, trans. John Farrell (Stanford University Press, 2005), p. 4.

[13] Stéphane Mallarmé, 'The Evolution of Literature' in *Selected Prose, Poems, Essays, and Letters*, trans. Bradford Cook (Baltimore, MD: Johns Hopkins University Press, 1956), p. 21.

[14] Stéphane Mallarmé, 'Music and Literature' in *ibid.*, p. 49.

only in a world that at least looks ordered', as Jonathan Loesberg comments. 'Because he has destroyed the logic that would allow one to see that the world is in fact ordered, he replaces that claim with one of appearance . . . His aesthetics will give value to accepting appearance and accepting it as mere appearance.'[15] To wrest an appearance of order from a world increasingly seen as disordered will become the seductive promise of works of art that, for reasons dramatically visible in the social and political upheavals associated with the Industrial Revolution in the nineteenth century, aim to suppress any reference to extraneous reality. Thus, for Gustave Flaubert, 'The only way not to be unhappy is to shut yourself up in art, and count everything else as nothing';[16] for Mallarmé, Wagner's music 'offers us protection against our own insufficiency and the mediocrity of nations; it lifts the ardent to the heights of certainty . . . Thus will our minds be kept in isolation from the incoherence which pursues them.'[17] Similarly, Walter Pater – who would have abhorred the ornamental aspects of Kant's example of free beauty – assumed that 'all disinterested lovers of books' would look to art 'for a refuge, a sort of cloistral refuge, from a certain vulgarity in the actual world'.[18]

While documenting a view of the aesthetic as radically departing from its mimetic or didactic function in the eighteenth century, Kant's list of merely decorative free beauties – from wallpaper and designs *à la grecque* to music – foreshadows, but does not legitimize, such 'escapist' developments. Although for Kant music did not possess the kind of autonomy that it would develop later and that would divest the aesthetic of the ethical symbolism it still had for Kant,[19] 'music not set to words' became for many poets and writers of the nineteenth century – from the German Romantic Novalis to Poe to Mallarmé to Verlaine to Pater to Wilde – the exemplary genre for the kind of non-referential language to which poetry should aspire.

What in the realm of *literary* autonomy best exemplifies Kant's idea of free beauty, to use Walter Pater's representative view on this aesthetic ideal, is lyric poetry, for in the lyric the distinction between matter and form is 'reduced to its *minimum*'. Pater's declaration that '*All art constantly aspires towards the condition of music*' insists that literary perfection is attained by reducing the semantic aspects of language so that meaning will reach us 'through ways not distinctly traceable by the understanding'. Such experience is attained only in those 'consummate moments' when 'form and matter, in their union or identity', represent an

---

[15] Jonathan Loesberg, *A Return to Aesthetics: Autonomy, Indifference, and Postmodernism* (Stanford University Press, 2005), p. 54.

[16] Quoted in Buckler, *Pater*, p. 407.

[17] Stéphane Mallarmé, 'Richard Wagner' in Cook, *Selected Prose*, p. 78.

[18] Pater, 'Style', pp. 400–1.    [19] Bowie, *Aesthetics*, p. 30.

'imaginative reason'.[20] While Pater's language here echoes the harmonizing of the mental faculties in the Kantian aesthetic experience, Kant would
have stressed the merely formal aspects of the aesthetic devoid of content. Moreover, in the near century that lies between Kant's and Pater's
aesthetics, Kant's claims for a universal validity of subjective taste have
gradually receded. For Pater, aesthetic taste is entirely subjective: 'Beauty,
like all other qualities presented to human experience,' he writes in the
preface to *The Renaissance*, 'is relative; and the definition of it becomes
unmeaning and useless in proportion to its abstractness.' The 'true student of aesthetics', Pater declares in overt opposition to Kant, is to find
beauty 'not in the most abstract but in the most concrete terms possible,
to find, not its universal formula, but the formula which expresses most
adequately this or that special manifestation of it'.[21] While Pater radically
relativizes the universal claims of Kant's aesthetic, he also avoids the danger inherent in those claims of replicating the 'abstract, serialized subject'
of the very commodity culture that Kant's aesthetic was to oppose.[22] It is
this moral potential of the aesthetic, which is to oppose the dehumanizing
effects of an emerging industrial capitalism, that Friedrich Schiller, in the
aftermath of the French regicide and reign of terror, seeks to develop in
his *Letters on the Aesthetic Education of Man* (1795).


## 2


As for Kant, for Schiller beauty 'accomplishes no particular purpose,
neither intellectual nor moral; it discovers no individual truth, helps us
to perform no individual duty and is, in short, as unfitted to provide a
firm basis for character as to enlighten the understanding' (Letter XXI).
But precisely in its infinity of potential, and simultaneous absence of any
purpose, the aesthetic remains the ideal of a freedom, a potential for
self-determination that, Schiller hopes, will affect political reality. With
express indebtedness to Kant – 'I will not conceal that my assertions will
chiefly be based on Kant's principles' (*Kantische Grundsätze*) (Letter I) –
Schiller claims that 'if man is ever to solve the problem of politics in
practice he will have to solve it through the problem of the aesthetic,
because it is only through Beauty that man makes his way to Freedom'
(Letter II).[23] By mediating the conflicting demands of the material drive

[20]  Walter Pater, 'The School of Giorgione' in Buckler, *Pater*, pp. 156–8 (Pater's italics).
[21]  Walter Pater, 'Preface' to *The Renaissance* in Buckler, *Pater*, p. 71.
[22]  Terry Eagleton, *The Ideology of the Aesthetic* (Oxford: Blackwell, 1990), p. 98.
[23]  All German terms and quotations are from Friedrich Schiller, 'Über die ästhetische
      Erziehung des Menschen' in *Werke und Briefe*, 12 vols., ed. Rolf-Peter Janz (Frankfurt:
      Deutscher Klassiker, 1992), vol. VIII, pp. 556–676.

(*Stofftrieb*) and the formal drive (*Formtrieb*) in the synthesizing play drive (*Spieltrieb*), the aesthetic, Schiller argues, resists the fragmentation and alienation imposed by civilization. The play drive – clearly related to Kant's free play of the faculties in aesthetic experience – manifests itself in the 'living form' (*lebende Gestalt*) that is the work of art,[24] exemplified in the supreme autotelism of the figure of Juno Ludovisi: 'The whole figure reposes and dwells in itself, a creation completely self-contained, and, as if existing beyond space, neither yielding nor resisting; here is no force to contend with force, no frailty where temporality might break in' (Letter XV).

And yet, despite this figure's ideal autotelism, we can never escape our dependence on external determinations; a work of art, Schiller writes, is to be judged as great in relation only to its approximation to the ideal. Such an ideal must necessarily minimize the content – referring as it does to material constraints and determinations – in favour of form alone. 'In a truly successful work of art the content should effect nothing, the form everything' (Letter XXII). However, even as early as in the tenth letter Schiller had warned that 'Precisely because taste pays heed to form and never to content, it finally gives the soul a dangerous tendency to neglect all reality entirely and to sacrifice truth and morality to an attractive façade.' In the same letter, Schiller notes the troubling fact that in almost any historical age where art and taste are cultivated, one finds humanity debased, and that not one example could be adduced to demonstrate that aesthetic culture would lead to political emancipation and social virtue.

While Schiller's attempt to lay the 'firm ground' for a historically relevant aesthetic thus leads us 'for a time' away from familiar historical examples (Letter X), his argument finally cannot lead us *back* to historical reality either. Although he had intended to add to Kant's *a-historical* aesthetic a *historical* dimension, Schiller's theory of art – although retaining a critique of historical reality – finally survives only by negating that reality – and defines itself, as Hans-Georg Gadamer has shown, through that negation.[25] In the very last paragraph of the twenty-seven letters on the aesthetic education, Schiller asks whether such a state of beautiful appearance exists at all, and where it would be found. He answers his question by radically minimizing and relegating the earlier, more ambitious historical relevance of the aesthetic to precisely the few select circles (*wenigen auserlesenen Zirkeln*) composed of fine-tuned souls, all opposed

---

24   All English translations of Schiller are from Friedrich Schiller, *On the Aesthetic Education of Man*, trans. Elizabeth M. Wilkinson and L. A. Willoughby (Oxford: Clarendon Press, 1967).
25   Hans-Georg Gadamer, *Wahrheit und Methode: Grundzüge einer philosophischen Hermeneutik* (Tübingen: Mohr, 1986), p. 88.

to moralizing and uninspired imitation, just as one would find them in the rarefied gatherings of the Symbolists or the Victorian Decadents.

Schiller's concept of 'play' as autonomous performance is contradicted by what Gadamer reveals as the term's anthropological grounding.[26] On the one hand, play is 'a return to that negative state of complete absence of determination' (Letter XXII); on the other hand, play is also a particular response to existential and historical human predicaments. Thus, in its rejection of determination, play can be understood as a radical critique of those material realities. It is, as Theodor Adorno points out, in the immanence of literary form that the unresolved antagonisms of social reality play themselves out, and it is in the absorption of these antagonisms that literary autonomy differs from the undialectical negativity of 'art for art's sake'.[27] When Mallarmé's persona in 'The Evolution of Literature' announces that 'the poet can only go on strike against society, and turn his back on all the contaminated ways and means that are offered him', he may well exemplify the escapist predispositions of art for art's sake. 'For anything that is offered him is necessarily inferior to his ideal and to his secret labor.'[28] When, on the other hand, one of Oscar Wilde's characters in *The Importance of Being Earnest* declares that 'style, not sincerity, is the vital thing',[29] he reflects Wilde's resistance to the moral obligations and economic incentives that would compromise, precisely, a writer's sincerity. 'What must then be emphasized', Terry Eagleton concludes, 'is the contradictory nature of an aesthetic which on the one hand offers a fruitful ideological model of the human subject for bourgeois society, and on the other hand holds out a vision of human capacities by which that society can be measured and found gravely wanting.'[30]

## 3

In France (as well as in other European countries and the United States), Kant's, Schiller's, Schelling's, the Schlegels' and von Humboldt's writings on the aesthetic had been popularized by Germaine de Staël's (1766–1817) immensely successful *De l'Allemagne*. Although the book does not treat Kant's philosophy in detail, or in depth, it was de Staël's affinities with German Romanticism, rather than with the French Revolution, that promised a new aesthetic idealism. 'Kant, a German, was thus not directly

[26] *Ibid.*, p. 88.
[27] Theodor Adorno, *Ästhetische Theorie* (Frankfurt: Suhrkamp, 1973), p. 16.
[28] Mallarmé, 'Evolution of Literature', p. 22.
[29] Oscar Wilde, *The Importance of Being Earnest*, ed. Ruth Berggren (New York: Vanguard Press, 1987), p. 164.
[30] Eagleton, *Ideology*, p. 118.

tied to the Revolution, to the rejected past', as John Claiborne Isbell notes; 'that key fact makes it easier for him to represent a new future.'[31] Heinrich Heine's introduction of 'an entirely new type of literature' in his book *The Romantic School* aims to offer 'a kind of continuation of Mme. de Staël's book *De l'Allemagne*' that, as Heine writes in his opening sentence, 'is the only comprehensive information the French have received concerning the intellectual life in Germany'.[32]

The contradictions and dialectical tensions inherent in aesthetic autonomy – exemplified in Heine's concomitant allegiance to both poetry and politics – are henceforth borne out in individual literary practices as much as in broader ideological positions. While the so-called 'Young Germans', including Heine (self-exiled in Paris from 1831 to 1856), soon perceived the idea of literary autonomy as an obstacle to political emancipation, in France it was the very progressivism exemplified in this idea that opposed the reactionary dogmatisms of a Désiré Nisard, Saint-Marc Girardin or Gustave Planche, while in England literary autonomy would not become a viable aesthetic position until the second part of the nineteenth century in the writings of Swinburne, Pater and Wilde.

If Heine's stance represents a vexed and ambivalent commitment to literary autonomy, Théophile Gautier's manifesto for the art for art's sake movement – his preface to his erotic novel *Mademoiselle de Maupin* (1835) – advances, unequivocally, its rebuttal of 'the moral journalists' and 'the utilitarian critics' by allusion to Kant's famous definition of the work of art as a purposeful purposelessness: 'a book cannot be turned into gelatin soup, a novel is not a pair of seamless boots, a sonnet [is not] an automatic syringe, a drama is not a railway – all of which things are essentially civilising and carry mankind along the road of progress'.[33] But Gautier's protest against utilitarianism – 'the most useful place in a house is the water-closet' – is not, finally, a call to abandon all reality (to repeat Schiller's warning) but rather to renounce truth and morality when these are nothing but dogmatic conventions (*WTG*, vol. i, p. 82).

Not surprisingly, given the merely consumerist habits of the rising bourgeoisie after the French Revolution, Gautier's sarcasm in his preface is aimed at the utilitarian values fostered by technological and economic progress, especially the 'useful, virtuous and progressive periodicals' (*WTG*, vol. i, p. 78) that published serial chapters of novels, thus

---

[31]  John Claiborne Isbell, *The Birth of European Romanticism: Truth and Propaganda in Staël's De l'Allemagne* (Cambridge University Press, 1994), p. 164.

[32]  Heinrich Heine, 'The Romantic School' in *Heinrich Heine: Selected Works*, trans. and ed. Helen Mustard (New York: Random House, 1973), p. 129.

[33]  Théophile Gautier, 'Preface to Mademoiselle de Maupin' in *The Works of Théophile Gautier*, trans. and ed. F. C. de Sumichrast, 24 vols. (New York: George D. Sproul, 1900), vol. i, p. 77. Hereafter cited as *WTG*.

relegating poetry to the marginal economic and social status it has
retained to this day. In succumbing to their commercial success, Gautier
declares elsewhere – and with not a little Nietzschean *ressentiment* –
novels are not only inferior to poetry but also 'horribly dirty things'. In
an unpoetical age, poetry does not sell, but then again, 'The finest things
are neither saleable nor purchasable' (*WTG*, vol. XXIII, pp. 219–20).

The uselessness of poetry is finally a notion that reflects for Gautier
the analogous gratuitousness of human existence in a world that esteems
shoes above poetry, cabbages above tulips: 'There is mighty little use in
our being on this earth and living' (*WTG*, vol. I, p. 80). If the uselessness
of life is nevertheless a necessity, it is so because it is as inexpendable
as the beautiful. 'Flowers might be suppressed without the world suffering materially from their loss, and yet who would be willing that there
should be no more flowers?' However, despite its appeal as an axiomatic
truth, Gautier's apology for a 'spiritual' rather than 'material' value of
literature can only be advanced through caricature of either side of this
dialectic: 'The spiritual use is that when one is reading novels one is asleep,
instead of reading useful, virtuous and progressive newspapers, or other
indigestible and degrading drugs' (*WTG*, vol. I, p. 81). Gautier can only
allude to the kind of 'firm ground' Schiller, too, had failed to provide in
his attempt to articulate a transcendental aesthetic value not contingent
on the material. Like Kant, Gautier cannot say what the beautiful is other
than what it is not: 'There is nothing really beautiful save what is of no
possible use (*WTG*, vol. I, p. 80). Gautier's rhetorical questions 'What
is the use of women's beauty?' and 'What is the use of music?' (*WTG*,
vol. I, p. 82) remain unanswerable. His manifesto for an '*art sacré*'[34]
remains devoid of the kind of mysticism that Baudelaire and Mallarmé
would embrace.

### 4

When Baudelaire, in his essay on Gautier, attacks the doctrine of the
indivisibility of beauty, truth and goodness as nothing but foreign (i.e.
German) sophistry,[35] he was probably referring to Victor Cousin's lectures at the Sorbonne, published in 1853 under the title *Du vrai, du beau,
et du bien*. Cousin's aesthetic neo-Platonism is indebted to the German
Romantic philosopher Friedrich Schelling, for whom beauty is a transcendental, timeless moment. 'This idea of the perfect moment', as Kai
Hammermeister notes, 'that reveals the true nature of the object, transcends time, and eternalizes the object in art, will inform many poetic

[34] See his essay 'Du beau dans l'Art' (1856).
[35] Charles Baudelaire, *L'Art Romantique*, ed. Edmond Jaloux (Geneva: Albert Skira, 1945), p. 164.

theories of modernist writers, as in James Joyce's theory of epiphany, Virginia Woolf's "moment of being", or Marcel Proust's *moment privilégié*.'[36] To this list one might want to add that eminent theorist of the transcendent moment, Walter Pater, for whom the aesthetic experience in its fugitive transience represents the pinnacle of all human aspiration by 'set[ting] the spirit free for a moment'.[37] The same neo-Platonic aesthetic informs what W. K. Wimsatt and Cleanth Brooks call the 'diffuse and vaporous Kantian elements'[38] in Edgar Allan Poe's essay 'The Poetic Principle' (1850) – a manifesto that greatly influenced Baudelaire and Mallarmé – where beauty, being 'an immortal instinct', affords brief glimpses of a 'Loveliness whose very elements, perhaps, appertain to eternity alone'.[39]

Despite his indebtedness to Poe, Baudelaire advocated an aesthetic in which transcendence was to be reduced to correspondence, idea to sense, meaning to structure, signification to configuration. This conversion of a vertical to a horizontal aesthetic is exemplified in Baudelaire's declaration that the beautiful is foreign, bizarre, contorted, intense, ephemeral. Rather than being desublimated, as it is in Gautier, the Platonic ideal has here been orientalized, as Jenine Abboushi Dallal points out, to become what she calls a 'colonial aestheticism'.[40] 'One reason', she writes, 'why aestheticism gained currency particularly in France lies in the points of convergence between aestheticism and French imperial ideology. Shared by both is the principle of autonomy from the material world: in aestheticism, the separation of the Beautiful from the realm of use, corporeality, and worldliness; in French imperialism, the independence of culture from geography and the course of history.'[41] Dallal thus reads Baudelaire's aestheticism – along with Gautier's and Flaubert's – as a gesture of cultural and corporeal renunciation: symbolized, for Gautier, in the city of Paris in cinders; for Baudelaire, in the conflagration of the beautiful; for Flaubert, in suicide;[42] for Mallarmé, we might add, in the effacing of signification. Prefiguring all of these images of a self-immolating aesthetic is Poe's ideal poetic subject, the death of a beautiful woman, where the exotic, the colonial, the carnal are simultaneously invoked and repressed. What remains in the wake of such self-cancellation – itself an image of autonomy – is an epistemology of the beautiful similar to Gautier's (or Schiller's) aesthetic where art and history affirm each other only through mutual negation.

36  Hammermeister, *German Aesthetic Tradition*, p. 79.
37  Walter Pater, 'Conclusion' to *The Renaissance* in Buckler, *Pater*, p. 219.
38  William K. Wimsatt and Cleanth Brooks, *Literary Criticism: A Short History*, 2 vols. (University of Chicago Press, 1983), vol. II, p. 478.
39  Poe, 'Poetic Principle', p. 77.
40  Jenine Abboushi Dallal, 'French Imperialism and the Aesthetics of Extinction', *Yale Journal of Criticism*, 13 (2000), p. 244.
41  *Ibid.*, p. 242.    42  *Ibid.*, p. 248.

But if for Gautier roses are beautiful because they are not cabbages, in Baudelaire the beautiful is more mystically, more romantically, a matter of intimate correspondences. While Gautier and the Parnassians practise a 'pictorial and descriptive objectivism', and while they renounce 'the search for a reciprocal penetration of mind and nature', as Pierre Bourdieu explains, Baudelaire invokes 'a sort of mysticism of sensation enlarged by the game of language: an autonomous reality, with no referent other than itself, the poem is a creation independent of creation, and nevertheless united with it by profound ties that no positivist science perceives'.[43] Baudelaire's poem 'Carrion' exemplifies this autonomous reality. Although its opening line, 'Remember, my soul, the thing we saw', seems at first to tip the balance of reciprocity towards pictorial objectivism, and although a rotting cadaver would seem an inappropriate playground for the autotelic game of language, Baudelaire will transform the cadaver into a beautiful, morbid world unto itself, capable of emitting the 'strange music' that is Baudelaire's poetry.[44] In Baudelaire, Kant's proposition of a harmony of subject and object in the aesthetic judgement is thus rephrased as intimate correspondences between all things fair and foul.

Baudelaire's poet – backstreet picker of rags, urban flâneur, dandy, lover of graveyards – returns, in 'The Painter of Modern Life', 'from the valley of the shadow of death'. His moribund state ought to assure aesthetic disinterest, but he is drunk with forms and colours.[45] The latter implies a telling departure from Kant's warning that 'the colors that illuminate the outline belong to charm' (*Reiz*; §14). If charm impairs the judgement of taste, Baudelaire's poet practises an aesthetic that, as Kant might say, 'though vivid to sense... cannot make [the object] beautiful and worthy of being beheld' (§14). The poet in Baudelaire's 'The Painter of Modern Life' will thus not aspire to a transcendental aesthetic; the difference between design and colour is the difference between idea and matter, between form and content, between a vertical and a horizontal aesthetic.

## 5

Swinburne, who reviewed *Les Fleurs du mal* in the *Spectator* (6 September 1862) after it had been censured for obscenity, remarks that 'a poet's business is presumably to write good verses, and by no means to redeem

---

[43] Pierre Bourdieu, *The Rules of Art: Genesis and Structure of the Literary Field*, trans. Susan Emanuel (Stanford University Press, 1995), p. 107; cf. Kant, *Critique of Judgment*, §49.

[44] Charles Baudelaire, *Les Fleurs du mal*, trans. Richard Howard (Boston: Godine, 1983).

[45] Baudelaire, 'The Painter of Modern Life', p. 8.

the age and remould society', and further 'that the art of poetry has absolutely nothing to do with didactic matter at all'.[46] Nevertheless, he also points out that 'there is not one poem of the *Fleurs du Mal* which has not a distinct and vivid background of morality to it. Only this moral side of the book is not thrust forward in the foolish and repulsive manner of a half-taught artist.'[47] Baudelaire himself insists, after all, in the same commentary on Poe where he had declared that poetry has no other purpose than itself, 'I am not attempting to say that poetry does *not* ennoble morals.'[48]

That autonomous literature, despite its refusals and renunciations, should still have a moral function is not surprising. In Kant's aesthetic theory, fine art, although radically autonomous, has 'nevertheless' (*dennoch*) eminent social relevance in 'advancing the culture of the mental powers in the interest of social communication' (§44); this view is similar to Schiller's aesthetic in which the beautiful engenders moral dispositions. Kant's (or Schiller's) theory of aesthetic autonomy should thus be dissociated from the practice of the Parisian bohemians, who, as Pierre Bourdieu puts it, 'also claim the values of independence but in order to legitimate either transgressions without properly aesthetic consequences or pure and simple regressions to the facile and the "vulgar"'.[49] Kant's advocacy of aesthetic autonomy is not an invitation to disregard either moral or aesthetic constraints. Although Kant states: 'We regard free art [as an art] that could only turn out purposive (i.e. succeed) if it is play, in other words, an occupation that is agreeable on its own account', he distinguishes such free art not only from craft, which he considers 'mercenary', but also from art promoted by 'recent educators [who] believe that they promote a free art best if they remove all constraint from it and convert it from labor into mere play' (§43). Even in free art, 'there is a need for something in the order of a constraint, or, as it is called, a *mechanism*' (§43). 'Lawless freedom' of the imagination, Kant writes, 'produces nothing but nonsense' (§50). When he concludes that 'the beautiful is the symbol of the morally Good' (§59), it is clear that for Kant, the beautiful is not analogous but *subordinate to* the good.

It is in the levelling of this hierarchy, in the equation of the good with the beautiful, that Gautier, Baudelaire and Flaubert differ from Kant, and it is the inversion of this Kantian hierarchy that earns Swinburne, Pater and Wilde the label of Decadent Victorians. If beauty, for Kant, is the symbol of the morally Good, 'Beauty', declares Wilde, 'is the symbol of

46  Algernon Charles Swinburne, 'Critique of Charles Baudelaire's *Les Fleurs du Mal*' in *Swinburne as Critic*, ed. Clyde K. Hyder (London and Boston: Routledge & Kegan Paul, 1972), p. 28.
47  *Ibid.*, p. 32.     48  Baudelaire, 'Further Notes on Edgar Allan Poe', p. 107.
49  Bourdieu, *Rules of Art*, p. 77.

symbols.'[50] Wilde's refusal to attribute any moral value to the aesthetic can be seen not only as an affirmation of Schiller's aesthetic, radically void of any social determinants or moral commitments, but also as a refusal to put precisely this autonomy into the service of an ultimate moral purpose.

'Form is amoral', as Theodor Adorno cautions,[51] echoing Schiller's warning about the 'dangerous tendency' inherent in the concept of aesthetic form. But only radical autonomists – Mallarmé or Swinburne or Wilde – would be implicated in such wholesale sacrifice of morality to what Schiller had called 'sheer verbal façade' – not Baudelaire, not Flaubert. The latter's painstakingly deliberate attention to the 'centripetal force' of his prose opposed the economic and social commodification of the novel. Books that advocate style over content, Flaubert wrote to Louise Colet (16 January 1852), have been banned by past oriental despots as they will be banned by future socialist governments. Schiller would have agreed.

6

Symbolist poetry invokes transcendental idealism often in morbid invocations of an escape from life, as in Mallarmé's poem 'Windows', where, 'seized with disgust for the man of hard heart',

> Je fuis et je m'accroche à toutes les croisées
> D'où l'on tourne l'épaule à la vie, et, béni,
> Dans leur verre, lavé d'éternelles rosées,
> Que dore le matin chaste de l'Infini
> Je me mire et me vois ange! et je meurs, et j'aime
> – Que la vitre soit l'art, soit la mysticité –
> A renaître, portant mon rêve en diadème,
> Au ciel antérieur où fleurit la Beauté!

> I flee, clinging to all the window frames,
> From where one can turn one's back on this shit;
> And blessed in their glass, bathed in eternal rains,
> In the chaste morning of the Infinite,
> I look at myself and see myself as an angel! And I die, and I yearn
> – Be the window pane art, be its mysticism –
> To be reborn, bearing my dream for a diadem,
> In the former sky where Beauty flourished.[52]

[50] Oscar Wilde, 'The Critic as Artist' in *The Complete Works of Oscar Wilde*, ed. Josephine M. Guy, 4 vols. (Oxford University Press, 2007), vol. IV, p. 158. Hereafter cited as *OW*.
[51] Quoted in Hammermeister, *German Aesthetic Tradition*, p. 202.
[52] Stéphane Mallarmé, *Collected Poems*, trans. Henry Weinfield (Berkeley: University of California Press, 1994), pp. 11–12.

For Mallarmé, however, this is the ironic performance of an attempted escapist aesthetic that serves to remind that only the material is real, 'But, alas! Here – below is master'; the aesthetic – safe shelter (*cet abrî sure*) – is only to assure the impossibility of transcendence. Mallarmé's poet, with his two featherless wings, resembles here Baudelaire's allegorical albatross, whose giant wings famously prevent him from walking – both allegorical fowls casting doubt on Gautier's claims that poets, unlike novelists, can both fly and walk.[53] Mallarmé thus embraces Romantic aspirations only in their ineffability; despite the excessively self-referential arabesques of his style, the aesthetic totality of his vision is to converge into metaphysical purity, such as silence or nothingness. The glittering, lonely, naked peaks of 'the Absolute', he writes in his homage to Wagner, are 'doubtless never to be reached by man'.[54]

Prophetic of twentieth-century poststructuralist views on the opacity of language, Mallarmé points to the intrinsic deficiency of any language to coincide with what it seeks to name. In order to achieve 'the pure work', the poet not only 'rejects natural materials as too crude', but also is himself to disappear, yielding 'the initiative to words, through the clash of their ordered inequalities; they light each other up through reciprocal reflections like a virtual swooping of fire across precious stones'.[55] In advocating anti-Romantic anonymity, Mallarmé anticipates T. S. Eliot's (and the New Critics') theory of impersonality; in his foregrounding of the disharmonious clash of words, he predicts the Formalism of the New Critics and their love of paradox and ambiguity; in his reference to the arbitrary correspondence between words and things and his attention to the opaque materiality of language, he foreshadows the supreme autonomy of deconstructive textuality. 'The miracle of great poetry', he writes in 'Solemnity', is that 'it can replace all things, simply because all things are absent'.[56]

And yet, despite his Modernist and postmodern declarations *avant la lettre*, Mallarmé retains belief in the transcendental, restorative power of poetic speech. 'I am convinced', he proclaims in 'Music and Literature', 'that the constant grasp and realization of this ideal constitutes our obligation to Him Who once unleashed Infinity – Whose rhythm (as our fingers longingly seek it out among the keys of our verbal instrument) can be rendered by the fitting words of our daily tongue.'[57] The spiritual,

---

53  Théophile Gautier, 'On the Excellence of Poetry' in *WTG*, pp. 210–18.
54  Stéphane Mallarmé, 'Richard Wagner, Revery of a French Poet' in Cook, *Selected Prose*, p. 78.
55  Stéphane Mallarmé, 'Crisis of Verse' in *Divagations*, trans. Barbara Johnson (Cambridge, MA: Harvard University Press, 2007), pp. 207–8.
56  Stéphane Mallarmé, 'Solemnity' in Cook, *Selected Prose*, pp. 70–1.
57  Mallarmé, 'Music and Literature', p. 49.

hermetic autonomy of the book, moreover, preserves the secret formula
for the composition of rhythms, sovereign gestures, miracles that proclaim the unleasher of infinity. The symbolic thickness of the pages of a
book – in contrast to the flat depthlessness of a newspaper – amounts, for
Mallarmé, to 'a tomb in miniature for our souls'; within that tomb, or
more literally within the darkness enclosed by the 'folding of the paper',
all that is revealed is the opacity of language: 'that darkness scattered
about in the form of black characters'. The task of the book, then, is to
preserve 'the secret contained in its pages'. Since its foldings are tantaliz-
ingly 'virginal', Mallarmé advises that the least violent form of reading
would be to hear the book's language as if it were music. 'Poetry, accompanied by the Idea', writes Mallarmé, whose debt to Poe is here audible,
'is perfect Music, and cannot be anything else.'[58]

If this correspondence of music to the autonomy of art does not exactly
reflect Kant's example of free beauty as music *not* set to words, it is
because of the affinity of Symbolist poetry with programme music as
Mallarmé – or Verlaine, who advocated music above all things – would
have found it discussed in the *Revue Wagnerienne*.[59] In his tribute to
Richard Wagner, Mallarmé thus speaks of the felicitous interpenetrations
that music and drama perform in Wagner's opera, whose 'invisible folds
of musical texture'[60] are closely related to Mallarmé's own aesthetic ideal.
Poetic form, he writes in his letter to François Coppée (5 December 1866),
is as self-referential as the notes on a scale:

once we have perfectly defined poetic form, our principal aim should be to make
the words of the poem self-mirroring (since they are sufficiently autonomous to
begin with and need no outside impression) to such an extent that no one of
them will seem to have a color of its own, and all of them will be merely the
notes of a scale.[61]

Claims to aesthetic autonomy are totalizing on both the smallest and
the largest scales. In the former, such totalizing claims are exemplified
in Mallarmé's image of the book as a tomb that compels the reader to
perform as the forensic specialist he is to become in the New Critical
revival of the autonomous text studied 'in miniature'; in their vaster,
universal dimensions, the totalizing claims of autonomism are implied in
Mallarmé's 'magic concept of the Work'. The book in which 'all earthly

[58] Stéphane Mallarmé, 'The Book: A Spiritual Instrument' in Cook, *Selected Prose*,
pp. 25–7.
[59] John Porter Houston and Mona Tobin Houston (eds.), *An Anthology of French Symbolist Poetry* (Indiana University Press, 1980), p. 11.
[60] Mallarmé, 'Richard Wagner, Revery of a French Poet', p. 75.
[61] Stéphane Mallarmé, Letter to Francois Coppée, 5 December 1866, in Cook, *Selected
Prose*, p. 93.

existence must ultimately be contained' is there described as 'a hymn, all harmony and joy; an immaculate grouping of universal relationships [that] come together for some miraculous and glittering occasion'.[62] The idea of the autonomous literary work thus applies not only microscopically, involving the minute particulars of the text, but also macroscopically by envisioning the world as text, a world that constitutes itself as a perpetually self-engendering, self-contained aesthetic organism.

The German Romantic poet Novalis prefigures such ideas of the world as text, or text as world, when he writes that language, like mathematics, is its own world, in which 'the world-soul express[es] itself'.[63] In the fifth part of his *Hymn to the Night*, the poet thus imagines 'one eternal poem... within the face of God', just as Mallarmé would envision his inconceivable *Gesamtkunstwerk* as a 'supreme language' collectively aspired to by all writers, a totality of universal correspondences. 'All holy games of art', writes Friedrich Schlegel, 'are only distant imitations of the endless play of the world, of the work of art which constantly forms itself.'[64]

Wordsworth's emphatic declarations in his 'Preface to *Lyrical Ballads*' that 'Poetry is the breath and finer spirit of all knowledge', that 'it is the impassioned expression which is the countenance of all Science', and further on that 'the Poet binds together by passion and knowledge the vast empire of human society, as it is spread over the whole earth, and over all time',[65] project the elements of such universalized autonomous literary composition – its claims to totality, its form, its origin in the inspired genius – onto a world that Schiller could not find.

## 7

Romantic conceptions of a dynamic interrelation, correspondence or confusion of world and language must logically include the claim made by Schlegel, Novalis, Baudelaire, Mallarmé, Pater and Wilde that criticism is not a rupture of art's self-completion but an extension of its autonomy. Thus, Schlegel can say: 'Every art and every science that operates by means of discourse, if it is practiced for its own sake as art, and if it achieves the highest summit, is poetry.'[66] Similarly, for Novalis, the

---

[62] Mallarmé, 'The Book: A Spiritual Instrument', pp. 24–5.
[63] Bowie, *Aesthetics*, p. 65.    [64] *Ibid.*, p. 67.
[65] Wordsworth, 'Preface to *Lyrical Ballads*' in *The Prose Works of William Wordsworth*, eds. W. J. B. Owen and Jane Worthington Smyser, 3 vols. (Oxford: Clarendon Press, 1974), vol. I, p. 140.
[66] Herbert Lindenberger, 'Literature and the Other Arts' in *The Cambridge History of Literary Criticism. Vol. v: Romanticism*, ed. Marshall Brown (Cambridge University Press, 2000), p. 372.

word for criticism is 'to romanticize', which amounts to a qualitative extension of poetry. '[C]riticism', Walter Benjamin comments, 'is therefore the medium in which the restriction of the individual work refers methodically to the infinitude of art and finally is transformed into that infinitude.'[67] The work of art that permits and sustains such qualitative enlargement, or such transformation into infinity, exemplifies formal perfection and testifies to its own microcosmic totality. Such claims are echoed in Wordsworth's pronouncement that poetry's is 'the empire of human society', or in Shelley's famous declaration that 'Poets are the unacknowledged legislators of the World.'

Not least because of the formal perfection by which it resists the limiting commodifications of knowledge or pleasure, poetry thus extends its purview to become a collective term for all knowledge,[68] including literary criticism that, as Friedrich Schlegel puts it, should therefore abdicate its rhetorical function. Like the poet, the ideal critic, according to Schlegel, 'doesn't try to make any particular impression on [the reader], but enters with him into the sacred relationship of deepest symphilosophy or sympoetry'.[69] That criticism and art together form one homogeneous whole, that they are extensions of each other, is of course part of Baudelaire's identity as prose-poet or poet-critic, as it is part of Mallarmé's inclusion of the reader – he thought of the convergence of text and reader as 'nuptials' – in the poem's performative process. The Mallarméian reader thus replicates, in the act of reading, the poem's hermetic totality.

At the end of the nineteenth century these issues are famously taken up in Oscar Wilde's 'The Critic as Artist', where Wilde's persona Gilbert declares that

> It is through its very incompleteness that Art becomes complete in beauty, and so addresses itself, not to the faculty of recognition nor to the faculty of reason, but to the aesthetic sense alone, which, while accepting both reason and recognition as stages of apprehension, subordinates them both to a pure synthetic impression of the work of art as a whole, and, taking whatever alien emotional elements the work may possess, uses their very complexity as a means by which a richer unity may be added to the ultimate impression itself.
>
> (*OW*, pp. 160–1)

Both Kant and Pater make their appearance in this passage, Kant in the subordination of recognition and reason to the 'aesthetic sense alone'; Pater in the completion of the work of art through the critic's 'impression',

---

[67] Quoted in Alfredo De Paz, 'Innovation and Modernity' in *ibid.*, p. 37.
[68] Brown, *Cambridge History*, p. 372.
[69] Friedrich Schlegel, 'Philosophical Fragments', quoted in Jon Klancher, 'Criticism and the Crisis of the Republic of Letters' in *ibid.*, p. 310.

a word which implies the subjective, provisional nature of interpretation that should result not in finality but in reverie.

In the vein of Novalis's, Schlegel's or Mallarmé's claims of a cosmic aesthetic universalism, beauty, for Wilde's Gilbert, 'reveals everything, because it expresses nothing. When it shows us itself it shows us the whole fiery-coloured world' (OW, p. 158). Paradoxically, such effects are achieved, as they are in Baudelaire or Mallarmé, because of the indeterminacy of all artistic expression, its overt avoidance of any mimetic or moralistic intent, its promise thus to allow mystical visions of 'a wider world' that make Wilde's ideal critic, somewhat Byronically, 'brood and dream and fancy'. 'This is the reason why music is the perfect type of art', explains Wilde's persona; 'Music can never reveal its ultimate secret' (OW, p. 160). All of this renders for Wilde (or for Mallarmé, whom he here resembles) the interminability of the critic's interpretative activity analogous to the infinity of the vast world intimated in the hermetic totality of art. Surveying that world 'from the high tower of Thought', Wilde's aesthete transfers the autonomy of beauty into the critic's wholly autonomous subjectivity, the harmonious agreement of the mental faculties into supreme moral indifference: 'Calm, and self-centered, and complete, the aesthetic critic contemplates life, and no arrow drawn at venture can pierce between the joints of his harness . . . Is such a mode of life immoral?' asks Gilbert: 'Yes: all the arts are immoral' (OW, p. 179).

The arts are immoral because morality, as Wilde keenly experienced in his trials and imprisonment for 'indecency', is as socially constructed as is truth or nature. As opposed to Victorian moralism as to literary Realism as to scientific objectivity, Wilde demands that Arnold's critical imperative 'to see the object as it really is' be revised to read: 'to see the object as in itself it really is not' (OW, p. 159). Lying has decayed, as Wilde declares in 'The Decay of Lying', because we have forgotten that all seeing is perspectival, that all claims to truth are fictions; Realism – the prose of Stevenson, James, Maupassant, Zola – represses the fictional nature of language. When Wilde chides Dickens for arousing 'our sympathy for the victims of the poor law-administration', he opposes Dickens's appeal to established, and thus merely imitated, values instead of their radical revaluation as advocated in Wilde's famous mandate that life imitate art. 'We have mistaken the common livery of the age for the vesture of the Muses, and spend our days in the sordid streets and hideous suburbs of our vile cities when we should be out on the hillside with Apollo' (OW, pp. 82–3). Life can only be justified aesthetically.

In order to avoid merely imitating and universalizing given cultural values, prejudices and biases, the highest aesthetic ideal for Wilde, as it was for Schiller, must be an art defined in purely formal terms, an art that 'never expresses anything but itself', that 'reveals her own perfection', that 'rejects the burden of the human spirit', an art that with supreme autonomy 'develops purely on her own lines. She is not symbolic of any age. It is the ages that are her symbols' (*OW*, p. 97). However, such timeless, transcendent aesthetic principles, symbolic as they are of the particular burdens of Wilde's own Victorian age, contradict Wilde's own fiercely held convictions that all truths are socially constructed. The aesthetic remains one of the unexamined lies in his essay. If the autonomy of the aesthetic makes the aesthetic epistemologically useful, even necessary, to define Wilde's subversive position, it also controverts his claim that 'as long as a thing is useful or necessary to us, or affects us in any way, either for pain or for pleasure, or appeals strongly to our sympathies, or is a vital part of the environment in which we live, it is outside the proper sphere of art' (*OW*, p. 82).

Kant's subjective universality of taste, Schiller's beautiful appearance, Baudelaire's intimate correspondences, Mallarmé's supreme language, Wilde's immoral art, all seem to testify that the idea of literary autonomy can be maintained only as a contradiction. 'The Truth in art', concludes Wilde in 'The Truth of Masks', 'is that whose contradictory is also true' (*OW*, p. 228). Nevertheless, the moral and epistemological negotiations necessitated by the contradictory nature of the aesthetic also make possible a lingering, a hesitation, a scepticism on the threshold of history. It is in the aesthetic moment that history can be something other than itself, and that moment enables us to recognize history as such. 'The end of life', Pater concludes his essay on Wordsworth, 'is not action but contemplation – being as distinct from doing – a certain disposition of the mind', whose moral education, as in Kant, Schiller or Arnold, is attained through a withdrawal from 'the mere machinery of life'. In such (for Pater always only momentary) reprieves, 'what is desirable in itself' can be glimpsed. And what is desirable in itself is finally, as Kant and Schiller advocated, nothing other than what enables the moral sympathies, such as Pater admires in Wordsworth's depictions 'of man suffering, amid awful forms and powers'.[70]

---

[70]  Walter Pater, 'Wordsworth' in Buckler, *Pater*, pp. 428–9.

# 12

# Hegel's aesthetics and their influence

## M. A. R. Habib

'Whether we know it, or like it, or not, most of us are Hegelians... Few thinkers have so many disciples who never read a word of their master's writings.' These are the words of Paul de Man regarding Hegel's aesthetics and their influence on our thinking about literature.[1] Hegel's philosophy in general stands at the centre of modern Western thought. Conservative and left-wing critics alike have long acknowledged that Hegel's system integrates major intellectual developments, such as the various streams of Enlightenment and Romanticism, into its own formidable synthesis. Moreover, many of the modern European systems of thought arose as modifications of, or reactions against, Hegel's dialectic: Marxism, Absolute Idealism, existentialism, positivism and analytic philosophy, not to mention the more heterologous streams running from Schopenhauer through Nietzsche to Derrida and beyond. In brief, Hegel has enabled our worlds of thought on many levels, philosophical, logical, political, historiographical, theological and aesthetic.

G. W. F. Hegel (1770–1831) was born in Stuttgart, capital of the duchy of Württemberg, to a father who was a minor civil servant. He studied theology at the famous seminary in Tübingen, where he became acquainted with the poet Friedrich Hölderlin and the philosopher Friedrich Schelling. He worked as a private tutor in Switzerland and then began teaching at the University of Jena in 1801. In 1816 he became Professor of Philosophy at the University of Heidelberg; and in 1818 he was invited to assume the Chair of Philosophy at the University of Berlin, where his reputation reached its height. Hegel's first major publication was *The Phenomenology of Spirit* (1807), followed by his three-volume *Science of Logic*, published between 1812 and 1816. His subsequent *Encyclopedia of the Philosophical Sciences* was a recapitulation of his philosophy as a whole; and his final work published in his lifetime was *Philosophy of Right* (1821). After his death, his students and disciples edited and published his lectures on diverse subjects, including *Lectures on the*

---

[1] Paul de Man, 'Sign and Symbol in Hegel's "Aesthetics"', *Critical Inquiry*, 8 (1982), p. 763.

*Philosophy of History*, *Lectures on Aesthetics*, *Lectures on the Philosophy of Religion* and *Lectures on the History of Philosophy*.[2]

Hegel's system was initially inspired by the French Revolution of 1789, which for him betokened the revolutionary struggle of the bourgeois class throughout Europe to gain supremacy over the feudal aristocracies and the clergy, and to replace the decaying and irrational hierarchies of feudalism with a society based on reason, where both political institutions and the human community embodied a rational outlook. Revolutionary bourgeois ideals received their most articulate expression in Hegel's work. In this sense, Hegel is a product of the Enlightenment, stressing as he does the supreme value of reason, which he brings into confluence with the other main impulse of Enlightenment philosophy, empiricism. However, Hegel's system, while not itself Romantic, is also deeply informed by certain attributes derived from Romanticism: a commitment to the idea of unification or totality and a concomitant belief that subject and object, the human self and the world, are mutually created and determined. Hegel insisted that this unity of subject and object, mind and nature, was not intuitive but rationally comprehensible.[3]

## Hegel and history

Hegel was the most articulate proponent of what was later called 'historicism', the belief that we must understand phenomena – people, nations, events and objects – as shaped internally by their specific historical contexts, often driven by inexorable laws. Hegel sees human history as a movement of consciousness towards self-conscious freedom and rationality. As consciousness moves to higher levels, it perceives increasingly that what it previously took as the external world, as something alien and foreign to it, is in fact essentially constituted, at its deepest rational core, by its own operations. What was previously confronted as *substance* is now recognized as *subjectivity*. Hegel sees this movement from substance to subject as a process that works both in the logical workings of consciousness and in the progression of consciousness through history.

The Hegelian dialectic, central to Hegel's thought at all levels, is a way of thinking about any aspect of the world in a dynamic manner, in three broad stages. Initially an object is viewed in its given particularity as self-identical and independent. In the second stage the object's 'identity'

[2] For an account of Hegel's life in its intersections with his thought, see Terry Pinkard, *Hegel: A Biography* (Cambridge University Press, 2001); for an account of the development of Hegel's thought, see Charles Taylor, *Hegel* (Cambridge University Press, 2008).
[3] G. W. F. Hegel, *Hegel's Phenomenology of Spirit*, trans. A. V. Miller (Oxford: Clarendon Press, 1979), pp. 11, 29–32. Hereafter cited as *PS*.

is viewed as externalized or dispersed through its social and historical relations, which effectively constitute 'it'. It is here viewed in its universal aspect. In the third stage the object's identity and unity are viewed as mediated (rather than immediately given), embodying its relations, and embodying the universal in the particular. Hence the dialectic is a way of thinking which acknowledges that the self and the world stand in necessary connection, that thought is not a static system of classification but a self-criticizing process, and that the world as simply given to our senses does not merit the designation 'reality'. Things in the world are to a large extent defined by their relations; hence they cannot be understood in isolation, abstracted from their connections with other things, and must be understood within their historical contexts. As Hegel states in his *Philosophy of Right*, 'What is rational is actual and what is actual is rational.'[4] Reality is not simply a vast and possibly incoherent assemblage of unrelated and unalterable facts (as crude empiricism would have it); rather, in its core, it is rational, historically progressive, and potentially unified, answering to the deepest demands of our own rational selves. Hence the dialectic is a mode of thought that is not only rational but relational and historical.[5] In fact, the dialectic as formulated by Hegel is a historically cumulative process, harmonizing a number of broad dispositions in modern philosophy, empiricist, rationalist and Romantic, as he explains in his *Lectures on the History of Philosophy*.[6] Hegel sees this movement towards freedom operating historically, from the oriental world, where only 'one' – the emperor – is free, to the Greek and Roman world, where 'some' are free, to the modern world, where 'all' are free.

## Hegel's aesthetics

Hegel's lectures on aesthetics were delivered in Berlin in 1823, 1826 and 1828–9. The first edition, in three volumes, was published between 1835 and 1838. As noted by several scholars, Hegel had a keen interest in the arts, informed by a mastery of ancient texts in their original languages.[7] His aesthetics are closely tied to his philosophy of history. Hegel sees art as one of the stages traversed by the Absolute Idea or spirit on its journey

4 *Hegel's Philosophy of Right*, trans. T. M. Knox (1952; rpt Oxford: Clarendon Press, 1967), p. 10.
5 *Hegel's Science of Logic*, trans. A. V. Miller (London and New York: George Allen & Unwin/Humanities Press, 1976), pp. 128–32, 479. Hereafter cited as *SL*.
6 *Hegel's Lectures on the History of Philosophy*, vol. III, trans. E. S. Haldane and Frances H. Simson (London and New York: Routledge & Kegan Paul/Humanities Press, 1963), pp. 217–18, 295, 363–9, 427–8. Hereafter cited as *Lectures*.
7 See, for example, the introduction to *Hegel: On the Arts*, intro. and trans. Henry Paolucci (Smyrna, DE: Griffon House, 2001), pp. x–xi.

towards freedom and rationality. Art, like religion and philosophy, is one
of the modes through which spirit manifests or expresses itself.

Hegel begins his *Aesthetics* by maintaining that art is higher than
nature. The beauty of nature, he says, is merely a reflection of spiritual
beauty.[8] Like Kant, Hegel sees art and beauty as a realm that belongs to
'*sense*, feeling, intuition, imagination'. Its sphere is essentially different
from that of thought, and 'the source of works of art is the free activity
of fancy which in its imaginations is itself more free than nature is' (*Aes*,
p. 5). In a later section, Hegel distinguishes between 'fancy' (*Phantasie*),
which is truly creative, and what he considers to be the 'purely passive
imagination' (*Einbildungskraft*) (*Aes*, p. 281); this distinction – inasmuch
as it is consistent in Hegel – appears, on the surface, to invert Kant's usage
of the terms for the 'productive' and merely 'reproductive' imagination.
T. M. Knox believes that Hegel uses the words 'fancy' and 'imagination'
interchangeably (*Aes*, p. 5n), rather than refining the distinction between
them as Coleridge was to do. Other scholars believe that Hegel does, in
fact, differentiate the terms.[9] All that needs to be stated here is that, for
Hegel, the creative imagination can use the formations of nature but can
also go beyond them in its free activity (*Aes*, p. 6).

Hegel insists that true art must be free: 'in this its freedom alone is
fine art truly art, and it only fulfils its supreme task when it has placed
itself in the same sphere as religion and philosophy, and when it is simply
one way of bringing to our minds and expressing the *Divine*, the deepest
interests of mankind, and the most comprehensive truths of the spirit'
(*Aes*, p. 7). The point here seems to be that art must fulfil the same functions and ends as these other disciplines in its own way, and stand with
relative independence, rather than its purpose falling within those other
disciplines. Art is unique in its ability to embody even the most abstruse
ideas in sensuous form: it reconciles the worlds of sense and intellect.
In fact, art helps us to perceive reality by allowing us to understand the
'true meaning' of appearances, which would otherwise be chaotic and
contingent, as they are for ordinary perception and even for history (*Aes*,
p. 9). Hegel is careful to point out, however, that art is not the highest
mode of expressing the truths of the spirit; in this function, it is superseded by both religion and philosophy (*Aes*, pp. 9–10). In the present era,
says Hegel, art no longer affords the satisfaction of spiritual needs that

[8] G. W. F. Hegel, *Aesthetics: Lectures on Fine Art*, vol. 1, trans. T. M. Knox (Oxford
University Press, 1975), p. 2. Hereafter cited as *Aes*.
[9] See, for example, Jennifer Ann Bates, *Hegel's Theory of Imagination* (Albany: SUNY
Press, 2004), pp. 110–13. See also Jay Miller, 'Irony and Sincerity: Rethinking Hegel's
Critique of Romantic Aesthetics', unpublished PhD thesis, University of Notre Dame
(in progress), esp. ch. 4, p. 151 n.13 (available online at www.jasonmatthewmiller.com/
uploads/5/7/5/9/5759941/ch._4_-_the_politics_of_phantasie.pdf).

earlier ages had sought in it: in our world, thought has developed into a necessity, whereby we employ 'general considerations and . . . regulate the particular by them' (*Aes*, p. 10).

Like Kant, Hegel distinguishes the realm of art from, on the one hand, the realm of practical desire and utility, and, on the other hand, the purely theoretical realm of science. Hegel explains here, as he does in the *Phenomenology*, that our basic mode of relating to the world is *desire*, whereby we refashion objects and the world generally in our own deepest image. We do not, however, relate to art in this way: we leave it 'free as an object to exist on its own account'. In other words, our engagement with it is purely contemplative and we do not *use* its sensuous features. For example, we do not usually use a poem to convey a practical message; we regard the poem as an object in its own right; in this way, our relationship to it is not one of desire (*Aes*, p. 37). Nor, on the other hand, do we adopt a scientific view towards art, a view that will evince only what is universal in it, for in engaging with a work of art, we cherish its individual and sensuous aspect (*Aes*, p. 38). A work of art, says Hegel, 'stands in the *middle* between immediate sensuousness and ideal thought'. The sensuous aspect of art is itself ideal, since it is elevated above purely material nature: this sensuous element is not present for its own sake; it does not presume to independence, but is an embodiment of spiritual or ideal interests. Hegel speaks of the 'essential figurativeness and sensuousness' of art, whose function is to exhibit the 'profoundest and most universal human interests in pictorial and completely definite sensuous form' (*Aes*, pp. 39–40). Hegel rejects the centuries-old notion that the aim of art is imitation, or that art awakens or purifies one's feelings and passions (*Aes*, pp. 47–9). Art's vocation, he says, 'is to unveil the *truth* in the form of sensuous artistic configuration, to set forth the reconciled opposition [between the worlds of thought and sense] . . . and so to have its end and aim in itself' (*Aes*, p. 55). What is interesting here is that, within the context of Hegel's overall thesis that art must express the truths of spirit, he nonetheless insists on the autonomy of art: its manifestation of spiritual truth does not serve the interests of pleasure, morality or instruction; rather, this expression of truth is an end in itself, the end and purpose of art.

Hegel commends Kant's notion of art as achieving a union between the worlds of spirit and nature (*Aes*, p. 56). But he rejects Kant's view that aesthetic judgement somehow bypasses the conceptual understanding and is based on the 'free play of Understanding and imagination'. Hegel's objection is that we would not then have knowledge of the actual nature of the work of art (*Aes*, p. 58). He applauds Kant's definition of aesthetic judgement as 'disinterested', universally valid, and unclouded by desire or practical motives. He also concurs with Kant's notion of beauty as 'purposive' inasmuch as it reveals a harmony of means and

ends (*Aes*, pp. 58–9). But he believes that Schiller progressed beyond
Kant in attempting to grasp intellectually the essence of art as the unity of
'universal and particular, freedom and necessity, spirit and nature' (*Aes*,
p. 62). In this context, Hegel also considers the notion of irony as formulated by Friedrich von Schlegel. He sees this irony as grounded in the
philosophy of Fichte, which established the ego as the fundamental principle of knowing, and viewed all aspects of the world as modifications of
it (*Aes*, pp. 64–5). For Schlegel, the *artistic* ego undertakes a procedure of
irony, viewing itself as detached from the conventions, laws and morals
that it expresses, and whose validity it questions (*Aes*, pp. 66–7). These
observations furnish the immediate background of Hegel's own aesthetic
views.

According to Hegel, art fulfils an important function in giving sensuous
form to a concrete spiritual content, but philosophy constitutes a higher
mode of representing spirit. Hence in his larger scheme of the progress
of consciousness, Hegel assigns to both religion and philosophy a place
higher than art. These disciplines can articulate what art, limited by its
sensuous form, cannot. For example, art can represent the Greek gods
since they are closely related to the natural, human form; but it cannot
adequately express the profundity of the Christian notion of God, which
can only be conveyed by thought (*Aes*, pp. 72–3).

Corresponding to this evolution of the Idea, as well as of the development of its particular configurations in art, Hegel divides the 'science' of
beauty into three parts: the first deals with the 'universal Idea of artistic
beauty as the ideal'; the second deals with the various artistic forms in
which the Idea has been presented; and the final part considers the various
arts as divided into their genera and species. Under the first heading, that
dealing with the ideal of beauty, Hegel makes it clear that art is intrinsically related to truth: the highest art presents not just any content in a
form suitable to it; rather, it embodies and presents the truth of the Idea.
In turn, the Idea itself generates from within itself the appropriate artistic
configurations for its own expression. In other words, artistic form is not
just an external appendage to the content of the Idea but must derive
from the very nature of the Idea (*Aes*, pp. 74–5).

In the second part, Hegel considers how the Idea has been manifested
historically in particular forms of art. He identifies three progressive
stages of art: symbolic, classical and Romantic. In the first stage, that
of *symbolic* art, the spiritual content or idea is still indefinite, obscure,
and has not yet achieved individuality. The sensuous artistic form which
attempts to embody such vagueness is itself defective. Spiritual significance is attached randomly to objects in nature, and there is no true
correspondence between content and form. For example, a block of
stone might symbolize the Divine but it does not truly represent it. The

spiritual idea distorts natural phenomena into grotesque and huge shapes in its endeavour to express itself through them. But the spirit itself, says Hegel, 'persists sublime above all this multiplicity of shapes which do not correspond with it' (*Aes*, pp. 76–7). He characterizes this stage as the 'artistic pantheism' of the orient (*Aes*, p. 77).

Hegel identifies the second stage as that of *classical* art, which abrogates the two signal defects of symbolic art: both the indeterminate nature of the Idea and its inadequate form of embodiment (*Aes*, p. 77). Classical art, in contrast, 'is the free and adequate embodiment of the Idea in the shape peculiarly appropriate to the Idea itself in its essential nature' (*Aes*, p. 77). For Hegel, the most adequate embodiment of the Idea or spirit is the human form, his reasoning being that God, or the 'original Concept', created the human form as an expression of spirit. Classical art, then, is marked by anthropomorphism and personification (*Aes*, p. 78), which also, however, indicate the limitation of such art: 'here the spirit is at once determined as particular and human, not as purely absolute and eternal' (*Aes*, p. 79). While the human form is the form most suitable for expressing spirit, it is nonetheless limited, burdened as it is by its own material nature and particularity.

This limitation necessitates a transition to a higher stage, the *Romantic* form of art. The unity achieved in classical art between the Idea and its reality is here sublated once again: their opposition is reinstated, though at a higher level than that which had marked symbolic art. Hegel avers that the classical mode is the 'pinnacle' of artistic form, and its limitation is inherent in art *per se*, which must use sensuous forms to convey a spiritual content. The limitation here is that the Idea or spirit is not 'represented in its *true nature*'. For spirit, Hegel reminds us, is 'absolute inwardness' or 'infinite subjectivity' of the Idea; in other words, spirit is pure thought or ideality which cannot be constrained or expressed by external, sensuous means (*Aes*, p. 79).

Romantic art, then, annuls the 'undivided unity' of classical art precisely because it expresses a higher content, that is, spirit or Idea at a higher stage of its development. This content is correlative with Christianity's view of God as spirit, in contrast with the Greek conception of the gods. In classical Greek art, the Idea is presented as an *implicit* unity of human and divine natures: the Greek god is known by 'naive intuition and sensuous imagination, and therefore his shape is the bodily shape of man. The range of his power and his being is individual and particular' (*Aes*, p. 79). At a higher stage of spirit's development, this unity, which was merely implicit and sensuously embodied, is elevated into 'self-conscious knowledge' (*Aes*, p. 80).

Spirit at this higher stage can no longer be expressed in a medium that is sensuous and material; this medium must be, as Hegel puts it, the '*inwardness of self-consciousness*'. Christianity conceives of God not as an individual spirit but as absolute spirit, and therefore takes spiritual inwardness, not the human body, as its medium of expression. The unity of human and divine must be realized only by spiritual knowledge, freed from material existence. In this way, Romantic art is actually the 'self-transcendence of art'. It effectively transcends the sphere of art since the latter by definition is a presentation of spirit in sensuous form. In this third stage, 'the subject-matter of art is *free concrete spirituality*, which is to be manifested as *spirituality* to the spiritually inward' (*Aes*, p. 80). By this Hegel means that the subject matter of art is subjectivity itself, the inner world of thought, emotion and spirituality. The artist no longer expresses what is in the world but what lies at the depth of the human self. In this way, 'Inwardness celebrates its triumph over the external... whereby what is apparent to the senses alone sinks into worthlessness' (*Aes*, p. 81).

How can the Romantic artist express human subjectivity without using a material, sensuous medium? Hegel's answer is that, although an external material medium is employed, it is acknowledged to be 'inessential and transient', a mere expedient, which utilizes devices of the imagination such as plot, character and action. This external medium, and the external world in which it is grounded, are viewed as having their essence not in themselves but in the spirit that uses them for its expression (*Aes*, p. 81). Hegel appears to be saying here that aspects of the external world are not used for their intrinsic meaning. The phenomena of nature, such as autumn or mountains or skylarks, are used symbolically to convey human thoughts and emotions; they are acknowledged as merely contingent occasions for exploring the inner world of subjectivity, without any regard for their own status as objects in nature. Hence, in Romantic art the separation of Idea and form, their mutual indifference and inadequacy, emerge once again; the difference is that now the Idea is perfected in its development, and in this perfection it can suffer no adequate union with what is external; its true reality and manifestation lie within itself. In general, Hegel characterizes the symbolic, classical and Romantic forms of art as consisting, respectively, in the 'striving for, the attainment, and the transcendence of the Ideal as the true Idea of beauty' (*Aes*, p. 81). The centre of the entire world of art, for Hegel, is the 'region of divine truth, artistically represented for contemplation and feeling' (*Aes*, p. 83).

In the next section of his *Aesthetics*, Hegel explains that these three general forms of art – symbolic, classical and Romantic – are realized in the specific arts of architecture, sculpture, painting, music and poetry. Each of these arts, he says, primarily embodies one of the general art forms: for example, classical art is orientated towards sculpture, and Romantic art towards poetry. These affiliations are not always clear cut:

epic poetry, for example, expresses classical objectivity, and poetry in general can embody each of the three forms (*Aes*, p. 82).

The first (and most rudimentary) art is architecture, which manipulates the external world, attempting to make it conform with art, and to imbue it with spiritual qualities. But the world that architecture confronts is a world of mass which is subject to mechanical laws, in which spirit cannot be realized or embodied. Hence architecture is the fundamentally symbolic art since it uses material things merely as emblems of spirit. But, in Hegel's terminology, architecture nonetheless works on nature to free it from 'the jungle of finitude and the monstrosity of chance', thereby creating a 'path' for spirit. It levels a space for the god and builds his temple, an enclosure for spiritual community (*Aes*, p. 84). The way is now open for the next phase of art, sculpture: into this temple, the 'god enters himself as the lightning-flash of individuality striking and permeating the inert mass' (*Aes*, p. 84). In sculpture, 'the spiritual inner life, at which architecture can only hint, makes itself at home in the sensuous shape and its external material'. Sculpture, then, fundamentally expresses the classical form of art, since it houses spirit in bodily form, being in immediate unity with it. What Hegel appears to be saying here is that the material mass processed by sculpture is no longer manipulated according to its mechanical qualities alone, but rather driven by a conception of the ideal forms of the human figure in all three spatial dimensions. This spatiality, however, is 'abstract' since it portrays an ideal human form extricated from the contingent circumstances of the world (*Aes*, p. 85).

Now that architecture has founded the temple, and sculpture has erected within it the image of the god, this sensuously present god must interact with the *community*: the 'compact unity in itself which the god has in sculpture disperses into the plurality of the inner lives of individuals whose unity is not sensuous but purely ideal. And so only here is God himself truly spirit, spirit in his community' (*Aes*, pp. 85–6). In other words, once a human community of worship is formed, the god is freed from his immediate immersion in a bodily medium and 'is raised to spirituality and knowledge ... which essentially appears as inward and as subjectivity'. In this third stage, then, spirit ascends to a higher level: escaping the restrictions of material form, the god assumes the form of spiritual knowledge, passing into the collective subjectivity of the community, into its beliefs, thoughts and feelings; it is these beliefs, not the act of physically congregating, that unites the community in an 'ideal' way, furnishing its subjectivity. God is seen as alternating between his own 'inherent unity' and his realization in the knowledge and beliefs of the community. This third phase of God's development coincides with Romantic art, for the object of artistic representation is now the inner world of human thought and feeling (*Aes*, p. 86).

Romantic art must use a sensuous material appropriate to the expression of inner subjectivity. Hegel states that this material is of three types: colour, musical sound, and 'sound as the mere indication of inner intuitions and ideas' ('signs'). The modes of art correlative with these materials are, respectively, painting, music and poetry. In general, these arts express a more intimate connection between spirit and matter than was exhibited in architecture and sculpture: the sensuous medium is now posited as spiritual and ideal, hence these arts conform to the Romantic mode (*Aes*, pp. 86–7). In each of these arts, the world of matter is raised to an ideal and spiritual status: it is significant not in itself but only in terms of the human subjectivity it embodies or expresses. The first of these arts, painting, represents pure 'visibility', which is particularized as colour. Unlike architecture, painting does not consider mechanical qualities of objects; and unlike sculpture, it does not depict their 'sensuous spatiality'. Rather, it subjectivizes the quality of visibility and posits it as ideal. Painting frees art from the spatiality of material things by restricting visibility to the dimensions of a plane surface. On the other hand, the content of painting can attain the 'widest particularization', extending over the entire world of particular existence, including the full range of human emotion (*Aes*, p. 87).

Music is the second art which realizes Romantic form. This art probes still deeper into subjectivity and particularization. According to Hegel, music further negates and idealizes space by concentrating it into the isolated unity of a single point, a movement or tremor of the material body in relation to itself. In music, the ideality of matter appears no longer as spatial but as a temporal ideality, an ideality of sound or tone. Succession in time, says Hegel, is more 'ideal' than coexistence in space, since the former appertains to consciousness alone. The abstract visibility of matter, as presented in painting, is modulated into audibility: 'sound releases the Ideal, as it were, from its entanglement in matter'. Music marks the point of transition between the 'abstract spatial sensuousness' of painting and the 'abstract spirituality' expressed in poetry (*Aes*, p. 88).

Hegel sees poetry as the third and highest realization of Romantic art, because it completes the liberation of spirit from materiality that was begun by painting and music. Hegel states: 'For sound, the last external material which poetry keeps, is in poetry no longer the feeling of sonority itself, but a *sign*, by itself void of significance... Sound in this way becomes a *word* as a voice inherently articulated, the meaning of which is to indicate ideas and thoughts.' In this stage, the poet, as a self-conscious individual, 'unites the infinite *space* of his ideas with the *time* of sound'. Anticipating certain Romantics and Russian Formalists, Hegel states that poetry does employ sound, but only to express ideas, 'only as a sign in itself without value or content'. The audible, like the visible, is relegated to being 'a mere indication of spirit'. Hegel sees the proper element of poetic representation as the imagination, and poetry itself as 'the universal art of the spirit', which is not bound by sensuous material but instead 'launches out exclusively in the inner space and the inner time of ideas and feelings'. This is the stage at which 'art now transcends itself... and passes over from the poetry of the imagination to the prose of thought'. In general, Hegel characterizes architecture as an 'external' art and sculpture as 'objective', while he designates painting, music and poetry as 'subjective' (*Aes*, pp. 88–9).

## Characteristics of poetry in general

Hegel's detailed treatment of literature in the second volume of his *Aesthetics* comprises an analysis of three genres of poetry: epic, lyric and dramatic. He begins by offering an account of the general features of poetry. The fundamental subject matter of poetry, he reaffirms, is not the external world but our inner, spiritual life, the world of human passion, thought and action. The outside world enters into poetry only in a humanized form, as embodying and expressing our inner world. According to Hegel, there are certain essential differences between poetry and prose. To understand these, we must recall that in his *Lesser Logic*, Hegel had distinguished three basic modes of thought: Understanding, which views the world as static and composed of discrete particular things; Dialectic, which ascertains the contradictory and dynamic nature of things, but is unable to reconcile these contradictions; and Speculation, or 'Positive Reason', which 'apprehends the unity of terms... in their opposition'.[10] The most important difference between poetry and prose is that the latter treats actuality according to the restricted thinking of the Understanding, whose categories (such as cause and effect, or means and end) regard every particular thing in the world as 'falsely independent', unrelated by any inner unity. Equally, 'ordinary' thinking has no concern with the unity or essence of things and events: it takes these as accidental, as possessing no intrinsic meaning. Poetry, in contrast, sees in phenomena what is rational, substantial and true. In fact, the poetic imagination is akin to Speculative thought in philosophy, which apprehends the unity and totality of particulars, discerning what is universal in them. But there is a crucial difference: poetry must 'take speculative thinking into the imagination and give it a body'. Given its innate tendency to particularization,

[10]  *Hegel's Logic: Being Part One of the Encyclopaedia of the Philosophical Sciences (1830)*, trans. William Wallace, 3rd edn (1873; rpt Oxford University Press, 1982), p. 119.

poetry must present the universal not in philosophical abstractness but in its particular manifestations; it must represent 'reason individualized'. As such, in analysing poetry, we must take into account its national character, era and even the 'subjective individuality' of the poet. But poetry cannot remain sunk in mere particularity: all its national and cultural variety must be underlaid by a 'universal human nature.'[11]

Like Kant, Hegel sees poetry as straddling the world of sensation and the world of thought and feeling. Imagination (*Vorstellung*) draws on both spheres, and allows particulars to coexist with relative independence in the overall unity they otherwise comprise (*Aes* II, p. 1035). It should be stressed that in Hegel's concept of poetic unity, although every particular element contributes to the creation of an organic whole, that element remains interesting 'on its own account'. Poetry 'lingers' over what is individual and particular, even as it uses it to mirror our inner thoughts and feelings. The 'harmonious totality' achieved by poetry must be expressible *only* in a given configuration of particulars, which in turn embody one fundamental idea as their origin (*Aes* II, pp. 980–2). Poetry thereby expresses the 'inner meaning and essence' of particulars as they appear in the world (*Aes* II, p. 1003). By way of analogy, Hegel observes that music achieves harmony only if each note is allowed 'its independent and free' sound. This relative independence of each particular means that the harmonizing unity in poetry remains merely 'inner' and implicit. Such unity is least evident, says Hegel, in epic, which offers a wider depiction of external reality; in drama, the unity is more concentrated, and in lyric poetry it is highly variable (*Aes* II, pp. 985–6). Here, as so often, Hegel is accommodating Aristotle's views to his own scheme.

Given that poetry voices not merely the 'abstract essence' of a thing but its 'concrete reality', its language is figurative. It does not present things with the 'literal accuracy', definiteness and clarity of prose, which is concerned only with meaning. Like Locke, Hegel regards metaphorical and figurative language as relatively 'unclear and inaccurate'. He points out, however, that poetry does not aim for 'abstract accuracy'; it endeavours rather to present a concrete vision of appearances. Indeed, poetry must take pains to avoid the commonplace language of prose and the clear-cut distinctions and relations of the Understanding. Having said all this, Hegel acknowledges that the boundary between poetry and prose 'can only be drawn with difficulty' (*Aes* II, pp. 1002–7).

A third characteristic of poetry, in addition to its essential expression of subjectivity and its 'figurative' achievement of a unity which concretely embodies the universal, is its autonomy. Echoing

---

[11]  G. W. F. Hegel, *Aesthetics: Lectures on Fine Art*, vol. II, trans. T. M. Knox (Oxford University Press, 1975), pp. 972–8. Hereafter cited as *Aes* II.

Kant – without, however, developing Kant's elaborate concept of 'purposiveness' – Hegel states that the unity of poetry is 'not purposeful'. But Hegel is equally, if not more, insistent on the 'freedom and right of the imagination' (*Aes* II, p. 996). On numerous occasions, he emphasizes that poetry creates 'a totality complete in itself' (*Aes* II, p. 973), an 'independent . . . and . . . closed world on its own account' (*Aes* II, p. 980). Poetry must avoid every aim beyond art and live 'for its own sake alone'. It must not provide purely religious or moral instruction or engage in political agitation; poetry can be effectively used for all these purposes, but they should not be explicit and should be subordinated to artistic ends. Equally, however, poetry should not be isolated; it must 'enter into the midst of life', offering insight into the deeper, inner meaning of events and actions. Again echoing Kant and also anticipating Arnold's notion of 'disinterestedness', Hegel urges that poetry should be free from practical ends, 'with an eye calmly and freely surveying all existence whether subjective or objective' (*Aes* II, pp. 995–9).

## The genres of poetry

Before proceeding to his treatment of the specific genres of poetry, Hegel offers a useful summary of their characteristics and differences. Epic poetry depicts actions and events objectively and in their wholeness; the lyric expresses not the object but the subject's inner world of thought and feeling; drama combines these two modes, offering an objective account of the development of an action and also its origin in the hearts of individuals (*Aes* II, pp. 1037–9). Turning to the epic, which he sees as historically prior to the lyric and drama, Hegel defines this as the expression of 'the world outlook and objective manifestation of a national spirit presented . . . as an actual event'. This totality includes not only the religious consciousness of a people but also its political and domestic life. The action presented by an epic is not any 'single casual deed' but 'an action ramified into the whole of its age and national circumstances', requiring 'the portrayal of this world in its entirety'. But the epic's depiction of this national spirit must also embody what is universally human (*Aes* II, pp. 1044–8, 1057). And, although the epic presents an objective world, in which the poet's subjectivity is effaced, it is nonetheless characterized by the 'free individuality' of its heroic figures, who must be depicted as 'whole men' with a range of passions and in a variety of situations. Indeed, it is a single character, such as Achilles, who influences the course of the chief event. Though these characters possess individuality, the freedom of their actions is nonetheless subject to the workings of fate (*Aes* II, pp. 1053, 1067).

Hegel situates the development of epic within a broad historical context. An epic, he says, expresses the 'childlike consciousness' of a people where the relations of ethical life and the bonds of family and nation have been framed but have not yet developed into the form of rational and universal institutions and laws (*Aes* II, p. 1052). In historical terms, an epic action typically presents a 'productive collision', as in the Trojan War, which sets a whole nation in motion and which brings about a turning point in world history, leading to a higher stage of civilization. The Greek victory, for Hegel, represents the triumph of West over East, of European rationality over 'Asiatic brilliance' and 'patriarchal unity' (*Aes* II, pp. 1059–62). Hegel acknowledges that his contemporary world is not conducive to epic and needs another form. Much later, Georg Lukács will argue that this new form was the novel, which is the 'epic' of the godless modern world. Still, Hegel is able to envision a future epic, taking root in America, which might describe 'the victory . . . of living American rationality over imprisonment in particulars' (*Aes* II, p. 1062). Hegel, who had never seen America, would have been surprised to learn that the most popular 'epic' in that country today – the *masnavi* – was penned not by Whitman or any other American poet but by the Islamic mystical Persian poet Rumi (1207–73).

Hegel in fact dismisses Rumi's poetry as effectively 'burying' the epic art of Persia, which had received its foremost embodiment in the *Shahnamah* of Firdausi (940–1020). In general, Hegel's comments on Eastern literature – uninformed by any knowledge of the Arabic or Persian languages or their literary conventions – are desultory and somewhat confused. For example, he says at one point that the love songs of the Persian poet Hafez (c.1325–c.1389) express the 'whole living individuality' of the poet; later, he cites the same poet as an example of the oriental poet's mind being 'sunk' in externality (*Aes* II, pp. 1121, 1148). Applying Western literary conventions to the canons of Eastern poetry, he confidently concludes that the Greek and Roman epic is the ideal embodiment of 'epic proper', just as Greek poetry affords the 'perfect example' of the lyrical form (*Aes* II, pp. 1098–9, 1150).

The lyric is characterized by Hegel as a form of poetry which displays a subjective disposition or, as Hegel terms it, the 'self as individual', with all the relevant details of a person's unique situation and concerns. Here again, Hegel insists on artistic autonomy: the lyric poem creates 'a new poetic world of subjective meditation and feeling', which is not portrayed as resulting in any practical activity or dramatic conflict. But the subjective or particular, cautions Hegel, is of no interest by itself, and must express what is universally human. Moreover, the poet must objectify human passion and extricate it from all accidental circumstances. As Hegel puts it – so elegantly – subjectivity draws 'the objectively existent world' into itself. That world becomes internalized, with any given external situation being grasped in its 'deeper essential character'. In this manner, the lyric poet *can* describe external life, revealing 'himself as existent objectively as well as subjectively' (*Aes* II, pp. 1111–14, 1120–1, 1127). Whereas the epic tends to disperse itself through descriptions of the external world, the principle of lyric poetry is concentration (*Aes* II, pp. 1133–4). The unity of lyric derives from an 'inwardness' of mood or reflection, a mood which is recreated in the reader (*Aes* II, pp. 1115–16).

The lyric form, says Hegel, can flourish in any historical period, but is characteristic especially of a later stage of civilization than the epic, a stage where the individual has become independent and self-reflective and can see the world from his own perspective. As Hegel has it, this is a stage where the individual is increasingly aware of her inner life in an increasingly 'prosaic' world. He acknowledges, however, that subjective inner life can broaden and deepen into a vision of 'the whole world' (*Aes* II, pp. 1122–3). We might think of the poetry of Whitman or T. S. Eliot as aspiring to such breadth. Hegel offers some interesting insights into the ability of poetry to rise to a comprehensiveness of outlook. The lyric, he says, need not exclude general views as long as these are accommodated to the form of the imagination. Indeed, lyrical poetry should approach the condition of music. In general, it should strike a medium between 'almost dumb conciseness' and 'eloquent clarity' (*Aes* II, pp. 1134–7).

The highest stage of poetry, and of any art generally according to Hegel, is reached in drama, which unites lyric subjectivity with epic objectivity, the inner life and its external realization in action (what Hegel terms subjective and objective 'pathos'). Drama exhibits a complete action which, however, enshrines not a single aim but a collision of aims and their resolution. In this resolution it reveals the 'real inner essence of human aims, characters, and conflicts' and the 'accomplishment of what is absolutely rational and true' (*Aes* II, pp. 1158–60, 1162–3). Hegel's views of tragedy specifically are considered in more detail below.

Unlike epic poetry, drama does not describe the external environment; it must 'strip externals away', omit any incidental scenes, and show the 'self-conscious and active individual' as the cause of events. Nor does it present an entire world view like the epic, but is, rather, concentrated into the 'simplicity of specific circumstances' (*Aes* II, pp. 1160–1). Like Aristotle, Hegel views the unity of drama as more concise than that of the epic. Concerning the traditional dramatic 'unities', Hegel recommends flexibility regarding the unity of time and of place. The truly inviolable unity, he says, is that of action, which must be grounded in the 'total movement' of conflict and resolution (*Aes* II, pp. 1164–8).

As with the other genres, Hegel insists that the language of drama must rise above mere prose and conventional speech; it must be suited to individuals in their '*substantial* significance', their embodiment of what is universal (*Aes* II, pp. 1171–2). He also emphasizes that drama must take account of its audience and exhibit universal interest, vitality of characters and ultimately the realization of what is 'absolutely rational and true' (*Aes* II, pp. 1175–9). Discussing the role of the actor, he suggests that this was minimal in ancient drama, where the actor was merely the instrument of an author, and more pronounced in modern drama, which relies on an actor's individuality, though Hegel acknowledges the existence of various schools of thought on this subject (*Aes* II, pp. 1188–9).

Since conflict – between characters and between their aims – is central to drama, the dramatic genres, says Hegel, must be distinguished by the 'relation of individuals to their aim' (*Aes* II, p. 1193). In tragedy, as seen above, an individual identifies her aim with one of the 'spiritual powers' or 'substantive spheres' of life such as family love or patriotism. In this sense, the character is a living representative of a given sphere. In tragedy, the eternal powers emerge as victorious in reconciling these conflicting aims, and displaying the one-sidedness of opposed individuals who 'destroy themselves'. In comedy, however, the individual survives and we witness the victory of her 'own subjective personality'. In this lies the general ground of comedy: it depicts a world where 'man . . . has made himself completely master of everything that counts to him . . . as the essence of what he wills and accomplishes'. The aims of that world are self-destructive because they are unsubstantial (*Aes* II, pp. 1193–9). Interestingly, Hegel regards a failed democracy, exemplifying such a world, as comic in this respect:

Nothing can be done, for example, to help a democratic nation where the citizens are self-seeking, quarrelsome, frivolous, bumptious, without faith or knowledge, garrulous, boastful, and ineffectual: such a nation destroys itself by its own folly.
(*Aes* II, p. 1199)

Comedy, Hegel is careful to point out, must be distinguished from mere 'laughter', which can be inspired by the portrayal of vices, follies, silliness and contravention of norms. True comedy, according to Hegel, implies 'an infinite light-heartedness and confidence' of someone secure enough to bear the frustration of his aims. More specifically, comedy offers certain contradictions, as, for example, between a character and his aims, between unsubstantial aims and the seriousness with which they are pursued, or between the character's aims and external circumstances. Given its contradictory essence, comedy is in even more stringent need of resolution than tragic action. Ultimately comedy too must present the triumph of the 'absolutely rational', which reveals the folly, unreason and contradictions of the human behaviour in the finite world (*Aes* II, pp. 1200–2).

Hegel identifies a third genre between tragedy and comedy, which includes Roman satiric drama and tragicomedy. This mixed genre attempts to reconcile the difference between the tragic and the comic: the characters have aims which, as in tragedy, are substantial, but their intransigence is softened and they are more disposed to reconcile. Such a mingling of aims is characteristic of much modern drama where subjective individuality becomes dominant, pushing even the substantive spheres of the ethical powers into the background. Other dramas are motivated primarily by the desire to create theatrical effects or to highlight the inner nature of an individual. Hegel observes that the boundaries of this genre are not firm and that it risks departing from the requirements of genuine drama altogether or lapsing into prose (*Aes* II, pp. 1202–4).

## Hegel on tragedy

It is worth considering in a little more detail Hegel's influential theory of tragedy, which is expressed in many of his works, including the *Phenomenology* as well as his lectures on the philosophy of religion and history. His most mature account, to be expounded briefly here, occurs in his lectures on aesthetics.[12] As seen above, according to Hegel, drama accords a central place to the conflict or collision between various characters and their respective aims. In tragedy, this conflict occurs as follows: the overall ethical order, as Hegel sees it, consists of a number of powers or dimensions – family love, political life and religion; the characters identify with one substantive sphere of this overall undifferentiated ethical order – for example, Antigone with family loyalty and Creon with religious obligation, each acting as a representative of the chosen sphere. The essence of tragedy is that these spheres, now differentiated from one another, come into opposition. Each side, each character, is justified but one-sided, its allegiance to one sphere of the ethical order, contravening another sphere. The third phase of tragedy is the resolution, which supersedes and abrogates the one-sided particular perspectives and allows us a glimpse of 'eternal justice', of the ethical order in its undivided totality.

Hence tragedy consists of characters and their aims which come into conflict, thereby dividing an initial unity (the ethical order) which is then restored at a higher level (even at the expense of the death or suffering of the protagonists) (*Aes* II, pp. 1193–7). As Hegel sees it, the main kind of conflict, exemplified in *Antigone*, is that between two aspects of ethical

---

[12]   A compilation of Hegel's writings on tragedy is available in *Hegel on Tragedy*, ed. and intro. Anne and Henry Paolucci (1982; rpt Smyrna, DE: Griffon House, 2001).

life: state and family. Antigone honours the bonds of kinship while Creon honours Zeus, the dominating power over public life (*Aes* II, p. 1213). A second type of conflict, portrayed most beautifully in *Oedipus Tyrannus* and *Oedipus Coloneus*, is the justification of what an individual has self-consciously willed and done as against what he was fated by the gods to do (*Aes* II, p. 1214). 'The tragic complication', says Hegel, 'leads finally to no other result or denouement but this: the two sides that are in conflict with one another preserve the justification which both have, but what each upholds is one-sided, and this one-sidedness is stripped away and the inner, undisturbed harmony returns in the attitude of the chorus which clearly assigns equal honour to all the gods' (*Aes* II, p. 1215). This harmony can return in different ways. The most perfect classical example, in Hegel's eyes, is in *Oedipus Coloneus* where Oedipus expunges his inner discord.

Hegel makes some interesting general observations on tragedy. Truly tragic action, he suggests, presupposes a concept of individual freedom or at least of independence and responsibility. Predictably, he sees genuine drama as beginning in Greece and not in what he calls the oriental world (*Aes* II, pp. 1205–6). We can see that Hegel's analysis of drama is characteristically dialectical, whereby an initial unity is differentiated and then restored at a higher level; it also accords with his general historical scheme as a movement towards rationality and freedom. Indeed, tragedy reveals the underlying rationality of the ethical order, even if in its resolution individuals are sacrificed: 'only with such a conclusion can the necessity of what happens to the individuals appear as absolute rationality'. We are shattered by the fate of the heroes but repose in the knowledge of ethical harmony (*Aes* II, p. 1215).

Hegel's distinction between ancient and modern drama has aroused much interest and controversy. He observes that the conflict in ancient tragedy is not a collision between individuals but a 'battle between the essential powers that rule human life' (*Aes* II, p. 1206). Given that the basis of such tragedy is the ethical order or what Hegel calls the 'substance of ethical life', the depths of individuality and personality remain undeveloped (*Aes* II, p. 1222). In contrast, modern tragedy, as with all poetry of the 'Romantic' modern period, adopts the principle of subjectivity. Its content is the individual's passion and inner life and subjective personal ends. The collision of actions in modern tragedy does not rest on conflicts extrapolated or introjected from the ethical order but is accidental, though substantive moral ends may be engaged in a contingent manner. Our poetic interest lies in the greatness and depth of the characters (*Aes* II, pp. 1206, 1223–6). The spectacle offered by modern drama is that of 'the modern individual with the non-universal nature of his character' (*Aes* II, p. 1231). The most poignant 'portrayal of concretely human individuals and characters' occurs in Shakespeare, who 'stands at an almost unapproachable height...on the infinite breadth of his "world-stage"' (*Aes* II, p. 1227). Shakespeare's *Hamlet* is the greatest example in this regard. The 'collision' here turns strictly 'not on a son's pursuing an ethically justified revenge and being forced in the process to violate the ethical order, but on Hamlet's personal character...he eventually perishes owing to his own hesitation and a complication of external circumstances' (*Aes* II, pp. 1225–6). And so with Shakespeare's portrayal of character in general: 'this progress and history of a great soul, its inner development, the picture of its self-destructive struggle against circumstances, events, and their consequences – all this is the main theme in many of Shakespeare's most interesting tragedies' (*Aes* II, p. 1230).

Interestingly, as seen above, this assertion of subjectivity reaches even greater extremes in comedy (both ancient and modern), which presents a world governed by subjectivity, a world whose aims are 'self-destructive because they are unsubstantial' (*Aes* II, p. 1199). Hegel's theory of tragedy, and of drama in general, is in effect an accurate microcosm of the dialectical and historical nature of his aesthetics in general: a movement from an external and objective though naïve harmony with Spirit (here as the ethical order) towards subjectivity and dislocation from Spirit, from the universal, and from ethical justification into the more ironic and particularized postures of modern Romanticism.

## Hegel's influence

Hegel's aesthetics have had a pervasive influence on both literature and criticism. First, as noted by many scholars, they mark a decisive break from the centuries-old aesthetics of representation and specifically of imitation of nature which dominated neo-classical poetics. Breaking with such ahistorical rationalism, Hegel provided a ground and inspiration, like Kant, for many Romantic conceptions of literature (though neither philosopher was a Romantic).

A second area of influence – and contention – has concerned the importance that Hegel attaches to art. Some have noted that, where previous thinkers such as Plato and Aquinas had gravely demoted the spheres of poetry and art, Hegel effectively raised art into confluence with the endeavours of religion and philosophy. He saw art as an index of a people's profoundest beliefs and ideas. Far from being a trivializing or corrupting influence, art is, like religion and philosophy, concerned with ultimate truth. As William Maker puts it, art for Hegel 'addresses the very core of our being', though it no longer occupies the central place it once held in human experience.[13] Maker notes that for Hegel, art is a means

---

[13] William Maker, 'Introduction' in *Hegel and Aesthetics*, ed. Maker (SUNY, 2000), pp. vii–viii.

of resolving the restrictive opposition between the inner private sphere and the outer domain of nature; it is also emancipatory in enabling us to rise above a merely consumptive and desirous relation to material things; and, perhaps most importantly, it expresses something universally true about humanity; and because it expresses a sensuous manifestation of the intelligible, it expresses truth in its own unique mode.[14] Conversely, many commentators on Hegel's aesthetics have remarked on the apparently low status he assigns to art. Peter Szondi attributes this, and Hegel's general 'myopia' in poetics, to his 'inadequate conception' of language.[15] Marxist critic Terry Eagleton sees this low status as testifying to the fact that Hegel 'gravely underestimates the ideological force of sensuous representation'.[16]

A third stream of influence derives from the comparative and historicist nature of Hegel's treatment of art. Henry Paolucci points out that Hegel's aesthetics, comprehensive and accommodating various conceptions of beauty, effectively opened up for comparative study the cultural legacy of the peoples of the Near and Far East, including studies of Judaism and Buddhism, as in the work of archaeologists such as W. F. Albright, Emil L. Fackenheim and Kurt F. Leidecker.[17] The late nineteenth-century thinker and aesthetician Wilhelm Dilthey was profoundly influenced by Hegel in his historicism; the major modern aestheticians Benedetto Croce and Giovanni Gentile developed many of Hegel's insights. His work enabled the aesthetics of the Anglo-American Idealists such as Bernard Bosanquet, who saw Hegel's insistence that art deals with the ideal (rather than, say, nature) as 'the greatest single step that has ever been made' in aesthetics.[18] Bosanquet's own analyses of Dante and Shakespeare are vitally informed by this insight.

Fourth, Hegelian aesthetics have a highly ambivalent relationship to poststructuralism and what has generally passed for postmodernism. These recent tendencies have rejected the Enlightenment 'grand narratives' of reason, progress and freedom, viewing them as tainted by ideological subtexts of race, culture and imperialism. Such rejection has effectively reversed Hegel's prioritization of religion and philosophy over art: art, foundationless and irrational, remains to proclaim the death of philosophy (religion having allegedly expired much earlier). We see this procedure in thinkers across a wide spectrum from Schopenhauer and Nietzsche through Matthew Arnold before it reaches twentieth-century

---

[14] *Ibid.*, pp. xiii–xiv.    [15] Quoted in De Man, 'Sign and Symbol', p. 765.
[16] Terry Eagleton, *The Ideology of the Aesthetic* (Oxford: Blackwell, 1990), pp. 142, 144, 150.
[17] Paolucci and Paolucci, *Hegel on Tragedy*, pp. xv–xvi.
[18] Bernard Bosanquet, *A History of Aesthetic* (1892; rpt London and New York: George Allen & Unwin/Humanities Press, 1966), p. 342.

thought. But, as already indicated, many of the proponents of Modernism, postmodernism and poststructuralism (not to mention Schopenhauer and Nietzsche) had inevitable recourse to Hegelian notions in the very formulations of their strictures on philosophy. Carl Rapp points out that what Hegel sees as the end of art, the dissolution of Romantic art, is actually an indefinite process, and that the condition described by Hegel as Romantic irony was proleptic of the conceptions of subjectivity in modern literature, a subjective focus maintained in the work of thinkers such as Derrida, Foucault and Richard Rorty.[19] Jere Surber also sees Hegel's aesthetics as anticipating Modernist developments and specifically as opening the way for art to express philosophical issues and perspectives.[20] Hegel anticipated some of the insights of Freud concerning the development of identity, and the insights of Saussure concerning the nature of language. Others have reminded us of the influential nature of Hegel's notion that art is linked to the endeavours of religion and philosophy, while recognizing that political problems cannot countenance merely aesthetic solutions.

Finally, just as Hegel's dialectic obliquely anticipates philosophies such as existentialism and attitudes such as deconstruction, so his views of tragedy anticipate even the more modern fragmented stage of 'absurdist' playwrights such as Beckett, Ionesco and others. It was the renowned Shakespearean critic A. C. Bradley who introduced Hegel's theory of tragedy to the English-speaking world in a famous lecture of 1909, stating that, since Aristotle, Hegel was the only philosopher to have treated tragedy 'in a manner both original and searching'.[21] Nonetheless, Hegel's reflections on Shakespeare have been relatively neglected in Anglo-American letters, whereas his writings on the foremost European literary masters have markedly influenced literary scholars in Germany, France and Italy, informing the pages of such figures as Taine and De Sanctis. In 1969 the critic Leonard Moss argued that Hegel's theory of tragedy had in fact exerted a widespread but unacknowledged influence. Though some thinkers such as Kenneth Burke and Sidney Hook explicitly attempt to come to terms with Hegel's theory, most commentators ignore or explicitly dismiss it while unwittingly propounding variants of it, most of them not having read Hegel.[22] Subsequent commentators,

19   Carl Rapp, 'Hegel's Concept of the Dissolution of Art' in Maker, *Hegel and Aesthetics*, pp. 15–21.
20   Jere Surber, 'Art as a Mode of Thought: Hegel's Aesthetics and the Origins of Modernism' in Maker, *Hegel and Aesthetics*, p. 46.
21   A. C. Bradley, 'Hegel's Theory of Tragedy' in *Oxford Lectures on Poetry* (1909; rpt New York and London: St. Martin's Press/Macmillan, 1965), p. 69.
22   Leonard Moss, 'The Unrecognized Influence of Hegel's Theory of Tragedy', *Journal of Aesthetics and Art Criticism*, 28 (1969), pp. 91, 93–5.

such as Mark William Roche, Kirk Pillow and Brian K. Etter, have taken up Moss's call for a more responsible and careful assessment of Hegel's notions.[23]

One of the most concerted attempts in the late twentieth century to develop a dialectical literary criticism on a Hegelian basis (albeit modified by its Marxist extrapolation) has been made by Fredric Jameson, who identifies a number of broad elements which might orientate such a criticism. These elements include a shift from a focus on the object to a focus on the connection between subject and object, whereby criticism reflects upon the contribution of its own perspective and intellectual instruments to the overall perceptual situation.[24] Dialectical criticism is deeply aware of human beings and the world as mutually constructive. It is also intrinsically anti-systematic, in the sense that the initial categories of analysis used by criticism are recognized as provisional and ever shifting in their mutual relations (*MF*, pp. 311, 336, 362). Dialectical criticism is diachronic and intrinsically comparative: its understanding of a work or author is differential, and it views form as the result, inwardly shaped, of a given content (*MF*, pp. 332, 380). It integrally involves sublation (*Aufhebung*, abrogation and preservation in a higher synthesis) of its own perspectives, and the reconciliation of 'inner' elements with 'outer' elements, a work's existence with its history (*MF*, p. 416). Interestingly, in this view, literary autonomy itself becomes a dialectical phenomenon (*MF*, p. 313). All in all, Jameson sees Hegel's work as still the most complete description of how transformations in social life affect the arts (*MF*, p. 352). He acknowledges that the totalizing and relational impulse of Hegelian criticism has been opposed by the various traditions of empirical realism in both literature and philosophy (*MF*, p. 368).

Much recent criticism has also reacted against what it sees as the totalizing nature of Hegel's vision, stressing instead the local, the particular and the notion of 'difference'. For example, many of Derrida's notions rest on an arresting of the Hegelian dialectic at its second stage, that of externalization, the stage where the identity of any entity is viewed as pure difference, as entirely consumed by its relations to other entities. But the insights that are characteristically attributed to modern literary theory – the critique of essentialism, the discrediting of correspondence

[23] See Mark William Roche, *Tragedy and Comedy: A Systematic Study and a Critique of Hegel* (SUNY Press, 1998); Kirk Pillow, *Sublime Understanding: Aesthetic Reflection in Kant and Hegel* (London and Cambridge, MA: MIT Press, 2000); Brian K. Etter, *Between Transcendence and Historicism: The Ethical Nature of the Arts in Hegelian Aesthetics* (SUNY Press, 2006).

[24] These insights are offered in a chapter entitled 'Towards Dialectical Criticism' in Fredric Jameson, *Marxism and Form: Twentieth-Century Dialectical Theories of Literature* (Princeton University Press, 1971), p. 308. Hereafter cited as *MF*.

theories of truth and meaning, the deconstruction of identity, the exhibition of the constructed nature of subjectivity and objectivity, the emphasis
on the constitutive role of language in that construction, the arbitrariness
of the sign, and the idea of otherness or alterity as it informs much modern thought – had already been discovered by many thinkers, including
Locke, Hume, Kant, Schopenhauer, Nietzsche, Bergson and Heidegger.
But it was in the works of Hegel – in his general philosophy and his
aesthetics – that they received their most profound and comprehensive
articulation.

# 13

# Marx, Engels and early Marxist criticism

## MACDONALD DALY

In 1971, Fredric Jameson, possibly the most influential Marxist critic of the late twentieth century, recommended 'a relatively Hegelian kind of Marxism' to the literary critical world. Those only partly acquainted with Marxism might have been forgiven for wondering why a political and philosophical doctrine which had so long prided itself on 'overcoming' Hegel, on having turned Hegel on his head, on having morphed Hegel's Idealist dialectic into the apparently quite contrasting doctrine of historical materialism, was itself seemingly being cast back into the politically conservative swamp from which it usually claimed to have rescued not only German philosophy but the entire modern world. Jameson dated the emergence of Hegelian Marxism to a short period of about fifteen years, the pertinent milestones being, in the German-speaking world, 'Lukác's *History and Class Consciousness* in 1923, along with the rediscovery of Marx's *Economic and Philosophical Manuscripts of 1844*' (first published, incompletely, in Russian in 1927, and completely, in German, in 1932) and, in France, 'the Hegel revival there during the late thirties'.[1] Jameson did not need to be explicit that this was also the definitive period of developing anti-Stalinist revulsion in Western Europe. Our speculative reader may legitimately have surmised from Jameson that the fledgling Marxist criticism of the late nineteenth and early twentieth centuries, which had taken its stand on Marx's own oft-repeated sense that Hegelianism was a political dead end, was now itself ironically considered to have been a grand tour down a most disappointing methodological cul-de-sac.

Indeed, Jameson, like almost every other modern Marxist aesthetician of note, neglects many of the figures who will make an appearance in this chapter, like Franz Mehring, William Morris, Antonio Labriola and Georgi Plekhanov.[2] But the reader more familiar with Marxist modes

---

[1] Fredric Jameson, *Marxism and Form: Twentieth-Century Dialectical Theories of Literature* (Princeton University Press, 1971), p. ix.

[2] All of them are likewise ignored by as influential and as recent a selection as Terry Eagleton and Drew Milne (eds.), *Marxist Literary Theory: A Reader* (Oxford: Blackwell, 1996), which presents selections from Marx and Engels and thence leaps boldly ahead to Lenin without even a further nod at the nineteenth century.

of argumentation would have little problem with the proposition that a thing can turn into its opposite, or that a negation can be negated, without any return to the *status quo ante* being effected. Dialectical deftness is the stock in trade of Hegelianism and Marxism alike. The young pre-Marxist Marx, in a note appended to his doctoral thesis of 1841, in which he clearly had Hegel in mind, already had a definite grasp of the method:

It is conceivable that a philosopher should be guilty of this or that inconsistency because of this or that compromise; he may himself be conscious of it. But what he is not conscious of is that in the last analysis this apparent compromise is made possible by the deficiency of his principles or an inadequate grasp of them. So if a philosopher really has compromised it is the job of his followers to use the inner core of his thought to illuminate his own superficial expressions of it. In this way, what is a progress in conscience is also a progress in knowledge. This does not involve putting the conscience of a philosopher under suspicion, but rather construing the essential characteristics of his views, giving them a definite form and meaning, and thus at the same time going beyond them.[3]

It is with reference to this description of the proper relation between a philosopher and his followers that this chapter will ultimately offer an assessment of nineteenth-century literary critics who attempted to elaborate and/or practise a Marxist aesthetics. Did they, as Marx put it, 'use the inner core of his thought to illuminate his own superficial expressions of it' in the aesthetic field? Or, as the relative silence concerning them of Jameson and many other commentators perhaps suggests, did they fail in this task? And if they failed, did any do so less ingloriously than others?

We must first of all, then, uncover the 'inner core' of Marx's thinking with respect to art and literature, a task which virtually all who are fit to comment have acknowledged as difficult on account of the very 'superficial expressions' of it which Marx left, not to mention the scattered textual locations in which they arise. There is, to be sure, the ultimate gift horse Marx gave us, namely his 'Preface' to *A Contribution to the Critique of Political Economy* (1859), in which he explicitly includes the 'aesthetic' in his list of examples of 'ideological forms' comprising the 'superstructure' of society:

In the social production of their life, men enter into definite relations that are indispensable and independent of their will, relations of production which correspond to a definite stage of development of their material productive forces. The sum total of these relations of production constitutes the economic structure of society, the real foundation, on which rises a legal and political superstructure

---

[3] *Karl Marx: Selected Writings*, ed. David McLellan (Oxford University Press, 1977), p. 13.

and to which correspond definite forms of social consciousness. The mode of
production of material life conditions the social, political and intellectual life
process in general. It is not the consciousness of men that determines their being,
but, on the contrary, their social being that determines their consciousness. At a
certain stage of their development, the material productive forces of society
come in conflict with the existing relations of production, or – what is but a legal
expression for the same thing – with the property relations within which they
have been at work hitherto. From forms of development of the productive forces
these relations turn into their fetters. Then begins an epoch of social revolution.
With the change of the economic foundation the entire immense superstructure
is more or less rapidly transformed. In considering such transformations a
distinction should always be made between the material transformation of the
economic conditions of production, which can be determined with the precision
of natural science, and the legal, political, religious, aesthetic or philosophic – in
short, ideological forms in which men become conscious of this conflict and
fight it out. Just as our opinion of an individual is not based on what he thinks
of himself, so can we not judge of such a period of transformation by its own
consciousness; on the contrary, this consciousness must be explained rather
from the contradictions of material life, from the existing conflict between the
social productive forces and the relations of production.[4]

It has seldom been noted how repetitious this passage is. Marx hardly
builds an elaborate or complex argument here: rather, he reiterates a
central idea in varied phrasing in a manner typical of someone intent on
persuading a reader of a novel notion (for Hegelians an heretical notion).
The same three-element relation, of actually quite simple subject–verb–
object expressions, is described in three different ways: (1) (subject) the
*economic structure of society* or *the mode of production of material
life* or *social being* (2) (verb) *gives rise to, conditions* or *determines* (3)
(object) the *legal and political superstructure*, the *social, political and
intellectual life process in general*, or *consciousness*, respectively. In the
English translation quoted, the three different formulations depict almost
the same relation, being hardly at semantic variance with one another
except in the verbs. But it is in the hazards of those verbs that markedly
variant and incompatible versions of the relations between 'base' and
'superstructure' (and consequently between Marxism and art) have taken
root.

The crucial three sentences read, in Marx's original,

Die Gesamtheit dieser Produktionsverhältnisse bildet die ökonomische Struktur
der Gesellschaft, die reale Basis, worauf sich ein juristischer und politischer
Überbau erhebt, und welcher bestimmte gesellschaftliche Bewusstseinformen
entsprechen. Die Produktionsweise des materiellen Lebens bedingt den sozialen,

---

[4] Karl Marx and Frederick Engels, *On Literature and Art* (Moscow: Progress, 1976),
p. 41.

politischen und geistigen Lebenzsprozess überhaupt. Es is nicht das Bewusstsein der Menschen, das ihr Sein, sondern umgekehrt ihr gesellschaftliches Sein, das ihr Bewusstsein bestimmt.[5]

The German verb *bedingen* in the second sentence is delicately nuanced: *bedingt* here could justifiably have been Englished (in ascending order of strength) as 'presupposes', 'conditions', 'causes', 'necessitates' or 'determines', although many would argue that had Marx had the last in mind he would probably have reached for a stronger verb. The verb so translated, which he does use in the following sentence, is *bestimmen*, which is even more varied in application: thus *bestimmt* could mean any of 'modifies', 'influences', 'conditions', 'decides', 'defines', 'designates', 'fixes', 'determines' or 'predetermines'.

Now, there are clear differences of interconnectedness indicated by the causative verbs 'gives rise to', 'conditions' and 'determines'. The first defines a weak relation in which (a) simply creates the preconditions for (b); the second implies a stronger causative relation in which (a) influences or sets limits to the form of (b); the third might imply that (a) is the thoroughly controlling and moving force behind or within (b). If, for heuristic purposes, one leaves aside the complex social phenomena which Marx is actually describing, and replaces them with simpler correlates, as Marx himself does with the example of (a) 'an individual' and (b) 'what he thinks of himself', then the differences of interconnectedness are easier to appreciate. Take the alternative example of (a) a person's body and (b) a person's character. In this case, the first proposition is surely a universally acceptable one: it amounts to little more than a statement of the obvious, namely that to have a character one must possess a body. The second proposition would also probably pass without major disagreement: all that would be questioned is the degree to which character is affected by physiology. The third proposition, that character is controlled thoroughly and at all times by the operations of bodily reflexes, organs, genetic programming and so on, might gain the assent of certain neuroscientists and behaviourists, but is unlikely to meet with the approval of too many others, scientists included, not least because it seems to render the very concept of 'character' (if it is merely an epiphenomenon) worthless: all talk of character can simply be reduced to physical terms in such a case.

The passage is evidently an example of what the soon-to-be Dr Marx had already diagnosed as a 'deficiency of ... principles or an inadequate grasp of them' because the three propositions are not mutually compatible: to leave all of them open as possibilities is precisely a 'compromise',

5 *Marxismus und literatur: eine dokumentation in drei bänden*, ed. Fritz J. Raddatz, 3 vols. (Hamburg: Rowohlt, 1969), vol. i, p. 152. I would like to thank Professor Svenja Adolphs for confirming some particulars of the original German.

here no doubt made for the sake of the non-Idealist, anti-Hegelian emphasis which Marx felt was required at the moment. Marx himself never
went 'beyond' them, although the early Marx demonstrably believed the
opposite. It is worth recalling that the man who wrote 'It is not the consciousness of men that determines their being, but, on the contrary, their
social being that determines their consciousness' two decades earlier 'criticised Democritus' strict determinism and came out in favour of Epicurus'
position of freedom of man's consciousness to change his surroundings'.[6]

The sheer number and extent of Marx's casual and formal comments
on art and literature, the pleasure he took in them and the value they
obviously possessed for him, give the lie to any charge of philistine dismissal of the aesthetic or its importance. But only a decade previously,
in the *Manifesto of the Communist Party* (1848), he could write, 'Does
it require deep intuition to comprehend that man's ideas, views and conceptions, in one word, man's consciousness, changes with every change
in the conditions of his material existence, in his social relations and
in his social life? What else does the history of ideas prove, than that
intellectual production changes its character in proportion as material
production is changed?'[7] Earlier still, *The German Ideology* (1846), a
text written jointly with Engels which from the very first page is a bold,
lacerating and unrelenting attack on Hegel and his contemporary followers, is replete with formulations which seem to vacillate between the
uncompromisingly 'deterministic' and pliably 'conditional' versions of
base–superstructure relations, but ultimately veer towards the former:
'The phantoms formed in the brains of men are also, necessarily, sub-
limates of their material life-process, which is empirically verifiable and
bound to material premises. Morality, religion, metaphysics, and all the
rest of ideology as well as the forms of consciousness corresponding to
these, thus no longer retain the semblance of independence.' But the same
text also continually stresses that this is not how humans *live* their relation to the world: on the contrary, they seem always and everywhere to
have acted as if the reverse were true, imagining that the moving principle
of the world really is thought: 'If in all ideology men and their relations
appear upside-down as in a *camera obscura*, this phenomenon arises just
as much from their historical life-process as the inversion of objects on
the retina does from their physical life process.'[8]

Writing in 1852, in *The Eighteenth Brumaire of Louis Napoleon*, he
could still say, 'Upon the different forms of property, upon the social
conditions of existence, rises an entire superstructure of distinct and peculiarly formed sentiments, illusions, modes of thought, and views of life.

---

[6]  David McLellan, *The Thought of Karl Marx* (Basingstoke: Macmillan, 1979), p. 7.
[7]  Marx and Engels, *On Literature and Art*, p. 73.      [8]  *Ibid.*, p. 43.

The entire class creates and forms them out of its material foundations and out of the corresponding social relations.'[9] But it did not fail to dawn on Marx that these apparent illusions were *socially produced* (always a key concept for him) and socially potent. 'Production not only provides the material to satisfy a need,' he wrote in the late 1850s, 'it also provides the need for the material ... An *objet d'art* creates a public that has artistic taste and is able to enjoy beauty.'[10] But if the appetite for beauty can become a *need*, akin to appetites more traditionally conceived of as physical, where does the material end and the non-material begin?

There is no linear development in these sometimes contradictory, sometimes complementary thoughts. Variations on these themes, unpredictably inflected towards or between the various versions of the base–superstructure motif, can emerge at different points in Marx's *œuvre* with something approaching randomness. As early as 1844 he could ferociously satirize capitalism's denial of the enjoyment of luxury, its imperative to save rather than spend, as one of its morally worst features, and in doing so he notably made no distinction between 'material' and 'non-material' activities: 'The less you eat, drink and buy books; the less you go to the theatre, the dance hall, the public house; the less you think, love, theorise, sing, paint, fence, etc., the more you *save* – the *greater* becomes your treasure which neither moths nor rust will devour – your *capital*.'[11]

It is important to note that the few texts in which we find Marx attempting to work out the implications of his theory of determination for specific forms of art show that he was in difficulty. Above all, there is the famous (or notorious) 1857 draft 'Introduction' to *A Contribution to the Critique of Political Economy* (which was not published until 1903), in which he embarks upon a disquisition concerning the long-lasting appeal of ancient art, stimulated by questions such as, 'Is the conception of nature and of social relations which underlies Greek imagination and therefore Greek [art] possible when there are self-acting mules, railways, locomotives and electric telegraphs?' His answer to the conundrum of the ongoing social value of Greek art was, 'Does not the child in every epoch represent the character of the period in its natural veracity? Why should not the historic childhood of humanity, where it attained its most beautiful form, exert an eternal charm because it is a stage that will never recur?'[12] This was a desperately bad stab at a good question, but more important than its bathos is the fact that Marx's response reverts to categories which are entirely non-Marxist. This may be one reason why he chose not to publish the draft.

9 Karl Marx and Frederick Engels, *Collected Works*, 50 vols. (London: Lawrence & Wishart, 1979), vol. XI, p. 128.
10 Marx and Engels, *On Literature and Art*, p. 129.
11 *Ibid.*, p. 133.    12 *Ibid.*, pp. 83, 84.

The least satisfactory response to the shortcomings of Marx's thinking on these matters, however, is to wave aside his inadequately worked out positions as merely nugatory. Marx was too influential a thinker for the tradition of aesthetic criticism he inspired to be ignored in this way. He himself, as we have already seen, described a more intellectually effective procedure. Did his followers attempt to construe 'the essential characteristics of his views, giving them a definite form and meaning, and thus at the same time going beyond them'? It is certainly possible, at this distance, to identify the 'inner core' of Marx's thought with respect to aesthetics. This essentially posits the truth that the human capacity to produce art is dependent on an economic system in which such production (and its consumption) is made possible, that art itself is a 'secondary' phenomenon which bears the ineradicable traces or marks of its economic dependency (and is thus highly historically variable), but that it also creates new needs which themselves lead to the diversification of the product and thus (logically) would seem to intervene in the 'primary' economic system. One might paraphrase Marx's thinking along these lines as prompting a number of questions which he himself is unable to answer but which provided a working agenda for his followers. Among these questions might be the following: *in what specific ways* do economic conditions 'influence' the production of art in concrete cases?; *how much* is art influenced by economic conditions?; is there any way in which art can be said to be *relatively free* of such influence?; if so, can some arts, or some aesthetic texts, be said to be *more or less free* than others?; if not, is art, in the final analysis, *reducible to* economic categories?; or is it possible that the influence might also work *in reverse*, art precipitating modifications in economic life?

Some of these questions were tackled while Marx himself was still alive, but not by Marx. It is too little acknowledged that, in the aesthetic field at least, Engels, *pace* his own self-characterization, did not simply play second fiddle to Marx as the latter's popularizer. He not only supplemented Marx's general reflections on art, but considerably enlarged upon them, and even introduced quite new emphases and lines of thought. This is nowhere more patent than in his espousal of Realism as his preferred aesthetic form. According to Stefan Morawski, 'The word "realism" does not appear in any text by Marx.'[13] Later Marxist aestheticians' preoccupation with Realism, which can be found as late as Georg Lukács and Raymond Williams, is almost entirely due to Engels. In its earliest emergence in his writing, this concern seems driven by the fact that the 'reality' depicted by certain works of art coincides happily

---

[13]  Lee Baxandall and Stefan Morawski (eds.), *Karl Marx and Frederick Engels on Literature and Art* (New York: International General, 1973), p. 30.

with Marx's historical materialist theory of 'the real foundation', or, in an even more pedestrian manner, with the mere practical necessities of spreading the socialist message. In 1844, for example, Engels articulated his enthusiasm for a contemporary painting by Karl Hubner, 'The Silesian Weavers', which he praised in terms that referred to little other than its politically emotive content and its consequent efficacy as a piece of propaganda: it 'made a more effectual Socialist agitation than a hundred pamphlets might have done'.[14] But the very fact that Engels even saw fit to hail a painting as a notable contribution to the early progress of the socialist movement is eloquent testimony to his sense of art's social importance.

Engels soon overcame (if indeed he ever held) the simple belief that the merit of a work of art is merely an index of the effectiveness with which it encapsulates a socialist politics, and this is why it would be unfair to lay the responsibility for the later, grotesque Stalinist doctrine of 'Socialist Realism' at his door. It is in his correspondence, not Marx's, that we first encounter a perspective on Realism which acknowledges it both as a set of aesthetic conventions and as a social form with especial resonance for Marxism. In April 1888, in a draft letter to responding to the author of a novel of working-class life, he famously announced, 'Realism, to my mind, implies, besides truth of detail, the truthful reproduction of typical characters under typical circumstances', and criticized the work because it had failed to meet the criteria of circumstantial typicality, in that it omitted to depict the working class as much more than a passive mass.[15] It would be easy to dismiss this seemingly sweeping criticism of a large corpus of fiction as a product of Engels' highly politicized disposition, but to do so would fail to attend to its remarkable originality. We may now be used to authorial class allegiance, ideological tendency and unconscious motivation as they can be found to operate in literary texts, but no one, before Engels, was prepared to articulate their putative effect *and* simultaneously establish a political dimension for evaluation of the aesthetic results.

Moreover, Balzac's work is here appropriated for Marxism in a way that vitally undermines the vulgar Marxist notion that art be produced to a political prescription and its evaluation firmly subordinated to socialist ends. We may distinguish four implicit, associated points: first, literary writing is not an 'opinionated' discourse and cannot be evaluated by the same standards as, for example, a political polemic; second, this is

---

14   *Ibid.*, p. 105. The painting is in the Kunstmuseum, Düsseldorf: a monochrome reproduction can be found in Margaret A. Rose, *Marx's Lost Aesthetic: Karl Marx and the Visual Arts* (Cambridge University Press, 1984), p. 105.
15   Marx and Engels, *On Literature and Art*, pp. 91–2. On 'tendency writing', see further Engels's letter to Minna Kautsky, 26 November 1885, quoted in *ibid.*, pp. 87–9.

not to say that art is non-ideological, but that it is not (or should not be) *expressly* so; third, the ideological nature of an art work cannot be equated with the (conscious) ideology of the artist, and indeed may be in conflict with it; and, fourth, it therefore follows that classical or bourgeois art cannot simply be dismissed on the assumption that it is ideologically reactionary. The fact that these points raise further questions which are not answered by Engels only demonstrates how they enlarge the scope of Marxist inquiry into art, its evaluation and its functions. What stance should a Marxist critic take on classical or bourgeois works of art that cannot be read 'against the grain' in the way that he reads Balzac? If analysis shows that the work is indeed reactionary, in however subtly tangential and aesthetically pleasing a manner, should Marxist critics thereafter simply wash their hands of it? Or should they embark on a critique of its content while praising its form? In short, how much is Marxist theory willing to separate the aesthetic value of a work of art from its ideological outlook?

Just as Engels's comments on Balzac initiated a search for solutions to these problems, so too did they encourage speculation as to the issue of Realism and its relation to Marxist 'reality'. It is clear from his closing remarks that Engels is praising the Realist mode in which he chose to write as much as he is praising Balzac himself. One cannot imagine, for example, a Symbolist or a Surrealist method being used to produce a 'chronicle-fashion' history of society of a kind which might attract equivalent approbation from Engels. But does this amount to the proposition that Marxism privileges Realism above other artistic modes? Is aesthetic verisimilitude the inevitable correlative of Marx's conceptualization of 'reality'? Is it thus inherently 'progressive' and other representational modes inherently conservative?

Marx had died in 1883. It is arguable that, in the twelve years remaining to him, Engels did considerably more than popularize the pre-existing conceptual and textual legacy Marx had bequeathed. As the surviving member of the partnership and keeper of the flame, Engels was increasingly looked to by growing numbers of younger Marxist intellectuals as the greatest living authority on the doctrine, and this gave him the privilege of being permitted to amplify its silences and smooth its rough edges. This did not occur when he and Marx worked alongside one another. A unique moment in intellectual history occurred in 1859, when, within a month of each other, Marx and Engels both wrote separate letters to Ferdinand Lassalle, each adversely criticizing with identically insincere courtesy Lassalle's recently published drama, *Franz von Sickingen*.[16] Each letter represents the closest reading of a single literary text Marx

---

[16]  *Ibid.*, pp. 98–107.

and Engels seem ever to have committed to paper, but their content and tone are so similar that it is hard to distinguish one from the other. Marx wrote several times to Engels in the intervening month, during which one suspects Engels became aware of and consciously echoed what he knew Marx already to have written.[17]

How different things were when Engels found himself by default to be the (intestate) Marx's intellectual heir. Called upon to act as Marx's editor, executor and exegete, he did not hesitate to reconfigure Marx's concepts in the light of new political and economic circumstances, most important of all the rise of social democracy in Germany. His most profound innovation was the concept of mediation, promulgated in a letter to Franz Mehring in July 1893:

The ideologist who deals with history (history is here simply meant to comprise all the spheres – political, juridical, philosophical, theological – belonging to society and not only to nature) thus possesses in every sphere of science material which has formed itself independently out of the thought of previous generations and has gone through its own independent process of development in the brains of these successive generations. True, external facts belonging to one or another sphere may have exercised a codetermining influence on this development, but the tacit presupposition is that these facts themselves are also only the fruit of a process of thought, and so we still remain within that realm of mere thought, which apparently has successfully digested even the hardest facts.[18]

An analysis which demonstrates 'mediation', then, is one which traces 'false' ideological consciousness to its 'true' source in material interests, but does so without denying the social effectivity of ideology.

With regard to art, the case has since regularly been made that aesthetic productions are important purveyors of ideological concepts and values. Marx himself was fond of showing that Shakespeare was radically insightful with regard to the relations between material interests and ideology, famously citing in *Economic and Philosophical Manuscripts of 1844* the 'Gold? Yellow, glittering, precious gold?' soliloquy from *Timon of Athens* to show how 'Shakespeare excellently depicts the real nature of money',[19] its ability to make real what can otherwise only be imagined, but also its capacity to transform, dictate or determine ideological consciousness. Engels's outline theory of mediation, then, would seem similarly to encourage analysis (or critiques) of conservative artistic works as ideological constructions producing 'false consciousness'. The analysis

---

[17]  Marx and Engels, *Collected Works*, vol. XL, pp. 418–46.
[18]  Robert C. Tucker (ed.), *The Marx–Engels Reader*, 2nd edn. (New York: Norton, 1978), p. 766.
[19]  Marx and Engels, *On Literature and Art*, p. 136.

or critique would presumably show how this 'false consciousness' is a mediation of 'true' material interests, and demonstrate and evaluate (perhaps condemn) the degree of historical effectiveness of such works. Conversely, 'radical' art would by implication tend to expose the material sources in which all ideological consciousness is rooted, thus producing a 'true' (in Marxist terms, non-ideological or scientific) picture of the world.

This proposed application of Engels's sketchy theory is obviously tendentious, not least in its suggestion that not all art, but only conservative art, is ideological. But it is a significant advance from a fairly rudimentary 'reflection' theory (in which art [in the superstructure] merely *reflects* history [the base]) to a more sophisticated 'mediation' theory (in which art *both reflects and has the capacity to alter* history). However limited or crude such nascent insights may seem now, they give Engels an important place in Marxist literary critical thought: in the aesthetic field at least, it was he who rendered the Marxist analytic method dialectical. 'Mediation' was to remain a key concept for Marxists until as recently as Louis Althusser.

The recipient of Engels's letter, Mehring, has the distinction of writing what is acknowledged to be the first sustained volume-length study in Marxist aesthetics, *The Lessing Legend* (1893). Originally a series of journal articles, this began as a rebuttal of a particularly tendentious study of Lessing by the bourgeois critic Eric Schmidt, but grew into a spirited attack on an entire phalanx of German literary historians who linked the German literary renaissance of the eighteenth century to the rise of Prussia, thus associating the reign of the absolutist Frederick II and the birth of classical German literature. Engels's letter was primarily written to thank Mehring for having sent the book, which he had already told Karl Kautsky he considered 'first-rate',[20] but as Engels's compliments to Mehring demonstrate, he considered the book's value to lie in its historical rather than its aesthetic analysis, as have most other commentators. To this day *The Lessing Legend* has been translated into English only in a radically abbreviated form, which has itself been long out of print, and consequently Mehring remains a literary critic whose reputation has made little impact on the Anglophone world.[21] This is a sad fact, given

[20] *Ibid.*, p. 64.
[21] Franz Mehring, *The Lessing Legend*, trans. A. S. Grogan (New York: Critics Group Press, 1938). Very little of Mehring's work (other than his epoch-making biography of Marx, published in English in 1936) is available in English. This may be the appropriate point to note that Marxist writers of this period have, however, been astonishingly well served by the internet generation: Mehring is only one of the many Marxist writers rescued from almost complete oblivion, for example by the extraordinary site www.marxists.org.

his prodigious, incessant and highly scholarly activity. As we shall see, Mehring's association with Rosa Luxemburg proved to be his historical undoing at the hands of Stalin.

Mehring came to Marxism later than most, in his forties, with his aesthetic perspective already somewhat formed and fully Kantian, which, to say the least, would seem *prima facie* to pose a considerable Idealist problem for a Marxist. (Indeed, there is a history of Marxist aesthetics waiting to be written along the lines that the principal advances in the field came from those, from Benjamin to Sartre to Williams, who came to Marxism from Idealist humanist background which they stubbornly refused fully to renounce.) Far from recanting his Kantian past, Mehring set about adroitly attempting to fuse the Marxist theory of ideology with Kantian (and Schillerian) aesthetics. For example, in one of the best-known of his 'Aesthetic Ramblings' (a regular column he contributed to the journal *Die Neue Zeit*, edited by Kautsky, in 1898–9), he resynthesized the Kantian theory of aesthetic judgement from a materialist point of view.[22] In so doing, he was the first to imply that Marxism had inherited a great deal from classical German aesthetics in particular as well as classical German philosophy in general. It took half a century for this emphasis to be taken up again by Herbert Marcuse and, ironically, the man who was to do Mehring's reputation most damage, Lukács (on which see the end of this chapter).

It is surprising, given the fact that Marx and Engels spent most of the later parts of their lives in London, that only William Morris, in this period and from this part of the world, made a noteworthy and lasting contribution to Marxist aesthetics. (The temptation to include in this survey that even more famous frequenter of London Marxist circles – George Bernard Shaw – has been resisted. Shaw's early commitment to Marxism is indisputable, but it was decidedly on the wane from 1884, when he joined the Fabians and, predictably, took a socialist path that was, by definition, rather lukewarm towards Marxism. Most of his creative and critical work postdated this conversion and did not appreciably contribute to Marxist aesthetics strictly conceived.)[23] Yet many of Morris's voluminous essays on art, literature and aesthetics were for long as

---

[22] The discussion can be found in Maynard Solomon (ed.), *Marxism and Art: Essays Classic and Contemporary* (Detroit: Wayne State University Press, 1979), pp. 102–6.

[23] Readers interested in pursuing Shaw's politics and its place in his work are referred to Gareth Griffith, *Socialism and Superior Brains: The Political Thought of George Bernard Shaw* (London: Routledge, 1993). Likewise a number of European initiatives which took place under the sign of anarchist socialism, but were only questionably Marxist, are not accounted for here: see, for example, Eugenia W. Herbert, *The Artist and Social Reform: France and Belgium 1885–1898* (New Haven, CT: Yale University Press, 1961).

hard to get hold of as they are difficult to do justice to in the restricted scope of the present chapter.[24]

More importantly, Morris's unique utopian concerns and emphases take us back, as no other critic of the period does, to the influence on the early Marx of Fourier and Feuerbach. The following passage, for example, from the text of a lecture, 'Art under Plutocracy', originally delivered in the University of Oxford in November 1883, seems to bear all the marks of a writer who is familiar with Marx's *Economic and Philosophical Manuscripts of 1844*:

art is founded on what I feel quite sure is a truth, and an important one, namely that all art, even the highest, is influenced by the conditions of labour of the mass of mankind, and that any pretensions which may be made for even the highest intellectual art to be independent of these general conditions are futile and vain; that is to say, that any art which professes to be founded on the special education or refinement of a limited body or class must of necessity be unreal and short-lived. Art is man's expression of his joy in labour.[25]

But Morris could not possibly have known Marx's writings of 1844, which did not see the light of day in any form until 1927, and were not published in full until 1932. His Marxist textual influences seem principally to have been Marx's *Capital* and Engels's *Socialism: Utopian and Scientific* (the pamphlet which laid bare to a larger than usual audience the utopian influences on the early formation of Marxism), both of which he read in French translation in the 1880s. Morris probably arrived at this Marxist juncture via non-Marxist sources such as Ruskin (who chaired the meeting at which the words above were first spoken) and that great influence on Ruskin, Carlyle, who was in the main responsible for plugging the British of the nineteenth century into classical German aesthetics of the eighteenth.

It is difficult to imagine how novel it must have seemed, in the industrial English Midlands of January 1884, to attend a lecture at the Leicester Secular Society (later published as 'Art and Socialism', Morris's best-known essay), and hear Morris open with the words, 'My friends, I want you to look into the relations of Art to Commerce': note the 'you', which turns what would otherwise be a statement of intent into an exhortation.[26]

[24] Even today most readers can assemble Morris's critical *œuvre* only mosaic-like from a number of rather obsolete selections: see William Morris, *Stories in Prose, Stories in Verse, Shorter Poems, Essays and Lectures*, ed. G. D. H. Cole (Bloomsbury: Nonesuch Press, 1934), particularly the section 'Letters and Essays'; *The Unpublished Lectures of William Morris*, ed. Eugene D. Lamire (Detroit: Wayne State University Press, 1969); *Selections from the Prose Works of William Morris*, ed. A. H. R. Ball (Cambridge University Press, 1931), esp. the section 'Art and Social Reform'; and *Political Writings of William Morris*, ed. A. L. Morton (London: Lawrence & Wishart, 1979).
[25] Morton, *Political Writings*, pp. 66–7.   [26] *Ibid.*, p. 109.

Morris's preference for addressing and encouraging his audiences to action, appearing in person before them, was a form of praxis all its own, and rather different from the mode of address of Marx, who usually preferred, when addressing popular audiences, to remain behind the screen of the printed journalistic word. But what 'Art and Socialism' does have in common with Marx, although seemingly worked out semi-independently, or by extrapolation from certain sections of *Capital*, is a sure grasp of the 'alienated labour' thesis. What Morris does that is new is quite specifically to relate two apparently disparate practices, art and labour, in defence of the proposition that 'the world of modern civilization in its haste to gain a very inequitably divided material prosperity has entirely suppressed popular Art':

the cause of this famine of Art is that whilst people work throughout the civilized world as laboriously as ever they did, they have lost – in losing an Art which was done by and for the people – the natural solace of that labour; a solace which they once had, and always should have, the opportunity of expressing their own thoughts to their fellows by means of that very labour, by means of that daily work which nature or long custom, a second nature, does indeed require of them, but without meaning that it should be an unrewarded and repulsive burden.[27]

Of course there is something quite idiosyncratic about this: Marx only very occasionally looked back to the Middle Ages as benignly as Morris habitually did, and Morris seemed incapable of convincingly explaining how the process of the eradication of popular art by commerce was to be reversed. In these respects Morris bumped into and did not go beyond the limits of the utopianism which Marx had had to leave behind long before. In his own diverse artistic practice, for which he is rightly better known than his essays on art, Morris often seemed simply to be trying to revive the practices of the feudal past. But the fact that he was not practised in the ways of the historical materialist dialectic is not sufficient reason for such a rich body of work to have such a limited audience today.

Morris's plentiful writings on art and its problematics within capitalism are one indication that, by the *fin de siècle*, Marxism, even in the aesthetic field, had started to spread far beyond German borders. Engels's initiative on 'mediation', for example, was almost immediately taken up, probably in acknowledgement of Engels's direct encouragement of him, by Antonio Labriola, a Professor of Philosophy at the University of Rome, in *La concezione materialistica della storia* (*Essays in the Materialistic Conception of History*). This book, published in Italian in 1896, was quickly to enjoy pan-European influence, being translated into a number of languages by

[27]  *Ibid.*, p. 110.

the end of the century, including a French edition introduced by Georges
Sorel and read early by Lenin, who encouraged a Russian translation,
which duly appeared in 1898. Trotsky too read the book in the 1890s.

Labriola attempted in this book to distinguish what might be considered 'direct' ideological projections of economic facts (like politics
and law) from 'indirect' correspondences (like art and religion), claiming
'that in artistic or religious production the mediation from the conditions
to the products is very complicated';[28] warned against the reduction of
the former to the latter; and drew attention to the fact that, despite all
social organization, humans remained fundamentally rooted in a physical
nature which changed slowly enough to be considered a permanent fact:
in this fact, by implication, might be the solution to Marx's conundrum
as to the long-lasting appeal even of 'outdated' art forms. Labriola moreover called for a social psychology which might explicate what he was
confident enough to depict as a full-blown dialectical scenario: 'forms
of consciousness, even as they are determined by the conditions of life,
constitute themselves also a part of history... there is no fact in history
which is not preceded, accompanied and followed by determined forms of
consciousness, whether it be superstitious or experimental, ingenious or
reflective, impulsive or self-controlled, fantastic or reasoning'.[29] Althusser
was hardly the first to point out that Engels's famous 'last instance', in
which 'the economic movement finally asserts itself' as the prime mover
'amid all the endless host of accidents' of history, never came.[30]

Labriola did not engage directly with works of art or literature, but
Georgi Plekhanov, who introduced him to a Russian audience by means
of a critical essay published in September 1897,[31] certainly did. At this
time Plekhanov, founder of the Russian Social-Democratic Party, was the
theoretical leader of Russian communism, having not yet been eclipsed by
Lenin, with whom he was to break in 1905 over their differences on armed
insurrection. His major work, *Art and Social Life* (1912), attempted to
apply Marx's general theory, as adapted by Engels and Labriola, to specific works, and remained enormously influential, despite Plekhanov's
dwindling political fortunes, well into the Stalinist era. Two of the main
reasons for his sustained popularity, even after his death in 1918, were no
doubt his fairly mechanical 'reflection theory' (which seemed to return art
to a subsidiary role as a passive 'reflector' of primary economic developments) and his hostility to literary and artistic experimentalism (Cubism
in particular attracted his ire), both of which meant that he offered no

[28] Antonio Labriola, *Essays in the Materialistic Conception of History*, trans. Charles H.
Kerr (Chicago: Charles H. Kerr, 1908), p. 217.
[29] *Ibid.*, p. 113.    [30] Tucker, *Marx–Engels Reader*, p. 760.
[31] Solomon, *Marxism and Art*, p. 92.

threat to the Stalinist promotion of Socialist Realism and its counterpart, implacable opposition to Modernism. But *Art and Social Life* remains one of most learned and wide-ranging examples of early Marxist literary criticism and theory, as do Plekhanov's other major essays, such as that on Ibsen and on French drama and painting of the eighteenth century.[32] Solomon offers a generous but well-balanced account of Plekhanov's historical importance, in particular his importation into Marxism of Karl Bücher's theory of the relation between primitive art and the labour process.[33] Plekhanov's influence shows, however, that the centre of gravity of Marxist intellectual work had shifted from Germany even before the accommodation of German social democrats to the Great War definitively robbed them of any claim they may have had to be the natural inheritors of Marxist theory.[34]

Marx's nineteenth-century heirs undoubtedly fleshed out his suggestive remarks on general aesthetic questions and attempted to show how they might accord with (or need to be adjusted to fit) his political and economic theories. In this respect they have been unduly neglected. They made a significantly lesser contribution to the analysis of specific literary texts, but the explanation for their omission from many narratives of Marxist aesthetics lies not in their empirical shortcomings but in a later historical development which engulfed them. By the end of the century the epicentre of all Marxist debate, including that around aesthetics, was moving decisively to Russia.

The turning point was undoubtedly Lenin's essay 'Party Organisation and Party Literature' (1905), which stated that 'everyone is free to write and say whatever he likes, without any restrictions',[35] but reserved the right to expel from the Bolshevik Party those whose exercise of this freedom brought them into conflict with the Party line. Lenin made it explicit that his strictures applied to literary artists as well as writers on politics. He justified such a policy because the Party was a 'voluntary association' whose ideological integrity was in need of protection if it was to fulfil its aims. Once it had done so and actually became the governing

[32] Plekhanov has been much better served in English translation than the arguably more deserving Mehring: see Georgi Plekhanov, *Art and Social Life*, ed. Andrew Rothstein (London: Lawrence & Wishart, 1953). For the essays on Ibsen and on the eighteenth century in France, see Georgi Plekhanov, *Art and Society and Other Papers in Historical Materialism* (New York: Oriole Editions, 1974).
[33] Solomon, *Marxism and Art*, pp. 119–24.
[34] It is worth noting that 1914 is also the point at which Kautsky's participation in Marxism, which had cast a very long shadow for several decades, effectively ended. Kautsky is not discussed in any detail in this chapter, because his discussions of literary topics were few and perfunctory. His real aesthetic interest was in the visual arts, on which he wrote a great deal for the Viennese journal *Zeitschrift für Plastik* in the 1880s.
[35] Solomon, *Marxism and Art*, p. 181.

party in 1917, a little later making itself coterminous with the state, such a policy applied to art was obviously full of repressive potential.

The evaluation of art according to its political tendency was never originally intended by aesthetically inclined Bolsheviks to preclude other kinds of evaluation or to legitimize what eventually took place under Stalin. But when, in 1931, Stalin attacked Rosa Luxemburg and her associates for being precursors of Trotskyism in his article 'Some Questions Regarding the History of Bolshevism', the rewriting of the history of the nineteenth-century beginnings of Marxist literary criticism was one of the inevitable, if minor, consequences. Those who had endeavoured in that period to enlarge the range and scope of Marxist aesthetics would soon be past their sell-by date as a result, unless they were so intellectually compromised (or capable of being so) as to be worthy of honour in Stalin's philistine polity. Mehring in particular, having been lauded by Luxemburg, was viciously attacked by many who now occupied places in the aesthetic division of the bureaucracy – none more ardent to damn him than Georg Lukács, the man who, Jameson reminds us, was foremost among those responsible for reorientating critics towards 'a relatively Hegelian kind of Marxism'.[36]

---

[36] The details of this sorry revisionist episode are recounted by Solomon in *ibid.*, pp. 101–2.

IV

# *Later nineteenth-century developments: Realism, Naturalism, Symbolism and Decadence*

# 14

# Realism, Naturalism and Symbolism in France

ROSEMARY LLOYD

The proliferation of newspapers in France during the second half of the nineteenth century – a result of the development of cheaper materials, the incorporation of advertisements to pay for the bulk of the production costs, the rise of literacy, and a general, although by no means constant, relaxation of censorship laws – led to a corresponding explosion in critical writing. Daily, weekly and monthly publications included at more or less regular intervals their feuilleton, devoted to reviews of art, theatre, music and literature. Addressing a mass readership about works that had only just appeared accustomed critics to the cut and thrust of a more dynamic and often more vituperative debate than that of the academy. For critics writing for the volatile readership of the daily paper, the temptation to entertain by skewering a work of literature on the tip of an acid pen was frequently too great. Seeking out grammatical or factual errors, finding slips in Latin quotations, or merely deriding the mechanics of plot or the central objects of interest selected, remained the method of choice for the majority of critics and was not disdained even by the best of them.

That different dynamic is a frequent presence in criticism of this period, even when it was collected in volume form and published at a temporal remove from the hurly-burly of production. At the same time, the close intellectual and social relationships among writers, musicians and artists encouraged critical exploration of numerous common themes across different genres. While critics working from within the academy were predictably more conservative, they also brought to bear a wider perspective, freed from the need to make instant judgements on works of the moment. Some of the best critics of the period, moreover, were also creative writers, who frequently used their critical articles to explore themes, experiment with techniques or analyse approaches they would use in their own literary productions.

Public enthusiasm for popularized science – embodied by the natural history museum in the *jardin des plantes* – in turn engendered among writers and critics a desire to make their own work appear more scientific. Medical analyses, a desire for accurate observation, claims of impartiality, the use of abundant documentation, the description of species of animals all find parallels in creative writing, from Honoré de Balzac's

determination to reveal 'species' within contemporary humans, to Emile
Zola's claims for the novel to have the same experimental nature as
chemistry or biology, and this in turn fostered among critics an aspiration towards a more scientific form of criticism, one less open to claims
of arbitrariness and partiality.

Nevertheless, if writers and critics often shared this enthusiasm for
science, they more frequently clashed over the writers' desire to capture
contemporary life, to reveal it warts and all, in ways that touched both
political and moral nerves in critics. Setting the tone for this debate is
the critic Hippolyte Castille's (1820–86) accusation that Balzac favoured
depictions of evil over representations of good, to which Balzac made the
following well-known and in many ways typical riposte: 'Moralizing the
age is the aim all writers must set themselves, under pain of being mere
*crowd pleasers*: but can criticism point out new procedures for doing
so to those writers condemned of immorality? Well, the time honoured
procedure has always been to show the wound.'[1]

Despite this apparent acceptance of Castille's central argument,
Balzac's programme was, predictably, far broader and more imaginative
than a mere showing of the wound. In his preface to *The Human Comedy*,
Balzac sets out an ambitious programme which will allow literature to
rival science in its exploration and analysis of the real world. In the wake
of work carried out by such scientists as Buffon, Cuvier and Geoffroy
Saint-Hilaire in defining animal species, he posits the existence of social
species such that a soldier is as different from a worker, an administrator
from a lawyer, as wolves are from lions or sheep from crows. Moreover,
while the lioness may be briefly depicted once the lion has been described,
in society, he asserts, the woman is not always merely the female version
of the male. In addition, humans reflect their individual characteristics by
the objects they accumulate, and the houses in which they live. Thus, any
attempt to convey the whole of contemporary society must have a triple
form, one which focuses on men, women and objects. To carry out such
a project demanded a particularly complex use of literary styles. Here
Balzac draws on the example of Walter Scott, whom he greatly admired,
to justify an amalgam of drama, poetry, landscape descriptions and philosophical analyses. For him, in other words, verisimilitude resulted not so
much from a painstaking evocation of the real but from a cunning blend
of the marvellous and the realistic, the poetic and the epic.

Balzac's theoretical writing, which can be found embedded in his novels, especially *Lost Illusions*, as well as in more conventional locations,
such as prefaces or newspaper articles, makes frequent reference to the
language of the visual arts, especially where the presentation of character

---

[1] Honoré de Balzac, *Ecrits sur le roman* (Paris: Librairie générale française, 2000), p. 318.

is concerned. He contends, for example, that some characters have to be depicted in close-up, others merely sketched in, still others kept simply as vague figures in the background of one novel, only to leap into the foreground in a different novel. This technique demands from the reader a different response, based on reading not just a single novel, but a closely integrated series of novels. Balzac placed additional demands on his reader by using that integrated series, as he argues in various prefaces, within his scientific or at least would-be scientific framework.

While Balzac's insistence on the writer's need to place truth above all other criteria, in the smallest details as well as in the overall picture, led many of his followers to focus on the scurrilous, destructive or even trivial in everyday life, his own image of what came to be known as Realism ranged much more widely, with emphasis placed also on the uplifting, self-denying and exceptional in human nature and in contemporary society. Nevertheless, for many critics the process of 'showing the wound' assumed unacceptable dimensions as a result of the rise of the so-called Realist school, associated with the painter Gustave Courbet (1819–87) and the now largely forgotten writers Champfleury (1821–89) and Duranty (1833–80). In a response to the critic Louis Peisse (1803–80), who wrote for several newspapers and was curator for the collections of the prestigious but largely conservative Ecole des Beaux-Arts, Courbet insisted in characteristically bellicose terms: 'Yes, Peisse, we must drag art down from its pedestal. For too long you have been making art that is pomaded and "in good taste". For too long, painters, even my contemporaries, have based their art on ideas and stereotypes.'[2] He is equally forthright in responding to a charge by the journalist André Garcin (1821–1906) that he was a socialist painter: 'I accept that title with pleasure, I am not only a socialist but a democrat and a Republican as well – in a word, a partisan of all the revolutions and above all a Realist. But this no longer concerns M. Garcin, as I wish to establish here, for "Realist" means a sincere lover of the honest truth.'[3] He further clarifies his view of Realism in a letter to young artists published in the *Courrier du dimanche* on 29 December 1861, where he insists on the physical nature of the language of painting and promotes the power of perception, arguing that 'Imagination in art consists of knowing how to find the most complete expression of an existing thing, but never of inventing or creating the thing itself.'[4] The power of perception itself, rather than the nature of the object perceived, as the essential factor in beauty began to dominate not just Realist art but Realist writing, too.

---

[2] Gustave Courbet, *Letters of Gustave Courbet*, ed. and trans. Petra ten-Doesschate Chu (University of Chicago Press, 1992), p. 88.
[3] *Ibid.*, p. 103.   [4] *Ibid.*, p. 204.

For his part, Champfleury began his Realist manifesto with an outright attack on critics and on what he perceived as the parasitic nature of criticism, paradoxically revealing the essentially symbiotic relationship that had developed between the creative and critical:

> The best way of proving one's power is shown by works rather than discussions. But works are not always studied with the application that an author has the right to demand; the writer disappears behind the novel, which is open to a thousand contrasting interpretations, and to criticize them you have to be as powerful as the writer, you have to have gone through the same variations, doubts, uncertainties, travails, and studies as the writer before you can express a judgement. Critics are not built like that: being a critic is performing a job, carrying out a profession that is easily learnt and that leaves you with a tranquil spirit.[5]

For Champfleury, Realism was a product of the Revolution of 1848, which brought an end to the French monarchy and briefly ushered in a republic before enabling the *coup d'état* of the future emperor, Napoleon III. As such, Realism was the observation and representation of the contemporary without recourse to social or aesthetic hierarchies, an image of art and literature where a carrot would be as important and as inspirational as a love affair, while the majority of critics, Champfleury asserted, were 'cataloguers, embalmers, taxidermists and nothing more'.[6] The challenge Champfleury issued to critics was, therefore, that of assessing without assassinating, exploring without exterminating.

Gustave Flaubert (1821–80) would doubtless have been convulsed with mocking laughter at the thought of contributing to standard journalistic criticism – indeed he considered it essential that a writer remain in an ivory tower, nose amid the stars, as he only half-mockingly puts it in a letter of 20 June 1853 to Louise Colet. Significantly, when he jokingly imagines himself as a professor at the Collège de France, it is only to devote an entire course to the question of boots in literature. It was, rather, in his voluminous letters that he revealed his ideas about writing. In them, he insists on the essential separation of the writer from the objects observed: 'the greatest and rarest writers', he argued in 1846, as he would throughout his life, are those who 'sum up humanity without bothering either about themselves or their own passions. Setting aside their personality to become absorbed in those of others, they reproduce the Universe which is reflected in their works, sparkling, varied, multiple, like an entire sky reflected in the sea with all its stars and all its

---

[5] Jules-François-Félix Husson, known as Champfleury, *Le Réalisme* (Paris: Michel Lévy, 1857), p. 1.
[6] Champfleury, *Réalisme*, p. 6.

azure.'[7] Impersonality was central to his artistic credo. In several slightly different formulations, he was adamant that the writer needed to be like God in the universe, present everywhere but visible nowhere. Balzac's authorial interventions predictably irritated Flaubert, who sought rather to leave the reader to draw his or her own conclusions.

Extremely sensitive to the sound of the words he used, Flaubert frequently urged those friends who wrote asking for his advice on their manuscripts to focus more on the rhythm of their phrases, the need to avoid distracting jingles, or repeated sounds, and to force their thought into more tightly expressed language, rejecting anything verbose or lacking muscle. His painstaking critiques of the minor poet Louise Colet, who was also his lover at the time when he was working on *Madame Bovary*, or of his friend the now largely forgotten poet and playwright Louis Bouilhet, reveal just how much weight he placed on precise definitions of words, on the importance of carefully controlled metaphor, on the determined rejection of commonplace expressions and thought. Poetry, he asserted, had to be every bit as precise as geometry.

Flaubert also placed considerable weight on the structure of a work, insisting that every element in it must be conceived for its contribution to the overall effect. Dante's *Inferno*, for example, is admired for its great inspiration, but condemned for its lack of a plan and its repetitions, while in regard to his own work he argues that a deviation of a single line could make him miss his goal entirely. The role of art, he frequently argues in his letters, is not to make its audience laugh or cry, but to make them dream, a goal achievable only if everything follows inexorably the predetermined course of events. This could be attained, he argued in a letter to Mademoiselle Leroyer de Chantepie, only if art were made to rise above the personal and to reach, through a pitiless method, the precision of the physical sciences.

This stress on modelling art after science creates a strong contrast between Flaubert and the poet Charles Baudelaire (1821–67), although Baudelaire was to write the most perceptive contemporary review of *Madame Bovary*. Baudelaire, who insisted on the need to portray the heroism of the modern world, argued indeed that the best criticism was not rational and even-handed, but to the contrary impassioned and unashamedly grounded in personal preference. His critical writing, both artistic and literary, was to set new standards, as much in the quality of the prose as in the intensity of the arguments. His own approach as a critic depends above all on a reading of the work that reveals its central preoccupations, and on an analysis of what the writer set out to achieve,

7 Gustave Flaubert, *Correspondance*, ed. Jean Bruneau, 5 vols. (Paris: Gallimard, Bibliothèque de la Pléiade, 1973), vol. I, p. 396.

which is also in many cases an experiment with how that aim might be reached by other means. Refusing to be limited by generalized concepts of what literature should do, he insisted that the dominant goal of a work of art was to create beauty, regardless of its moral values, and regardless, too, of any truth external to the work itself. Focusing on contemporary publications, he reveals astonishing sensitivity to the aims of such diverse writers as the poet Théophile Gautier and the novelist Flaubert, and he also explores such conflicting current trends as Realism and the neo-paganism of Gérard de Nerval and his coterie. Through brilliant pastiches he is able simultaneously to reveal and analyse a writer's style. If personal preferences or simple envy prevent him from fully appreciating writers such as Victor Hugo, his critical writing has all the intensity promised by his programme of passion and partiality.

Predictably, Baudelaire took exception to Champfleury's truculent assertions, in an unfinished article entitled 'Since Realism Exists', in which he depicted the label as a mere advertising stunt on the part of Courbet and Champfleury, but went on to affirm that every good poet had always been a Realist. Poetry, he laconically insisted, is 'what is most real, what is completely true only in another world', adding: 'this world, a hieroglyphic dictionary'.[8] For Baudelaire, imagination was the queen of faculties, the essential element needed for any reading of such a dictionary.

This notion that the external world had to be deciphered in order to reveal its true reality, an image based at least in part on popular enthusiasm for the transcription of Egyptian hieroglyphs on the Rosetta stone, carried out by the Frenchman Champollion, is also central to another outspoken proponent of Realism, the art critic and novelist Edmond Duranty (1833–80). In an insightful study entitled *The New Painting* (*La Nouvelle peinture*, 1876), Duranty, whose thinking was deeply influenced by the development of photography, draws on Balzac's assertions of the close relationship between dwellings and their inhabitants, to suggest a mode of viewing paintings which is also applicable to responding to literature: the language of an empty apartment should be sufficiently clear to allow us to deduce the character and habits of those who live there, and the street will say through its passers-by what hour of the day it is, and what moment of public life is being depicted.[9] For him, one of the great attractions of reality was its eternal variety, its impromptu nature.

Finding a way of understanding that eternal variety is what dominates the work of the influential writer and thinker Hippolyte Taine (1828–93). This programme is especially evident in the scintillating preface to

<hr/>

[8] Charles Baudelaire, *Œuvres completes*, ed. Claude Pichois, 2 vols. (Paris: Gallimard, Bibliothèque de la Pléiade, 1976), vol. II, pp. 58–9.
[9] Edmond Duranty, *La Nouvelle peinture* (Paris: Dentu, 1876), p. 28.

his history of English literature. A philosopher and historian by training, Taine nevertheless found his greatest inspiration in literature. The history opens with this triumphant affirmation of critical faith:

The study of history has been transformed over the last hundred years in Germany and the last sixty years in France. This took place as a result of the study of literature. It was found that a work of literature was not a simple game of the imagination, the isolated caprice of a hot head, but a copy of the surrounding behaviour and the indication of a state of mind. The conviction was that one could, on the basis of monuments of literature, rediscover the way in which human beings felt and thought many centuries ago. Put to the test, the hypothesis succeeded.[10]

If you look at a manuscript, a parchment, a published work, he asserts, it is as if you were looking at a fossilized shell: you want to rediscover the animal that inhabited it and gave it shape. Today, he adds, 'history, like zoology, has found its anatomy, and whatever may be the historical branch we choose, philology, linguistics or mythology, it is this route one takes to make it produce new fruit'.[11]

Drawing his inspiration in large part from Darwin, whose *Origin of Species* had been published in the previous decade, Taine famously asserts that three different sources contribute to the production of a person's elementary moral state: race, milieu and moment,[12] adding that once we have considered these three elements, that is to say 'the inner forces, the pressure from outside, and the impulsion already present, we have exhausted not only all the real causes but all possible causes of movement'.[13] Taine's publications were to have a profound influence on the work of many critics and writers, most famously, perhaps, that of Emile Zola, even if he later acknowledged or at least asserted increasing differences between himself and the historian. In the search for a telling formula that could sum up a writer and his or her work, Taine was inevitably led to simplify, to iron out the knotty complexities and unpredictable idiosyncrasies that mark creative writing. Nevertheless, his arguments and the underlying ambition to make criticism less arbitrary and personal, and its conclusions more scientifically justifiable, provided significant impetus to critics for the rest of the century and beyond.

Indeed, many other critics were also tempted to move criticism away from the anecdotal and partial and towards a more exact discipline, even while their main focus was on more traditional functions of criticism, such as the promotion of classical literary standards and the rejection of what were seen as immoral works. The journalist and academic Désiré

---

[10]  Hippolyte Taine, *Histoire de la littérature anglaise*, 5 vols. (Paris: Hachette, 1866), vol. I, p. iii.
[11]  *Ibid.*, p. xii.      [12]  *Ibid.*, p. xxiv.      [13]  *Ibid.*, p. xxxiv.

Nisard (1806–88), for instance, reflects such an ambition in the painstaking definitions he offers in *Studies in Literary Criticism* (*Etudes de critique littéraire*, 1858). Focusing first on the nature of contemporary criticism, in which he discerns four main types – that which sought to make literary criticism into a new kind of history, that which concentrated on the writer's personal attributes, that which judged literature through the morality it conveyed, and that which saw criticism as at least potentially an exact science – he argues for a critical approach which demands that literature abandon the desire to please (this he castigates as facile literature) and set instead moral standards for its readers, as he argues the great classical texts have always done. As might be predicted from this, Nisard, who wrote for such widely read papers as the *Journal des débats* and the *Revue des deux mondes* among other periodicals, was a virulent critic of the Romantics, hotly defending classical literature throughout his career.

It was not, however, merely those critics who disliked the literature of their age who found Taine's scientific turn of thinking appealing in the way in which it seemed to offer a degree of certainty and predictability in an area dominated by impression and opinion. Among the most notable of those attracted to contemporary writing was the gifted critic and translator Emile Hennequin (1858–88), whose life was cut tragically short, and who set out in his *Critique scientifique* (1888) to found a scientifically based criticism which he called 'aesthopsychology'. This he defined as 'the science of the work of art as sign'. He opposed the importance placed by Charles-Augustin Sainte-Beuve (1804–69) and Taine on the writer's personality, biography and milieu, and focused instead on the work itself, claiming that it was through the 'scrutiny of the work alone' that the critic could discover 'the clues necessary for the study of the author's thought'.[14]

In the posthumously published *Some French Writers* (*Quelques ecrivains français*) of 1890, Hennequin brought that scrutiny to bear on such exponents of what he called Realism as Flaubert and Zola. Exploring the work of art as sign enabled him to reach such incisive judgements as the following:

In contrast with the classical technique of describing in a few general terms, and with the Romantic technique, which describes in a few specific words, in conformity with the act of vision which is a synthesis of a thousand elementary perceptions, Zola, together with all the Realists, creates his tableaux through the enumeration of an infinite number of details, occasionally summed up in a view of the whole. Each spectacle is depicted in its constituent parts, each marked by a colourful adjective corresponding to the way in which it is perceived; then, in a generalizing sentence, the whole is taken up again with terms dominated by the

[14] Emile Hennequin, *La Critique scientifique*, 3rd edn (Paris: Perrin, 1894), p. 65.

shape and shade that can be found in the majority of the elements making up the whole. Monsieur Zola's descriptive masterpiece, *Le Ventre de Paris*, abounds in passages applying this theory.[15]

The sharp attention paid to the work itself also enables such contrasts as the following, which exemplifies Hennequin's critical skills:

Flaubert's prose is beautiful through the beauty and exactness of the words, their tenacious liaisons, the clear brilliance of the images; but in addition it charms the voice and ears through the harmony that arises from the skilful dose of strong and weak terms... The only specific characteristic possessed by Zola's vocabulary is abundance, a quality that belongs to all those who have rubbed shoulders with the Romantics, and, here and there, a smoky colouration.[16]

Taine's critical thinking also inspired one of the most highly regarded journalistic critics of the last half of the century, at least in his lifetime, the pugnacious Jean-Jacques Weiss (1827–91). In his essays on the history of French literature, first published in volume form in 1865, Weiss was above all stimulated by the way in which Taine's method consisted in 'seeking the story of a people's transformations through the series of literary types that people has created'.[17] A nation's literature, he believed Taine to have shown, was the only thing that could teach us to judge its institutions correctly. No doubt this sense of the kinds of judgement that could be made on the basis of literary texts propelled his sense of indignation when, in 1857, he perceived what he described as an outpouring of 'brutal art', notably Flaubert's *Madame Bovary* and Baudelaire's *Les Fleurs du Mal*. But he took exception to certain elements in the thinking of both Taine and the historian Ernest Renan, especially what he saw as their refusal to grant individuals the power of free will, which he believed could be stronger than the forces of race, milieu and moment.

Exploring Flaubert's novel and Baudelaire's poetry in the context of a society he saw as dominated by money, he pointed to an eclipse of the ideal, which he argued had been replaced by cynicism and misanthropy. In a typically ferocious passage, Weiss argued that unlike Balzac showing the wound:

Baudelaire does not say: 'This is debauchery'. He forages in by-ways and gutters, he besmirches grace, beauty, love, youth, freshness and spring time, and in the hoarse voice of orgies which nevertheless retains its gaiety, he cries: 'This is the human race'. And don't try to argue with him! M. Baudelaire will accuse you of screwing up your face:

Hypocrite reader, my double, my brother!

[15]  Emile Hennequin, *Quelques ecrivains français* (Paris: Perrin, 1890), p. 71.
[16]  *Ibid.*, pp. 69–70.
[17]  Jean-Jacques Weiss, *Essais sur la littérature française* (Paris: Calmann Lévy, 1891), p. iii.

He has taken this rhetorical precaution, as early as his preface, against those sissies who turn away from breathing in the scent of his dear little flowers.[18]

As a drama critic, especially writing for the *Journal des débats* in the final years of his life, Weiss continued to uphold literature's role as moral guide, in a series of frequently sparkling and highly erudite reviews.

As Realism moved more towards Naturalism, with its even greater infusion of the scientific and its sharper emphasis on the sordid, Guy de Maupassant (1850–93), best known for his short stories, offered in the guise of a preface to his novel *Pierre et Jean* a study of the novel as genre and of its critics which stands in sharp contrast to the opinionated writing of critics like Weiss. The aim of the writer, Maupassant argued, was not to tell us a story or to amuse, guide or move us, but to force us to reach an intelligent understanding of the deep meaning hidden in the events narrated. As a result, a writer's proficiency had nothing to do with the evocation of emotion or the creation of some poignant misfortune, but lay 'in the skilful grouping of small constant facts from which the definitive meaning of the work comes to light'.[19] Just as writers were held to observe external reality without interposing their own convictions or values, so critics, he argued, must, 'without prejudice, preconceived opinions, or ideas based on those of a school, understand, distinguish, and explain all tendencies however much opposed they may be to each other, as well as the most varied temperaments, and admit the discoveries of the most diverse forms of art'.[20]

Writing without prejudiced and preconceived opinions, as Maupassant no doubt knew perfectly well, was, however, not a characteristic of most nineteenth-century critics. The novelist and critic Joris-Karl Huysmans (1848–1907), who at the outset of his career was closely connected with Zola and the Naturalist movement, was a trenchant commentator on contemporary art and literary movements. His critical writing is infused with his understanding of scientific discoveries, from those of the psychologist Charcot to those of the eye-specialist Galezowski. He combines this knowledge with a strong desire for art – painting and fiction – to represent the contemporary world and to do so by focusing on the life and work of ordinary people. All of modern life, he argues in his account of the Impressionist exhibition of 1880, is still to be studied:

only a few of its many faces have been seen and noted. Everything is still to do: the official galas, the salons, the balls, the corners of familiar life, the life of artisans and the bourgeoisie, the shops, markets and restaurants, the cafés and

[18]   *Ibid.*, p. 179.
[19]   Guy de Maupassant, *Pierre et Jean* (Paris: Albin Michel, 1984), p. 21.
[20]   *Ibid.*, pp. 15–16.

bars, in a word all of humanity, whatever social class it belongs to and whatever function it performs, at home, in the hospices, the open-air dance floors, the theatres, the squares, the poor streets or those vast boulevards whose American look provides the necessary framework for the needs of our age.[21]

And he continues, in words that take their initial impulse from Baudelaire and find their fulfilment in Zola: 'all the work of humanity in factories and workshops; all that modern fever that the activity of industry sets before us, all the magnificence of machines, all that is still to be depicted and will be depicted provided that Modernists worthy of the name agree not to allow themselves to be diminished and mummified in the eternal reproduction of the same subject'.[22]

The exhortatory nature of Huysmans's criticism, imbued with a deep knowledge of the visual arts and considerable enthusiasm for contemporary science, finds a parallel of sorts in Zola's partly serious, partly tongue-in-cheek manifesto to which, inspired by Claude Bernard's method of investigating hypotheses through experiments, he gave the title *The Experimental Novel (Le Roman expérimental)* (1880). The novelist, he insists, is composed of an observer and an experimenter, the observer providing the facts as they are perceived and establishing the groundwork for the characters, while the experimenter places his characters in a particular series of incidents and events in order to show that things will unfold according to the particular phenomena under study.[23] He singles out Balzac's novel *La Cousine Bette* as a prime example of an experimental novel, in this scientific sense, because Balzac not only observes but experiments by placing his character in specific situations to see what will transpire. The problematic nature of the changes brought about by the intervention of the writer is dismissed with a breezy wave of the hand: 'what must be stressed', he argues, 'is the impersonal nature of the method'.[24]

Zola was fascinated by the ways in which different family members, placed in different environments and faced with varying situations, react in vastly different ways and develop along starkly contrasted lines. It is this fascination that not only underlies the theoretical writing of *The Experimental Novel* but also and more profoundly underpins the whole of his novel series *Les Rougon-Macquart*. All the writer has to do, he asserted (and thus all the critic has to judge), is to 'take facts from nature and then study their mechanism by modifying the circumstances

[21] Joris-Karl Huysmans, *L'Art moderne/Certains* (Paris: Editions 10/18, 1975), pp. 140–1.
[22] *Ibid.*, p. 141.
[23] Emile Zola, *Le Roman expérimental* (Paris: Garnier-Flammarion, 1971), pp. 63–4.
[24] *Ibid.*, p. 89.

and the milieus in which they find themselves, without ever failing to adhere to the laws of nature'.[25]

Always energetic in his expression and trenchant in his judgements, Zola devoted a range of critical essays, published first in periodicals before being collected under the umbrella title of *The Experimental Novel*, to questions such as the role of money in literature, the adaptation of the theatre to naturalism, the sense of the real, and the nature of contemporary criticism. As a critic he reveals an openness of mind, an infectious enthusiasm and a lively informality of style that set him apart from his more tendentious – in part because less gifted – contemporaries. Take, for example, the opening paragraph to his review of the first work published by Léon Hennique:

A first book is a form of virginity. Before cutting the pages, you feel a sense of the unknown. Who knows? Perhaps this volume contains the first cry of a great talent. A veiled woman passes by; your heart beats faster, you follow her; heavens above, what if she's the one you've been waiting for! I know that women and books bring much disillusionment; the woman turns out to be ugly, the book puts you to sleep. No matter, you have experienced the charm of hope.[26]

That charm of hope runs through his critical writing, pulling the reader along, forcing us to enter into the ambitions of those writers on whom he focuses. Where many of his contemporaries devoted their criticism to deriding and denouncing, Zola, even when he is expressing his antagonism towards certain writers or certain aspects of their work (Balzac's depiction of high society, for instance), manages to convey the impression that there is still much that is admirable in what they have to offer. Above all, in reading Zola's critical essays, one is left with the conviction that here is someone who loves reading and wants his readers to share his passions.

For many critics, Naturalism, while it ran the risk of cynicism, also opened up the possibility of renewing not just the novel but the theatre. Thus, in a series of talks given in the 1890s, Henry Becque (1837–99) focused on what he depicted as positive recent developments. Becque was a prolific and energetic dramatist who also wrote as a drama critic for a range of different periodicals including *L'Union républicaine*, *Le Théâtre du XIX siècle* and *Le Peuple*. In a lecture on French theatre since 1830, he modestly claimed that he possessed neither the seriousness nor the assurance necessary for criticism, and indeed his criticism is marked less by a desire to judge than by the suavely personal tones of an amateur eager to convey his own sense of pleasure or his own hesitations. After asserting

---

[25] *Ibid.*, p. 64.    [26] *Ibid.*, p. 237.

that the preface to *Cromwell*, where Hugo expresses his theory of theatre and more generally of literature, is unreadable now, he adds: 'I am telling you this in passing to let you know one of my favourite ideas. There are no theories. Theories are empty, confused, almost always fabricated by someone in order to explain the talent he or she has or believes they have. All we have are works, and it is the person who wrote those works who at the same time found the formula for them.'[27] Becque's literary model was the dramatist Victorien Sardou (1831–1908), whom he admired for his familiarity with the habits of his times and for his willingness to do no more than depict them rather than analyse or assess them, but Becque's work as both critic and dramatist was influenced above all by the energetic, open-minded and ebullient director Antoine, the founder of the Théâtre Libre. Antoine's aim, like those of his writers, insists Becque, was to come as close as possible to the representation of life and of truth.[28]

Francisque Sarcey (1827–99), who was drama critic for, among other newspapers, the *Opinion nationale*, made no bones about the ephemeral nature both of the plays on which he wrote and of his writing itself, using this fact to justify the importance he placed on success as a leading criterion. He argued that such success indicated revealing links between the play and the current tastes of the audience. When he came to offer what he calls his aesthetics of the theatre, however, he too revealed the influence if not of scientific discourse, at least of the popular admiration for vulgarized science: 'I shall attempt to create a work of science, for aesthetics is a true science, and like all sciences, is based on closely observed facts.'[29] He goes on to argue that:

It cannot be repeated too often, for there is a terrible prejudice that has the whole university behind it, that aesthetics is not charged with making masterpieces grow more quickly or more abundantly any more than it can prevent them coming into being. Its mission is not even to make them more agreeable and to increase in this way the total of our pleasures. Aesthetics consists purely, uniquely and absolutely in the study of the facts it analyses in order to extract laws from them. It is chemistry applying its analytical procedures to those kinds of entities called plays...The aesthetician is a chemist.[30]

As one might assume from this argument, Sarcey's prime consideration was the realistic nature of the play, leaving him closed to more experimental theatre and especially that of the Symbolists, but it also led

---

[27]  Henry Becque, *Œuvres complètes*, 7 vols. (Paris: G. Crès, 1926), vol. VII, p. 39.
[28]  *Ibid.*, p. 65.
[29]  Francisque Sarcey, *Quarante ans de théâtre* (Paris: Bibliothèque des annales politiques et littéraires, 1900), p. 122.
[30]  *Ibid.*, p. 124.

him to reject the use of theatre to convey a primarily moralizing lesson. Responding to Dumas *fils*'s assertion that theatre's primary aim should be moralistic, Sarcey argues that any play that puts a higher priority on moralizing than on recreating reality will fall into preaching and from there into boring, 'the most mortal poison known to humanity'.[31] The play then becomes frozen in the forced attitude imposed by the thesis that has to be upheld, which clogs all the springs of movement and suppresses life.

Yet if Sarcey sought to bring the aura of science even into what he depicts as an ephemeral art, doubts about the possibilities and limits of scientific criticism can be found in such disparate and influential voices as those of Ferdinand Brunetière (1849–1906), Ernest Renan (1823–92) and Edmond Scherer (1815–89). Brunetière, an academic and frequently vituperative critic, argued in his *Questions de critique* ('Critical Questions') of 1889 that not only did science lack the degree of certainty and objectivity with which it was generally credited (after all, he reminds his readers, Cuvier, not so long ago, affirmed that species never change), but that even if it were to acquire that certainty, it would be as a result not of its methods, but of the object it studied.[32] Attacking Hennequin's theory, he affirms, with characteristic truculence, that 'the work of art, before being a "sign", is a work of art, existing on its own and for itself, which fact alone makes it impossible to compare it with works of nature. Its meaning is linked to that of all the works which have preceded it and as a result it cannot be removed from history to be placed in the abstract.'[33] He admits that art can be used for other purposes, such as reaching a deeper understanding of humanity, but he sees the critic's primary role as deciding the extent to which a work of art has realized its most important purpose, which is 'to imitate life, then to complete life and finally to idealize it'.[34] And in his *Evolution des genres* (1890), Brunetière attacked Taine for ignoring questions of aesthetics and regarding works of literature as if they were identical with archival documents. Nevertheless, in *Nouvelles questions de critique* ('New Critical Questions', 1890), Brunetière wrote more approvingly of Taine, and especially of his 'fine lessons on the ideal in art', and spoke of Hennequin's work as 'rich in detail, curious and *suggestive*'.[35] Moreover, in differentiating between the Naturalists, as those who saw the imitation of nature as the final purpose of art, and Idealists, as those who used the 'means of nature' to express their idea of what could or should be, Brunetière claims that these definitions

---

[31]  *Ibid.*, p. 177.
[32]  Ferdinand Brunetière, *Questions de critique* (Paris: Calmann Lévy, 1890), p. 319.
[33]  *Ibid.*, p. 323.    [34]  *Ibid.*, p. 323.
[35]  Brunetière, *Nouvelles questions de critique* (Paris: Calmann Lévy, 1890), p. 303.

have the advantage of transforming an aesthetical question, plagued by partiality and prejudice, into a matter of science.[36]

The historian and philosopher Ernest Renan, in a precocious work written in the late 1840s but not published until 1890, *L'Avenir de la science* ('The Future of Science'), argued of criticism in the widest sense of the word that:

the skill worthy of this name is possible only under conditions of the most perfect autonomy. Criticism does not admit respect. Criticism sees neither prestige nor mystery, but breaks all charms and tears aside all veils. This powerful irreverence, turning on all things a firm and analytical eye, is guilty, by its very essence, of divine and human treason. It is the only authority that is not subject to any outside check; it is Saint Paul's spiritual being, judging everything and judged by no one. The cause of criticism is the cause of rationalism and the cause of rationalism is the cause of the modern mind.[37]

The judgement he associates with criticism is, by its very nature, profoundly different from that of science. Criticism, he concludes, with the kind of pithy formula that is typical of his thinking, is the 'inspirational discussion of all that had previously been believed without sufficient examination, in the aim of extracting from it a purer and more advanced truth'.[38]

For his part, the Geneva-born Edmond Scherer presented Taine's theories as too dry, too general and too mechanistic to convey the complexity, richness and variability of literature. The tone of his criticism, warmly personal and marked by close attention to the text, is conveyed in the following affirmation about Fromentin's novel *Dominique*: 'this tale', he affirms, 'has enjoyed a kind of half-success, precisely that which I would have wanted for it, the half-success that a lover prefers for the woman he loves, fearing to see her the object of too strident an admiration'.[39] At its best, Scherer's criticism offers a beautifully nuanced appreciation of the work in question, but it pointed the way to the kind of subjective and impressionistic criticism that dominates the work of the novelist and critic Anatole France.

A prolific writer, France (1844–1924) denied the possibility of any form of objectivity. 'As I understand it,' he argued, 'criticism, like philosophy and history, is a kind of novel aimed at canny and curious minds, and every novel, correctly considered, is an autobiography. The good critic tells the story of the adventures his soul experiences on reading

---

36  *Ibid.*, p. 285.
37  Ernest Renan, *L'Avenir de la science* (Paris: Calmann Lévy, 1890), p. 45.
38  *Ibid.*, p. 62.
39  Edmond Scherer, *Etudes sur la littérature contemporaine*, 10 vols. (Paris: Calmann Lévy, 1891), vol. II, p. 17.

masterpieces.' There is, he adds, 'no objective criticism as there is objective art, and all those who flatter themselves that they are putting something other than themselves into their work are dupes of a fallacious illusion. The truth is that one never steps outside oneself. It is one of our great miseries.'[40] We are all immured within ourselves, he argues, which means that neither Idealist art nor Naturalist art sees more clearly than the other. Zola's view of humankind is as valid, he admits, as George Sand's, but since truth belongs exclusively to neither, why not prefer images of 'grace, beauty and love'?[41] As a result, the worth of criticism, according to France, depends entirely on the personality of the critic.

Writing in a conversational style and with considerable lightness of touch, he is above all an entertainer rather than an analyst, a critic who is happy to affirm that the three great qualities of French writing are clarity, clarity and clarity.[42] Occasionally maliciously gossipy, as when he recounts the protest five of Zola's former disciples had published on the publication of *La Terre* ('The Earth'), France is at his happiest moving with ease, in ways that reveal the influence of Sainte-Beuve, from Maupassant's character to the nature of his writing, establishing close and transparent connections between the two:

He writes as a good Normandy landowner lives, economically and joyously. Wily, scheming, benevolent, pretty much of a mocker, somewhat of a braggart, ashamed of nothing except his broad innate goodness, careful to hide the exquisite elements of his soul, full of firm and lofty reason, not a dreamer, giving little thought to what might happen after death, believing only in what he can see, counting only on what he can touch, he is one of us, someone from our own province![43]

That linking of person and production, a legacy of Sainte-Beuve, is also at the heart of the critical writing of Jules Lemaître (1853–1914), who opens his critical survey of his contemporaries with this revealing quotation from Sainte-Beuve's *Joseph Delorme*:

The critical mind is by nature . . . a great and limpid river that undulates and unfolds around the works and monuments of poetry, as around cliffs, fortresses, hills carpeted with vineyards and leafy valleys bordering its banks. While each of these things stays in its place and concerns itself hardly at all with the others, the river goes from one to the other, bathing them without harming them, embracing them with a living flowing water, understanding them, reflecting them, and when the traveller seeks to know and visit these various sites the river takes him to them in a boat, bearing him smoothly and showing for him one after the other all the elements of this changing spectacle.[44]

[40] Anatole France, *La Vie littéraire* (Paris: Calmann Lévy, 1925), pp. iii–iv.
[41] *Ibid.*, p. 343.  [42] *Ibid.*, pp. 54–5.  [43] *Ibid.*, p. 55.
[44] Jules Lemaître, *Les Contemporains: études et portraits littéraires* (Paris: H. Lecène & H. Oudin, 1886), p. i.

Like France, Lemaître sees criticism as a meeting of friends, and argues that it is with sympathy and love that a critic should approach those contemporaries who are not beneath the attention of criticism. First, as a critic you should analyse the impression the book makes on you – an assertion in which the idea of impression outweighs the notion of analysis – and from that basis you should attempt to define the authors you discuss, revealing their temperament, image of the world, degree of sensitivity and so forth. This leads you to identify so closely with the writers that if they commit serious errors, it causes you real pain, but at the same time you understand why they have done so and forgive them.[45] Among the most tolerant of critics of this period, despite his ability to indulge at times in ferocious arguments, Lemaître enjoined his readers to accept anything from writers except boredom and mediocrity.

An even more outspoken critique of Realism and Naturalism came from French Symbolism, whose manifesto was written by Jean Moréas in 1886. The Symbolist movement included the poets Jules Laforgue, Henri de Régnier and Gustave Kahn, Huysmans and the dramatist Maurice Maeterlinck. However, the beginnings of French Symbolism can be traced back to Baudelaire, and its aesthetics were further developed by Paul Verlaine (1844–96), Arthur Rimbaud (1854–91), Stéphane Mallarmé (1842–98) and the critic Remy de Gourmont (1858–1915). Partly through Arthur Symons's book *The Symbolist Movement in Literature* (1899), French Symbolism exerted a profound impact on early twentieth-century writers such as W. B. Yeats, T. S. Eliot, James Joyce, Virginia Woolf and Marcel Proust; its influence extended to later literary theorists such as Roland Barthes, Jacques Derrida and Julia Kristeva. Symons had described the Symbolist movement in general as a 'revolt against exteriority, against rhetoric, against a materialistic tradition'.[46]

The Symbolists inherited from Baudelaire an overarching concern with poetic form, language and the evocation of subjective states, as well as the notion of synaesthesia between the various senses. Influenced by Plato, they viewed the sensible world as an imperfect imitation or expression of a higher, infinite realm which could be suggested by symbols. They rejected the literal and allegedly scientific language of the Realists and Naturalists in favour of a more allusive and symbolic mode, highlighting the visual and aural dimensions of poetry and aligning it primarily with music. Above all, they shared Baudelaire's view that the material world is merely a 'dictionary of hieroglyphics' pointing to a transcendent world beyond.[47] Baudelaire's well-known sonnet 'Correspondances' offers a

---

45  *Ibid.*, p. 250.
46  Arthur Symons, *The Symbolist Movement in Literature* (1908; rpt New York: Haskell House, 1971), p. 9.
47  Baudelaire, *Œuvres complètes*, vol. II, pp. 87–8.

poignant expression of his aesthetic, depicting the sensible world as a 'forest of symbols' gesturing towards an ideal realm. The Symbolist poets and critics would extend his conviction that earthly phenomena should be considered as correspondences of a higher realm, some, like René Ghil (1862–1925) in his *Traité du verbe* ('Treatise on the Word'), taking this credo to extraordinary lengths, insisting on direct correspondences among letters, sounds and colours.

Jean Moréas's manifesto had seen Symbolism as rejecting not only the descriptive language of realism and naturalism, but also the precise and chiselled language of the Parnassians, principally Théophile Gautier and Charles Marie René Leconte de Lisle. Mallarmé's *Divagations* (1897) was another important document of Symbolist aesthetics. Mallarmé spurned the notion that language refers to any external world or that it expresses a poet's subjectivity. Instead, anticipating Lacan, he saw the poet as entering a linguistic structure which in fact shaped his world: 'If the poem is to be pure, the poet's voice must be stilled and the initiative taken by the words themselves.'[48] The poetic imagination, he said, must aspire to the condition of music, extricating itself from the 'unceasing immobility' of our conventional intellectual operations. Interestingly, these statements anticipate important insights of Henri Bergson. Mallarmé highlighted the material aspects of language, its sound, its rhythms and its various patterns and shapes. The poet should not represent an object but convey its essence: 'To *name* an object is largely to destroy poetic enjoyment, which comes from gradual divination. The ideal is to *suggest* the object. It is the perfect use of this mystery which constitutes symbol.'[49] Mallarmé offers a famous example of this procedure: 'When I say: "a flower!" then from that oblivion to which my voice consigns all floral form, something different from the usual calyces arises, something all music, essence, and softness: the flower which is absent from all bouquets.'[50]

A major later theoretical voice of French Symbolism was that of Gourmont, who entirely rejected the ideals of impersonality and objectivity. He asserted that 'only mediocre works are impersonal'[51] and promoted a 'pure art' which was 'concerned exclusively with self-realization'.[52] Gourmont's subjective Idealism was founded on Schopenhauer's statement that 'the world is my representation', which

---

48  Stéphane Mallarmé, 'Crisis in Poetry' in *Mallarmé: Selected Prose Poems, Essays, and Letters*, trans. Bradford Cook (Baltimore, MD: Johns Hopkins University Press, 1956), p. 40. Hereafter cited as *Mallarmé*.

49  'The Evolution of Literature' in *Mallarmé*, p. 21.

50  'Crisis in Poetry' in *Mallarmé*, p. 42.

51  Remy de Gourmont, *Selected Writings*, trans. and ed. Glenn S. Burne (New York: University of Michigan Press, 1966), p. 124.

52  Remy de Gourmont, *Decadence and Other Essays on the Culture of Ideas*, trans. William Bradley (1922; rpt London: George Allen & Unwin, 1930), p. 31.

Gourmont held to be 'irrefutable'.[53] In general, the highly subjectivist stance of the Symbolists betokened their sense of social alienation and withdrawal from a world they viewed as sordidly materialistic. As Mallarmé said, 'Whenever the masses are being herded indiscriminately toward self-interest, amusement, or convenience, it is essential that a very few disinterested persons should adopt an attitude of respectful indifference toward those common motivations.'[54]

This was also a period of considerable activity in terms of comparative criticism. The great comparatist thinker Philarète Chasles (1798–1873) begins his exploration of literary England with this exordium:

Goethe was correct to say shortly before his death that Europe was now just one great literary country. The spirit of place, which belonged to the Middle Ages, and was so forcefully developed by the subdivisions of feudalism, is gone today. Europe is now nothing but a single literature, subject to several philosophical influences and above all to very diverse political tendencies, but freed from the bonds of ancient nationalism.[55]

Casting his net wider than many of his contemporaries, whose focus was France and often more specifically still Paris, he clearly relishes the task of summing up the contemporary state of, say, the novel, using this summary to move into either a close analysis of a particular work or a careful comparison of works by writers of different nationalities. Modern literature, he argues in his introduction to Thackeray's *Vanity Fair*, accords a significant and legitimate place to the novelist, for it is the novelist alone who can reproduce 'the singular complexity of these times of decadence, their bizarre characteristics, their mingled nature, their strange arabesques and scrolls, their varied reflections. The novelist is the tale-teller, the analyst, the epic poet in prose of times that, stripped of simplicity, grandeur and unity, hide mysterious depths and fearful gulfs.'[56] But modern publishing trends, especially those of the serialized novel, led, he insisted, to so fluid a mould and such an absence of constraints that even the great writers like Scott and Dickens fell victim to these traits.

In addition to his skill at broad-sweep summary, Chasles has the knack of the pithy comparison, as when he puts Balzac and Thackeray side by side. Balzac, he argues, analyses above all the corrupt details and delights in them, whereas Thackeray merely permits us to guess their presence, 'letting the mermaid's tail dive into the depths of the water where she embraces corpses and slides over corruption'. Balzac 'delights in dragging

---

53  Gourmont, 'The Roots of Idealism' in *Decadence*, pp. 209–10.
54  'Music and Literature' in *Mallarmé*, p. 56.
55  Philarète Chasles, *Voyage d'un critique à travers la vie et les livres: l'Angleterre littéraire* (Paris: Charpentier., 1876), p. i.
56  *Ibid.*, p. 190.

us into those depths, and certainly no one could bring to such a work more talent and powerful sagacity. Thackeray's cunning pleasure is to indicate what he does not show.'[57]

A period of remarkably diverse critical stances, the second half of the nineteenth century thus bore the stamp of those twin literary and artistic movements, Realism and Naturalism, even when it attempted to deny, deride or reject them. Above all, it reflected the growing fascination with science and a longing to emulate it, born either of the despair that the sciences would far outstrip the popularity of literature, or of the conviction that in scientific progress lay the key to more general human progress. While many of those critics who dominated opinion during their lifetime are now forgotten, their influence stamped much contemporary literature so profoundly that no understanding of nineteenth-century writing is complete without an awareness of their legacy.

[57] *Ibid.*, p. 230.

# 15

# Symbolism and Realism in Germany

## Martin Swales

Nineteenth-century German literature has often been regarded as suffering from the disabling condition of provincialism. This shortcoming is felt with particular urgency, so the argument runs, in respect of the literary genre that, across Europe, emerges as the central expression of modern life from the late eighteenth century on: the Realistic novel. When viewed in the company of Balzac, Jane Austen, Stendhal, Dickens, the Brontës, Flaubert, George Eliot, Tolstoy and Turgenev, German prose does, admittedly, look strangely marginal. It seems concerned with modest lives and circumstances, it seems underpowered emotionally, tentative in its perceptions and diagnoses of the tensions that inform and deform modern life.

The standard explanation for this state of affairs goes as follows: prior to 1806 the German-speaking lands do not constitute a unified nation state. Rather, they exist as that patchwork of cities, principalities and small territories that make up the Holy Roman Empire. Even after the Napoleonic reforms of the early nineteenth century, the German Confederation numbers something over thirty territories. In consequence, then, the day-to-day demographic reality of life in the German-speaking lands during the great age of European Realism was dominated by a climate of particularism and, by that token, provincialism. There was no great capital city, no metropolis to which, for good and for ill, the cultural life of the nation referred and deferred. Indeed, the nation as a whole did not exist on the ground; rather, it was located in language, in culture, in inward, spiritual experience rather than in robustly outward, practical affairs. Hence, Germany fails to provide Realism in the European mould.

This somewhat generalized picture has a certain cogency and truthfulness. But it conceals as much as it explains. And one aspect that frequently gets overlooked is the fact that German culture does reflect on and explore the aesthetics of modern prose writing in ways that are more sophisticated and telling than any comparable debates occurring elsewhere in Europe. Admittedly, much of the critical and theoretical discussion in Germany is scattered and fragmentary, located in prefaces, reviews, letters, notes and jottings. But there is, as I shall endeavour to show, a consistency to the terms and forms of the debate that is genuinely fruitful.

When Goethe dies in 1832, Heine and his contemporaries register a profound sea change: the period of high art has closed (marking the 'Ende der Kunstperiode'), and what follows is a more down-to-earth, a more prosaic cultural condition. Much German criticism and theory in the subsequent decades is devoted to the attempt to understand that prosaic condition. The issues extend to both drama and poetry, as we shall see; but the forefront of attention is occupied by the forms of prose narrative – particularly the novel and the *Novelle*. An all-important and remarkably early statement of the central issues is offered by Hegel in his aesthetics. He registers, in effect, two contextual instances that help intertextually to define the birth and nature of modern prose. One is the medieval epic, and the other is Goethe's novel *Wilhelm Meister's Apprenticeship*. Hegel writes as follows:

This essence of the novel is knight errantry which has become a serious matter again and which constitutes a genuine thematic concern... It is primarily young men who are these new knights and who have to find a way through the ways of the world which tends to realize its own purposes rather than their ideals, and who regard it as a major misfortune that there are such things as family, bourgeois society, the state, laws, business concerns etc., because these substantial facts of life with their constraints range themselves cruelly against the ideals and the eternal rights of the heart... These struggles, then, are nothing more than the years of apprenticeship, the education of the individual at the hands of existing reality, and acquire their true meaning in this context. For the end of such years of apprenticeship consists in the protagonist getting licked into shape... However much he or any of his kind may have had his quarrels with the world or been pushed around, in the last analysis he tends to get his girl and some sort of job, marries and becomes a philistine just like all the others... One of the most recurrent conflicts, and it is one that is most appropriate to the novel, is, therefore, that between the poetry of the heart and the countervailing prose of circumstances.[1]

This passage is sustained by a sophistication and differentiation of theoretical debate and a critical purchase that have not, as far as I am aware, been equalled anywhere in European letters of the time. Hegel registers the intertextual persistence of an epic model in the modern novel. Heroes (and most usually it is heroes rather than heroines who are at the centre of attention) have their tasks to perform, their journeys to undertake, their obstacles to overcome. But the modern novel is a site of disenchantment. There is little grandeur or exoticism in evidence: there are no giants or sorceresses, no magic transformations, no visions, no revelations. Rather,

---

[1]  Quoted in Hartmut Steinecke (ed.), *Romanpoetik in Deutschland: von Hegel bis Fontane* (Tübingen: Narr, 1984), pp. 44–6. Translations from the German are the author's own throughout.

the bourgeois hero has to cope with a philistine family, and has to do battle with the institutions of modern social life – the school, the army, the professions. Hence, in his perception of the modern novel as the successor to the ancient epic, Hegel registers a degree of impoverishment; the prosaic condition, it seems, is omnipresent and all-powerful, and Hegel seems to regret the banalization of the epic form. Yet he is nothing if not ambivalent. At times he seems to welcome the fact that the idealistic young protagonist gets licked into shape by inexorable practicalities. On the other hand, he seems to regret the triumph of philistinism that is entailed. In any event, there are possibilities of growth and change. And here the second intertext is all-important. Hegel's use of the term *Lehrjahre* (apprenticeship) makes clear the reference to Goethe's celebrated novel *Wilhelm Meister's Apprenticeship*, which has often been felt to inaugurate the line of the so-called *Bildungsroman*. A word of explanation is appropriate at this juncture.

The *Bildungsroman* is often claimed to be a particularly German novel form. At one level, it has at its centre an experiential focus that is familiar from a number of key works of European Realism, for it explores the processes by which a young person is initiated into the ways of the world. In many of the major Realistic novels of the nineteenth century (Dickens's *Great Expectations* would be a classic example) that theme is explored in terms of the sheer practicality of the issues involved; matters such as money, job and marriage are very much to the fore. Yet the German *Bildungsroman* is less interested in outward, practical affairs; rather, it is animated by a philosophical agenda, one that is concerned with (and for) the definition of the human self in its fullness, with the relationship between reflection and activity, between knowing and being. Put most simply: most *Bildungsroman* protagonists – and this is certainly true of Goethe's Wilhelm Meister – never have to ask themselves seriously where the next meal is coming from; whereas their counterparts in mainstream European Realism do.

Goethe's novel was enormously influential in Germany throughout the nineteenth century, and many subsequent writers and commentators felt that they had in one way or another to take issue with it. Novalis initially loved it, but then decided that it was a small-spirited and prosaic work, an attack on the very spirit of poetry. Friedrich Schlegel, the great Romantic critic and theoretician, praised it for its sovereign irony. The point we need to note here is the following: Goethe's novel and the critical response to which it gave rise (particularly from Hegel) establish a theoretical and stylistic framework within which the condition of modern prose can fruitfully be debated. The terms of this debate are dialectical in that we have on the one hand poetry, ideals, art, fine feeling, the holiness of the heart's affections; and on the other prose, conformity, acquiescence in practical affairs. The thematic dialectic generates a stylistic dialectic: the novel is both a narrative constituted of symbolism, inwardness, reflectivity, concept and idea and also a recognizable instance of social, cultural and institutional mimesis. For both Goethe and Hegel, then, ambivalence is the inalienable birthright of the modern novel.

This dialectical energy runs throughout nineteenth-century German theorizing on the novel, and I shall endeavour to trace some of the stages through which the debate passes. But at the outset I want to highlight the extraordinary durability of Hegel's insights. In 1857 Friedrich Theodor Vischer, in his *Aesthetics or the Science of the Beautiful*, writes the following about the novel (I quote in extracts):

> The basis of the modern epic, of the novel, is reality acknowledged through experience, that is to say a world that is no longer endowed with myths and miracles. In parallel with the growth of this worldview, mankind has introduced into the world the prosaic organization of human affairs... The hero is no longer outwardly active; rather, he pursues, within the experiential world available to him, the growth process of his life in which love plays a major part, and the conflicts of soul and spirit take the place of deeds... The *bourgeois* novel is ultimately the normal species of the novel... The family hearth and home is the true centre of the world picture in the novel and it only acquires its full significance when the emotions cluster round it and modulate the hard truths of life into the gentler string sounds of an expanded spiritual world.[2]

Vischer is manifestly aware of his sources – Goethe's *Wilhelm Meister* and Hegel. And he offers a wide-ranging commentary that addresses both thematic and stylistic questions. Above all else, he is at pains to stress the aesthetic and socio-political historicity of the novel genre. Its irresolution, its uneasy hovering between the poetic and the prosaic condition, is the measure of its diagnostic relationship to modern culture.

A similar – and similarly urgent – sense of the spiritual condition of the modern novel can be heard from Georg Lukács in his early work *The Theory of the Novel* (1920). One thinks of a passage such as the following:

> The novel is the epic of the world abandoned by God. The psychology of the novel hero is the daemonic; the objectivity of the novel is the mature manly insight that meaning can never fully penetrate reality, but that, without meaning, reality would dissolve into insubstantiality. All this means one and the same thing. It defines the inwardly derived, productive limitations of the novel's structural possibilities and it also unambiguously highlights the historico-philosophical moment in which great novels are possible, in which they unfold to achieve the symbolic instantiation of the essential things that need to be said. The ethos of the novel is one of mature manliness; and the characteristic

[2] Quoted in *ibid.*, pp. 159–64.

structure of its theme is the discreet way in which it handles the separation of inwardness and adventure.[3]

Manifestly Lukács's whole argument is full of a Hegelian sense of the historical specificity of literary forms, of the dialectical processes by which the grand epic model becomes reduced to the story of the soul of man (and it is most usually the man – the gender issue extends from Hegel to Lukács in an unbroken continuity) under bourgeois capitalism. Yet even in that reduced condition – and here the Hegelian dialectic comes into play – the work of art, in this case the novel, is not merely a symptom but also a diagnosis of, perhaps even a protest against, the fracturings and discontinuities of the modern world. The human disarray in, and the aesthetic disarray of, the modern novel are the deepest truth it has to offer its readers.

These are admittedly headily metaphysical ruminations. Many of the arguments advanced by the less adventurous – and less Delphic – theo-reticians of the prose form in Germany are also helpful, even if they are nowhere near as probing and thoughtful. In any event, the lesser figures do sustain an important and ongoing debate, one invariably couched in terms of the dialectic of poetry and prose. And they contribute signifi-cantly to the legitimation of the novel as a serious literary genre. It should, after all, be remembered that in the early years of the nineteenth century in Germany the novel is regarded with both suspicion and misgiving – as a somewhat shapeless, untidy, episodic, vulgar form. But it is remarkable how swiftly these attitudes change. The immense enthusiasm for Walter Scott in the 1820s in Germany produces a breakthrough in respect of historical fiction in particular. One issue is highlighted with particular urgency: in the historical novel the protagonist no longer has to be a remarkable (as one might put it, poetically endowed) individual; rather, he can best serve the purposes of the narrative project in which he figures if he is average – a representative of his class or group or clan, and not an exceptional personality in his own right.

This is the first stage on the road that leads to the emergence of the social novel in Germany. Already by the 1830s the mass appeal of the novel starts to be perceived as a virtue. It is a genre that can speak not only of a society but also *to* a society. One key witness here is Wolfgang Menzel, who stresses that the popularity of the novel's thematic concern does not necessarily diminish its poetic quality. He writes: 'It seems that this strange undervaluing of a poetic form, which in spite of everything remains the most popular one, is based on an old prejudice.'[4] Robert

---

[3]  Georg Lukács, *Die Theorie des Romans* (Darmstadt and Neuwied: Luchterhand, 1971), p. 77.
[4]  Quoted in Steinecke, *Romanpoetik*, p. 64.

Prutz hopes for a fusion of prosaic immediacy with poetic uplift, citing *Don Quixote* as a model of what can be achieved:

The novel must incorporate the narrative poem, the narrative poem must incorporate the novel. The first process would free the novel, without it thereby becoming untrue to reality, from the prosaic tendencies that in large measure continue to be part of its substance and would lift it into that serene realm of fantasy and beautiful play which is by no means closed to the novel.[5]

That call for a reconciliation of poetry and prose, both for referential, narratively mediated abundance and a poetry of theme (inwardness) and mode (symbolism), is taken up by the key theoreticians of Poetic Realism: Julian Schmidt and Gustav Freytag.

Both Schmidt and Freytag begin in 1848 to work for the literary journal *Die Grenzboten* ('The Border Messengers'). They advocate a Realism that allows poetic and prosaic imperatives to intersect. In a commentary on English fiction, Schmidt at one point writes: 'The realism of poetry will then lead to pleasing works of art as long as it concentrates on pleasing aspects.'[6] Schmidt is aware that Scandinavian literature is committed to Poetic Realism; and it is a tendency that he advocates in respect of his own country. Moreover, he buttresses his arguments with a lively sense of intertextual debate. The great writers of the German classical period (particularly Goethe) were, according to Schmidt, animated by ideals; whereas the coming tendency is one which will insist that Idealism and Realism are two sides of the same coin: 'The belief of past ages was that ideals were the enemy of reality and cancelled it out. But our belief is that ideas realize themselves in reality, and we take this belief to be the basis of future art.'[7] Compared with the major narrative achievements of English and French prose in the nineteenth century, such sentiments may sound somewhat conciliatory, timorous even. And, admittedly, some of the actual prose texts that might be taken to enshrine these principles – such as Otto Ludwig's *Between Heaven and Earth*, Theodor Storm's *Immensee* and the egregiously doctrinaire best-seller *Debit and Credit* by Gustav Freytag – seem worlds apart from the referential and stylistic reach of Dickens or Flaubert. Yet, if they do nothing else, they contribute to that sea change in European cultural opinion that allows prose fiction, and especially the novel, to become the dominant expression of bourgeois society. Freytag, writing in the 1880s, has no doubt which genre constitutes the cardinal achievement of his age. He suggests 'that at some future stage people will regard the novel in prose, such as it emerged with

---

[5] Quoted in *ibid.*, p. 139.    [6] Quoted in *ibid.*, p. 155.
[7] Quoted in Gerhard Plumpe (ed.), *Theorie des bürgerlichen Realismus: eine Textsammlung* (Stuttgart: Reclam, 1985), p. 124.

Walter Scott and unfolded through the cultures of Europe, as the greatest and most characteristic advance achieved by nineteenth-century poetry'.[8]

By the end of the nineteenth century, the challenge of Naturalist theory and practice starts to make itself felt. Friedrich Spielhagen echoes the growing enthusiasm for a more 'scientific' literary mode when he advocates objectivity in the novel. Similar views are expressed by the Hart brothers and M. G. Conrad. And Wilhlem Bölsche insists on, to quote the title of his famous treatise, 'the scientific bases of poetry'. Yet Bölsche is no mere ideologue, for in his *Natural History of the Modern Novel* he insists that Zola's creative achievement goes well beyond the scientific pretensions of his much-quoted essay 'Le Roman expérimental'. Bölsche stresses Zola's passion, the sheer luridness of his prose, and highlights the powerful eroticism that fires his imagination. And he contrasts Zola's impassioned, shocking worldliness with the sheer timorousness of German prose fiction throughout the nineteenth century. There is, of course, a measure of truth to his criticism. The need to poeticize the prosaic does in many respects move German prose writing away from the critical, exploratory energies of European Realism. Yet that is not the whole story.

There is one aspect of that whole German obsession with the dialectic of prose and poetry which Bölsche overlooks. It is that, in its finest products, German narrative fiction engages with and achieves a particular Realism of mentality, concept and idea that is a profound enrichment of European letters. The key figures in this context are Gottfried Keller and Theodor Fontane.

Two theoretical remarks by Gottfried Keller are decisive for any understanding of his creative achievement; and they are remarks that derive from the whole conceptual framework of thinking about prose narrative in the German-speaking lands that we have been discussing. One remark expresses an impassioned vindication of the poetic principle in defiance of all that might, in the modern world, seem to conspire against it – and this includes the inroads of modern technology. Keller coins the phrase 'poetry's privileged right of access', and he goes on to define it as 'the right at any time, even in the age of frock coats and railways, readily to make contact with parables and fables'.[9] The term 'right of access' is itself significant because it invokes a principle of governance within the Holy Roman Empire by which rulers of territories, however small and provincial, had direct access to the emperor. Keller knows, then, that the defence of poetry may have something slightly nostalgic or quixotic about it.

[8]  Quoted in Steinecke, *Romanpoetik*, p. 238.
[9]  Gottfried Keller in a letter to Paul Heyse of 27 July 1881.

Keller concedes as much in the second remark I wish to quote, which acknowledges the full force of historical-cum-scientific realism:

In a word: there is no individual sovereign originality in the sense advocated by the geniuses of capriciousness or the vain subjectivists. Only that which emerges from the dialectics of cultural movement is new in a good sense.[10]

Here he makes clear that inherited values and norms and aesthetic conventions can only express themselves in the present by means of a dialectical debate with the energies of historical change.

These two observations – the defence of the traditional rights of poetry on the one hand, and the insistence on the dialectics of cultural movement on the other – spell out the parameters of Keller's achievement. In his great novel *Green Henry* he gives us the portrait of the artist as a young man and middle-aged failure. Heinrich Lee aspires to a career as a painter; but his own lack of talent, compounded by the emergence of a culture of market-driven philistinism, dooms him to a resigned and despondent old age. At this level of argument, then, *Green Henry* is a Realistic novel about the unyielding demands of practical social reality. But, at another level, it takes seriously the claims of the quickened imagination. It shows, with an intensity that is fully worthy of Dickens, how the pressures of social conformity and the authoritarianism of clumsy teachers can conspire to damage the child's inner life. Increasingly Heinrich allows his imagination to repudiate all practical involvements, all social and ethical commitments. In the process, he damages himself both inwardly and outwardly. The price paid is cruelly high – not least because, as the novel constantly shows, the socio-cultural reality that human beings inhabit is a world made up of both practical and imaginative allegiances.

Keller's *Green Henry* offers, then, a superlatively rich and complex understanding of the ways in which and the extent to which society is constituted not just of material things, but also of mental processes, of ideas, assumptions, values and symbolizations. Precisely this differentiated range of understanding is a recurrent feature of German prose, in my view. The dialectic of prose and poetry can, of course, generate works that are merely timid, provincial and escapist. But in the hands of its finest practitioners it can make possible a Realism of mental and imaginative life that is nothing short of remarkable.

This applies with particular force to the novels of Theodor Fontane. He began only late in life to write novels. In his earlier years he was active as a journalist and a critic. His observations on contemporary literature allow us to witness the gradual emergence of the novelist that he was later

---

[10]  Gottfried Keller in a letter to Hermann Hettner of 26 June 1854.

to become. His most famous definition of the novel is a wholehearted commitment to a Realism of setting, character and event:

It seems to me that the task of the modern novel is to depict a life, a society, a circle of people in such a way that there emerges an undistorted mirroring of the life that we lead. The best novel will be the one whose figures so merge with figures from real life that we in recollection no longer know whether they are fictional or living personages.[11]

This sturdy declaration sounds, on the face of it, very unreflective. Yet elsewhere in his criticism Fontane shows himself much more able to consider matters of technique, to attend to the processes of artistic mediation by which a social world is expressed through fictional narrative.

Issues having to do with that mediation come to the fore, for example, in Fontane's discussion of Zola. In many ways, Fontane was not unsympathetic to Naturalism, as is attested by his positive response to the early dramas of Gerhart Hauptmann. But he was stung by the brutality of Zola. In part his reproach is thematic – Zola is simply too fascinated by ugliness for his (Fontane's) taste. But there was also the issue of artistic mode. He comments:

His *realism* or *naturalism*. There are all kinds of good things to be found, but not realism. On occasion he depicts ugliness. But these ugly things are not realism. Realism is the *artistic re-creation* (and not mere copying) of life. Hence – honesty, truth: I sorely miss these great virtues.[12]

What is at stake here is, as Fontane puts it, art as stenography versus art as aesthetic transformation.

In theoretical terms, the categories within this binary opposition are somewhat crude. But, once heard in the context of Fontane's practice as a novelist, they take on richness of implication. Fontane's novels of contemporary life are remarkable above all for their exploration of social conformity. There are neither rebels nor fanatics in his world. Rather, all depends on, as he once put it, 'conventions and agreements'. Fontane is incomparable in his understanding of the mechanisms of socialization and repression. And his narrative art finds the appropriate form for the exploration of this theme; he is the master of subtextual statement. Behind the seemingly undemanding foreground of casual conversation and social occasions there is a dense network of echoes and patterns that generate a critical, indeed diagnostic illumination of the experiences put before us. Fontane's art is as restrained as are the lives of his characters. But the artistic subtext knows better than do the characters. The 'poetry' (i.e. the artistic sophistication) of his prose is, then, no prettifying agency; rather, it embodies a matchless understanding of those socio-psychological

---

[11]  Quoted in Steinecke, *Romanpoetik*, pp. 227–8.    [12]  Quoted in *ibid.*, p. 217.

processes by which institutional and social rules are enforced. Once again, both the theory and the practice of German prose Realism achieve a mental history of social life. It is worth noting that at the very threshold of the twentieth century German literature produces a novel which brings this achievement to its full flowering: Thomas Mann's *Buddenbrooks*. In that story of family decline, material and mental concerns interlock to provide a richly complex picture of motivation and causality.

I have spent a great deal of time considering issues to do with the evolution of the German novel in the nineteenth century – primarily because, in any account of aesthetic theory and literary criticism of the time, the novel takes pride of place. But it should be noted that there is also at the time an intense theoretical discussion (particularly within Germany) of the shorter prose form known as the *Novelle*. Two issues are salient here. One is the thematic notion that the *Novelle* constantly explores and worries about the issue of artistic totality because it seeks to mediate between individual, specific, exceptional experience on the one hand and the laws of generality and continuity on the other. That thematic argument finds its correlative in stylistic and narrative theories which draw attention to the fact that historically (this means from Boccaccio on) the *Novelle* has tended to be a gregarious form. That is to say, it has often existed as a group of tales told by and to a small community of people who are both tellers and listeners. From that constellation emerges the sense that the *Novelle* often thematizes the mediations involved in the narrative process – mediations between a single voice and its public, between the expression of unique and exceptional things on the one hand and the discourse of established, corporate, social understanding on the other. In the multiple tensions (both thematic and structural) which it enshrines, then, the *Novelle* embodies many of the dilemmas and aporias of bourgeois individualism.

These dilemmas and the artistic uncertainty to which they give rise also inform the theory and practice of both drama and lyric poetry. As regards the drama, three creative talents are central to the German nineteenth century: Georg Büchner, Friedrich Hebbel and Gerhart Hauptmann. All three understand human experience as being inalienably anchored in, perhaps even in large measure determined by, the socio-historical world in which the characters find themselves. Yet drama – and particularly tragedy – by tradition aspires to a measure of grandeur; it seeks to do more than simply replicate forms of social interaction.

Friedrich Theodor Vischer writes:

The true home of modern drama is the un-magical reality of history. Drama steps into the centre of the conditions and circumstances of reality and extends its concern right into the intricate spheres of family and private life which give the ideals of the new world their warmth and inner vitality. Like the novel, so too the drama has to highlight those places where the genuinely prosaic order of history (or what is generally taken to be prosaic) is shattered, opens itself up and offers an image of freer movement.[13]

We register here terms familiar from the discussion of prose fiction; above all, the need for poetry to challenge the tyranny of prose. The dilemma is acute and can be felt in the theory and practice of Germany's major nineteenth-century dramatists. Büchner in *Woyzeck* and *Danton's Death* thematizes a determinism that will become second nature to the Naturalists at the end of the century. But he also seeks to vindicate – or at the very least to grieve for – a realm of human choice and autonomy. Hebbel, in his theory and his practice, seeks both to acknowledge the omnipresent conditioning agencies of history, and also to reveal the possibility for explosive change. The suffering of the tragic protagonist becomes meaningful in that it derives from and illuminates the motor forces of historical conflict and development. At each juncture of profound crisis the conflict serves to move the world forward. Stylistically Hebbel finds himself caught between the language of the unregenerate condition of the entrapped creature on the one hand and on the other the privileged, visionary rhetoric of the self that apprehends meaning and purpose. The upshot may be a profound uncertainty of style and diction. But the uncertainty is the measure of the creative disturbance at the heart of Hebbel's work.

By the end of the nineteenth century, with the early work of Gerhart Hauptmann, Naturalism carries all before it: the conditioning factors of 'race, milieu, moment' hold almost total sway. Yet poetry will not be banished forever, because the later Hauptmann will seek to create poetic, visionary, mythic drama. The movement he enacts from Naturalism to (for want of a better word) Symbolism is something he shares with Ibsen and Strindberg.

Similar tensions inform the debate about, and the production of, lyric poetry in Germany. Hermann Marggraff speaks for many when he registers the inroads of the modern industrial world into the traditional domain of lyric poetry:

In German lyric poetry there has admittedly been much misuse of springtime and love, of moonlight and sweet smelling flowers; but how low the standing of all these themes has sunk we hardly need to say.[14]

Yet the implied critique of traditional lyric utterance goes hand in hand with a certain unease at the prospects for modern poetry:

---

[13] Quoted in Plumpe, *Theorie*, p. 287.    [14] Quoted in *ibid.*, p. 304.

Our poets of the future will perhaps find the smoke of a chimney, the piercing whistle of a steam engine, the deafening clamour of a train much more poetic and amenable to poetic song than the wisp of fog in the mountain gorge, the uplifting notes of the posthorn or the secret rumbling of a romantically hidden water mill; the perfumes which roses and lilies emit will strike them as less pleasurable than the mixed odours of a factory that processes herrings, tallow, and fish oil.[15]

In many ways the crucial witness to the European dilemma as regards poetry comes from an earlier writer: Heinrich Heine. At one level, he is the no-nonsense advocate of a post-Romantic, post-Goethean world, in which journalism and politics are much more important than any attempt to keep the Muses alive and well and active. Yet at another level Heine loved the things he despised – particularly the (Romantic) poetry of mood, of privileged emotion, of longing. He also had an immense facility as a writer of verse. And this enabled him both to serve and to ironize the lyric impulse. He can be sweet, tender, tawdry, cheap, scurrilous, facile, and profound. In his very irresolution he is one of the absolutely central voices of European poetry. Marggraff is no doubt thinking of Heine when he writes: 'For a time German lyric poetry seemed to be in danger of losing itself in mere negation and witty irony.'[16] Much of Heine's negative and ironic temper can be felt in his remarkable critical study *The Romantic School*. Yet in his creative work the irony and the negation became necessary thematic and stylistic components within his complex articulation of the hazardous condition of modern poetry. Poetry, we might say, if it is to be true to itself and true to its age, has to acknowledge the condition of prose.

The gain and loss endemic to that acknowledgement were at the heart of nineteenth-century German writing about the theory and practice of literary endeavour – in prose, drama and poetry, as we have seen. The irresolution that can be felt at every turn is precisely what makes the German contribution to the literary expression of modernity through the course of the nineteenth century so decisive.

[15] Quoted in *ibid.*, p. 305.    [16] Quoted in *ibid.*, p. 307.

# Nineteenth-century British critics of Realism

ELAINE FREEDGOOD

When a Realist writer depicts a dressmaker, G. H. Lewes wrote, she 'must be a young woman who makes dresses, and not a sentimental "heroine", evangelical and consumptive; she may be consumptive, she may also be evangelical, for dressmakers are so sometimes, but she must be individually a dressmaker'.[1] This dictum is more complex than it would first appear: a dressmaker may not be a recycled fictional type – like the consumptive, evangelical, sentimental heroine. We see right away that a convention of Realism is that it abstains from literary convention, or from *previous* literary conventions (it will necessarily create its own). A Realistic dressmaker may have some of the qualities of a typical fictional heroine, since any real dressmaker might have evangelical beliefs or pulmonary ailments, but she must be 'individually' a dressmaker.

And yet 'a dressmaker' is not an individual: the word denotes a member of an occupation, not a particular person. It marks class, gender and a set of social conditions: it is a job, for example, in which it was thought, in the nineteenth century, that a young woman had a greater chance of remaining chaste than she would have if she worked in a factory; one in which women frequently went blind; a life of long hours and hard, repetitive, 'sweated' labour. To give a character in a novel this job, then, as Elizabeth Gaskell, for example, gives it to the eponymous heroine of *Mary Barton* (1848), is to give that character certain highly specific social characteristics through metonymic association. We learn that John Barton, Mary's father, wanted his daughter to become a dressmaker because he assumes that his sister-in-law has become a prostitute from the loose ways she learned while working in a cotton mill. What is crucial to note is that the Realistic novelist relies on the metonymic associations of the dressmaker in the actual social world, not on the literary conventions with which such characters have previously been connected. The Realistic dressmaker is connected to the world, in short, not to the literary past. The process of becoming an individual, in British Realism and in nineteenth-century critical views of it, is a complex combination of

---

[1] *Literary Criticism of George Henry Lewes*, ed., Alice R. Kaminsky (Lincoln: University of Nebraska Press, 1964), p. 89.

becoming a single, remarkable, apparently non-literary character through
becoming a recognizable member of an actual, historical, social group.

This is because, in the view of its nineteenth-century British critics,
Realism is responsible for representing social and individual experience
as it really occurs in the world outside the novel. And it must do so
through the most mundane, material means: if 'in French fiction dinner
is understood – in the English it is a main business, during which the
capabilities of the host are fully developed'.[2] Nothing can be taken for
granted: social life and individual character are found in the most basic
details of everyday life; none can be spared, all must be fully accurate. In
the essay 'Silly Novels by Lady Novelists', George Eliot complains about
the appalling lack of empirical veracity purveyed by said novelists: 'their
intellect seems to have the peculiar impartiality of reproducing both what
they *have* seen and heard, and what they have *not* seen and heard, with
equal unfaithfulness'.[3] The novelist must be true to her own experience
of the word: a lack of such fidelity is a fictional sin of vast proportions
in Eliot's Realistic ethic. Similarly, George Meredith recommends what
he describes as comedy (the genre he ascribes to his novel *The Egoist*)
because it 'keeps the minor writer to a definite plan, and to English'.[4]

In the most famous apostrophe on Realism in the nineteenth-century
British canon on the subject, Eliot pauses in the narration of *Adam Bede*
to assure her readers that

my strongest effort is to . . . give no more than a faithful account of men and
things as they have mirrored themselves in my mind. The mirror is doubtless
defective; the outline will sometimes be disturbed, the reflection faint or
confused; but I feel as much bound to tell you as precisely as I can what that
reflection is, as if I were in the witness-box narrating my experience on oath.[5]

Eliot is not naïve about the necessary distortions that perception will
introduce into representation, but her effort will be towards an absolute
fidelity to what is really *there*. Note the simile that Eliot draws between
Realistic novel writing and testifying under oath: the *experience* the novelist supplies ought to be of the quality of a sworn truth. Binding herself
to this standard of truth in fiction, Eliot opens up a paradox about fiction

---

[2] Henry Southern, 'French Novels' in *A Victorian Art of Fiction: Essays on the Novel in British Periodicals. Vol. I: 1830–1850*, ed. John Charles Olmsted (New York: Garland, 1979), pp. 131–2.
[3] *Essays of George Eliot*, ed. Thomas Pinney (New York: Columbia University Press, 1993), p. 304.
[4] George Meredith, 'On the Idea of Comedy, and of the Uses of the Comic Spirit' in *George Meredith's Essay on Comedy and Other New Quarterly Magazine Publications: A Critical Edition*, ed. Maura C. Ives (Lewisburg, PA: Bucknell University Press, 1998), p. 145.
[5] George Eliot, *Adam Bede* (Harmondsworth: Penguin, 1982), ch. 17, p. 221.

that many Victorian writers seemed to have lived with quite comfortably. Fiction may or may not be a *re*-presentation of certain specific 'men and things', but it is a portrait of the kinds of men and the kinds of things that the author has encountered, and encountered regularly. These types have mirrored themselves in her mind. She is not, like silly lady novelists (and undoubtedly some silly male ones Eliot failed to notice or chastise), writing in a state of reckless disconnection from reality.

In her 'Dialogue on Novels', the late nineteenth-century novelist and critic Vernon Lee makes the perplexed French interlocutor Marcel observe that '[i]t is extraordinary how aesthetical questions invariably end in ethical ones when treated by English people'.[6] We can understand this link between the aesthetic and the ethical when we think carefully about the cultural work that the British novelist was expected to perform, especially after the mid-century. The Realistic novelist was something of a sociologist and news reporter, a chronicler of the present and the recent past, a commentator on the contemporary world. Indeed the work of the Realist novel, as it is evaluated by nineteenth-century British critics (a group that includes many novelists themselves), often sounds more like that of social science, history or governmental investigation than it does like that of an artistic or aesthetic form. Realism was expected to be pedagogical; it was expected to teach its readers about the world they were living in but experiencing in a necessarily limited way.

Many novelists were clearly as interested in shaping reality as they were in reflecting it. Dickens is perhaps the most wide-ranging novelistic reformer: he represented the plight of the urban poor such that readers will pity its membership and reserve judgement for the conditions that produce poverty; he satirized the bureaucratic processes of chancery and the cruelty of debtors' prisons; he helped invent the idea of childhood to which we now adhere. Thackeray skewered social life so that his readers might renounce its worst falsenesses. Gaskell hoped to bring upper- and middle-class readers into a kinder relationship to the labouring class that surrounded them: she warns of the consequences that might befall Britain if the urban poor begin to think in terms of revenge instead of resignation. Margaret Oliphant surely critiques the condition of women and the law of property inheritance, although Victorianist scholars cannot decide whether or not she is a feminist. Anthony Trollope shows us the human wreckage produced by financial fraud, and develops a devastating critique of the vagaries of the British financial system in the Victorian period in his representations of those who exploited it. Eliot aims to produce 'sympathy' for ordinary characters: a high ideal in Eliot, an all-purpose social

---

6 Vernon Lee (Violet Paget), 'A Dialogue on Novels' in *Victorian Criticism of the Novel*, eds. Edward M. Eigner and George J. Worth (Cambridge University Press, 1985), p. 235.

and political balm. Late in her career, she became more ambitious and
tried to help readers, with the publication of *Daniel Deronda*, imagine
a Jewish state into existence. Kipling's record of Britain's imperial and
colonial relation to India is full both of the jingoism we associate with
his worst poems and, *avant la lettre*, of the pains and possibilities that
inhere in the postcolonial theorizing of hybridity. Representations of the
tragedy of human sexuality by writers like Thomas Hardy, Oscar Wilde
and Eliza Lynn Linton may have much to do with how we think of
modern sexuality.

   If this entry seems to be unduly focused on the novel it is because
in the literary criticism of the period, 'Realism' is broadly coincident
with the novel itself, which is defined, as it often is now, against the
'romance'. Writing in 1842, George Moir notes that instead of 'mar-
velous and uncommon incidents', the novel is concerned with the 'ordinary train of events', 'the modern state of society'. The 'impression of
verisimilitude' is created by the accretion of 'many particulars', 'minute
traits of character' and 'descriptions of external scenery'.[7] Moir brings
together the visual, the social and what we would now call the psychological dimensions of novelistic representation in his definition of what
creates verisimilitude, or the effect of the Realistic. Indeed, 'inner' reality
is often as important to critics of the novel as the depiction of outward
reality: Lewes remarks that *Jane Eyre* '*is* an autobiography, – not perhaps, in the naked facts and circumstances, but in the actual suffering and
experience'.[8] This is the same standard of Realism that Eliot applies to
her own fictional production in *Adam Bede*: fidelity to experience makes
for something that seems like contact between representation and reality.

   How much reality was the writer to represent? Dickens was roundly
castigated by critics for a too-lively depiction of 'the haunts, deeds, language, and characters of the very dregs of the community' in *Oliver Twist*:
it is 'a hazardous experiment to exhibit to the young these enormities',
Richard Ford complained in the *Quarterly Review*.[9] Another critic contended that the 'vigour and power' of these representations creates 'in
the public a morbid interest in such heroes and their mode of life'.[10]
It was not until the last third of the century, Catherine Gallagher has
argued, that British Realism could catch up with a fundamental insight
of Flaubert: 'that the object of representation could be deprived of value
in the very process of representing it and that the value thus subtracted

[7] George Moir, 'Modern Romance and Novel', cited in Eigner and Worth, *Victorian Criticism of the Novel*, p. 22.
[8] G. H. Lewes, 'Recent Novels: French and English' in Olmsted, *Victorian Art of Fiction*, p. 570.
[9] See Olmsted, *Victorian Art of Fiction*, p. 291.
[10] Thomas Cleghorn, 'The Writings of Charles Dickens' in *ibid.*, p. 455.

from the thing depicted could be appropriated by the representation'.[11] One of the writers from this later period, George Gissing, characterizes Dickens as precisely not a Realist. In a discussion of the fairy-tale quality of the scene in *Dombey and Son* (1848) in which Florence mixes a mug of grog for Captain Cuttle, Gissing notes that 'no one can for a moment believe that two such persons were ever in such relations'. But a 'spell is laid upon us' by such scenes. Gissing concludes that 'Dickens never puts his genius to better use than in his idealization of English life and character.'[12]

The paradox, of course, is that fiction would be the realm in which to carry out what became an extremely convincing representation, or creation, of social reality. Historians have not shied away from using the 'evidence' of Realism: Dickens's *Little Dorritt* has long been a source for information on Victorian debtors' prisons; the historian of marriage, the family, domesticity and gender relations cannot avoid the accounts of hearth and home found in the Realistic novel from *Pride and Prejudice* at the nineteenth century's beginning to the feminist and anti-feminist New Woman novels of its end. Perhaps this paradox about the truth or reality to be found in fiction is one for the postmodern reader and not the nineteenth-century one: in the nineteenth century, the largest possible vision of recent and contemporary social reality would perhaps be most available to readers in novels like *Vanity Fair, Mary Barton, Jane Eyre, David Copperfield, Middlemarch, The Way We Live Now* or *Jude the Obscure*. The sociological study had yet to be invented; the investigation into problematic living and working conditions is just getting under way as a genre (and is often as popular as the novel); the multiple media on which we rely for news of the world are all mostly a long way off. One major information technology that did develop alongside Realism – photography – held its prose counterpart to a high standard of empirical accuracy. The 'competition' from photography demanded that the Realist novel, recent critics have argued, offer its readers a particularly vivid world, which could easily and happily come to seem like *the* world.[13]

Nineteenth-century critics were not particularly naïve about Realism, although their Modernist descendants often accuse them of this failing: Lewes well understood that every representation is 'not the thing itself'

[11]  Catherine Gallagher, *The Industrial Reformation of English Fiction 1832–1867* (University of Chicago Press, 1988), p. 266.

[12]  George Gissing, *Charles Dickens: A Critical Study* (New York: Dodd, Mead, 1901), p. 218.

[13]  See Nancy Armstrong, *Fiction in the Age of Photography: The Legacy of British Realism* (Cambridge, MA: Harvard University Press, 1999), and Jennifer Green Lewis, *Framing the Victorians: Photography and the Culture of Realism* (Ithaca, NY: Cornell University Press, 1996).

and 'must necessarily be limited by the nature of its medium; the canvas of the painter, the chords of the musician, and the language of the writer'.[14] Eliot, similarly, often pauses in her fiction to reflect on the way in which the writer chooses what to represent, creating a sense of reality out of a process of selection in which much is left out. She knows that the 'mirror' in her mind on which the world casts its shadows is not a perfect reflector. Perhaps equally aware of the ways in which readers may construct their own realities out of novelistic details, Eliot's narrators famously guide our interpretative processes minutely, as if to forestall the readerly construction of a novelistic reality not in perfect accord with her own. This is the kind of reflectiveness that we often associate with the postmodern novel and its criticism: indeed, the postmodern novel relies on an idea of Realism that is often too simple given the rich self-reflection of Realist writers themselves, and the ample thinking on the subject by critics in the period, who knew that reality was hard to know and that Realism was a difficult, and often treacherous substitute for it. Reading Realism was a way of having a relationship with the world in the nineteenth century, when the world was not at the multimedia-possessing fingertips of its inhabitants, but only very partially available to the eyes and hands of eager readers: hence the profound responsibility placed on the Realist writer to deliver that world with as little distortion and interference as possible. That such distortion and interference were inevitable was of course well understood: it was itself part of the relationship between the reader, the author, the novel and the world that Victorians began to theorize in their reflections on writing, reading and the ethics of literary representation.

[14]   G. H. Lewes, 'Realism and Idealism' in Kaminsky, *Literary Criticism of George Henry Lewes*, p. 87.

# 17

# American literary Realism

CAROL J. SINGLEY

'I don't care for what people call "art"', William Dean Howells wrote to S. Weir Mitchell, whose new novel Howells praised in 1885, 'I like nearness to life.'[1] Thus Howells, acknowledged 'Dean of American letters', established the parameters for Realism, a literary style that flourished in the years bracketed by the end of the American Civil War (1865) and the beginning of the First World War (1914). Howells, an influential critic, novelist and editor, helped to shape the perception – which continues today – of Realism as an objective or transparent representation of ordinary life. An aesthetically complex literary form, Realism developed partly in response to certain accelerated social and economic changes in American culture. It ranges from good-natured, even sentimental, renderings of manners to psychologically dense and near fatalistic representations of human strivings. Realism somewhat resembles Naturalism, a style of writing that reached its height in the 1890s and portrays literary subjects as powerless in the face of external or internal forces. Popularly understood, Realism is the literature of the average and everyday, the result of viewing the world neither with the rose-tinted spectacles of Romanticism nor with the dark shades of Naturalism, but with the clear lenses of scientific objectivity and photographic accuracy. Realism was less concerned with formal qualities than with social context and arguably produced more notable fiction than poetry, although critics such as Henry James worked to define a poetics of Realistic fiction.

American Realism has its roots in Europe, dating from the fifteenth century. These roots include quattrocento Realist painting; the more general impact of the ideologies behind representational political institutions and the revolutions of 1776 and 1789 in America and France respectively; the increasing emphasis on empirical science; and the growth of historical narrative. As Paul Schellinger notes, Realism is not the rendering of detail and the ordinary but experimentation with a single coordinated system or single-point perspective that produces the illusion of neutrality. In

[1] W. D. Howells to S. Weir Mitchell, 20 October 1885, in *William Dean Howells, Selected Letters. Vol. 3: 1882–1891*, ed. Robert C. Leitz III (Boston: Twayne, 1908), pp. 134, 152.

Realism, authors present action and issues as shared, objective or true.[2]
For nineteenth-century writers in England, France and Russia, these verities could be found in previously unexplored aspects of social life. In
England, the popularity of Dickens's Realistic, sometimes melodramatic,
depictions of factories, slums and prisons expanded the definition of
what constituted appropriate subject matter for literature. In France,
Balzac's stories and novels set new standards for literary observation,
while Flaubert's *Madame Bovary* (1857) demonstrated artful style in
combination with Realistic detail. Russian writers Turgenev, Tolstoy and
Dostoevsky influenced generations of American Realist writers with their
depictions of class and their concerns with social justice.

Most influential were the writings of Zola, whose doctrine of Naturalism, formulated in 'The Experimental Novel' (1880), studied human
behaviour as if it were under a microscope, subject to the same forces of
nature as all functioning organisms. Borrowing ideas from science and
medicine, Zola equated the writer's world with the laboratory. Novelists,
he wrote, by their 'observations and experiments' seek 'to possess a
knowledge of the mechanism of the phenomena inherent in man, to show
the machinery of his intellectual and sensory manifestations under the
influences of heredity and environment'.[3] A focus on the deterministic
qualities of natural and social conditions has led critics to equate
Naturalism with fatalism, although technically Naturalist writers are
concerned with exploring causes and effects. In Europe and the United
States the terms 'Realism' and 'Naturalism' have sometimes been used
interchangeably, but critics debate whether Naturalism is merely Realism
in extreme form or a distinct literary mode. 'Realism' is often used to
describe the fiction of Howells and James in the 1870s and 1880s, and
'Naturalism' that of Frank Norris and Theodore Dreiser in the 1890s.
Such designations, however, inadequately account for the work of
writers such as Stephen Crane, Edith Wharton and Kate Chopin, which
displays elements of Realism and Naturalism. Nor do they fully describe
the voluminous regional literature produced by African Americans and
Native Americans during this time.

American Realistic writers developed an interest in documenting the
world around them in conjunction with their experience of profound
changes in society at the end of the nineteenth century. In general,
American Realism is defined more by history than by ideology, as it
is in Europe. Industrial development was advancing at an unprecedented

---

[2] 'Realism' in *Encyclopedia of the Novel*, ed. Paul Schellinger, 2 vols. (Chicago: Fitzroy
Dearborn, 1998), vol. II, pp. 1073–4.
[3] Emile Zola, *The Experimental Novel and Other Essays* (New York: Haskell House,
1964), pp. 17, 20–1.

pace, and with it a new commercialism and an unparalleled growth of cities, whose populations swelled with immigrants from Europe and with African Americans from the South. Westward expansion added to a sense of incessant mobility, while a post-Darwinian emphasis on science rather than religion, as well as technological advances, fundamentally changed the character of knowledge and communication. Realistic literature is in constant dialogue with professional discourses of the time – scientific, reformist, legal and commercial – and uses these ways of knowing as reference points. Writers reflect not the Romantic idealism of previous decades but the contemporary pragmatic Realism of Charles S. Peirce and John Dewey. They examine ideas as solutions to specific problems that occur within a social context, and they develop theories of knowledge based on empirical observation of facts and actualities rather than on deductive truths.

Attention to the pressures of everyday reality not only characterizes Realistic fiction but also points to literature as a vehicle for social reform and social awareness. Regardless of their orientation towards their subjects, Realistic writers shared a belief in the social consequences of reading and writing literature. They took it upon themselves to investigate the workings of society, making Realism as much social critique as social observation. Implicit in their work is the notion that literature serves not just an aesthetic but a public function. There was a close relationship between fiction and journalism at this time, evidenced by the fact that many writers, such as Twain, Crane and Dreiser, worked as reporters as well as novelists. Their visits to slums, factories, railroad operations and meat-packing plants constituted empirical research for their works of art.

The notion that literature, like the democratic ideals which are sometimes related to Realist aesthetics, could redeem or improve human character is demonstrated in the writings of William Dean Howells (1837–1920). As editor of the influential magazines the *Nation*, the *Atlantic Monthly*, *Harper's Monthly* and *Cosmopolitan*, and as the author of numerous novels, Howells played a major role in advancing the careers of dozens of writers, including Twain and James, as well as regional and ethnic minority writers such as Sarah Orne Jewett, William Chesnutt and Abraham Cahan. Howells's *Criticism and Fiction* (1891) celebrated literature of the commonplace, as in his declaration that 'the talent that is robust enough to front the every-day world and catch the charm of its work-worn, care-worn, brave, kindly face, need not fear the encounter'.[4] His preference for the ordinary and his concomitant suspicion of aristocratic leanings aligned Realism with a nineteenth-century tradition of

4 W. D. Howells, 'Criticism and Fiction' in *Criticism and Fiction and Other Essays*, eds. Clara Marburg Kirk and Rudolf Kirk (New York University Press, 1959), p. 67.

Jeffersonian and Jacksonian faith in vigour and common sense. Although Howells's later fiction was criticized for being too genteel, he eschewed the romantic and the sentimental, and he facilitated the linkage between literature and social justice. Whether recording the social and moral quandaries of business or divorce, Howells believed that moral purpose was essential to good art. In well-known novels such as *The Rise of Silas Lapham* (1885) and *The Hazard of New Fortunes* (1890) as well as in his criticism, he demonstrates both optimism and objectivity, exhibiting an evolutionary faith in social progress and in characters' abilities to remake themselves.

Some Realist writers made it a point to depict the middle and lower classes of society, often in a spirit of egalitarianism. Describing this tendency, Charles Dudley Warner noted in 1883 that Realistic fiction leads us to examine the 'seamy' side of life and 'force[s] us to sup with unwholesome company'.[5] In 1893 Maurice Thompson similarly noted that in Realistic poetry and fiction 'we are hobnobbing with persons with whom we could not in real life bear a moment's interview'.[6] Defenders of Realism such as Hamlin Garland (1860–1940) found nobility in the commonplace, argued for authenticity, and promoted Realism as a vehicle for democracy and social progress. Advocating literature based on experience in *Crumbling Idols* (1894), he lambasted Easterners who wrote about the West without ever having visited it. His views, reflecting a lingering Emersonian and Whitmanian idealism, helped unite the local and national aspects of Realist literature. Theodore Dreiser (1871–1945) joined Garland in criticizing those who turn away from the more mundane or distasteful aspects of life, going so far as to suggest that their refusal to see life as it truly is reflected blindness and denial of parts of themselves. In *Sister Carrie* (1900) and *The Financier* (1912), he describes the ill-fated dreams of characters defeated by circumstances.

For Realist Edith Wharton, however, the demand that fiction address the commonplace created its own tyranny. Wharton objected to the dictum 'that only the man with the dinner pail shall be deemed worthy of attention' and rebelled against such prescriptions in her portrayals of the elite New York society of her childhood.[7] Her descriptions of characters ruled by social convention and her bleak endings are vivid reminders that environment and biology affect all ranks of society. In *The House of Mirth* (1905), Lily Bart is oppressed by wealth as well as by poverty:

[5] Charles Dudley Warner, 'Modern Fiction', *Atlantic Monthly*, 51 (1883), 464–74; rpt in Donald Pizer (ed.), *Documents of American Realism and Naturalism* (Carbondale: Southern Illinois University Press, 1998), p. 41.
[6] Maurice Thompson, *The Ethics of Literary Art* (Hartford Seminary Press, 1893); rpt in Pizer, *Documents of American Realism*, p. 126.
[7] Edith Wharton, *A Backward Glance* (New York: Scribner's, 1934), p. 206.

the links of her sapphire bracelet 'seemed like manacles linking her to her fate'.[8]

Recent critics have elaborated on Realism's capacity also to record and exert power within arenas not expressly political. As Nancy Bentley writes, both literary Realism and ethnography strove to document events in a way 'that gives the observer mastery over a cultural territory'.[9] Amy Kaplan explores the role Realism played in helping middle and upper classes distinguish themselves from the lower classes. Kaplan writes that Realism 'has turned into a conservative force whose very act of exposure reveals its complicity with structures of power'.[10] Marxist critic Fredric Jameson notes the Realist novel's role in 'a properly bourgeois cultural revolution...whereby populations...are effectively reprogrammed for life and work in the new world of market capitalism'.[11] Alan Trachtenberg charts the growth of a corporate business system that was welcomed by the genteel classes and resisted by populists and the working classes.[12] And Phillip Barrish explains how literary Realism conferred intellectual prestige and cultural distinction on its practitioners.[13]

Realistic writers with a penchant for Naturalism, in addition to Dreiser and Wharton, include Frank Norris (1870–1902), Stephen Crane (1871–1900) and Jack London (1876–1916). They subscribe to a darker form of Realism as found in the writings of Zola, which depicts characters devoid of agency and overpowered by biological and environmental forces. As Presley, in Norris's novel *The Octopus* (1901), reflects, 'Men were nothings, mere animalcules, mere ephemerides that fluttered and fell and were forgotten between dawn and dusk.'[14] Norris developed a theory of Romantic Naturalism in which writers represent the actuality of life commonly associated with Realism but also go beyond the surface value of experience to seek a greater truth, such as the kind found in romance. Some of Norris's works combine sordid details with what Richard Gray terms 'an almost poetic celebration of the primal rhythms that...drove through nature and the primal urges that pulsed through man'.[15] London

8  Edith Wharton, *The House of Mirth*, ed. Cynthia Griffin Wolff (New York: Penguin, 1988), p. 7.
9  Nancy Bentley, *The Ethnography of Manners: Hawthorne, James, Wharton* (Cambridge University Press, 1995), p. 2.
10 Amy Kaplan, *The Social Construction of American Realism* (University of Chicago Press, 1988), p. 1.
11 Fredric Jameson, *The Political Unconscious: Narrative as a Socially Symbolic Act* (Ithaca, NY: Cornell University Press, 1981), p. 152.
12 Alan Trachtenberg, *The Incorporation of America: Culture and Society in the Gilded Age* (New York: Hill & Wang, 1982).
13 Phillip Barrish, *American Literary Realism, Critical Theory, and Intellectual Prestige, 1880–1995* (Cambridge University Press, 2001), pp. 1–7.
14 Frank Norris, *The Octopus: A Story of California* (New York: Bantam, 1963), p. 425.
15 Richard Gray, *A History of American Literature* (Oxford: Blackwell, 2004), p. 300.

sets *The Call of the Wild* (1903) in the Klondike and depicts the brutal indifference of nature to human aspiration. Crane similarly documents the power of environment as well as the moral hypocrisies of society in his deterministic novella *Maggie: A Girl of the Streets* (1893), about a girl in the Bowery who 'blossomed in a mud puddle'.[16] Reliance on the force of natural laws in Realistic fiction produces pessimistic endings that some readers found morally objectionable or in bad taste. It also prevented characters from self-reflection, a fact that led Henry James to charge that Zola strikes the reader as 'magnificent' but 'ignorant'.[17]

Social changes in late nineteenth- and early twentieth-century society set writers seeking the presumed stability and permanence found in local life. Realism developed alongside an interest in regionalism, which represents customs, values and language patterns of a particular geographic area. Often small-town life is presented through the central consciousness of an urban outsider, whose cosmopolitanism serves as counterpoint to the local experience. Sarah Orne Jewett, for example, writes in *The Country of the Pointed Firs* (1896) about towns in Maine depopulated because of Civil War casualties and westward or urban migration. Her accounts of coastal life – simple, profound and often elegiac in tone – convey deep respect for individuals and their communities, past and present; her unadorned prose anticipates the minimalism of Modernism. Mark Twain produced a complex form of Realism that combines humour and social satire in his fiction about antebellum Southern life. His attention to dialect and detail in *The Adventures of Huckleberry Finn* (1884) captures the innocence of childhood as well as the brutal effects of slavery. Twain eschewed sentimentalism, but Huck's questing spirit, *naïveté* and yearning for nature make the novel Romantic as well as Realistic. Kate Chopin focused on Creole society and sexual politics in her controversial novel *The Awakening* (1899), which explores a woman's restless desire to escape the bonds of marriage and motherhood. Not strictly a regionalist, Louisa May Alcott (1832–88) wrote of genteel poverty and childhood challenges in her best-selling *Little Women* (1868–9), set in Concord, Massachusetts.

A focus on local colour, in the opinion of critic Alfred Kazin, fostered a sense of belonging to a native way of life and promoted an 'elementary nationalism'.[18] However, some critics judge these claims to be simplistic and find in regional writing a resistance to dominant economic and social systems. Whereas industrial society homogenizes difference and destroys

---

[16] Stephen Crane, *Maggie: A Girl of the Streets* (New York: Bantam, 1986), p. 16.
[17] Henry James, 'The Art of Fiction', *Longmans*, 4 (1884), p. 21.
[18] Alfred Kazin, *On Native Grounds: An Interpretation of Modern American Prose Literature* (New York: Harcourt Brace, 1942), p. 17.

localities, regionalist writing keeps the local alive. Working from marginal positions, these writers add alternative, sometimes subversive, voices to those of the mainstream. Judith Fetterley and Marjorie Pryse, as well as Josephine Donovan and Kate McCullough, argue that female local colourists were actually proto-feminists whose work was undervalued because it challenged the status quo.[19] They describe an 'antihegemonic strain of regionalist discourse' that Tom Lutz finds 'through the genre's entire history'.[20] Cautions against literary tourism appear in Garland's writings as well as in recent work by Richard Brodhead and Amy Kaplan, who charge regional writers – more educated and sophisticated than their subjects – with violating or appropriating local material in order to serve the tastes of an urban, elite readership.[21] Lutz places regionalism in dialogue with cosmopolitanism in a manner designed to include the values of both.

Nowhere are issues of appropriation more salient than in writings about racial and ethnic minorities, especially African Americans. Joel Chandler Harris (1845/8–1908) earned praise for his depictions of ante-bellum plantation life and his Uncle Remus character, but in juxtaposition with writing by African American regionalist Charles W. Chesnutt (1858–1932), Harris's renderings can seem sentimental, even whitewashed. In *The Conjure Woman and Other Conjure Tales* (1899), Chesnutt presents the Old South through the eyes of an ex-slave, Uncle Julius McAdoo, whose savvy, subversive struggles against white power undermine any romantic myths of chattel slavery. African American writer Frances E. W. Harper wrote realistically about post-Civil War family life. Julia A. J. Foote (1827–1900) and Pauline Elizabeth Hopkins (1859–1930) experimented with several genres, Foote sometimes returning to earlier literary forms such as the spiritual autobiography, and Hopkins relying on more contemporary forms of writing.

Mexican American writers expressed resistance to white domination with the *corrido*, a narrative form with roots in the romances of medieval Spain. Native Americans also tried to counter racial and ethnic injustice.

---

[19] Judith Fetterley and Marjorie Pryse, 'Introduction' in *American Women Regionalists, 1850–1910: A Norton Anthology*, eds. Judith Fetterley and Marjorie Pryse (New York: Norton, 1992), pp. xiii–xiv; Josephine Donovan, *New England Local Color Literature: A Women's Tradition* (New York: Frederick Ungar, 1983), pp. 2–10; Kate McCullough, *Regions of Identity: The Construction of America in Women's Fiction, 1885–1914* (Stanford University Press, 1999), pp. 5–9.

[20] Tom Lutz, *Cosmopolitan Vistas: American Regionalism and Literary Value* (Ithaca, NY: Cornell University Press, 2004), p. 25.

[21] Richard Brodhead, *Cultures of Letters: Scenes of Reading and Writing in Nineteenth-Century America* (University of Chicago Press, 1993); Amy Kaplan, 'Nation, Region, Empire' in *Columbia History of the American Novel*, eds. Emory Elliott *et al.* (New York: Columbia University Press, 1991).

Ponca chief Standing Bear (1829–1908) delivered a momentous speech
protesting the removal, or relocation, of Indian populations; tribal performances of Ghost Dance Songs announced a vision in which injustices
enacted by the US government would be redressed; and Charles Alexander
Eastman (1858–1939) and Zitkala-Ša (1876–1938) described experiences
of dislocation and assimilation in white boarding schools. Illinois-born
Mary Austin (1868–1934) migrated westward and described the West's
liberating landscape as well as the clash of Anglo, Native American and
Spanish cultures.

Immigrant literature appeared in fictional and non-fictional forms.
Abraham Cahan (1860–1951), Mary Antin (1881–1949) and Anzia
Yierzerska told the story of Jewish immigration; Upton Sinclair featured a
Lithuanian immigrant in his muckraking novel about the stockyard, *The
Jungle* (1906); and sisters Winnifred Eaton (1875–1954) and Edith Maud
Eaton (1865–1914) narrated Chinese immigrant experiences. 'Realism' is
a historically accurate term for these writings, but issues of social justice
rather than matters of literariness predominate in their construction.

The literary forms of American Realism were profoundly shaped by
Henry James (1843–1916), whose critical theories and works of fiction
became more influential in the twentieth century than those of Howells.
Friends as well as fellow writers committed to the craft, Howells and
James talked endlessly to settle 'the true principles of literary art'.[22] Matters on which they agreed included writing about the ordinary; eschewing
romance, melodrama and exoticism; appealing to the higher faculties of
the reader; and relying on character rather than plot for effects. However,
whereas Howells focused on American life, James pursued an international theme and was absorbed by European theories of art and representation. If Howells was taken by the commonplace, James was affected by
'the special case'[23] and delved deeply into the psychological complexities
of human experience in order to arrive at truth for a given character or
situation. A fundamental difference in attitude towards the masses also
distinguishes their work. According to Howells, the problems of modern
society stemmed from a failure of fraternity and unity that could bring
all Americans together. The Realist, Howells wrote in *Criticism and Fiction*, 'feels in every nerve the equality of things and the unity of men'.[24]
James, on the other hand, instinctively fled the masses despite his best
democratic intentions, suspecting the grossness of their judgements and
aesthetic sensibilities.

[22]  W. D. Howells to E. C. Stedman, 5 December 1866, in *Selected Letters of W. D.
    Howells. Vol. I: 1852–1872*, eds. George Arms *et al.* (Boston: Twayne, 1979), p. 271.
[23]  Gray, *American Literature*, p. 287.
[24]  Howells, *Criticism and Fiction*, p. 15.

James also differs from Howells in his devotion to craft. Whereas Howells relied on the tools of the reporter or journalist, James experimented with narrative technique. He became an innovator in the articulation of inner consciousness. There is 'no more nutritive or suggestive truth...than that of the perfect dependence of the "moral" sense of a work of art on the amount of felt life concerned in producing it', he wrote in the Preface to *The Portrait of a Lady* (1881).[25] Point of view was essential in order to convey this quality of 'felt life', and James worked assiduously in his fiction to clarify the positions from which his characters saw and experienced the world. 'The house of fiction', he explained, 'has...not one window, but a million...every one of which has been pierced, or is still pierceable...by the need of the individual vision and by the pressure of the individual will.'[26] His aesthetic theories privileged perspective, which ultimately not only shaped but also defined character, and led to fiction that became increasingly nuanced and psychological. Although not a relativist, James was influenced by contributions in modern psychology, including those of his brother William James, who argued in *The Varieties of Religious Experience* (1902) that an idea has meaning only in relation to its consequences.

Realism in the United States owes a debt to European models, but historical and social forces in the post-Civil War era, including political corruption, westward expansion, immigration and the legacy of slavery, contributed to the construction of distinct literary forms and themes. American Realistic writers not only chronicled and interpreted but also sought to change the dimensions of the rapidly altering society in which they were immersed. Their work is not easily summarized or generalized, but Henry Adams (1838–1918), who wrote that the world into which the child of 1900 was born 'would not be a unity but a multiple', conveys the sense of mobility, diversity and social uncertainty to which American Realistic writers responded.

[25]   Henry James, Preface, *The Portrait of a Lady* (Oxford University Press, 1995), p. 7.
[26]   *Ibid.*, p. 8.

# 18

# Decadence and *fin de siècle*

RAY FURNESS

The terms 'Decadent' and 'Decadence' are acknowledged to be protean, mutable: Decadence is both a literary or aesthetic label and a moralizing evaluation, a movement in art and literature denoting an anti-naturalist, mannered cultivation of deliberate artifice as well as a castigation of all that was deemed to be perverse or questionable in contemporary life. Decadence was associated and frequently overlapped with Aestheticism in a blurred symbiosis; the Decadent would emerge as a specific type, a dandy, a cultivator of recondite attitudes, an exquisite, frequently degenerate and often associated with aberrant sexuality. The concept is associated above all with *fin de siècle* Paris, also London, with the yellow paper covers of the novels published by Charpentier, with the 1880s and also the 1890s, this last as the 'yellow' or 'mauve' decade, but its historical provenance is long, indeed venerable.

The word 'décadence' appeared in France in the fifteenth century as a loan word from Latin displacing the earlier 'déchéance'; French authors of the eighteenth century popularized it, and the authors of the 1880s and the 1890s will find the term, with its connotations of decline, over-refinement and unwholesomeness, ready to hand. Montesquieu had used it in 1734 when discussing the rise and fall of Rome; Rousseau, using concepts such as corruption and dissoluteness, argued that society was degenerate, associated as it was with dissipated sophistication; Voltaire lamented, in 1770, 'les temps de la plus horrible décadence' ('this age of the most appalling decadence') and emphasized that decadence was symptomatic of a society sated with beauty and rejoicing in 'le goût du bizarre' ('a predilection for the bizarre'). Some sixty years later the literary historian Désiré Nisard, in his study (1834) on late Latin poetry ('les poètes latins de la décadence'), insisted on the similarities between the poets of his own times and the Silver Age: the concept of a 'littérature de décadence' is here adumbrated; critics and journalists such as Maxime Ducamp and Claude-Marie Raudot will further embellish the term, pointing above all to the hyper-sophistication, extreme ornamentation and decrepitude in contemporary art scarcely concealed by a glittering surface. The association of decadence with modern literature is now at hand, the linking of art with high artifice and amorality, with its practitioners as dandies or degenerates, aesthetes whose sole aim was the cultivation of arcane beauty.[1]

The begetter of French and, later, English literary decadence is Théophile Gautier. *Mademoiselle de Maupin* (1835) exults in an infatuation with the visible world at the expense of ethical values: the aesthete Chevalier d'Albert, an immoralist who dreams of igniting cities to illuminate his celebrations, who seeks to be a woman to experience new sensual pleasures, who rejects the Christian doctrine of sinfulness and who refuses to contemplate the ugly and the banal, will prepare the way for many of the figures in this study. Baudelaire's later description of the dandy (1863) as belonging to a new aristocracy, a haughty and exclusive sect resisting the rising tide of democracy, is anticipated by Gautier, as is Barbey-d'Aurevilly's portrayal of the dandy as the androgyne of history, as are Oscar Wilde's antics. The cruelty of aestheticism is also implied in Gautier's novel, as is its association with hermaphroditism and homosexuality; languor and total indifference to all that the bourgeoisie holds dear are also fashionable. But it was the appearance, in 1867, of Baudelaire's *Notes nouvelles sur Edgar Poe* (a preface to the second part of Baudelaire's translations of the American writer) which offered a new evaluation, a most decisive formulation of the terms 'Decadent' and 'Decadence'. It is here that Baudelaire transmutes these labels, hitherto pejorative, into positive terms of approval: those critics who had rejected Poe for being morbid and bizarre failed to realize, Baudelaire insisted, that Poe aimed at being unnatural, for the natural had no appeal for the modern mentality, neither had a belief in progress and happiness. It was not the rising, but the setting sun which was now invoked, an age moving towards dissolution.

Baudelaire's position would be admirably summed up by Gautier, who, in the 1868 edition of the *Fleurs du mal*, argued that Baudelaire loved that which had been called 'le style du décadence', that is, art of an extreme sophistication characteristic of dying civilizations, ingenious, complex, knowing and full of neuroses, a poetry aware of exhaustion and yet seeking out the most abstruse terminology, delighting in a self-referential play on the edge of extinction. *Mademoiselle de Maupin* had announced that all art was useless, having no meaning outside itself; its author now sees in Baudelaire the paradigm of modernity in his rejection of moral precepts, his connoisseurship of sickly sensations, his sophisticated complexity and his flirtation with neurosis and depravity. As Baudelaire had extolled this in Poe, so Gautier extols it in Baudelaire, and that which is formulated in Paris in the 1860s will become the literary slogans of the 1880s and

[1] Erwin Koppen, *Dekadenter Wagnerismus* (Berlin and New York: De Gruyter, 1973), pp. 6–25.

1890s: Aestheticism, *l'art pour l'art*, Decadence and *fin de siècle*. To claim that an awareness of, and a wayward delight in, Decadent exhaustion was a manifestation of some national malaise in France resulting from defeat at the hands of the Prussians at Sedan is misleading: the praise of decline and arcane exclusivity, and the rejection of bourgeois norms, have deeper roots. And even Emile Zola, later to be rejected alongside his Naturalist programme for his banausic and stultifying portrayals of drab reality, could also admit (in *Mes haines*, 1866) that his taste was depraved, and that he loved those works associated with Decadence where a pathological sensibility ousted the rude health of earlier centuries.[2]

We are arguing that those literary tropes associated with decay which are under discussion here predate the defeat of 1870, and yet it is also undeniable that a growing awareness of impotence, of weariness, of living within a deliquescent civilization, of being helplessly vulnerable to, and perversely in love with, the inevitability of cultural decline increasingly permeated the literary circles in France: the century was dying, and the malady experienced became defined by the term *fin de siècle*. It is no coincidence that Schopenhauer's pessimism became extremely fashionable at this time. On 23 May Verlaine's sonnet 'Langueur' appeared in the *Chat noir*: its first line, 'Je suis l'Empire à la fin de la Décadence', seemed to many to inaugurate a new mentality. The same year saw Paul Bourget's *Essais de psychologie contemporaine* with its chapter on 'Théorie de la décadence'; Baudelaire is the dedicatee. Three years later, in conversation with Anatole Baju, editor of the journal *Le Décadent* and author of *L'Ecole décadente* (1887), Verlaine would claim that he loved the word 'decadence', glinting with reflections of purple and gold; to the journalist Jules Huret, in 1889, he would explain, much as had Baudelaire, that the epithet 'Decadent' had been thrown as an insult; he had picked it up and thrown in back as a war cry. The term, as we have noted, is both aesthetic label, denoting degenerate over-refinement, and pejorative insult; the figure of the Decadent is delightfully parodied in *Les déliquescences d'Adoré Floupette, poète décadent* ('The Deliquescent Dissolutions of Adoré Floupette, Decadent Poet') by Henri Beauclair and Gabriel Vicaire in 1885.

It was, however, the appearance, in May 1894, of Joris-Karl Huysmans's *A rebours* ('Against Nature'), a novel hailed by Barbey-d'Aurevilly in a review on 29 June as one of the most Decadent works of the Decadent century, which seemed to many, and not only in France, to be the ultimate crystallization of the Decadent mode, its guidebook and truest examplar. It achieved notoriety in London after the publication in book

[2] Emile Zola, 'Mes haines' in *Œuvres complètes*, ed. Henri Mitterand, 15 vols. (Paris: Cercle du livre précieux, n.d.), vol. X, p. 62.

form of Oscar Wilde's *The Picture of Dorian Gray* in 1891 and during
the trial of 1895: it was held to be the poisonous yellow book given to
the young Gray by the languid aesthete Lord Henry Wotton, and Wilde,
under cross-examination, hinted that it was so (Dorian Gray had procured
from Paris nine large, paper copies of the first edition, bound in different colours to suit his various moods). Duc Jean Floressas des Esseintes
was based to a large extent on Robert, Comte de Montesquiou-Fezensac,
dandy and aesthete; it is also of interest that Wilde, in an earlier draft of
his novel, gave the poisonous book a name, *Le Secret de Raoul*, by one
'Catulle Sarrazin', a conflation of Catulle Mendès and Gabriel Sarrazin,
both of whom Wilde knew in Paris; the name of 'Raoul' is also found
in Rachilde's *Monsieur Vénus*.[3] Dorian Gray acknowledges the unnamed
volume as the strangest book that he had ever read, a book of exquisite
raiment and the delicate sound of flutes, a book where the sins of the
world passed in dumb show before him.

Huysmans had earlier written staid descriptions of proletarian life, but
Edmond de Goncourt had encouraged him to turn to the exploration
of cultured beings and exquisite things: pose and self-stylization now
become paramount in Huysmans, artifice and self-reflexive discourse.
Des Esseintes is the aesthete *par excellence* in his desire to cultivate the
most *outré* sensations, yet he is also, in his sterile cultivation of all that
is against nature, all that is bizarre, exhausted and perverse, a Decadent
archetype. A breviary of Decadence, then, particularly memorable for its
description of Gustave Moreau's *Salomé*; this *femme fatale* would inspire
countless variations, and the ambiguity of many of Moreau's figures,
their hermaphroditism and lascivious sexlessness, when filtered through
Huysmans's jaded prose, would haunt many a decadent imagination.
Mario Praz has written at length on this, also on the importance for
Huysmans of Mallarmé's *Hérodiade*.[4] *A rebours* is certainly a Decadent
concoction, but the exploration of synaesthesia and the 'dérèglement de
tous les sens' ('derangement of all the senses') are the preoccupations of
the *symbolistes*; portrayals of estrangement and existential *Angst* also
prefigure twentieth-century concerns.

In the novel des Esseintes links the Marquis de Sade with Barbey
d'Aurevilly as two writers who exhibited demoniac erotomania and the
creation of sensual monstrosities: Barbey's *Les Diaboliques*, a collection
of six stories, had appeared some ten years before and the blasphemies,
the tortured awareness of sin and delight in the repugnant and grotesque,
became part of the stock in trade of the French Decadent canon of the

---

3 Richard Ellmann, *Oscar Wilde* (London: Hamish Hamilton, 1987), p. 298.
4 Mario Praz, *The Romantic Agony*, trans. Angus Davidson, 2nd edn (Oxford University
  Press, 1951), p. 303.

1880s. Villiers de L'Isle Adam's *Contes cruels* are also recommended in *A rebours*: there is horror in these tales reminiscent of Edgar Allan Poe, together with the obligatory *femme fatale* (Queen Akëdysseril). As the century drew to a close the French literary imagination manifested itself in an ever-increasing desire to shock and repulse: Jean Lombard's *L'Agonie* (1888) exulted in sensational descriptions of Heliogabalus and his debauchery, sodomy and delight in murder, and in the following year Rachilde (that is, Marguérite Vallete), in her *Monsieur Vénus*, luxuriated in descriptions of androgynous necrophilia. (She had also, in 1886, published her *Marquise de Sade*.) Such offerings showed French *fin de siècle* letters in a lurid light, utterly remote from the cultivation of aesthetic sensibilities associated more with England; it must have seemed to Oscar Wilde, after having met Maurice Rollinat, a Baudelaire epigone who had achieved notoriety with a repugnant collection of sordid poems entitled *Névroses* (1883; 'Le succube' may serve as an example), that the Aestheticism which he, Wilde, a pupil of Walter Pater, had hitherto celebrated for its sensitive refinements had exhibited baleful formulations: the 'curiously jewelled' style which had ravaged Dorian Gray, the elaborate paraphrases which had characterized 'the work of some of the finest artists of the French school of *symbolistes*',[5] had been fractured by a sensational cult of posturing stridency and debased to an absurd Grand Guignol.

In England the cult of Aestheticism, a cult which overlapped with, and was tinged by, certain aspects of French Decadence, derived largely from Walter Pater; a generation was saturated with Pater's writing, a writing suffused with a love of beauty but also aware of the fascination of corruption. Pater, like Swinburne, had learned much from Pre-Raphaelitism and he expressed his admiration for William Morris in *Aesthetic Poetry* (1869), his delight above all in Morris's portrayal of medieval Provence, of people of 'a remote and unaccustomed beauty, somnambulistic, frail, androgynous, the light almost shining through them'.[6] Pater's style is characterized by lassitude, a muffled delight in portraying quiet, meditative introspection; he is aware of 'that subtle and delicate sweetness which belongs to a refined and comely decadence'.[7] In Pater the aesthete is not an artist so much as a connoisseur celebrating each delicious impression in an effortless recollection, recalling the beauty of strange colours, strange dyes, the touch of cool water upon ardent flesh, the face of a friend.

[5] Oscar Wilde, *The Picture of Dorian Gray* (Paris: Charles Carrington, 1908), pp. 201–2.
[6] Walter Pater, *Essays on Art and Literature*, ed. Jennifer Uglow (London: Dent, 1973), p. 97.
[7] In the preface to Pater's *Studies in the History of the Renaissance*. The reference is to the style of late Provençal poets.

Pater's *Studies in the History of the Renaissance* (first edition 1873)
was Wilde's golden book, a book which, he admitted in *De Profundis*,
had had such a strange influence on his life. Wilde seized eagerly upon the
exhortation to experience each transient moment as an aesthetic manifestation or epiphany, for it is only as an aesthetic phenomenon (as Nietzsche
knew) that life may be justified. The book's tacit epicureanism, hinting
at a quasi-homosexual hedonism (particularly in the essays on Leonardo
and Winckelmann), its comments on the fascination of corruption, the
startling analysis of the Mona Lisa (her vampire-like knowledge of the
secrets of the grave) and the insistence that all art constantly aspires to
the condition of music – this was fascinating for the young Wilde in his
first term at Oxford. It was the conclusion above all that struck him
with the force of revelation (a conclusion which Pater omitted from the
second edition of the book as a possible danger to young men): life can
only have meaning if one retains an ecstasy, a rapt awareness of life's
beauty, and the only energy needed is the ability to burn as a hard, gem-
like flame. Listlessness may now be tempered by a recollection of beauty,
however transient. Lord Wotton knew this, as did Dorian, and the young
ephebe of Wilde's novel will seek to cultivate a life where yellow satin
can console for all that is tawdry and base. Dorian becomes as languid as
his mentor and seeks to emulate des Esseintes, but the desire to become
perfect by the worship of beauty fails, and the life of mere sensation is
unmasked as being jejune and self-destructive: he becomes 'aestheticism's
first martyr'.[8]

Wilde will later feel the need to analyse the phenomenon of aestheticism
in his essays 'The Critic as Artist' and 'The Soul of Man under Socialism',
where, it is claimed, the artist forces the world towards a self-recognition
which might imply change; but the prodigious success of *The Picture of
Dorian Gray* meant, inevitably, that Wilde was hailed as the worshipper
of beauty above all who, in Lionel Johnson's Latin poem written in
gratitude for the gift of the novel, loves forbidden fruits and plucks strange
flowers: 'Here are apples of Sodom, here are the very heart of vices, and
tender sins. In heaven and hell be glory of glories to you who perceive so
much.'[9]

Wilde was fêted in Paris; he met Verlaine and sundry young Decadents
(Rollinat) and attended Mallarmé's *mardis* or Tuesday gatherings. The
French master, another recipient of Wilde's now famous novel, could
not fail to approve of Dorian's praise of that mysterious book which
held his, Mallarmé's, poetry in such high esteem (an aphorism in the

[8] Ellmann, *Oscar Wilde*, p. 297.
[9] Quoted in *ibid.*, p. 306: 'Hic sunt poma Sodomorum; hic sunt corda vitiorum; et peccata dulcia. In excelsis et infernis, tibi sit, qui tanta cernis, gloriarum gloria.'

preface to *The Picture of Dorian Gray* also insisted that art was at once surface and symbol; Mallarmé would share too Wilde's belief that poetry should exist in its own right, not for some extrinsic purpose, neither should it be vulgarized by contact with the masses). Wilde was drawn irresistibly towards Mallarmé's unfinished *Hérodiade* with its bejewelled, sterile creature lost in sick fantasies, and also towards the description in *A rebours* of Gustave Moreau's notorious picture; Wilde's play *Salomé*, appearing in French in book form in 1893, elicited the praise of Mallarmé, Maeterlinck and others, and also linked his name indissolubly to that of Aubrey Beardsley. It would also harvest the opprobrium of Victorian guardians of decency who saw it as a work of unashamed Decadence, morally suspect and impure. A version in English was planned, and Wilde was drawn to Beardsley's portrait of Salome holding the severed head of John the Baptist on a salver from which hung skeins of coagulated blood.

Beardsley will play a not inconsiderable role in Wilde's biography, and it has been argued that in the years leading up to Wilde's arrest the term 'Decadence' acquired a specific meaning as a description of the aesthetic movement associated specifically with Wilde and Beardsley, becoming largely a personality cult defined virtually by the two.[10] Beardsley's hectic and precocious energy (an energy driven by the tuberculosis that would kill him at the age of twenty-five), his cadaverous appearance and cult of the dandy, his insistence that fine raiment and the music of Richard Wagner were his two passions, were quintessentially of the English 1890s. His drawings have much of the French rococo about them, yet he learned a great deal from the Pre-Raphaelites; his world is also grotesque with its effete courtiers, catamites, androgynes and perverts, a gallery of tainted excrescences from a very late phase of culture. It is a self-contained world of esoteric and dubious sexual personae, of artifice and façade, masks, cosmetics and mirrors, self-referential and sterile.

To many, Beardsley was simply Wilde's acolyte, but he and Wilde went separate ways; Wilde had no part in Beardsley's plan for the *Yellow Book*, an outlet for contemporary writing. This organ would reflect the preoccupations of the 'yellow' nineties, that is, French Decadent literature, the supremacy of artifice and the dandyism of the Regency. (*A propos* the colour: the decade was frequently assigned the colour mauve, a colour akin to violet which, in its transition from red to blue, apparently represented the colour of women no longer fruitful, also of priests living in celibacy.) The inaugural dinner of 1894 was attended by contributors both actual and potential and included George Moore, John Davidson,

---

[10] Jerusha Hull McComack, *John Gray: Poet, Dandy and Priest* (Hanover, NH, and London: Brandeis University Press, 1991), p. 109.

Lionel Johnson, Ernest Dowson and W. B. Yeats (Henry James was also present). Art was to be the artist's protest against nature, and French portrayals of lubricity and degeneration were to be emulated. Beardsley's skilful compositions in black and white ('The Wagnerites' of the third *Yellow Book* had been sketched during a performance of *Tristan und Isolde* at the Paris Opéra in May 1893) delighted in expressions of cruel aesthetic reception, and the design for the prospectus of the *Yellow Book* similarly conveyed the impression in the elegance of the glove and the haughty mien of the female browser that the material on offer was intended to convey a certain *frisson*. But the arrest of Oscar Wilde with a yellow bound volume under his arm, albeit a French novel and not Beardsley's illustrated quarterly, caused a scandal that signified the end of Beardsley's venture, associated as it was with unwholesomeness and unclean practices.

Beardsley's resilience, however, is seen in his indifference to calumny and his contribution to another journal, the *Savoy*, a periodical of an exclusively literary and artistic kind. 'For us', Arthur Symons wrote in an editorial note of the January 1896 number, 'all art is good which is good art'.[11] But the *Savoy* came to rely too heavily on Beardsley, whose health was failing; its future was jeopardized. It did, however, publish Beardsley's *Under the Hill*, a prose concoction delighting in fey improprieties (it was a milder version of *Venus and Tannhäuser*, whose explicit pornotopia would never have passed the censor). *Under the Hill* is a frivolous and amusing variation on Wagner's *Tannhäuser* in which the Chevalier, in silk, lace and spangled muslin, dallies in Venus's realm, indulging in preposterously salacious antics. (Swinburne, it should be noted, also provided a version of the Tannhäuser legend in his 'Laus Veneris', a far more earnest portrayal of entrapment and suffocation.) The manuscript remained unfinished: the 'Fra Angelico of Satanism' (as Roger Fry described Beardsley) died in Mentone in 1898, a convert to Catholicism and arguably the most original amongst the gallery of Decadent talents we are attempting to describe.

Decadence has also been described as 'an exceptionally self-reflexive discourse, alert to the allusive, representational function of aesthetic and other tastes'.[12] Arthur Symons attempted to analyse it, together with Aestheticism and Symbolism (he was, in fact, the first to use the term 'decadence' in English literary circles in any systematic way, in *Harper's New Magazine* in 1893). In describing the 'decadent' or '*symboliste*' tendencies in modern French literature Symons interprets Decadence as an

---

[11] Quoted in Stanley Weintraub, *Beardsley* (London: Penguin, 1972), p. 160.
[12] Emma Sutton, *Aubrey Beardsley and British Wagnerism in the 1890s* (Oxford University Press, 2002), p. 27.

intense self-consciousness, a restless curiosity in research, an oversubtle insistence on complexities of refinement and a spiritual and moral perversion. Later, in 1899, he would argue, in *The Symbolist Movement in Literature*, that the term 'decadent' is only appropriate in a discussion of style: we recall that des Esseintes was ravished by the excesses of Mallarmé's syntax and the exhausted sterilities of late Latin. Symons also insisted that Decadence should be seen as a preliminary stage or anticipation of Symbolism; again, the two terms are awkwardly juxtaposed. Symons was a gifted critic, widely read in several languages and keen to display his knowledge of French literature; his book on Symbolism discussed the poetry of Rimbaud, Laforgue and Verlaine as well as Mallarmé: it was dedicated to W. B. Yeats. The Irish poet encouraged Symons to concentrate on an occult understanding of Symbolism, freed from Decadent posturing, for literature was to become a form of religion with the duties and responsibilities of a sacred ritual. Symons may have sought to distance himself from the decadents but he had also struck poses in the *Yellow Book*, and Lionel Johnson had parodied Symons's less wholesome love lyrics in *Pageant* (1897) under the title 'A Decadent Lyric', where the joys of coitus are sung. John Lane, finally, the most important publisher of the Decadent movement, strove likewise to define the term 'decadence': it was a form of *fin de siècle* licentiousness. W. B. Yeats, more poetically, spoke of Decadence as being 'the autumn of the flesh'.[13]

Was not Bunthorne a 'pallid and thin young man, a haggard and lank young man'? (W. S. Gilbert). Andrew Lang, also writing flippantly of poets such as Ernest Dowson (in *Critic*, xxxvii [1900]), singled out the cult of debility, the world-weariness and the flirtation with suicide which characterized many of the poets of the day. Dowson was the quintessential late Victorian *poète maudit* ('stricken poet') who died in his thirties, as did Lionel Johnson; John Davidson committed suicide by drowning in 1909. Yeats and Symons were associated with a group of poets including Dowson and Johnson who formed the so-called Rhymers' Club; Yeats would later describe the group and their preoccupations in *The Oxford Book of Modern* Verse (1936), their revolt against Victorian rhetoric and moralizing and their admiration for the literature of France, above all for 'daycadongs' (this was Dowson's coining; he had met 'our dear and incomparable Verlaine' in London). Yet compared to the achievements of Paris the Rhymers' verses are pallid indeed, wilting and world-weary despite the desire to live life as a pure, 'gem-like flame' (Pater). There is nothing of the intensity of Baudelaire despite much talk of sinfulness

---

[13] 'The Autumn of the Flesh' in *Literary Ideals in Ireland* (1898). Quoted in Richard Ellmann, *Yeats: The Man and the Masks* (Oxford University Press, 1973), p. 211.

and affliction: Dowson's *Cynara* well exemplifies this, where a diction gleaned from Swinburne or Rossetti struggles for conviction in an attempt to convey erotic confusion.

Many exhausted souls, ravaged by an imagined surfeit, longed for liturgy and acceptance into the church, for candles, incense, vestments; Johnson's melancholy 'The Church of a Dream' may be cited, also David-son's 'A Ballad of a Nun', which portrays the predictable tension between spirit and flesh (it was skilfully parodied by Owen Seaman as 'A Ballad of a Bun', whose first line explains that 'A decadent was dribbling by'). Lionel Johnson, in his essay 'The Cultured Faun' (1891), wittily summa-rizes the attitudes of those who sought to parade their Decadent leaning, those 'Elects of Beauty, saints and sinners, devils and devotees . . . Romans of the Empire and Italians of the Renaissance. Fin de siècle! Fin de siècle! Literature is a thing of beauty, blood and nerves.'[14]

The century was indeed coming to an end, and with it reassuring Vic-torian certainties, but the Rhymers exhibited little in the way of Neronian decadence or the monstrous degeneration of the Borgias in their wistful cult of naughtiness; they were, rather, those tired hedonists whom Wilde, tiring of self-conscious aesthetes without talent or wit, lampooned in *The Decay of Lying*, those who wore faded roses in their buttonholes and cultivated an admiration for the ruthlessness of the emperor Domitian. To be 'part lewd, aesthetical in part, and *fin de siècle* essentially' (Symons) may well have been the goal; the overall impression, however, is one of velleity and pose, the pose of the 'greenery-yallery, Grovesnor-gallery, foot-in-the-grave young man' (Gilbert). Is Decadence only to be associ-ated with physical lassitude and psychological and moral perversion? Or bizarre ornamentation and ultra-refinement in style? Another voice, not from France but from Germany, enters the debate.

Two months before his collapse into clinical insanity Nietzsche wrote from Turin to his friend Malwida von Meysenbug that 'I am, in mat-ters concerning *décadence*, the highest authority at present on earth.'[15] A startling claim, perhaps, from a thinker normally associated with mythopoeic giganticism, a philosopher with a hammer exulting in energy, power and imperious will. But the hammer does not merely shatter, it tests that which is whole and that which is hollow. It became increasingly clear to Nietzsche that he was living in an age whose values he could not accept, and that a vast transvaluation of all hitherto accepted norms and precepts must be undertaken. That which encourages and enhances life must be extolled; any form of morbidity must be swept away. If the will

---

[14]  Quoted in *Poetry of the Nineties*, ed. R. K. R. Thornton (London: Penguin, 1970), p. 18.
[15]  Friedrich Nietzsche, *Werke in drei Bänden*, ed. Karl Schlechta, 3 vols. (Munich: Hanser, 1954–66), vol. III, p. 1322.

is sapped, and healthy instincts are crippled by introspection, sickliness, perverse egomania, then man becomes an invalid, or neurasthenic. It is Christianity above all which is castigated by Nietzsche for its insistence on original sin and a consequent denial of earthly joy; he will contribute an original and controversial voice to the discussion of *fin de siècle* degeneration. If religion, morality and Christian thinking are all unmasked as symptoms of life-denying *décadence* (Nietzsche preferred to use the term in French), then it is art which may provide an antidote. But if art does not affirm life, then it too is sick. And the artist who exhibited most clearly those symptoms of *décadence* which Nietzsche now deplored, and who was at bottom a neurosis, *une névrose* (a term Nietzsche had found in Paul Bourget), was Richard Wagner.

Nietzsche's polemical essay *Der Fall Wagner* (1888) has been called by Thomas Mann the most important piece of writing, as far as the history of ideas is concerned, in the philosopher's whole output. This 'case history' expresses the argument with great pungency: Wagner's art is sick. The problems he brings to the stage are all hysterical ones, and the convulsive nature of the passions demonstrated by his characters, their instability and excessive posturing, betray clearly, Nietzsche explains, that their creator was neurotic. Looked at from a psychological point of view it becomes quite clear that Wagner's heroes and heroines were nothing more than a gallery of invalids, mentally disturbed patients ripe for treatment. As Bourget had included Baudelaire in his gallery of bizarre and solitary neurotics, so Nietzsche, speaking as a cosmopolitan *homme de lettres*, uses the French term for neurosis to describe Wagner. And if, Nietzsche impishly suggests, Wagner's characters were changed into contemporary figures, then the result would indeed be remarkable: once the historical trappings were removed, then the Wagnerian heroines become exact images of Emma Bovary. 'Yes, by and large Wagner only seems to be interested in the problems which today preoccupy the little Parisian *décadents*. Only five steps away from the hospital! Nothing but very modern problems, nothing but the problems of a big city.'[16] Wagner was not to be hailed, then, as a national composer of a grandiloquent *Reich*: he was a French Decadent.

Nietzsche stresses Wagner's affinity with *fin de siècle* morbidity; he had been aghast at *Parsifal* yet also fascinated by it, its highly questionable fusion of Christian mysticism and blatant sexuality, its holy grail and gaping wound, its images of spear and chalice, its castration, flower maidens and cult of blood. The sultry pseudo-religiosity of this work, the death-intoxicated eroticism of *Tristan und Isolde* and the glorification of incest in *Die Walküre* could not fail to enrapture and appal: *Tannhäuser*, likewise, as we have noticed, made a profound impression on the

---

[16] *Ibid.*, vol. II, pp. 322–3.

generation we have been describing. It is unlikely that Nietzsche had read any of the numbers of the *Revue wagnérienne*, founded in 1885 by Edouard Dujardin, but the contents would not have surprised him, for the journal was not an academic organ seeking an objective appraisal of Wagner but one which used his name as a magic cipher for the exploration of recondite worlds: Mallarmé contributed his act of homage, as did Huysmans and Verlaine. Nietzsche intuitively grasped that Wagner subsumed Modernism: an age preoccupied with an abnormal cultivation of the self, a guilt-ridden sexuality and the expression of psychic disturbance must needs submit to the latter's (Wagner's) hegemony. 'It is the problem of *décadence* that most concerns me. Very well! Like Wagner I am a child of this age, that is, a *décadent*, but differ from him in that I understood it, and fought against it.'[17]

Schopenhauerian pessimism, Christian self-laceration (with Christ as 'this most interesting *décadent*') and all forms of histrionic posturing are rejected by Nietzsche, who sought at the end of his mental life the 'Great Midday', a state beyond decadence where art is neither sickly self-indulgence nor morbid debasement but an act of life-affirmation, cleansed of sterile artifice, a light, clear, Claude Lorrain landscape away from the cloudy north, from Wagnerian weight and turmoil, from the nihilism which the Decadents loved, from the lure of extinction to which many of Wagner's heroes, like pilgrims, aspired.

In the same year that Nietzsche's essay was written, 1888, the Austrian critic, poetaster and *littérateur* Hermann Bahr visited Paris and witnessed the contemporary artistic milieu with which we are now familiar: a 'nervous Romanticism', Bahr learned, was now in vogue, replacing the superficialities of Naturalism. Some six years later, in his *Studien zur Kritik der Moderne*, Bahr would formulate for his Viennese readers what the fashionable preoccupations were (artifice, Wagnerism, contempt for bourgeois normality, etc.); Bahr also stressed the link between the preoccupation of the young writers and certain aspects of German Romanticism: the concept of neo-Romanticism now emerges.

Bahr, like many others, indiscriminately uses that familiar trinity of ill-defined terms (Symbolism, Aestheticism, Decadence) but also insists that certain Romantics had prepared the way for the later probing into subrational darkness and the flirtation with disease and cruelty; Vienna, heart of an over-ripe and vulnerable empire, was a more appropriate retort for dubious and fascinating experiments than brash and triumphalist Berlin, and Bahr's descriptions of Parisian poisons were avidly read in the coffee houses. The Viennese Felix Dörmann was eager to portray the rank and fetid corners of the psyche, insisting in his *Neurotica* (1891) and *Sensationen* (1896) that his love for all that was abnormal and sick was to

---

[17] *Ibid.*, p. 903.

be applauded (it is tempting to see Dörmann in the caricatured Viennese *fin de siècle* dandy who, becoming increasingly frail, limp and phthisic, is finally scooped up by his companion and flung around her neck as a boa).

A writer of the stature of Hugo von Hofmannsthal had also absorbed the world of *fin de siècle* Vienna. His early lyric dramas abound in amoral hedonism and the beauty-and-blood cult of some imaginary Renaissance world; familiar topoi in the poetry are the crystal, metallic garden and the rank, enervating hot-house. But Hofmannsthal's meditations on the relationship between art and life undergo a profound change: in *Der Tor und der Tod* ('The Fool and Death', 1892) the aesthete is made to admit that he has never experienced the joy of true artistic creation, and the young hero of the story *Das Märchen der 672 Nacht* ('The Fairy-Tale of Night Number 672', begun in 1894) likewise acknowledges before his brutal end that his former life of beauty had been a fragile shell. A darker note enters Hofmannsthal's work, where Aestheticism is now held to be sterile, a desperate charade to conceal life's horror: the artists of his age may have arrogated to themselves an almost quasi-divine status in their contempt for banal reality, but they were sick eagles, absurd in their posturing and pitiful to behold.

Hofmannsthal's name is inextricably linked with that of Stefan George, another acolyte of Mallarmé's and one who had returned from Paris with a sense of mission: the cultivation of *l'art pour l'art* within a German literary setting. His early poetry rehearses the familiar topics and setting; the Algabal poems represent the German contribution to the *fin de siècle* obsession with the degenerate Roman emperor. They were dedicated to the memory of King Ludwig the Second, an iconic figure who represented for many the triumph of art over stultifying banality. The year 1892 saw the publication of the first number of George's periodical *Blätter für die Kunst* ('Pages Concerning Art'), a journal modelled on the *Ecrits pour l'art* ('Writings of Art') and one which insisted on beauty as the highest ideal (Ernest Dowson was one of the contributors). Many young men felt attracted, even magnetized, by the hieratic nimbus which surrounded George; a homoerotic subtext was also apparent. The sacerdotal ritual, the pose of high priest of art, would increasingly achieve imperious tones, and George's deification of a youth after his sudden death alienated many within the circle. George's later striving to become master of a secret Germany, the guarantor of some spiritual rebirth, falls outside the scope of this section: suffice it that the young poet who had flirted with the accoutrements of Decadence later sought in art the highest epiphany and, in the years leading up to his death in 1933, in heroic male beauty the godhead itself.

'Whatever else the slogan *fin de siècle* might mean (a slogan so very prevalent in Europe then): neo-catholicism, satanism, intellectual criminality, the over-ripe tradition of nervous intoxication – at any rate, it was a formula for a finale of some kind, the all too fashionable and somewhat foppish formula for the awareness that something was coming to an end, the end of an age, the end of the bourgeoisie.'[18] In his auto-biographical essay *Meine Zeit*, written in 1950 when he was seventy-five years old, Thomas Mann looks back on the turn of the century, on the *fin de siècle* age of Aestheticism and Decadence, and finds much that is for ever fascinating, despite its rejection of that bourgeois age which had nurtured him and which he had always loved.

A brief comparison with Max Nordau is enlightening. Nordau's pee-vish and pompous diatribes against *fin de siècle* attitudes (in *Entartung*, 1892/3, translated as *Degeneration* in 1895) had sought to defend ordered progress and the foundation of nineteenth-century bourgeois culture, but Nordau had stooped to vulgar diatribe in his attack on writers such as Verlaine and Mallarmé (Verlaine is reviled as a repulsive degenerate with an asymmetrical skull and mongoloid physiognomy; Mallarmé's long, pointed earlobes are also castigated, these being ostensibly a fea-ture typical of criminals and madmen). The chief culprit for Nordau is Richard Wagner, the paradigm of Decadence, an artist both degen-erate and harmful whose grandiose visions were but histrionic gestures poised above incandescent decay and springing from a diseased sexual-ity: Wagner was, in short, the last fungoid growth on the dunghill of Romanticism.[19] Nordau sought to be an advocate of health and sanity but his crude vilification betrays a shallow intellect.

A writer like Mann may well have mourned the passing of nineteenth-century certainties and looked back with nostalgia, but knew also that he, as a writer, would never be able to shake off the fascination of decay and depravity. He belonged, he explained in the *Betrachtungen eines Unpolitischen* ('Observations of a Non-political Man', 1918), 'intellectu-ally to that breed of writers spread out all over Europe who were rooted in *décadence*; they were appointed to be chroniclers and analysts of the movement and yet, at the same time that they carried within their hearts the determination to *deny* decadence they realized the half-heartedness of such a denial and only *experimented* with it'.[20] Wholesome fare or poi-soned tinctures? Ethical banalities or aesthetic phosphorescence? Thomas Mann had lived for many years in Munich and been a close associate of Arthur Holitscher, author of the novel *Der vergiftete Brunnen* ('The Poisoned Well', 1900) with its obligatory portrayal of Wagner's Venus-berg bacchanal, this time performed in a conservatory choked with rank

---

[18] Thomas Mann, *Gesammelte Werke*, 13 vols. (Frankfurt: Fischer, 1990), vol. XII, p. 201.
[19] Max Nordau, *Degeneration*, trans. George L. Mosse (Lincoln and London: University of Nebraska Press, 1968), p. 128 (on Verlaine), p. 131 (on Mallarmé), p. 194 (on Wagner).
[20] Mann, *Werke*, vol. XII, p. 201.

vegetation; also of Kurt Martens, the title of whose *Roman aus der Décadence* ('Novel from the Realm of Decadence', 1898) would well have suited *Buddenbrooks* (Mann uses in the subtitle the word *Verfall*, 'decay', rather than repeating the fashionable catchword). The questionable aspects of Aestheticism had never failed to fascinate Mann, those attitudes which were not life-enhancing in a Nietzschean sense but sprang from an alluring sickness. Yet beauty itself, Mann suspected, beauty which transcends moral precepts, is inherently suspect for, in appealing to the senses, it presupposes sensual entrapment and erotic charge: the earnest scholar who succumbs to the blandishments of physical loveliness is as vulnerable as the knowing connoisseur.

It is Venice which is singled out by many *fin de siècle* writers as the ultimate *mise-en-scène* for salacious, even lethal, adventures, and to Mann it seemed the only possible setting for the death of Gustav von Aschenbach. Mann knew of Wagner's description of cholera and the sinister appearance of black gondolas in the city; he knew that Wagner had composed much of the music of *Tristan und Isolde* there and, above all, that Wagner had died there. Mann was also acquainted with the writings of the homosexual poet August von Platen, whose most famous sonnet, 'Tristan', links the worship of beauty indissolubly to abandonment and death.[21] Wagner, Venice, homoerotic longing and dissolution: the chronicler and analyst of Decadence, in his portrayal of an afflicted lover gazing out at the waters after his soul has lost itself to a vision of beauty inseparable from death, has given the most movingly perceptive apotheosis in German literature of *fin de siècle* artistic vulnerability; an oblique reference to distant rumblings of war hint that not only Aschenbach, but bourgeois culture itself, was moving towards extinction.

'The most monumental figure of the Decadent Movement, the figure in which the various European currents of the second half of the nineteenth century converged, was given to the world not by France, but by Italy.'[22] This characteristically extravagant statement by Mario Praz must finally give us pause. In Gabriele D'Annunzio the pallid and neurasthenic elements of Decadence give way to flamboyance and the cult of the superman, and a disturbing synthesis of death-intoxication and triumphalism prepares the way for that 'aestheticising of politics' which Walter Benjamin will associate with fascism.[23] In Italy the term *decadenti*, used

---

[21] The first verse of Platen's poem ('He who has beheld Beauty with his eyes...') is used as a motto for Philippe Jullian's *Esthètes et magiciens* (Paris: Librairie académique Perrin, 1969). This has been translated into English by Robert Baldick as *Dreamers of Decadence* (London: Phaidon Press, 1971).
[22] Praz, *Romantic Agony*, p. 385.
[23] Walter Benjamin, 'Das Kunstwerk im Zeitalter seiner technischen Reproduzierbarkeit' in *Gesammelte Schriften*, eds. Rolf Tiedemann and Hermann Schweppenhaeuser, 7 vols. (Frankfurt: Suhrkamp, 1980), vol. II, p. 467.

first by Vittorio Pica in the Turin journal *Gazzetta Letteraria* (November 1885), was applied to Verlaine and his circle, those who represented, Pica argued, a reaction against nineteenth-century ideals of progress and who fought against creeping democratization. They attacked positivism and sought the cultivation of the artificial and the exceptional: this has a very familiar ring.

'Decadence' describes a way of life, not a formal stylistic construction: this is seen in Luigi Gualdo's novel *Decadenza* (1893), whose hero predictably despises bourgeois norms. In Gianpietro Lucini's anthology *Figurazioni ideali* ('Ideal Figurations'), *decadenza* again appears as a symptom of dissatisfaction with science, religion and politics: an aristocratic disdain is encouraged. In the early poetry of D'Annunzio the topoi of Decadence are frequently present: a good example is the collection *Intermezzo*. George Arthur Greene, an early acquaintance of W. B. Yeats, translated parts of this in his anthology *Italian Lyricists of Today* (1893) and disseminated an awareness and appreciation of contemporary Italian poetry amongst the members of the Rhymers' club. Echoes of the poetry of Dante Gabriel Rossetti ('Due Beatrici', for example) and a sadomasochistic fixation on the figure of St Sebastian (he would later supply Debussy with material for the musician's *Le martyr de Saint Sébastien*) make D'Annunzio very much a child of his time.

Interwoven with images of beauty, decay and suffering, however, a strand of debased Nietzscheanism appears, not Nietzsche as psychologist but Nietzsche–Zarathustra as *Übermensch* preaching self-fulfilment, creativity and the destruction of morality. Voluptuousness and brutality come to the fore in D'Annunzio, a synthesis derided by Thomas Mann, who despised D'Annunzio's lewd Aestheticism, his bombast and his later political aspirations, the aspirations of a buffoon, of 'Wagner's monkey': his, Mann's, deep devotion to Wagner and profound indebtedness to Nietzsche's subtle probing of Decadence must mean a rejection of the Italian's rodomontade and theatrical gestures. There is much attitudinizing in *Il trionfo della morte* ('The Triumph of Death', 1894), a highly wrought erotic novel where the score of *Tristan und Isolde* acts as stimulus and warning: in cruel abandonment the young hero hurls himself, with his mistress locked in a fierce embrace, to destruction. The book begins with an aphorism from Nietzsche's *Jenseits von Gut und Böse* ('Beyond Good and Evil') on the dangers caused by certain works of literature and ends in Wagnerian rapture and obliteration.

Wagner is even more present in *Il fuoco* ('The Flame of Life', 1900), the most complete instance to be found in literature of Wagnerian nervous strain, where another young aesthete ardently exults in the composer's gigantic achievement. (It is tempting to see D'Annunzio's determination to give music and theatre a supreme status in Fiume as stemming from Wagner's example.) There is death and transfiguration in this novel, but also a hollow theatricality, culminating in the famous set piece where six rapt acolytes carry Wagner's draped coffin on to a waiting gondola beneath wintry skies. The Roman laurels laid upon the bier ostensibly hint at the supremacy of Italian culture;[24] D'Annunzio, irredentist, aviator and future adviser to the Duce, will become a figure of derision, advocate of a debased aesthetic radicalism, turning politics into bad opera. The true adherent of the doctrine of *l'art pour l'art* would never prostitute his art to the demands of vulgar jingoism.

The literature of the *fin de siècle* is a raree-show containing many fascinating exhibits, many exotic blooms, some poisonous, others tainted; Nordau's banal strictures of reproof, however, cannot be allowed to stand. The writers discussed here played with solipsism and detachment but they also pushed out the boundaries of what was commonly acceptable, and they contributed to the transition from late Victorian convention to the more unsettling adventures of twentieth-century Modernism. Dorian Gray may have longed for the 'fin du globe' ('the end of the world') because life was felt to be a great disappointment: his creator, however, and a florilegium of like-minded writers, made sure that their decade would be remembered as the culmination of an age which, deriving much from Pater and the French, had the courage to be extravagant and to dream strange dreams, to indulge in spiritual corruption and yet also to seek to fix the last fine shade, the most delicate nuance. They provided the drop of poison which can improve the health of an organism, an exotic spicing to enhance the taste of the blandest offering, and they paradoxically ensured that the end of their century was anything but moribund: the inventions of the literary imagination have rarely betrayed such resilience and lavish prodigality.

---

[24]  John Woodhouse, *Gabriele D'Annunzio: Defiant Archangel*, 2nd edn (Oxford University Press, 2001), p. 123.

# 19

# The avant-garde in early twentieth-century Europe

### ROGER CARDINAL

The military term 'avant-garde' designates a detachment of elite troops which ventures into alien territory to carry out swift raids aimed at destabilizing enemy defences and hastening the subsequent advance of the army proper. Nowadays, critical convention applies the term to literary and artistic groups which challenge the cultural status quo through unprecedented modes of creative expression.

This chapter offers a succinct account of avant-garde activity in Europe during the first decades of the twentieth century. This was an extremely complex cultural phase, when Modernist innovations seemed to occur simultaneously in different cities and to ramify swiftly across national borders. Commentators have even found it necessary to speak of avant-gardes in the plural, and thus of *Futurisms* or *Dadaisms* rather than a single, neatly integrated Futurism or Dadaism. Further, avant-gardists were drawn to a wide range of expressive modes: poetry, fiction, recitation, performance, dance, drama, film, music, architecture and the visual arts. Further still, individuals were often adept in more than one of these. Given such a plethora of variations, this chapter seeks simply to identify the main avant-garde groups in the period, along with their characteristic manifestations.

The generation which matured during the last decade or so of the nineteenth century was acutely sensitive to technological change. Yet, as industrialization and urbanization rushed forward, political and cultural control was seen still to lie in the hands of elderly leaders whose thinking was judged to be stifling, corrupt and thoroughly outdated. As the new century unfolded, young avant-gardists engaged in robust ideological skirmishes which announced their determination to blaze a fresh and progressive path. In truth, their recoil from dull conformity reflected idealistic yearnings dating back to Romanticism, while a propensity for scandal had already marked the last years of the nineteenth century. In a sense, the avant-garde's fixation upon novelty and surprise represents a virulent continuation of the dissenting practices of certain outstanding iconoclasts of previous decades, such as the writers Charles Baudelaire, Alfred Jarry, Arthur Rimbaud, August Strindberg and Oscar Wilde, the artists Paul Gauguin, Vincent van Gogh and Edvard Munch, the

musicians Richard Wagner and Gustav Mahler, the philosophers Arthur
Schopenhauer and Friedrich Nietzsche, and the political theorists
Mikhail Bakunin and Karl Marx. Their lessons were absorbed within the
nascent ideologies of the Expressionists, the Futurists, the Dadaists and
the Surrealists, inspiring them to reject conventional materialism and
to confound the inherited orthodoxies of Realism and Naturalism. The
decisive event of the First World War led to the collapse of the German
and Austro-Hungarian empires and the consequent emergence of new
Central European states whose young intellectuals and artists were eager
to enter the arena of modernity.

In France, and especially in Paris, artistic innovation had been nurtured
since at least the 1880s, under the aegis of Decadence, Symbolism and
Impressionism. Refined literary and musical circles had opened up original experimental paths. But progress seemed slow. Having invented a new
way of painting the outer world, Impressionism had become a repeatable
formula. The audience for the arcane sonnets of the Symbolist master
Stéphane Mallarmé was restricted to a circle of devotees, and although
they believed fervently in a concerted Aestheticism, their declarations
lacked the combative thrust which would characterize the avant-garde
proper. Musicians were responding to the challenge of Wagnerian chro-
maticism, as witness Claude Debussy's *Prélude à l'après-midi d'un faune*
('The Prelude to a Faun's Afternoon', 1894), indebted to Mallarmé but
transformed into a work of explosive primitivism when Vladimir Nijin-
sky danced it at the Ballets Russes in 1912. In painting, the brief heyday
of Fauvism (c.1905–6) liberated artists such as Henri Matisse, André
Derain and Maurice de Vlaminck from any lingering commitment to
realistic colour, although their loose collective lacked an organizational
structure. It fell to the Polish Italian poet Guillaume Apollinaire to codify
the aspirations of his generation under the banner of what he dubbed
*l'esprit nouveau* ('the new spirit').

In his youth, Apollinaire had espoused the languorous aesthetic of
Symbolism, but now reinvented himself as a modern Orpheus and advocate of daring experiment. From his Parisian headquarters, he played the
part of commander-in-chief, keeping track of avant-garde interventions
across the European cultural map. His influential *The Cubist Painters*
(1913) focuses on the experimental still lifes of Pablo Picasso, Georges
Braque and Juan Gris, which subverted the established conventions of
spatial representation. Later, Apollinaire was to float the concept of
Orphism, a lyrical variant of Cubism associated with the art of Robert
Delaunay (who himself preferred to speak of Simultanism). By now,
new groups and new slogans were proliferating at bewildering speed.
Apollinaire enjoyed the status of honorary Futurist, corresponding with
Marinetti's Italian group and writing poems such as 'Zone' that offer a

model for avant-garde writing in their visionary evocation of modernity, mirrored in the disruption of traditional form and the abolition of punctuation. Cubist poets such as Pierre Reverdy, Max Jacob and the Chilean Vicente Huidobro would follow suit, as indeed would the later Surrealists, specialists in volatile images and baffling intersections of meaning. Just before his death in 1918, Apollinaire retreated to a less belligerent position, arguing that adventurousness needed to be offset by some element of orderliness. Nevertheless, the reverberations of *l'esprit nouveau* had begun to energize avant-garde circles across the continent.

As the deeds of the Cubists were bruited beyond French borders, so their bold precedent intersected with foreign developments of varied complexion and terminology, involving not only literature and painting but also sculpture, photography and architecture. The Czech brand of Cubism (sometimes labelled Cubo-Expressionism) drew sustenance from many sources, including French Fauvism and Cubism and German Expressionism, not to mention the work of isolates such as the Norwegian Edvard Munch and the contemporary craze for African tribal art. By 1911, Emil Filla, Bohumil Kubišta, Josef Čapek and others had established the Skupina group in Prague, and were mounting exhibitions of work by Picasso, Braque, Kirchner, Heckel and Munch, and placing the Cubist aesthetic at the service of uplifting social and spiritual goals. Despite its professed cosmopolitanism, Czech Cubism evinced a strong nationalist streak, occasioned by its structural need for a firm identity. Once the new republic of Czechoslovakia was established in 1918, the movement splintered into smaller factions, the most important being the Devetsil group, which met in a Prague café to discuss Surrealism, cinema and jazz. Its adherents included the poets Vitězslav Nezval and Jaroslav Seifert, as well as the anti-Naturalistic photographers František Drtikol, Josef Sudek and Jaroslav Rössler. Their collective efforts would later produce a distinctively Czech brand of Surrealism.

Within Germany and Austria, a whole generation of youthful creators concurred in recognizing the need to sever all continuity with a constricting cultural inheritance. The mood of rebellion was exacerbated by the experience of trench warfare in the First World War, which gave a dramatic impetus to cultural change. The widespread movement known as Expressionism produced works marked by an extreme sense of social, psychological and metaphysical alienation, and by a hyperbolic and uncompromising tone. Affecting the arts at large in the Germanophone countries, the movement was rich in individual creativity, yet sponsored few of those small and intense collectives which typify what I shall call the 'classic' avant-garde. Two groups emerge as outstanding cases of avant-gardism, even though they broke ground in contrary directions.

In Dresden, and later in Berlin, the group styling itself Die Brücke ('The Bridge') advocated a dynamic new approach to art-making, backed by a social programme cemented by close personal friendships and communal living. Rejecting his academic training, the group's leader, Ernst Ludwig Kirchner, opted for a raw and vehement style which conveys an immediate physicality, while his associates Erich Heckel, Karl Schmidt-Rottluff and Emil Nolde developed similarly anti-beautiful strategies in hastily executed, even garish pictures. Unlike the city-based majority of avant-gardists, the Brücke artists made regular sorties into the countryside, confirming group solidarity through communal holidays by sea or lake, where the habit of unabashed nakedness encouraged a favourite motif in their art.

By contrast, the Munich-based group Der blaue Reiter ('The Blue Rider') was altogether more intellectually nuanced and rigorous in its search for fresh perspectives. The expatriate Russian Vassily Kandinsky and the German Franz Marc co-edited *The Blue Rider* (1912), an 'almanac' comprising essays and a picture album of contemporary European art-styles. Kandinsky argued that art-making was the locus of spiritual emancipation in a period of cultural decadence, and contended that creative expression springs from an 'inner necessity'. His treatise *Concerning the Spiritual in Art* (1911) became a founding text of painterly abstraction.

In 1922, Kandinsky joined the Bauhaus in Weimar, a school of art and design established by the architect Walter Gropius. (It later moved to Dessau and then to Berlin.) Other staff members were experimental artists like Paul Klee, Lyonel Feininger and Lászlo Moholy-Nagy. The Bauhaus cultivated an aesthetic of harmony and formal austerity, associated with geometric abstraction and the pan-European idiom of Constructivism. Despite its air of a breakaway utopian community, it was a serious pedagogic institution with no ambition to provoke or scandalize the public: indeed it enjoyed financial support from the provincial government, and as such showed no signs of the self-reliant truculence of the classic avant-garde.

By the 1930s, the enforcement of National-Socialist culture led to the suppression of all experimental art. Intolerant of a Modernism which it saw as unhealthy and suspect, Hitler's regime propounded a retrograde aesthetic of Aryan neo-Classicism. In 1937 the Haus der Kunst in Munich mounted an exhibition of Nazi-style heroic Realism, while the infamous Degenerate Art exhibition was held nearby, with artworks by the likes of Emil Nolde and Kurt Schwitters hung derisively alongside those of mental patients and non-European tribal carvers. The charge of degeneracy effectively outlawed avant-gardism within the Third Reich, and Kirchner committed suicide in 1938 when he learned that 600 of his paintings had been removed from public collections and destroyed.

Emerging in a country marked more than most by classical culture, Italian Futurism was adamant in proclaiming the bankruptcy of tradition. The first avant-garde movement to assert itself through a concerted publicity campaign, it stands out through its extravagant enthusiasm for the machine age. The Futurist ambition was to translate the marvels of technology into artistic form by foregrounding the principles of speed and surprise. Its brutal disavowal of the past implied the extinction of museum culture: a racing car, insisted Filippo Tomaso Marinetti, is intrinsically more beautiful than a classical statue such as the *Victory of Samothrace*. Thus were born 'the primitives of a new sensibility', as the painter-sculptor Umberto Boccioni put it.[1] The latter gave symbolic shape to the avant-garde onslaught in an astonishing bronze, *Unique Forms of Continuity in Space* (1913), which shows a heroic figure dashing along with greatcoat flapping in the wind. When the architect Antonio Sant'Elia joined the group, he abandoned professional caution and, in his 'Manifesto of Futurist Architecture' (1914), outlined plans for a city 'agile, mobile and dynamic in every detail' which would contain 'an architecture whose sole justification lies in the unique conditions of modern life'.[2]

Italian Futurism owed its unmistakable style and momentum to its charismatic leader, Marinetti, who issued 'The Founding and Manifesto of Futurism' in 1909 and remained its tireless spokesman until his death in 1944. His impudent bombast offered a telling model for avant-gardists at large, while his manipulation of the press ensured that Futurist antics were never far from the public eye, whether in Italy or abroad. From 1909 through to the late 1930s, Futurism issued a stream of manifestos outlining its policies with regard to poetry, painting, sculpture, music, photography and film. Moreover, it stretched its purview to all kinds of cultural and social issues, including fashion, cookery, sexual relations, industry and patriotic feeling. It was as if every aspect of life were subject to a new aesthetic definition. Futurism's eclectic passions even extended to warfare, which – in contrast to nearly all other contemporary movements – it celebrated as the most glamorous and intensely fulfilling of experiences. 'We intend to sing the love of danger, the habit of energy and fearlessness', proclaimed Marinetti, who went so far as to court the fascist leader Benito Mussolini, offering the services of Futurism to the

---

[1]  Umberto Boccioni, 'Futurist Painting and Sculpture' (1914) in *Futurist Manifestos*, ed. Umbro Apollonio (London: Thames & Hudson, 1973), p. 176.

[2]  Antonio Sant'Elia, 'Manifesto of Futurist Architecture' (1914) in Apollonio, *Futurist Manifestos*, pp. 170, 169.

right-wing political cause.[3] Despite these overtures, the dictator never for-malized an alignment with the Futurists, although some of his ministers underwrote certain of their initiatives.

In Russia, Futurism emerged at much the same time as in Italy and was just taking shape as reports of new styles came flooding in from the West. The main centres were St Petersburg and Moscow, though avant-gardism extended to several other cities in the Russian territories, including Baku (Azerbaijan), Tbilisi (Georgia) and Vitebsk (Belarus). In Tbilisi and later in Moscow, the poet Alexei Kruchenykh pioneered the notion of an original language called *zaum*, based on the expressive poten-tial of unadorned sounds. He was seconded by Velimir Khlebnikov, a poet who drew inspiration from folk literature and the babbling of chil-dren. The proto-Futurist Hylaea group issued its manifesto in Moscow in 1912, calling for Pushkin, Dostoevsky and Tolstoy to be thrown over-board from 'the Ship of Modernity'; the group later adopted the ban-ner of Cubo-Futurism. Its membership comprised the poets Khlebnikov, Kruchenykh and Vladimir Mayakovsky, the painter-poet David Burliuk and the artists Mikhail Larionov and Natalia Goncharova. The latter pair went on to establish their own variant movement, Rayonism, a colourful visual enactment of dynamic motion, rendered in lavish dabs and streaks. After settling in Paris, they produced set designs for Serge Diaghilev's Ballets Russes.

As a Cubo-Futurist in Moscow, the painter Kazimir Malevich produced *The Knife-Grinder* (c.1912), a work implying the harmony of man and machine, a theme less alarming than the Italian celebration of fast cars and aeroplanes. By 1915, Malevich had abandoned representation, adopting the banner of Suprematism and painting purely geometric shapes: these were envisaged as objects of spiritual contemplation, much in the spirit of the traditional Russian ikon. From 1919, he ran an independent art school in Vitebsk and, with El Lissitzky, founded a Suprematist group called Unovis. Lissitzky in turn developed his own version of Suprema-tism, dubbed Proun, which involved both painting and three-dimensional installation. Both artists later visited Germany and had dealings with Dadaists and Constructivists alike, thereby demonstrating that theoreti-cal differences between Modernist trends were not always absolute.

The war in Europe and the Bolshevik Revolution of 1917 brought a dramatic impetus to the Russian avant-gardists, who strove to assert their relevance to the contemporary situation. In fact, the pragmatic politics of the Bolsheviks set them an impossible challenge, pressurizing them to justify their art-making. In truth, experimental paintings and spiritual

[3] Filippo Marinetti, 'The Founding and Manifesto of Futurism' (1909) in Apollonio, *Futur-ist Manifestos*, p. 21.

themes were of no interest to a population engaged in building a post-revolutionary society. The poet Mayakovsky sought in vain to popularize his writings. For a couple of years, the Futurists agitated under the banner of LEF (the Left Front for the Arts), bending their ideas to the social ideal. But their efforts were always treated with suspicion, and once Josef Stalin came to power, the state doctrine of Socialist Realism outlawed all avant-garde experimentalism. Mayakovsky's career foundered on the rocks of official contempt, his suicide in 1930 signalling the end of an era of attempted compromise. Ironically, this totalitarian abolition of avant-garde activity coincided with its similar suppression in Nazi Germany.

Vorticism in England was a brief and rather self-conscious offshoot of Italian Futurism. Its inception dates back to a notorious lecture which Marinetti delivered in London in 1910. An English group took shape when the polemical artist and writer Percy Wyndham Lewis set up the Rebel Art Centre as a site for Modernist experiment. The painter C. R. W. Nevinson had befriended Marinetti, and the two co-authored a manifesto in 1914; but Lewis refused to kowtow to Italian influence, preferring the intellectual sponsorship of the American poet Ezra Pound, who coined the term 'Vorticism'. In tune with Futurist practice, Lewis exploited an eye-catching typeface in a foundational manifesto signed by ten follow-ers, among them the painter Edward Wadsworth and the French sculptor Henri Gaudier-Brzeska. The document called for a Futurist-style cleans-ing of cultural dross, designating as enemies the foremost figures of British establishment culture. Though its text echoes the Italian passion for the machine, Vorticism was in practice more drawn to an aesthetic of geo-metrical precision, diverging from the Italian obsession with speed-thrills. Unfortunately, the First World War halted the group's momentum, divert-ing its artists into military action and claiming several lives, including that of its major talent, Gaudier-Brzeska. Lewis enrolled as an official war artist, Wadsworth designed 'dazzle' camouflage for merchant ships (a rare practical application of a Futuristic style), and Nevinson drove a front-line ambulance before becoming a war artist. The horrors of the trenches cut short any inclination to celebrate modern warfare, while the armistice hastened a return to tradition. Despite Lewis's efforts to revive 'the great English Vortex', it was effectively dead by 1920.

In Spain, the movement known as Ultraismo emerged in Madrid during 1919–23. Activated by the arrival from Paris in 1918 of the freewheel-ing poet Vicente Huidobro, advocate of what he called Creacionismo, a poetry abjuring orthodox representation and formal constraints, the movement flourished under the aegis of the poet Guillermo de Torre, sec-onded by the Argentinian Jorge Luis Borges. Implementing a bold typog-raphy, it preached the doctrine of autonomous metaphor and developed Apollinaire's theme of the ecstatic subject possessed by visions of the modern metropolis. Madrid would later see the emergence of a Spanish Surrealism in the persons of Luis Buñuel and Salvador Dalí, while Barcelona produced the Cubist sculptor Pablo Gargallo and the Surrealist painter and sculptor Joan Miró.

The short-lived phenomenon known as Dadaism represents a case of an almost ubiquitous European avant-garde movement. In general terms, the Dadaist project was both extreme and imprecise: its main objective was the definitive abolition of all inherited artistic, cultural, political and philosophical assumptions. Arising during the First World War, its ideas reflected a widespread frustration and jadedness at a time of economic and psychological depression; but what was striking about Dadaism was that it formulated its protest with exceptional gusto and abrasive humour. The movement pinned its aspirations to the seemingly absurd watchword 'Dada', a passe-partout phoneme whose very opacity promised a gamut of alternative meanings. While destruction and negation were immediate priorities, an ill-defined utopia appeared to be posited beyond the horizon, still hazy in outline because of the smoke and din of the immediate battle.

One of Dadaism's defining characteristics was its antagonism to the narrow nationalism which underlay the conflicts of the war. Based on neutral territory in Switzerland, a Zurich-based collective brought together various émigré artists: Romanians (Tristan Tzara, Marcel Janco), Germans (Hugo Ball, Emmy Hennings, Sophie Täuber), an Alsatian (Hans Arp) and an Austrian (Walter Serner). They operated at the Cabaret Voltaire in the old town, where raucous poetry readings, masked dances and barbarous drumming produced a nightly unleashing of dark forces in ritual celebration of the death of art and rationality. Less immediately obvious was the fact that art-making of considerable inventiveness was proceeding in the daytime. Arp's wood reliefs and collages dictated by chance, Täuber's suavely hued canvases, Ball's mystico-philosophical musings and Tzara's disjointed yet imperious poems would, in retrospect, appear to imply immense possibilities for positive creativity.

A more politically orientated Dadaism arose in Berlin, with writers such as Richard Huelsenbeck and Raoul Hausmann and the chaotic collage-maker and architect Johannes Baader, self-styled *Oberdada* or President of the Globe. Huelsenbeck had been party to the Dada agitations in Zurich, and arrived in Berlin in 1917 to implement what he had learnt. His group organized reading tours through Germany and Czechoslovakia and manifested a trenchant commitment to left-wing politics, siding in the postwar confusion with the Spartakists, the communists or the anarchists, more or less at whim.

In Cologne, the artist Max Ernst and the writer-painter Johannes Baargeld formed the 'Dada Conspiracy of the Rhineland', a spoof terrorist operation professing left-wing ideals but essentially dedicated to

mischief-making. Hans Arp joined them in a 1920 exhibition of collaborative painting and sculpture; it was held in a courtyard accessible only via
the toilet of a café. In Hanover, the collage-maker and poet Kurt Schwitters ploughed a lone furrow as a kind of one-man Dada group. Under the
idiosyncratic rubric of 'Merz' (another nonsense word), his experiments
resulted in typographical innovations, sound-poems, collages made from
detritus, and an enigmatic quasi-architectural installation known as the
*Merzbau*.

It was in 1922 that an unusual confluence of impulses gave rise to
the so-called Dada–Constructivist Congress. Held in Weimar, it brought
together the Dadaists Arp, Schwitters and Tzara and the Constructivists
Lissitzky, László Moholy-Nagy and Theo van Doesburg, leader of the
Dutch group De Stijl. Here would seem to be a clash of artistic trends and
temperaments, although it is arguable that all delegates were in agreement
about making a clean break with the cultural past. What is most paradoxical is that the resolutely abstract painter Van Doesburg had adopted the
pseudonym I. K. Bonset in order to write Dada poetry and edit the Dada
journal *Mécano* from Leiden. In truth, international Constructivism was
essentially a pervasive design style whose sobriety was altogether remote
from the aggressive militancy of Dadaism. Undoubtedly, Constructivism
exerted a wide influence in the fields of painting, assemblage, sculpture
and architecture; yet, in judging its historical role, one might categorize
this austere trend – perhaps in common with Cubism – as a stylistic and
aesthetic option sufficiently diffuse and self-engrossed to have shunned
the jostling vortex of the classic avant-garde group.

In Paris, Dadaism began when a circle of poets launched an eclectic
magazine called *Littérature* and gradually turned it into an outlet for
Dada expression. The poets André Breton, Louis Aragon and Philippe
Soupault, and later Paul Eluard and Benjamin Péret, were prime movers,
but it took Tristan Tzara's arrival from Zurich in January 1920 to set
in motion a concerted schedule of exhibitions and demonstrations. The
Dada Festival mounted by Tzara in a concert-hall in May 1920 was
expressly designed to antagonize the public and the press.

The Dada virus affected several other cities, such as Brussels (Clément
Pansaers) and New York (Marcel Duchamp, Man Ray), as well as
Budapest, Leiden, Mantua and Zagreb. The painters Marcel Duchamp
and Francis Picabia were only loosely affiliated to Paris Dada. Duchamp
had emerged from a Cubist phase to become an ironic observer of the
avant-garde scene, flouting aesthetic protocol with his own brand of lazy
art, epitomized in the readymade, which shocked public taste by assigning aesthetic virtue to bottle-racks, ceramic urinals and the like. For his
part, Picabia attached girls' names to diagrams of machine parts, and
contributed to Dada publications from a studied distance. When Paris

Dada foundered, he tried to relaunch it under the banner of Instanta-neism, though his efforts amounted to no more than a single issue of his magazine *391*.

Paris Dada having run its course, Breton and his friends passed through a torpid period which Aragon dubbed *le mouvement flou* (the amorphous movement). Short-lived pacts were made with other groups, including the left-wing Clarté group and the mystically inclined Le Grand Jeu. Little by little, a distinctive pattern of ideals and practices arose. Breton it was who took command of operations, articulating the surrealist project in the first 'Manifesto of Surrealism' in 1924. (Be it noted that Apollinaire had coined the term *surréalisme* several years before.) Breton proposed a model of the psyche indebted both to Sigmund Freud's psychoanalytic theory and to the example of Spiritualist mediumism. Automatism was to become the fundamental of Surrealist doctrine, a channel for 'selfless' self-expression characterized by spontaneity and non-rational fluency. Literary automa-tism, with its propensity to generate outlandish images, was the starting point for the poetry of Paul Eluard, Benjamin Péret, Robert Desnos and René Char. It very soon emerged that the visual arts were no less a privileged Surrealist medium. Major painters of the early period include Giorgio de Chirico – who later founded the Pittura metafisica ('Meta-physical Painting') school in Ferrara with the one-time Futurist Carlo Carrà – André Masson, Max Ernst, Yves Tanguy and Salvador Dalí. By the late 1930s, Surrealism had established itself as an international art movement which regularly organized its own idiosyncratic exhibitions, notably in Paris (1933, 1938, 1947) and London (1936).

Surrealist groups soon sprang up in other cities. In Brussels, a closely knit collective consisted of the writers Paul Nougé, Camille Goëmans, Marcel Lecomte and Louis Scutenaire, along with the painter René Magritte and the composer André Souris. It maintained a restless and occasionally acerbic dialogue with Paris Surrealism and followed a stealthier, less overtly political strategy which sought to undermine obtuse perceptions of social life and to establish a revelatory outlook upon the everyday. Unlike the Parisians, the Brussels group showed a marked inter-est in music. Elsewhere, a smaller group of Walloon Surrealists emerged under the aegis of the poet Achille Chavée. In Prague, a tenacious group led by Vitězslav Nezval and Karel Teige, veterans of Devetsil, included the artists Jindrich Styrsky and Toyen. Avant-garde activities began in Belgrade from the 1920s, with the establishment of a Surrealist group by the 1930s. In Bucharest, a small group emerged in the 1940s, with the poets Gellu Naum and Gherasim Luca. In London, a less vigorous circle developed around the Belgian collage-maker E. L. T. Mesens. Another group flourished in Cairo during 1937–48, led by the poet Georges Henein.

Despite a fluctuating membership – several key members went over to the rival Documents group, led by the dissident writer Georges Bataille, while others deserted to communism – the Paris group was the most disciplined and durable of all twentieth-century avant-garde groups. (The last gasp of formal Surrealism in Paris occurred as late as 1969, and even today sporadic manifestations of Surrealism continue to crop up in cities worldwide.) It represented a collective lifestyle, a radical cultural front and a forum for the production of intriguing artworks. The group espoused a flexible aesthetic, embracing such extremes as Oceanic tribal art and the drawings of lunatics. It took a firm stand against Catholicism and colonialism, and in 1925 demonstrated against the military repression of native populations in North Africa. Through the 1920s, its taste for radical politics encouraged long and troubled negotiations with the French Communist Party; however, Stalin's show trials in the 1930s would in due course necessitate a final noisy break with communism.

Breton's tireless theorizing elaborated an ethical doctrine based upon a neo-Romantic vision of a reality renewed by the imagination, the central faculty which had the power to channel the secret impulses of the unconscious and to liberate man from social and psychological inhibitions. The Surrealist conception of love encompassed both the subjective-emotional and the flagrantly erotic, and was subsumed within a wide-ranging conception of human desire. While critics dismissed it as nebulous and utopian, Surrealism insisted on the primacy of the creative life, and arguably defended the most positive of avant-garde ideals.

Being tied to a specific linguistic, social and political context, each avant-garde group tended to develop a distinctive character and pattern of behaviour. Many groups voiced adamant claims to total self-sufficiency, even to the point of deriding rival groups and denying obvious influences. Fortunately, there remains some latitude for generalization, and what follows is a review of those fundamental traits or tendencies that support the notion of a typical avant-garde group.

As recent research has begun to emphasize, several eminent female artists were affiliated to the early avant-garde: an especially impressive number emerged in the Surrealist orbit from the 1930s onwards. Nonetheless, few of these women can be regarded as dominant activists, for it cannot be denied that the majority of avant-gardists were impatient young males eager to assert their talents. Of course, avant-garde battles were – despite a few instances of exuberant fisticuffs – fought not on a literal battlefield, but on the virtual battlefields of culture, namely print publications and such public sites as the art gallery, the theatre and the café.

Indeed, though a few avant-gardists, Kandinsky and Kirchner among them, thrived in the countryside, the vast majority were urbanites. In Germany, the café culture of pre-war Berlin offered an alternative to the

bourgeois home to young tearaways hungry for creative dialogue. The
Cubo-Futurists of St Petersburg met regularly at the notorious Stray Dog
café. In wartime Zurich, Dada's home was the Café Voltaire, hidden
amid the narrow alleys of the old town. In postwar Paris, the Dadaists
convened at the Café Certâ, a nondescript bar in a rundown passageway,
chosen for its lack of pretension; it is lovingly evoked in Aragon's *Paris
Peasant* (1926). Later, the Paris Surrealists used a succession of cafés as
their headquarters and stronghold, each member being expected to sip
the evening *apéritif* and contribute to the ongoing debate.

Lively tussles with the established cultural order typify the classic avant-
garde campaign, success being measured by the disapproval of a conservative press. Throughout the Dada months in Zurich, Tristan Tzara
subscribed to a press-cuttings service and had amassed over 8,000 notices
by late 1919. A favourite guerrilla weapon was the collective tract, distributed across the city in multiple copies. Its tone was invariably pungent
and confrontational, and is epitomized in the title of the Russian Futurists' 'A Slap in the Face of Public Taste' (1912). On 8 July 1910, the
Italian Futurists climbed the Campanile in Venice to scatter thousands of
leaflets onto the Piazza San Marco, broadcasting a scathing critique of the
city's smugness about its venerable past. In 1913, Apollinaire created a
minor scandal with his mischievous 'The Futurist Antitradition' (1913), a
tract listing supposed enemies and allies under the headings 'Shite to...'
and 'Flowers to...'. A similar format was adopted by Wyndham Lewis
in the first issue of *Blast*, while a referendum held by the Paris Dadaists in
1921 allocated negative or positive marks to a roster of cultural figures
from Homer to Picasso.

Early Paris Surrealism revelled in scandal and was not averse to exploiting sheer bad taste, as witness its 1924 pamphlet 'Un Cadavre' ('A
Corpse'), which insulted the recently deceased establishment author Anatole France. The outspoken Antonin Artaud addressed inflammatory open
letters to the pope, the Dalai Lama and the directors of prisons and lunatic
asylums. Though composed by one person, the tract was normally signed
by all group members, which meant that it took on the secondary function
of an instrument for testing allegiance. Inevitably this brought dissent into
the open and often hastened an individual's angry (and painful) departure.

The tract is cousin to the manifesto, the very paradigm of avant-garde
expression. Marinetti ensured maximum impact for 'The Founding and
Manifesto of Futurism' when it appeared on the front page of the Paris
newspaper *Le Figaro*. By 1916, Italian Futurism had generated over fifty
manifestos, many tied to personal projects: thus Luigi Russolo wrote
'The Art of Noises' (1913) to explain his research into acoustics, while
the photographer and cineast Anton Giulio Bragaglia issued 'Futurist
Photodynamics' (1911) to herald a photography expressive of vibrant

movement. Russian Futurism likewise marked its progress in a succession of confident manifestos. In 1912, Khlebnikov joined with the poet Vladimir Mayakovsky to produce a text establishing the Russian Futurist platform. A year later, Khlebnikov and Kruchenykh collaborated on 'The Word as Such', which was at pains to deride Italian Futurism as all hot air and no artistry. Kruchenykh issued his manifesto on *zaum*, the 'Declaration of the Transrational Language', at Baku in 1921. Malevich's later 'The Non-Objective World' (1927) announced art's abstractive victory over a reality rendered obsolete.

Among the Dadaists, Richard Huelsenbeck shrewdly observed that 'the manifesto as a literary medium answered our need for directness'.[4] His 'Dadaistic Manifesto' of 1918 brushes aside Expressionism as being weak-kneed and salutes Dadaism as 'the international expression of our times'. Tristan Tzara recited his 'Dada Manifesto 1918' before a Zurich audience: bursting with virulent invective, it is spellbinding in its sheer dynamism. Insisting that 'I am against systems, the one acceptable system is to have no system on principle', Tzara builds to a breathless climax: 'Freedom: DADA DADA DADA, howling of painful seizures, interlocking of opposites and all contradictions, grotesques and inconsequences: LIFE.'[5] In Zagreb, the 1921 'Zenithist Manifesto', signed by the poets Ljubomir Micić, Ivan Goll and Boško Tokin, announced a scheme for the fusion of Cubist, Expressionist and Futurist aspirations, based upon the 'aestheticisation of all dynamisms and mysticisms'.[6]

Historians of Surrealism often see a symptomatic shift in the brief manifesto 'Lâchez tout' ('Drop Everything') which André Breton issued in 1922. Its pithy message was essentially aimed at his fellow Dadaists, whom he exhorted to abandon everything and 'set forth on the roads'. A couple of years later, his far weightier 'Manifesto of Surrealism' (1924) laid down a dictionary-style definition of the movement, along with a tribute to the power of the imagination and a report on the recent achievements of his team.

The *Blue Rider* almanac represents a striking composite of manifesto and anthology. It contains essays by the Russian Futurist David Burliuk and the Austrian composer Arnold Schönberg. The longest piece is Kandinsky's influential 'On the Question of Form', while the German

---

[4] Quoted by Hans Richter from Richard Huelsenbeck's 'First Dada Speech in Germany' (1918) in Hans Richter, *Dada: Art and Anti-Art* (London: Thames & Hudson, 1965), p. 103.

[5] Tristan Tzara, 'Dada Manifesto 1918' in Tristan Tzara, *Œuvres complètes*, ed. Henri Béhar, 6 vols. (Paris: Flammarion, 1975), vol. 1, p. 367.

[6] 'The Zenithist Manifesto' in *Between Worlds: A Sourcebook of Central European Avant-Gardes, 1910–1930*, eds. Timothy O. Benson and Éva Forgács (Cambridge, MA, and London: MIT Press, 2002), p. 291.

painter August Macke contributed the pithy 'Masks', invoking the coexistence and universality of a portrait by Van Gogh, a Benin bronze, a medieval gothic sculpture and a child's drawing. The 140-odd illustrations in this landmark publication maximize the range of reference across space and time and reflect an unusual sensitivity to marginalized or forgotten works from the past.

Certain eclectic avant-garde journals offered a broad international platform, such as the Romanian *Contimporanul* ('The Man of the Present'), whose pages were generously opened to Expressionist, Futurist, Dadaist and Constructivist concerns. In Germany, the many organs of Expressionism, such as the weeklies *Der Sturm* ('The Storm') and *Die Aktion* ('Action'), fostered progressive ideas and contained argumentative essays as well as creative writing. Cubism in Paris was represented by *Nord-Sud* ('North-South', 1917–18), edited by Pierre Reverdy, who invited contributions from the young Dadaists. But the more characteristic forum for an avant-garde group was its own named magazine, its title usually embodying a watchword or mission statement. Such a publication cemented group unity, allowing established members to exhibit their latest writings and pictures, and newcomers to justify themselves to their seniors. Tzara was the effervescent editor of *Dada* in Zurich during 1917–20 and of *Cœur à barbe* ('Bearded Heart') in Paris in 1922. Solo-authored Dada magazines were not uncommon: Paul Eluard's *Proverbe*, Picabia's *391*, Kurt Schwitters's *Merz*. Paris Surrealism communicated its evolving message through a succession of journals, starting with *La Révolution surréaliste* ('The Surrealist Revolution', 1924–9). Always outspoken, its publications were rarely censored, though an inflammatory issue of *Coupure* ('Cutting') was banned during the May Events of 1968.

The Russian Futurists were the most energetic proponents of an avant-garde theatre, managing to persuade the distinguished professional director Vsevolod Meyerhold to mount Mayakovsky's plays *Mystery-Bouffe* (1918) and *The Bed Bug* (1929). As it turned out, Kruchenykh's opera *Victory over the Sun* (1913), with sets and costumes by Malevich, remains a rare instance of a large-scale theatrical project executed uniquely by avant-gardists. More typical of avant-garde expression was the mischievous, half-improvised happening that tended to attract and then to snub its audience. Futurist *soirées* in rented theatres took place in Rome, Turin and other Italian cities from 1913 and comprised jeering speeches by Marinetti, the showing of artworks and the recital of insolent poems. The self-taught musician Russolo proposed an art based on the sounds of everyday life, and especially of machinery; after the war, he put on several concerts in Paris, using electrical whistles, roarers and his bizarre invention, the *russolofono* of 1929. The resulting cacophony was a direct challenge to the audience, whose indignant catcalls were deemed integral to the event. In like fashion, the Paris Dadaists under Tzara staged a cycle of theatrical events, daring the public to come and be shocked by their inconsequential playlets, their parodies, their outrageous promise that Charlie Chaplin would be present (a bare-faced lie). The climax came one evening in 1920 when the baying customers threw eggs and vegetables at the actors, who, looking back, were, to Tzara's delight, no longer able to discern which was the auditorium and which the spectacle. A year later, André Breton tired of empty provocation and forced a showdown with Tzara by mounting a mock trial of the right-wing novelist Maurice Barrès, who was represented in court by a dummy. When called to testify, Tzara refused to take the event seriously, while Breton fulminated in earnest about Barrès's alleged 'conspiracy against the security of the mind'. The clash marked the watershed between a moribund Dadaism and a militant Surrealism.

It is noticeable that a majority of avant-garde groups were preoccupied with linguistic innovation. The Expressionist poetry of Georg Trakl constantly veered towards bleak and estranging formulations, while August Stramm developed a half-strangulated idiom governed by a jagged syntax that corresponded perfectly to the experience of front-line combat, which claimed his life in 1915. Within Surrealism, Duchamp, Desnos and Michel Leiris engaged in syllabic word-play, while Surrealist poetry at large pursued an idiom of extreme semantic incongruity, which, though faithful to traditional syntax, was deemed to possess oracular qualities and to reflect the workings of the unconscious mind. In extolling the principle of 'words set at liberty', Marinetti called for a 'wire-less imagination' dedicated to 'the absolute freedom of images or analogies'. His 1914 poem 'Zang Tumb Tumb', ostensibly describing the Siege of Adrianopolis (which he had observed first-hand in 1912), was above all a visual experiment in disposing letters freely across the page. Typographical adventurism is an unmistakable feature of avant-garde expression, as witness the experiments of Apollinaire, as well as those of Ultraismo, Futurism and Dadaism.

But it was recitation which best suited the Dadaist temperament. Mind-numbing confusion was created by the simultaneous recitation of multilingual poems at the Cabaret Voltaire. Yet Hugo Ball's magisterial rendering of the sound-poem 'Gadji beri bimba' in Zurich in July 1916 was a telling instance of nonsense modulating into meaning, for Ball found himself intoning his daft text as though it were a sacred litany. In his solo recitals, Schwitters achieved a fusion of non-referential utterance and musicality when he hummed and squealed the four movements of his *Ursonate* ('Primal Sonata', 1922–32). In turn, the Russian Futurists Kruchenykh and Khlebnikov pioneered the transrational idiom of *zaum*, a random mixture of glossolalia and onomatopoeia. In his 1918 lecture 'On

Madness in Art', Kruchenykh argued that insanity could conduce to creativity, and insisted that the impenetrable syllables of *zaum* always carried
latent meanings. Khlebnikov asserted his right to implement neologisms,
malapropisms and other lexical anomalies. His famous poem 'Enchantment through Laughter' (1910) exploits neologisms extrapolated from
the basic word 'laughter' (*smekh*). Kruchenykh's play *Zangezi*, staged by
Vladimir Tatlin in 1923, posits a language of the gods, incomprehensible
to man because it consists purely of sounds.

Despite a general antipathy to formalized religion, a good many avant-
garde circles were intrigued by spiritual and mystical ideas. The Theo-
sophical Society founded by Helena Blavatsky in 1875 offered a seductive
vision of the interplay of philosophy, science and religion; its doctrines
were later subsumed by Rudolf Steiner within Anthroposophy, a spiritual science purporting to attune the individual to the universe. An invisible dimension made visible through art became a guiding concept for
artists like Kandinsky, Alexej von Jawlensky, Mondrian and others. The
Paris-based Czech painter František Kupka saw himself as a prophet who
could communicate on the spiritual plane through his rhythmical abstract
designs. In Russia, the mystic philosopher Peter Ouspensky influenced the
Cubo-Futurists, while Malevich's abstractive aspiration to transcend the
three dimensions was pursued by his several disciples in Suprematism.
Popular interest in clairvoyance and telepathy grew during the war years
and was deemed compatible with Albert Einstein's thesis on the fourth
dimension. This last was invoked in Apollinaire's *The Cubist Painters*
(1913) and given a specifically occult twist by Boccioni in Italy. In 1915,
Giacomo Balla and Fortunato Depero produced 'Futurist Reconstruction
of the Universe', promising 'to give skeleton and flesh to the invisible, the
impalpable, the imponderable and the imperceptible'.[7] Esoteric notions
of magical insight and of a reality transfigured inform the creations of
many avant-gardists, such as Balla's *Iridescent Interpenetrations*, paintings whose mesmerizing colour units were designed to mirror infinity. The
ultimate basis for these waves of occult thinking was the conception of
the artist as a seer who lays bare hidden mysteries through unprecedented
structures of understanding.

In their principled refusal of conformity, avant-garde artists found
dozens of ways to singularize their art. Inspired by the autodidact styles
of Van Gogh and Gauguin, the Brücke artists cultivated a slapdash manner, with Kirchner producing sketches of wilful gaucheness, arguing that
they were not scrawls but 'hieroglyphs' capturing the true essence of the
depicted object. In Surrealism, non-rational improvisation or 'automa-
tism' was revered as the privileged conduit of subjective expression,

[7] Giacomo Balla and Fortunato Depero, 'Futurist Reconstruction of the Universe' (1915)
in Apollonio, *Futurist Manifestos*, p. 197.

expressly at variance with Realism: André Masson's drawings of the early 1920s were deemed genuine transcripts of unconscious process. The technical variants to which automatism gave rise – such as *frottage* and decalcomania, which elicited meaning from arbitrary textures and smudges – were prized as markers of Surrealist authenticity; albeit a cooler technique – as it were the illusionistic depiction of oneiric fantasies – underlay the more popular styles of painters such as De Chirico, Magritte and Salvador Dalí, the master of insidious *trompe l'œil*.

Wilful deviation from traditional art-practices is essential to the avant-garde. It adopted anomalous colour from Fauvism and fractured shapes from Cubism. Taking its cue from the *papiers collés* ('pasted papers') of Braque, Picasso and Gris, it developed collage as a medium of discovery. The format helped Malevich on his path to abstraction, and inspired Max Ernst as he moved from Dada to Surrealism. The collage principle means disposing dislocated visual fragments within a single frame, recycling old images to produce startling new combinations. The variant of photomontage (the deployment of scissored segments of photographic prints) was pioneered by the Dadaist John Heartfield and the Constructivist Alexander Rodchenko.

When Kandinsky made his first abstract watercolour in 1910, its fluid, organic style represented the most radical break with Realism. Later, his abstractions became highly geometrical and meticulously finished, veering towards the anti-Naturalistic or geometric ideal of Constructivism. Other avant-gardists preferred an approach which privileged the hand, retaining a certain unevenness and palpability. For example, the handmade woodcut, favoured by both Gauguin and Munch, became a favourite medium of Die Brücke; Kirchner even issued the group's founding manifesto (1906) in woodcut form. Gaudier-Brzeska made his own tools before fashioning handmade sculpture from discarded materials. Although Hans Arp's later sculptural works in plaster and stone are more polished, his Dada reliefs in wood are a further instance of the handmade as a token of authenticity. Conversely (and perversely), Duchamp launched the idea of the *readymade* by nominating certain industrial (machine-made) artefacts and simply labelling them as art, not necessarily even handling them himself.

A final emphasis must be laid upon the frequency of collaboration between individuals. Tzara's poems and Arp's woodcuts met in the joint publication *Cinéma calendrier du cœur abstrait* ('Cinematic Calendar of the Abstracted Heart', 1920). The Prague poet Nezval and the designer Karel Teige co-published *Alphabet* (1926), a synthesis of verbal and visual expression which exemplified their doctrine of Poetism. Surrealist poets frequently solicited illustrations from their painter friends. But perhaps the most telling case of collaboration is the Russian Futurist book. Its texts were printed on cheap lithographic pages, stapled or left loose, and included illustrations by Malevich, Larionov, Goncharova and

Olga Rozanova. *Mirskontsa* ('Worldbackwards', 1912) placed images by Goncharova, Larionov and Tatlin alongside facsimiles of handwritten texts by Kruchenykh and Khlebnikov, complete with spelling mistakes and no punctuation. Perhaps the most touching Futurist publication was *Pomada*, a set of poems by Kruchenykh with pictures by Larionov: it was printed on wallpaper and bound in sacking.

I have emphasized the notion of the classic avant-garde group as a tightly knit fighting unit committed to change. Its fierce demands prioritize the right to uncensored expression and result in startling artworks and actions which defy the cultural establishment – whose disapproval seems necessary to the group's identity and self-esteem. Individual ambition might coincide with the collective dynamic, or diverge from it. Many avant-gardists joined a group because it offered a supportive context for their private experiments, but departed in anger, or simply drifted away, once required to adhere to an explicit ideology. Italian Futurism, Suprematism, Vorticism and Paris Surrealism were defined and energized by a single charismatic leader. By contrast, other groups functioned with little sense of hierarchy, following – more or less instinctively – an anarchist model of collaboration. Huelsenbeck insisted that Dada was a club each of whose members enjoyed the same status – that of president. Reconciling individualism with collective purpose, the Futurist Gino Severini envisaged subjectivity as 'a centre of universal irradiation' and 'the point where centripetal forces converge'.[8]

As regards the vexed issue of political commitment, Surrealism provides the most instructive example. As they themselves acknowledged, the Paris Surrealists of the 1920s and 1930s were struggling to reconcile two perfectly distinct goals: a Rimbaud-inspired liberation of the artistic sensibility and a Marxist social revolution. That the only political force in France at all capable of implementing the latter, namely the French Communist Party, should deride the first as a bourgeois luxury grew to be the stumbling block which eventually prompted the group's abandonment of overt politicking in favour of less public (and, in truth, more enjoyable) avenues of action and expression. After the Second World War, some French surrealists did collaborate with anarchist groups; and it can be conjectured that a tacit orientation towards anarchistic rebelliousness and an ideal of order-amid-lawlessness is the strongest political strand in avant-garde ideology.

In general, the early avant-garde defined itself in contradistinction to a rather amorphous enemy, usually equated with the contemporary social system at large. However, more often than not, the immediate target of its iconoclasm was a specific *arrière-garde* composed of conformist

[8]  Quoted by Umbro Apollonio in his 'Introduction' to *Futurist Manifestos*, p. 11.

artists, reactionary critics, an inflexible educational system and a complacent bourgeoisie. In fact, the pertinence of the avant-garde metaphor diminishes if one expects it to denote a guerrilla unit eager to facilitate the advance of more orthodox forces. Despite some successful skirmishes, no avant-garde group or movement ever acquired sufficient bulk or impetus to achieve permanent victory: the most it could hope for was to bequeath an inspiring legend to a subsequent generation of rebels. Of course, a century on, cultural consecration has taken place, most obviously manifested in the current flood of books and retrospectives. Some now envisage the early avant-garde as outdated, its cutting edge blunted by time. Others still treasure its example, mindful of its enduring virtues: its risk-taking; its zestfulness and imaginativeness; its cosmopolitanism; its delight in improvisation, incongruity and surprise; its resistance to dogma and routine.

# Some major critics of the period

# 20

# Charles-Augustin Sainte-Beuve (1804–1869)

## WOLF LEPENIES

### A life and a method

Charles-Augustin Sainte-Beuve was born on 23 December 1804 in Boulogne-sur-Mer. At the age of fourteen, he was sent to Paris to continue his studies. He attended lectures at the Medical Faculty from 1824 to 1827. Although he soon gave up medicine for literature, he retained a penchant for the scientific method. Swept along by the Romantic movement, he wrote articles in the *Globe* – the equivalent of today's *Nouvel observateur* – and became a comrade in arms of Victor Hugo, falling out with him in 1834. Sainte-Beuve wrote verses and even published them – like so many critics, he saw literary criticism as a sacrifice to be offered to poetry; he completed one novel (*Volupté*) and planned more; but what made him famous were the weekly articles he wrote for the great Parisian newspapers: the *National*, the *Revue de Paris*, the *Revue des deux mondes*, the *Constitutionnel*, the official *Moniteur* and finally the oppositional *Temps*. From 1837 to 1838 he gave lectures in Lausanne, and these formed the basis of his masterpiece *Port-Royal*, a fascinating multi-volume account of the world of Jansenism whose empathetic intensity can still transport the reader today. From 1848 to 1849, he taught in Liège; the fruit of this sojourn was his compendious later book on Chateaubriand and his circle (*Chateaubriand et son groupe littéraire sous l'empire*, 1861). Sainte-Beuve, who denied that he had any *esprit de corps* and was proud of his distance from institutions, made his way through all the major French (that is, Parisian) institutions: he was Conservator at the Bibliothèque Mazarine and held the Chair of Latin Poetry at the Collège de France, where rebellious students limited his activity to his inaugural lecture. He taught at the Ecole Normale Supérieure, was elected to the Académie Française in 1844, and was appointed a Senator by Napoleon III in 1865. He died on 13 October 1869 in Paris.

This chapter is based on Wolf Lepenies, *Sainte-Beuve: Auf der Schwelle zur Moderne* (Munich: Hanser, 1997); French translation, *Sainte-Beuve: Au seuil de la modernité* (Paris: Gallimard, 2002).

Sainte-Beuve was perhaps the greatest critic in an epoch rightly called
the age of criticism. In the judgement of George Steiner, he is the only
critic who still retains interest as an author. For a long period in his life,
his literary production was tied to a strict working routine, culminating
in an article published each Monday morning – hence the title *Causeries
du lundi* ('Monday Chats') and later *Nouveaux lundis*. Such were the
gravity and length of these articles that not even a weekly, let alone a
daily, newspaper would print them today. On three days – Tuesday,
Wednesday and Thursday – he dictated initial sketches to his secretary.
On Friday, he wore ear-plugs: not even the slightest noise should disturb
him in the final editing of his articles in what was then still a rural Rue du
Montparnasse. On Friday evening, he received the first galley proofs, and
on Saturday morning his secretary read out to him the original text of the
manuscript, which he now corrected and amplified. On Sunday morning,
a second version was sent to the editorial office. Sainte-Beauve read a
third set of proofs in the editorial office on Sunday afternoon. Then he
was free – until Tuesday morning. Such was the life of a literary labourer
who has rightly been described as a worldly Benedictine. These articles
were not improvised reflections that flowed casually from Sainte-Beuve's
pen. Many of them were the products of real research and run to twenty
or thirty pages in the book version of today; to write them, Sainte-Beuve
had to visit a number of libraries and archives. In many cases, members
of the family of the author to whom he wished to dedicate his next *Lundi*
brought him completely new material which had to be read, checked and
worked into the respective article.

Sainte-Beuve is one of those authors who make us regret that there is
no discipline devoted to historical time and motion studies. It remains
unimaginable how a literary production of this intensity and compass
could be maintained for decades. Sainte-Beuve had a secretary, but the
latter had to write by hand each new version of the article, which risked
being swamped and rendered illegible by the author's additions and cor-
rections. Couriers took the proofs from the author to the editorial office
and back. But this author also wrote many letters every day, some of them
several pages long, and regularly received visitors; and even a bachelor
occasionally needed to satisfy what Auguste Comte would have described
as 'needs of the heart'. It was also his normal practice to dine at length
in company in the evening. This routine, maintained for decades, and
the magnitude of his output remain a wonder, and Sainte-Beuve, who
deplored the industrialization of literary production, was one of the nineteenth century's first literary wage labourers, often close to exhaustion
and constantly complaining of weariness.

The nineteenth century is a century of melancholy; it saw melancholy
as its defining property, describing it as the *mal du siècle*. This was a

symptom of the malaise of modernity, a discontent which found expression in Sainte-Beuve's criticism. He accorded literature a privileged status, because he saw it as the only intellectual province in which order could be preserved in the chaos of fragmenting value systems and the heady turmoil of an idea of progress that had lost all fixed standards in both life and letters. The instrument for restoring order was literary criticism. With its aid, the history of literature could be written as a series of acts of retribution that – like all true retribution – would seek to restore tranquillity and balance, that is, retributive justice. Sainte-Beuve's attitude towards modernity is conservative, but not reactionary: he regretfully recognized the processes that were shaping modern urban and industrialized society with its scientific and egalitarian tendencies, but he knew that these processes are irreversible.

## The melancholy of modernity

Sainte-Beuve's father died before his birth. His mother spent the last months of her pregnancy deep in mourning. This is partly why he spoke of melancholy as a trait imparted to him at birth. For Sainte-Beuve, who early foresaw that literature would be his life, it was important to associate himself with melancholy, because it was traditionally attributed to members of the thinking elite. 'Mélancolie. Signe de distinction du cœur et d'élévation de l'esprit', one reads in Flaubert's *Dictionnaire des idées reçues* ('Dictionary of Received Ideas'). One is not only born as a melancholic, one also knows why this is so. As Joubert wrote, melancholy may be a sadness that finds no words, but it always has its reasons.

At the same time, Sainte-Beuve realizes that melancholy is a psychological state that has a lot to do with national character or, more precisely, with the nation-specific integration or containment of certain feelings. Wordsworth, to take just one example from literary history, is not understood in France, where the *mal du siècle* is at home – because he seems too happy. What is advantageous in England becomes a problem in France. Wordsworth is a 'regular', a 'monk in an order', who must be reproached for not having suffered enough. This is why Sainte-Beuve, who likes Wordsworth, does his best to turn him into an elegiac poet who can become naturalized on the continental side of the English Channel. He turns him in fact, into an English Lamartine. In an age that translated everything, it was precisely Wordsworth whose work the French Romantics neglected to translate. Sainte-Beuve made up for this omission through his criticism.

In the nineteenth century, anyone who wanted to launch a career in intellectual life and the arts had to adopt the symptoms of the *mal du siècle*. Sainte-Beuve, the contemporary of Auguste Comte, was a covert sociologist who knew that even the most intimate desires have to find recognized forms in a society and tradition that help them to gain full expression and social recognition. However sad sadness is, it does not become unbearable unless others fail to perceive it. Sainte-Beuve knew when one had to be deeply sad in order to be in tune with the present.

Consequently, Sainte-Beuve's portrait of a great melancholic, La Rochefoucauld – written in 1840, around the middle of his life – takes on special importance. He saw the composition of this portrait as the turning point of his life. Sainte-Beuve was a positivist in an epoch in which even the literary intelligentsia was interested in physiology; he originally wished to become a physician. But in 1830, on the eve of the July Revolution, he was caught up in a profound crisis; without ever having committed himself to the Romantic movement, he felt the urge to live out a mystically inclined romanticism. This is testified by the first two volumes of *Port-Royal*, a volume of poetry titled *Les Consolations* (1830), and especially the novel *Volupté*. Without ever distancing himself from these works, at the end of his life Sainte-Beuve saw a mental illness in the mood that gave rise to them. His portrait of La Rochefoucauld was the first step to intellectual recovery. It was a turning away from Catholicism and a return to positivism, but one shaped less by the will to change the world than by a scepticism based on worldly experience.

One cannot read the portrait of La Rochefoucauld as anything other than a contribution to Sainte-Beuve's autobiography, for, as he himself said, the key to every *homme de lettres'* biography could be found in his bibliography. Not that Sainte-Beuve hid behind La Rochefoucauld; he uses him to lend his self-image sharper contours. Sainte-Beuve gives La Rochefoucauld's life history an interpretation that can be understood only against the background of his own life's project.

Moved by La Rochefoucauld's 'unbelievable sadness', Sainte-Beuve speaks – like La Rochefoucauld himself and most of his biographers – of the schism in this life, which fell into two contrary halves, the first devoted to ambition and gallantry and the second, after the final failure of the Fronde, that uprising of the French nobility against the monarchy, to devotion and penance. But he mentions this only to undercut this dichotomy by subtle means. To Sainte-Beuve, La Rochefoucauld's fate seemed preordained: the latter became a wise man when he could no longer have any effect in the world of politics, finding his fulfilment in failure. The *Maximes et réflexions* (1664) are not compensation for an inhibited *vita activa*, they are the climax of a single, coherent life and the naturally predetermined crowning of a literary career. In this sense, Sainte-Beuve was convinced that Nature had destined him, too, to become a critic.

## Literature from the spirit of natural history

In his youth, Sainte-Beuve had been a positivist – a positivist with a warm heart and full of enthusiasm. This is why it was easy for him to switch camps to Romanticism. The portrait of La Rochefoucauld shows how Sainte-Beuve turned back to positivism without returning to his youthful views. Rather, his positivism is now post-Romantic and sceptical; it is modest in its expectations and demands and fuelled by a cool head. The corresponding view of humanity owes its merciless aspects to La Rochefoucauld's insights. For the moralist, man is no longer a sinner and subject; in the era of great disappointments, nothing remains of him but a sensitive apparatus that must be analysed without religious or political apologetics. La Rochefoucauld views humanity with a disinterested curiosity that recalls Descartes and Mme Lafayette's novel *La Princesse de Clèves*; he observes humankind like an intellectual precursor of that rebellious materialism that helped to shape the Enlightenment and that would form the *idéologues* of the Directoire and the Napoleonic age.

Sainte-Beuve sees himself as a naturalist whose *Lundis* strive to compile a human herbarium and whose 'histoire naturelle littéraire' aims at a complete classification of intellectual types. In this, he is close not only to the naturalist Buffon (1707–88) and his gay science, the 'science sereine', but also to the *Comédie Humaine* of his antagonist and literary adversary Balzac; and as with Buffon and Balzac, ambition and modesty are combined in him.

Modesty is a typical stance of the observer and classifier in natural history. The naturalist Sainte-Beuve wants to systematize; he is a decided adherent of classification. But he sticks close to the facts; he prefers to admit exceptions to his system rather than distort reality to make them fit. In the middle of the century of Darwin, Sainte-Beuve is thoroughly convinced that literary criticism is still in the epoch of Linnaeus and Cuvier, that it can at any rate become a kind of natural-historical typology, and that the age of overarching syntheses is far from over. Sainte-Beuve sought to combine charm with a sense of reality in his criticism; poetry and physiology should not be mutually exclusive. Buffon could have described the goal of his *Histoire naturelle* (1749–88) in similar terms.

When we speak of Sainte-Beuve's naturalism and his 'histoire naturelle littéraire', we speak of a natural history in the spirit of Buffon. The naturalist who remained a writer and the critic who allied himself with a modest natural science move towards each other in the history of the mind. Sainte-Beuve's proximity to Buffon is obvious – but, for that very reason, not very revealing. It is more productive to see him in conjunction with Linnaeus.

In his early studies, Sainte-Beuve accused the historians of the French Revolution of subjecting human activity to rigid rules that yoked people to the cart of an inexorable fate, thereby all too thoughtlessly releasing the historian from the duty of despising the oppressor, sympathizing with the victim, and having all the feelings that bring colour and life into history. Sainte-Beuve distanced himself from historical determinism; he rejected interpretations of the past whose linear sequence no longer permitted any conclusions to be drawn about an uncertain and vacillating present. When Sainte-Beuve yet again grew angry with one of these systematic views of history in which the cold and artificial order of a this-worldly *deus ex machina* ruled, he promptly reverted to the 'original', that is, Bossuet (1627–1704), who was at least honest enough to write his world history as a history of salvation. Or he would open a volume of Cardinal de Retz's memoirs to discover real life once more – the life of intrigues and the human masquerade.

But what may initially look like an uncompromising criticism of historical determinism – a calm but firm plea for an empirical historiography that sees the rule in the exceptions and that accepts the incongruities of the historical process because they are an expression of human, all-too-human weaknesses – is in reality a sign of burning doubt and deep yearning. For only an agnostic who does not raise the issue of his unbelief is sure of his position. But an obsession which constantly speaks of what it supposedly does not want betrays a desire and a deeply felt lack that must look for compensation. In truth, Sainte-Beuve remained a determinist in his innermost heart, and it is the old-fashioned nature of this view that exerts such a pull on us today. It can be summed up in the assertion that, for Sainte-Beuve, in an age of growing disorder, literary criticism becomes an instrument of an all-encompassing, order-creating retribution.

Sainte-Beuve stands on the threshold of modernity. He perceives the other side, the costs of the great processes shaping modernity – science's triumph and secularization, industrialization, urbanization and democratization – and he does it with a mixture of astonishment and mourning, rejection and fascination, whose stoicism resembles that of Jacob Burckhardt. The world falls into disorder, the overview of the whole is lost, and because the beginning of this process coincides with the French Revolution, the intellectuals, especially in France, believe they are acting on the main stage of world history.

But Sainte-Beuve does not tend to the tragic: he does not resist developments that the human intellect can no longer plan and human hands can no longer prevent. He remains conservative and reminds himself and his readers of the epochs – especially the great seventeenth century, the age of Louis XIV and Boileau – in which order and taste still ruled, but he is no reactionary: the individual is still permitted to invoke the good

old days, but individual yearnings offer no foundation for a political programme. The more insecure politics and the more opaque the general
power relations in human society become, the greater importance literature takes on for Sainte-Beuve. In a time of growing disorder, it remains
the sole province of the human spirit in which order can be established.
The instrument creating order is criticism. Revenge and retribution are
its methods.

   In the field of natural history, Buffon and Carl Linnaeus (1707–78) are
seen as the great antipodes.[1] Buffon resists every artificial classification: he
still attempts to grasp the whole of nature in the form of an observation-
based description of the living world. This is an aristocratic attitude:
it takes for granted that the world can be experienced and controlled.
Linnaeus is different – a bourgeois by birth and only later raised to
nobility, he is convinced that we require an artificial system in order to
apprehend the plenitude of the natural world.

   Sainte-Beuve's judgement that, in the middle of the nineteenth century,
one was still in the epoch of Linnaeus and Cuvier shows how alive the traditions of natural history had remained for him. Sainte-Beuve compared
himself to Buffon: he wished to create a natural history of literature. Yet
classification became a central feature of his method: the critic Sainte-
Beuve, whom no less than Marcel Proust reproached for his personality
cult and his undisciplined *causeries*, believes he can do justice to the
individual author only by identifying him precisely as a member of a specific family, as an example of a species. In his addiction to classification,
Sainte-Beuve is much closer to Linnaeus than to Buffon, who sought only
to observe and describe. And he is particularly close to Linnaeus when
he attempts to transpose the views and methods of natural history to the
world of writers in order to create a kind of zoology of *Homo sapiens
scribens*.

## Criticism and retribution

When Sainte-Beuve discusses literary criticism, it is conspicuous that his
language is strongly moulded by metaphors from the sphere of law.
In his own words, he had long behaved like an attorney; but he ultimately wanted to be a judge as well. There is nothing he admires more
than poetic justice, and few remarks can have flattered him as much as
the verdict of Laure Surville (Balzac's sister, of all people), who called

---

[1]  Cf. Wolf Lepenies, *Das Ende der Naturgeschichte: Wandel kultureller Selbst-
    verständlichkeiten in den Wissenschaften des 18. und 19. Jahrhunderts* (Munich and
    Vienna: Hanser, 1976).

him the 'grand justicier de la littérature française'.[2] Sainte-Beuve turned
the history of literature into a tribunal; for him, it is a this-worldly
history of revenge and injustice, of charges and restitutions, of confessions and perjury, of exonerations and judicial errors, of convictions and
appeals.

Sainte-Beuve yearns for the 'douceurs de la stabilité littéraire' ('the
sweetness of literary stability'), but, precisely in literature, stability is hard
to achieve, because here there are no legally binding judgements: literary
history is a process that remains open, an unending series of revisions
and rehabilitations. The production of justice and balance accordingly
exceeds the powers of any individual, it requires institutional support
and anchorage, and France can consider itself more fortunate than any
other country because Richelieu had early created a literary tribunal and
'supreme court' in the Académie Française.

Sainte-Beuve was convinced – and Baudelaire shared this conviction –
that every author is characterized by a key word. Once we discover this
word, the œuvre opens up and reveals its secret. This key word is also
present in Sainte-Beuve. It is the word *vengeance*. Literary history is the
tribunal of literature. Before this tribunal not only many petty cases are
enacted, but also the great dramas of revenge and retribution in which La
Rochefoucauld and Mme de Longueville, Voltaire and Joseph de Maistre,
Pascal and Montaigne, but above all – in *Port-Royal* – the Jansenists and
the Jesuits confront each other.

Literature is always a matter of settling old accounts, 'de régler les
comptes'. Even if Sainte-Beuve used this expression only with reference
to his *Cahiers intimes* (which are revealingly called *Mes poisons*), this is
not merely a manner of speaking; his entire work can be described as an
'arsenal des vengeances'.[3]

In this context, the spheres of revenge range from gossip, the indispensable medium of communication of a society in which writers and
readers spent most of their time in the world of the salons, through the
political controversies of the day, to the philosophy of history. 'Uncle'
Sainte-Beuve, as his admirers called him, took part in the orgies of gossip
of his age – the Goncourt brothers spoke in this connection of his 'petites
vengeances' – and he still provides his readers with abundant material for
gossip today.

Sainte-Beuve not only registered the acts of vengeance, he also constantly evaluated them. There was a 'vengeance permise' ('permitted

---

[2] Laure Surville to Sainte-Beuve, 26 August 1850, in Charles-Augustin Sainte-Beuve, *Correspondance générale*, ed. J. Bonnerot, 19 vols. (Paris: Stock, 1935– ), vol. VIII, p. 177.
[3] Charles-Augustin Sainte-Beuve, *Mes poisons: cahiers intimes inédits*, ed. Victor Giraud
(Paris: Editions d'Aujourd'hui, 1977), p. 3.

vengeance'), embodied in his eyes especially in the behaviour of La Rochefoucauld, but there was also a purely destructive revenge and that, in the realm of politics, had calamitous consequences: thus, for Sainte-Beuve, the future welfare of France was decisively prejudiced by the excess of revenge exacted by the revolutions of 1789 and 1830. Unlike the physicotheologians, and unlike those historians who believed in a this-worldly providence, Sainte-Beuve was no longer convinced that, in the course of political history, individual acts of revenge added up to a balance and compensation and ultimately created a great system of retributive justice. He no longer believes in the *vengeance divine*, the *Nemesis Divina*, that brings the world to its senses; in his essay on Guizot, he approvingly quotes the verses of the 'great Corneille', in which his early doubts about providence become manifest:

> Mais l'exemple souvent n'est qu'un miroir trompeur;
> Et l'ordre du Destin, qui gène nos pensées,
> N'est pas toujours écrit dans les choses passées.
> Quelquefois l'un se brise où l'autre s'est sauvé,
> Et par où l'on périt un autre est conservé.[4]

> An example is often a mirror that deceives,
> And the working of Fate that discomforts our thoughts
> Is not always written in past events:
> Sometimes one is broken, when another other is saved,
> And what destroys the one preserves the other.

For Sainte-Beuve, Corneille's verses expressed the one true philosophy of history, a view of history that no longer knew any absolutes and in which experience was constantly questioned. For Sainte-Beuve, there was revenge in world history, but no longer any comprehensive retribution. Literature, by contrast, was the realm where each work was entitled to its 'juste rétribution' and hope remained that appropriate criticism would produce the compensatory justice of comprehensive retribution. Revenge is the key word in Sainte-Beuve's œuvre, retribution the key word of his thinking.

In *Contre Sainte-Beuve*, Marcel Proust speaks of him as the 'Buffon de la critique'. But if Proust had known Linnaeus's work, he would have called Sainte-Beuve, more justifiably, the 'Linnaeus of criticism'. For Proust himself had placed Sainte-Beuve in a context that makes his proximity to Linnaeus's convictions obvious.

Proust claims not to take Sainte-Beuve's scientific method seriously – not because Sainte-Beuve was not doing science, but because science made it impossible for him to see what is crucial for literature. The literary world

---

[4] Corneille, *Cinna*, II,1:388–92; trans. John Farquhar.

is impoverished, not enriched, by the scientific analyses that a Sainte-Beuve mimics. But Proust did not write about Sainte-Beuve as one writes about someone one dislikes, but as one writes about someone one must keep at a distance, to prevent him from coming too close. Proust saw more clearly than anyone else how natural history and morality become closely linked in Sainte-Beuve's criticism. Proust also recognized Sainte-Beuve's originality in his attempt to write a natural history of literature.

The crucial passage in Proust's struggle with Sainte-Beuve is ambiguous. It reads:

Just as we have seen how Sainte-Beuve believed that the life of the salons, of which he was fond, was indispensable to literature and accompanied it over the centuries – here at the court of Louis XIV, there in the select circle of the Directory – so also did this creator who worked all week, often without rest even on Sundays, and received his honorarium each Monday from the pleasure he gave to good judges and the blows he administered to the wicked, conceive of all literature as a series of *Lundis* which might perhaps be re-read, but which, in order to please, had to be written for their own time, with the opinion of good judges in mind and without too much concern for posterity. *He sees literature in terms of the category of time.*[5]

Proust, the harsh critic of Sainte-Beuve, had an inkling of the resoluteness with which the critic Sainte-Beuve tried to restore literary justice by means of retribution and to preserve the order of literature in a world full of disorder.


## The church of the intellectuals

The revolutionary upheavals of the nineteenth century offered Sainte-Beuve more than one opportunity to take a position on the development of literature and intellectual policy, the *politique de l'esprit*, as Paul Valéry would later call it. The tone of these essays is elegiac; what Sainte-Beuve describes are stages in a history of decay. 'The old ones have finally lost the game against the modern ones', he once says – and counts himself among the former. But his laments are not unbridled: 'To avoid being intimidated by the word', he advises when 'littérature industrielle' is first mentioned, 'and to combat better the matter it refers to, one must first of all exaggerate nothing.'[6] Discipline, in any case a prominent characteristic of Sainte-Beuve, always makes his laments comprehensible and gives

---

[5] Marcel Proust, *Contre Sainte-Beuve* pref. de Bernard de Fallois (Paris: Gallimard/folio essais, 1994), p. 139.
[6] Charles-Augustin Sainte-Beuve, 'De la littérature industrielle' (1 September 1839) in *Portraits contemporains*, 5 vols. (Paris: Calmann-Lévy, 1881–2), vol. II, p. 446.

even his polemics a rational character since they are calculated and well considered.

Sainte-Beuve sees in the decadence of literature, in the slump of literary morality, a consequence of the general industrialization and democratization that affected all areas of modern society and can no longer be stemmed. Literature has turned from a vocation into a profession, and he who takes as his slogan *Vivre en écrivant!* ('to live by writing') is no longer announcing an intellectual programme, but merely providing evidence of employment:

> One must come to terms with the new habits, with the invasion of literary democracy together with the rise of all the other democracies. It makes no difference that this situation is particularly crassly expressed in literature. To write and have something published is less and less something special. At least once in his life, everyone will have his page, his discourse, his publisher's brochure, his toast, everyone will be an author once. From there it is just a small step until everyone writes his own feuilleton. Why not me too? everyone asks. Respectable motives are also present. After all, one has a family, one has married for love, of course one's better half will also write under a pseudonym . . . I, too, write, one must tell oneself when one writes about those who also write a little in order to live.[7]

The decline of literary taste and the shift in the centre of gravity of the literary genres can usually, in the age of payment by the line, be traced to trivial causes: 'There are authors who only write their feuilleton novels in dialogue form now, because that way there is a pause after every sentence and sometimes after every word and one easily gains an extra line.' This is why one must take care not to suspect deep political convictions where the only point is to generate literary added value in the most elementary sense: 'A wag who was once of the profession joked that the word *révolutionnairement*, because it was so long, had particularly profited him.'[8] Now all at once everyone able to write can call himself an *homme de lettres*: the title has lost all its value, and the writer has become a worker, indeed a proletarian, driven by need to produce incessantly.

No one bemoaned the industrialization of literature as emphatically as Sainte-Beuve; yet no critic adapted his own mode of production to this process of industrialization as fully as he did. Sainte-Beuve is a worker harnessed every week to the production of his workpiece, those famous articles that then appeared on the literary market on Monday – even on the holiday Monday that is called 'Saint Lundi' in France. Sainte-Beuve's

---

7 *Ibid.*, p. 454.
8 Charles-Augustin Sainte-Beuve, 'Quelques vérités sur la situation en littérature' (1 July 1843) in *Portraits contemporains*, vol. III, pp. 308–9.

method of literary production is also both modern and pre-modern, because it is a cottage industry: he works as if on a private assembly line, manufacturing his product and then, in a dramatic turnaround, presenting this workpiece to a large, educated public on Monday. Thus, the *Lundis* take on great symbolic significance and testify to the exceptional position of their producer: they appear on the first working day of the week – the worker Sainte-Beuve's only day off.

Saint-Beuve lived the life of a proletarian, as he once wrote to Flaubert, but he would not have wished it otherwise: he had found his calling. Literary activity also ennobled the worker precisely because it was no caprice or pastime, but became hard work. Sainte-Beuve, who, as a reader, loved the society of the seventeenth-century nobility so much, is consciously bourgeois in the act of writing. *Homme de lettres* may no longer be a title of honour in bourgeois society, but it is still an honourable professional title to be earned with great effort and at the price of constant fatigue – another word that appears again and again in Sainte-Beuve's letters. Beyond that, literary work is a compensation for lack of success in private life and for manifold setbacks – it is a strict regime that admirably testifies, though always only part of the time, to control of the emotions.

For Sainte-Beuve, literature was revenge, but it was also succour. Revenge and succour, perhaps salvation – such words embody a religious view of literary life. The misfortune of not being able to believe explains the religious tinge of this intellectual life. It is the age of compensations. In April 1831, Sainte-Beuve wrote to Victor Hugo that he might soon become a Saint-Simonian – in the way one joins a church. Then he would believe in God, be moral and love other people. His words contain no irony. The late faith of the Catholic Sainte-Beuve is of this world; it is orientated not towards the salvation of the soul, but towards the right way to live on earth. Not in his private life, which is not for us to judge, but in the formulation of his basic intellectual ideas, Sainte-Beuve recalls Spinoza, who once said of himself that, since he was an atheist, he must at least live like a saint.

Sainte-Beuve's description of literature and criticism as work, exertion and strain always has a theological colouring. It is not just the work of an individual, it is an individual's work in solitude; it is not just the work of a worker, but of a monk – carried out, in the age of the steam engine, at high speed. A monastic existence under the conditions of industrial society – this is also how Sainte-Beuve understands the context of his intellectual production.

The image of the cloister appears in his writings as often as the image of the worker: these are leitmotifs in his letters, which often seem like epistles. Politically tending to conformity and yet never free of suspicion towards politics, whenever Sainte-Beuve must enter the 'place publique', he tries to cross it as fast as possible, to get back to his cell and his work again.

The nineteenth century was an age in which science and secularization proceeded, but for that very reason it was also an age of compensation, in which many intellectual and artistic activities took on religious qualities. Sainte-Beuve coined an expression for this that can only really be used in French: in connection with Ernest Renan's *Vie de Jésus* ('Life of Jesus'), he speaks in 1863 of the tendency, indeed the necessity, to 'religionize'. In the context of increasing distance from religion and of crises of faith, attitudes with religious features develop everywhere in intellectual Europe.

Typical of these is the key term coined by Coleridge in England: *clerisy*. It meant the community of intellectuals comprising a this-worldly church – *en*-clesia as opposed to *ec*-clesia. This self-description of the intellectual community remained influential down to Julien Benda's *clerc* and the literary Catholicism of a T. S. Eliot. We find a similar concept in Sainte-Beuve. On 15 May 1867, the aged and increasingly coura-geous Sainte-Beuve took a stand in the Senate on the dispute then raging in France on freedom of instruction. One month earlier, he had reso-lutely defended Renan's appointment to the Collège de France, which the Catholic right wing had massively attacked. Sainte-Beuve spoke, not without irony, of the 'grand diocèse' that shaped the intellectual life of France:

Gentlemen, there is a grand diocese, without a precisely defined circle of believers, that extends across all of France, indeed throughout the world, and that has its branches and enclaves even in the congregations of the prelates themselves; it is a diocese that, without violence and scandal, gains importance and grows ever larger, and that, in its breadth and expansion, counts in its number spirits of varying degrees of emancipation, but who all agree on one point: that the most important thing is to free oneself from absolute authority and blind submission; it is an immense, or if you prefer, an indeterminate and unbounded diocese that counts as its own thousands of deists, spiritualists, and adherents of so-called natural religion, pantheists, positivists, realists . . . sceptics and researchers of every kind, proponents of common sense, and sectarians of pure science: this diocese (or whatever you wish to call this province) is everywhere to be found . . .

Gentlemen, this grand diocese, this great province of the mind and of reason has neither priests nor bishops, it is true, and no consistorial president – but what use are titles here – or head who could speak in its name, but each of its members has the duty, when the opportunity arises, and feels compelled by his conscience to defend the rights of truth, science, and free research.[9]

9  Charles-Augustin Sainte-Beuve, quoted after Maxime Leroy, *La Pensée de Sainte-Beuve* (Paris: Gallimard, 1940), pp. 105–6.

Sainte-Beuve's words express clearly and incisively the mood of a European intelligentsia that has lost its faith and no longer feels bound by ecclesiastical ordinances, but is filled instead with all the stronger a yearning for community. He knows he is in agreement here with such people as Coleridge, Carlyle and Matthew Arnold. But in addition, Sainte-Beuve has a premonition of attitudes that will shape the intellectual climate of the turn of the century and the 1920s.

Sainte-Beuve's criticisms look forward to and prefigure Julien Benda's *clerc* and the socially free-floating intelligentsia of Karl Mannheim. Sainte-Beuve himself perceived his own time as an interval between two long waves, 'an interlude of chaos and confusion', but he saw himself as one of a generation which, in social isolation and intellectual independence, had not yet succumbed to the great confusion.

Here lie Sainte-Beuve's ambition and fate, which typify those of the European intellectuals. Their attempt not only to preserve an inner independence, but also to develop it into a kind of intellectual community, is courageous and admirable. But the hope was illusory that they could thereby create a society within society. Literary people like Sainte-Beuve played coquettishly with their distance from society and their lack of social influence – but, individually and as a group, they were also convinced that they had insights whose implementation could change the very foundations of modern life. Melancholy and utopia are interlinked. In the nineteenth century, the intellectuals' wishful thinking had not yet been tested; its effects were purely regional. Not until the twentieth century did the great secular religions – fascism and communism – offer the *clercs*, who had supposedly repudiated every faith and every church, the possibility of taking an active part in realizing the new communal utopias that ended in ideological terror. It now became clear what a fall threatened the intellectuals, who had seen no risk, only an exclusive chance to further their knowledge, in their free-floating existence. Carried along by their active contemporaries, intellectuals became the most effective and banal accomplices of evil. Today, after the fall of communism, intellectuals are gradually beginning to realize that they are not betraying their calling when they join a culture of compromise, and to understand that unrestricted thought, and action with a medium-term perspective, need not be antitheses. Our world may thus become more boring, but it will be a happy boredom after the catastrophes that the twentieth century unleashed. However distant he may otherwise appear to us, we are reminded of this by the great literary critic, Charles-Augustin Sainte-Beuve.

# 21

# Hippolyte Taine (1828–1893)

## HILARY S. NIAS

From his early youth Hippolyte Taine's ambition was to be a philosopher. He would probably have shrugged his shoulders in stoical resignation to see that his posthumous fame was that of a critic of literature and of art. He did not hold a high opinion of the traditional critic, whom he compared to a surgeon working, scalpel in hand, to dissect a body. In a student essay, he had asked, 'What would you say of a doctor who, wishing to demonstrate the life and beauty of a creature, began by killing it?' On the threshold of the Second Empire, however, Sainte-Beuve was promoting a new form of criticism where, rather than 'resembling a pirate and rejoicing in shipwrecks', the critic became 'the pilot who comes to the aid of those overtaken by the storm as they leave port'.[1] Incorporating ideas from Chateaubriand and Mme de Staël, who in *Mémoires d'outre-tombe* and *De L'Allemagne* respectively, had argued for an examination of literature based on its cultural roots in the country of origin, he advocated a greater objectivity in criticism. Literary works were now to be judged not according to rigid rules, but in 'psychological' terms and within their historical context. Criticism should move away from the emotively charged and judgemental stance of Voltaire towards a more objective and professional assessment of both the good and bad points in a work. For Taine, then, the emphasis was on rational analysis of the ideas and historical context of the author. Rules in literature, he argued, are not constant but fluctuate with changes in social and cultural history.

Taine had a stormy career at the Lycée Bourbon, and subsequently his thesis on 'Les Sensations', expounding a new theory of the Self, was rejected by the Sorbonne. After three tedious years of intellectual exile teaching in provincial schools, he returned to Paris, where he apparently abandoned his philosophical ambitions and turned his hand to journalism, contributing a series of articles to the *Revue des deux mondes* and the *Revue de l'instruction publique*.

As with his contemporaries, among them Prévost-Paradol, Renan, Sarcey and Suckau, Taine's strategies for intellectual survival may have

---

[1] Charles-Augustin Sainte-Beuve, *Les causeries du lundi*, 16 vols. (Paris, Garnier frères, n.d.), vol. XV, p. 373.

been a response to historical and sociological factors. First, there was a powerful cultural prejudice that elevated art above religion. Second, rapid scientific advance was generating a view that almost everything was susceptible to scientific analysis. The positivist school of philosophy, inaugurated by Comte, had laid the groundwork here for extending the methods of natural science to the world of ideas (though Taine himself seems unlikely to have encountered Comte's writing before 1860).[2] Finally, the new historical writing of the period, informed by the findings of geological, archaeological and philological research, also played a part in this transformation of the self-understanding of intellectuals and the erosion of their self-confidence. Deeper insights into the psychology of the past helped to relativize modern certainties. All this took place in a time of strong reaction against revolutionary thought: in sixty years, France had endured three revolutions, and a general mood of retreat from confrontation and disorder echoed the attitude of its intelligentsia.

In Taine's case, however, conformity with the current trend was based not on political conviction but on a conscious strategy for intellectual survival. To the essayist Jean-Jacques Weiss, he had confessed his inability to make his philosophical ideas palatable, and had written to his friend Suckau of his unwillingness to espouse the 'banalité officielle' and his decision instead to employ a subterfuge: he consequently applied his psychological and philosophical theories indirectly in his literary criticism, by first examining in detail how a given author or thinker had reached his conclusions in a text, then measuring his own ideas against theirs.[3] The approach was new, as was his principal theory that all human endeavour is inescapably defined by the historical moment in which it was created, by the cultural setting in which it took shape and by the national characteristics of its author. Taine called his analysis according to these criteria his 'method', and its ground rules are adhered to throughout his writing, whether in works of literary criticism such as his essay on Livy, the *Philosophes français du XIXe siècle* (1857), the three volumes of *Essais de critique et d'histoire* (1858, 1865, 1894 posth.), and the *Histoire de la littérature anglaise* (completed in 1864), or in other studies such as *Philosophie de l'art* (1865) and *Les Origines de la France contemporaine* (1875–93). These ground rules have their roots in his earliest aspirations to draw up a new definition of the nature of the self within the metaphysical tradition but expressed in the new language of scientific inquiry, a definition he would not publish until 1870 in *De l'intelligence*, the work that he valued above all his others.

---

[2] D. G. Charlton, *Positivist Thought in France during the Second Empire* (Oxford University Press, 1959), p. 21.
[3] *H. Taine: sa vie et sa correspondance*, 4 vols. (Paris: Hachette, 1905–8), vol. I, p. 281. Hereafter cited as *VC*.

The examiners of his doctoral thesis on La Fontaine (1853) seem to have been oblivious to the fact that Taine had managed, using this method, to slip in two philosophical theories which betrayed the increasing influence of science on him: literature, he argued, was a system of literary types, and poetry was the supreme type within this system. As he claimed in an introductory broadside, 'criticism can be turned into a kind of philosophical research' and the essay effectively becomes, as Simon Jeune suggests, 'a profession of anti-conformist faith, hostile to traditional religious positions and moral justifications'.[4] Sainte-Beuve recognized Taine's approach as an 'artifice with surprising results', for what the thesis actually provided was an indirect method of discussing the nature of Taine's hobby-horse: the self. Leaving aside his youthful search for the mysterious origin or hypothetical purpose of the self, Taine here claims to offer a 'scientific' analysis of its operation through the imagination and the language of the poet.[5] From the outset, he justifies drawing general conclusions about beauty from the particular beauties of an individual fable by pointing out that zoologists have discovered general natural laws by studying a single insect. He argues that, in this manner, the essential nature of a work can be established. The language he uses is, however, far from scientific. Poetry's spontaneous, involuntary organization of the world is caused, he says, by the poet's 'internal idea', by his 'obscure internal wisdom'. The expression betrays Taine as a 'dissatisfied romantic'[6] and there are echoes, too, of Hegel's distillation of the absolute or essence out of the particular. Taine nevertheless described Hegel's system as 'artificial' and 'useless'; it produced, he claimed, no more than 'a pyramid of ideas' (letters of 25 February 1852 and 28 March 1853). The academics, meanwhile, criticized him for an *over*-emphasis on science, an exaggerated systematization and too great a levity of tone. Nonetheless, they could not deny the authority and novelty of Taine's critical approach and awarded him the coveted doctorate.

In 1853, with some of his confidence restored and in a bid for greater recognition, Taine submitted a massive 'essay' on Livy for a competition at the Académie Française. It is here that he first uses the term for which he is perhaps best known, the *faculté maîtresse* or master faculty, to describe the central characteristic in a given author and his work. But Taine's style was overwhelmingly systematic and historical, and his 'method' so transparent and dominant that it was only after many revisions that the essay was eventually published in 1856.

[4] Simon Jeune, 'Taine et la guerre de 1870' in *Les Ecrivains français devant la guerre de 1870 et la Commune* (Paris: A. Colin, 1972).

[5] Hippolyte Taine, *Essai sur les fables de La Fontaine* (University of Michigan Library, 2009), pp. 19, 122.

[6] Simon Jeune, *Poésie et système: Taine interprète de La Fontaine* (Paris: Armand Collin, 1968), p. 137.

Soon after this, the Librairie Hachette decided to publish as a single volume the essays on French nineteenth-century philosophers which
Taine had been contributing piecemeal to the *Revue de l'instruction
publique*. *Les Philosophes classiques du* xixe *siècle en France* (1857),
as this work would subsequently be known, finally brought him fame.
In it, he restated his claim that no work can be judged exclusively as
the product of an artist's genius, but that it is fundamentally constrained
on the one hand by his own character, and on the other by the race,
culture and times (*race, milieu, moment*) that he lives in, which combine
to define his 'dominant faculty'. Taine's 'method' and the topoi *faculté
maîtresse* and *race, milieu, moment* would become hallmarks of his writing. *Les Philosophes classiques* appeared in the same year as Flaubert's
*Madame Bovary*. Both became *causes célèbres* and were seen as gestures of defiance towards the intellectual and artistic establishment. The
tenor of Taine's book was so consonant with contemporary aesthetic,
scientific and historical thought that it found an immediate resonance
in many among Taine's audience, and he found himself launched on a
full-blown career as a literary critic, having finally attained the fame he
sought:

My sole aim is to gain notoriety: when I write my psychology, I should like at
least part of the public to say to itself: here is an animal with two feet and
equipped with a pen, with ideas of such and such a colour and such and such a
style; that biped may say some clear and novel things on the subject. Let's read
[him].[7]

Adhering to his method in *Les Philosophes classiques*, Taine systematically dissects a group of recognized thinkers of the preceding generation, known as the Eclectics. The distinguishing characteristics of
Laromiguière, Royer-Collard, Maine de Biran, Cousin and Jouffroy are
each in turn defined psychologically and within the context of their
Frenchness, their eclecticism and the fact they were writing in the early
part of the nineteenth century, before a minute inspection of their philosophies culminates in their comprehensive demolition. The essays challenged Eclectic thought with brilliant but ruthless criticism, allowing
Taine at the same time to elaborate his own ideas. He maintains that
he will expound not a new philosophy, but merely a method, one which
has already been advanced by Hegel and which combines the best of both
the spiritualist and positivist thinkers of the day. A note accompanying
a copy of the work, sent to his friend Ernest Renan, makes his intention
clear: 'One of your collaborators... offers a little book of criticism to a
critic, a little book of philosophy to a philosopher, who under the pretext

---

[7] Letter to Suckau, 8 July 1856, VC, vol. II, p. 135.

of avoiding philosophy, includes it everywhere . . . a little book of history to the one who introduces psychology into history' (*VC*, vol. II, p. 147).

The Hegelian method to which Taine refers is one in which history evolves by a dialectical process, a process that can be clearly observed, for example, in Taine's analysis of the introspective Maine de Biran, who, through excessive metaphysical thinking and misuse of language, creates out of the self a separate being; he is described as one of those thinkers who 'bear the imprint of their own faculties; whose method manifests the nature of their mind. If their mind is flawed, so is their system.'[8] Writing about Victor Cousin, Taine declares that philosophies, being a human product, have a cause; that they can be explained only by their 'milieu' and that the style in which a mind expresses itself reveals its 'dominant quality' – in this case, that of moral oratory (*Phil. class.*, pp. 80–1). Both thinkers are shown to be the product of the metaphysical thought of the eighteenth century, in which they were born. Taine still maintains adamantly: 'I do not claim to have a system: I am at most following a method. A system is an explanation of the whole, and indicates a work that is complete; a method is a way of working and indicates a work to be achieved' (*Phil. class.*, p. 153). He concludes his study of the Eclectic philosophers in language more redolent of philosophy than of literary criticism, declaring that 'The exterior expresses the interior, history uncovers the psychology and the face reveals the soul' (*Phil. class.*, p. 340); if it is possible to make manifest the 'dominant faculty' of a people, so it should be possible, following this kind of analysis, to deduce a *loi génératrice* or supreme law governing existence.

The success of *Les Philosophes classiques* was underlined by the fact that the doyen of literary journalism, Charles-Augustin Sainte-Beuve, devoted admiring articles to Taine in two of his *Causeries du lundi* in successive editions of *Le Moniteur* in 1857, acknowledging the originality of Taine's notion of *race, milieu, moment* as a framework for literary criticism. Despite the mild reproof of his dogmatic tone and disregard for the feelings of those he criticized, Taine's reputation was made.

Taine's method is marked by a number of influences, giving rise over the years to an assessment by some of his contemporaries that he lacked originality, one of his fiercest critics, Elme Caro, even charging that his 'system' was merely a repackaging of Diderot's materialism with an admixture of Spinoza, Condillac and Hegel. Taine's thinking was unquestionably informed by his reading of philosophy both at the Lycée Bourbon and at the Ecole Normale, and its development can be followed in the letters that he wrote to teachers and friends, both at this time and subsequently.

---

[8] Hippolyte Taine, *Les Philosophes classiques du* XIXe *siècle en France* (Paris: Hachette, 1912), p. 62. Hereafter cited as *Phil. class.*

A formidably industrious student, Taine worked his way through the great philosophers and found each, in turn, to be wanting. It has often been stated that the determinism of Spinoza and the historicism of Hegel were the great influences on his thought, but it is important to recognize that, as he studied them, the flaws in each caused him bitter disillusionment. At the age of twenty-one he wrote to a fellow student condemning the errors he had detected in Spinoza: 'He is only my master in part. I believe him to be wrong on several fundamental issues' (*VC*, vol. 1, p. 75). Later the intoxication of reading Hegel, who was 'a Spinoza multiplied by Aristotle' (*VC*, vol. 1, p. 154), would lead him to exclaim:

I shall probably never again experience impressions equal to those which he gave me... When for the first time one scales the heights of the *Logik* and the *Encyclopaedia*, one experiences emotions similar to those felt at the summit of a great mountain. The air is thin, one's vision is disturbed... one could believe oneself to have reached the summit of science and a view over the entire world.

(*Phil. class.*, pp. 132–3)

Hegel too, though, would fall from grace. 'Alas, there goes another illusion!' cried Taine; 'it is grand, but it is not true metaphysics; the method is artificial, and the much vaunted construction of the absolute is useless' (*VC*, vol. 1, p. 217).

In the preface to a later (1868) edition of *Les Philosophes classiques*, Taine declares that all he is seeking to do is to justify and to apply Hegel's idea of nature as 'an order of forms which depend on one another and which compose an indivisible whole'. And it can be argued that his method includes elements of Hegel's dialectical and historical approach: a thesis meets with an antithesis, and out of this arises a synthesis, which in turn serves as the new thesis, and so on. It is not difficult to see how, at the simplest level, such a formula informs Taine's criticism. In *Les Philosophes classiques*, as we have seen, the arguments of each thinker are first put forward and their good points extolled. Subsequently, a contrasting approach – Taine's – is suggested and a new synthesis proposed. This scarcely amounts to a wholehearted endorsement of Hegel, and any Hegelian or Spinozist elements in his thought may have been less a consequence of his conviction of their rightness and more the result of what his old teacher, Charles Bénard, described in Taine as a 'wonderful power of assimilation'. This absorbent capacity accords well with Taine's own description of the determination of an individual by his nature and context. It also explains the many contemporary ideas that abound in his work, although a Darwinian explanation might equally well be posited, expressed in the language of evolution, adaptation and relativity.

The success of *Les Philosophes classiques* encouraged the Librairie Hachette to publish in 1858 a further collection of critical and historical essays, *Essais de critique et d'histoire* (1858). Often these were part of a reciprocal exercise in which Taine and his contemporaries promoted each other's work by writing positive reviews, but in many cases Taine found occasion to raise and discuss philosophical issues. In the preface to these essays, he defends a prescriptive criticism which sees the creative artist as 'a machine consisting of ordered wheels' driven by a 'dominant faculty' – a factor determined by the great weight of history. Jules Michelet, for example, was a historian in whom the poetic faculty, influenced by the Romantic passion of his times, encouraged a greater concern for 'the pathetic' and 'the interesting' than for truth. This theory, Taine repeats, is one already proposed by Aristotle and Hegel and not by himself; he is merely applying it. Against his objectors, he argues in the preface that this is the correct approach for a critic who wishes to philosophize. For he is not an artist appreciating the beauty of a creation, but a philosopher, and 'If it is beautiful to expose a person, it may [also] be interesting to make him understood.' The central question for him is not 'who?' but 'why?' As his contemporary Renan wrote: 'The duty of the critic should not be to regret that men have not been different from what they were, but to explain what they were.'[9] The whole of the previous century concentrated on seeking out the essential nature of things; history ceased to lose itself in a plethora of detail and sought rather to trace events and characters back to the dominant force of the age from which they came. Only by mastering this method, claims Taine, shall we be able to foresee the future.

In the concluding page of his preface Taine speaks of the vision that may be attained by his method of tracing the faculties and passions which in ourselves are only meagre, but which in great figures and great movements can become sublime. An essay on Balzac, first published in the *Journal des débats* in the same year, sets out very clearly the ideas underlying Taine's theory of criticism. First, he describes the essential nature of the individual writer:

What we call the mind of a man is his ordinary way of thinking. There is in each of us a certain habit that leads us on, obliging us to look first there, then here, lingeringly or briefly, slowly or quickly, suggesting here images, there philosophy, further on mockery, to the point that we will always fall into [this way of thinking] whatever work we are doing, inevitably, because this necessity has become our nature, our will and our inclination. Scientists call this a method; artists, a talent.[10]

Balzac had wanted, Taine says, to write a 'natural history of Man' (*Nouveaux essais*, p. 17). Taine admires his 'systematic' approach. He is not

---

9   Jeune, 'Taine et la guerre de 1870', p. 137.
10  Hippolyte Taine, *Nouveaux essais de critique et d'histoire* (Paris: Hachette, 1909), p. 15. Hereafter cited as *Nouveaux essais*.

spontaneously creative; writing for him is hard work. It is not until he
escapes from the scientist in himself that he becomes an artist, at which
point his creation becomes, in Taine's word, a 'hallucination' (p. 28). In
contrast with a moralizing poet like Corneille, Balzac, the naturalist, sees
cause and effect: something moves the 'spiritual automaton' within him
and thus activates the rest. For the naturalist writer 'virtue is a product
like wine or vinegar . . . fabricated like any other, by a series of established
processes with a measurable and certain effect' (p. 60). But Taine would
have liked to see this deterministic imagery carried further and applied
not just to the frailties of man but also to his more elevated forms of
thought. With another echo of Hegelian thought, he bewails the lack of a
historical sense in Balzac which might have encouraged him to trace the
origins and consequences of the characteristics he observed. What he saw
was an 'optical illusion' that both guided him and led him astray.

Over the next few years Taine would gradually publish, in the *Revue
des deux mondes*, the essays that would eventually make up his ambitious
*Histoire de la littérature anglaise* (the first three volumes of which were
published in 1863). The introduction to this work is notably different in
style and content from the *History* itself and could stand alone as a manifesto for Taine's concept of criticism. It offers the most familiar exposition
of his theory, as he elaborates his method of interpretation according to
the now familiar 'dominant faculty' and '*race, milieu, moment*':

> The primitive impetus will always prove to be some very general disposition of
> the mind and the soul, either innate and naturally related to the race, or
> acquired and produced by some circumstance affecting the race . . . So that the
> total movement of each individual civilization can be considered as the effect of
> a permanent force that, at any moment, varies its influence by modifying the
> circumstances under which it operates.[11]

He emphasizes the fundamental causal importance of the physical and
historical context in creating what he calls the elementary moral state of
a people. This context, he says, is like a 'lake' or 'profound reservoir'
into which the centuries have poured their contribution; geography and
climate together with the social conditions resulting from the prevailing
religion also contribute. The national character that arises from these
determining factors does not then operate on a 'tabula rasa', but on a
'tabula' already bearing the traces created by previous artistic works.
The result is that one *idée maîtresse* arises and then fades and dies, to
be followed by another which in turn is conditioned and directed by
its predecessor. The operation of this intellectual process, he says, is a

[11] Hippolyte Taine, *Histoire de la littérature anglaise*, 5 vols. (Paris: Hachette, 1866–71),
vol. I, pp. xxii–iii. Hereafter cited as *Hist. angl.*

mechanical one and the only difference between it and physical processes is that its properties are more difficult to quantify (*Hist. angl.*, vol. 1, p. xxiii).

   The forcefulness of Taine's diagnosis derives in part from its mechanical and scientific imagery and the assertion that it is the scientific method that will bring the greatest advances in understanding human psychology. The contemporary fascination with new scientific discoveries had also led other thinkers to attempt to apply the language and method of the new disciplines to less 'positive', or concrete, areas of enquiry. Renan in particular had called, in his *De l'origine du langage* (1848), for the search for an 'embryogeny' of the human spirit (a neologism coined as recently as 1836), in language very close to Taine's aspiration to a 'zoology of the human spirit, with psychology as its physiological and anatomical principle' (*VC*, vol. 1, p. 120). By now, the second and more liberal decade of the Second Empire was unfolding, and radical writers like Taine felt emboldened to express their avant-garde views more freely. Thus, as Taine pursued this 'scientific' line with increasing emphasis on psychology as his instrument of inquiry, he portrays Bacon, for example, as enjoying remarkable self-confidence, Shakespeare as inspired by a 'clear-sighted madness', Dickens as driven by an intense imagination verging on monomania, and Byron as afflicted with a peculiar disposition towards extreme emotions, which sometimes induced madness and sometimes the sublime.

   The most controversial claim in the introduction to the *Histoire de la littérature anglaise*, however, and the one that generated the strongest reaction, was Taine's contention, harking back to his essay on Balzac, that 'Whether facts are physical or intellectual... they are always caused by something... Vice and virtue are products like vitriol and sugar' (*Hist. angl.*, vol. 1, p. xv). The language here was not new, but the very determinism that attracted Taine to Balzac now became a source, in his own work, of strong opposition from fellow thinkers and writers. There was an immediate outcry from the religious camp on the part of the bishop of Orléans, Monseigneur Dupanloup, who claimed that Taine's teaching was liable to encourage materialism and atheism in the young, and even in the world of letters there was disquiet. The young Emile Zola, who would adopt Taine's aphoristic 'le vice et la vertu sont des produits comme le vitriol et le sucre' as the epigraph to his novel *Thérèse Raquin* (1867), evidently admired both the language and the scientific aspect of his approach, claiming Taine as the leader of the Naturalist movement (a distinction Taine firmly rejected). In *Mes haines* (1866), however, Zola condemned Taine's over-systematic and mechanical method, maintaining that it reflected and arose out of Taine's personality, and was too rigid to reach the truth. He also criticized Taine for affording, as a result, too little importance to the individual personality, arguing that he had been overwhelmed by the 'crazy [desire] of our century to know everything and to reduce everything to equations'.[12]

Nevertheless, the primary effect of the publication of the *Histoire de la littérature anglaise* was firmly to establish Taine's credentials as a leading figure in the world of letters. He was duly appointed, in 1864, to the chair of art and aesthetics at the Ecole des Beaux-Arts where he was followed down the street, after his inaugural lecture, by a cheering crowd of admiring students. True to form, Taine declared that, although art appears to be the most arbitrary and spontaneous of human works, it is in fact, like all human works, subject to 'precise conditions' and 'fixed laws': 'My whole duty, is to expose the facts to you and to demonstrate to you how they are produced.'[13] The students regarded him as a revolutionary and applauded his break with the traditionalist and conventional teachings of his predecessor, Viollet-le-Duc.

An apparently ineluctable determinism permeates the collected essays of the *Histoire de la littérature anglaise*. As Taine treats successive literary periods, he demonstrates how each one was the necessary condition for the emergence of the literary figures he describes and how they in turn could not have been different. Of Bacon, for example, he states that his ideas could not have prospered in a time of discouragement and decadence (*Hist. angl.*, vol. I, p. 396), but that equally, he was unable to follow them through, for 'methods and philosophies arise out of the spirit of an age' (vol. I, p. 401) and Bacon and his century were still enmeshed in scholastic thought. Shakespeare, too, was 'of his great generation and of his great century'; he was also conditioned by the fact that, in common with his contemporaries, he had learned to overcome the onslaught of passion and enthusiasm, allowing his genius to exploit his billowing imagination, rather than being overwhelmed by it, so that it became 'a flowering rather than a sickness' (*Hist. angl.*, vol. II, p. 184). As for Byron: conditioned from the outset by a heredity in which intemperance, madness and violence were very pronounced, he represented more than any other the contemporary *maladie du siècle* – the belief underlying all the art and religion of the century that there is 'some monstrous disproportion between the parts of our make-up, and that all human destiny is vitiated by this discord' (*Hist. angl.*, vol. IV, p. 420). In the final pages of his essay on Byron, Taine gives full voice to his persuasion that science now offers the true route to knowledge and the understanding of human nature, as he reiterates his deterministic mantra:

[12] Hilary Nias, *The Artificial Self: The Psychology of Hippolyte Taine* (Oxford: Legenda, 1999), p. 123.

[13] Hippolyte Taine, *Philosophie de l'art*, 2 vols. (Paris: Hachette, 1903), vol. I, p. 14.

Up till now, in our judgement of Man, we have taken as our masters
revelationists and poets, and like them we took as certain truth the dreams of
our imagination and the imperious suggestions of our hearts... At last science
approaches, and approaches Man; it has overtaken the visible and palpable
world of stars, stones and plants, where it was scornfully confined; armed with
the precise and penetrating instruments, of which three hundred years of
experience have demonstrated the precision and measured the reach, it takes on
the soul. Thought and its development... its deep corporeal roots, its infinite
vegetation through history... are now the object [of its inquiry...] [Man] is a
product, like anything else.                      (*Hist. angl.*, vol. IV, pp. 421–2)

And it is not only man that is material for such treatment, for Taine
asserts that it can equally well be applied to art, morality, politics and
religion.

Despite his dogmatic tone, there is at the end of this passage a curious note of mitigation perhaps, rather than apology, as he attempts to
communicate an almost Romantic yearning for a softer and vaguer explanation and a desire to portray science in this light. Describing how virtue
and human reason are just as susceptible to analysis as any other part of
our being, he asks:

Who can be indignant at a living geometry? Who on the other hand will not be
moved to admiration by the spectacle of the grandiose powers which, situated at
the heart of things, are constantly growing in the limbs of the old world,
spreading the wave over the infinite network of the arteries and unfurling over
the whole surface the eternal flower of youth and beauty.

Such purple prose is more than a genuflection towards those of his readers who were resistant to his otherwise overwhelming scientism. It also
reflects a personal discomfort with the geometrical analysis of the non-
geometrical. He may have felt that it was more likely to be successful in
reaching the truth than the 'Chinese puzzle' of Hegel's language, but he
could sense that it failed to convey his own intellectual excitement. Similar effusions are to be found throughout his work and eventually come to
his rescue in his *magnum opus* on the self, where scientific analysis finally
lets him down.

In 1866 a second edition of the *Essais de critique et d'histoire* was published, with a second preface. Here, Taine again addresses criticism of
what is now being called his 'system'. He reaffirms that he will admit to
no more than a 'method', to which, he believes, anything from individuals
to philosophy and the state can legitimately be subjected for analysis. In
this way, it will soon become apparent that no event is ever more than a
movement in a current. Answers uncovered in this way are not, however,
'abstract formulas', but living forces which govern the world of matter
in the same way that they govern the mind. From this, argues Taine, it

follows that the self remains free and responsible in spite of predeter-
mination: it has the power to influence and change the development of
things by locating their cause.

It is not difficult to see how in 1870, before the stability of the Second Empire was shaken to its roots by the Franco-Prussian War, Taine
was at last emboldened to publish his major work of psychology, *De
l'intelligence*. Here he employs the same methodical and painstaking
scientific analysis, invoking the same historical process with the same
overtones of German Romanticism. His lectures at the Ecole des Beaux-
Arts were published gradually in successive volumes: in the first of these,
*Philosophie de l'art* (1865–9), Taine subjects great artists through the
ages to the same categorization according to their country of birth, the
culture of their age and their historical moment.[14]

Meanwhile, criticism of Taine was mounting on moral, political and
philosophical fronts. Bourget deplored the irreligiosity of Taine's views
and Elme Caro joined the attack from his position in the academic establishment, deploring the lack of moral leadership in Taine's philosophy.
But most relevant to this study is the attack made by Henri Bergson in
1888. Without actually naming Taine, he criticized both the determinism
of Taine's exegesis and the mechanistic language he employs in his 'psychology', saying that the use of concrete imagery to describe the immate-
rial loses sight of the deeper, inexpressible self, that the words falsify the
intuitive sense. The complaint echoes that of Zola twenty years earlier
and foreshadows what today is seen as the one of the most distinctive –
and most debated – characteristics of Taine's critical writing. If Taine
is today considered by some to be an unsatisfactory literary critic – too
methodical, too generalizing and not sufficiently attentive to the text –
this is not surprising, for reasons that have been examined. Indeed, he
said of himself: 'I am not an artist. My whole aim is to write my idea.
As to the format, it is simply a way of making myself better understood'
(20 December 1859, *VC*, vol. II, p. 183). It was already clear from his
declaration in the preface to his first volume of essays that Taine's interest
lay with the author and not with the text – a fact that has contributed
to his posthumous renown. He pays little attention to the actual texts
of the works he uses in his studies of various authors. He may cite a text
to exemplify the rhetorical turn of Livy's mind, or one by Shakespeare
to demonstrate the fertility of the playwright's imagination. But he was
preoccupied with the process by which the creative urge in the author,
conditioned by his *race, milieu, moment*, produces the work of art, rather

---

[14] Taine's art criticism is examined in more detail in Hilary Nias, 'Hippolyte Taine' in *Key
Writers on Art: From Antiquity to the Nineteenth Century*, ed. Chris Murray (London:
Routledge, 2003), pp. 212–18.

than with its composition and content. In a review of Camille Selden's 'L'esprit moderne en Allemagne' of 1869, he stated that the value of words was only to be understood in psychological terms,[15] and in the preface to the *Histoire* he reiterates that the value of a text is measured by its psychological depth (*Hist. angl.*, vol. I, pref., p. xlvii). He would have been mystified by the notion that a text should be considered in isolation from its author.

Taine's 'idea' concerned the nature of the self. His ambition was to be a philosopher but his 'method' of inquiry was that of science and he applied it to all aspects of humanity, to literature, to art, to history and, above all, to psychology. His approach was prescriptive and the templates of a *faculté maîtresse* and of *race, milieu, moment* were applied rigorously and relentlessly in all his research. In the work he prized most, *De l'intelligence*, he sought to define the essence of man by deducing a central and unalterable element, the *faculté maîtresse*, that lay at the root of all thought and all action and which was subsequently modified by external effects. In the essays on criticism and the *Histoire*, he demonstrated how this same essential quality explained the nature of each author's work and how it was influenced by the geography, culture and history in which the individual under scrutiny lived. In art the process was identical: the creations of all great artists were explained as the direct result of an internal agent whose temperament was qualified by the cultural tradition, climate and environment of their place of birth. And in history, the process was identical: all events and all historical figures were the end product of the combination of these factors.

Seen by his contemporaries as the dominant intellectual figure in France in the nineteenth century, Taine fell into comparative obscurity for a long time after his death in 1893. More recently, interest in Tainian criticism has revived, and in 1992, Jean-Thomas Nordmann published a lengthy study of Taine, identifying him as one of the founders of comparative criticism.[16] Biography is a *sine qua non* of much modern criticism, and the national and cultural influences on an artist are often highlighted. It may be argued that Taine was instrumental in introducing the now familiar hermeneutical approach to art expounded by Dilthey and Gadamer. The insistence, in their teaching, on the importance of context in the study of literature is one that is today taken for granted, but it was as new in Taine's day as his young admirers claimed, and he contributed significantly to its modern acceptance, inspiring a modern psychological analysis of the artist half a century before Freud appeared on the scene.

[15]  Hans Aarslef, 'Taine et Saussure', *Yale Review*, 68 (1978), p. 71.
[16]  Jean-Thomas Nordmann, *Taine et la critique scientifique* (Paris: Presses Universitaires de France, 1992).

# 22

# Francesco De Sanctis (1817–1883)

RENATE HOLUB

Two remarks are of particular interest to historians of nineteenth-century Italy. One was made by Prince Metternich (1773–1859), major architect of the Treaty of Vienna (1818), in which he denied Italy the 'principle of nationality' as pre-Napoleonic absolutist monarchical regimes and policies were restored. The prince famously declared: 'Italy is a geographic expression.'[1] The second remark was by Massimo d'Azeglio (1798–1866), one of the leading politicians and public intellectuals of the national unification movement, who in 1860 asked: 'L'Italia è fatta, ma chi farà ora gl'italiani?' ('We have made Italy, but who will now make the Italians?').[2] Both remarks capture not only the extraordinary complexity of Italy's birth as a sovereign nation state in nineteenth-century Europe, but also the formidable obstacles encountered by the 'risorgimento', the struggle for Italy's independence, constitutional liberty and unity, which had been pursued by various nationalist groups since 1796.

The pace of this historical process was contingent on a series of interrelated factors. In the first place, Italy had a subaltern status vis-à-vis Europe's great powers and the shifting alliances between the Russian Empire, Prussia, the Habsburg Empire, England, France and the Ottoman Empire in the East. Moreover, Italy had been colonized since the middle of the sixteenth century, resulting in an extraordinarily fragmented and decentralized political system. Colonization had also produced recurrent cultural and political resistance in all corners of Italy, often spearheaded by reform-minded intellectuals. Another crucial factor was the cultural hegemony of the papacy, a powerful administrative apparatus which had wielded great ideological, moral and spiritual power on the peninsula for centuries. And finally, there was the 'Napoleon effect', encompassing not only Napoleon's impact on the organization of a modern infrastructure in Italy and his direct ideological links with the French Revolution of

---

[1] Quoted in Nicola Badaloni, *Storia d'Italia. Vol. III: dal primo settecento all'unità*, 6 vols. (Turin: Einaudi, 1973), vol. III, pp. 240, 1213.
[2] Quoted in E. J. Hobsbawm, *Nations and Nationalism since 1780: Programme, Myth, Reality* (Cambridge University Press, 1990), p. 44.

1789, but also, and more importantly, his sweeping reforms of judicial systems, and the constitutional and administrative changes introduced by the Code Napoléon. His occupation of Italy, which lasted almost twenty years, had thus participated in the modernization and secularization of the peninsula. Few social groups escaped these influences – not least the intelligentsia, which, despite its social and cultural heterogeneity, had at the end of the Napoleonic era taken upon itself the task of creating modern political institutions. As a result, the quest for Italian independence and sovereignty was increasingly associated with the need to limit absolutist power by means of constitutions and parliaments. The life's work of Francesco De Sanctis illustrates the Italian quest to secure full sovereignty, national identity and a liberal citizenry.

De Sanctis was born on 28 March 1817 close to the city of Naples into an educated family of artisans.[3] He was thus a subject of the absolutist Bourbon kingdom of Naples and the Two Sicilies, the largest monarchy in Italy, which, until the arrival of the Napoleonic regime, had been economically, politically and juridically controlled by some of the largest feudal landowners, both papal and secular. De Sanctis's father and uncles were Freemasons. Membership of Freemasonry was not unusual among the educated urban and rural classes since this fraternity constituted a progressive political force; as such it was systematically persecuted by the feudal and absolutist regimes of papal and dynastic princes.[4] In order to continue his education, the young De Sanctis moved to Naples, which had been the historical scene of countless uprisings, revolts and revolutions against all manner of imperialist, feudalist and absolutist dynastic rulers from Spain, Austria, France and the Papal States. Here, he studied literature and history for five years and then continued his secondary studies with an emphasis on European philosophy and literature of the seventeenth century; in short, he followed a humanistic rather than a scientific vocation.

By 1834 De Sanctis had studied law, and he worked closely with his former teacher, the influential liberal aristocrat and pedagogue Masilio Puoto, preparing scholarly editions of early Italian literary figures and revising a book on elementary rules of the Italian language (1839). As instructor at the military college of Ninziatella, De Sanctis taught grammar and the theory and history of literature, including minor literary

3  The biographical data are taken from a variety of sources, including Francesco De Sanctis, *Scelta di scritti critici*, ed. Gianfranco Contini (Turin: Unione Tipografica-Editrice, 1959) and De Sanctis's extensive correspondence in *Epistolario*, eds. Muzio Mazzocchi Alemanni, Giovanni Ferretti *et al.*, in Francesco De Sanctis, *Opere di Francesco De Sanctis*, ed. Carlo Muscetta, 23 vols. (Turin: Einaudi, 1958), vols. XVIII–XXIII (1956).
4  Oreste Dito, *Massoneria, Carboneria ed altre societa segrete nella storia del Risorgimento italiano* (Turin and Rome: Casa Editrice Nazione, Roux & Viarengo, 1905).

figures, non-Italian writers and Romantic literature. During this period, he met Giacomo Leopardi, one of Italy's greatest nineteenth-century poets, who had distanced himself from the Romantic literary tradition typical of the European restoration. De Sanctis's brilliant analysis of Leopardi's poetry would later become one of the pillars of his historical science of literature, in which the practice and theory of literary criticism converged. Indeed, it was during his time as a young professor in Naples that De Sanctis developed his theoretical programme: in the service of the struggle for nationality, independence and constitutionalism, it combined an aesthetic theory of Italian language and literature with a nationalist theory of literary criticism. In De Sanctis's programme, both aesthetic theory and literary criticism functioned as tools in the hands of the 'literary scientist', with the help of which humanist intellectuals undertook the cultural education of Italians for a future nation state and enlightened citizenry.

To this end, De Sanctis developed a programme of militant criticism according to which the intellectual theorist examines the relations not only between literary forms and historical epochs (historical literary criticism), or between the content and form of a poem (aesthetics), but also between the writer or thinker and his or her political environment, and the degree to which such persons promote a 'national principle'. In other words, as a critical theorist, De Sanctis investigates the writer's partiality in the project of the national struggle. Hence De Sanctis's critical theory is underlain by a 'principle of realism', his distinct legacy to subsequent generations of theorists. When Mazzini called for insurrection against the tyranny of absolutism, De Sanctis's participation was a foregone conclusion, for he considered his role to be that not of an observer, but of an actor in the historical process, a role which his theory of literary criticism systematically endorsed.[5]

De Sanctis climbed the barricades of Naples in the spring of 1848 with his students, when uprisings against the restoration regimes throughout Italy had begun. It was the year in which 'all of old Europe entered into a holy alliance to exorcize the spectre of communism', as Marx famously commented.[6] De Sanctis's active resistance to the Bourbon regime had serious consequences. He was arrested, was liberated, sat as parliamentary candidate, served as secretary of a provisional commission of a ministry of education, and was suspended from his post when the *ancien régime* of the Bourbons returned. He fled to the southern city of Cosenza,

---

[5] Luciano Russi, *Nascita di una nazione: ideologie politique per l'Italia (1815–1861)* (Pescara: Clua Editrice, 1981).

[6] Karl Marx and Friedrich Engels, 'Manifesto of the Communist Party' in *The Marx–Engels Reader*, ed. Richard C. Tucker (New York and London: Norton, 1978), pp. 469–501.

only to be arrested in 1850. About 5,000 others shared his fate. In solitary confinement, he found solace in his intellectual interests. He studied German, translated from German a *General History of Poetry*, the *Logic* of Hegel and parts of Goethe's *Faust*, and wrote an essay on Schiller. By 1853, De Sanctis was exiled and ordered to live in North America. But he made his way instead to the northern city of Turin, capital of Piedmont, where the uprisings of 1848 had led to a constitutional monarchy.

De Sanctis survived as freelance lecturer on the subject of Italian literature and emigrated to Zurich, where he taught Italian literature at the university. There, he had the opportunity to meet intellectuals from all over Europe, among them Richard Wagner, Franz Liszt and Jacob Burckhardt.[7] But his encounters with Mazzini and Manzoni were of much greater significance, as the former represented the main republican-democratic faction, and the latter the main Catholic-liberal faction in the risorgimento of nineteenth-century Italy.

With the amnesty of 1860 in Naples, De Sanctis hurried back to Italy. During the risorgimento, the Catholic-moderate wing of the national movement had defeated the secular, republican and democratic wing. De Sanctis, first nominated by Garibaldi as governor of his native province of Avellino, soon became director of public instruction in Naples, in which capacity he reformed the university by hiring 'new men' for the 'new Italy', among them his students Bertrando Spaventa (1817–83) and Pasquale Villari (1827–1917). Both of these would become leading figures of Italy's intellectual culture, the former in the field of nationalist Hegelianism that inaugurated the Marxist tradition in Italy, and the latter in the area of demography and the positivistic social sciences.[8] Both in turn influenced De Sanctis by energetically promoting, in a highly illiterate society, state intervention in educating the popular masses.

In 1861, De Sanctis began his service in the first cabinet of the new sovereign kingdom, and as deputy in the Italian parliament he would serve until his death. He made his living as a freelance scholarly journalist, writing for important journals such as *Il politecnico* and *La nuova antologia* until late in life. His famous *History of Italian Literature* is in part a compilation of essays he expressly wrote for income. His 'La prima canzone di Giacomo Leopardi' was published in the *Nuova antologia* of 1869, as was his 'Boccaccio e le sue opere minori' in 1880. But he also revised for publication the lectures he had given on Italian literature in Naples, Turin and Zurich. A Neapolitan edition of his *Saggi*

---

7 Gramsci has a beautiful paragraph in his *Prison Notebooks* which potentially sheds light on the intellectual nature of the Burckhardt–DeSanctis relationship: see Antonio Gramsci, *Quaderni del carcere*, ed. Valentino Gerratana (Turin: Einaudi, 1975), p. 1908.

8 For an overview of the history of Marxism in Italy, see Paul Piccone, *Italian Marxism* (Berkeley: University of California Press, 1983).

*critici* appeared in 1866, his *Saggio critico su Petrarca* in 1869, and his masterpiece, *Storia della letteratura italiana*, in 1870–1.

As a Southerner, De Sanctis engaged in important social initiatives affecting the South. With Vincenzo Gervasio (1844–1909), he launched educational reforms for a region which was up to 95 per cent illiterate. He then assumed the editorship of *L'Italia*, an important daily newspaper, the purpose of which was to build a centre-left constitutional opposition party. He became a member of the first new government of a unified Italy because of his membership of the moderate wing of the 'Historical Right' party (*Destra Storica*). And he became convinced that a new society required a new policy; known as 'trasformismo' or transformation, this also reflected the political dimension of De Sanctis's 'realism'. He dedicated himself to the organization of a new centre-left party, thereby contributing to the formation of a 'Historical Left' (*Sinistra Storica*) while simultaneously occupying a chair in comparative literature at the University of Naples in 1872.[9] De Sanctis's lectures regularly appeared in Neapolitan newspapers. Among his students were Francesco Torraca and Adolf Gaspary, who would subsequently become important literary historians.

Retiring from public service in 1880, De Sanctis had served his young nation state as a member of parliament, minister of education and professor of a state university. When he died on 29 December 1883 in Rome, Italy lost not only a newspaper editor, essayist, journalist, freelance writer and founder of modern literary criticism in Italy, but also a public intellectual whose projects combined politics with literature and education. 'My life,' he wrote, 'has two pages, one literary, and one political, and I have no intention of tearing up either of them: these are my two duties and I will continue to attend to them until the end.'[10] And so he did. As politician and public intellectual, he had contributed to the 'making of an Italian citizenry'.

Italy's public spheres had been considerably expanded by the third quarter of the nineteenth century through an increase in the circulation of newspapers, journals and other publications. This could only expedite De Sanctis's indefatigable efforts as educator of the educators of the people.[11] In the Italian context, Vittorio Alfieri had already promoted the

---

[9] Arnold Apweiler, *Begründer der italienischen Komparatistik: Francesco De Sanctis und Arturo Graf* (Aachen: Shaker, 1997).

[10] Cited and translated from Giovanni Spadolini, 'Il profeta dell'italia laica' in Francesco De Sanctis, *Lettere alla 'nuova antologia'*, ed. Giovanni Spadolini (Florence: Le Monnier, 1983), pp. 5–13: ('la mia vita ha due pagine, una letteraria, l'altra politica, ne penso a lacerare nessuna delle due: sono due doveri che continuerò fino in fondo').

[11] As far as De Sanctis's respect for d'Azeglio is concerned, see his essay on him in *Nuovi saggi critici* (Naples: Morano, 1901), pp. 279–91.

idea that only a cultural revival in Italy could lead to a political revival.[12] De Sanctis's theory of literary criticism and his political programme of public education combined the historical study of Italian literature in all of its forms with a political theory of aesthetics. Its purpose was fourfold: (1) to link aesthetic experience to political education; (2) to read literature as social history; (3) to teach through literature and aesthetics the extraordinary achievements of Italian culture; and (4) to relate the cultural defects of past civilization to those of present-day Italy.[13]

There is considerable coherence between De Sanctis's theory of literary criticism, his practice of it and his aesthetic theory. These are all largely indebted not to Idealist aesthetics, but to Hegel's philosophical idealism, in particular his *Phenomenology* and *Logic*. De Sanctis appropriated the Hegelian concept of a dialectic of content and form. While he differentiates form and idea along Hegelian lines, he sometimes identifies idea with content, and at other times, he dialectically relates both idea and form to content or reality. For De Sanctis, literary criticism which focuses only on the content of the literary text, or only on its formal qualities, is inadequate and fails to serve a civilizing function.[14] This is the case with the *l'art pour l'art* movement, in which the content of art is not 'life' but art, where 'life' denotes a material reality which is social and collective. The materiality of art is also stressed in his famous essay on Petrarch, in which he declares that the aesthetic world is substance, not appearance, reality, not idea, and that the poet's function is to 'naturalize art, and not to turn nature into art'.[15] In this statement, De Sanctis gives ontological priority to 'the real'. Poetic production is not separable from 'reality', and the more successfully the poet is able to reproduce that reality in form, 'to naturalize art', the greater the poet will be. Yet inasmuch as the poem's function is to 'naturalize art', the act of 'naturalization' that grasps content yields merely an approximation, an idea about reality and not reality itself. In this interpretation of the Hegelian dialectic, there are limits to the poet's ability to render reality.

Similarly, in his essay on Dante, De Sanctis states that 'the argument of a work of art is not empty, a tabula rasa; it already possesses the conditions of its existence according to which it is destined to evolve in a particular

12 See Vittorio Alfieri, *Del Principe e delle lettere*, ed. Giorgio Barberi Squarotti (1789; rpt Milan: Serra & Riva, 1983).

13 The role of literature and literary criticism in liberation movements or in the formation of a new and more liberal political era is also relevant to nineteenth-century Russia. See Georg Lukács, 'The International Significance of Russian Democratic Literary Criticism', in *Studies in European Realism*, intro. Alfred Kazin (New York: Universal Library, 1964), pp. 97–125.

14 Francesco De Sanctis, *La crisi del Romanticismo* in *Opere*, vol. IV (1973), pp. 376–7, 380–1.

15 De Sanctis, *Nuovi saggi critici*, p. 278.

form'.[16] In this interpretation of the dialectic, there is a paradox between form as a fixed idea of reality, and form as representing the fluidity of reality (content). In the former case, forms grasp the essential content of reality in an idea. In the latter case, the fluidity of reality is interpreted by means of creative or formal expression. Hence, there subsists a tension between form as self-becoming, and form as determined by structural conditions. De Sanctis's appropriation of Hegelian dialectics in his own aesthetic theory reflects a logical tension in the content–form relationship.

De Sanctis did not generate this tension. He inherited it from Hegel's work, where it is present from the beginning, as in the 'Preface' to his *Phenomenology*. It is also present in subsequent philosophical systems inspired by Hegel, as in the various Marxist traditions. When structure determines agency, it potentially deprives the dialectical model of its historical possibilities. This creates significant difficulties for a liberational theory of history, which Italian Hegelians attempted to overcome. A possible solution was to turn to a different logical model of historical transformation, that of the Spinozistic-atomistic tradition, for example, which was indeed adopted by Arturo Labriola, a follower of Bertrando Spaventa and De Sanctis. In this model, the speed of historical motion, like that of the motions of atoms, is uneven, and the resulting consequences of encounters from multiple directions of particles or particulars are neither predetermined nor predictable. New combinations, occasions, opportunities emerge for pacing or directing historical transformations. This is the conceptual model which, via Gramsci, was adopted in France by Althusser. It is an antidote to Hegelian-Marxist historical linearities and predictabilities, and a powerful analytical tool for intellectuals theorizing historical transformations outside the constraints of European-Transatlantic history.[17]

No wonder, then, that De Sanctis would vacillate in his aesthetic theory between a model of subjective self-becoming and a model of structural determinacy. This vacillation is also apparent in his theory of literary criticism. To begin with, he views literary expression as a reflection of social history, and the critic's task as assessing the capacity of art to grasp the essentials of the historical content, and considering the stage

[16] For Gramsci's interest in the structure–agency relationship as outlined by De Sanctis's aesthetic theory, see the former's *Quaderni del carcere*, pp. 514–17; see also Francesco De Sanctis, *Lezioni e saggi su Dante* in *Opere*, vol. v, ed. Sergio Romagnoli (1967), pp. 392–4.
[17] The work of Kojève and Hyppolite is particularly interesting in this context. See Jean Hyppolite, *Genesis and Structure of Hegel's Phenomenology of Spirit*, trans. Samuel Cherniak and John Heckman (1946; rpt Evanston, IL: Northwestern University Press, 1974); Alexandre Kojève, *Introduction to the Reading of Hegel: Lectures on the Phenomenology of Spirit*, ed. Allan Bloom, trans. James H. Nichols, Jr (1947; rpt Ithaca, NY: Cornell University Press, 1980).

reached by a collective consciousness of the status of human rights. In the current case, this content was Italy's march towards independence, liberalism and sovereignty. Thus, for instance, the poetry of Leopardi reflects the tensions, suffering and contradictions of a particularly painful historical moment in Italy's social and political evolution. As such, his poetry reflects not only a formal dialectic of form and content, but also a particular feature of historical life – the lack of liberty and justice. Leopardi, as great poet, was able to represent, through his philosophical scepticism, the collective psychology of a shared historical experience. Hence his greatness resides above all in his advocacy, as an intellectual, of a liberal political evolution in Italy.[18] In contrast, Romanticism may reflect significant features of an epoch, but does nothing to promote liberalism.

According to De Sanctis, a literary tradition can grasp the spirit of an epoch through the use of particular poetic instruments. In Parini's work, for example, irony is used to underscore the discrepancies between appearance and reality: Parini unconsciously portrays a corrupt and decaying aristocratic society, thereby hinting at the formation of new social strata. While De Sanctis can appreciate Parini's unconscious representation of a historical movement towards modern liberty and justice, he is much more drawn to the more explicit ideological orientation of figures such as Leopardi. In contrast to Parini, who focuses on the morality and sentiments of a particular social class, Leopardi is able to grasp a plurality of contradictory sentiments, moralities and spiritualities in a society comprising many social and cultural groups. Italy is not, for De Sanctis, a society of elites, but one of culturally diverse and stratified groups.

De Sanctis's historicist framework also satisfies his 'Realist' demand for a relation between 'life' and 'art', where 'life' is always understood as social and political life. His concept of 'Realism' is informed by Hegel's philosophy of history inasmuch as the *Zeitgeist* reflects the innate desire of a collective consciousness for justice and liberty, and hence for an expansion of political rights. For De Sanctis, artists and intellectuals have a critical function in Italy's political project of state formation. He highlights the poet's moral agency in the ordering of the actual world.

The principle of political intentionality in De Sanctis's 'Realist' literary theory is particularly apparent when we compare his theory of literary criticism to Lukács's aesthetic theory. Both espouse a concept of 'Realism', since both have appropriated aspects of Hegel's historical dialectic in which the 'idea' or consciousness of rights is linked to a particular historical 'reality', and in which a particular form reflects a particular

---

[18] On Leopardi and his republicanism see De Sanctis, *Nuovi saggi critici*, pp. 105–27, and *Scelta di scritti critici* in *Opere*, vol. x, ed. Gianfranco Contini (1949), pp. 633–42.

consciousness of rights in history. While Lukács, as a Marxist, sees this historical reality primarily as the struggle between classes, De Sanctis views it more broadly, as the complex social and political history of Italy caught between the liberties of the pre-Renaissance era, the decadence of the Renaissance, and the struggle for national unification in the risorgimento. What is interesting is that De Sanctis makes the representation of a 'mass of social sentiments' one of his criteria of poetic success, as delineated in his essay on Leopardi. He thereby anticipates, in the 1860s, aspects of Lukács's concept of 'totality'. But De Sanctis also presciently anticipates the controversies on the political nature of art between Lukács and members of the Frankfurt School of critical theory during the 1920s and 1930s.[19]

De Sanctis himself did not fall into the trap of a non-negotiable either–or position, as in the debates on aesthetics among classical Marxists and neo-Marxists. It was important for him to draw on as many artistic, philosophical and intellectual energies as possible, as long as they could be accommodated in a larger national-liberal project. For instance, he appreciated Zola's Naturalist novels and, by extension, Italian versions of Naturalism known as 'verismo'. He was interested by the documentary character of such writing, as it could not fail to address the indifference to poverty on the part of the bourgeoisie, while simultaneously pointing to the origins of criminality in social and economic deprivation. Naturalism represented a new literary genre which responded to new social-historical developments such as the emergence of a *Lumpenproletariat* in nascent capitalism.

In his *History of Italian Literature*, De Sanctis would again draw on Hegel's *Phenomenology* in interpreting that history as a reflection of Italy's historical consciousness on the march towards political and cultural modernity. Intended as a manual for teachers and a textbook for students (mostly male and upper middle-class), the *History* was written in accessible Italian, with a thorough pedagogical awareness of its particular readership: the young generation of a young Italy. As it turned out, it would become a favourite book of many Italian generations in search of literacy. In this work, De Sanctis tells the story of Italy's long march towards nationhood and secularization. In doing so, he involves his readers in dialogue, inviting their opinion on historical events or cultural icons, and addressing them directly.

The *History* begins with the poets of the courtly culture of Frederick II in Sicily (*Scuola Siciliana*), moves on to the great poets before the autonomous communes in northern Italy lost their independence, and

---

[19] See Renate Holub, *Antonio Gramsci: Beyond Marxism and Postmodernism* (London: Routledge, 1992), chs. 2–3.

depicts the socioeconomic crisis that ended the Renaissance. It follows the struggle for Enlightenment values and their impact on the risorgimento. De Sanctis portrays these developments against the background of the most important figures of Italian cultural history, including Dante, Petrarch, Machiavelli, Guiccardini, Campanella and Vico. It is an intellectual history of two civilizations: those of the Middle Ages and of modernity. Whereas the Middle Ages of autonomous city states constitute a Hegelian thesis affirming the spirit of liberty, the post-humanist era generates an antithesis, or negation of that spirit. Through Vico's Enlightenment and the risorgimento, a new emancipatory synthesis emerges. De Sanctis compares this history with the processes of modernization in the rest of Europe. He strikingly portrays the work of Machiavelli as that of a Luther in Italy, a move which allows him to highlight similarities in the conditions in Germany and Italy in the formation of a modern liberal consciousness. Machiavelli becomes for him Italy's first modern thinker, displaying a modernity of spirit which Vico appropriates and transmits to Italian Hegelianism.

De Sanctis's poets and writers are, as public intellectuals, the conscious bearers of the evolution of a modern theory of justice and the makers of a modern nation state. In linking intellectuals to the formation of that state, De Sanctis prefigures Antonio Gramsci's lifelong interest in the role of intellectuals in the political destiny of Italy. The purpose of the *History of Italian Literature* was to remind its readers, on the one hand, that all obstacles notwithstanding, the moment of a new liberty and nationhood had arrived; it thereby celebrated the triumph of reason. But it also reminded them that Italy had also known its dark ages, that periods of true poetry, energy and optimism (Dante) had been followed by periods of mere artistry, melancholy and dissolution (Ariosto and Tasso), admonishing them that the new nation should never again fall into despair, and play second fiddle in the orchestra of European nations.[20] The past still weighed heavily on the living.

De Sanctis himself saw his *History* as an animated and popular piece, a preliminary history of literature of sorts. The real work of writing a history of Italian literature still remained to be accomplished. It would have to be a complex enterprise, including the history of Italian languages and dialects. The real historical project would consist of monographs on writers and artists, examining their poetics and aesthetics. Much empirical work would have to be done to this end.[21] But meanwhile, with his *History of Italian Literature*, De Sanctis had practised what he had

[20] Francesco De Sanctis, *Storia della letteratura italiana*, ed. Maria Teresa Lanza (Milan: Feltrinelli, 1970), p. 865.
[21] De Sanctis, *Nuovi saggi critici*, p. 252.

prescribed in his cultural politics. The historian of literature, as literary critic, was called upon to participate in a project designed to engage prospective citizens with the languages, cultures, histories and literatures of the country as a whole. Although the nation state in Italy was *de facto* established by the 1860s, De Sanctis, like d'Azeglio, knew that 'Italians had to be made' – that the formation of a national identity had to overcome the enormous differences among the population with respect to political values, moral sentiments and perceptions of justice, liberty and equality, in addition to enormous disparities in levels of literacy. The epicentre of De Sanctis's cultural politics thus lay in the recognition not only of the multicultural complexion of the social classes in Italy, but also of the plurality of sentiments, values, customs and habits of thought represented in the history of Italian literature.[22] Gramsci greatly appreciated De Sanctis's programme, which had promoted cultural pluralism. Benedetto Croce, one of the leading intellectuals in Italy during the first half of the twentieth century, redirected cultural policy along the lines of a 'high culture' through his promotion of 'cultural refinements'. For this reason, Gramsci viewed De Sanctis as a much more effective cultural critic than Croce, particularly with respect to the Italian South, in which all three intellectuals had grown up.

The concept of a 'national popular' culture is one of De Sanctis's distinguishing marks as an aesthetic and cultural theorist. Nowhere is he more deeply immersed in Italian cultural history, however tacitly, than in his conception of philology or textual criticism as an act of political reconstruction. For him, as for countless intellectuals in Italy before him, literary criticism is not an end in itself, but a means to a political end. It can liberate from superstitions, falsifications and distortions; it can lay bare the fundamentals of dogma, theocratic claims and absolutist pretensions; it can sovereignly challenge, on the grounds of both philology and philosophy, all varieties of 'authoritarian reason'.[23] This is the art of literary criticism which Lorenzo Valla practised when, in the fifteenth century, he unmasked as forgeries certain ancient manuscripts which the papacy had used to lay claim to vast territories in Italy.[24] This is equally the art of literary criticism which Giambattista Vico practised several centuries later when, in his *Scienza nuova della commune natura delle*

---

[22] See Francesco De Sanctis, *La giovinezza: Memorie postume seguite da testimonianze biographiche di amici e discepoli* in *Opere*, vol. I, ed. Gennaro Savarese (rpt 1972). This contains elements of a 'critical pedagogy'.

[23] Nicola Badaloni, in his magisterial essay on major cultural trends from 1700 to 1860, uses the term 'ragione signorile' or 'seigneurial reason' when discussing the conceptual obstacles to democratic thought in Italy's moral and intellectual history. See his 'La cultura' in *Storia d'Italia. Vol. III*, pp. 699–984.

[24] Lorenzo Valla, *La falsa donazione di Costantino*, ed. Aldo Arminante, trans. Gerardo Fortunato (Salerno: Edisud, 1997).

*nazioni* (1725, 1744), he refuted by empirical means the claim that there was a single source for the world of justice, equality and liberty. This combination of philology with political philosophy is also at work in De Sanctis's project, in which the study of past literary texts contributes to the formation of national public opinion in nineteenth-century Italy.

A few years after De Sanctis's death in 1883, Antonio Labriola (1843–1904), one of his students and a follower of Bertrando Spaventa, began to read Marx. The Italian industrial working class had meanwhile begun to organize itself under the leadership of the socialist party, and Benedetto Croce, likewise a student of Spaventa, had written against Marx around the turn of the century. Ten years later, from within the socialist camp, the first fascist intellectuals emerged. As patriotic organizer of the modern nation state, as Hegelian literary critic and cultural theorist, De Sanctis proved useful not only to the liberal intellectual Croce and the fascist philosopher Gentile, but also to the important Marxist thinker and activist Antonio Gramsci. What Croce, Gentile and Gramsci had in common was their comparative approach to Italian intellectual culture, an approach which allowed them to compare intellectual developments in Italy to those of the dominant modernizing forces in Europe. Interestingly, as the foregoing remarks indicate, it is in the work of Antontio Gramsci that one discerns most affinities with the legacy of De Sanctis.

After the second World War, awareness of the educative function of intellectuals in raising the nation's cultural consciousness had never quite disappeared in Italy. It was incorporated into the programme of political parties, left and right alike.[25] Under the impact of the student movement and the working-class movement, and the power of the left-wing political parties, intellectual critics began to rewrite Italian history from a Marxist perspective. As a result, important literary histories were published in the 1960s and 1970s, among them those by Giuseppe Petronio, Carlo Salinari and Alberto Asor Rosa.[26] It was in this context that De Sanctis's work underwent a renaissance, for his history of Italian literature could still serve as an inspiration. Significant monographs on his work also appeared during this period. With the transition of Italy's predominant intellectual cultures from Marxism to liberalism, a transition it shares with the Western world, interest in De Sanctis has somewhat diminished.[27]

[25]  See Renate Holub, 'The Cultural Politics of the CPI from 1944–56', *Yale Italian Studies*, 2 (1978), 261–83; and Renate Holub, 'Towards a New Rationality? Notes on Feminism and Current Discursive Practices in Italy', *Discourse*, 4 (1982), 89–107.

[26]  Giuseppe Petronio, *Invito alla storia letteraria* (Naples: Guida, 1970); Carlo Salinari, *La critica della letteratura italiana* (Naples: Liguori, 1973); Alberto Asor Rosa, *Sintesi della storia della letteratura* (Florence: La nuova Italia, 1972).

[27]  Renate Holub, 'Post-War Intellectual Cultures: From Marxism to Cultural Studies' in *The Cambridge History of Literary Criticism. Vol. IX: Twentieth Century Historical,*

De Sanctis's life project combined the cultural organization of a nascent nation state with service as minister of education and parliamentarian in a new government. He undertook these tasks after enduring the typical experiences of risorgimento intellectuals: political persecution, trial, imprisonment and exile. In some ways, his biography is reminiscent of the work of intellectuals today in many global regions. De Sanctis's project can still be inspirational in that he refused, in his study of Italian history, to submit his thinking to a dualistic model in which the past history of a 'nation' is interpreted only as a process of victimization, subordination and domination imposed by outside forces. 'Collective psychologies', his work suggested, are never at a standstill, for they can expand or contract according to the status of liberty, solidarity and justice. This insight can still inform the creation of new cultural spaces in our world.

*Philosophical and Psychological Perspectives*, eds. Christa Knellwolf and Christopher Norris (Cambridge University Press, 2001), pp. 133–45.

# 23

# Matthew Arnold (1822–1888)

## Clinton Machann

Matthew Arnold (1822–1888) was probably the most influential British critic of the Victorian period. This is ironic since he had relatively little to say about the rapidly developing and popular genre of the novel, but in his essays he introduced and applied an expanded concept of 'criticism' that continues to influence literary and cultural critics today. His central ideas and reputation were somewhat controversial in his own time – especially with regard to his biblical or religious criticism. Arnold's literary career is distinctive because of his status as a major poet as well as critic. He began to write important poems as a student at Oxford, and his later transition from poet to critic was to some extent motivated by personal tensions and frustrations in his own poetic work. His professional career as an inspector of schools was also influential in his development as a critic. In large measure, his success as a writer and intellectual was due to his ability to negotiate the various and sometimes conflicting traditions and influences he inherited from his family and from the British society of his day.

## Family background, education and early career

Matthew Arnold was the eldest son of the famous preacher and pedagogue Thomas Arnold, headmaster of Rugby School.[1] His cosmopolitan outlook was encouraged by both his mother's sympathies for French egalitarian ideals and his father's interest in German scholarship.

Arnold's years at Balliol College, Oxford (1841–4), strongly influenced his subsequent literary career and the formation of his mature thought. Although he was only a mediocre student of the classics at this time, he was reading and absorbing a great deal of literature by writers who would influence his work for the rest of his life: Carlyle, Emerson, George Sand and Goethe. Winning the Newdigate prize for his poem *Cromwell*

---

[1] Two modern biographies of Arnold are Park Honan's *Matthew Arnold: A life* (Cambridge, MA: Harvard University Press, 1983) and Nicholas Murray's *A Life of Matthew Arnold* (London: Hodder & Stoughton, 1996).

in 1843 provided the impetus he needed to pursue poetry as a vocation. Most of his important poems would be written within the next ten years. Also, the tradition of Oxford University itself as a force in English culture would become central to Arnold's identity as a writer and thinker.

Although Balliol itself was a centre of resistance to the Tractarians, who were making their influence felt throughout the University at this time, Arnold joined the students who went to hear John Henry Newman preach. Arnold admired the sermons for their charm and intellectual power, but, unlike his brother Tom, he was never drawn into the Oxford Movement. Instead, in the midst of the very serious religious debates raging at Oxford, he adopted a detached attitude and avoided definite allegiance to either the social-activist Broad Church Anglicanism of his father or the High Church party of Newman and E. B. Pusey. It would later become clear that Arnold was in fact closer to his father than to Newman on the key issue of recognizing the English church as a fundamental national institution. Arnold's complicated grounding in religious controversy at Oxford is an important factor in his development as a critic.

While still at Balliol, Arnold wrote several of the poems he would include in his first published volume. In 1847, he was appointed personal secretary to Lord Lansdowne, a leading Whig statesman. The position was a kind of sinecure which allowed him ample time to write poetry. *The Strayed Reveller* appeared in 1849. The major themes of Arnold's mature poetry were already present in this first volume: the need for stoic detachment, the buried self, the primacy of universal law over personal desire, the inadequacy of human love, the transiency of human life, the exhaustion produced by inner division.

Arnold had absorbed Romantic ideas about poetry that elevated the status of the poet while ensuring that he would always face his limitations. As he would later put it, 'The grand power of poetry is its interpretative power; by which I mean...the power of so dealing with things as to awaken in us a wonderfully full, new, and intimate sense of them, and of our relations with them.'[2] The poet has the power to open up his readers to increased consciousness and the possibility of a unifying self-knowledge grounded in human experience, but this 'criticism of life', as he would call it, involves a constant struggle. Long after his own poetic powers had diminished, Arnold kept this belief in the power of poetry to transcend common speech and scientific discourse at the centre of his literary criticism.

[2] *The Complete Prose Works of Matthew Arnold*, ed. R. H. Super, 11 vols. (Ann Arbor: University of Michigan Press, 1960–77), vol. III, pp. 12–13. Further references to this standard collected edition of Arnold's prose works are cited within the text as *CPW*.

In 1851 Arnold was appointed Inspector of Schools by Lord Lans-downe, and this appointment cleared the way to his marriage with Frances Lucy Wightman. Arnold began a long and apparently happy marriage and also his thirty-five-year career of travelling widely, inspecting elementary schools and training colleges conducted by Nonconformists and Methodists. He was broadly sympathetic to the wide range of society with which his inspectorship brought him into contact and idealistic about the overall 'humanizing' and 'civilizing' effects of education. His experiences as a school inspector would help to generate the socio-political ideas of *Culture and Anarchy*.

Though he had nagging doubts about the direction he was taking as an artist and thinker, Arnold wrote one important poem after another, including 'Empedocles on Etna', the title poem of his 1852 collection, considered by many critics to be his most important and successful poem, an honest exploration of deeply felt contradictions and inadequacies. Arnold saw the plight of the ancient philosopher as analogous to that of the Victorian intellectual. Among the traits of 'modern consciousness' are scepticism as to ultimate truths, acute self-consciousness, a sense of isolation and loneliness, suspicions of 'pure' intellectualism, the desire for 'wholeness' and nostalgia for a lost world. The confusion and folly of the world are too much for Empedocles, who becomes 'dead to every natural joy' and finally escapes his conflicted life in a suicidal plunge into the crater of the volcano.

Arnold's preface to his 1853 volume of poetry interprets his own poem as symptomatic of the morbid preoccupation with the self that he thought characterized modern poetry, and he calls for a more impersonal mode that he associated with the 'grand style' of the great classical poets. He based his 1853 poem 'Sohrab and Rustum' on an incident from the heroic legend of Rustum, a figure from Persian mythology. 'Balder Dead', completed the next year, was based on the story of a Scandinavian sun god. Most ambitiously, he studied the plays of Sophocles and attempted to recapture the grandeur of ancient Greek tragedy in his own verse drama *Merope* (1858), but critics were unkind. A few of the poems from the 1850s, eventually published in *New Poems* (1867), have been considered among his best, notably 'Dover Beach' and 'Stanzas from the Grande Chartreuse', but these stoic, meditative poems about the loss of an 'age of faith' are not in the new impersonal mode that Arnold was trying to develop. Nevertheless, he had become a highly visible writer. By calling into question the relation of the poet to his times and by forcefully rejecting the personal, lyrical mode that had dominated English poetry since the ascendancy of the Romantics, he invited debate and made himself a target for controversy. His flair for probing sensitive aesthetic and cultural issues would lead to a major shift in the direction of his literary career.

Arnold was elected Professor of Poetry at Oxford in May of 1857 (for the first of two successive, five-year terms), and he used his new forum to explain and defend the approach to literature to which he was now committed in his creative work. He was the first holder of the post who was not an ordained minister and the first to lecture in English rather than Latin. In his inaugural lecture, 'On the Modern Element in Literature', delivered in November 1857, he further developed his idea that classical literature is 'modern' when it manifests tolerance, a critical spirit and intellectual maturity. Arnold's critical attempts to justify his own failing poetic programme led him away from poetry to concentrate on criticism itself.

Arnold's work as school inspector, though it required a rigorous schedule that left him little free time to devote to literary study, caused him to travel across England by rail to a greater extent than any previous literary man had ever done, and this experience would be an important influence on his prose. Another important influence would be the foreign travel made possible by his position. This reinforced and opened up the expression of tendencies in Arnold's thinking that had been present from his early years: his cosmopolitan outlook; his comparative, dialogic habits of mind; and his sensitivity to large social and political issues, lately expanded by his involvement in the fledgling, chaotic educational institutions of his country, and contact with large numbers of people from various backgrounds and social classes. Arnold took advantage of this European tour to meet leading French educationists as well as intellectuals and literary men such as Ernest Renan, Charles-Augustin Sainte-Beuve, François Guizot and Victor Cousin.

Arnold's essay 'Democracy', originally a preface to his report on French education, begins with the assumption that democracy is both desirable and inevitable, and he emphasizes his commitment to the ideal of equality. Arnold sharpened his concept of the *state* – which he defined, following Edmund Burke, as '*the nation in its collective and corporate character*' (*CPW*, vol. II, p. 26). Arnold's clarified sense of audience is as important as his evolving social mission: he is speaking primarily to the middle-class English, who must shed their narrow and provincial views in order to lead their nation to a more enlightened future.

In November 1860, Arnold gave an Oxford lecture entitled 'On Translating Homer', and what was intended to be one grew into a series of three lectures, the last of which was presented in late January 1861. These lectures are the bridge to the major essays in which he would fashion a new critical tradition in English. As Arnold reached an impasse in his own poetic efforts, the issue of literally *translating* the great classical works so that they might live again for modern readers acquired an ever greater significance for him. Any successful English translation of

Homer, the greatest classical writer, would have to capture his special qualities of language – his rapidity, plainness and directness in thought, his nobility – but Arnold believed that the recent translation by Francis W. Newman (brother of J. H. Newman) failed to do that. In attacking Newman's inept translation, and then answering the pamphlet Newman published in response, Arnold found his critical voice. *On Translating Homer: Three Lectures* was published by Longman in January 1861.

Arnold as a critic does not use his public forum primarily to argue for and against particular issues or even particular doctrines or systems of thought. Instead he attempts to express a certain way of looking at things that represents his true or 'best' self and at least potentially appeals to the true or best selves of his audience. In the Homer lectures he began to develop the critical language which culminates at the end of the decade in *Culture and Anarchy*, combining elements of social satire, journalism, religious sermons, philosophical dialogues and literary lectures. In his altercation with Newman, Arnold focused on the role of the critic: 'The "thing itself" with which one is here dealing, – the critical perception of poetic truth, – is of all things the most volatile, elusive, and evanescent... The critic of poetry should have the finest tact, the nicest moderation, the most free, flexible, and elastic spirit imaginable' (*CPW*, vol. 1, p. 174). This is recognizably the Arnold of *Essays in Criticism* and *Culture and Anarchy*, the prose classics of the 1860s that are still considered to be his most important literary productions. Twentieth-century scholars emphasized the significance of his literary persona, his tone, his *voice*. John Holloway articulated well the subtle qualities of the Arnoldian style when he wrote that 'his work inculcates not a set of ultimate beliefs... but... a certain temper of mind'.[3] 'Attitudes', 'habits', a 'frame' or 'temper' of mind, rather than a precise philosophy or set of doctrines, are said to inform Arnold's prose writings. For some critics, 'flexibility' is the key term.[4] Arnold's critical voice is one of the most significant innovations in nineteenth-century English letters.

## Essays in Criticism (1865)

Beginning with the series on Homer, nearly all of Arnold's lectures were published, initially as essays in journals. The first lecture destined for *Essays* was on the French poet Maurice de Guérin. Arnold made Guérin representative of the artistic temperament, and he generalized about two formations of that temperament: 'Poetry is the interpretress of the natural

---

[3] John Holloway, *The Victorian Sage* (New York: Norton, 1965), p. 203.
[4] Most notably, William Robbins in *The Arnoldian Principle of Flexibility* (Victoria, BC: University of Victoria, 1979).

world, and she is the interpretress of the moral world; it was as the interpretress of the natural world that she had Guérin for her mouthpiece' (*CPW*, vol. III, p. 30).

During the period 1863–4, additional Oxford lectures found their way into print. 'Pagan and Christian Religious Sentiment', where Arnold introduces the concept of an 'imaginative reason' that appeals both to intellect and to a religious sense, was published in the *Cornhill*, as was 'The Influence of Academies on National Spirit and Literature', a subject suggested by an essay Renan wrote on the French Academy. Finally, Arnold's lecture on 'The Functions of Criticism at the present Time' (later entitled 'The Function . . .') was the last one destined for the 1865 *Essays*, serving as its introduction.

In his publishing activities in the early-to-mid-1860s Arnold quickly worked his way into the expanding world of literary journalism. Avoiding the well-established and predictable journals such as the *Quarterly* and *Edinburgh*, he concentrated on new or renovated journals that were reaching out to new audiences more open to intellectual change. This expanding 'higher journalism' was helping to bridge the distance between the discourse of cognoscenti and that of the popular press. Especially important for Arnold were the recently reorganized *Fraser's Magazine*, under the editorship of Arnold's old Oxford acquaintance J. A. Froude, and *Macmillan's Magazine* and the *Cornhill Magazine*, both of which had been launched in 1859.

Arnold deplored the level of discourse in the English literary journals of his day, but he realized that they had become the chief source of intellectual influence in England. The development of his critical prose can be understood only in the context of the reviews and periodicals that were a major force in shaping popular taste and ideas, even on the higher levels of literary culture. Macmillan brought out *Essays in Criticism* early in 1865. The most essential essays in defining the Arnoldian critic at this stage of development are those on Heinrich Heine and literary academies as well as the introductory 'Function of Criticism'. For Arnold, Heine carried on Goethe's most important line of activity – as 'a soldier in the war of liberation of humanity' (*CPW*, vol. III, p. 108). Like his greater precursor, Heine embodied the modern spirit, and Arnold admires his 'life and death battle' with *Philistinism*. With this key term provided by Heine, Arnold names his own English enemies, the 'narrow' Philistines who value 'practical conveniences' over ideas and reason, and he would make great use of this satirical nickname for the English middle class.

Goethe and Heine had rejected 'routine' thinking by placing the standard for judgement 'inside every man instead of outside him' (*CPW*, vol. III, p. 110). The essay on academies seems to be arguing for the value of a central authority like that of the Académie Française in establishing high standards of British literary taste – especially in prose – but Arnold is ultimately interested in the articulation of a common culture, not a formal institution. The real authority will emerge from a social bond developed collectively by individuals who transcend their provincialism and 'the two great banes of humanity', 'self-conceit and the laziness coming from self-conceit' (*CPW*, vol. III, p. 232). This idea clearly anticipates Arnold's argument for *culture* as authority in *Culture and Anarchy*.

'The Function of Criticism' is by far the most important essay in Arnold's 1865 volume and perhaps the single most important essay of its kind in Victorian literature. Drawing on his own powerful impressions of the *secular* side of J. H. Newman's legacy – the ideal of knowledge for its own sake – Arnold helped to lay the groundwork for disparate future developments such as late nineteenth-century Paterian Aestheticism, early twentieth-century liberal humanism, and the late twentieth-century ascendancy of 'criticism' over 'literature' in academia. Like the volume as a whole, 'Function' relies heavily on Arnold's adaptation of French sources, especially Renan and Sainte-Beuve. Renan is surely one of Arnold's models for the ideal critic, though Arnold believed his own primary purpose of inculcating intelligence, as opposed to Renan's purpose of inculcating morality, corresponded to the contrasting needs and deficiencies of the English and French readers of the day. From Sainte-Beuve Arnold adapted his central idea of disinterestedness. Characteristically, when Arnold finally gives his 'definition' of criticism late in the essay, it is a very broad and inclusive one: '*a disinterested endeavour to learn and propagate the best that is known and thought in the world*' (*CPW*, vol. III, p. 283).

*Essays in Criticism* was widely reviewed. The comments on Arnold's *literary* criticism *per se*, the essays on the Guérins and Joubert, were almost universally positive. However, many reviewers, while not as censorious as Leslie Stephen, were unhappy with the *social* criticism – Arnold's assaults on English complacency and his ridicule of figures like Sir Charles Adderly and J. A. Roebuck, who celebrated 'Our old Anglo-Saxon breed, the best in the whole world!' His critics wondered why Arnold had to be so negative about English society and why he had not confined himself to literary matters, where his knowledge and authority were obvious. However, social criticism was not peripheral but central to his critical project. He did not limit his subject to taste; his concern was with the totality of human experience as it was interpreted by a national culture. An aesthetic sense was important not primarily in itself but rather in its relation to knowledge and to religion.

His last important volume of new poetry was published by Macmillan in July 1867. *New Poems* is an interesting amalgamation of old and new materials. Although he still strove for *disinterestedness* in his critical prose, he had given up his search for the calm and repose that he associates with the greatest poetry. Between *Merope* in 1858 and *New Poems* in 1867, Arnold had published a total of four poems, all in journals. 'Empedocles' could now be seen, retrospectively, as representing a stage in the development of a poet who had had his say. 'Dover Beach', on the other hand, was a jewel that Arnold had (uncharacteristically) kept to himself since the beginning of his married life. Although it was not immediately appreciated by Victorian readers, it was destined to be read by later generations of readers as an important poem in its own right and representative of Victorian consciousness. In the final poem of the 1867 volume, 'Obermann Once More', Arnold finally rejects Romantic melancholy, which has been one of the great driving forces behind his poetry, and acknowledges mankind's profound need for a 'joy whose grounds are true'. The poem anticipates his religious criticism of the 1870s.

Arnold wrote an especially interesting letter to his mother in which he offered his best-known overall assessment of his own poetry: 'My poems represent, on the whole, the main movement of mind of the last quarter of a century, and thus they will probably have their day as people become conscious to themselves of what that movement of mind is, and interested in the literary productions which reflect it' (5 June 1869).[5] The fact that Arnold had published *Culture and Anarchy*, his most influential book of social criticism, earlier in 1869 helps to establish the outline of his career as an active writer. Although nearly all of his important poems were now behind him, Arnold's reputation as a poet would grow during the final two decades of his life.

## *Culture and Anarchy* (1869), *Friendship's Garland* (1871)

After publishing *Essays in Criticism* in 1865, Arnold abandoned literary criticism *per se* for an entire decade. For Arnold, Britain's failure to provide the kind of strong, unified school systems he saw in Prussia and France was only part of a much larger and more comprehensive cultural and political problem, but his European tour served to strengthen his opinion that his own country was badly in need of educational reform. Arnold's Taunton Commission report on French, Italian and Prussian secondary schools and universities was published by Macmillan in March 1868, as *Schools and Universities on the Continent*. While writing his report he was also creating the character of Arminius, the fictional German visitor he used to satirize British society in *Friendship's Garland*.

---

[5]  The most extensive collected edition of Arnold letters is *The Letters of Matthew Arnold*, ed. Cecil Y. Lang, 6 vols. (Charlottesville: University of Virginia Press, 1996–2001).

In June 1867 Arnold delivered his final Oxford lecture, 'Culture and Its Enemies'. This was the beginning of *Culture and Anarchy*. Arnold is reluctant to define exactly what he means by 'culture', but it is clear that he does not mean a precise body of knowledge or art but rather a psychological attitude of mental freedom, driven by the motive of intellectual curiosity. His fundamental egalitarianism is evident here. Culture 'seeks to do away with classes' and 'make the best that has been thought and known in the world current everywhere' (*CPW*, vol. v, p. 113). The 'enemies' of culture are a 'mechanical and material civilisation' that stifles the inner life of the individual, an unsympathetic spirit of competition, and an 'intense energetic absorption' in specialized pursuits. Later renamed 'Sweetness and Light' as the first chapter of *Culture and Anarchy*, 'Culture and Its Enemies' adapts Jonathan Swift's metaphor of the bee from *The Battle of the Books*, making sweetness stand for beauty of character and light for intelligence, with the additional connotation of spiritual illumination.

Arnold's part in developing the modern usage of the term 'culture', which has become ubiquitous in literary and socio-political discourse, is one of his most important contributions as a man of letters, and it is intimately tied to his own growth and development as a writer.[6] Use of the term was already fairly common among English writers and intellectuals in the 1850s, but it was closely associated with the German word *Bildung* and its English equivalents, self-development and self-cultivation. That is, 'culture' usually meant 'self-culture', and for many it had negative connotations of amorality, egoism and an unhealthy Aestheticism.

'Culture and Its Enemies' was Arnold's first unambiguous essay in social and political criticism. In writing this kind of criticism he was following the precedent of Carlyle, whose first social and political essay, 'Signs of the Times', had appeared in the *Edinburgh Review* of June 1829, during the period of social disturbance prior to the First Reform Bill in 1832. Carlyle's critique of the 'Age of Machinery' provided Arnold with one of the basic metaphors of *Culture and Anarchy*: the Englishman's unwarranted faith in (institutional) machinery. The total number of 'culture' articles grew to six and were collected in a book manuscript with the subtitle 'an essay in political and social criticism'. Arnold wrote at a time of social disturbances and general unrest. The Second Reform Bill, increasing the electorate from one-fifth to two-fifths of the adult male population, was passed in August 1867, but civil strife continued. In

---

[6] For a concise account of the evolving meanings of 'culture' in nineteenth-century England and Arnold's role in this process, see David J. DeLaura, 'Matthew Arnold and Culture: The History and the Prehistory' in *Matthew Arnold in his Time and Ours: Centenary Essays*, eds. Clinton Machann and Forrest D. Burt (Charlottesville: University of Virginia Press, 1988) pp. 1–16.

February 1868, Disraeli succeeded Lord Derby as Tory prime minister, but in April he was defeated on the Irish Church question. In November a general election under the provisions of the reformed franchise returned a liberal Parliament, and *Culture and Anarchy* was published just before the new Parliament convened in February 1869.

Arnold's second chapter, 'Doing as One Likes', sets the limited ideal of personal liberty – which, if undirected, leads to anarchy – against the interests and authority of the state in its Burkean sense. But how does the individual reach beyond his personal and class loyalties to the idea of the 'whole community'? By our 'everyday selves' we are 'separate, personal, at war'. When 'anarchy presents itself . . . we know not where to turn'. According to Arnold, the ideal of culture suggests that beyond his everyday self the individual at least potentially has a *best self*; 'by our *best self* we are united, impersonal, at harmony' (*CPW*, vol. v, p. 134). This extension of his earlier idea of critical disinterestedness in 'The Function of Criticism' is still the most intriguing and controversial aspect of his cultural ideal: that through 'culture' an individual is capable of rising above his individual and class interests. In other words, culture is resistant to ideology.

The third chapter develops Arnold's playful tripartite classification of the 'Barbarians, Philistines, Populace' (aristocracy, middle class and working class) in British society, each with its distinctive qualities. Barbarians have a 'high chivalrous style' but also a 'fierce turn for resistance' and inaccessibility to ideas; Philistines have honesty and energy but also provincialism and narrowness; the Populace is the 'vast residuum', emerging as a force to augment that of the Philistines but still undeveloped, 'marching where it likes, meeting where it likes, bawling what it likes, breaking what it likes' (*CPW*, vol. v, p. 143). Underlying class differences, however, is a common human nature as well as the common English defect of imagining 'happiness to consist in doing what one's ordinary self likes' (*CPW*, vol. v, p. 145). Although Arnold as social critic usually concentrates his energies on the Philistines, the class with the most power and influence, here he looks at society as a whole: '[I]n each class there are born a certain number of natures with a curiosity about their best self, with a bent for seeing things as they are, for disentangling themselves from machinery, for simply concerning themselves with reason and the will of God, and doing their best to make these prevail; – for the pursuit, in a word, of perfection' (*CPW*, vol. v, p. 145). He uses the ironical term 'aliens' for those special individuals who come to terms with their best selves in order to be led by a general humane spirit and thus liberate themselves from the blinders of class ideology, and he believes that the number of aliens 'is capable of being diminished or augmented' (*CPW*, vol. v, p. 146). It is clear that Arnold identifies himself as one of these aliens and that his goal as a social and political critic is to increase the number of independent-minded aliens who, like him, will dedicate themselves to the 'pursuit of perfection'. He wants to perform in his text the very critical acts he is describing and that he wants his audience to emulate.

In his fourth chapter, 'Hebraism and Hellenism', Arnold asks his reader to join him in probing beneath the habits and practice that prohibit one from understanding the fundamental problem in English society that Arnold has already identified: action with insufficient light, the constant emphasis on doing rather than knowing. Both Hellenism and Hebraism aim at the goal of human perfection or salvation, claims Arnold, but 'by very different courses. The uppermost idea with Hellenism is to see things as they really are; the uppermost idea with Hebraism is conduct and obedience' (*CPW*, vol. v, p. 165). Appealing to a cyclical view of history, Arnold argues that both principles play a part in the development of civilization, and 'by alternations of Hebraism and Hellenism, of a man's intellectual and moral impulses... the human spirit proceeds' (*CPW*, vol. v, pp. 171–2). Early Christianity was the great triumph of Hebraism, the Renaissance was that of Hellenism. However, in England the Hellenic impulse of the Renaissance was 'prematurely' checked by the reactionary cross-current of Puritanism in the seventeenth century. This 'unnatural' state of affairs has impeded progress towards Hellenic 'spontaneity of consciousness' and imposed an overemphasis on 'conscience and conduct', an 'imbalance' towards the moral, Hebraic side.

The 'one thing needful' in the fifth chapter, 'Porro Unum est Necessarium', is of course the Hellenistic corrective to the Puritan moralism dominant in British society. In pointing out what he takes to be the misinterpretation of St Paul's writings by British Puritanism – taking the key terms used by Paul in a 'connected and fluid' way and using them in an 'isolated, fixed, mechanical way, as if they were talismans' – Arnold sets the stage for his first book of religious criticism, *St. Paul and Protestantism*. In the final chapter, 'Our Liberal Practitioners', Arnold applies his ideas to some 'practical operations' of the day, including the disestablishment of the Irish Church, the Real Estate Intestacy Bill and the Deceased Wife's Sister Bill, all of which point to the *mechanical* nature of conventional political thinking.

In his Conclusion, Arnold returns to a higher style and makes his most sweeping claims for culture in stating his conviction 'that the endeavour to reach, through culture, the firm intelligible law of things... that the detaching ourselves from our stock notions and habits, that a more free play of consciousness, an increased desire for sweetness and light, and all the bent which we call Hellenising, is the master-impulse even now of the life of our nation and of humanity' (*CPW*, vol. v, p. 229). At the heart of *Culture and Anarchy* is a tension between apolitical individualism and desire for community. In his poetry Arnold had explored the question of the individual's authentic or true self and had implied that even though we assume it exists, it may be buried or cut off from ordinary consciousness. Now he equates the 'best self' with 'right reason'.

Since the summer of 1866, Arnold had been publishing a series of satirical letters on political and cultural issues in the *Pall Mall Gazette*. One was written in response to a letter written by the historian and critic Goldwin Smith on England's position in the Austro-Prussian War. Arnold thought that Smith's opinions in favour of an English alliance with Prussia revealed the blind hatred of France and generally shallow understanding of European matters that was typical of Liberal thought. Arnold's satiric response to Smith became the first of thirteen 'Arminius' letters to the *Pall Mall Gazette*; Arnold interrupted the series after the seventh letter in the spring of 1867 and resumed it again during the period 1869–71. The Arminius letters would be published along with 'My Countrymen' and 'A Courteous Explanation' in 1871 as *Friendship's Garland*. In the Arminius letters Arnold writes his most outrageous and funniest satire, drawing heavily on the literary precedents of Swift, Voltaire, Heine and Carlyle. He used the device of the transparent literary hoax whereby a foreign visitor offers critical comments on English institutions, to the dismay of a naïve English friend who attempts to explain their virtues. The visitor in this case is an arrogant young Prussian named Arminius, Baron von Thunder-ten-Tronckh, grandson of the character described by Voltaire in *Candide*. While searching for a living descendant of the optimistic philosopher Dr Pangloss, Arminius visits his English friend 'Matthew Arnold', a Grub Street hack.

For a time in the late 1860s, Arnold was working concurrently on his foreign education report, his 'Culture and Anarchy' essays and the Arminius letters, using three separate but interrelated literary modes to express his ideas and opinions. His essays were a familiar topic of discussion in journals such as the *Saturday Review*, the *Spectator*, the *Fortnightly Review*, *Macmillan's Magazine*, the *Quarterly Review* and the *Edinburgh Review*, as well as in *The Times*, the *Daily Telegraph*, the *Daily News* and other newspapers. By the late 1860s his public image had solidified as the 'Apostle of Culture' and, increasingly, both friends and opponents had strong opinions about him. Arnold uses irony not only as a weapon to undercut his adversaries but in a self-deprecating manner to establish his own modesty, openness, lack of dogmatism. His consistent refusal to *systematize* his ideas – a quality that irritated the philosopher Frederic Harrison and other critics – was at least partially a legacy from Arnold's father, who observed in his Oxford lectures on history 'how little any real history is an exact exemplification of abstract principles'.[7]

One early and important instance of the influence of Arnold's cultural criticism was in the Renaissance essays of Walter Pater, the first of which was published in November 1869. But at this point in his career Pater was interested only in the aesthetic dimension of Arnold's thought. According to David DeLaura, 'If there is a "moment" when the Keatsian artist announces an ultimate severance from the hope of affecting nineteenth-century life, it may be in Pater's first essays of the late sixties, as Matthew Arnold's great "critical effort" is systematically reshaped into the catchwords of the new aestheticism.'[8] Like Arnold, Pater was seeking to modify and transform traditional religious categories, but without Arnold's increasing social and ethical motivation. An even more unexpected sign of Arnold's influence came in 1871 with the publication of E. B. Tylor's *Primitive Culture*, a pioneering work in anthropology. Tylor adapted the term that Arnold had popularized for use in a newly developing field of science and applied it in evolutionary and hierarchical senses.

Arnold wrote his seminal essays on culture during a time of personal anguish and grief. His infant son Basil, not yet two years old, died in January 1868, just as Arnold was finishing the second 'Culture and Anarchy' article for the *Cornhill*. He was a dedicated and affectionate father, and the premature death of three of his four sons was the greatest sorrow of his life. His search for meaning in life in the face of this personal suffering helped motivate his religious writings of the 1870s.

### *St. Paul and Protestantism* (1870), *Literature and Dogma* (1873), *God and the Bible* (1875), *Last Essays on Church and Religion* (1877)

Arnold's religious and biblical criticism grows directly out of his writings about culture. His critique of the English Dissenters begins with 'My Countrymen' in 1866, and he refers to St Paul repeatedly in the essays of *Culture and Anarchy*. To Arnold, St Paul represents the best of the Christian 'Hebraic' tradition because, up to a point, he incorporated Hellenism, a free flow of consciousness, into his thinking about morality. The English Puritans, however, treated his teachings in a mechanical way, much like the mechanical way that the Jews treated the Mosaic law in

---

[7] Thomas Arnold, *Introductory Lectures on Modern History* (Oxford University Press, 1842), p. 180.
[8] David J. DeLaura, *Hebrew and Hellene in Victorian England: Newman, Arnold, and Pater* (Austin: University of Texas Press, 1969), p. 230.

Paul's day. Observers who have watched Puritanism 'handle such terms as *grace, faith, election, righteousness*' must feel that these terms 'have for the mind of Puritanism a sense false and misleading' and that 'this sense is the most monstrous and grotesque caricature of the sense of St. Paul, and his true meaning is by these worshippers of his words altogether lost' (*CPW*, vol. v, p. 182). In addition, Arnold wanted to challenge the Dissenters' claim to the historical justification of their separation from the English Church. His line of thought led to *St. Paul and Protestantism* (1870), *Literature and Dogma* (1873), *God and the Bible* (1875) and *Last Essays on Church and Religion* (1877).

Arnold attended religious services regularly and defended the Church of England as a national institution. He wanted the Dissenters to come back into the fold. As he suggested in the Preface to *Culture and Anarchy*, being raised in the national church provides 'a lesson of religious moderation, and a help towards culture and harmonious perfection' (*CPW*, vol. v, pp. 239). He thought it was essential to preserve the English Bible as poetry and as the repository of collective wisdom from the past. However, he assumed that religion cannot remain dogmatically stationary in the face of a great revolution in scientific knowledge and that, in order to remain vital, sacred texts must be interpreted anew by each age.

In *St. Paul* Arnold assumes that there is in the flux of things a 'universal order which the intellect feels after as a law and the heart feels after as a benefit' (*CPW*, vol. vi, p. 9). He also assumes that there is a '*stream of tendency by which all things seek to fulfil the law of their being*' (*CPW*, vol. vi, p. 10). Paul is dealing with this kind of knowledge and feeling, but the reader cannot understand him unless he grasps the essential metaphorical nature of religious language. *St. Paul* was the first of Arnold's books to reach a second edition within a single year, and the critical response was much more lively than it had been to *Culture and Anarchy*, though many of the reviews were ambivalent or negative. Critics claimed Arnold was undermining traditional Christian values with his ideal of culture. However, after decades of absorbing wide-ranging influences from Wordsworth, Goethe and Carlyle, from the *Imitation of Christ* and the *Bhagavad-Gita*, from Spinoza, John Henry Newman and Renan, Arnold remained an Anglican ritualist who felt he was in a meaningful way continuing the work of his Broad Church father.

Encouraged by the response to *St. Paul*, Arnold began a new manuscript on 'literature as it regards dogma', and Smith published it in February 1873 as *Literature and Dogma: An Essay Towards a Better Appreciation of the Bible*. Reaching a wider audience than any of his other books, Arnold's last substantial, original book of any kind was a 'bestseller' in an age of religious controversy. *Literature and Dogma* was also the first of Arnold's books to be translated, appearing as *La Crise religieuse* in France (1876). Coverage by the periodical press – in England, America and Europe – was correspondingly substantial, the most extensive that Arnold had ever received. In *Literature and Dogma* he attempts to rescue Christianity from anthropomorphism and other vulgar errors of popular theology. Following Spinoza, he assumes that miracles must be discounted. The language of the Bible is the poetry of old Israel, 'thrown out' to express experience that otherwise could not be expressed. In addition to his continental influences, Arnold may have found a source for his approach in the works of his father's friends Richard Whately and R. D. Hampden, the 'Oriel Noetics', who made a distinction between the symbolic language of scripture and the explicative language of dogma. Arnold uses the German term *Aberglaube*, 'extra-belief', to describe much biblical language. Always speaking as a literary and cultural critic rather than a theologian, he does not attempt a precise or fixed definition of religion, but he does describe it as *'morality touched by emotion'* (*CPW*, vol. VI, p. 177). In order to improve morally, one must consult one's conscience. His term for God is *'the enduring power, not ourselves, which makes for righteousness'* (*CPW*, vol. VI, p. 200).

Early in his career, Arnold had used the term *Zeitgeist*, which he picked up from Goethe and Carlyle, to refer to current intellectual fashion or the spirit of the age, as opposed to the universal verities of human experience. Now in the mid-1870s, Arnold argued that the *Zeitgeist* had made it impossible for traditional religious belief in miracles, plenary inspiration and a personal God to stand. In order to preserve the Bible as an essential religious guide in the new scientific age, the biblical critic must interpret it in terms that would allow a 'real experimental basis' for its claims. Most critics with ecclesiastical affiliations, both Protestant and Catholic, tended to condemn Arnold on the grounds that he was not competent to deal with theological issues and in any case was no friend of Christianity.

However, in Arnold's view the English public simply did not understand the extent to which the modern spirit in Europe had dissolved the authority of the Bible as a practical source of wisdom. Unless his essentially conservative critical effort were successful, the Bible in Britain would be doomed to the same fate, and it was his English critics that he felt compelled to answer. He did so in a series of articles for the *Contemporary Review*, published by Smith and Elder as *God and the Bible* in November 1875. In his opening chapters, Arnold amplifies his position that there is no evidence for supporting the belief in an anthropomorphic God: 'men do not know enough about the Eternal not ourselves that makes for righteousness, to warrant their pronouncing this either a person or a thing'

(*CPW*, vol. VII, p. 160). For Arnold, the discerning reader knows when to read the Bible literally, when it speaks of righteousness as salvation, and figuratively, when it refers to God as a talking, thinking being. Arnold devotes the second half of the book to the question of the authenticity of the Book of John. For him, this was another opportunity to demonstrate clearly how a 'disinterested' literary critic could resolve certain biblical questions more effectively than could traditionalist theologians or German specialists 'carried away by theorizing'. Arnold decides that the final version of the gospel is not by John himself but rather a redaction based on *logia* or sayings of Jesus composed by a later Greek Christian editor.

Although Arnold wrote as an intellectual, he was committed to a *popular* transformation of religious thought in England. During the Renaissance, many 'cultivated wits' had lost the Bible, but the 'great solid mass of the common people kept it'. Now *'the masses'*, *'the people'* are losing it and thus 'can no longer be relied on to counteract what the cultivated wits are doing' (*CPW*, vol. VI, p. 362). After the success of *Literature and Dogma*, Arnold had high expectations for its sequel, but was disappointed in sales. Although *God and the Bible* was seen as somewhat derivative of and less significant than the previous book, it extends Arnold's range as a literary critic, especially in its investigation of John, and Arnold believed that it contained some of his best prose (*CPW*, vol. VII, p. 439). It was in fact his last unified book-length project of any kind, although his production of critical essays continued unabated. He was determined to return to the subject of 'literature proper' but could not easily pull himself away from religious studies, continuing to lecture and publish articles on religious topics in the mid-1870s, including two *Contemporary* articles on Joseph Butler, the eighteenth-century bishop who resisted Deist philosophy. Arnold identifies with this man and 'his argumentative triumph over the loose thinkers and talkers of his day' (*CPW*, vol. VIII, p. 29). In terms of Arnold's familiar psychological dualism, this English theologian – whom his father had studied before him – balances the more exotic Spinoza as a major influence on his religious thinking.

Arnold's concentrated study of the Bible as literature had had a fundamental effect on his views about the *status* of poetry. Announcing his 'career shift' in the Preface to *Last Essays* he wrote, '[I]n returning to devote to literature, more strictly so-called, what remains to me of life and strength and leisure, I am returning, after all, to a field where work of the most important kind has now to be done, though indirectly, for religion.' Arnold believed that the essential transformation of religion could only be accomplished by applying the 'literary' qualities of 'flexibility, perceptiveness, and judgment' (*CPW*, vol. VIII, p. 148). Although all his important poetry was in the past, his reputation as a poet continued to grow.

## Poems of Wordsworth (1879), Mixed Essays (1879), Irish Essays (1882), Discourses in America (1885), Essays in Criticism: Second Series (1888)

Arnold's introduction to Macmillan's 1879 edition of Wordsworth's poetry became one of his most important contributions to literary criticism. His goal was to make Wordsworth's poems as widely read as Milton's. Regardless of his insistence on classical genres, Arnold's nineteenth-century cosmopolitanism is evident in his attempt to place Wordsworth in the context not of English poetry merely but of European poetry as well. Arnold used the project to adjust his stance in relation to the best of the Romantic heritage once again. It seemed to revive his old delight in the natural world: 'The effect of reading so much Wordsworth lately has been to make me feel more keenly than usual the beauty of the common incidents of the natural year, and I am sure that is a good thing' (CPW, vol. IX, p. 339). While dismissing didacticism in poetry, Arnold adapts his old definition of poetry as a criticism of life (now 'under the conditions fixed for us by the laws of poetic beauty and poetic truth'), and argues that *moral* ideas are a 'main part of human life'. Like other great poets, Wordsworth focuses on the question *how to live* (CPW, vol. IX, p. 45). Although Arnold and his ideal of disinterestedness had been a major influence on Pater's formulation of Aestheticism, here Arnold is distancing himself from that concept, and the Arnold of 'Wordsworth' was much less attractive to Aesthetes like Pater and Swinburne than the earlier Arnold had been.

Other projects undertaken by Arnold in the late 1870s and early 1880s showed that he was re-examining and elaborating his views on poetry and literature. He wrote the general introduction for T. Humphrey Ward's anthology entitled The English Poets (1881). Later entitled 'The Study of Poetry', it contains some of his best-known pronouncements about poetry and poets. It is pre-eminently an essay of judgement and evaluation. Arnold begins by making a very large claim for poetry:

The future of poetry is immense, because in poetry, where it is worthy of its high destines, our race, as time goes on, will find an ever surer and surer stay. There is not a creed which is not shaken, not an accredited dogma which is not shown to be questionable, not a received tradition which does not threaten to dissolve. Our religion has materialised itself in the fact . . . and now the fact is failing it. But for poetry the idea is everything; the rest is a world of illusion . . . the idea *is* the fact. The strongest part of our religion to-day is its unconscious poetry.

(CPW, vol. IX, p. 161)

This passage, closely related to Arnold's Bible criticism, would draw responses, both positive and negative, from future generations of scholars and literary critics, but Arnold wrote primarily for a general, middle-class audience (*CPW*, vol. IX, p. 379). He employed some of the critical formulations that had become familiar in his work and reintroduced and elaborated some of the ideas he had introduced in the 1860s, beginning with the early Homer essays. Poetry is a criticism of life. The reader must see the poetic object as it really is, thus avoiding the fallacies of the merely personal and the merely historical estimate. Even Arnold's notorious 'touchstone method' is anticipated by his use of quotations in the Homer lectures – the best way to know 'truly excellent' poetry when we see it is 'to have always in one's mind lines and expressions of the great masters, and to apply them as a touchstone to other poetry' (*CPW*, vol. IX, p. 168).

To an even greater extent than in 'Wordsworth', Arnold was concerned with ranking the English poets, or rather with deciding which ones should be singled out as truly 'classic', and some of his judgements were controversial. He praises Chaucer, yet decides that the fourteenth-century poet lacks 'high seriousness' and thus is not one of the 'great classics'. Burns falls short for a similar reason. Arnold's most striking evaluations concern the eighteenth century, which, he decides, was an age of prose, not of poetry. Although they may be masters of the art of versification, 'Dryden and Pope are not classics of our poetry, they are classics of our prose' (*CPW*, vol. IX, p. 181). Gray, on the other hand (to whom Arnold also contributes a separate essay in the anthology), 'is our poetical classic of that literature and age'. In this essay Arnold considers no poet later than Burns – because 'we enter on burning ground as we approach the poetry of times...near to us – poetry like that of Byron, Shelley, and Wordsworth – of which the estimates are so often not only personal, but personal with passion' (*CPW*, vol. IX, p. 187).

And yet Arnold had been eager to write his essay on Wordsworth, and early in 1880, he was planning not only essays on the Romantic Keats as well as the eighteenth-century Gray for the same anthology but also a selected *Poetry of Byron* with its own critical introduction. Arnold argues that Keats is not 'ripe' for 'that faculty of moral interpretation which is in Shakespeare...But in shorter things, where the matured power of moral interpretation, and the high architectonics which go with complete poetic development, are not required, he is perfect' (*CPW*, vol. IX, p. 215). Arnold was more interested in securing the reputation of Byron, an important early influence on his own poetry, whom in his 1850 elegy on Wordsworth he had honoured (along with Wordsworth and Goethe) as one of the three poets who had most set the tone for their age (*CPW*, vol. IX, p. 236).

While he was completing his retrospective study of the English Romantics, Arnold continued to write and lecture on miscellaneous topics. *Irish*

*Essays*, brought out by Smith and Elder in February 1882, included seven new pieces that had been previously published in the *Nineteenth Century*, the *Fortnightly Review* or the *Cornhill* during the period 1879–81. Arnold was sensitive to the 'hateful history of conquest, confiscation, ill-usage, misgovernment, and tyranny' in English–Irish relations (*CPW*, vol. IX, p. 312) and he advocated policies that would promote *'healing'* in Ireland. One of the most significant aspects of Arnold's *Irish Essays* is his use of Burke. Although Arnold sometimes disagreed with Burke's Conservative politics, he found much to admire in Burke's essays and used sentences and phrases from Burke as 'touchstones' to test the truth or moral value of ideas about the English character and the English nation. Arnold's positive experience of editing Wordsworth and Byron probably contributed to his idea of publishing a collection of Burke's principal writings on Ireland, and *Edmund Burke on Irish Affairs* was brought out by Macmillan in June 1881, nearly a year before *Irish Essays*.

Another important development in Arnold's career in these years grew out of a kind of public debate he had with a formidable but amicable adversary. T. H. Huxley, the pre-eminent spokesman for science in Victorian England, had been Arnold's friend since the 'Culture and Anarchy' period, but the two men disagreed about the position of science in culture and education. Huxley had attacked the classical literary curriculum entrenched in English universities. He accepts Arnold's idea that 'a criticism of life is the essence of culture' but insists on the centrality of modern scientific knowledge to that criticism. Arnold's answer, eventually published in the August *Nineteenth Century* as 'Literature and Science', in some ways the culminating statement of his claims for literature, is also, along with J. H. Newman's *Idea of a University*, one of the classic defences of the humanities or liberal arts in education. Arnold argues that 'those who are for giving to natural knowledge ... the chief place in the education of the majority of mankind, leave one important thing out of their account: the constitution of human nature'. 'Human nature' is 'built up' by 'the power of conduct, the power of intellect and knowledge, the power of beauty, and the power of social life and manners' (*CPW*, vol. X, pp. 61–2). He insists that only in the study of literature is knowledge related to 'the sense in us for conduct, and to the sense in us for beauty' (*CPW*, vol. X, pp. 64–5). That is, in literature, the Hellenic 'sweetness and light' emphasized in *Culture and Anarchy* is related to the Hebraic conduct emphasized in the religious books. Scientific knowledge, by itself, is finally 'unsatisfying, wearying' to the majority of mankind.

'Literature and Science' would prove to be popular with Arnold's audience in his American lecture tour of 1883–4. In the spring of 1882, Arnold wrote 'A Word about America', published in the *Nineteenth Century*. Making references to his recent reading of Henry James's novel

*Roderick Hudson*, Arnold describes the American population as made up of Philistines, just like British Philistines (with the Barbarians left out entirely and the Populace nearly). Although he focuses on the need for greater 'cultivation' in America, Arnold maintains an amiable tone – no doubt preparing for his American audience – and sounds a familiar refrain when he recommends reform of secondary education as 'the really fruitful reform to be looked for in America' (*CPW*, vol. x, pp. 22–3).

'Numbers; or The Majority and the Remnant' was the first lecture Arnold would deliver in America. Drawing on both Isaiah ('Many are called, few chosen') and Plato ('The majority are bad'), he challenges what he thought to be the not uncommon fallacy among Americans that the majority is always right. The third and most controversial lecture was 'Emerson'. Expressing his admiration for Emerson since his Balliol days, Arnold asserts that Emerson is finally superior to Carlyle, and his essays are the most important work done in prose, just as Wordsworth's poetry is the best work done in verse. Yet Arnold does not refrain from pointing out Emerson's limitations: he is not a 'great poet' and, furthermore, 'his style has not the requisite wholeness of good tissue' to qualify him as a great writer or man of letters (*CPW*, vol. x, p. 172). Everywhere he went, Arnold was hounded by the American press, which he considered vulgar and intrusive. But despite the hostile press during his 1883–4 tour, in the long run Arnold made a greater impact on America than any other British or European critic.

Arnold published 'A Word More about America' in the *Nineteenth Century* for February 1885. This anticipates the more developed treatment of his views on America in 'Civilisation in the United States'. He had decided that the 'political sense' was sounder in America than it was in England. Unlike the English, Americans had solved the 'political and social problem'. However, in Arnold's opinion the Americans had not yet solved the 'human problem', and the quality of life in the United States was such that an Englishman of taste would rather live in continental Europe.

Arnold left behind him one last book publication project in nearly final form, a 'purely literary' volume entitled *Essays in Criticism: Second Series*. Most important among Arnold's later essays is 'Tolstoi'. He had met Tolstoy briefly in 1861, when the Russian was taking a tour of English elementary schools. Later, Tolstoy, who like Arnold rejected the supernaturalism of the gospels, read Arnold's critical and religious writings, and Arnold developed an interest in Tolstoy's novels, especially *Anna Karenina*, which he read avidly in 1887. Arnold contrasted the Russian Realism of Tolstoy – which he associated with the profound soul-searching of Tolstoy and his character Levin – to the 'petrified feeling', the 'atmosphere of bitterness, irony, impotence' he found in the works of the French Naturalists (*CPW*, vol. XI, pp. 292–3).

Emphasizing the realism of Tolstoy and helping to establish Tolstoy's reputation in English-speaking countries, Arnold – near the end of his life – displayed an especially progressive aspect of his critical intelligence. In a larger sense, Arnold's cosmopolitan point of view, combined with his innovative but controversial ideas about critical disinterestedness and the vital importance of literature and culture in human life, would continue to influence future generations of critics.

# 24

# Henry James (1843–1916)

## DONALD STONE

In 1864 Henry James, perhaps already dimly aware at the age of twenty-one that he would one day become the greatest of American novelists and critics, began a historic relationship with Charles Eliot Norton. As editor, together with James Russell Lowell, of the *North American Review*, Norton had just accepted the young man's first review essay. The book under scrutiny, promisingly titled *Essays on Fiction*, disappointed James for failing to be a definitive 'critical treatise' designed 'to codify the vague and desultory canons' of the novel.[1]

In decades to come James would write several classic essays on novelists and on the novel, showing it to be a genre that defies codes and canons: 'the most independent, most elastic, most prodigious of literary forms' (*LC*, vol. II, p. 1321). He would, in time, authoritatively consider such issues as the importance of novelistic form, the use of point of view, the morality of fiction and the need for authorial freedom. But in 1864 he was still a literary hopeful, assuring Norton that he could write on subjects other than the novel although admitting 'that that kind of criticism *comes most natural*'.[2] For the next few years James contributed to the *North American Review*, the *Nation* (a new journal also edited by Norton) and the *Atlantic Monthly* (subedited by James's friend William Dean Howells) review articles on authors as various as Epictetus, Goethe, Victor Hugo, Walt Whitman, Anthony Trollope, Charles Dickens, George Eliot, Matthew Arnold and the unfortunate creator of *Essays on Fiction*.

By 1867 James was describing to his friend T. S. Perry his desire 'to do for our dear old English letters and writers *something* of what Ste. Beuve and the best French critics have done for theirs'. Far from his mind, at this point, was the thought that he would ever permanently leave America. Born in New York and intellectually nourished in New England, James felt that being an American was 'an excellent preparation for culture'. Unlike writers from other countries, Americans, he wrote,

---

[1] Henry James, *Literary Criticism*, eds. Leon Edel and Mark Wilson, 2 vols. (New York: Library of America, 1984), vol. I, p. 1196; hereafter cited as *LC*. In 1864 James also published his first tale, 'A Tragedy of Errors'.

[2] Henry James, *Letters*, ed. Leon Edel, 4 vols. (Cambridge, MA: Harvard University Press, 1974–84), vol. I, p. 57.

have the freedom to 'pick and choose and assimilate and in short (aesthetically etc.) claim our property wherever we find it'. Americans, to be sure (he added), 'have something of our own', something deep 'in our moral consciousness'.[3]

Born into a remarkable family, which roamed about Europe and eastern America during his formative years, James exhibited signs of precocity early on. In his autobiography, he chronicled his discovery, at the age of about eleven, that a hyperactive consciousness and restless curiosity such as his had a value that could be put to critical use. Attending a staging of *Uncle Tom's Cabin*, James recalled 'the thrill of an aesthetic adventure': watching the performance and also critically *watching* himself watching, receiving 'his first glimpse of a "free play of mind" over a subject which was to throw him with force at a later stage of culture, when subjects had considerably multiplied, into the critical arms of Matthew Arnold'.[4] Norton's invitation that he review Arnold's *Essays in Criticism* (1865) was remembered by James as a turning point in his life. As he read the ink-stained proofsheets, he recalled being 'transported, as in a shining silvery dream, to London, to Oxford, to the French Academy, to Languedoc, to Brittany, to ancient Greece' (*LC*, vol. I, p. 172). In addition to opening up a multitude of foreign worlds, Arnold demonstrated how criticism satisfies a moral, aesthetic and civil claim; he showed that the critic's function, in large part, is 'to exalt the importance of the ideal' ('poetic feeling subserving the ends of criticism'), while he also revealed powers of acute observation and sympathy in the form of a charming style. James also took to heart Arnold's strictures on the need to avoid 'provincialism' and, in order to sustain a 'free play of mind', to maintain an attitude of 'disinterestedness' with regard to the practical world (*LC*, vol. I, pp. 711–19).

Like Arnold, James looked to France for critical guidance. 'In that country', James later wrote, 'criticism is not only a profession, it is a power.'[5] Among his early reviews are pieces on French critics Edmond Schérer, whom James praised for his 'positive' morality (*LC*, vol. II, pp. 802–11), and Hippolyte Taine (pp. 826–56). Although the latter's

3 *Ibid.*, pp. 76–7.
4 Henry James, *Autobiography*, ed. F. W. Dupee (New York: Criterion, 1956), pp. 96–7. For Arnold's (as well as Sainte-Beuve's) influence on James, see Sarah B. Daugherty, *The Literary Criticism of Henry James* (Athens: Ohio University Press, 1981); Vivien Jones, *James the Critic* (New York: St. Martin's Press, 1985); Morris Roberts, *Henry James's Criticism* (Cambridge, MA: Harvard University Press, 1929); Donald Stone, *Communications with the Future: Matthew Arnold in Dialogue* (Ann Arbor: University of Michigan Press, 1997).
5 Henry James, 'The Letters of Delacroix', rpt in *The Painter's Eye*, ed. John L. Sweeney (London: Rupert Hart-Davis, 1956), p. 200.

'dogmatism' repelled James, Taine's belief in the importance of historical conditioning influenced James's own views.

Taine's impression that the British mind 'is indifferent and even hostile to ideas' (p. 837) is one that Arnold shared and that James would acquire once he decided to settle in England. In the mid-1870s, when he was living in Paris, James also took note of an Arnoldian favourite, Ernest Renan, a stylist second only to Sainte-Beuve. In an 1883 tribute, James approvingly cited Renan's proto-Arnoldian view, 'The essence of criticism is to be able to understand states very different from those in which we live' (p. 643). However, for James as a young aspirant, the French critic of most importance – 'the acutest critic the world has seen', James called him in 1875 (p. 669) – was Charles-Augustin Sainte-Beuve. In the first of several pieces devoted to him, James in 1868 noted the multiplicity of his talents: 'He is a little of a poet, a little of a moralist, a little of a historian, a little of a philosopher, a little of a romancer.' His 'insatiable curiosity' (p. 668) was particularly welcome to an author who, both as critic and novelist, would urge writers and readers alike 'to be one of the people on whom nothing is lost!' (*LC*, vol. i, p. 53).

'The disparagers of culture make its motive curiosity', Arnold observes at the beginning of *Culture and Anarchy*; but for a critic like Sainte-Beuve, Arnold avows, curiosity is the prerequisite for intelligence: curiosity fuels the desire 'to see things as they are'.[6] For Arnold and James this means that the critic, no less than the artist, has a responsibility to see life as clearly and fully as possible. Invited in 1891 to join a forum on 'The Science of Criticism', James contributed the only essay he ever devoted to the function of criticism. He shortened the imposing 'Science of Criticism' title used by the host journal, the *New Review*, to 'Criticism' when he reprinted it in his 1893 collection, *Essays in London and Elsewhere*. Following Arnold's lead in 'The Function of Criticism at the Present Time' (best known of the *Essays in Criticism*), James asserted the need for serious criticism in a time, like his, lacking in standards.

Unlike the situation in France, where critics looked exclusively at works worthy of notice, the situation in England was such that an overflow of negligible publications had led to a proliferation of mindless reviews. 'What is the function in the life of man', James asks, 'of such a periodicity of platitude and irrelevance?' (*LC*, vol. i, p. 96). Beginning on a sarcastic note, he builds towards a deeply felt defence of the 'high utility' of criticism, criticism that 'proceeds from deep sources, from the efficient combination of experience and perception. In this light [James] sees the

---

[6] Matthew Arnold, *The Complete Prose Works*, ed. R. H. Super, 11 vols. (Ann Arbor: University of Michigan Press, 1960–77), vol. v, pp. 90–1. Hereafter cited as *CPW*.

critic as the real helper of the artist' (Arnold's argument in 'The Function of Criticism').

Moreover, with his 'curiosity and sympathy', his openness to all 'impressions' and his ability to act upon the 'liveliest experience', the critic is also 'brother' to the artist. 'He only knows that the more impressions he has the more he is able to record, and that the more he is saturated, . . . the more he can give out' (pp. 98–9). By 1893 James knew very well that criticism is anything but a science. 'No theory is kind to us that cheats us of *seeing*', he had written to Robert Louis Stevenson two years earlier.[7] Good criticism is the expression of a percipient consciousness. 'Just in proportion as he is sentient and restless, just in proportion as he reacts and reciprocates and penetrates, is the critic a valuable instrument' (p. 98). In this short, remarkable essay James defends criticism as an art form that holds its own alongside the art of fiction.

Following Norton's death in 1908, James paid tribute to his New England mentor's 'civilising mission', his effort to bring culture to 'a young roaring and money-getting democracy, inevitably but almost exclusively occupied with "business success"'. Professor of Fine Arts at Harvard, a Dante scholar and the friend of John Ruskin, Norton had pleaded in behalf of beauty and 'style' while also pleading for 'substance'. He sought, as an enlightened 'son of the Puritans', 'to lose himself in the labyrinth of delight while keeping hold of the clue of duty'; he addressed himself 'to the moral conscience while speaking as by his office for our imagination and our free curiosity'.[8] This same combination of aesthetic appreciation and moral concern was to motivate James throughout his literary career. Arnold had famously called these contending forces 'Hellenism' and 'Hebraism', '*spontaneity of consciousness*' versus '*strictness of conscience*'; and he had argued the need for both faculties.[9] In practice, however, the one faculty often thrives at the expense of the other; and in the period of James's creative and critical apprenticeship, extending from 1864 to 1879 and culminating in the novels *Roderick Hudson* (1875) and *The American* (1877) and in the collection *French Poets and Novelists* (1878) and the *Hawthorne* (1879), we see a running battle between James's aesthetic and his moral predilections. In his second period – the mature years that produced *The Portrait of a Lady* (1880) and his finest critical effort, *Partial Portraits* (1888), containing the great essay 'The Art of Fiction' – James balanced the two forces with increasing success. But even in the last phase – the period of the great trilogy, the wonderful

[7] James, *Letters*, vol. III, p. 325.
[8] Henry James, 'An American Art-Scholar: Charles Eliot Norton' in *Notes on Novelists* (New York: Charles Scribner's Sons, 1914), pp. 414–15, 422.
[9] Arnold, *CPW*, vol. I, p. 165.

essay 'The Future of the Novel' (1899), and the prefaces to the New York Edition of his fiction – James never abandoned the moral imperatives of Norton. Meanwhile, his capacity to appreciate expanded enormously in his later years; and he accordingly urged his readers to expand their consciousness for moral as well as aesthetic reasons.

*

To Norton's sister Grace, who suffered from depression, James wrote in 1883 an important statement of his personal beliefs. 'I don't know *why* we live', he admitted, but he felt that life was worth holding on to for as long as there were new impressions to be absorbed. 'In other words', he affirmed, 'consciousness is an illimitable power, and though at times it may seem to be all consciousness of misery, yet in the way it propagates itself from wave to wave, so that we never cease to feel, though at moments we appear to, try to, pray to, there is something that holds one in one's place, makes it a standpoint in the universe which it is probably good not to forsake.'[10] James was well aware of life's miseries, and part of the appeal of Ivan Turgenev and the French writers lay in their refusal to gloss over this reality. Guy de Maupassant, he wrote in a superb essay (1888), 'sees human life as a terribly ugly business'; and James contrasted this view to the 'optimism' served up in the English novel, an 'optimism of ignorance as well as of delicacy' (*LC*, vol. II, pp. 536, 540). As early as 1868, James decried James Anthony Froude's facile view 'that the world is built somehow on moral foundations; that in the long run it is well with the good [and]...ill with the wicked'. 'If there is one thing that history does not teach', James contends, 'it is just this very lesson.' For the future author of *The Princess Casamassima* and *The Wings of the Dove*, history is a record of 'the indifference of events to man's moral worth or worthlessness' (*LC*, vol. I, pp. 1014–15). It was art's task to create a bulwark against life's misery and wastefulness; this was a task Joseph Conrad would applaud (and emulate) when he spoke of the artist as 'the preserver, the keeper, the expounder of human experience' and when he lauded James as 'the historian of fine consciences'.[11]

For James human ideals, no less than artworks, are willed into being; and he often dwells in the early essays on the importance of ideals. Whitman, for example, is castigated in 1865 for his failure to suppress his ego on behalf of 'an idea' (*LC*, vol. II, p. 633). A decade later James asserts that the 'fatal charmlessness' of Flaubert's novels constitutes 'an eloquent

---

[10]  James, *Letters*, vol. II, p. 424.
[11]  Joseph Conrad, 'Henry James: An Appreciation' (1905); rpt in *Henry James: A Collection of Critical Essays*, ed. Leon Edel (Englewood Cliffs, NJ: Prentice Hall, 1963), pp. 11–17.

plea for the ideal' (*LC*, vol. II, p. 290). In the earliest of his five essays on Trollope, James complains that the Victorian novelist is 'true to common life' at the expense of higher, more imaginative, flights (*LC*, vol. I, p. 1314). (He would subsequently revise this judgement.) But James also denounces the vapid 'new-fashioned idealism' of American novelists who would do well to 'study the canons of of the so-called realist school' in France (p. 607).

As early as 1867 James sketched out one of the basic ideas of 'The Art of Fiction', that the novelist should treat her subject in the manner of a 'historian'; and he cites Balzac ('The novelist who of all novelists was certainly the most of one') as the supreme exemplar, 'the historian of contemporary manners' (p. 1155). Reading the early James reviews is to remember that even the best critics sometimes err – in, for example, the dismissive notices of Dickens's *Our Mutual Friend* (1865) or Hardy's *Far from the Madding Crowd* (1874), or in the curiously mixed reaction to George Eliot. (But Sainte-Beuve, as James noted, consistently underestimated Balzac.) In the 1874 essay on Turgenev, James declares, 'The great question as to a poet or a novelist is, How does he feel about life? What, in the last analysis, is his philosophy?' (*LC*, vol. II, p. 992). In this respect, Dickens is found wanting: 'He must know *man* as well as *men*, and to know man is to be a philosopher' (*LC*, vol. I, p. 857). Yet while James ranks the 'philosophic' Eliot alongside Turgenev as writers who 'care for more things in life' than other novelists (*LC*, vol. II, p. 972), he repeatedly faults her for being so philosophical and for neglecting artistic form. It is apropos of Eliot that James, in 1866, pompously proclaims, 'The critic's first duty in the presence of an author's collective works is to seek out some key to his method, some utterance of his literary convictions, some indication of his ruling theory' (*LC*, vol. I, p. 912). Thirty years later James would satirize this presumption in his tale about the imperceptiveness of most reviewers, 'The Figure in the Carpet'. James acknowledges Eliot's power of delineating human characters and her 'extensive human sympathy' (p. 907), traits she shares with Turgenev. But *Middlemarch* is characterized as 'a treasure-house of details, but . . . an indifferent whole' (p. 958).

Two more quotations from early reviews are worth citing here to illustrate Jamesian views that remained constant in his criticism. The first, from his first signed essay, 'The Novels of George Eliot' (1866), asserts that 'the writer makes the reader very much as he makes his characters. When he makes him ill, that is, makes him indifferent, he does no work; the writer does all' (*LC*, vol. I, p. 922). The second, from 1868, and showing the influence of Sainte-Beuve, declares contritely, 'The day of dogmatic criticism is over, and with it the ancient infallibility and tyranny of the critic. No critic lays down the law, because no reader receives the law ready made. The critic is simply a reader like all the others – a reader who prints his impressions' (p. 223). If James found so much to criticize in Eliot this was perhaps because she was the English novelist he most looked forward to reading; and he would eventually pay proper homage to her not in a critical essay but in *The Portrait of a Lady* when he transformed her Dorothea Brooke (from *Middlemarch*) and Gwendolen Harleth (from *Daniel Deronda*) into Isabel Archer. In the best of the ten essays he devoted to her work, 'Daniel Deronda: A Conversation' (1876), James divided his mixed feelings towards her among three characters who have just read her latest novel. Constantius, who is conscious of Eliot's best and worst qualities, compares her to Turgenev: 'One is a poet, the other is a philosopher. One cares for the aspect of things and the other cares for the reason of things' (p. 983). Luckily, the house of fiction has room for both occupants. In the end, Constantius declares in grand Arnoldian fashion, 'Yes, I think there is little art in *Deronda*, but I think there is a vast amount of life. In life without art you can find your account; but art without life is a poor affair. The book is full of the world' (p. 992).

In 1875 James settled in Paris for a year to work at novel writing. He supported himself, in part, by writing scores of articles and reviews of books of every possible sort, including travel books extending from Mexico to Egypt to China. He also revealed a talent for writing about the fine arts and the theatre. Many of the review articles were devoted to French writers, including Prosper Mérimée, Stendhal, Hugo, Emile Zola. Before moving to Paris, James penned an eloquent appreciation of Turgenev (1874); and now he had the chance to meet the object of his admiration. Turgenev, in turn, introduced him to his friends among the French Realists, Flaubert, the Goncourt brothers, Alphonse Daudet. James's first impression was not flattering: 'They are extremely narrow', he wrote to his mother, 'and it makes me rather scorn them that not a mother's son of them can read English.' To his sister Alice, James described the mixture of pleasure and disappointment he received reading *Deronda* in Paris: 'The English richness of George Eliot beggars everything else, everywhere, that one might compare with her.'[12] Two months later, in one of the letters from France that he contributed to the *New York Tribune*, James mentioned for the first time a particularly 'unclean' member of the Flaubert circle, Zola: 'the most thorough-going of the little band of the out-and-out realists' (*LC*, vol. II, p. 861).

By late 1876 James had crossed the channel to London, having decided, as he wrote Grace Norton, that London was, for an 'observer', the 'place where there is most in the world to observe'. In the same letter, however,

---

[12]   James, *Letters*, vol. II, pp. 20, 30.

he noted the lack of cosmopolitanism in 'the average Briton of culture'.[13] Perhaps thinking to correct that provincialism, as Arnold had attempted to do in his *Essays in Criticism*, James decided to collect some of his best essays on French authors into a single volume.

*French Poets and Novelists* (1878) helped launch James in the eyes of British reviewers as a devotee and follower of French Realism. Of the twelve essays in the volume, one was on the Russian Turgenev; another on the *Théâtre Français*; two on minor French notables, written in imitation of Sainte-Beuve; and two on the French poets Alfred de Musset and Charles Baudelaire. If James's remarks on Baudelaire and Flaubert seem uninformed or misguided, his tributes to Théophile Gautier, Balzac, George Sand and, above all, Turgenev show his new strengths as literary critic: his talent for appreciation and his deftness of phrasing. The Baudelaire and Flaubert essays are unsatisfying because of James's squeamish and patronizing attitude; they seem written to placate British Philistinism. 'It is not in the temper of English vision', he says approvingly, 'to see things as M. Flaubert sees them' (*LC*, vol. II, p. 168). It is to James's credit that he would return to Flaubert in future essays and try to be just to an author he disliked but whose best work he knew to be a 'masterpiece' (p. 171). In the case of Baudelaire, James refused to take seriously a poet who admired a poet James could not take seriously, Edgar Allan Poe; and he refused to see Baudelaire's sense of evil as anything other than superficial, 'something outside of himself' (p. 155).

James is on surer ground in the Gautier essay, having already praised him in an earlier essay for being 'the poet of the look of things' (p. 353). The 1873 tribute, written soon after Gautier's death, acknowledges Gautier's remarkable 'Athenian' (i.e. Hellenic) gifts: his 'extraordinary' 'faculty of visual discrimination' (p. 357). The apostle of '*l'art pour l'art*' is, for James, an unsurpassed literary painter; and only at the end of the essay does he imply that Gautier's great virtue was also a weakness. In a subtly powerful, lusciously written, critique of Gautier's aestheticism, James reveals how much closer he is, by contrast, to writers like Eliot and Turgenev:

He could look every day at a group of beggars sunning themselves on the Spanish Steps at Rome, against their golden wall of mouldering travertine, and see nothing but the fine brownness of their rags and their flesh-tints – see it and enjoy it for ever, without an hour's disenchantment, without a chance of one of those irresistible revulsions of mood in which the 'mellowest' rags are but filth, and filth is poverty, and poverty a haunting shadow, and picturesque squalor a mockery.                                                         (p. 374)

---

[13]  *Ibid.*, vol. II, p. 135.

James's momentary revulsion is a reminder of how the future creator of Gilbert Osmond, in *The Portrait of a Lady*, and Gabriel Nash, in *The Tragic Muse*, could criticize the aesthetic side of his own nature.[14]

In the Turgenev essay James salutes another 'attentive observer' of life (*LC*, vol. II, p. 972). But unlike Gautier, Turgenev sees deeply into life: 'He has a passion for shifting his point of view, but his object is constantly the same – that of finding an incident, a person, a situation, *morally* interesting' (p. 973). As a creator of men and women Turgenev seemed to James without an equal. (In the New York Edition preface to *The Portrait of a Lady*, James recalled how 'this beautiful genius' invariably began with a 'vision' of an individual, who then lent himself to a 'situation' suitable to his particular nature [pp. 1072–3].) And Turgenev was as much an artist as Flaubert, albeit one capable of mingling 'realism and idealism' (p. 978). James warmed to Turgenev's 'philosophy', which echoed his own melancholy views but which was based on more substantial experience than James's. For Turgenev, life was a 'battle', 'Evil... insolent and strong; beauty enchanting but rare; goodness very apt to be weak; folly very apt to be defiant; wickedness to carry the day; imbeciles to be in great places, people of sense in small, and mankind generally, unhappy.' Yet, James added, this world is all we have: 'we can neither forget it nor deny it nor dispense with it'. And here James's aesthetic and moral sides draw closely together: 'We can welcome experience as it comes, and give it what it demands, in exchange for something which it is idle to pause to call much or little so long as it contributes to swell the volume of consciousness' (p. 998).

Reading James's Turgenev essays and Balzac essays side by side, one might well be baffled by his lifelong preference for Balzac as the supreme novelist. But he was smitten by Balzac's 'overmastering sense of the present world', 'his huge, all-compassing, all-desiring, all-devouring love of reality' (*LC*, vol. II, pp. 49, 66–7). The sheer audacity of Balzac's plan – the creation of a *comédie humaine* – overwhelmed James's critical faculties whenever he wrote on Balzac; and novelistic weaknesses that he deplored in other writers he applauded in Balzac. 'He is an extraordinary tissue of contradictions', James admitted.

He is at once one of the most corrupt of writers and one of the most naïf, the most mechanical and pedantic, and the fullest of *bonhomie* and natural impulse. He is one of the finest of artists and one of the coarsest. Viewed in one way, his novels are ponderous, shapeless, overloaded; his touch is graceless, violent, barbarous. Viewed in another, his tales have more colour, more composition, more grasp of the reader's attention than any others.

---

[14] For James's complicated attitude towards Aestheticism, see Jonathan Freedman, *Professions of Taste: Henry James, British Aestheticism, and Commodity Culture* (Stanford University Press, 1990).

In James's secular world, Balzac ruled as artistic deity. (He cites, approvingly, Taine's claim for Balzac as, 'after Shakespeare,... our great magazine of documents on human nature' [p. 67].) In the paper 'The Lesson of Balzac', which he delivered during his 1902 return visit to America, he admitted having 'learned from him more of the lessons of the engaging mystery of fiction than from any one else' (p. 121). But the influence was more of an inspirational than pedagogic nature: he was encouraged, for example, to esteem the materiality of life, and to view the world as a laboratory for the artist. Unlike American novelists such as Hawthorne and James, born into a barren social and cultural atmosphere, Balzac had the good fortune to draw on a richly stratified and dazzlingly solid and variegated social world. Moreover, he had 'the morality of the Catholic Church' to provide him with 'an infinite *chiaroscuro*' (p. 45).

James included a second essay on Balzac in *French Poets and Novelists*, this one devoted to the recent publication of his letters. (A significant number of James's publications, including the great story 'The Aspern Papers', were inspired by collections of letters.) But Balzac's letters reveal an absence of 'ideas' and practically no hint 'of the world he lived in'; they reveal only the literary worker, the creator (for James) of the most solid 'intellectual work... ever... achieved by man' (*LC*, vol. II, pp. 81–2, 89). By contrast, James's essay on George Sand dwells far more on her appeal as a Romantic figure than as a writer. Her romances are easy to read, but not worth rereading; they lack Balzacian 'exactitude'. She is, unlike Turgenev, neither 'observant' nor a 'moralist' (p. 733). Like Arnold and others of their generation, James had been intrigued by her 'optimism' and 'idealism' (as well as by her amatory escapades); but such optimism may now be out of place. 'Something even better in a novelist', he concludes, 'is that tender appreciation of actuality which makes even a single coat of rose-colour seem an act of violence' (p. 734).

If Sand's predilection for romance seemed ultimately wanting, for James, what could be said on behalf of an American romancer whose life did not offer the compensation of notoriety? Agreeing to write on Hawthorne for the new English Men of Letters series, James confronted his greatest predecessor among American writers, one who (like James) had visited Europe but proved to be one on whom everything was lost. Applying Taine's principle of the importance of milieu to an artist's development, James managed to find occasion for praising Hawthorne despite the absence in his native New England of anything resembling Balzac's worldly support system.

Hawthorne's career, James says at the outset, is proof of the 'moral... that the flower of art blooms only where the soil is deep, that it takes a great deal of history to produce a little literature, that it needs a complex social machinery to set a writer in motion' (*LC*, vol. I, p. 320). Hawthorne's own awareness of the deficiencies in his 'dear native land' leads James into the famous passage where he chronicles 'the items of high civilization' found in other countries that are lacking in America:

No sovereign, no court, no personal loyalty, no aristocracy, no church, no clergy, no army, no diplomatic service, no country gentlemen, no palaces, no castles, nor manors, nor old country-houses, nor parsonages, nor thatched cottages nor ivied ruins; no cathedrals, nor abbeys, nor little Norman churches; no great Universities nor public schools – no Oxford, nor Eton, nor Harrow; no literature, no novels, no museums, no pictures, no political society, no sporting class – no Epsom nor Ascot!'                                          (pp. 250–2)

(It is typical of James's sly humour to sandwich 'novels' somewhere in between Eton and Epsom.) In the absence of such material paraphernalia, Hawthorne was sometimes obliged to turn to artistic devices such as allegory and symbolism, devices deplored by James for their lack of realism. Nevertheless, the author of *The Scarlet Letter* had two strong points to draw upon: he had a knowledge of the 'deeper psychology' (p. 368); and he possessed, thanks to his Puritan heritage, a sense of sin that could be transmuted (like Balzac's Catholicism) into art.[15] Hawthorne, James maintains, used the 'Puritan conscience' not for 'moral and theological' purposes but rather 'as a pigment' (p. 363). When *Hawthorne* was published in America, there were outcries against James's negative image of his native land. He admitted to Howells that he had used 'the word provincial too many times'; but he challenged his friend to name an American novelist (aside from the two of them) 'belonging to the company of Balzac and Thackeray'.[16]

The most compelling passage of the biography, however, refers not to Hawthorne but to those modern Americans who had lost the innocence of earlier generations in the wake of the Civil War. This traumatic event, James writes, 'introduced into the national consciousness a certain sense of proportion and relation, of the world being a more complicated place than it had hitherto seemed, the future more treacherous, success more difficult'. The modern American will necessarily 'be a more critical person than his complacent and confident grandfather'. And 'he will be, without discredit to his well-known capacity for action, an observer' (*LC*, vol. I, pp. 427–8). James's modern American, having learned the melancholy truth of Turgenev's philosophy, will be an observer, critic, reader and novelist like Henry James.

---

[15]  In the Baudelaire essay, James compared the French poet, who presented a superficial 'treatment of evil', with 'Hawthorne, who felt the thing at its source, deep in the human consciousness' (*LC*, vol. II, p. 155).
[16]  James, *Letters*, vol. II, pp. 266–7.

*

The 1880s were a particularly rich period in James's career as critic and novelist.[17] In 1882 he was saluted by Howells as the 'chief exemplar' among the new 'school' of novelists who combine the psychological analysis of Eliot and Hawthorne with the formal demands of the French Realists. 'In one manner or other,' Howells contended, 'the stories were all told long ago; and now we want merely to know what the novelist thinks about persons and situations. Mr. Henry James gratifies this philosophic desire.'[18] Howells's comments annoyed Walter Besant, a popular writer of the period, who (as we will see) made a contending claim for the novel which inspired, in turn, James's 'The Art of Fiction' (1884). As the decade began, however, James looked benignly upon all the possibilities open to artists. 'Art', he said in 1880, 'is really but a point of view, and genius but a way of looking at things. The wiser the artist, and the finer the genius, the more easy will it be to conceive of other points of view, other ways of looking at things, than one's own.'[19]

In the same year James wrote his fullest tribute to Sainte-Beuve, the French critic most adept at making his point of view (a compound of 'scholar', 'observer', 'moralist' and 'psychologist') an art of appreciation. 'He valued life and literature', James wrote, describing his own practice, 'equally for the light they threw upon each other'(LC, vol. II, p. 681). James also wrote, in the 1880s, generous studies of Renan (1883) and Arnold (1884), finding qualities in each (Renan's delicacy of style, Arnold's 'largeness of horizon' [LC, vol. I, p. 723]) that compared favourably to Sainte-Beuve.

In the great collection of essays from this period, *Partial Portraits* (1888), James took his place among the company of his critical predecessors. While invoking Sainte-Beuve's method of literary portraiture, James was inspired again by the *Essays in Criticism* (a second series of which also appeared in 1888 following Arnold's death). Arnold had described his aim in the *Essays* as trying to 'approach truth on one side after another';[20] and so he celebrated a contrasting group of truth-seekers: Marcus Aurelius, St Francis, Spinoza, the Guérins, Heine, Byron, Wordsworth. In *Partial Portraits*, James, while paying tribute to a number of artists particularly dear to him, also holds up the novelist as the supreme truth-teller. The novel's value, he affirms (in the Turgenev essay), 'lies in its power to tell

17 See Donald Stone, *Novelists in a Changing World: George Meredith, Henry James, and the Transformation of English Fiction in the 1880s* (Cambridge, MA: Harvard University Press, 1972).
18 W. D. Howells, 'Henry James Jr.', *Century Illustrated Monthly Magazine*, 3 (1882), 25–9; rpt in *Henry James: The Critical Heritage*, ed. Roger Gard (London: Routledge & Kegan Paul, 1968), pp. 126–34.
19 James, 'Letters of Delacroix', p. 183.      20 Arnold, *CPW*, vol. III, p. 186.

us the most about men and women'. James acknowledges, however, that some readers will be less interested in men and women than in finding 'a good story' (LC, vol. II, p. 1023).

In a review of Zola's Nana (1880) James described the novel as 'the most human form of art'; but he criticized both the French novelist's disregard for the finely human side of life and the English reading public's disregard for art and life. 'Reality is the object of M. Zola's efforts', James remarks, 'and it is because we agree with him in appreciating it highly that we protest against its being discredited' (LC, vol. II, pp. 867–8). In the English-speaking world, meanwhile, 'Half of life is a sealed book to young unmarried ladies [the novel's target audience], and how can a novel be worth anything that deals with only half a life? How can a portrait be painted (in any way to be recognizable) of half a face?' (p. 869). James's highest praise, in Partial Portraits, is thus lavished on writers who write truly about life, writers as different from each other as Trollope and Maupassant, Turgenev and Stevenson. His criticism is directed, in relatively gentle fashion, towards those writers who were deprived of 'certain chords': Emerson, for example, who lacked an aesthetic sense. The only non-artist included among the 'portraits', Emerson is perhaps here to remind us of Hawthorne's similar deficiency. 'Emerson's personal history is condensed into the word Concord', James drily observes, 'and all the condensation in the world will not make it look rich' (LC, vol. I, pp. 269, 250).

A sadder case for James was his favourite English novelist, George Eliot, whose posthumously published letters reveal a 'provincial strain' (p. 997) and a shocking disregard for Balzac. For the novel's future, James suggests, it is best to look to novelists who observe reality without being constrained by aesthetic limitations or philosophic preoccupations. A work such as Romola, for James 'the finest thing she wrote', is 'overladen with learning, it smells of the lamp, it tastes just perceptibly of pedantry' (p. 1006). Eliot is compared negatively to Daudet, for whom 'the personal impression, the effort of direct observation, was the most precious source of information for the novelist' (p. 1009).[21]

James's portraits of Trollope and Daudet were written just before 'The Art of Fiction', while he was thinking his way towards that essay, while the later portraits of Maupassant and Stevenson contain James's afterthoughts. A line from the Stevenson essay summarizes James's main principle: 'The breath of the novelist's being is his liberty, and the incomparable virtue of the form he uses is that it lends itself to views innumerable and diverse, to every variety of illustration' (LC, vol. I, p. 1248).

---

[21]  Perhaps to counterbalance the negative effects of the Eliot essay, James also included in Partial Portraits the delightful 1877 'Daniel Deronda: A Conversation'.

James's tribute to Trollope (for whom he had expressed 'a partiality' two decades earlier) is one of his finest essays, probably the best account ever devoted to the chronicler of Barsetshire. Although not standing 'on the very same level as Dickens, Thackeray and George Eliot, . . . he belonged to the same family' (p. 1331), James contends; and moreover he is one of the few English novelists who can be compared to Balzac. He too created a fictional world with recurring characters; and although he usually focused on commonplace reality, he was capable, in works like *He Knew He Was Right*, of tragic pictures 'worthy of Balzac' (p. 1351). Although Trollope observed a typically British 'decorum', he was never 'mawkish' or 'prudish', and he possessed 'a certain saving grace of coarseness' (another Balzacian trait). 'If he was in any degree a man of genius (and I hold that he was), it was in virtue', James says, of his 'happy, instinctive sense of human varieties' (pp. 1334–5). Like Balzac, he believed in the novelist's responsibility (which he practised himself) to create characters who 'stand on their feet'; and he chose to write novels of 'character' rather than novels of 'plot', knowing 'that character in itself is plot' (p. 1336). This anticipates the famous passage in 'The Art of Fiction' where James skewers the absurdly artificial opposition set up by inept critics who demand novels with 'stories' rather than novels about 'persons and situations' (the kind of novels Howells had praised James for writing). 'What is character but the determination of incident? What is incident but the illustration of character?' (p. 55).

James also calls attention to Trollope's cosmopolitanism. Thanks to his work for the postal service, he has 'a spacious geographic quality' – a knowledge of all of England and much of the globe – plus a familiarity with 'all sorts and conditions of men' that puts the insular French novelists to shame (p. 1346). In almost every respect, Trollope seems their superior. 'In spite of his want of doctrinal richness', James observes, 'he tells us, on the whole, more about life than the "naturalists" in our sister republic'; and he ranks high among the British novelists who are 'more at home in the moral world' than Zola and company (p. 1348). James does fault Trollope's 'suicidal satisfaction in reminding the reader that the story he was telling was only, after all, a make-believe'; and James utters apropos of Trollope one of the few canonical ideas to be found in 'The Art of Fiction': 'It is impossible to imagine what a novelist takes himself to be unless he regard himself as an historian and his narrative as a history' (p. 1343). But a historian, paradoxically, is exactly what Trollope is. He possessed, like Balzac, a 'great apprehension of the real' (p. 1336); and 'So much of the life of his time is reflected in his novels that we must believe a part of the record will be saved' (p. 1353).

It may be that James's greatness as literary critic is more evident in the Trollope essay than in 'The Art of Fiction'. It is a generous tribute by a

critic who has learned how novels are put together, and by a novelist who
has mastered the art of criticism as a form of intelligent appreciation.
But that is to say that James is essentially a descriptive, non-dogmatic
critic like Sainte-Beuve, not a prescriptive critic like Walter Besant. In the
genial essay on Daudet, written soon afterwards, he overlooks the French
writer's lack of 'system' or 'philosophy' (*LC*, vol. II, pp. 235, 248). It is
enough for James that Daudet's poetically (but also realistically) observed
'representations' of life are appealing to him. 'The success of a work of
art', he offers by way of explanation for his partiality, 'to my mind, may
be measured by the degree to which it produces a certain illusion; that
illusion makes it appear to us for the time that we have lived another life –
that we have had a miraculous enlargement of experience. The greater the
art the greater the miracle' (p. 242). Novels are so many 'representations'
of life, and for some readers, James concedes, the 'illusion' offered by
Ouida is preferable to that offered by Jane Austen. Here, as in 'The Art of
Fiction', he is intentionally vague in defining the novel precisely because
he has no wish to burden the novel with definitions.

In the original 1884 text of 'The Art of Fiction' James described the
novel as competing with life; in the 1888 version (which appears in *Partial Portraits*) he changed the wording (under the influence of Stevenson's
essay 'A Humble Remonstrance') to 'The only reason for the existence
of a novel is that it does attempt to represent life' (p. 46). This restates
the position taken in the Daudet essay. The least satisfactory sections of
'The Art of Fiction' are the various earnest attempts to define the novel –
whether as a 'representation' of life; as a kind of 'history' with a search
for 'truth' analogous to Gibbon's (p. 46); as a 'personal, a direct impression of life' (this anticipates the position in the Maupassant essay); or
as a kind of living 'organism' in which each part contains 'something of
each of the other parts' (p. 54). (It is in this last definition that James disposes of the novel of 'character' versus novel of 'incident' controversy.)
Tony Tanner wittily, and admiringly, speaks of James's 'authoritative
vagueness'; and he rightly observes that 'James's critical writing discovers and demonstrates the hopeless inadequacy of *any* theory to account
for and describe the countless, unaccountable ways in which writing can
attract, take, and hold us. Criticism is not, and cannot be, a theory. It is
an art.'[22]

In 'The Art of Fiction', James was intent not on writing a theory of
fiction but rather on defending an art form that resists regulations. The
occasion for his essay was Besant's published lecture 'The Art of Fiction',
which contained, amid helpful advice for the would-be novelist, a number

[22] Tony Tanner, *Henry James and the Art of Nonfiction* (Athens: University of Georgia
Press, 1995), p. 41.

of maxims. 'First, and before everything else', Besant postulates, 'there is the Rule that everything in Fiction which is invented, and is not the result of personal experience and observation, is worthless.' Another rule is that, in spite of 'this new school' of novelists who disdain storytelling, 'the story is everything'. Moreover, the 'modern English novel... almost always starts with a conscious moral purpose'.[23] James, for his part, welcomes Besant's paper, whose title he appropriates, and he takes the occasion to make a plea for 'serious' discussion of the novel as a major art form.

'Art lives upon discussion', James says at the outset, 'upon experiment, upon curiosity, upon variety of attempt, upon the exchange of views and the comparison of standpoints' (LC, vol. 1, pp. 44–5). He then politely faults Besant for dictating 'what sort of an affair the good novel will be'. For James, the novel must 'be perfectly free. It lives upon exercise, and the very meaning of exercise is freedom' (p. 49). To demand that the writer draw only upon personal experience is to ignore the internal and intuitive dimensions of experience: 'It is the very atmosphere of the mind; and when the mind is imaginative... it takes to itself the faintest hints of life, it converts the very pulses of the air into revelations.' It includes 'the power to guess the unseen from the seen, to trace the implication of things, to judge the whole piece by the pattern, the condition of feeling life in general so completely that you are well on your way to knowing every corner of it'. 'Experience', in other words, 'consists of impressions' and thus 'impressions *are* experience'. The good novelist is one possessed of an active consciousness, one 'on whom nothing is lost' (pp. 52–3). As for the need to write 'stories', James concedes that while tales may take up part of the novel, they are inextricably linked to the form of the novel. 'The story and the novel, the idea and the form', he observes, 'are the needle and the thread', and neither can survive without the other (p. 60). But novels can be made out of psychological dramas no less than out of adventures. Almost the 'only obligation' James lays on the novel is that it be 'interesting' (p. 49).

As for Besant's (and the English public's) view of the morality of fiction, James eloquently speaks in behalf of the artist's freedom: 'The essence of moral energy is to survey the whole field' (p. 63). Earlier in the essay, James suggests that the novelist's 'taste' would help guide him in the choice of material (p. 59); but James also recognizes that the novelist's 'intelligence' is crucial in the decision of what to write about:

There is one point at which the moral sense and the artistic sense lie very near together; that is in the light of the very obvious truth that the deepest quality of

[23]  Walter Besant, *The Art of Fiction* (New York: Brentano's, 1902), pp. 34, 66–7, 57.

a work of art will always be the quality of the mind of the producer. In proportion as that intelligence is fine will the novel, the picture, the statue partake of the substance of beauty and truth. To be constituted of such elements is, to my vision, to have purpose enough. No good novel will ever proceed from a superficial mind; that seems to me an axiom which, for the artist in fiction, will cover all needful moral ground.                                    (pp. 63–4)

He described his essay to Stevenson as 'simply a plea for liberty';[24] but in his conclusion, he also noted, 'This freedom is a special privilege, and the first lesson of the young novelist is to be worthy of it.' Pointing to Zola's 'prodigious effort' in France, James warns that such work can be undermined by narrow views. 'If you must indulge in conclusions', he concludes, 'let them have the taste of a wide knowledge' (p. 65).

Despite the touch of New England moralism in that last remark, James in the 1880s was moving to a higher appreciation of the French Naturalists than he had possessed earlier. To Howells, in 1844, he complained of the 'floods of tepid soap and water which under the name of novels are being vomited forth in England'; and he described the current efforts of Zola and company as 'the only kind of work . . . that I respect'.[25] The essay on Maupassant (1888) salutes the work of one who looks unflinchingly at reality but who also writes with the highest artistry.

Maupassant and his *confrères*, moreover, 'treat of that vast dim section of society' (*LC*, vol. II, p. 547) studiously ignored by English writers. (James had just published a magnificent but largely ignored novel set in the lower classes, *The Princess Casamassima*, drawing on the methods of the French Naturalists.)[26] James grants Maupassant his right to stress the 'erotic element' in his works, although he notes a tendency in *Pierre et Jean* to allow characters with 'an air of responsibility' (pp. 548, 546). But if the French writers seem to explore the 'carnal side of man' at the expense of man's higher nature, English and American novelists ignore this side altogether.

This brings James back to 'the famous question of morality, the decency, of the novel'. In the finale to the Maupassant essay, he restates the thesis of 'The Art of Fiction' with fiery conviction:

Hard and fast rules, *a priori* restrictions, mere interdictions (you shall not speak of you shall not look at that), have surely served their time, and will in the nature of the case never strike an energetic talent as anything but arbitrary. A healthy, living and growing art, full of curiosity and fond of exercise, has an indefeasible mistrust of rigid prohibitions. Let us leave this magnificent art of the novelist to itself and to its perfect freedom.                         (pp. 548–9)

---

[24] James, *Letters*, vol. III, p. 58.    [25] *Ibid.*, p. 28.
[26] See Lyall H. Powers, *Henry James and the Naturalist Movement* (East Lansing: Michigan State University Press, 1971).

This celebration of Maupassant's right to his point of view constitutes James's finest tribute to the novel form.

Maupassant, Stevenson and Pierre Loti were James's favourites among the younger generation of writers whom he saluted for bringing fresh impressions to the novel. He welcomed Maupassant's (and Zola's) description of the novel as 'simply the vision of the world from the stand-point of a person constituted after a certain fashion' (*LC*, vol. II, p. 523), but transformed it into the metaphor of the 'novelist [as] . . . a particular *window*, absolutely – and of worth in so far as he is one' (this from a letter to Howells in 1890).[27] (In the preface to the New York Edition of *The Portrait of a Lady*, James amends the metaphor of novelist as window, describing him now as a figure gazing out of one of the million windows in the 'house of fiction' and forming 'an impression distinct from every other' [p. 1075].) When asked by the Deerfield Summer School for his views on the novel, James urged the students to 'do something from your point of view; . . . do something with the great art and the great form; do something with life. Any point of view is interesting that is a direct impression of life' (*LC*, vol. I, p. 93). This is advice that would be heeded by most of the leading modern novelists, whether they acknowledged their debt (from Conrad and Ford Madox Ford to Philip Roth and Orhan Pamuk) or unknowingly or unwillingly profited from his example (from Edith Wharton and Virginia Woolf to Kazuo Ishiguro and Ian McEwan). James showed that a serious art form could be made out of the author's singular point of view, and he also showed how novels could be created by focusing on the point of view of one or more characters.

*

James published two more collections of critical essays during his lifetime: *Essays in London and Elsewhere* (1893) and *Notes on Novelists* (1914). The earlier volume contains the 1891 essay on 'Criticism' in which he complains of the flood of indiscriminate reviews, signs of a debased modern taste, and in which he looks to the critical spirit (in Arnoldian fashion) to help foster a better intellectual and artistic climate. In the late essay 'The New Novel' (1914), part of the later collection, James describes the 'effect, if not the prime office, of criticism' as making 'our absorption and our enjoyment of the things that feed the mind as aware of itself as possible, since that awareness quickens the mental demand' (*LC*, vol. I, p. 124). But even as James surveyed the contemporary deluge of shoddy offerings, he remained hopeful about 'The Future of the Novel' – the title he gave in 1899 to one of his best late essays. Novels will continue to

---

[27] James, *Letters*, vol. III, p. 282.

be written, he affirms, because of mankind's 'general appetite for a *picture*'. We all have an aesthetic instinct as part of our human nature, and thus we take pleasure in reading an art form that is 'of all pictures the most comprehensive and the most elastic', The novel has 'for its subject, magnificently,...the whole human consciousness' (p. 102).

On a sombre note, James also speaks of man's destructive impulse, his 'incomparable faculty for...mutilating and disfiguring' what comes to hand (p. 109). But as long as art thrives, man thrives. 'The future of fiction is intimately bound up with the future of the society that produces and consumes it...A community addicted to reflection and fond of ideas will try experiments with the "story" that will be left untried in a community mainly devoted to travelling and shooting, to pushing trade and playing football' (p. 106). Whereas Arnold had once looked to culture as the panacea for mankind, James's great 'anodyne' was the novel. Only when people are thoroughly sick of life will they stop reading novels, he avows, and even then, the collapse of mankind will provide one last story. Until then, until 'the world is an unpeopled void there will be an image in the mirror' to sustain the survivors (pp. 109–10).

James, in the late novels (*The Ambassadors*, *The Wings of the Dove*, *The Golden Bowl*) as well as in the late criticism, looked to the values that endure amid the wreckage of modern history. In these essays he cited the 'lessons' to be learned from novelists such as Turgenev, Zola, Flaubert and, above all, Balzac. Although Turgenev's Russian colleague Tolstoy took on a more ambitious subject in his novels ('all human life!'), Turgenev had the edge in that more intimate sphere, 'the world of our finer consciousness' (*LC*, vol. II, pp. 1030, 1034). Reacting to the death of Zola, in 1902, James finally gave the creator of the ambitious series of Rougon-Macquart novels (landmarks of French Naturalism) credit for having 'pulled it off' (p. 896). James conceded that Zola had been '*obliged* to be gross, on his system, or neglect to his cost an invaluable aid to representation'; and so he could not 'withhold [his] frank admiration from the courage and consistency with which [Zola] faced his need' (pp. 878–9).

James, in his middle and late essays, carried the art of appreciation to its highest level. Few critics have proved capable of such sensitivity and generosity, and none could write so beautifully. Only in his very late study of 'The New Novel' (1914) did his taste fail him. As he took stock of the new generation – Conrad, H. G. Wells, Arnold Bennett, Edith Wharton, D. H. Lawrence – he found it hard to see how such writers, each 'immersed in his own body of reference' (*LC*, vol. I, p. 128), could keep the vessel of fiction afloat. But from the past masters he found increasing sustenance: from Flaubert's heroic battle with artistic form, from Balzac's love for reality and for his characters. Thirty years after dismissing the author of *Madame Bovary* as a failure, James now saw the perfection of that novel. 'The work is a classic', he wrote in 1902, 'because the thing, such as it is, is ideally *done*, and because it shows that in such doing eternal beauty may dwell' (*LC*, vol. II, p. 325). Balzac may not have been 'totally an artist', in the manner of Flaubert, but he had an 'unequalled power of putting people on their feet' (pp. 94–5). What better lesson could Balzac provide, James declared in 'The Lesson of Balzac' (1905), than love for all his characters, the worthless no less than the worthy. 'It was by loving them...that he knew them' (p. 132).

It was out of the generous desire to share his own lessons, acquired from over forty years of reading and writing, that James wrote the great prefaces for the New York Edition of his selected fiction. He described his intentions to Howells as 'a sort of plea for Criticism, for Discrimination, for Appreciation on other than infantile lines' – a continuation and expansion of what he had been doing all along in his essays. (He was also following in the tradition of George Sand and Daudet, who had attached to editions of their works prefaces explaining the works' 'origins' [*LC*, vol. II, pp. 718, 232].) According to Leon Edel, these works, 'dictated at intervals between 1906 and 1908, show in their colloquial ease and flow the embodied truths of the art of fiction as James had practiced it and the distillation of a lifetime of close reading of major and minor novelists of the West'.[28] They are certainly among his most appealing works. In addition to the practical comments on his use of point of view in his novels, and on his struggle (not always successful, he admits) positioning the 'organic center' of his works (p. 1109), James provides personal reminiscences of how each work came into being. He also conveys his delighted reaction upon finding himself not only the writer but the reader of his own fictions.

The eighteen prefaces can be read as a kind of narrative in which James shows how the pursuit of the right form for each novel finally coincides with the choice of the right 'reflector' or point of view. (James does not advocate a specific form for all novels, only the one that works best for each 'particular case' [p. 1141]. In *The Tragic Muse*, for example, he aimed at a kind of pictorial organizational principle inspired by a Tintoretto painting, while in *The Awkward Age* he drew upon the theatre for inspiration.) And when form and point of view come together the novel achieves a moral significance as well.

---

[28] Leon Edel, *Henry James: The Master, 1901–1916* (Philadelphia: Lippincott, 1972), pp. 332–3.

In the case of the earliest novel under consideration, *Roderick Hudson*, James recalls the difficulty of developing his characters in a credible but contained manner. In real life, James notes, 'relations stop nowhere, and the exquisite problem of the artist is eternally but to draw, by a geometry of his own, the circle within which they shall happily *appear* to do so' (*LC*, vol. II, p. 1041). James subsequently decided to tell the tragic history of his artist-hero as it is perceived by an intelligent secondary character. 'The centre of interest throughout "Roderick"', he notes, 'is in Rowland Mallet's consciousness, and the drama is the very drama of that consciousness' (p. 1050). This allowed James not only to dispense with the Victorian convention of the omniscient narrator, but also to draw the reader and the reflector together in a shared experience. We as readers are sharing a learning experience, expanding our consciences along with Rowland; just as in subsequent James novels we will be learning alongside Isabel Archer and Lambert Strether. James's search for the right form for the novel and his decision to advance the story through Rowland's point of view are artistic choices with profound moral implications. For in life as in books, we are what (and how) we perceive. James's aim in showing the drama of consciousness in his novels points up the necessity of our becoming 'finely aware' readers in real life.

When James concluded his 1902 essay on Flaubert by asking, 'Are we not... pretty well all novelists now?' (*LC*, vol. II, p. 346), he was (jovially) underscoring this kinship between novelist and character and reader. His choice of characters was determined by their ability to grow in consciousness. Isabel Archer's story, in effect, is her coming to awareness. The old question of whether novels are about 'character' or 'incident', which James had deftly answered in 'The Art of Fiction', becomes a question of larger consequence: what is character really but the possession and growth of consciousness? 'What a man thinks and what he feels are the history and the character of what he does', James says in the preface to *The Princess Casamassima* (p. 1092); and elsewhere in the same preface he notes 'that the figures in any picture, the agents in any drama, are interesting only in proportion as they feel their respective situations; since the consciousness, on their part, of the complication exhibited forms for us their link of connexion with it'. James praises characters such as his Hyacinth Robinson for getting the '"most" out of all that happens to them and who in so doing enable us, as readers of their record, as participators by a fond attention, also to get most. Their being finely aware – as Hamlet and Lear, say, are finely aware – *makes* absolutely the intensity of their adventure, gives the maximum of sense to what befalls them' (p. 1088). Hence, James never sees 'the *leading* interest of any human hazard but in a consciousness... subject to fine intensification and wide enlargement'

(p. 1092). But the 'mass of mankind', he sadly observes in the preface to *What Maisie Knew*, 'are banded, probably by the sanest of instincts, to defend themselves to the death against any such vitiation of their simplicity' (p. 1169).

In the 1888 Maupassant essay, James had applauded the French Realists for looking at places from which English writers and readers avert their heads, the lower depths, for example; and in the preface to *Princess*, he pointed to his own attempt to depict an aspect of London ignored by the middle classes, the dingy 'underworld' of the 'disinherited' (p. 1096). This was the novel for which James had taken intensive notes, in the manner of the French Naturalists. More importantly, he had also drawn on his own 'sense of life' and his 'penetrating imagination', without which one is a 'fool in the very presence of the revealed and assured', but being 'so armed you are not really helpless, not without your resources, even before mysteries abysmal' (p. 1102).

The possessor of such knowledge – whether a percipient character, novelist or reader – is armed with the 'critical impulse' (a faculty most professional critics lack, as James ruefully notes in 'The Figure in the Carpet'). 'To criticise', he says, 'is to appreciate, to appropriate, to take intellectual possession, to establish in fine a relation with the criticised thing and make it one's own' (*LC*, vol. II, p. 1169). Thus, the prefaces collectively argue the value and necessity of the 'penetrating imagination', even as they acknowledge its rarity in life. Similarly, James writes eloquently of the need for formal coherence in the novel precisely because coherence is difficult to find elsewhere. Life, he argues in the preface to *The Spoils of Poynton*, is 'nothing but splendid waste. Hence the opportunity for the sublime economy of art, which rescues, which saves' (p. 1139), which transforms bits of throw-away life into something that endures.

James elaborates, in the preface to *The Tragic Muse*, on the need for artistic 'composition' in the novel. 'There is life and life', he explains (having alluded to the 'loose baggy monsters' of Tolstoy, Dumas and Thackeray, 'with their queer elements of the accidental and the arbitrary'), 'and as waste is only life sacrificed and thereby prevented from "counting", I delight in a deep-breathing economy and an organic form' (pp. 1107–8). These lessons – on the need to be 'finely aware', on the need to rescue and preserve life by turning it into 'the sublime economy of art' – are the lessons of the prefaces; and they are lessons that have been appropriated by James's literary progeny from Virginia Woolf in *To the Lighthouse* (trying 'to make of the moment something permanent') to Ian McEwan in *Atonement* and Colm Tóibín in *The Master*. The protagonist of David Lodge's recent novel *Author, Author* is Henry James, who, when asked if he has religious beliefs, appropriately replies, 'Consciousness is my religion, human consciousness. Refining it, intensifying it – and preserving it.'[29]

After James's death many of his ideas about novelistic form were taken up by critics like Percy Lubbock, in *The Craft of Fiction*, or were condemned by writers like E. M. Forster, in *Aspects of the Novel*. In his preoccupation with Jamesian point of view (which he saw as a purely formal device without moral implications) in the prefaces, Lubbock overlooked what Wharton saw as James's stress on 'moral values ("importance of subject")' in the novels.[30]

In 1918 T. S. Eliot famously saluted James's ideological purity; and the praise of Eliot, Lubbock and R. P. Blackmur (who called the prefaces 'the most eloquent and original pieces of literary criticism in existence') helped enshrine James's position among the New Critics, the proponents of formal purity.[31] As we have seen, James's views on criticism and the novel were never based on theory but on what he called 'experience', or more precisely, on fine consciousness. While some recent critics have thereby seen him as a precursor of phenomenology (or, more radically, of psychoanalytical, feminist or even Marxist 'critical theory'),[32] it may be just as true to say that he was only articulating the practice of Sainte-Beuve. James was original in his stress on the reader's active role in the literary process. In this respect he encouraged the very different rhetorics of fiction advocated by Wayne Booth and J. Hillis Miller. The view that 'Literature must be in some way a cause and not merely an effect' is true for James, but not in the deconstructive manner endorsed by Miller. Closer to the truth is Tony Tanner's claim that 'James's central intention is . . . to stress the primacy of the receptive and transformative consciousness.'[33] In a much-quoted letter to H. G. Wells in 1915, written during a war that confirmed his worst fears of human destructiveness, James made a claim for the creative process that has never lost its relevancy: 'It is art that *makes* life, makes interest, makes importance, for our consideration and application of these things, and I know of no substitute whatever for

[29] David Lodge, *Author, Author* (New York: Viking, 2004), p. 91.
[30] Percy Lubbock, *The Craft of Fiction* (1921; rpt New York: Viking, 1957); Millicent Bell, *Edith Wharton and Henry James* (New York: Braziller, 1965), p. 1965.
[31] R. P. Blackmur, *Studies in Henry James*, ed. Virginia A. Makowsky (New York: New Directions, 1983); T. S. Eliot, 'In Memory of Henry James', *Egoist*, 5 (1918), 1, rpt in *Critical Essays on Henry James*, ed. Peter Rawlings (Aldershot: Scolar Press, 1993).
[32] Paul B. Armstrong, *The Phenomenology of Henry James* (Chapel Hill: University of North Carolina Press, 1983); John Carlos Rowe, *The Theoretical Dimensions of Henry James* (Madison: University of Wisconsin Press, 1984).
[33] J. Hillis Miller, *The Ethics of Reading* (New York: Columbia University Press, 1987), p. 5; Wayne C. Booth, *The Rhetoric of Fiction* (University of Chicago Press, 1961); Booth, *The Company We Keep: An Ethics of Fiction* (Berkeley: University of California Press, 1988); Tanner, *Henry James and the Art of Nonfiction*, p. 34.

the force and beauty of the process.' But this was to restate the wisdom of his early mentor, Charles Eliot Norton, for whom (as James wrote six years earlier) 'Art' with a capital 'A' was 'the most beneficial of human products'.[34]

34  James, *Letters*, vol. IV, p. 770; James, *Notes on Novelists*, p. 422.

# 25

# Georg Brandes (1842–1927)

## POUL HOUE

I

A native of Denmark, Georg Brandes was the most prominent and controversial critic of Danish literature and culture during the late nineteenth and early twentieth centuries. The gifted and worldly young Brandes refused to acquiesce to the unholy alliance of the homely (Biedermeier) version of late Romantic idealism, a watered-down Christian orthodoxy, and the political resignation of the Danish cultural elites after their nation's cession of its southern provinces to Germany in 1864. An empathetic student of Danish Romantic literature and so-called golden age culture, Brandes nevertheless spearheaded a modern breakthrough in Danish letters, intended to bring his nation up to date with European modernity.

Although his efforts as a gadfly on the national scene were temperamental, spectacular and untiring, they were only moderately successful. Resistance from the prevailing political, religious and cultural powers was fierce and rendered Brandes a *persona non grata* in establishment circles for decades. His call for progress was largely muted and, despondent about his cultural impact, he gradually abandoned his hopes for a broad revival of *citoyen* virtues and retreated instead to the hero-worshipping of great individuals.

On the other hand, the small number of Brandes's followers and victories in the Danish culture wars of the 1870s and 1880s belies his actual significance. Over time, his radical positions and critical alertness did meet with greater, if never unanimous, approval. But more importantly, his front-line struggles were admired by such luminaries as Norway's Henrik Ibsen and Sweden's August Strindberg. For all the discomfort stirred by Brandes nationally, his voice was heard throughout Scandinavia, and his criticism made an enduring impression on a memorable array of Scandinavia's best authors. Never before or since have the literatures of the Nordic countries been in such close and lively contact with one another.

Moreover, Georg Brandes's role as an independent modern intellectual extended to the European scene. His introduction of Nietzsche to Scandinavian culture, with reverberations in Germany, is but one example of his critical range. A remarkable network of progressive

464

politicians, authors and intellectuals interacted with Brandes. And while, discontented with the response of his fellow Danes to the work of his youth, he went into voluntary exile for years and later embarked upon a cult of the artistic genius, his socio-political sensibilities were never dulled; in fact, he increasingly embraced the causes of oppressed individuals, minorities and entire peoples across Europe, and vigorously opposed all the warring factions of the First World War.

Such a stance towards the war inevitably gave pause to many a cultured European admirer of Brandes's literary prowess. Respect for his intellectual courage was once again contested by powerful and popular sentiments deploring what appeared to be the great man's disrespect for conventional wisdom and traditional values. At the same time, socialist and other opponents of the bourgeois order chastised him as an insider and an unreliable ally. Brandes was an outspoken champion of women's rights, yet his treatment of particular women writers – in life and work – has been fiercely contested, especially by younger feminist critics and scholars.

Notwithstanding its formal brilliance, Georg Brandes's critical work has not fared much better. It has been habitually accused of falling below scholarly standards, and most of it has faded from public view. Supposedly a proponent of positivist modernity, Brandes was never the dispassionate scientific observer; and his essayistic approach has been deemed both naïve and outdated by proponents of later critical theorists, including formalists and structuralists. The politically minded have typically found him too aestheticist, while aestheticists have rejected the political tenor of his work. Brandes habitually showed little respect for conventional cultural and critical sensibilities. It is no surprise that an era so saturated with latent anti-Semitism would seek to smoke this assimilated Jew out of his Danish and European identity.

These are among the reasons why Brandes's reputation has remained that of the lonely, activist, perennial critic. Yet his criticism integrated and transmitted a broad range of critical impulses: from Hegel, Kierkegaard and German biblical scholars, as well as from his beloved French teachers Taine and Sainte-Beuve. It was also informed by a series of influences stretching from Greek Antiquity through the Italian Renaissance and Shakespeare to French Classicism and Romanticism. It can truly be said that he extended the critical enterprise well beyond its academic confines.


II


Georg Brandes was raised in Copenhagen, Denmark, in a Jewish middle-class home with no religious affinities, by a doting mother and an unsuccessful wholesaler father. The precocious youngster matriculated at the age of seventeen as a law student at Copenhagen University, but three years later, already steeped in literature and philosophy, changed his focus to aesthetics. He received his master's degree with distinction only two years later, in 1864, the same year in which his country was emasculated by Prussia. In 1866 he went to Paris on the first of his many travels abroad, and after completing his inaugural dissertation four years later, on Taine and contemporary French Aestheticism, he spent sixteen months in France, England and Italy, before returning to Copenhagen. His critical breakthrough came in 1871–2 with his university lectures on the main currents in nineteenth-century literature.[1]

Henning Fenger concludes his own inaugural dissertation on Brandes by noting that he 'recognized that he had been a romanticist spending all his life in fighting romanticism'.[2] As Paul V. Rubow has shown, this was certainly true of Brandes's take on the English and French Classicists, whom he long viewed from a Romantic perspective and whose achievements in the theatre he valued most. Gradually, via studies of English and German Romantics, he came to appreciate the French classics for their bearing on French Romanticism; but even so, he continued to view Classicism from a modern viewpoint, an approach confirmed by the incipient influence of Taine. Over time Brandes did reverse his criticism of Racine, but not of Corneille, whose order, clarity and intellectual precision he continued to view as poor classical substitutes for Romantic imagination. But he was more sympathetic, as in his later monograph on Voltaire, to the French Enlightenment Classicists, whom he saw as preparing the way for the brilliance of the nineteenth century.

The Romantic in Brandes also defined his relation to Roman and Greek Antiquity. He rejected the Romans as unpoetic (an attitude he shared with N. F. S. Grundtvig) and elevated the Greeks, whom he viewed through Goethe. His Homer is that of Werther, his Hellas the Italian version concocted by Winckelmann. It is the same humanism, marked by 'edle Einfalt und stille Grösse' ('noble simplicity and quiet greatness'), that permeates

[1] For these formative years of Brandes's intellectual development as a literary and cultural critic and historian, see Paul V. Rubow, *Dansk litterær kritik i det 19. århundrede indtil 1870* (Copenhagen: Munksgaard, 1921), *Georg Brandes' briller* (Copenhagen: Levin & Munksgaard, 1932), *En studie-bog* (Copenhagen: Gyldendal, 1950), *Herman Bang og flere kritiske Studier* (Copenhagen: Gyldendal, 1958); Henning Fenger, *Georg Brandes' læreår: læsning ideer smag kritik 1857–1872* (Copenhagen: Gyldendal, 1957); Harald Rue, *Om Georg Brandes* (Århus: Sirius, 1973); Bertil Nolin, *Den gode europén: studier i Georg Brandes' ideutveckling 1871–1893* (Stockholm: Svenska Bokförlaget, 1965); Sven Møller Kristensen, *Georg Brandes: kritikeren liberalisten humanisten* (Copenhagen: Gyldendal, 1980); Jørgen Knudsen, *Georg Brandes: frigørelsens vej 1842–77, I modsigelsernes tegn 1877–83, Symbolet og manden 1883–95, Magt og afmagt 1896–1914, Uovervindelig taber 1914–27* (Copenhagen: Gyldendal, 1985–2004).
[2] Fenger, *Georg Brandes' læreår*, p. 474.

the derivative sculptures of Bertel Thorvaldsen. Eventually, this idealized Hellenism was replaced by more realistic inclinations. As French Realism began to influence Brandes's tastes, his main attraction became life, rather than imitation, and the appeal of Thorvaldsen faded. So did that of Winckelmann as Brandes came to appreciate the very Renaissance that was anathema to Winckelmann's Hellenism. Thorvaldsen had circumvented Michelangelo at his peril, and Brandes's objective was no longer to parrot Antiquity, but to serve as midwife for a rebirth of its classics. This new Hellenism underlies the critique of dualism to which Brandes would devote his first book, *Dualismen i vor nyeste philosophie* ('The Dualism in Our Newest Philosophy', 1866).

Brandes's Hellenism was informed by Kierkegaard's vision of Antiquity, though it was more conventional. His Kierkegaard phase lasted from the early to mid-1860s and was inextricably linked to a personal and religious crisis. Kierkegaard was transmitted to Brandes through different channels by his two professors Hans Brøchner and Rasmus Nielsen. But his impact was on a twenty-year-old, hypersensitive, mother-dominated virgin, steeped in idealism and Platonic love, susceptible to religious emotions and intimations of the demonic, unhappily in love with Christianity and his own poetic bent, and in the throes of Johannes Climacus's theology.

Brandes's book on dualism reflects his conflictual relationship to Kierkegaard. Both the mid-nineteenth century's faddish harmony of faith and knowledge and Kierkegaard's attack on this are criticized by Brandes, who eventually abandoned Kierkegaard's absolutism. His philosophical antidotes were Spinoza, the left Hegelians and Taine, and with his dissertation on Taine he was finished not only with Kierkegaard, but also with his own philosophical production. His encounter with John Stuart Mill in England may have boosted this departure from Kierkegaard. At the same time, the critic in Brandes found affinities among artistic Realists such as Ibsen. Brandes the Romantic who fought Romanticism was also a Kierkegaardian who fought Kierkegaard.

### III

Georg Brandes's main competitor as the pre-eminent Danish literary critic in the 1860s was the conservative Clemens Petersen. Whereas Petersen could be quite critical of the older Romantics and even their later imitators, Brandes was as generous towards his parents' generation as he was systematically opposed to its present-day heirs. Contemporary literature, he thought, should not recast the rhetoric and models of the classics and Romantics, but should grasp instead the poetry and novelty of real-life experience. In a famous essay on Shakespeare, 'The Infinitely Small and the Infinitely Great in Poetry', from his collection *Kritiker og portraiter* ('Criticisms and Portraits', 1870), Brandes rejects Heiberg's negative estimate of Shakespeare, whom Brandes himself sees as an individualistic and naturalistic alternative to the declamatory and periphrastic style of artistic formalism in Denmark.

In appraisals like this, Brandes appears as a literary psychologist who rejects current ethical positions like Petersen's in favour of an objective aestheticism which holds that ethical and topical issues undergo aesthetic transformation in a work of art. Hence the critic should be a philosopher, not a moralist. This is not to say that Brandes immediately put traditional criticism behind him. His submission for the university's gold medal in 1862–3 (published in 1868) was an old-fashioned academic treatise on the concept of tragic fate whose treatment of its subject – and of the comic – was much in the vein of Heiberg's dialectical logic; but it was no more than a stepping stone from the methodologies of the past – and the idealism of Greek Antiquity – to the Naturalism, materialism, positivism and pluralism now emerging in literary studies in Europe.

A pivotal figure in this change of direction was Taine, the subject of Brandes's doctoral dissertation of 1870. Taine's historical comparisons of works of art with their underlying subject matter were echoed in Brandes's essay on Shakespeare, later incorporated in his longer work *William Shakespeare* (1895–6); and this method was refined to characterize the unity of an author's entire production, in terms of choice of subjects, ideas and their realization. Though by most accounts not a great psychologist himself, Brandes was not persuaded by Taine's historical system with all its typology and dispassionate logic, and so his main objective was rather to emulate the individualized portraits of Sainte-Beuve and to identify the aesthetic laws inherent in individual works and genres. In fact, his own approach became for a time more empathetic and less judgemental, as in his landmark essay on Hans Christian Andersen.

As Henning Fenger states, Brandes's literary programme drew on the obligatory canon of French and English revolutionary Romanticism, and his philosophical programme, formulated in slogans advocating free thought, summed up his fifteen years of study in German Hegelianism, French positivism and English utilitarianism. Nevertheless, his overall programme was anachronistic from the outset, in contrast to the genuine Naturalism of Flaubert and Zola; and with his quasi-Romantic sensibility Brandes remained less convinced by his new ideological tenets than by the aesthetic Hellenism and Kierkegaardian philosophy of religion of which, according to Rubow, he had officially taken leave. Symptomatically, the admired Taine was now a waning star. Accordingly, Brandes's *Hovedstrømninger* ('Main Currents', 1872–90) and the modern breakthrough it was set to usher in became a house divided; Brandes's biographer Jørgen Knudsen reads the six volumes as an incantation on behalf of a godless humanity's loneliness and hope for salvation.[3]

The celebrated introduction to volume I (1872) outlines the dramatic plan and didactic purpose of the entire series. Volumes I (on the so-called French emigrant literature inspired by Rousseau), II (on Germany's semi-Catholic Romantic school) and III (on French authors supporting orthodoxy, clergy and legitimacy) chart the developing artistic reaction to revolutionary progress. In volume IV of Brandes's account, progressive literature, centred on Byron in England and his heroic death in the war of Greek liberation, finally regains momentum; and subsequently, in volume V, preceding the July Revolution in France, major French writers form their own Romantic school, stimulating a renewed progress, which finally culminates in Germany, in volume VI, where Jewish liberal writers like Heine pick up the inspiration of Byron's war in Greece and the July Revolution.

The lesson to be learned by the work's primarily Danish audience was that a modern literature thrives not by virtue of its abstract idealism, but by the presence of current political debates at its centre. Unlike the great Danish romanticist Adam Oehlenschläger, whose dramatic hero Aladdin was merely a genius without a cause and whose anti-Aladdin, Noureddin, was but a Faust devoid of inspiration (two instances of purely inner freedom), Brandes sought an outer and political liberty. In his view, the time for cautious reaction to revolutionary excess was over; the enlightened spirit of a free humanity must rise once again.

As Valdemar Vedel has argued, volume II, on the Romantic school in Germany, cemented Brandes's complicated relationship – a marriage of convenience – with the German spirit in general.[4] The volume's design and inspiration issued from Herder and the German tradition, rather than from Taine and the French. German readers embraced it wholeheartedly, both for its intrinsic merit and for the novelty its author could offer as a perceptive outsider. Yet despite its refreshing style and realistic sensibility, it soon became a dated work. Its many comparisons between German and Danish Romanticism were chiefly to the advantage of the Germans; but Brandes did not mince his words about the evils of the old Romantics' mishmash of mysticism, irrationality and egocentric indulgence.

The contrast between the volume's content and Brandes's personal appreciation of facets of modern Germany became further pronounced

[3]  Cf. Hans Hertel, *Litteraturens vaneforbrydere: kritikere, forlæggere og lystlæsere – det litterære liv i Danmark gennem 200 år* (Copenhagen: Gyldendal, 1999), p. 77.

[4]  Valdemar Vedel, 'Georg Brandes og Tyskland' in *Tilskuerens festskrift til Georg Brandes* (Copenhagen and Christiania: Gyldendal, 1912), pp. 67–80.

during his five years of voluntary exile in Berlin (1877–83), where he went in order to escape some ugly conflicts afflicting him and his radical movement in Copenhagen. His admiration for the vigour of Bismarck's new state almost overcame the resentment he had harboured towards Germany since 1864; and his self-assumed role as critical intermediary between Nordic and German culture was clearly animated by the vitality of social life in the new German capital.[5]

Prominent among his subjects were, of course, Nietzsche, his main discovery, as well as the Heine of his last volume of *Hovedstrømninger*. Yet for all his affection towards both, he found in each writer elements that echoed his misgivings about the new Germany. The fall of liberalism and the rise of racism and militant anti-Semitism were that nation's Achilles' heel. Both Heine and Nietzsche had celebrated greatness and espoused a defiance of uniformity that delighted and troubled Brandes in equal measure. Vedel rightly observes how much of German culture had actually escaped Brandes's attention in the two *Hovedstrømninger* volumes on the German literature of 1800–50, and how his marriage of convenience to Germany was destined to break up as a result of an incompatibility of temper.[6]

Such discord was conspicuous by its absence in his account of so-called Naturalism in England, in volume IV, which, after his large monograph on Shakespeare (and a much shorter one on Disraeli), was his only major work on English literature. Here, if anywhere in *Hovedstrømninger*, individuality – as defined in Brandes's new image of himself – rises above the petty concerns of the present. As Otto Jespersen suggests, the Hegelian scheme of things is on its way out and 'The Great Personality, the Source of Culture' (1890) is about to take its place.[7]

## IV

Criticism of *Hovedstrømninger* was so widespread in Denmark (as opposed to Sweden, for example) that Brandes felt called upon to write a book in which he explained and defended himself: *Forklaring og forsvar: en antikritik* ('Explanation and Defence: An Anti-Critique', 1872). Charged, for instance, with using free thinking as code for immoral thought, Brandes declared that free thinking is simply the spirit of progress. Besides, he is neither a materialist socialist nor an

[5] See Georg Brandes, *Berlin som tysk Rigshovedstad: Erindringer fra et femaarigt Ophold* (Copenhagen: Gyldendal, 1885).
[6] Vedel, 'Georg Brandes og Tyskland', p. 80.
[7] Otto Jespersen, 'Brandes og engelsk Litteratur' in *Tilskuerens festskrift*, p. 86.

idealist Scandinavianist, for no such categories are compatible with independent thinking, which, unlike received knowledge, means thinking from first principles. While Brandes acknowledges that various cultures are informed by universal factors – climate conditions, family structures, moral conduct – he is nonetheless a cultural relativist who attributes national peculiarities and variations to local circumstances. This is the posture of a European social critic who self-assuredly criticizes outdated and narrow-minded habits in his small native country in order to open its national culture to modern independence; it is not the position of someone merely attempting to subvert his own culture. In fact, *Forklaring og forsvar* is proof that Danish culture is the *sine qua non* of this 'good European', as both Nietzsche and Thomas Mann described Georg Brandes.

Vilhelm Andersen estimated in 1912 that one-third of Georg Brandes's literary production had Danish subjects, and that most of these titles were structured and composed around the battlefield of *Hovedstrømninger* (1872–90).[8] A fragmented body of work, it is held together mainly by the author's personality, whose intellectual development it documents. Preceding the multi-volume centrepiece *Æstetiske studier* ('Aesthetic Studies', 1868) and *Kritiker og portraiter* ('Criticisms and Portraits', 1870), the latter including the essay on H. C. Andersen, chart the transition from abstract aestheticism to characterizations of individual authors in the manner of Taine and Sainte-Beuve, which in turn reflects Brandes's move from Hegel's and Heiberg's speculative aestheticism, and from the German Romantic concern with beauty, to Taine's and Sainte-Beuve's French historical criticism and its concern with truth.

Alongside *Hovedstrømninger*, Brandes published *Søren Kierkegaard* (1877), *Danske digtere* ('Danish Authors', 1877) and *Det moderne gennembruds mænd* ('The Men of the Modern Breakthrough', 1883). Kierkegaard is the driving force behind the anti-Kierkegaardian *Hovedstrømninger* volumes I and II, and serves as a scapegoat for the bitterly criticized German Romantics in the latter. In the 1877 monograph the avowed utilitarian rationalist continues his assault on the paradoxical absolutist, who is now alleged to be more categorical than God himself. But the vindictiveness of the attack issues from the subject itself. Kierkegaard's philosophy of choice and personal responsibility served Brandes's modern breakthrough well, but only when uncoupled from religious authority; and Kierkegaard's radicalism was also a point of identification, but only when deprived of its own dialectics. In the same way that Brandes preserved Romanticism by relegating it to noble memory,[9]

[8] Vilhelm Andersen, 'Georg Brandes og dansk Litteratur' in *ibid.*, pp. 11–17.
[9] Cf. Rue, *Om Georg Brandes*, p. 97.

he now seeks to appropriate Kierkegaard's tormented genius for his own causes, at a safe distance from his own Kierkegaardian crises.[10]

The chapters on older Danish authors in the second title of 1877 are by Brandes's own account linked directly to the first volumes of *Hovedstrømninger*. Vilhelm Andersen points to parallels between this work's later volumes and *Det moderne gennembruds mænd*, which deals with the front line of Danish and Norwegian radical writers – conveniently excluding such lesser militants as the eminent Realist Herman Bang, whose own *Realisme og realister* ('Realism and Realists', 1879), a programmatic equivalent to Brandes's work, offered a far more generous treatment of its opponents, and a far more advanced Modernism than the traditional Romantic version espoused by Brandes.[11] Yet, as *Hovedstrømninger*'s six-volume *tour de force* approached its conclusion, Brandes had actually renounced his popular revolution in favour of a humanized version of Nietzsche's superhuman: an aristocratic radicalism founded upon the work of great personalities, regarded as the sources of culture.

Brandes's ultimate dissatisfaction with the Danish literary scene[12] was reflected in an essay on Goethe and Denmark, published in *Mennesker og værker i nyere evropæisk literatur* ('Men and Works in Recent European Literature', 1883), which belittles every Danish writer one could conceivably measure against the towering German. Only the Norwegian-born playwright Holberg, whom Brandes celebrated in his anniversary monograph of 1884 and an essay of 1887,[13] stands out – as Brandes himself, in his own opinion, stood out – in the crowd of Danish Lilliputians. Vilhelm Andersen, who found Brandes lacking as a historian of (Danish) literature because he was an agitator whose principal ambition was to use the past for present purposes, willingly admits that, with all his biases and other limitations, he was the foremost Danish literary critic. In many respects an inheritor of the late Romantic norms he so publicly combated, Brandes was unparalleled in his critical precision and poignancy, largely as a result of his cosmopolitan perspective on the Danish scene. Andersen identified the circumstances under which the mature Brandes would reign supreme as a culture critic, with his selected heroes and broad humanitarian causes as incompatible bedfellows.

[10] For the observations in this paragraph, see Finn Hauberg Mortensen, 'Var Brandes moderne?' in *The Modern Breakthrough in Scandinavian Literature 1870–1905*, eds. Bertil Nolin and Peter Forsgren (University of Gothenburg, 1988), pp. 291–4.
[11] Peer E. Sørensen, 'Georg Brandes, Herman Bang, Johannes Jørgensen og Goethe' in *Georg Brandes og Europa*, ed. Olaf Harsløf (Copenhagen: Det kongelige Bibliotek/Museum Tusculanums Forlag, 2004), pp. 184–90.
[12] Cf. the piece on J. P. Jacobsen in Brandes's *Essays: Danske personligheder* (Copenhagen: Gyldendal, 1889), p. 274.
[13] Rpt in *ibid.*, pp. 1–48.

V

Years before these undertakings, Brandes had written a number of major studies on the range of European literature and culture cited above, including *Esaias Tegnér: en litteraturpsychologisk studie* ('Esaias Tegnér: A Literary-Psychological Study', 1878), *Benjamin Disraeli, Jarl af Beaconsfield: en litterær charakteristik* ('Lord Beaconsfield: A Study of Benjamin Disraeli', 1878) and *Ferdinand Lassalle: en kritisk fremstilling* ('Ferdinand Lassalle: A Critical Presentation', 1881). An essay written for Tegnér's 100-year anniversary and included in *Mennesker og værker* summarizes Brandes's approach to his subject. Tegnér, he says, was greater as a man than as a poet, and the way to apprehend him is not through aesthetics but through literary psychology, practised dispassionately as a natural science. Accordingly, this free-thinking bishop re-emerges as a French Classicist rather than a German Romanticist like his Danish counterpart Oehlenschläger, and as a far more worldly individual; a lover of freedom and truth, of light, clarity and reason: altogether a man to Brandes's taste.

As for Disraeli, his conservatism intrigued Brandes. How did he resist modernity's dissolution of tradition? How did his inscrutable politics reveal itself in his novels? And how did he cope with the anti-Semitism he suffered, whose rise his biographer witnessed at first hand in Berlin? In contrast to Disraeli's Semitism, Brandes was opposed to explicit Jewishness, and advocated the assimilationist view that Jews should render their identity invisible by accepting 'the all-embracing modern religion of humanity'. If Disraeli was a distinguished Jew, as Brandes acknowledged, he would also be 'the last Jew'.[14] The book on Lassalle was also about a Jew and also written in Berlin. A pioneering work, its shortage of source material was nonetheless a liability that made it too easy for the author to superimpose his personal dilemmas on his subject. Brandes had twofold misgivings – about the politics of the bourgeoisie he came from and the socialist leanings of the working class – and he always kept socialism at arm's length, though within intellectual reach. His reluctant approval of Lassalle's impossible cause and his admiration for his intellectual defiance were no doubt a product of his own political experiences.[15]

Three essays written on Ibsen between 1867 and 1898, collected in book form as *Henrik Ibsen* (1898), mark the last phase before Brandes's

---

[14] Salo W. Baron, 'Georg Brandes and Lord Beaconsfield' in *Lord Beaconsfield: A Study of Benjamin Disraeli*, trans. Mrs George Sturge (New York: Thomas Y. Crowell, 1966), p. xiii.
[15] Jørgen Knudsen, 'Georg Brandes', Forfatterportræt/Arkiv for Dansk Litteratur, http://adl.dk/adl_pub/fportraet/cv/ShowFpItem.xsql?nnoc=adl_pub&ff_id=2&p_fpkat_id=fskab (accessed 18 May 2012).

final and heroic humanitarian period as a critic and writer. Brandes's Ibsen is an intellectual exile who is only at home in homelessness, a detached genius whose only faith is in the supreme individual personality, in Kierkegaard's single individual, a misanthropist (though not a misogynist) with many questions and few answers, a disillusioned moralist who finds mankind miserable rather than evil, and whose sinister universe is depicted with indignation rather than compassion, informed by the belief that suffering purifies. Freedom, for Ibsen, is not a collective possession but the fruit of individual effort, a form of spiritual superiority remote from real-life commitments to which even Brandes seems attached. As a modern writer, Ibsen is averse to democracy as an ideology, and he scoffs at majority freedoms bought at a discount. Unlike Bjørnson, who is a poet and everything else, Ibsen is a poet and nothing else (except an ardent collector of medals and good will).[16] Both of them intellectual aristocrats in exile, Ibsen and Brandes were polarized products of the modern era, sharing only a solitude that Ibsen cherished and Brandes feared.

The books about Tegnér, Disraeli and Lassalle, according to Rubow, were all preceded by a careful study of Sainte-Beuve's *Chateaubriand*, which affirmed and identified with its subject. Initially Brandes himself warned against such involvement, but as his feelings of isolation, abandonment and disappointment mounted during the 1880s, his reservations concerning authorial subjectivity waned and made even Sainte-Beuve look detached from his topic in comparison. Similarly, the distance between Brandes's *Tegnér* and *Shakespeare* is nearly negligible, with each text connected to its author as a city to its Trojan horse.[17] In Shakespeare's case, psychopathology was Brandes's means of identifying (with) his subject. Like Renan, who created images that encompassed his own possibilities, Brandes created his Shakespeare in the image he had moulded of himself and transferred to this creation his own ideal of *Bildung*, his inclination to hero-worship, selection of subject matter and aversion to moralism. He was completely blind to Shakespeare's tragedies and their affinity with the baroque stage; this is a Shakespeare romanticized by a reader who uncritically monumentalizes and mythologizes Romanticism as if it were the Renaissance and makes rash comparisons between the author of *Hamlet* and Cellini, Raphael, Cervantes, Rabelais and, not least, Michelangelo.

Not surprisingly, as Rubow makes clear, Brandes's large volumes on *Michelangelo Buonarroti* (1921) are yet another exercise in the hero cult whereby the author identifies his own legend with the greatest figures in world literature and history (ignoring, for instance, Michelangelo's homosexuality).[18] This particular mutual glorification rests

[16] Cf. Rubow, *En studie-bog*, p. 124.
[17] This paragraph is heavily indebted to Rubow, *Georg Brandes' briller*, pp. 210–32.
[18] Cf. Rubow on Brandes and his homosexual friend Emil Petersen in *Herman Bang*, p. 53.

on the simplistic dogma that the Renaissance was the golden age of individualism, the breeding ground for superhumans and demigods, with Michelangelo himself at the summit of art history thanks to his giving rebirth to the naked human being in sculptural form; such glorification, as Taine might see it, rests on the expression of one compelling human attribute rather than a complex depiction of reality.

Between *Shakespeare* and *Michelangelo* appeared the hastily written works on *Goethe*, vols. I–II (1915) and *Voltaire*, vols. I–II (1916), the latter once again challenging religious dogma. A subsequent book, *Caius Julius Caesar* (1918), featured a man betrayed by the very masses which modern developments were meant to favour. Next came *Homer* (1921) and then, in smaller volumes, *Sagnet om Jesus* ('Jesus: A Myth') *Petrus* ('Peter') and *Urkristendom* ('Original Christianity'; 1925, 1926 and 1927), in which he put the new radical Bible criticism to polemical use against New Testament dogma and portrayed Jesus as a purely mythical figure concocted by Paul on the basis of Old Testament prophecies. By way of contrast, Brandes once again evoked the harmonious spirit of *Hellas* (1925), which proclaims that Greece, not Palestine, is the holy land – a typically divisive claim in the name of harmony from an ageing, rabble-rousing Classicist.

## VI

For all his continued productivity, Georg Brandes's work as a literary critic reached its peak before the First World War. His most original contributions – which included a wealth of theatre reviews and lectures on drama, a uniquely rich correspondence with scholars, artists and intellectuals across Europe, and personal advice to a number of Scandinavia's and Europe's emerging writers, many prominent women among them – had already been written, and his subsequent heroic monographs have mostly become epitaphs. But his countless travels in Europe, even America, led to several travel books of more lasting interest – for example, on Germany, Poland and Russia – together with critical interrogations of the war and the armistice itself. Along with pamphlets and countless speeches advocating the rights of repressed minorities and persecuted individuals such as Dreyfus, these books show how the modern world, in whose literary development Brandes had a waning interest, reignited his combative and constructive spirit in the service of larger practical causes.[19]

This was not the first time Brandes engaged directly with current socio-political issues. His voice was heard resoundingly during the so-called great Nordic war of sexual morality in the 1880s; and, during the

---

[19] See Jørgen Stender Clausen, *Det nytter ikke at sende hære mod ideer: Georg Brandes' kulturkritik i årene omkring 1. verdenskrig* (Copenhagen: C. A. Reitzel, 1984).

constitutional struggle of this decade, he overcame his profound misgivings about political parties to side with the majority of liberals and farmers against the oligarchic landed aristocracy, although more to advance the cause of freedom than that of democracy in itself.[20] Though usually reserved about majority rule, Brandes saw no practical justification for withholding his support of such rule against the illegitimate terror of minorities. Nevertheless, his radicalism remained aristocratic rather than democratic in nature, and his deepest pessimism issued precisely from his doubts about the prospects for his vision.[21]

Yet the legacy of Brandes, the literary and cultural activist, European and Nordic critic, who so dominated the European scene between 1870 and the First World War, is questionable. The cultural radicals who considered themselves the natural heirs of the Brandes 'tradition' in Denmark were prominent during the interwar period and, as neo-radicals, in the 1960s and 1970s. But the Marxist polarization of the 1970s undermined their positions, and more recent developments have not revived them. Yet Brandesians like Olaf Harsløf and Hans Hertel doggedly insist even now on Brandes's indispensability.[22] The former imagines a 'postmodern Georg Brandes', whose polarizing interventions in his era's cultural and literary debates and struggles are instructive for today's less ideological and more situational collisions in the war for or against globalization. And the latter reminds us of Brandes's programmatic words, adopted as a motto by the Brandes school at Copenhagen University, concerning the need for reciprocal interaction and identification between ourselves and the other. Some would call this internationalism at its best, but others have seen it as a betrayal of one's own world in exchange for something completely foreign and only scientifically comprehensible. Hence the kind of cultural warfare in which Brandes was embroiled is a part of his enduring legacy.

Though he inspired the 'modern breakthrough', Brandes's view of Modernism was oddly dated; and, notwithstanding his early translation of Mill's work on the rights of women and his support of several female artists, he managed to ruffle a surprising number of female feathers. On the other hand, his inspiration has extended to the young writers of China, as scholars have testified.[23] Though he may not be a source of

---

[20]  Poul Houe, 'Georg Brandes between Politics and the Political', *Orbis Litterarum*, 62 (2007), 230–40.

[21]  Cf. Georg Brandes, 'Spørgsmaalet om den evropæiske Literaturs Fremtid', *Politiken*, 30 January 1921.

[22]  Olaf Harsløf, 'Den postmoderne Georg Brandes', *Politiken*, 7 November 2002; Hans Hertel, 'Uundværlige Georg Brandes', *Politiken*, 25 November 2004.

[23]  See Zhu Shoutong, 'Georg Brandes og Kina' and Lars Lönnroth, 'Brandes ut ur Victoria Benediktssons dödsskugga' in Harsløf, *Georg Brandes og Europa*, pp. 285–303 and 415–19, respectively.

theoretical inspiration for today's technologized and professionalized students of cultural studies, Brandes the activist – pedagogue, stylist and intellectual – continues to remind us of an era when cultural wars summoned the learned and unlearned to the same battlefield.

It has been argued, as by Carsten Jensen at an award ceremony in 2004 for Brandes's biographer Jørgen Knudsen,[24] that Brandes was not, after all, the maker of the 'modern breakthrough' but its product, mouthpiece and instrument. But gadfly that he was – or what Jensen calls an incorrigible jaywalker at the crossroads of established order – he never failed to question this order's *raison d'être*. Indeed, Knudsen's 2,756 pages all lead up to the Brandesian key word: why? And the answer is still blowing in the wind.

[24] Carsten Jensen, 'Midt i lyskrydset', *Politiken*, 31 December 2004.

# VI

## *Genre criticism*

# 26

# Theories of genre

STEVEN MONTE

## Theoretical preliminaries and the early nineteenth century

In order to take stock of genre theory from 1830 to 1914, it is necessary to have some sense of what genre means today. Whatever its status among theorists, genre as a term and concept is applied widely. Many literature departments have genre requirements for major subjects, for example, and many job listings are defined by genre. Though the triad of literary genres – fiction (narrative), poetry (lyric) and plays (dramatic) – is discernible in Renaissance thought if not in Plato and Aristotle, it is institutionally a nineteenth-century inheritance. Genre also serves today as a marketing label with aspirations to classification: bookshops are organized in ways that promote genres such as 'Self-Help', 'Poetry', 'Sports', and the wonderfully inclusive 'Literature'. Like triadic schemes of genre, the marketing trend in generic labels is largely a nineteenth-century inheritance. What genre signifies in the twenty-first century is fluid, but in so far as it is a classificatory term, two general meanings have emerged. Genre refers, on the one hand, to categories on the order of narrative, lyric and drama; on the other hand, to sub-genres such as detective fiction, the personal essay, romantic comedy, the gothic novel and pastoral elegy. Fundamental questions in genre theory include whether and how works fall into related groups and what the interpretative consequences of such groupings are.

Twenty-first-century scepticism about genre follows and differs from nineteenth-century questioning. Nineteenth-century writers tend to examine genre from an aesthetic perspective: originality, not typicality, is the aim of literature; genre should arise organically or through the poet's sensibility. This perspective was largely a reaction against prescriptive notions of genre, especially neo-classical rules. Debates about genre, like debates over Romanticism and Classicism, could also have a political dimension. This sort of understanding about the nature of genre – that genre is, in effect, something more than genre – continues into the twentieth and twenty-first centuries, albeit from a more sceptical and academic viewpoint. As bookshops amply demonstrate, genre distinctions have not been dissolved but reformulated, yet for many theorists genre is more

imaginary than real – a metaphor, if not something ideologically more
suspect.

Turning to early nineteenth-century theories, it can seem at times that
German thinkers laid the groundwork for later discussions of genre. Their
triadic views of genre alone have cast a shadow from which theorists
have yet to emerge fully. Triadic schemes of the Hegelian sort represent
a relatively new way of combining historical and essentialist approaches
to genre. Renaissance and neo-classical writers tended to recognize about
seven or eight principal genres in some sort of hierarchical order. A typical
ranking might be epic, tragedy, satire, epigram, ode, elegy and pastoral.
Pre-1800 triadic schemes tend to be based on elements of presentation
or style – modes and moods – from Plato's division of literary discourse
into 'authorial, figurative, and mixed' to rhetorical distinctions between
high, middle and low style.[1] The genres of nineteenth-century triads,
by contrast, are often associated with particular cultures or historical
periods and often viewed as kinds that develop from each other, from the
emerging spirit of the times, or from the dialectics of opposing aesthetic
and philosophical impulses. What makes the nineteenth-century situation
still more distinctive is the emergence of new hierarchies among the genres
and the proliferation of tripartite schemes.

The historical and progressive dimensions of nineteenth-century triads
invite the label 'Hegelian', but the trend towards triads might as easily be
traced to Goethe and contemporaries other than Hegel. In notes to his
*West-Östlicher Divan* (1819), Goethe distinguished between the 'natural
forms of literature' (*Naturformen der Dichtung*: epic, lyric and drama)
and the 'poetic kinds' (*Dichtarten*: ballad, epistle, fable, novel etc.). The
*Naturformen* are permanent entities; the *Dichtarten* change over time.
Biological metaphors for genre are thus present in nineteenth-century
thinking from the outset, if not in Goethe's *Naturformen*, then through
a common term for genre among German writers, *Gattung* ('species').
Goethe's early mentor, Johann Gottfried Herder (1744–1803), was critical of genre theory, emphasizing the individuality of works, the multiplicity of genres, and cultural and historical differences. At the same
time, he thought of genres as evolving from 'germs' (Homer planted the
epic germ, for example) and 'roots' (the ode is the root of elegy, lyric
and pastoral). Herder presented the development of genres as variously
a degeneration, a kind of progression and a cycle. Through dialogue
with Goethe, Friedrich Schiller (1759–1805) developed the notion that

---

[1] For a fuller history of triadic theories, see the title essay of Claudio Guillén's *Literature
as System: Essays Toward the Theory of Literary History* (Princeton University Press,
1971), esp. pp. 390–405.

epic deals with a completely past action while drama presents action as completely present. More originally, Schiller defined genres through modes of sensibility rather than through forms of presentation. He distinguished between three 'sentimental' modes of feeling (satire, elegy and idyll) and could describe Goethe's *Tasso* as an 'elegiac drama' and his own *Robbers* as a 'satirical tragedy'. 'Sentimental' here is a term that Schiller develops in his influential *On Naïve and Sentimental Poetry*. Among other things, it means modern and self-conscious, the opposite of 'naïve' or being at one with the world.[2]

Friedrich's and August Wilhelm Schlegel's distinctions between classical and Romantic owe something to Schiller's typology of naïve and sentimental. Generally speaking, the classical is represented by the Greeks and the Romantic by the moderns, though Friedrich Schlegel (1772–1829) allows for classical and Romantic tendencies in all eras. In discussing the Greeks, he develops an evolutionary theory of literary kinds: genres grow, blossom, mature, harden, dissolve. Still, for him, literature will never become extinct. He speaks of epic as 'atomistic' in comparison to drama, which is unified, and suggests that the former is concerned with contingency, the latter with fate. August Wilhelm Schlegel (1767–1845) elaborates on many of his brother's ideas in ways that became influential. He emphasizes the role of chance in epic, disputes Aristotle's distinction between epic and drama based on mode of presentation (epic narration versus dramatic dialogue), and argues that the novel aims at inclusiveness: it is the Romantic analogue to the classical epic – a new genre of modern poetry, not its end. Besides distinguishing between classical and Romantic, he sometimes speaks of *Naturpoesie* and *Kunstpoesie*, 'natural poetry' and 'artistic poetry'. For him, the lyric is subjective and the epic is objective, though at times epic is a synthesis of both modes. In contrast to some neo-classical theorists, but like his brother and like Schiller, he tends to privilege the drama over epic. Drama is now thought capable of performing important political and philosophical work.

F. W. J. Schelling (1775–1854) presents a generic system that is, in theory, highly structured. For Schelling, lyric, epic and drama form the 'ideal' series of types; music, painting and the plastic arts form the 'real'

---

[2] For the historical and philosophical relation between dyads and triads, see *ibid.*, pp. 388–90. My discussion of late eighteenth- and early nineteenth-century theories draws on Guillén, *ibid.*, and also Tilottama Rajan, 'Theories of Genre', and David Simpson, 'Transcendental Philosophy and Romantic Criticism' in *The Cambridge History of Literary Criticism. Vol. v: Romanticism*, ed. Marshall Brown (Cambridge University Press, 2000), pp. 72–91, and René Wellek, *A History of Modern Criticism 1750–1950. Vol. I: The Later Eighteenth Century* and *Vol. II: The Romantic Age* (New Haven, CT: Yale University Press, 1955).

series. All art combines the finite and the infinite; poetry differs from other
arts only in its 'ideal' medium. Nevertheless or additionally, lyric is like
music, epic like painting, and drama like sculpture. Lyric is subjective; epic
is objective; while drama synthesizes the particular and the universal – it
is the union of lyric and epic, representing the struggle between freedom
and necessity. There are three modes: the schematic, the allegorical and
the symbolic. The novel is akin to verse romance. Indeed, for Schelling
and most of his contemporaries, the novel is a species of fantastical,
not Realist, fiction. And the short story is a novel expressed in lyrical
form.

In his *Aesthetics* (1835), Hegel describes genre within a system that integrates theory and history. He classifies the arts according to a sequence of
historical stages of art, from the 'symbolic' (allegorical) in ancient India
and Egypt, to the 'classical' (union of content and form) in the Greeks, to
the 'Romantic' (a new division of content and form marked by subjectivity
and the dissolution of outer form). After Hegel and the German Romantics, theorists were obliged to take into account questions of generic progression and decline. Echoes of German thought are increasingly audible
after 1830 outside Germany, but the effects can be felt earlier. Percy
Bysshe Shelley's 'Defence of Poetry' (1821) is a riposte to Thomas Love
Peacock's 'The Four Ages of Poetry' (1820), which presents a narrative
of growth and decline, from an iron age (of folk ballads, romances and
the like) through a golden age (of epic and tragedy) to a silver age (of
derivative social verse, satire and rule-bound poetry). The fourth age, the
age of brass, in which the genres have been exhausted, is, in effect, a
non-age, a tactical addition to an essentially tripartite narrative. Shelley's
impassioned defence is haunted by the prospect of decline, political and
aesthetic, as when he speaks of poetry as always addressing itself 'to those
faculties which are the last to be destroyed' and of poetry's voice being
heard 'like the footsteps of Astraea, departing from the world'.[3] Presenting a more optimistic account of historical progression, Victor Hugo's
1827 preface to *Cromwell* nonetheless reads as a variation on German
schemes. Hugo describes an historical sequence of genres largely determined by the relation of art to society and religion.[4] Modern literature
has moreover introduced a new type to poetry, the grotesque, bringing
together the sublime and the comic, the beautiful and the ugly, tragedy
and comedy.

---

[3] Percy Bysshe Shelley, 'Defence of Poetry' in *Shelley's Poetry and Prose*, eds. Donald H.
Reiman and Sharon B. Powers (New York: Norton, 1977), p. 493.
[4] Victor Hugo, preface to *Cromwell* in *Œuvres complètes de Victor Hugo*, ed. Jeanlouis
Cornuz, 38 vols. (Paris: Editions Rencontres, 1967), vol. XI, pp. 13–19. All translations
of Hugo are mine.

# Nineteenth-century genre theory in Russia, Italy and France

The representative, or at least most prominent, genre critics from nineteenth-century Russia, Italy and France are arguably Vissarion Belinsky (1811–48), Francesco De Sanctis (1817–83) and Ferdinand Brunetière (1849–1906). Belinsky and De Sanctis are commonly acknowledged as the foremost critics of their national traditions, and Brunetière, though less renowned than Sainte-Beuve or Taine, was more directly engaged with genre theory. It is possible to see these writers as developing or correcting German theorists and invoking a broader historicism.

Belinsky's criticism can be viewed as Hegelian, taking into account his changing views towards Romantic idealism and his nationalism. In 'The Idea of Art', Belinsky presents a Hegelian version of history in which humankind passes through stages of myth, art and thought. In 'The Division of Poetry into Kinds', Belinsky interprets tragedy in Hegelian terms, drawing from *Antigone* the philosophical idea of 'the triumph of the eternal and general over the individual and particular'.[5] Though indebted to Romantic theory, Belinsky felt himself to be a member of a new generation. Unlike Hegel, he was politically liberal; and he shared neither Hegel's nostalgia for Greek art as an aesthetic summit nor his belief in the imminent demise of art; Belinsky harboured hopes for future Russian writers.

One of the more intriguing tensions in Belinsky's criticism stems from his simultaneous beliefs in the power of genius and in the power of history. History and nationality seem at times to determine the fate of an author or a genre; Belinsky can even hint at a narrative of decline. Ultimately, though, genres transcend history and the great writers seem capable of accomplishing anything in spite of their times.[6] Belinsky's concerns throughout 1835 included an emphasis on genius and permanent genres, which continues in his later criticism, though the force of history is acknowledged more. In his 1841 review of Lermontov's poems, he presents the progression from epic through lyric to drama as necessary, not only in history but within the development of each individual poet, and argues that objective poetry is no longer possible because of a general historical movement towards reflection and subjectivity. Russian criticism after Belinsky is even more invested in history's power and the social purpose of literature.

As with Belinsky's criticism, nationalistic concerns inform De Sanctis's thought, which is treated in detail in a separate chapter in this volume.

---

5 René Wellek, *A History of Modern Criticism 1750–1950*. Vol. III: *The Age of Transition* (New Haven, CT: Yale University Press, 1965), p. 252.
6 V. G. Belinsky, *Selected Philosophical Works* (Moscow: Foreign Languages Publishing House, 1956), p. 87.

Italy's struggle for independence is the subtext of De Sanctis's *History of Italian Literature*, his most famous work. He mentions genre in relation to various periods in his history, though it is hardly his focus. His emphasis is on the particular as against the universal and he is severely critical of art that aims to produce the typical. The history narrated is one of achievement, fall and slow, struggling recovery. In the early chapters, De Sanctis discusses themes and genres of medieval literature such as love lyrics, visions and mystery plays, but without relish; it takes Dante to synthesize all of these in the *Divine Comedy*. Petrarch's lyrics represent a fall into subjectivity, somewhat compensated for by an increased emphasis on the human. Boccaccio marks a high point after which the Italian Renaissance declines, with the partial exceptions of Machiavelli and Tasso. In more modern times, writers such as Leopardi stand out and presage future achievements.[7]

Many tensions in Belinsky are also evident in De Sanctis: the call for a writer simultaneously national and non-typical, a historical scheme that points towards future national achievements, and a belief that writers cannot fully transcend their times. For De Sanctis, forms or genres in the sense of Goethe's *Dichtarten* can pass away, but art and genres in the sense of lyric, epic and drama cannot permanently disappear.

Brunetière, a prominent nineteenth-century genre theorist, was influenced by Hippolyte Taine (1828–93), who was instrumental in bringing sociological concerns to literature.[8] Taine believed that the genres of a given period parallel other cultural phenomena of that period: the poetry and the costumes of the seventeenth century express a common *Zeitgeist*. Taine, though, is not really interested in genre so much as in representative works, to the point where he presents a scheme of value based on how representative a work is. He is also interested in types, especially the depiction of 'heroic' and forceful types of the Iago or Vautrin variety, and consequently or paradoxically in what constitutes the individuality of a person, a time period or a country. Many of his concerns touched on genre, but Taine did not formulate a theory. Brunetière used scientific models to develop his theory and thereby stands out among his contemporaries.

Brunetière, more particularly, takes up the 'doctrine' of the evolution of species. Biological metaphors are a staple of nineteenth-century genre theory, but Brunetière's specific understanding of species and its application is essentially unprecedented. He is careful to delineate what is

---

[7] Francesco De Sanctis, *History of Italian Literature*, trans. Joan Redfern, 2 vols. (New York: Barnes & Noble, 1968), vol. II, pp. 946–7. This passage was written around 1871.
[8] See Rané Wellek, *A History of Modern Criticism 1750–1950. Vol. IV: The Later Nineteenth Century* (New Haven, CT: Yale University Press, 1965), p. 36.

most central to the theory of evolution: 'the mother idea...of evolution' is, 'according to Herbert Spencer, "the passage from homogeneous to heterogeneous"' or, 'as Häckel says, "the gradual differentiation of primitively simple material"'.[9] Brunetière's theory may acquire rhetorical authority from science, but its true authority depends on its power to furnish a coherent explanation of literary facts.

Brunetière develops a rich theory: genres, like species, have their histories and, in tracing these histories, one arguably comes to understand the genres better than one would through definitions that seek to establish essential features of literary kinds. Brunetière also allows for cultural-historical influences on literature while maintaining focus on the literary:

The superior adaptability and power of survival of the new species are at once recognized and proved, indeed, in practice. It is in vain that the older species attempt to struggle: their fate is sealed in advance. The successors of Richardson, Molière, and Shakespeare copy these unattainable models until, their fecundity being exhausted – and by their fecundity I mean their aptitude for struggling with kindred and rival species – the imitation is changed into a routine which becomes a source of weakness, impoverishment and death for the species.[10]

Brunetière's explanation of the development of genres is generous in that it potentially includes 'interior' influence (such as Hegelian dialectics), 'exterior' influence (materialist and otherwise) and authorial invention (especially genius). What is more, his theory demonstrates the interdependence of literary criticism, history and theory.

Most critics today would maintain that genres cannot really be said to die out like species; for this reason, among others, the genre–species analogy and Brunetière's theory have become discredited – perhaps unfairly. True, writers can make use of generic forms that have fallen into disuse: genres, from this perspective, do not die. Other implications of Brunetière's analogy also call for scepticism and scrutiny: (1) that nature, and therefore literary history, does not make jumps; (2) that evolutionary narratives, and therefore generic genealogies, are teleologically structured and must take the form of inevitable progress and inevitable decline; and (3) that since every organism belongs to a single species, every literary work belongs to a single genre. One might maintain that Brunetière's theory can accommodate nature's jumps and criticism's revolutionary narratives, first by emphasizing how, in theories of evolution, mutations and other factors can help explain sudden developments in species, and second by noting that Brunetière allows for the sudden leaps of artistic

9  Ferdinand Brunetière, *Etudes critiques sur l'histoire de la littérature française*, 7 vols. (Paris: Librairie Hachette, 1925), vol. VI, p. 11. Translations from this work are mine.
10 Ferdinand Brunetière, *Manual of the History of French Literature*, trans. Ralph Derechef (New York: Hashel House, 1970), p. xvii.

genius. As for teleological narratives, they may or may not be problematic depending on one's philosophical perspective. It could be argued that all narratives are teleological in so far as they have an object – perhaps even in so far as they take up the story of something. From this point of view, if the story of a particular genre is worth taking up, then an account of its rise, teleological though it may be, potentially possesses as high a degree of accuracy and as much explanatory power as any historical account. A more fundamental problem with Brunetière's approach concerns the possibility that literary works might belong to more than one genre. His method encourages neo-classical notions of the purity of genres, if not in theory then in practice: his account of French tragedy's development and decline indicates that he considers nineteenth-century tragic dramas to be not tragedies but examples of some other genre. A genealogical approach to genre nonetheless remains viable today.

That Brunetière was of his time would be a dull lesson to draw from his criticism; for all its problems, his theory raises issues that have purchase today. As noted, he draws on science but is not beholden to it for his authority: one of his more significant theoretical moves is to distinguish the study of literature from other disciplines. The lines he draws between disciplines, like the lines he draws between genres, may be too sharp for twenty-first-century taste, but they call attention to important implications of his species–genre analogy: that literary studies is comparable to other disciplines (possessing its own authority as a discipline) and that genre has an ontological status comparable to species (generic classifications not necessarily being reducible to subjective, value-laden constructions). These notions challenge in subtle and obvious ways the orthodox scepticism of today's academy. What connects Brunetière's theory to nineteenth-century intellectual culture is his attention to scientific developments and his historicism. His theory looks forward to a scientifically based study of literature and to an historically based criticism. It may even anticipate psychological theories of literary history, such as Harold Bloom's, in its highlighting of authorial influence on genre.

## Anglophone theory

Nineteenth-century British and American writers tend to avoid the kind of abstract theory associated with German philosophy, sometimes to the point where their theories of genre seem little more than justifications of their own aesthetic preferences. Leigh Hunt's discussion of imagination and fancy in 'What is Poetry?' (1844), for example, ultimately serves to buttress an almost neo-classical hierarchy of literary kinds despite its use of Romantic concepts.[11] From this perspective, 'Imagination belongs to Tragedy, or the serious muse; Fancy to the comic' (pp. 21–2). Hunt also assigns roles to feeling, thought, and wit in literary creation, as when he asserts that 'Imagination . . . makes the greatest poets; feeling and thought the next; fancy (by itself) the next; wit the last' (p. 44). This expressive hierarchy quickly translates into a generic hierarchy: epic is the highest class of poetry, followed by serious drama, non-serious drama, the pastoral, the lyric, and contemplative poetry with more thought than feeling. Walter Bagehot's scheme of genres follows a similar pattern: while his genre theory is a recognizable variation on German schemes, his critical remarks regarding lyrical modes are obvious covers for aesthetic judgements. Like many of the Romantics, Bagehot sees poetry as a progression from ancient impersonality to modern personality, though he considers lyric to be the most recent genre, developing out of drama, which developed out of epic. The modern poet, however, is not really epic or dramatic or lyric: he depicts his mind as a whole.[12] In 'Wordsworth, Tennyson, and Browning' (1864), Bagehot divides all poetry if not all literary art into 'three principal modes', 'the *pure*, which is sometimes, but not very wisely, called the classical; the *ornate*, which is also unwisely called the romantic; and the *grotesque*, which might be called the medieval'.[13]

Other Anglophone writers, such as Edgar Allan Poe (1809–49), concentrate on one genre, though their arguments relating to genre theory as a whole deserve mention here. Poe's ideas about lyric, as developed in 'The Philosophy of Composition' and elsewhere, concentrate on the 'totality, or unity, of effect' and on the combination of music with a pleasurable idea.[14] Epics like *Paradise Lost*, in this view, are inevitably successions of poetic heights and prosaic plateaus. Poe's ideas about expression and originality owe something to Romanticism, but his emphasis on the purity of the genres and on unity is neo-classical. Novels, perhaps, gain something from a variety of incidents and effects, but unity remains the critical yardstick not only for stories but for drama. Genres are perpetually available, according to Poe; decline is not inevitable. Modern drama, in particular, has not declined, as he writes in 'The American Drama'; it has remained static while other human endeavours have progressed (pp. 357–8). Like all art, drama requires original treatment to move forward. Originality

---

11  Leigh Hunt, 'What is Poetry?' in *Imagination and Fancy* (New York: George P. Putnam, 1851), p. 20.
12  Wellek, *History of Modern Criticism*, vol. IV, pp. 183–4.
13  Walter Bagehot, 'Wordsworth, Tennyson, and Browning' in *Literary Studies, Essays and Belles-Lettres*, 2 vols. (New York: E. P. Dutton, 1902), vol. II, p. 317.
14  Edgar Allan Poe,'The Philosophy of Composition' in *Essays and Reviews*, ed. G. R. Thompson (New York: Library of America, 1984), p. 15.

should not imply mixing genres, however: 'a man of true genius... has no business with these hybrid and paradoxical compositions' (pp. 387–8).

William Dean Howells (1837–1920) is overt regarding his preferences for the novel among genres and for the realist novel among novelistic fictions. In 'Novel-Writing and Novel-Reading', a transcript of a lecture he delivered in 1899, Howells admits to enjoying history, biography, travel writing, poetry, drama and metaphysics, in order to confess more openly that he enjoys the aforementioned genres to the degree that they remind him of 'the supreme literary form', the novel.[15] He distinguishes three forms of fiction 'in order of their greatness': 'the novel, the romance, and the romanticistic novel' (p. 10). Howells is effectively enlarging the concept of the novel to include earlier kinds of fiction. He can even claim that the *Iliad* and the *Odyssey* are novels because the epic is a version of the novel's historical form (p. 24). Such a capacious notion of genre may lack explanatory power, but it represents a novel response, so to speak, to changing literary forms and fashions. The novel can now annex the epic instead of being accommodated by it.

Henry James (1843–1916) in fact meditates on the rise of the novel and the corresponding need for theoretical reflection on the new genre. He opens 'The Art of Fiction' (1884) by remarking that only 'a short time ago' the English novel 'had no air of having a theory, a conviction, a consciousness of itself behind it' and that it is only now beginning to be taken seriously.[16] Like Howells, James champions the Realist novel – he claims that the 'only reason for the existence of the novel is that it does attempt to represent life' (vol. I, p. 46) – and tends to find fault with novels that abandon Realist premises even while asserting that the reader 'must grant the artist his subject, his idea, his *donnée*' (vol. I, p. 56). At times James can make sharp generic distinctions and then blur them. In his preface to *The Awkward Age* (1908), he establishes almost neo-classical divisions, then allows for mixing: 'Kinds', he writes, 'are the very life of literature, and truth and strength come from the complete recognition of them'; nonetheless, effects can be achieved by renouncing 'utterly' the view of generic consistency (vol. II, p. 1131). In 'The Lesson of Balzac' (1905), James argues that generic mixture is built into the novel, asserting that 'the lyrical element' abides in the novelist and at least some novelists carry this element into their fiction writing (vol. II, p. 121). Even granting that James's arguments are geared towards specific occasions and that he saw his criticism on the novel as preliminary, it is

[15] William Dean Howells, 'Novel-Writing and Novel-Reading' in *Howells and James: A Double Billing*, eds. William M. Gibson, Leon Edel and Lyall H. Powers (New York: New York Public Library, 1958), p. 7.
[16] Henry James, 'The Art of Fiction' in *Literary Criticism*, ed. Leon Edel, 2 vols. (New York: Library of America, 1984), vol. I, pp. 44–5.

hard not to see his shifting positions as significant: he wants the novel to be on equal footing with other genres but does not want the novelist to be constrained by generic considerations other than representing life and the stylistic implications of the artist's chosen subject. Convincing his audience to take the craft of fiction seriously takes precedence over any specific theory of genre.

Surveying nineteenth-century Anglophone criticism in search of statements about genre, one finds mostly scattered comments in histories and assertions derived from Romantic thinkers. As early as 1831, J. P. Collier sought to write a genre history in his *History of English Dramatic Poetry up to the Time of Shakespeare* – to show how Renaissance tragedy emerges from morality plays and mystery plays. Later in the century, John Addington Symonds pursued this project more diligently. His *Shakspere's Predecessors in the English Drama* (1884) is in some ways the book that Collier was unable to write. Symonds shows in detail how, from 'the Miracles, Moralities, and Interludes, the earliest comedies of manners, the classical experiments of Sackville and Norton, Hughes, Gascoigne, Edwards, and their satellites, the euphuistic phantasies of Lyly, the melodramas of Kyd, Greene, and Peele, together with the first rude history-plays and realistic tragedies of daily life, emerges Marlowe' – and how, from Marlowe, emerges Shakespeare.[17] He mostly avoids source hunting by concentrating on generic lineages, but his theoretical framework is a dull blend of triadic thinking and biological metaphor. Symonds speaks teleologically of three stages of generic development (preparation, maturity and decadence), claiming that Greek dramatic art follows the same 'rule of triple progression' as English tragedy (p. 6).

In his essays on poetry from the 1830s, John Stuart Mill is averse to neither theory nor genre. His familiarity with historical theories is evident in 'What is Poetry?' when he asserts that kinds of poetry exist in early societies, even if they are of the 'lowest and most elementary' sort – ballads, stories and the like.[18] Mill's distinction between interest derived from incident and that derived from feeling helps him describe generic differences: the novel offers mostly the former interest, poetry mostly the latter. Drama, especially the drama of Shakespeare, offers both interests in union. Though Mill at times employs 'poetry' as something like a synonym for literature, he contributes to the modern sense of poetry as lyric, not only by defining poetry against the novel but also with his claim that epic is 'not poetry at all' in so far as it is narrative (p. 12). Mill's

---

17  John Addington Symonds, *Shakspere's Predecessors in the English Drama* (New York: Charles Scribner's Sons, 1906), p. 4.
18  John Stuart Mill, 'What is Poetry?' in *Essays on Poetry*, ed. F. Parvin Sharpless (Columbia: University of South Carolina Press, 1976), p. 7.

theory of genre is, in effect, psychological, though it has the appearance of being form- or content-based. Mill talks of there being almost separate audiences for novels and poems (as though the genres produced different pleasures or suited different sensibilities), and of there being different poetic natures. While idealist and materialist dialectics are amenable to the notion that genre performs psychological work, Mill's theory seems to partake of an alternative nineteenth-century trend that pits psychological and historical explanations of genre against each other.

One Anglophone theorist who drew more directly on Romantic thinkers was Jones Very (1813–80), a compatriot and admirer of Emerson. In 'Epic Poetry' (1837), Very argues for a literary history similar to that of German thinkers, but with perhaps more emphasis on the role Christianity has played in effecting changes in literature and sensibility. Very's sequence of and arguments about genres, like Mill's, emphasize interest: 'I shall... show that the taking away of the peculiarities of *epic* interest, and the final emerging of that interest in the *dramatic*, is the natural result of the influences to which the human mind is subjected.'[19] For Very, the shift from epic is occasioned by a growth of the human mind, the development of 'a stronger sympathy with the inner man of the heart' (pp. 10–11). At one point, Very claims that the 'epic poetry of the Greeks corresponds to sculpture (p. 12), which at first glance seems an adjustment of Schelling's or the Schlegels' claim that drama is like sculpture, or a variation on Hegel's claim that sculpture is the art form that epitomizes the classical. For Very, sculpture implies an aesthetic of an outward-directed mind. What has turned our mind inward, Jones claims in logic reminiscent of Hugo's, is Christianity: 'The effect of Christianity was to make the individual mind the great object of regard, and[,] transferring the scene of action from the outward world to the world within, to give all modern literature the dramatic tendency' (p. 20).

Though not widely known, the Anglophone critic most engaged in genre theory was perhaps Eneas Sweetland Dallas (1828–79). Dallas's *Poetics* (1852) calls for discussion first because of its scheme of literary kinds based on the triad 'play, tale, song', a formulation that may derive from Jean Paul.[20] Throughout his criticism, Dallas alludes to thinkers who have made use of tripartite schemes and shows himself to be fond of triads. He opens his discussion of 'The Kinds of Poesy' by citing the *Leviathan*, in particular Hobbes's three poetic divisions and their narrative and dramatic subdivisions.[21] Dallas refers to triads of literary kinds as

[19] Jones Very, 'Epic Poetry' in *The Romantic Tradition in American Literature*, ed. Harold Bloom (New York: Arno Press, 1972), p. 4.
[20] Wellek, *History of Modern Criticism*, vol. IV, p. 145.
[21] E. S. Dallas, 'The Kinds of Poesy' in *Poetics* (London: Smith, Elder, 1852), pp. 81–2.

'trinities', alluding to theological arguments for tripartite generic schemes (employed in criticism since the Renaissance) and shoring up the idea that there are 'at bottom' three kinds of literature, 'Dramatic, Narrative and Lyrical; Play, Tale and Song' (p. 82).

Dallas's theory is more sophisticated in *The Gay Science* (1866), a two-volume plea for criticism as science.[22] His criticism represents well two related trends in the second half of the nineteenth century: turning towards science, especially psychology, in response to historicism, and adjusting literary theory in response to practice. Like many of his contemporaries, Dallas acknowledges the importance of historicist thinking. As his insistence on generic triads suggests, though, the nineteenth century felt some need to ground literary kinds, or aspects of them, outside history. By placing the essence of genre in the mind – mental capacity, mode of attention, sensibility – nineteenth-century theorists liberate genre not only from neo-classicism but, in a sense, from history. This move can also be described as an aesthetic turn from imitation to expression: Dallas considered Aristotle's contention that poetry is imitation to be 'demonstrably false' (vol. I, p. 26). Dallas's theory is, in part, a reflection of changes in artistic practice, such as the increase of self-expression in lyric and the rise of Romantic or 'emotionally expressive' instrumental music: within a decade of *The Gay Science*, Walter Pater will remark that all art constantly aspires to the condition of music. Dallas's theory allows for generic distinctions based on how a work affects the reader. Earlier theorists had considered mainly the authorial dimension of expression.

## Late nineteenth- and early twentieth-century theories: psychology and historicism

Historicism's struggle with psychology is an underlying dynamic of late nineteenth- and early twentieth-century theories of literary kinds. In retrospect, this development seems natural. Historical considerations helped the Romantics view genre as something that could perform philosophical and psychological work. As thinkers began questioning Idealist theories, psychology became the complement of or alternative to historicism – not solely at the expense of philosophy, though, if only because psychology and philosophy were not distinct intellectual enterprises in the nineteenth century. As psychology's explanatory power became more recognized among genre theorists, psychological theories were directed towards not

[22] E. S. Dallas, *The Gay Science*, 2 vols. (London: Chapman & Hall, 1866), vol. I, pp. 175–6.

only the author but the reader, and tended more to oppose than to complement historicism. Such a history of ideas does not tell the whole story,
of course, however nicely it sets the stage for a discussion of figures like
Nietzsche, Dilthey and Croce. There was no sudden paradigm shift in
criticism towards a mixture of historicism and psychology.

In Italian theory, at least two critics deserve mention, Adolfo Bartoli
(1833–94) and Vittorio Imbriani (1840–86). Bartoli's seven-volume history of Italian literature stands out in part because it surveys genres such
as *fabliaux*, Goliardic poetry and burlesque satires in order to portray
the mentalities of various periods. In a sense, it is a history of genres
whose details serve the Hegelian aim of fleshing out the *Zeitgeist*. Like
many of his liberal compatriots, Bartoli considered himself a humanist and favoured Realism; he was secular and anti-clerical in outlook.
(Hegelian views of history tend to be associated with liberalism in Italy.)
Imbriani was in one respect more Hegelian than Bartoli: his triads pro-
liferate in ways that rival Dallas's trinities. In his *Laws of the Poetic
Organism and History of Italian Literature* (1869), Imbriani considers
great works as the organic products of national development. He offers
a progressive scheme of genres (epic to lyric to drama), corresponding
to three stages in Italian literature (Dante, Ariosto–Tasso, Alfieri) which
correspond to what appear to be psychic sources of expression (intuition,
imagination, characterization). Each stage even has its own poetic metre.
Though great art ultimately comes from the people (via unconscious individual creation), some writers can be said to represent the culmination of
certain genres (Petrarch of troubadour poetry, Boccaccio of *fabliaux*). For
all of its clunky schematic apparatus, Imbriani's theory is characteristic
of other theories of its time in combining historicism and psychology.[23]

Nineteenth-century Russian criticism, like Italian criticism, can be
divided into liberal and conservative camps, though the Russian critics influenced by Belinsky were more progressive in their politics than the
Italians influenced by De Sanctis. As genre theorists, the 'Russian radical
critics' (as Wellek dubs them) call for discussion, if only because of their
extreme positions. Nikolai Chernyshevsky (1828–89) heads the group,
though he has little to say about genre. In *The Aesthetic Relations of
Art to Reality* (1855), he measures different art forms, including literary
kinds, in relation to reality; art is at best a reminder of or primer for the
non-fictional world. Reality is the content of all art; content is separable
from form. Chernyshevsky considers sculpture useless, music that deviates from natural song inferior, and poetry especially lame because it does
not appeal directly to the senses but to the imagination – besides, poets

[23] My discussion of Italian genre criticism after De Sanctis is drawn from Wellek, *History
of Modern Criticism*, vol. IV, pp. 125–40.

really just write memoirs, as criticism has shown. His disciple, Nikolai Dobrolyubov (1836–68), repeats the argument about literature being
a mirror of life and is as sceptical as his mentor about art's ability to
change reality. Literature can quicken and give more fullness to social
work, though. Realism is Dobrolyubov's standard for all genres: 'naturalness' should take precedence over dramatic principles such as unity
and coherence; novels should not be fantastical.

Dmitri Pisarev (1840–68) backs Cherynshevsky's contention that form
and content are separable, arguing against art as inspiration or unconscious creation. In 'The Destruction of Aesthetics' (1865), he asserts that
content is what should matter and that then proponents of 'art for art's
sake' accord an undue priority to form over content. Only forms and
genres with social use deserve to exist. The 'ornamental' arts of music,
painting and sculpture ought to be discarded – drawing, Pisarev dead-
pans, may be preserved for such uses as sketching architectural plans –
and poetry as verse is fortunately already dying. Novels and plays can
have the social purposes of propaganda, but historical novels are useless.
Pisarev is trying to shock his audience, of course, even as he is earnest
about the eventual demise of art. Because views like those of Chernyshevsky, Dobrolyubov and Pisarev were later used to support the Soviet
aesthetic of Socialist Realism, it is worth noting that these three theorists
were not Marxist thinkers, for reasons that go beyond a lack of access to
Marx's writings: they were as influenced by utilitarianism as by historicism, and they were at least as interested in getting their political ideas
past the censor as in presenting theories of aesthetics and genre.

The influence of Hegel and historicism was perhaps strongest in
German-speaking countries, but some critics do not fit easily into theoretical trends. The Austrian poet Franz Grillparzer (1791–1872), for
example, was against aesthetic systems and against Hegel's view that
art was closely linked to history and tending towards its demise. For
him, genius could transcend history. Genre would seem to count for little
from this perspective. For Ludwig Uhland (1787–1862), by contrast, genres and history are extremely significant. In his posthumously published
writings on the history of poetry (1865–73), Uhland views literary development as organic and combines different historical considerations –
ideal, material and formal. He connects genres to the social status of
their producers, where the sequence 'religious legend, chivalric romance,
courtly love poetry, and didactic verse' corresponds to 'mythic folk, cleric,
knight, and burgher'. Hegelian triads within triads can be found in Karl
Rosenkranz's *History of German Medieval Poetry* (1830), where literature is said to develop in three general stages – from intuition (epic) to
sentiment (lyric) to thought (didactic poetry) – and in three specific stages
within each general stage. At the same time, some critics react strongly

against Hegelian approaches to art. In *On Hegel's Aesthetic Philosophy* (1844), Theodor Wilhelm Danzel argues for the individuality of every work of art and contends that philosophizing about a work separates content from form.[24]

The more renowned Georg Gottfried Gervinus (1805–71) presents his *History of German Poetry* (1871–4, originally *History of the Germans' National Poetic Literature*, 1835–42) as simply history, though he in fact adumbrates theoretical positions and makes critical judgements throughout the work. Like Hegel, Gervinus believes that poetic and national evolution go hand in hand; literature is in some sense constrained by history. Other than a vaguely Hegelian belief that Germany's age of great art is past, though, there is no clear progression in Gervinus's history and *Geist* does not account for all of history's constraints. Contrary to Hegel, Gervinus allows historical forms to recur, as when he points out that epic is not limited to ancient times. Epic can be a viable genre if the age which produces it possesses 'the character of a rebirth, a rejuvenation of national experience' and the work's material is 'taken from the youthful days of the nation or at least drawn from the sources of true folk epic'.[25] Gervinus is somewhat neo-classical in his taste, even as he draws on Romantic ideas. Epic and drama are among the highest genres (akin to the plastic arts); lyric is among the lowest genres (akin to music). Epic is objective and turned towards the past, whereas tragedy is subjective and focused on the present. Gervinus's views also have a historical dimension. Historical tragedy is the modern poet's highest aim. The Romantics were unsuccessful at tragedy and cultivated the lowly lyric because they turned inward, as befits a lesser age marked by quietism (p. 581).

Friedrich Theodor Vischer (1807–87) is in many respects more Hegelian than Gervinus, but nonetheless moves away from history towards philosophical-psychological notions of genre. One way to understand Vischer's theory of literary kinds is via the organization of his *Aesthetics* (1846–57), in particular the volume on literature (*Dichtkunst*, the language-based art). For Vischer, the literary genres are, unsurprisingly, 'Epic Poetry', 'Lyric Poetry' and 'Dramatic Poetry'. His organization thus signals that each genre's types are natural, or at least capable of being defined without reference to history. Though Vischer refers to the history of art forms, he tends to define kinds in terms of their philosophical and psychological function, as transhistorical entities.

At the levels of *Gattung* and *Zweig*, Vischer's theory is conventional. The plastic arts present the objective reality of beauty, music the

---

[24] My discussion of German-speaking writers in this paragraph is drawn from Wellek's 'German Critics from Grillparzer to Marx and Engels' in *ibid.*, vol. III, pp. 182–239.

[25] Georg Gottfried Gervinus, *Geschichte der Deutschen Dichtung*, 5 vols. (Leipzig: Wilhelm Englemann, 1853), vol. V, p. 446. All translations are mine.

subjective reality, and literature the subjective-objective reality. Epic moves towards the objectivity of the plastic arts, lyric towards the subjectivity of music, and drama towards a synthesis of objectivity and subjectivity.[26] Unlike Hegel and most nineteenth-century theorists, Vischer considers comedy as the highest genre, as 'the act of pure freedom of consciousness' (p. 1444). Though inspired by some comments of Schiller, this view stands out because many nineteenth-century theorists equate drama with tragedy.

The writings of Arthur Schopenhauer (1788–1860) belong to Hegel's time, though they became influential only later in the century. Like Hegel, Schopenhauer places art somewhere below philosophy, though art hardly comes across as less valuable than philosophy and is in a sense continuous with it. Music, for example, is championed as the direct expression of the will without mediation of ideas, and poetry 'is related to philosophy as experience is to empirical science'.[27] Like Aristotle, Schopenhauer considers poetry more philosophical than history; like writers in the Platonic tradition, he sees art as working through particulars towards universals. Schopenhauer's laudatory and philosophical views on music were unusual among his contemporaries and made him attractive to late nineteenth-century thinkers. Though his high regard of tragedy is conventional and his hierarchy of genres is a variation on contemporary views (the lowly lyric is subjective, high drama is objective), his views on the psychological effect of tragedy are anomalous for his time. For Schopenhauer, tragedy does not produce a catharsis; fear and pity are but means to the 'true tendency of tragedy', 'the summons to turn the will away from life' (p. 435). Such a negation represents the highest wisdom in Schopenhauer's philosophy. Comedy produces the opposite effect – it is 'an invitation to the continued affirmation of the will' (p. 437) – and is a less objective and therefore lesser genre. Schopenhauer is hardly unique in taking objectivity as an aesthetic touchstone, but for him objectivity is inward-looking, directed towards facts of human existence rather than facts of the world. Thus the romance or novel 'will be of a so much higher and nobler kind the more of *inward* and the less of *outward* life it portrays'.[28] Schopenhauer's thinking is driven by a need to confront and turn away from the self. It is psychological and pessimistic.

[26] Friedrich Theodor Vischer, *Aesthetik oder Wissenschaft des Schönen*. *Vol. v: Die Dichtkunst* (Stuttgart: Karl Mäckten, 1857), pp. xi–xii, 1259ff. (epic), 1322ff. (lyric) and 1375ff. (drama). All translations are mine.

[27] Arthur Schopenhauer, *The World as Will and Representation*, trans. E. F. J. Payne, 2 vols. (New York: Dover, 1958), vol. II, p. 427.

[28] Arthur Schopenhauer, 'On the Metaphysics of the Beautiful and on Asthetics' in *Selected Essays of Arthur Schopenhauer*, trans. Ernest Belfort Baz (London: Cheswick Press, 1912), p. 304.

Friedrich Hebbel (1813–63) presents a similarly pessimistic theory in
'My Word Concerning the Drama' (1843) and his preface to *Maria Mag-
dalena* (1844). Unlike Schopenhauer, Hebbel does not take the starkly
pessimistic view that tragedy urges us to deny a will to life, though he
does believe that tragedy reconciles us to our fate. Like Schopenhauer,
Hebbel adjusts Aristotelian ideas in order to place emphasis on tragedy
as something fundamental to the human condition. Tragic heroes do not
fall because of hubris or some other lack of measure but because they are
human. For Hebbel, drama is a master genre – it differs from epic only in
that it is directed in 'proper balance' towards life's 'being and becoming'
and because it 'represents the process of life... by bringing the situation
to be considered before our eyes'.[29] Hebbel suggests that all genres strive
for a similar aim though drama is the highest art form. Ultimately, it is the
'lyric drama' that most perfectly achieves drama's function, apparently
because the lyric element helps the audience visualize 'how the individual
gains his form and focus in the conflict between his personal will and
the universal one' (p. 19). Hebbel seems to desire the kind of heroism
represented in Schiller's tragedies, though for him the fulfilment of noble
aims is more uncertain.

Schopenhauer's and Hebbel's brands of pessimism have an analogue in
Victorian thought, not only with regard to religious doubt, but in genre
theory. When Matthew Arnold defends his classically inspired drama
*Merope* (1858), for example, he offers an essentially modern rationale
for Greek tragedy, claiming that it 'conducts us to a state of feeling which
it is the highest aim of tragedy to produce, to *a sentiment of sublime
acquiescence in the course of fate, and in the dispensations of human
life*'.[30] This sort of pessimism can also be linked to reactions against
ideas of progress and against the rise of middle-class genres, such as
*Bürgerliches Trauerspiel* ('domestic tragedy') and the novel.

In *The Birth of Tragedy from the Spirit of Music* (1871), Friedrich
Nietzsche (1844–1900) also reacts to his time and has much to say about
art's psychological effects, but argues that aesthetic experience can be a
way out of pessimism. Art can turn away from Christianity's 'hostility to
life', for 'existence and the world' can be justified – are only justified – 'as
an *aesthetic phenomenon*'.[31] Nietzsche's interest in the genealogical can

---

[29]  Friedrich Hebbel, 'My Word Concerning the Drama' in *Three Plays by Hebbel*, trans.
      Marion W. Sonnenfeld (Lewisburg, PA: Bucknell University Press, 1971), p. 18.
[30]  Matthew Arnold, 'Preface to Merope' in *The Complete Prose Works of Matthew
      Arnold. Vol. I: On the Classical Tradition*, ed. R. H. Super (Ann Arbor: University
      of Michigan Press, 1961), p. 59.
[31]  Friedrich Nietzsche, *The Birth of Tragedy from the Spirit of Music* in *The Birth of
      Tragedy and The Case of Wagner*, trans. Walter Kaufmann (New York: Random House,
      1967), pp. 23, 52.

be linked to Darwin, though Nietzsche's sequence of art-drives is arguably Hegelian, motivated by a kind of internal dialectic (from the Apollonian to the Dionysian to the Socratic). Nietzsche does not, however, predict a Hegelian demise of art in that he allows for a new kind of Dionysian art, a rebirth of tragedy.

It is easy to overlook the fact that *The Birth of Tragedy* presents a general theory of kinds, a scheme in which genres are transformations of earlier genres, evolving along with art-drives and associated psychological needs. Nietzsche's theory draws on conventional biological metaphors for genre, including organism, species and family, but applies them in startling ways: 'Greek tragedy... died by suicide... When a new artistic genre blossomed forth... it was noted with horror that she did indeed bear the features of her mother – but those she had exhibited in her long death-struggle' (p. 76). While the sequence 'epic–tragedy–comedy' is a recognizable variation of Romantic generic histories, *The Birth of Tragedy* is not limited by triads in its genealogies. New Comedy was not the only genre to come from Greek tragedy. Nietzsche scornfully argues that the primary Socratic genre was the Aesopian fable and that the Platonic dialogue was 'the barge on which the shipwrecked ancient poetry saved herself with all her children' (p. 90). Nietzsche also tends to see new genres as incorporating previous kinds: 'If tragedy had absorbed into itself all the earlier types of art, the same might also be said in an eccentric sense of the Platonic dialogue which, a mixture of all extant styles and forms, hovers midway between narrative, lyric, and drama, between prose and poetry' (p. 90). Nietzsche's aesthetic tastes are in evidence in his genealogies, especially when he asserts that the Socratic overemphasis on optimism and intelligibility eventually brings about 'the death-leap' of tragedy into 'bourgeois drama' (p. 91). While Socratic optimism answers a psychological need for clarity and consciousness, such psychic fulfilment will inevitably prove unsatisfying. Nietzsche suggests that aesthetic expression, in particular that which comes from a Dionysian urge, will always remain a deep human need. His theory of tragedy thus combines historical and transhistorical considerations.

Wilhelm Dilthey (1833–1911) explicitly confronts the difficulty of constructing a historicist poetics. In 'The Imagination of the Poet: Elements for a Poetics' (1887), he defines the problem by questioning rhetorically how 'processes grounded in human nature' yield a variety of poetic types 'separated according to nations and periods'.[32] By comparing kinds of literature from different times and places, Dilthey hopes to distinguish

[32] Wilhelm Dilthey, 'The Imagination of the Poet: Elements for a Poetics' in *Selected Works. Vol. 5: Poetry and Experience*, eds. Rudolf A. Makkreel and Frithjof Rodi (Princeton University Press, 1985), p. 35.

between what is universal and what is historical; he is especially interested in the typical. He builds on the idea that authors express different types of 'lived experience', reproduced to some degree in the reader. Lived experience as the basis for art corrects the Hegelian notion of art as expression of ideas (p. 137). To put it another way, lived experience 'cannot be expressed in any proposition'; when the spectator or reader is moved, 'everything comes together into a graphic, felt unity of the deepest life-experiences, and that is precisely the significance of poetry' (p. 139). For all of his conviction regarding lived experience, Dilthey is not entirely confident that psychology can sort through and explain the sources of all the literary forms (p. 133). He is willing to accept that there are three historically significant modes of expression – lyric, epic and drama – in order to focus his discussion on the psychological grounding of genres.

Given this focus, Dilthey makes good more on his promise to link genre to psychology than on his promise to deliver a historicist poetics. His description of tragedy, for example, emphasizes the imagination's struggle with its material: '*A powerful tragedy is produced when poetic creativity confronts external states of affairs, reports, stories, etc., as inexorable reality. Then the imagination strives to give unity, inwardness, and meaning to this reality*' (p. 139). Tragedy strengthens rather than purges emotions. Lyric tends towards states of equilibrium, though all poetry heightens feelings for life. To some extent, Dilthey is influenced by formal notions of genre. Yet formal elements, including figures of speech, ultimately issue from lived experience: 'Hyperbole and understatement are . . . merely the final and most palpable expressions of the laws according to which images are intensified or reduced, expanded or condensed, under the influence of feeling' (p. 160). Dilthey distinguishes between genre and form to shore up his historicist poetics, arguing that amidst the 'historical variability of poetic form . . . *stable lawful relationships* emerge' (p. 167) and that '*there exists a lawful sequence of style forms*' within a national literature (p. 168). Art's function is to express the 'content of life' by finding a new form adequate to its times, but this function has become harder to fulfil:

As life becomes more complex, as its constituents and their relations to one another grow more manifold, and especially as more and more emotionally impoverished technological factors intrude between those moments that we experience with feeling, it requires greater power to raise the content of life to poetic form . . . Genuine works of literature, which attain an integral form through artistic simplification, require an even greater degree of genius.

(p. 168)

This passage looks forward to Walter Benjamin's arguments about modernity, but it is also typical of its time: Dilthey argues that 'the novel alone can fulfill the old task of epic literature' and concludes that a 'theory of the novel' is 'by far the most pressing and important task of contemporary poetics' (p. 172).

Like Dilthey, Benedetto Croce (1866–1952) bases aesthetics on psychology, though he draws very different conclusions about genre from those of his German counterpart. For Croce, aesthetics is a branch of philosophy; works of art produce a kind of knowledge that cannot be expressed in concepts. Art begins in, or rather is, intuition, which for Croce includes both the psychic source of expression and expression itself (he sometimes prefers the term 'intuition-expression'). Artworks express a state of mind and cannot be reduced to logical terms or generic types, as Croce writes in his *Guide to Aesthetics* (1913).[33] His 'intuition' is akin to Dilthey's 'lived experience', though the former points to a tighter relation between content and form and to an artistic mind less dependent on history. Dilthey can allow for generic states of mind based on similar lived experiences; Croce sees intuitions as radically individual.

Croce's theories changed over the course of his career, but his thoughts on genre remained consistently negative. In the *Aesthetics* (1902), he attacks 'even the most refined of [generic] distinctions', including dualistic schemes that divide literature into 'subjective and objective genres'.[34] In the *Guide to Aesthetics*, he denies the philosophical validity of the conventional tripartite scheme: 'Epic and lyric, or drama and lyric, are scholastic divisions of the indivisible. Art is always lyrical, or, if you like, the epic and drama of feeling' (p. 25). In *Poetry and Literature* (1936), he discusses the impossibility of determining genres philosophically and makes fun of the proliferation of genres, sub-genres, and sub-sub-genres.[35] Generic divisions can facilitate the knowledge of art, but one should never confuse 'the indexes with reality . . . or the hypothetical imperatives with categorical imperatives' (*Guide*, p. 45). 'Every true work of art', moreover, 'has violated an established genre and in so doing confounded the ideas of critics' (*Aesthetics*, p. 41). If one genre theorist can be singled out as the object of Croce's ire, it is Brunetière, who 'was convinced that it was impossible to judge until all the magnificent evolutionary history, which he was putting together with great pain, was properly constructed' (*Poetry*, p. 191). This criticism seems odd because

33  Benedetto Croce, *Brevario di estetica*, trans. Patrick Romanell (Indianapolis: Hackett, 1965), p. 44.
34  Benedetto Croce, *The Aesthetic as the Science of Expression and of the Linguistic in General* [part of the *Estetica*], trans. Colin Lyas (Cambridge University Press, 1992), p. 41.
35  Benedetto Croce, *Poetry and Literature: An Introduction to its Criticism and History* [*La Poesia*], trans. Giovanni Gullace (Carbondale: Southern Illinois University Press, 1981), pp. 187, 191–2.

Brunetière was not shy about rendering judgements. Croce's objection
may ultimately stem from aesthetic disagreement.

In general, early twentieth-century theory is marked by a resurgence of
historicism with an emphasis on form. In *Meditations on Quixote* (1914),
the Spanish philosopher and critic Ortega y Gasset (1883–1955) attacks
critics like Croce who 'deny the existence of literary genres', claiming
that genres can be characterized via descriptions of form issuing from
content.[36] Hegelian elements in Ortega's thinking are particularly noticeable in statements such as 'Each epoch brings with it a basic interpretation
of man ... For this reason, each epoch prefers a particular genre' (p. 113).
The Russian Formalists – writing mostly in the 1910s and 1920s – are
Hegelian in that they often rely on some notion of a *Zeitgeist* or an evolution of forms even as they tend to see genre as a function of different
language uses.

In *The Theory of the Novel* (written in 1914–15), the Hungarian critic
Georg Lukács (1885–1971) develops a historicist theory of genre by drawing substantially on literary works and German philosophers of the nineteenth century, just as Mikhail Bakhtin will later. In his 1962 preface,
Lukács details his indebtedness to nineteenth-century philosophy, at one
point making special mention of Dilthey, as if to admit to a somewhat
conflicted idea of genre, at once historical and transhistorical.[37] Dual if
not conflicting aims are apparent in the organization of *The Theory of
the Novel*: the book's subtitle is 'A Historico-Philosophical Essay on the
Forms of Great Epic Literature'. Its first half considers 'forms of great
epic literature examined in relation to whether the civilization of the time
is an integrated or a problematic one', while the second half attempts 'a
typology of the novel form' in relation to historical circumstances surrounding specific novels. Before his criticism became overtly Marxist –
perhaps even after – Lukács attempted to develop a historicist theory that
aspired to transhistorical truths. Unlike later academic historicism, which
rhetorically if not conceptually eschews transhistorical claims, Lukács's
theory points openly to nineteenth-century aspirations.

## Nineteenth-century genre theory in practice

To place nineteenth-century genre theories in perspective, it helps to
examine the period's artistic practice. The nineteenth-century literary

---

[36] Ortega y Gasset, *Meditations on Quixote*, trans. Evelyn Rugg and Diego Marín (New
York: Norton, 1961), pp. 111, 113.
[37] Georg Lukács, 'Preface' in Ortega y Gasset, *Meditations on Quixote*, trans. Anna
Bostock (Cambridge, MA: MIT Press, 1971), p. 13.

marketplace urges sensitivity to generic labels, in effect encouraging a new conception of genre. Hawthorne's label 'romance', for example, frames his work's reception as much as it describes a type of novel. In his preface to *The House of the Seven Gables* (1851), Hawthorne suggests that this label should give an author latitude with regard to subject matter and to treatment of materials, though he is quick to add that the romance, like all art, follows strict rules. Hawthorne wishes to cultivate an audience for his work, not only among discerning readers, but among the public at large. His anxiety is typical, especially among authors making their living from writing, and illustrates that genre is in part a negotiation between author and audience or, more generally, between publishing and consuming agents in literary production.

While it is possible to make similar arguments about eighteenth-century artistic production, if not that of earlier times, nineteenth-century anxiety about the literary marketplace is more acute and manifests itself in ways more acknowledged at the time and more discernible in the works. Nineteenth-century writers with artistic ambitions recurrently expressed concerns regarding the effect of journalism on literature, for example, and resistance to journalistic prose could effect generic changes and mark generic differences. (French Symbolist and Parnassian poems come to mind, as do the late novels of James.) Hawthorne complained about 'scribbling women', anxious that others were encroaching on his generic turf or that his romances might be tainted by generically similar work. As though competing for segments of the reading public, French poets commonly attached generic or quasi-generic labels to their volumes: *Méditations, Consolations, Contemplations, Petits poëmes en prose*. One of Charles Baudelaire's motivations for 'inventing' the genre of prose poetry was to make money from his poetry in the face of competition from genres such as the novel. Whether or not it appears in nineteenth-century theories of literary kinds, the concept of genre as 'market niche' existed in practice.

Nineteenth-century literary practice also reveals more starkly the interrelation between interpretation and evaluation, especially in so far as a revolutionary model of artistic progression dominated. As Romanticism and Realism testify, aesthetic revolutions transform notions of what art can be. With works of art in familiar genres, interpretation and evaluation are relatively separable activities, in part because the evaluation of what constitutes the works as art is already established. In the case of art in unfamiliar genres, interpretation and evaluation tend to follow closely upon each other. If you do not recognize the Realist novel as art, you cannot interpret or evaluate it as art; from the moment you recognize it as art, you are already well on your way to interpreting and evaluating it. Because, for example, a work like *Moby-Dick* (1851) challenges generic

conventions, it remains largely unrecognized until conventions change in
ways propitious to it. *Moby-Dick*, after all, mixes genres in ways that
may be aesthetically more akin to *Ulysses* (1922) than to almost any
nineteenth-century novel. Melville's novel did not, in fact, receive wide
recognition until the twentieth century. At least one other sort of work
encourages the view that interpretation and evaluation go hand in hand:
a work challenging generic conventions in such a powerful way as to
become a new generic model – something like *Madame Bovary* (1857) or
*Les Fleurs du mal* (1857).

Even the ascendancy of the narrative–lyric–dramatic scheme in
nineteenth-century genre theory may owe something to literary practice,
despite the fact that the triad hardly describes the century's variety of
literature. If critics had been intent on developing purely descriptive theories of literary kinds, they would have sought out or discussed more kinds
not easily accommodated by the conventional triad – genres with historical pedigrees, such as the essay, and journalistic kinds that had voguish
success, such as the *physiologie*. But even when nineteenth-century triadic theories are meant to be descriptive, they tend to be commendatory,
delineating what literature ought to be. Would-be descriptive theories
with generic hierarchies and exclusions are not new to the 1800s, of
course, and theories of what literature is are linked historically if not
philosophically to theories of what literature ought to be, as defences
of poetry attest. Still, nineteenth-century commendatory theories develop
in a milieu in which the stakes of what literature is have changed significantly. A modern sense of the term 'literature' emerges in the period
along with the study of English literature at universities and increased
educational opportunities for women and working-class men. ('Literature' replaces 'poetry' as the preferred term for language-based art, for
example.) In such an environment, 'literature' clearly designates more
than Latin and Greek classics, but how inclusive ought the term to be?
At once capacious and discriminating, the narrative–lyric–dramatic triad
seems theoretically suited to responding to the new needs of the century
while preserving a sense of continuity with the past. From this perspective, the triadic scheme's long-term success can be linked to aesthetics, to
ideology and, less glamorously, to institutional and intellectual inertia.

Literary practice also helps place in perspective the fluctuation of
generic hierarchies among nineteenth-century theorists. In speaking of
a conventional nineteenth-century triad, it is easy to gloss over the fact
that 'narrative' is a less stable designation than 'lyric' or 'dramatic': variants include 'epic', 'fiction' and 'novel'. For neo-classical critics, epic or
drama is the highest genre. Nineteenth-century critics also tend to place
epic or drama at the top of the hierarchy, drama especially in the first
half of the century. As might be expected, epic begins to drop out of

the triad or to take on metaphorical meaning as the century progresses. Critics are reluctant to accord literary status, let alone high standing, to the upstart genre of the novel until at least the mid-century. Gradually theory responds to practice, though: 'narrative' and 'novel' emerge as preferred generic labels to 'epic'; manifestos for Realist and Naturalist fiction are written and demand attention; and more novels are regarded as 'serious'. Meanwhile, despite its theoretical prestige and its popular versions, nineteenth-century drama increasingly strikes us today as less aesthetically successful than nineteenth-century fiction and poetry. Lyric, even though and perhaps because it becomes less sellable, attains its own kind of prestige: it is felt to be more directly expressive of inner states, more powerfully expressive, more philosophical and closer to music than other literary genres. While some of the high regard in which poetry becomes held may be based on historical prestige or the more intense attention of a coterie audience, it lasts beyond the nineteenth century. As Virginia Woolf remarked in 1922, 'There still lingers among us the belief that poetry is the senior branch of the service.'[38]

Given the impact of historicism on nineteenth-century thought, why were theorists not drawn to changes in literary practice that seem grist to historicism's mill? One might expect nineteenth-century theorists to take up ideas such as 'genre as market niche'. One might especially expect historical materialists such as Marx to take them up. Marx in fact discusses genre in the *Grundrisse*, where he puzzles over why modern readers like himself enjoy Homer's epics. As he puts it: 'The difficulty is that [the Greek arts and epic] still afford us artistic pleasure and that they count as a norm and an unattainable model.'[39] Marx argues that epic's charm for modern readers stems from associating Greek society with childhood: 'Why should not the historical childhood of humanity, its most beautiful unfolding, as a stage never to return, exercise an eternal charm?' (p. 246). This unconvincing (if endearing) explanation owes more to Romanticism than to historical materialism; it also suggests that at least one genre can be described in terms of a psychological effect that is virtually transhistorical. It may be that all historicist theories rely on some transhistorical principles. Nineteenth-century historicism, at any rate, is not averse to employing such principles at a pinch and aspires to transhistorical truths.

---

38  Virginia Woolf, 'On Re-Reading Novels' in *The Essays of Virginia Woolf. Vol. 3: 1919–1924*, ed. Andrew McNeillie (London: Harcourt Brace Jovanovich, 1988), p. 337.
39  Karl Marx, *Grundrisse* in *The Marx–Engels Reader*, ed. Robert C. Tucker, 2nd edn (New York: Norton, 1978), p. 246.

## 27

# Theories of the novel

### NICHOLAS DAMES

The nineteenth century is traditionally acknowledged as the era of the unquestioned dominance of the novel in Western literary culture, an apex moment in which the breadth of the popular readership for novels and the height of the novel's cultural and artistic influence combined in an unprecedented, and unrepeatable, manner. All the more strange, then, that another literary-historical commonplace would have it that the nineteenth century produced no theories of the novel, no genre-wide accounts of its most characteristic and widespread literary form, only occasional, suggestive and disconnected reflections. Contemporary histories and anthologies of what now goes under the name 'novel theory' usually begin no earlier than the prefaces and articles of Henry James, thereby making the twentieth century the era of theorizing what the nineteenth century only unreflectively generated and consumed.[1] Such canonical examples of nineteenth-century thinking about the novel form that remain well known, such as the letters of Gustave Flaubert, the manifesto-like prefaces of the Goncourts or Guy de Maupassant, or selected narratorial digressions by George Eliot, suggest that 'novel theory', to the extent it existed, was scattered, gnomic and unsystematized, essentially a set of asides. The usual narrative, therefore, runs something like this: starting with James and his later disciples, such as Percy Lubbock in his 1921 *The Craft of Fiction*, the basic elements of novelistic form are defined, a canon of representative novels shaped and honed, and the aesthetic dignity of the novel decisively defended. 'Theory', that is, coalesces out of the fragmented writings of earlier practitioners. As the scholar of novel theory Dorothy Hale has recently put it, 'the Anglo-American scholarly record is virtually unanimous in crediting James and Lubbock as the forefathers

---

Translations are my own unless otherwise stated.
[1] See, for instance, the interestingly named *Theory of the Novel: A Historical Approach*, ed. Michael McKeon (Baltimore, MD: Johns Hopkins University Press, 2000), which essentially begins with Georg Lukács. Volumes III and IV of René Wellek's monumental *A History of Modern Criticism 1750–1950*, 8 vols. (New Haven, CT: Yale University Press, 1965) contain no section on 'theories of the novel', which is presumed not to have existed at such an early period.

of novel theory'.[2] Outside the Anglophone world, such early twentieth-century instances as Georg Lukács's 1920 *The Theory of the Novel* still seem to have no grounding in previous thinking about the novel form.

Many of the flaws of these early twentieth-century novel theories are well known now, particularly their tendency to ignore the role of women in the rise of the novel. Their most entrenched strategic move, however – the implicit claim that no 'theories' of the novel predate their work, only authorial musings or journalistic pieties – remains remarkably successful, given that only a handful of scholarly recoveries have cared to argue for the presence of any theories of the novel prior to this alleged *fin de siècle* golden age.[3] It is no accident that James's 1884 article 'The Art of Fiction' is often taken as foundational for novel theory, given that it argues for a pre-existing void in theoretical thinking: 'Only a short time ago it might have been supposed that the English novel was not what the French call *discutable*. It has no air of having a theory, a conviction, a consciousness of itself behind it – of being the expression of an artistic faith.'[4] It is important to stress from the start that James's claim of a general absence of critical consciousness about the novel is a shrewd and enabling tactic rather than a truth. The nineteenth century was a period of burgeoning, chaotic, innovative and often quirkily arcane attempts to formulate answers to the set of questions: what is a novel? What does a novel do? Why have novels secured such a hold on European culture?

Put another way: if James and his followers saw nothing resembling theories of the novel prior to their work, that is because they tended not to like the kinds of answers, and procedures for arriving at these answers, that previous critics had offered to these questions. James's enabling

---

[2] Dorothy Hale, *Social Formalism: The Novel in Theory from Henry James to the Present* (Stanford University Press, 1998), p. 22. For a version of the kind of opinion to which she alludes, see Edwin Eigner and George Worth's claim that one must 'read between the lines [of nineteenth-century writing on the novel] to find English theory almost reluctantly put forth in arguments whose avowed purpose was to protect the English novel from theoretical foreigners and their misguided native disciples'. See Eigner and Worth, 'Introductory Essay' in *Victorian Criticism of the Novel* (Cambridge University Press, 1985), p. 1.

[3] There are three notable examples, centred on Britain, that argue for a vibrant pre-Jamesian body of novel theory: Richard Stang, *The Theory of the Novel in England, 1850–1870* (New York: Columbia University Press, 1959); Kenneth Graham's *English Criticism of the Novel, 1865–1900* (Oxford: Clarendon Press, 1963); and John Charles Olmsted's three-volume *A Victorian Art of Fiction: Essays on the Novel in British Periodicals* (New York: Garland, 1979). For a revisionary account of nineteenth-century French theories of the Realist and non-Realist novel, see Margaret Cohen, *The Sentimental Education of the Novel* (Princeton University Press, 1999).

[4] Henry James, 'The Art of Fiction' in *Henry James: Literary Criticism: Essays on Literature, American Writers, English Writers* (New York: Library of America, 1984), p. 44.

blindness has become our disabling blindness, as by taking his definition of novel theory for granted, we remove ourselves from potentially
fruitful approaches to a study of the novel. A few opening characterizations might help to identify the recurrent tendencies of nineteenth-century
novel theory that, to James and his followers, seemed mistaken, misguided
or irrelevant, and that thus tended to get lost in subsequent novel theories. The first trait is a willingness to acknowledge the incoherence of the
novel form itself; so loose and disparate its practices seemed, so flexible
its potential shapes, that any theoretical approach had first to posit shape-
lessness – a kind of anti-formalist notion of form – as essential to the genre.
'Are there rules for writing a novel, outside of which a written narrative
ought to bear another name?' asks Guy de Maupassant in his manifesto-
like preface, entitled 'Le Roman' ('The Novel'), to his 1888 novel *Pierre
et Jean*. 'If *Don Quixote* is a novel, is *The Red and the Black* another? If
*Monte Cristo* is a novel, is *L'Assommoir* one? ... Which of these works
is a novel? Where are these famous rules?'[5] Maupassant summarizes here
several decades' worth of relatively non-prescriptive attempts to define
the novel form, attempts which generally aimed at descriptions of what
novels are, or even how they are read, rather than how they should be
composed.

In 'The Art of Fiction', James complained at length about this tendency towards broad, value-neutral schemas of the novel, betraying the
existence of novel theories he usually refused to acknowledge:

The novel and the romance, the novel of incident and that of character – these
clumsy separations appear to me to have been made by critics and readers for
their own convenience, and to help them out of some of their occasional queer
predicaments, but to have little reality or interest for the producer, from whose
point of view it is of course that we are attempting to consider the art of fiction.[6]

James's pungent 'of course' obscures his innovation here. Nineteenth-
century novel theorists, with various emphases, tended to treat fiction
from the reader's perspective – what we might now call a version of
'reader-response theory' – rather than from the perspective of composition. Their goal was not to elaborate a theory of aesthetic value, but to
describe the cultural force of a form – a goal better performed from the end
of reception than that of production. Thus the second trait of nineteenth-
century novel theory: its orientation towards how novels were consumed,
towards the affective and epistemological workings of novelistic narrative upon readers, rather than any questions of novelistic construction.
Confronted with the spectacular rise in novel reading dating from the late

---

[5] Guy de Maupassant, 'Le Roman', *Pierre et Jean* (Paris: Louis Conard, 1909), pp. vi–vii.
[6] James, 'Art of Fiction', p. 55.

eighteenth century, critics of the early and mid-nineteenth century tended to analyse novels as a cultural technology rather than simply a new literary form, a technology aimed at the new conditions of widespread privacy and literacy.

The result of this concentration upon reception and cultural influence is a disciplinary breadth to nineteenth-century novel theory that post-Jamesian novel theory largely eliminates. Some of the most important names in nineteenth-century novel theory – Hippolyte Taine, G. H. Lewes, E. S. Dallas, Ferdinand Brunetière, to name a few – were authorities, or well-read amateurs, in various sub-fields of the natural sciences, physiological psychology and evolutionary biology. The results of their work in such fields were, as we shall see, considered to be germane to their attempts elsewhere to define the shape and force of the novel. Even the novelists who produced theories of the novel tended to lean upon scientific epistemologies, as in Balzac's use of taxonomic natural history or Zola's use of experimental physiology.

A subsidiary result of this disciplinary breadth is the difficulty a present-day scholar has in finding the sources of their most important work. If twentieth-century novel theories tended to appear as well-shaped critical books, nineteenth-century versions, produced by scientists, journalists and novelists rather than members of a literary-critical profession, are scattered in such venues as occasional critical articles and reviews (in important journals such as the *Contemporary* in Russia or *Blackwood's*, the *Spectator* or the *Fortnightly Review* in Britain), prefaces to controversial novels (such as those by the Goncourts, Maupassant and Zola), theories of aesthetic sensation (Dallas's 1866 *The Gay Science*), theories of consciousness or mental processing (Alexander Bain's 1859 *The Emotions and the Will*), manifestos of literary-critical practice (Emile Hennequin's 1888 *La Critique scientifique* ['Scientific Criticism']) and national literary histories such as Taine's 1864 *Histoire de la littérature anglaise* (*History of English Literature*), David Masson's 1859 *British Novelists and Their Styles* or Charles-Melchior de Vogüé's 1886 *Le Roman russe* ('The Russian Novel'). Adding to the confusion, the most prominent and powerful literary critics of the nineteenth century – in France, Charles-Augustin Sainte-Beuve, and in Britain, Matthew Arnold – produced no general account of the novel. Located in no one kind of critical protocol, and linked to no one kind of disciplinary approach or master figure, the novel theories of the nineteenth century were often haphazard but nonetheless intriguing attempts to confront a new object of knowledge: the popular phenomenon of the novel and of novel reading.

One prerequisite of such an approach was an acceptance of the reading public that had made the novel form so dominant. Jeremiads about the disastrous cultural effect of cheap publication and the widespread consumption of fiction, as in such classics of the genre as Sainte-Beuve's 1839 'De la littérature industrielle' ('On Industrial Literature'), are largely absent in the work of the century's novel theorists, who start from the liberal presupposition that popular success is a datum to be taken into consideration rather than a dismal result of the novel's ephemerality. The result is a rough operating definition of the novel common to much nineteenth-century theoretical writing: the novel is a literary machine appropriate for the conditions of modern consumption, and designed to make its consumer feel and think in ways different from earlier literary genres.

The most common differentiation made was with drama, usually taken to be the novel's great predecessor as a popular literary art. As expressed in Edward Bulwer-Lytton's 1838 'On Art in Fiction', one of the earliest British novel theories, the contrast between drama and novel centres on their respective normal modes of consumption:

In our closets we should be fatigued with the incessant rush of events that we desire when we make one of a multitude. Oratory and the drama in this resemble each other – that the things best to hear are not always the best to read. In the novel, we address ourselves to the one person – on the stage we address ourselves to a crowd: more rapid effects, broader and more popular sentiments, more condensed grasp of the universal passions are required for the last... In the novel it is different: the most enchanting and permanent kind of interest, in the latter, is often gentle, tranquillising, and subdued. The novelist can appeal to those delicate and subtle emotions, which are easily awakened when we are alone, but which are torpid and unfelt in the electric contagion of popular sympathies.[7]

Generic distinctiveness – what we might call the key signature of genre – is in Bulwer-Lytton's account an affective fact (the 'passion' of drama replaced by the 'delicate and subtle emotions' of the novel), which is explicable by reference to the situation of consumption. Private, solitary reading, and the host of facts associated with it, becomes the datum that defines both the novel's function and its form.

If a value-neutral acceptance of solitary reading was the first hall-mark of the consumption-centred tendency of nineteenth-century novel theory, a further trait displayed by Bulwer-Lytton's analysis – one that twentieth-century novel theories tended to anathematize – is its interest in affect rather than epistemology, or, put another way, its concentration on how different literary genres aim at different sets of emotions rather than different ways of organizing knowledge. States of emotion or sensation are routinely discussed as the primary end products of novel reading, not

---

[7] Edward Bulwer-Lytton, 'The Critic – No. 2: On Art in Fiction', *Monthly Chronicle*, 1 (1838), pp. 144–5.

states of apprehension or comprehension. An early quasi-theoretical text of Stendhal's, his 1822 *De l'amour* ('On Love'), distinguishes between two functions of the novel: a lesser function, that of advancing 'the knowledge of the human heart', and a higher function, the production of 'reverie, which is the true pleasure of the novel'.[8] This stress on the novel's production of affective states, states unique to solitary consumption, rather than knowledge, would by the century's end metamorphose into the discourse of 'pure' art, which asserted the novel's necessary independence from dogma or ideology. In the early nineteenth-century moment of Stendhal and Bulwer-Lytton, however, the emphasis was on the novel as a technology of largely incommunicable emotional states: reverie, fleeting moods, diffuse and unfixed contemplations.

This discourse of receptive states meant that the study of the novel was peculiarly suited to psychological inquiry – an inquiry, that is, into the cognitive and physiological transactions of novel reading. If Stendhal's and Bulwer-Lytton's surmises were vague in their terminology ('delicate and subtle emotions'), the path was open to critics trained in more rigorous modes of psychological science. Hence the still little-understood determining fact of much mid-century novel theory and criticism: its reliance upon physiological psychology as a key methodological tool for prising open the secrets of novelistic form. By the 1850s Britain was at the forefront of European work on the physical and psychological laws of nervous receptivity, known generally as physiology; it would not cede this centrality until the opening of Wilhelm Wundt's psychological laboratory in Leipzig in 1879. As a result, the most important work on novelistic form and physiological response was produced by British critics trained in physiology; so relatively consistent was their approach to novel theory that it might be called a Victorian 'school' of thought on the novel.

The most famous practitioner of this school was G. H. Lewes, a major Victorian editor and critic who also achieved a considerable scientific reputation, despite his lack of professional credentials, on the basis of such psychological treatises as *The Physiology of Common Life* (1860). Lewes's statements on fictional form turned continually to the relation between form and readerly cognition. Attempting to summarize his procedure, Lewes explained in his 1865 series of articles *The Principles of Success in Literature* that his 'inquiry is scientific, not empirical; it therefore seeks the psychological basis for every [literary] law, endeavouring to ascertain what condition of a reader's receptivity determines the law'.[9] The critical process, as Lewes explained it, would work by balancing what

---

8   Stendhal, *De l'amour*, ed. V del Litto (Paris: Gallimard, 1980), p. 55.
9   G. H. Lewes, quoted from the later book edition *The Principles of Success in Literature*, ed. Fred Scott (Boston: Allyn & Bacon, 1891), p. 128.

we might call 'top-down' analysis, working from observed facts of literary form to the kinds of reading response they evoke, with 'bottom-up' analysis, which would proceed from the observed facts of novel-reading protocols – privacy, immersiveness, sympathetic identification – back to the literary techniques that seem adapted to those practices. The novel theorist, put another way, must become adept at the psychological study of reading, used to matching a precise account of the genre's usual style of reception to an equally precise account of the genre's typical form, explaining each with reference to the other.

In Lewes's influential criticism, dispersed among a set of review articles in the 1850s and 1860s, the crucial concept that linked literary form with reader reception was the term 'construction'. As he claimed in an 1859 article on Jane Austen:

> The art of novel-writing, like the art of painting, is founded on general principles, which, because they have their psychological justification, because they are derived from tendencies of the human mind, and not, as absurdly supposed, derived from 'models of composition', are of universal application. The law of colour, for instance, is derived from the observed relation between certain colours and the sensitive retina. The laws of construction, likewise, are derived from the invariable relation between a certain order and succession of events, and the amount of interest excited by that order.[10]

The formal concept of 'construction' is important for what, from the standpoint of twentieth-century novel theory, it does not include. As hinted here, it does not include notions of characterization; of the mimetic relation of fictional events or settings to real life; of prose style; of standard or recurrent themes; of authorial presence or absence. It is rigorously limited to the mechanics of plot, to 'a certain order and succession of events'. In the physiologically inflected British novel theories of the mid-nineteenth century, plot becomes the master datum that produces the conditions of a reader's receptivity. This bias towards plot study would largely determine the course of British novel theory for several decades.

Plot is important for physiological critics because of its temporality and linearity: like any nervous-system sensation, it moves in time, oscillating between acute shocks and periods of lassitude or quiescence. The close similarity between how sensation was understood (as a wave signature) and how plots were understood (as rhythmic alternations between sensational events and digressive rest periods) meant that plot came to be understood as the primary means by which a novel entered the minds, and affected the bodies, of its readers. This was taken to be so salient a

---

[10] G. H. Lewes, 'The Novels of Jane Austen', *Blackwood's Edinburgh Magazine*, 84 (1859), p. 108.

fact that the pre-eminent Victorian physiological psychologist Alexander Bain defined the novel, in his mid-century magnum opus *The Emotions and the Will*, as 'the literature of plot-interest', characterizing it by 'the mental attitude under a gradually approaching end, a peculiar condition of rapt suspense, termed Pursuit and Plot interest', which allied it to hunting, combat, sport and amorous affairs.[11]

In Bain's logic, the distinctive fact of the novel is its production of engrossed reading, and engrossment, otherwise known as 'the situation of pursuit', is a fact solely determined by the rapid alternations and successive shocks of plot. 'Pursuit' propels the reader through the narrative, but the action of the narrative must be a kind of periodically interrupted sensation:

Ordinarily the feeling [of the reader] is some good or evil in the distance, an ideal end prompting us to labour for realizing it; the regards are intent upon the end, and more especially when its approach is rapid and near. Such a moment is favourable to that entranced attention, under which the mind is debarred from feeling, and from all thoughts extraneous to the situation. Nevertheless, we remit, at short intervals, the objective strain, falling back into emotion or self-consciousness; we then experience the full intensity of the primary motive, until such time as we are once more thrown upon the outward stretch.[12]

This is a more physiologically elaborated notion of Lewes's 'construction': how the rhythm and order of plot events determine the contours and quality of a reader's engrossed attention. What is unique about Bain's approach – in fact, what has largely made his absence from standard histories of criticism inevitable – is his refusal to use the usual terminology of literary form. For Bain, the unique facts of novel reading called for a new set of analytic terms ('pursuit', 'engrossment') based on the temporal energies of plot.

One other major Victorian critic took Lewes's and Bain's emphasis on plot even further, claiming that the contemporary novel by its nature worked to sacrifice all other formal facts to the exigencies of tying successive events together. E. S. Dallas, an eminent critic and, throughout the 1860s, the major fiction reviewer for *The Times*, produced in *The Gay Science* an aesthetic-psychological treatise which, in its second volume, argued that the novel was the form of mass identity. Read by a faceless mass audience, produced by authors invisible to and unknown by their public, mediated by the mechanics of the modern publishing industry, the

---

[11]  Alexander Bain, *The Emotions and the Will*, 2nd edn (London: Longmans, Green, 1865), p. 148. The book was initially published in 1859; the 1865 edition became a standard reference work in Victorian psychology and is, in histories of psychology as a discipline, the edition usually cited.

[12]  *Ibid.*, p. 151.

novel's entire formal workings tended to stress what Dallas called 'the withering of the individual as an exceptional hero, and his growth as a multiplicand unit'.[13]

Taking Thackeray's *Vanity Fair* as his central instance, Dallas described its method as follows: 'Let any two characters be as dissimilar as possible; let the circumstances in which they are placed be as opposite as the poles, I will prove that their natures are the same, and I do not doubt that, spite of our censures, we in their places would have acted precisely as they did.'[14] Thackeray is for Dallas a paradigm rather than an exception; as he goes on to explain, even the sensation fiction of Wilkie Collins or Mary Elizabeth Braddon, a style seemingly distant from Thackeray's everyday Realism, produces the same effect of making the distinctiveness of character vanish before the overwhelming importance of plot. Sequence and rhythm of events – the formal facts that produce readerly interest and engrossment – triumph over the production of unique characters. If for Lewes and Bain this is largely a psychological fact (to produce private engrossment, one needs plot), for Dallas, in a daringly sweeping move, this is actually a cultural fact. The novel, for Dallas, is the central form of an atomized, post-heroic culture, where private individuals form a mass audience that looks remarkably homogeneous in its tastes and desires. The centrality of plot to the novel is only a way of registering the disappearance of personal distinctiveness in a mechanized and democratized world.

The novel is, for Dallas, less a literary genre and more a technology:

The stereotype, the photograph, wood-engraving, the art of printing in colour, and many other useful inventions have been perfected – making the printed page within the last thirty years what it never was before. At the same time the railway and the steamship, the telegraph and the penny postage, by daily and hourly bringing near to us a vast world beyond our own limited circles, and giving us a present interest in the transactions of the most distant regions, have enormously increased the number of readers, have of themselves created a literature, and through that literature have had a mighty influence upon the movement of the time.[15]

That 'literature', it needs scarcely be said, is the contemporary novel, which should take its place alongside other communications technologies as an instance of the depersonalizing, or what one might now call 'virtual', tendencies of modern life. Dallas's account of the novel is, however, far less pessimistic than this might suggest. What can read to modern ears as a lament is actually an unusually affirmative description of the potential of this new medium called the novel, with its habit of throwing off the obsolete accretions of such things as heroism, individuality, even selfhood.

[13]  E. S. Dallas, *The Gay Science*, 2 vols. (London: Chapman & Hall, 1866), vol. II, p. 287.
[14]  *Ibid.*, p. 289.     [15]  *Ibid.*, p. 312.

The syntax in the above passage is telling: Dallas veers occasionally in his discussion of the novel towards a kind of post-humanism, in which the ultimate author of the novel as a form is not a person but a set of technological inventions – the telegraph, the photograph, the printing press – which 'have of themselves created a literature'.

This British school of physiological speculation into the novel had its impact abroad. It is felt throughout Taine's *History of English Literature*, where, as in his account of the popularity of Dickens, we can detect the Victorian tendency to explain a novel or a novelist with reference to the workings of a reader's mind:

> The contrast, the rapid succession, the number of the sentiments, add further to [our soul's] trouble; we are immersed for two hundred pages in a torrent of new emotions, contrary and unceasing, which communicates its violence to the mind, which carries it away in digressions and falls, and only casts it on the bank enchanted and exhausted. It is an intoxication, and on a delicate soul the effect would be too forcible; but it suits the English public; and that public has justified it.[16]

The attempt here to balance formal facts of plot rhythm with a psychological language of readerly engrossment is firmly British in style, derived ultimately from the Lewes–Bain–Dallas mode of theory.

The influence of such British speculation finds its most devoted and intriguing exponent, however, in the work of Emile Hennequin, whose *Scientific Criticism* sought to advance British physiological speculations further by making them the basis for a whole critical practice called 'esthopsychologie', or the scientific study of aesthetic response. Hennequin's ingenuity was to attempt to solve a methodological problem that British physiological critics of the novel had ignored: can one found a critical method on reader reception if the reactions of individual readers are so notoriously variable? As Hennequin admits, 'a perception is not at all a simple, passive act, the same for all those facing an identical object; the highest faculties – memory, the association of ideas – take part...individual differences can become enormous'.[17] But he suggests that the problem is irrelevant for the novel, in which the large variations of individual response are habitually narrowed to their smallest point. 'We have taken realism, and the novel, as the foundations of our argument, because in these cases the individual character, mental faculties, and capacities of the reader seem reduced to their smallest importance.'[18]

If Hennequin's 'esthopsychologie' is warranted to take reception as the starting point of a critical practice, it is because the novel works as

---

[16]   Hippotyte Taine, *History of English Literature*, trans. H. von Laun, 4 vols. (Edinburgh: Edmonston & Douglas, 1874), vol. IV, p. 134.

[17]   Emile Hennequin, *La Critique scientifique* (Paris: Perrin, 1888), p. 136.

[18]   *Ibid.*, p. 137.

an effective control for the experiment, producing a large percentage of identical responses. The novel reader, in other words, is necessarily a 'general' reader, produced by the machinery of the genre that she consumes. The novel's appeal is to the most mechanical aspects of our cognitive apparatus. This is a version of Dallas's technological speculation taken to an extreme; it imagines the novel as a mode of contemporary cognitive activity that erases our differences, much as some media theorists today imagine viewing television as the washing away of individual response in favour of a passive intake. By pushing British physiological speculation, Hennequin exposes its limits: what is left to say critically about individual novels if, ultimately, they work identically as a technology of nervous-system sensation production?

The other limit of physiological novel theory's procedures was a historical one, and one it shared with much other novel criticism of the time: its remarkable presentism. Viewing the novel as a mode of contemporary cognition made any questions of its development difficult to answer. As a result, the historically and transnationally aware histories of the novel that appeared at the close of the eighteenth and opening of the nineteenth centuries, such as Clara Reeve's *The Progress of Romance* (1785), Anna Barbauld's 'On the Origin and Progress of Novel-Writing' (1810) or John Colin Dunlop's *The History of Fiction* (1814), vanish, only to be replaced by suddenly amnesiac histories of the novel, rigidly bounded by time and nation. David Masson's *British Novelists and Their Styles*, perhaps the first history of fiction produced by a literary academic, symptomatically begins its account with Sir Walter Scott. This is, however, not only a characteristic of novel theories informed by physiological speculation; it is to be found throughout most nineteenth-century accounts of the novel. What tend to supplant developmental theories are taxonomic theories – precisely those categorical descriptions that Henry James was to deride later as 'clumsy separations'. Here another major scientific practice pulled at the theory of the novel: taxonomic natural history.

Most nineteenth-century novel histories or theories attempted their own classificatory system, which, in the mode of scientific taxonomy, arranged specimens in an atemporal gallery of 'types'. Masson's book divided the novel into thirteen types, ranging from the 'Novel of Scottish Life and Manners' to 'The Art and Culture Novel' and 'The Historical Novel'.[19] The conservative Victorian critic Walter Bagehot divided the contemporary novel into the 'ubiquitous', 'romantic' and 'sentimental' varieties.[20] Even Maupassant, who insisted upon the illusory and

[19] David Masson, *British Novelists and Their Styles: Being a Critical Sketch of the History of British Prose Fiction* (Cambridge and London: Macmillan, 1859), pp. 214–27.
[20] See Walter Bagehot, 'The Waverley Novels' in *Literary Studies*, ed. R. H. Hutton, 3 vols. (London: Longmans, Green, 1895), vol. II, pp. 87–110.

shifting nature of literary genre, felt compelled to produce and describe the categories of the 'novel of pure analysis' and 'objective novel'.[21] One late-century effort, consciously influenced by the Darwinian transformation of taxonomical science, sought to find a law of generic development rather than a static catalogue of kinds: Ferdinand Brunetière's 1890 *L'Evolution des genres dans l'histoire de la littérature* ('The Evolution of Genres in Literary History'). Brunetière's developmental theory is rudimentary and strictly linear, however, suggesting only that each novelistic genre – the *chanson de geste*, the *roman épique* and the *roman de moeurs* or novel of manners – is a direct consequence of the previous type.[22] Literary history, that is, had a small impact on most nineteenth-century novel theories.

The effect of taxonomical natural history is best seen, however, in Balzac's famous 1842 'Avant-propos' to his *Comédie humaine*, where taxonomy becomes part of the novel's inner workings rather than just a critical method. Balzac's notion of the novelist's task is here explicitly compared to the work of a natural historian, particularly to that of the Comte de Buffon, the renowned eighteenth-century naturalist and author of the seminal *Histoire naturelle*; what links the natural historian to the social novelist for Balzac is the delineation of 'espèces' or categorical 'types': 'There exist – there have always existed – Social Types just as there are Zoological Types. If Buffon wrote a magnificent work that encompassed in one book the whole of zoology, might there not be a work of this sort dedicated to Society?'[23] In effect, the novel, best described through a catalogue of novelistic types, is itself an attempt to generate and describe 'types' of human social activity. The epistemological value of the type, in Balzac, is precisely its value in taxonomical science: a more accurate understanding of general truths too often obscured by less meaningful individual variations. The general truth pursued by the novel's generation of types Balzac calls 'manners': 'By drawing up an inventory of vices and virtues, by collecting the principal facts of passion, by choosing the principal events of Society, by forming types out of numerous homogeneous characters, perhaps I might begin to write the history forgotten by so many historians, that of manners.'[24] Novelistic composition here explicitly replicates the activities of natural history – collecting, making inventories, generating categories – and, in Balzac's description, aims at the identical goal of a complete, accurate and generally true description.

[21] Maupassant, 'Le Roman', p. xvi.
[22] Ferdinand Brunetière, *L'Evolution des genres dans l'histoire de la littérature: leçons professées à l'Ecole normale supérieure* (Paris: Hachette, 1898), pp. 5–7.
[23] Honoré de Balzac, 'Avant-propos' in *La Comédie humaine* (Paris: Gallimard, 1976), vol. I, p. 8.
[24] *Ibid.*, p. 81.

The discourse of 'type' had a persistent impact upon nineteenth-century criticism. It is most famously associated with Taine's concept of the 'ideal' or 'model' literary character, one that would represent the traits, instincts and values of a race, nation or historical period, although the concept can be traced back at least to the 1830s, in an influential essay by the novelist Charles Nodier called 'Des types en littérature'. In Russian criticism, so much more politically engaged and polarized than its French or British counterparts, the notion of the novelistic type had a more explosive career; evaluations of key contemporary novels often turned on the extent to which central characters could or should be read as typifying aspects of Russian national or political life. Significant work by radical critics such as Vissarion Belinsky, Nikolai Dobrolyubov or Dmitri Pisarev was devoted to the question of the categorical representativeness of such charged figures as the eponymous hero of Sergei Goncharov's *Oblomov* (1859) or the doomed nihilist Bazarov in Ivan Turgenev's *Fathers and Sons* (1862). A major strain of critical writing on the novel, one might say, took for granted that the truth-value the novel generated – its ability to reflect accurately upon contemporary human society as well as human psychology – was in a direct relation to its ability to produce a series of recognizable, generalizable character types. If physiological criticism looked primarily to plot, in other words, the kind of criticism and theory derived from natural history looked first to character as the engine of novelistic meaning.

By insisting upon 'types' as a requirement for the truth-value of fiction, novel theories based on taxonomic natural history posed a question of immense importance for critics of the form: how does the novel represent the real? The answer those theories provided – that the real was represented by valid general categories – was, however, quickly outmoded and insufficient. Novelists and critics who, starting in the 1850s, concerned themselves with the 'Realism' of the novel (a word whose currency, in France at least, dates only from the late 1840s and early 1850s), increasingly understood Realism as a scientific practice, much as Balzac had, but a scientific practice of minutiae, of difference, of peculiarity and above all of detail.[25] The manifesto-like preface to the first edition of *Germinie Lacerteux* (1864) by Edmond and Jules de Goncourt uses the vocabulary not of naturalist or zoological 'collection' but of biological 'research'; the novel becomes a 'study' or a 'clinical' object:

Today, when the Novel is growing and expanding, when it is beginning to be the serious, passionate, living form of literary study and social inquiry, when by analysis and psychological research it is becoming the moral history of our time;

[25] See Wellek, *History of Modern Criticism*, vol. IV, pp. 2–3, for the early history of the term 'Realism'.

today, when the Novel has submitted itself to the study and discipline of science, it can claim the freedom and rights of science.[26]

The novel as 'inquiry' implied a novel devoted, in an increasingly specialist manner, to the depiction of singular cases and precise details, unmoored from taxonomical categories. Maupassant's advice is paradigmatic of this new Realist discourse: 'The smallest thing contains something unknown. Find it... make me see, by one word, by what a cab-horse does not resemble the fifty others that follow or precede it.'[27]

The notion of Realism-as-detail had, in practice, countless different colorations, although those colorations can usefully be described as national styles, and critical debates about novelistic Realism often took the form of contrasting one national style to another. Between British and French theorists, contrasting notions of Realist detail duelled for much of the century. Zola's famously proto-scientific 1880 manifesto 'Le Roman expérimental' ('The Experimental Novel'), which claimed for the novel the status of an observational science, stated that novelists 'should go forward, even if a whole lifetime of effort ends but in the conquest of a small particle of the truth'.[28] In British discussions of novelistic practice this French dedication to scientific 'particles' of detail was pictured as an immersion in the unattractive, unredeemed rubbish of lower-class existence. One of the more explicit discussions of this aspect of novelistic Realism is found in George Gissing's New Grub Street (1891), where the novelist Biffen – a struggling writer with advanced, continental notions of technique – defines a project along Zola's lines, one that aims at 'absolute realism in the sphere of the ignobly decent' and that would 'reproduce verbatim' the tedium and 'paltry circumstance' of working-class life.[29]

In Gissing's novel Biffen's attempt represents both a heroic dedication to a literary ideal and a darkly comic failure: Biffen's Zolaesque novel goes largely unsold, and Biffen himself commits suicide. The description of his novel theory is, however, a hesitantly admiring version of the mainstream French notion of Realism from the Goncourts, Maupassant and Zola, filtered through a British discomfort with the aggressively political, even revolutionary, aspect of that notion: that novelistic Realism is essentially a tool of detailed journalistic exposé of working-class existence. 'This book', the Goncourts had proudly written of Germinie Lacerteux, 'comes from the street.'[30]

---

26 Edmond and Jules de Goncourt, Préfaces et manifestes littéraires, ed. Hubert Juin (Geneva: Slatkine, 1980), pp. 26–7.
27 Maupassant, 'Le Roman', pp. xxiii–xxiv.
28 Emile Zola, The Experimental Novel and Other Essays, trans. Belle Sherman (New York: Cassell, 1893), p. 18.
29 George Gissing, New Grub Street (Harmondsworth: Penguin, 1985), pp. 173–4.
30 Goncourts, Préfaces et manifestes, p. 25.

British notions of Realism, by contrast, tended towards a description
of Realist detail as homely, 'everyday' fidelity, an orientation towards
the domestic and private rather than towards the working-class world
*per se*. George Eliot's embedded Realist manifesto in *Adam Bede* (1859),
in the chapter entitled 'In Which the Story Pauses a Little', turns for a
model to Dutch genre painting, 'these faithful pictures of monotonous
homely existence', and issues what could be considered the central fiat of
British Realism: 'let us always have men ready to give the loving pains
of a life to the faithful representing of commonplace things – men who
see beauty in these commonplace things, and delight in showing how
kindly the light of heaven falls on them'.[31] The appeal to Dutch painting
is Hegelian in origin, deriving from the defence in Hegel's *Aesthetics* of
the 'rich detail of the phenomenal real world' in such art; the emphasis
on Realist art as a transfiguration of detail – as everyday epiphany rather
than political exposé – is Eliot's own, however, and aptly characterizes
the British preference for a domestic and psychological sense of Realism
rather than any more openly ideological or political concept.[32]

If a notion of scientific fact lurks in the French analyses of the Realist
novel, behind the British description of Realism lies a concept of general
'truth' or 'fidelity', as in Lewes's 1858 apothegm that 'Realism is thus
the basis of all Art, and its antithesis is not Idealism, but *Falsism*.'[33] The
uneasy dialectic between these two strands of thought about the Realist
novel – between everyday homely truth and the hidden facts of under-
class life – determined most thinking about Realism until well into the
twentieth century, and critics outside the Anglo-French tradition often
found themselves forging versions of compromise between the two positions. The powerful American critic William Dean Howells, in his articles
collected in *Criticism and Fiction* (1891), tended to belittle the notion
of Realism-as-exposé, calling it 'the ugly French fetich which has possessed itself of the good name of Realism to befoul it', while finding the
mainstream of British everyday Realism, such as Dickens, Thackeray and
Trollope, essentially outmoded compared to newly available translations
of Russians such as Tolstoy and Turgenev.[34]

One particular strand of this debate was to have crucial importance for
the development of later novel theories: the place of the authorial voice

---

[31] George Eliot, *Adam Bede*, ed. Valentine Cunningham (Oxford University Press, 1996),
    pp. 177–8.
[32] G. W. F. Hegel, *Aesthetics: Lectures on Fine Art*, trans. T. M. Knox, 2 vols. (Oxford:
    Clarendon Press, 1975), vol. I, p. 173.
[33] G. H. Lewes, 'Realism in Art: Recent German Fiction', *Westminster Review*, 70 (1858),
    p. 273.
[34] W. D. Howells, *Criticism and Fiction: And Other Essays* (New York University Press,
    1959), p. 128.

within realist narrative. Here a victor can more reliably be discerned, one that would essentially shape the theory we now know as Formalism. That victor was the assertion that a truly Realist novel dispenses with a guiding authorial presence, achieving the transparency and supposed objectivity of science or photography. Novelistic Formalism is essentially born of the desire, frequently voiced in the second half of the nineteenth century, to erase the voice of the author, with results that were as theoretically curious as they were practically influential. The claim goes back at least to Balzac's 'Avant-propos', where he explains his task as simply the transcription of social reality: 'French society was to be the historian, I had only to be the secretary.'[35] Such descriptions of the novelist as neutral filter are common, leading to Zola's extravagant argument, in 'The Experimental Novel', that the novelist is the recorder and tester of the deterministic laws of social and physical life. Objectivity of this sort, however, was more of an epistemological claim than a technical one, since it was not necessarily tied to any particular formal feature of novelistic practice; in its appeals to either sociology or biology, this brand of novelistic objectivity tried to erase the boundary between art and science, making any question of aesthetic choice beside the point.

The concept of authorial objectivity in the novel did, however, eventually generate not only an ethic but a particular aesthetic approach: that which came to be known, largely through the letters of Flaubert, as *impassibilité*, or 'indifference', 'impersonality'. The key dates in this theoretical movement cluster in the 1880s: the 1883 publication of the German novelist Friedrich Spielhagen's *Beiträge zur Theorie und Technik des Romans* ('Essays on the Theory and Technique of the Novel'); the 1884 publication, with a preface by Maupassant, of Flaubert's *Lettres à George Sand*, followed by a four-volume *Correspondance* in 1887; and James's 1884 'The Art of Fiction'. Spielhagen's essay collection insisted upon the author's responsibility never to address the reader directly, but instead to objectify every possible idea through a character's speech, a standard that few modern novels, in Spielhagen's opinion, successfully achieved. James's seminal essay had similar concerns about contemporary fiction, although his emphasis was on the shattering of the illusion of reality occasioned by authorial intrusions. James's rhetoric on the subject, when turning to Anthony Trollope, merges morality with narrative technique: 'He admits that the events he narrates have not really happened, and that he can give his narrative any turn the reader may like best. Such a betrayal of a sacred office seems to me, I confess, a terrible crime.'[36] Spielhagen's and James's uniqueness, in the early 1880s, was to change the terms of the discussion of novelistic objectivity: after their

35 Balzac, 'Avant-propos', p. 11.     36 James, 'Art of Fiction', p. 46.

work, objectivity was no longer a fact of scientific epistemology (as it is in Balzac and Zola) but a hard-won result of careful technical arrangement, an aesthetic process. It could only result from the careful elimination of the 'I', the authorial voice, from narrative art, in the interests of a kind of novel that would speak for itself.

Flaubert's letters, even more than his novels, provided the movement for *impassibilité* with memorable slogans. 'An author in his book must be like God in the universe, present everywhere and visible nowhere', one such claim runs.[37] Another requires the author to 'appear in his work no more than God in nature. The man is nothing, the work everything!'[38] As manifestos these formulations are telling: just as in James, *impassibilité* appeals more to theology than science, more to aesthetics than politics. If the risk run by Balzac or Zola was that the novel would become formless, a list of facts and observations rather than a narrative with rules of construction, the risk Flaubert's notion of impersonality runs is a slippage into ironic distance and even cynical detachment. Affectively, at least, the scientific objectivity of Zola and the impersonality of Flaubertian aesthetics can seem worlds apart, since Zola's notion of objectivity still left room for political and ethical engagement in a way that Flaubert's vanished author tended to prevent. The spectre of radicalism – the long association in France between scientific rationalism and leftist politics – is an important part of Zola's notion of the 'experimental novel', while the motivating force behind Flaubert's *impassibilité* is a question of aesthetic hierarchies; if the novel is purged of its tendency to preachiness and lazy discursivity, it could move up the ranks of literary genres.

Hence the birth of Formalism, which tended to generate categories to describe how novels avoid the indications of authorial presence. Spielhagen's idea of objectification through character became, in James's later criticism and critical prefaces, the idea of 'point of view', the mechanism by which information is imparted to readers without clumsy authorial exposition. A curious kind of circle emerges: while the novel had in Bulwer-Lytton's day been discussed as the alternative to and historical successor of the drama, in Spielhagen and James the term 'dramatic' becomes one of praise, as the point of novelistic technique suddenly becomes to move the novel towards dramatic 'scenes' and 'showing' rather than merely discursive 'telling'. The only Formalist approach to the novel at the end of the nineteenth century that took communication between author and reader as a fact to be described

---

[37] Gustave Flaubert, from a 9 December 1852 letter to Louise Colet in *The Letters of Gustave Flaubert, 1830–1857*, trans. Francis Steegmuller (Cambridge, MA: Harvard University Press, 1980), p. 173.
[38] Flaubert, from a 31 December 1875 letter to George Sand in *ibid.*, p. 227.

was the work of the British critic and aesthetician Vernon Lee, whose unjustly ignored articles 'A Dialogue on Novels' (1885) and 'On Literary Construction' (1895) make a case for novelistic technique as a managing of the reader's attention, interest and sympathy.[39] Otherwise, early Formalism took drama as its guide for the novel: an absent, invisible author, a darkened and barely visible audience, and a brightly lit stage where characters move in complicated choreography.

The theory of the novel in the nineteenth century began, to all intents and purposes, with the efforts of psychological and physiological criticism to study the novel's dematerialized audience: that virtual, invisible mass public that had made the novel the dominant form of its day. By the close of the century, the main topic of novel theory became the dematerialized author, as championed in the early Formalism of Spielhagen and James. The shift from reader to author would be decisive and long-lasting. It made any question of novel reading as an object of inquiry vanish until late in the twentieth century; it helped turn novel theory from a consideration of a cultural movement – the novel as a force in the world – to the elucidation of the inner workings of a small set of representative, canonical novels, novels that were increasingly judged by the criterion of authorial invisibility or what James would later call 'tact'. The results of this profound shift in emphasis have been mixed. It led to undeniably brilliant work on how novelistic meaning happens apart from authorial control, work that – as in James, Lubbock, Mikhail Bakhtin and many others – ended a long and generally unproductive tradition of judging novels by the biographical peculiarities of their authors. It also constricted the range of novels that novel theory could consider, and it segregated the novel from the technological and social developments that it had always been so integral to, at least in the minds of its earliest nineteenth-century theorists. Only recently has this limited canon, and separation of novelistic aesthetics from history, been prised open to the kinds of evidence and kinds of discussions that novel theory initially fostered.

---

[39] See Vernon Lee, 'A Dialogue on Novels', *Contemporary Review*, 48 (1885), 378–401; 'On Literary Construction', *Contemporary Review*, 68 (1895), 404–19. Several of Lee's important late nineteenth- and early twentieth-century articles on the novel were later collected in *The Handling of Words, and other Studies in Literary Psychology* (London: John Lane, Bodley Head, 1923).

## 28

# Theories of poetry

JOHN D. KERKERING

In the opening pages of his 1887 study 'The Imagination of the Poet: Elements for a Poetics' Wilhelm Dilthey offers an expansive yet sober assessment of the challenges confronting the criticism of poetry: 'Today', Dilthey writes, 'anarchy rules the wide field of literature in every country';[1] although the countries Dilthey goes on to mention are exclusively European, he attributes the 'anarchy' facing them as much to external forces impinging upon Europe as to internal disruptions. Here Dilthey identifies several emerging concerns that would inform the criticism of poetry from 1830 to 1914: the novel threatens to eclipse poetry as the 'epic of modern life'; this 'modern life' is located in 'cities' where large-scale cultural phenomena – crowds, markets, skyscrapers, anonymity – replace natural phenomena as a basis for the overpowering effects of the sublime; a monolithic 'East' – viewed as at once 'barbaric' and 'vital' – elicits the simultaneous fascination and revulsion characteristic of Orientalist exoticism; and an erosion of elite 'standards of evaluation' reduces judgements of taste to matters of 'personal feeling', thereby empowering the appetites of the thronging 'masses'.

The present chapter will focus on Dilthey's assurance that poetic theory – which was, for Dilthey, at the heart of the 'human sciences' that he helped to pioneer – is equal to the task of bringing this 'anarchic' field of literature under the critic's control. 'This anarchy of taste', he writes, 'can, however, not be permitted to last. And it is thus one of the vital tasks of contemporary philosophy, art history, and literary history to reestablish a healthy relationship between aesthetic thought and art.' Dilthey's confidence drew upon established concepts in nineteenth-century aesthetics: 'Aesthetics, and within it poetics, can be constructed from a dual perspective. The beautiful can be taken either as aesthetic *pleasure* or as artistic *production*. The capacity for this pleasure is called "taste" and for this productivity "imagination".'[2]

---

[1] Wilhelm Dilthey, 'The Imagination of the Poet: Elements for a Poetics' (1887) in *Poetry and Experience: Selected Works*, eds. Rudolf A. Makkreel and Frithjof Rodi, 6 vols. (Princeton University Press, 1985), vol. v, p. 30.
[2] *Ibid.*, pp. 30–1, 120.

Dilthey's 'dual perspective' on 'the beautiful' provides a partial outline for the discussion of poetic theories that follows. However, his response to 'anarchy' seems to be aligned not with 'taste' or 'imagination' but, instead, with the sublime, a category of aesthetic experience that A. C. Bradley pairs with, yet distinguishes from, the beautiful:

In 'beauty' that which appears in a sensuous form seems to rest in it, to be perfectly embodied in it, and to have no tendency to pass beyond it. In the sublime, even where no such tendency is felt and sublimity is nearest to 'beauty', we still feel the presence of a power held in reserve, which could with ease exceed its present expression.[3]

When a 'power' (such as Dilthey's 'anarchy') exceeds expressions, the resulting effect is not beauty but sublimity:

In *some* forms of sublimity, again, the sensuous embodiment seems threatening to break in its effort to express what appears in it. And in others we definitely feel that the power which for a moment intimates its presence to sense is infinite and utterly uncontainable by any or all vehicles of its manifestation. Here we are furthest (in a way) from sense, and furthest also from 'beauty'.[4]

In the discussion that follows, Bradley's notion of the sublime will complement Dilthey's notion of the beautiful: theorists of poetry use the language of 'the beautiful' to describe an object which can be delimited (either as a source of pleasure or as a product of imagination), and the language of 'the sublime' to denote the effect of an object that cannot be limited, as in a great or infinite power which exceeds expression.

The terms 'poem', 'poet' and 'poetry' convey – via their common root, the Greek word *poiesis* – a product, agent or activity of 'making', and a question that has consistently attended this notion concerns whether and how to segregate human creativity from that of the divine.[5] The theological orientation of the French philosopher Victor Cousin's theory of poetry led him to assert, 'Doubtless, in one sense, art is an imitation; for absolute creation belongs only to God.'[6] Although he subordinates poetry to religion, poetry yet occupies an exalted position for Cousin, who in his *Lectures on the True, the Beautiful, and the Good* (1836, 1854) declares 'poetry the type of the perfection of all the arts, – the art

---

[3] Andrew Cecil Bradley, 'The Sublime' in *Oxford Lectures on Poetry* (New York: St. Martin's Press, 1909), p. 58.

[4] *Ibid.*, p. 58.

[5] See Susan Stewart, *Poetry and the Fate of the Senses* (University of Chicago Press, 2002), p. 12; and Allen Grossman, 'Wordsworth's "The Solitary Reaper": Notes on *Poiesis*, Pastoral, and Institution', *Triquarterly*, 116 (2003), pp. 277–8.

[6] Victor Cousin, *Lectures on the True, the Beautiful, and the Good*, trans. O. W. Wight (New York: D. Appleton, 1854), p. 156. Hereafter cited as *TBG*.

*par excellence*, which comprises all others, to which they aspire, which none can reach' (*TBG*, pp. 176–7).

Cousin's conclusions about poetry arise within a scholarly project he terms 'eclecticism', which, in a notable departure from Dilthey, consults prior philosophical writings – both ancient and modern, domestic and foreign – in order to assemble what he considers the most compelling ideas of the intellectual tradition. 'We are eclectics', Cousin writes,

> in the arts as well as in metaphysics. But, as in metaphysics, the knowledge of all systems, and the portion of truth that is in each, enlightens without enfeebling our convictions; so, in the history of arts, while holding the opinion that no school must be disdained, that even in China some shade of beauty can be found, our eclecticism does not make us waver in regard to the sentiment of true beauty and the supreme rule of art.                    (*TBG*, p. 178)

In its conformity to this 'supreme rule of art' poetry, for Cousin, accompanies all the other arts: 'So, to express the ideal of the infinite in one way or another', he writes, 'is the law of art; and all the arts are such only by their relation to the sentiment of the beautiful and the infinite which they awaken in the soul, by the aid of that high quality of every work of art that is called expression' (*TBG*, pp. 165–6). But poetry nevertheless comes to stand apart from (and at the pinnacle of) the other arts as a result of its distinctive expressive medium, language: 'The first care of the artist will be...to penetrate at first to the concealed ideal of his subject...in order to render it, in the next place, more or less striking to the senses and the soul, according to the conditions which the very materials that he employs – the stone, the color, the sound, the language – impose on him' (*TBG*, p. 165). Language, as material, imposes the conditions relevant to the art of poetry, and Cousin finds these conditions to be the most conducive to the expressive ends of the arts generally: 'But the art *par excellence*, that which surpasses all others, because it is incomparably the most expressive, is poetry' (*TBG*, p. 175).

Cousin's expressivism would appear to coincide in many respects with the theory of poetry advanced by his younger compatriot, Charles Baudelaire, whose critical writings echo Cousin's 'supreme rule': 'It is this admirable, this immortal, instinctive sense of beauty', Baudelaire writes, 'that leads us to look upon the spectacle of this world as a glimpse, a correspondence with heaven.'[7] Baudelaire's emphasis upon 'a correspondence with heaven' informs not just his criticism but also his own poetry, as is evident in one of the best-known poems from his controversial collection *Les Fleurs du mal* (1857), 'Correspondances'.

[7] Charles Baudelaire, 'Further Notes on Edgar Poe' in *Baudelaire: Selected Writings on Art and Artists*, trans. P. E. Charvet (Cambridge University Press, 1972), pp. 204–5. Hereafter cited as *SW*.

Extending these views beyond Baudelaire to include his contemporaries in Britain, Lothar Hönnighausen writes, 'What unites Baudelaire's understanding of correspondence with that of [John] Keble or [John] Ruskin is his conviction that the poet does not create but interprets correspondences already in existence as part of a universal analogy.'[8] By bearing witness to these correspondences, poets and their poems testify to divinity in a manner comparable to that of a cleric. Elizabeth Barrett Browning extends this mediating role not only outside the ranks of the clergy but also outside the male sex through the female protagonist of her verse novel *Aurora Leigh*:

> There's not a flower of spring
> That dies ere June, but vaunts itself allied
> By issue and symbol, by significance
> And correspondence, to that spirit-world
> Outside the limits of our space and time,
> Whereto we are bound. Let poets give it voice
> With human meanings, – else they miss the thought,
> And henceforth step down lower, stand confessed
> Instructed poorly for interpreters.[9]

Of the larger, post-Romantic tradition in which Browning, Hopkins and Baudelaire participate, Hönnighausen writes, 'the concepts symbol, typology, and correspondence serve as the foundations for an international movement in both literature and the other arts in the nineteenth century'.[10]

Despite these points of contact, Baudelaire's synaesthetic fusion among various arts points to important differences from Cousin. For instance, while Cousin would give a place to 'sensationalism', but only as a subsidiary or servant to 'reason', the clear emphasis in Baudelaire is on sensation. Indeed, the scandal that met the publication of his *Les Fleurs du mal* places Baudelaire entirely at odds with Cousin's advice to his intended audience in *Lectures on the True, the Beautiful, and the Good*: 'Reject that enervating literature, by turns gross and refined, which delights in painting the miseries of human nature, which caresses all our weaknesses, which pays court to the senses and the imagination, instead of speaking to the soul and awakening thought.'[11] It should thus come as no surprise that Baudelaire derides Cousin's influential identification of

---

8 Lothar Hönnighausen, *The Symbolist Tradition in English Literature: A Study of Pre-Raphaelitism and Fin de Siècle*, trans. Gisela Hönnighausen (New York: Cambridge University Press, 1988), p. 25.

9 Elizabeth Barrett Browning, *Aurora Leigh*, ed. Margaret Reynolds (Athens: Ohio University Press, 1992), pp. 364–5, lines 120–8.

10 Hönnighausen, *Symbolist Tradition*, pp. 24–5.    11 Cousin, *TBG*, p. 11.

the true, the beautiful and the good as one of the 'heresies in literary criticism': 'The loudly-trumpeted doctrine of the indissoluble union between
beauty, truth and goodness is an invention of modern philosophical nonsense' (SW, p. 265).

In order to advance an alternative to Cousin's 'indissoluble union'
Baudelaire invokes the critical writings of Edgar Allan Poe. Citing Poe's
essay 'The Poetic Principle', Baudelaire writes that Poe 'divided the world
of mind into pure intellect, taste and moral sense, and he applied his criticism according to which of the three divisions the object of his analysis
belonged to'.[12] When the object of analysis is a poem, neither 'pure
intellect' nor 'moral sense' is to be employed, but only 'taste': 'Pure
intellect pursues truth, taste reveals beauty to us, and our moral sense
shows us the path of duty' (SW, p. 204). Poe had asserted these points
in the context of criticizing the poems of his immensely popular compatriot Henry Wadsworth Longfellow for 'the too obtrusive nature of
their *didacticism*',[13] a charge that Baudelaire applies more generally: 'A
whole crowd of people imagine that the aim of poetry is some sort of lesson, that its duty is to fortify conscience, or to perfect social behaviour,
or even, finally, to demonstrate something or other that is useful' (SW,
p. 203).

Baudelaire can be confident of his own success in avoiding didacticism
because he believes he has appropriately modified – which is to say entirely
abandoned – his own search for a critical method: 'I have tried more than
once', he confesses, 'to lock myself inside a system, so as to be able to
pontificate as I liked. But a system is a kind of damnation that condemns
us to perpetual backsliding' – that is, he fails in practice to abide by
his method, a failure rendered here by analogy to violations of religious
codes of conduct (SW, pp. 117–18). 'Under the threat of being constantly
humiliated by another conversion, I took a big decision. To escape from
the horror of these philosophic apostasies, I arrogantly resigned myself to
modesty; I became content to feel; I came back and sought sanctuary in
impeccable naïveté' (SW, 118). This naïveté is the affirmative correlate of
Baudelaire's negation of systematic critical method, and he accordingly
valorizes critics and readers who embrace the fluid ephemerality of 'the
modern'. 'Modernity', Baudelaire writes, 'is the transient, the fleeting, the
contingent', a condition best expressed, for him, through 'fashion' and
best exemplified by such figures as the 'dandy' and by an emphasis upon
artifice and ornamentation – via jewellery, clothing and makeup – that
Baudelaire associates with (elite) women (SW, pp. 403, 392, 419, 427).

---

[12]  Baudelaire, SW, p. 198; Edgar Allan Poe, 'The Poetic Principle' in *Selected Writings of Edgar Allan Poe* (Boston: Houghton Mifflin, 1956), p. 469.
[13]  Poe, 'The Poetic Principle', p. 435.

What is important about the dandy or woman, for Baudelaire, is that such figures are understood to have a 'burning desire to create a personal form of originality . . . a kind of cult of the ego', and he praises individual artists – for instance, Poe, Wagner, Delacroix and, in this case, Gautier – likewise in proportion as their inimitable style strikes him as atypical and irreducible, singular and unique: 'In the realm of poetry and art, the great discoverers rarely have precursors. Every flowering is spontaneous, individual' (*SW*, pp. 420, 122).

Baudelaire's emphasis on the singularity of these writers and their works has implications, he acknowledges, for the production of art history. Delacroix, for instance, is 'a unique artist, without a forerunner, without precedent, probably without a successor, a link so precious that none could be found to replace it; and if it were to be destroyed, assuming such a thing to be possible, then a whole world of ideas and sensations would vanish with it, and too big a gap would occur in the chain of history' (*SW*, p. 139). Here the uniqueness of artworks makes art history contingent upon the availability of the works themselves. In their absence, less distinguished works will fall short of achieving divine correspondences, instead managing only to serve a lesser, documentary function of illustrating their authors' historical contexts.

What Baudelaire here presents as a liability is viewed, instead, as an opportunity – that poetry might serve as a vehicle of access to history – in the writings of his contemporary and compatriot Hippolyte Taine, whose work is examined elsewhere in this volume. Here, it can simply be stated that, by rejecting literary works' singularity – their status as 'an isolated caprice' – Taine is able to lay claim to them as reliable documentary evidence, thus attributing to these works a referential Realism inimical to the Symbolist tendencies of Baudelaire.[14] 'Pondering on these modes of feeling and thought, men decided', writes Taine, 'that they were facts of the highest kind. They saw that these facts bore reference to the most important occurrences, that they explained and were explained by them, that it was necessary thenceforth to give them a rank, and a most important rank, in history.'[15] Here the 'references' in question are not the 'correspondences' Baudelaire observed between this world and heaven but are instead concerned with the more mundane practices of everyday life: 'What have we under the fair glazed pages of a modern poem? A modern poet, who has studied and traveled.'[16] Reasoning from poems to poets amounts, for Taine, to reasoning from effects to causes, and by extending this mode of inference – from poem to poet, then from

---

[14] Hippolyte Taine, *History of English Literature*, trans. H. Van Laun, 4 vols. (New York: Frederick Ungar, 1965), vol. I, p. 1.
[15] *Ibid.*    [16] *Ibid.*, p. 3.

poet to the poet's society, and from that society to its causal sources in what Taine famously summarizes as his three most general material determinants of human history, the 'three primordial forces' of 'RACE, SURROUNDINGS and EPOCH' – Taine seeks to associate the writing of history with the growing prestige of the natural sciences.[17]

Charles-Augustin Sainte-Beuve (whose work is also treated in a separate chapter) is concerned to use literary works to illuminate not a race, milieu or age but, instead, an individual writer, or what he calls 'a talent'.[18] 'I may enjoy a work, but it is hard for me to judge it independently of my knowledge of the man who produced it, and I am inclined to say, *tel arbre, tel fruit* – the fruit is like the tree. Thus the study of literature leads me naturally to the study of human nature.'[19] Sainte-Beuve sets out to 'place the superior or distinguished writer in his own country, among his own people. If we knew his lineage thoroughly, physiologically speaking, including his remoter ancestors, we should gain much light on the essential hidden quality of his mind.'[20]

While these critics, contrary to the advice of Baudelaire, embrace poetry's historical utility, other critics ascribe to poetry a practical role in the conduct of life – the psychic life of the individual in the case of John Stuart Mill and, in the case of Karl Marx, the historical life of an economic group or class. For Mill, poetry's ability to improve an individual's conduct became apparent to him through his own struggle with 'depression': 'This state of my thoughts and feelings', Mill writes in his *Autobiography*, 'made the fact of my reading Wordsworth for the first time (in the autumn of 1828) an important event in my life.'[21] Describing Wordsworth's 1815 collection as 'medicine for my state of mind', he attributes to poetry the power of a cure: 'The result was that I gradually, but completely, emerged from my habitual depression, and was never again subject to it.' Poetry can exert this influence upon readers, Mill argues, because of its similarity to, but ultimate difference from, mere 'eloquence': 'Poetry and eloquence are both alike the expression or utterance of feeling. But if we may be excused the antithesis, we should say that "eloquence is *heard*, poetry is *over*heard. Eloquence supposes an audience; the peculiarity of poetry appears to us to lie in the poet's utter unconsciousness of a listener."' Mill recasts this distinction in terms of a theatrical metaphor to argue that 'All

[17] *Ibid.*, p. 17.
[18] Charles-Augustin Sainte-Beuve, 'On Sainte-Beuve's Method' in *Sainte-Beuve: Selected Essays*, trans. Francis Steegmuller and Norbert Guterman (New York: Doubleday, 1963), pp. 281, 288.
[19] Sainte-Beuve, 'The Natural History of Minds', in *ibid.*, pp. 281–2.   [20] *Ibid.*, p. 283.
[21] John Stuart Mill, *Collected Works of John Stuart Mill. Vol. I: Autobiography and Literary Essays*, eds. John M. Robson and Jack Stillinger (University of Toronto Press, 1981), p. 149.

poetry is of the nature of soliloquy . . . The actor knows that there is an audience present; but if he act as though he knew it, he acts ill.'[22]

Even as Mill invokes this theatrical scenario, his most pressing concern is with the context in which poetry is most typically encountered, 'printed on hot-pressed paper and sold at a bookseller's shop': 'A poet may write poetry', then, 'not only with the intention of printing it, but for the express purpose of being paid for it'; poems, then, are commodified objects. Thus 'Poetry', writes Mill, 'is feeling, confessing itself to itself in moments of solitude, and embodying itself in symbols, which are the nearest possible representations of the feeling in the exact shape in which it exists in the poet's mind.'[23] This manner of achieving individuality – by being embodied in beautiful poetic objects – stands in contrast to an aesthetics of individuation achieved, as this chapter will suggest, via the objectlessness of the sublime.[24] Understood as beautiful objects, poems are part of what Marx called the superstructure of a society. From this perspective, even poetry that expresses overt hostility to the bourgeoisie – for instance, the stance that T. S. Eliot ascribes to Baudelaire, 'the rebel against society and against middle-class morality' – ultimately serves as an intensified expression of capitalism's isolated bourgeois individual. Indeed, this posture of contentious isolation – as Baudelaire writes, 'Certain types of minds, solitary amongst crowds, and sustained by their inner monologues, are quite indifferent to any question of refinement in their audience. In effect, it would seem to be a fraternal attitude, founded on contempt' – is in fact consistent with the political liberalism outlined in Mill's *On Liberty*, which seeks to disseminate such normative and valorized depictions of individual interiority, subjectivity, autonomy, affect and depth, thereby transforming discontent – what Mill calls 'the very soul of melancholy exhaling itself in solitude' – from a social problem to a valuable personal resource.[25]

These two accounts of poetry's utility to its readers – its ability to enhance historical scholarship's archival specificity and its ability to sustain the liberal subject's individual autonomy – would each come under explicit criticism in Matthew Arnold's essay 'The Study of Poetry' (1880). Arnold emphasizes that 'we are to adopt a real, not a historic, estimate of poetry', so while a 'historic estimate' will concern itself with the issue of poetry's development and progress – hence 'Chaucer is the father of our splendid English poetry; he is our "well of English undefiled"' – a

---

[22] *Ibid.*, p. 349.      [23] *Ibid.*, pp. 151, 153, 348–9.
[24] See Frances Ferguson, *Solitude and the Sublime: Romanticism and the Aesthetics of Individuation* (New York: Routledge, 1992), p. 67.
[25] T. S. Eliot, 'From Poe to Valéry' in *To Criticize the Critic and Other Writings* (Lincoln: University of Nebraska Press, 1965), p. 37; Baudelaire, *SW*, pp. 181–2; Mill, *Collected Works*, p. 351.

'real estimate' of Chaucer comes to a different, less laudatory conclusion: 'something is wanting, then, to the poetry of Chaucer, which poetry must have before it can be placed in the glorious class of the best'.[26] Just as Arnold both acknowledges and sets aside the 'historic estimate' in the study of poetry, so too does he acknowledge the 'personal estimate of poets' – for instance, the view expressed by Mill about the poetry of Wordsworth – only to urge that 'if we are to gain the full benefit from poetry, we must have the real estimate of it'.[27] Unlike the historical and personal estimates, Arnold's 'real estimate' associates 'supreme poetical success' with 'an essential condition... high seriousness; – the high seriousness which comes from absolute sincerity'.[28]

Arnold also seeks 'to point out a method' requiring the reader 'to have always in one's mind lines and expressions of the great masters, and to apply them as a touchstone to other poetry': by quoting 'classic' works in their original tongues, we body forth in and through these 'touchstone' passages what Arnold calls an 'accent' and 'power' that indicate not, as Taine had argued, the poem's moment in history but a 'criticism of life'. Anticipating that 'most of what now passes with us for religion and philosophy will be replaced by poetry', Arnold searches for poetic writings that will fill this void: 'In poetry, as a criticism of life... the spirit of our race will find, we have said, as time goes on and as other helps fail, its consolation and stay.'[29] Enlisting readers as partners in this search also enables Arnold to groom them – these 'multitudes of a common sort of readers', akin to the mass public prompting Dilthey's description of 'anarchy' – to become receptive to consolation in this form. Arnold employs the idiom of the beautiful to describe the form and content of poems that will come to offer consolations akin to those of sacred writings.[30] He engages in explicit debate with other poets regarding the appropriate themes of poetry, himself encouraging emulation of works from classical Antiquity because 'a great human action of a thousand years ago is more interesting to [us] than a smaller human action of to-day'.[31] By contrast, as Lothar Hönnighausen observes, 'Pre-Raphaelitism... under [Dante Gabriel] Rossetti's leadership,... attempt[s] to create a new symbolic suggestiveness by adopting escapist themes and stylized techniques from the Middle Ages'.[32]

[26] Matthew Arnold, 'The Study of Poetry' in *Poetry and Criticism of Matthew Arnold*, ed. A. Dwight Culler (Boston: Houghton Mifflin, 1961), pp. 315–18.
[27] *Ibid.*, pp. 320, 322; Mill, *Collected Works*, p. 153.
[28] Arnold, 'Study of Poetry', p. 325. [29] *Ibid.*, pp. 306, 307. [30] *Ibid.*, p. 313.
[31] Matthew Arnold, 'Preface' to first edition of *Poems* (1853) in *Poetry and Criticism of Matthew Arnold*, p. 205.
[32] Hönnighausen, *Symbolist Tradition*, p. 33.

Yet another view, in favour of matter drawn from the historical present, was advanced by Elizabeth Barrett Browning's Aurora Leigh, who asserts that poets' 'sole work is to represent the age, / Their age, not Charlemagne's, – this live, throbbing age'.[33] Charles Baudelaire and Walt Whitman, similarly, favoured treatment of modern themes – in Baudelaire's case, because 'in order that any form of modernity may be worthy of becoming antiquity, the mysterious beauty that human life unintentionally puts into it must have been extracted from it', and in the case of Whitman, because no theme could rival the importance he accorded to a New World nation that had decisively severed all ties with Old World tyranny and tradition: 'The United States themselves', Whitman wrote in the 'Preface' to the 1855 first edition of Leaves of Grass 'are essentially the greatest poem'.[34]

More controversial than the appropriate historical content of poetry was the question of whether some kinds of content might warrant censorship. While this concern was as old as Plato's Republic, it took on added urgency at this time due to anxieties about the effects some poetry might have on a mass public increasingly understood to be – as the above statements by Arnold make clear – poetry's consumers, readers whose tastes either would or should shun sexually explicit, religiously heterodox or politically volatile content. In addition to the excision of poems depicting lesbian sexuality from Baudelaire's Les Fleurs du mal, Robert Buchanan's The Fleshly School of Poetry (1872) mounted a scathing attack on the poetry of Swinburne and Rossetti (charging the former with 'the representation of abnormal types of diseased lust and lustful disease' and the latter with 'a veritably stupendous preponderance of sensuality and sickly animalism'), but offered a more measured critique of the explicit sensuality in Whitman's poetry.[35] The American poet's Boston publisher, however, ceased publication of his poems in response to charges of obscenity from the New England Society for the Suppression of Vice, a circumstance that prompted Whitman's compatriot Mark Twain to pen – but not publish – 'The Walt Whitman Controversy', an essay defending his compatriot by indicting the double standards of his accusers.

In addition to debating the appropriate subject matter of poetry, poets and critics in this period likewise addressed themselves to questions of manner and issues of form. Perhaps the most notable formal experiments of this period were new genres of poetry, including the dramatic monologue associated with Robert Browning, the prose poem associated with

33  Barrett Browning, Aurora Leigh, p. 368, lines 202–3.
34  Baudelaire, SW, p. 404; Walt Whitman, 'Preface 1855' in Leaves of Grass and Other Writings, eds. Michael Moon et al. (New York: Norton, 2002), p. 616.
35  Robert Buchanan, The Fleshly School of Poetry (London: Strahan, 1872), pp. 20, 67, 96.

Stéphane Mallarmé and the free-verse line introduced in Walt Whitman's *Leaves of Grass* (1855). These efforts at formal innovation were followed by critical efforts to codify the patterns of form in literary history, thereby establishing the standards against which innovation could be measured; important instances of this work include Edgar Allan Poe's 'The Rationale of Verse' (1848), Coventry Patmore's 'Essay on English Metrical Law' (1857), Sidney Lanier's *The Science of English Verse* (1880) and – most exhaustively – George Saintsbury's three-volume *History of English Prosody* (1906–10).

While much criticism of poetry from this period operated within the parameters of Arnold's distinction between a poem's matter and its manner, a few critics – perhaps most notably A. C. Bradley – challenged this very distinction. In the opening lecture of his *Oxford Lectures on Poetry* (1909), entitled 'Poetry for Poetry's Sake' (1901), Bradley wrote, 'These antitheses of subject, matter, substance on the one side, form, treatment, handling on the other, are the field through which I especially want, in this lecture, to indicate a way.'[36] Bradley's 'way' is effectively to refuse the distinction altogether by appealing to the reading experience itself:

> If you read the line, 'The sun is warm, the sky is clear', you do not experience separately the image of a warm sun and clear sky, on the one side, and certain unintelligible rhythmical sounds on the other; nor yet do you experience them together, side by side; you experience the one *in* the other ... And this identity of content and form ... is of the essence of poetry insofar as it is poetry.[37]

While Bradley's emphasis here is on readers' experience, his point is that the capacity to provide such experience is the basis for valuing poetry for its own sake rather than as a means to some other end: 'The words "poetry for poetry's sake" recall the famous phrase "Art for Art"', Bradley observes, and according to this view the 'nature [of poetry] is to be not a part, nor yet a copy, of the real world (as we commonly understand that phrase), but to be a world by itself, independent, complete, autonomous; and to possess it fully you must enter that world'; from this requirement it follows that 'an actual poem is the succession of experiences – sounds, images, thoughts, emotions – through which we pass when we are reading as poetically as we can'.[38] One consequence of this view, Bradley acknowledges, is that 'the habit so dear to us of putting our own thoughts or fancies into the place of the poet's creation' – the habit of paraphrase – becomes 'heresy' since the poem becomes a 'unique expression, which cannot be replaced by any other'.[39]

---

[36] Andrew Cecil Bradley, 'Poetry for Poetry's Sake' in *Oxford Lectures on Poetry* (New York: St. Martin's Press, 1909), p. 8.
[37] *Ibid.*, pp. 14–15.   [38] *Ibid.*, pp. 4, 5, 4.   [39] *Ibid.*, pp. 24, 26.

Bradley's emphasis upon the poem as experience anticipates not only Cleanth Brooks's injunction against 'the heresy of paraphrase' but also the centrality of readerly experience that Jennifer Ashton has identified as the antagonist of twentieth-century literary Modernism.[40] But for the sources of Bradley's experiential emphasis we must look, as Peter Kivy has suggested, to Walter Pater, whose *The Renaissance: Studies in Art and Poetry* (1866) opens by invoking a definition of criticism made famous by Matthew Arnold, then redirects that definition towards his own notion of 'aesthetic criticism': 'the first step towards seeing one's object as it really is, is to know one's own impression as it really is, to discriminate it, to realize it distinctly'.[41] For Pater, the virtue of arts such as poetry is their capacity to occasion experience consisting of impressions that warrant this intense mode of scrutiny, but such a project – an analysis pursuing ever more refined attention towards infinitesimally subdivided nuances of sensation – launches the critic upon a trajectory which culminates, as Jonathan Loesberg has observed in his study of Pater's aestheticism, in 'the dissolution of the self into discrete sensations'.[42] 'Pater's aestheticism', Loesberg writes, 'cannot impose an order on a chaotic reality, either an ideal order or a fictive one, because the form it perceives is that of chaos.'[43] The 'chaos' of perceptions occasioned by art objects, including poems, is thus itself the object of analysis for Pater's 'aesthetic criticism': 'Aesthetic perception... allows one to sense the act of sensation... Art for art's sake means, finally, the aesthetic perception of perception.'[44]

What Pater points to, then, is a phenomenon that Bradley himself, in his lecture 'The Sublime' (1904), identifies as a circumstance 'where we *attempt* to measure, or find limits to, the greatness of the thing. *If* we make this attempt, as when we try in imagination to number the stars or to find an end to time, then it is essential to sublimity that we should fail, and so fail that the idea of immeasurability or endlessness emerges.' Bradley's discussion of the sublime assigns this failure to one of 'two "aspects" or stages in it', a 'negative' stage – entailing 'a sense of our own feebleness or insignificance' – immediately followed by a 'positive' stage that he describes as 'a rush of self-expansion, or an uplifting'. In order to differentiate the 'negative' aspect's degrees of severity Bradley advises that 'we may conveniently use the adjective "unmeasured" so

[40] Jennifer Ashton, *From Modernism to Postmodernism: American Poetry and Theory in the Twentieth Century* (Cambridge University Press, 2007), pp. 7–10, 27.

[41] Peter Kivy, *Philosophies of Arts: An Essay in Differences* (Cambridge University Press, 1997), p. 97; Walter Pater, *The Renaissance: Studies in Art and Poetry: The 1893 Text*, ed. Donald L. Hill (Berkeley: University of California Press, 1980), p. xix.

[42] Jonathan Loesberg, *Aestheticism and Deconstruction: Pater, Derrida, and de Man* (Princeton University Press, 1991), p. 22.

[43] *Ibid.*, pp. 25–6.     [44] *Ibid.*, p. 25.

long as we remember that this means one thing where we do not measure at all, and another thing where we try to measure and fail'.[45] Bradley's distinction provides a helpful basis for differentiating two strands within this period's poetic theories, and this mode of calibrating the sublime's negative aspect – as either an absence of measurement or a failure of measurement – will structure the following account of those theories. While the latter emphasis on failed measurement will prove characteristic of French Symbolism, the former account of absent measurement will return us to Dilthey's *Poetics*, with which this chapter began.

The latter emphasis in Bradley's account of the sublime, with its focus on fracture or overwhelming of all representational vehicles, is consistent with the account Laurence Porter has offered of the broad 'movement' of French Symbolism: 'Instead of merely challenging the audience's preconceptions regarding what poetry should say, and how, Symbolism disrupted the very communicative axis linking sender to message to receiver, thus calling into question the very possibility of any communication whatsoever. The French Symbolist movement, then, was neither a coterie nor a system, but a crisis.'[46] This 'crisis', Porter observes, emerged out of 'a powerful aesthetic heritage, running from Kant to Coleridge to Poe to Baudelaire. By emphasizing the autotelic nature of poetry, its detachment from social and intersubjective concerns, this heritage enormously increased the burden on conventional language that was expected to convey unique and unconventional thought while remaining intelligible... Shedding its referents, poetry in this tradition becomes self-reflexive, focused on the poet and poetry.'[47]

We have already seen how Baudelaire and Barrett Browning 'increased the burden on conventional language' by pursuing divine 'correspondences'; Baudelaire sheds referents in his hostility to photography's mimetic fidelity, and the alternative of emphasizing the poet's relation to poetry is evident as he shifts the focus of Edgar Allan Poe's essay 'The Philosophy of Composition' away from Poe's concern – the poem's effect on readers – and towards the moment of the poem's composition:

For Poe, the imagination was the queen of the faculties; but by this word he understood something greater than what the ordinary run of readers understand by it. Imagination is not fantasy, nor is it sensibility, difficult though it would be to conceive of an imaginative man who was not sensitive. Imagination is a virtually divine faculty that apprehends immediately, by means lying outside philosophical methods, the intimate and secret relation of things, the correspondences and analogies.[48]

45 Bradley, 'The Sublime' in *Oxford Lectures*, pp. 51–4, 61.
46 Laurence M. Porter, *The Crisis of French Symbolism* (Ithaca, NY: Cornell University Press, 1990), p. 20.
47 *Ibid.*, p. 18.     48 Baudelaire, 'Further Notes on Edgar Poe', p. 199.

As Baudelaire and his successors intensified their demands upon language they began, according to Porter, 'to despair of the success of the communicative process altogether, since only the transcendent is worth communicating and since the poet's verbal vehicle must be the antithesis of transcendence [because 'the words available for embodying a transcendent poetic vision are conventions']. Such despair is what characterizes Symbolism proper... [A]ll the major Symbolist poets in France underwent a crisis of loss of faith in the communicative process.'[49]

The writer whose confrontation with representational crisis has come to be seen as the pinnacle of French Symbolist poetics is Stéphane Mallarmé, whose essay 'Crisis in Poetry' (1895) makes clear the weight of the demands being placed upon the materials of poetic creation: 'Languages', Mallarmé writes,

> are imperfect because multiple; the supreme language [of Baudelaire's divine 'correspondences'] is missing. Inasmuch as thought consists of writing without pen and paper, without whispering even, without the sound of the immortal Word, the diversity of languages on earth means that no one can utter words which would bear the miraculous stamp of Truth Herself Incarnate. This is clearly nature's law – we stumble on it with a smile of resignation – to the effect that we have no sufficient reason for equating ourselves with God.[50]

Having placed upon words the 'impossible' demand that – on the model of onomatopoetic words like 'bang' or 'crash', which would appear to embody the very sounds that they also represent – they be 'Incarnate' instances of the ideas to which they refer, Mallarmé then finds language inadequate to this end and makes use of it in a different manner, not referentially but symptomatically: 'It is not *description* which can unveil the efficacy and beauty of monuments, seas, or the human face in all their maturity and native state, but rather evocation, *allusion, suggestion*. These somewhat arbitrary terms reveal what may well be a very decisive tendency in modern literature, a tendency which limits literature and yet sets it free.'[51] This alternative, evocative use of language permits Mallarmé to continue his pursuit of 'Truth Herself Incarnate' with the understanding that the poem's language must have failed as language in order for the poem to succeed as poetry. Such uplifting failures exemplify the stronger version of the sublime described by Bradley, the version in which we measure and fail (rather than the one in which we do not measure at all). Comparable pressures on the medium of language help

---

49  *Ibid., Crisis*, pp. 11, 12, 11.
50  Stéphane Mallarmé, 'Crisis in Poetry' in *Mallarmé: Selected Prose Poems, Essays, and Letters*, trans. Bradford Cook (Baltimore, MD: Johns Hopkins University Press, 1956), p. 8.
51  *Ibid.*, p. 40.

explain other formal innovations of modern poetry – in particular, as Allen Grossman has compellingly argued, the 'free-verse' lines of Walt Whitman and the 'difficult' poetics of Hart Crane.[52]

In contrast to this account of poetic 'making', in which the sublime's overwhelming power situates poetry's imaginative activity upon the very brink of language's fragmentation and failure ('Symbolist poetry', writes Porter, 'is a poetry of failure'[53]), Wilhelm Dilthey expresses, as we have already seen, greater confidence in the structures that arise from the activity of poetic creation. When Mallarmé laments that 'the supreme language is missing', he treats this absence as a loss impossible to overcome (since 'we have no sufficient reason for equating ourselves with God'), whereas Dilthey understands the absence of a 'supreme language' not theologically but historically, as a circumstance arising in time and subject to a temporal resolution. This resolution – the eventual appearance of a supreme language – is to be observed, Dilthey writes, in and through the work of a poetic 'genius':

> But the *unity* of a period and a people that we characterize as the *historical spirit* of an age can only arise from these elements through the *creative power* and self-assurance of a genius . . . The genius of the ruler or the statesman forges isolated facts into a purposive unity which their coordination makes possible. The aim of this kind of genius is very different from that of the artist and the philosopher, but they are akin with respect to scope and greatness. *In religion and philosophy, in art and especially in poetry, the coordination of constituents which exists in a particular time . . . is connected through a historically creative process into a unity which transcends what is given.*[54]

Dilthey's attribution of 'scope and greatness' to a genius's creations exemplifies the more moderate version of the sublime that Bradley associated with the absence (rather than the failure) of measurement. From this unmeasured vantage point the genius's creative efforts obtain the status – both for the genius and for its audience – of what Dilthey calls 'an *acquired nexus of psychic life*'.[55] Literary criticism, taking such worldviews as its object of analysis, gave rise to a discipline of 'human sciences' that has much in common with the 'cultural poetics' characteristic of the 'new historicism' which arose a full century after the publication of Dilthey's *Poetics*.

[52]  Allen Grossman, *The Long Schoolroom: Essays in the Bitter Logic of the Poetic Principle* (Baltimore, MD: Johns Hopkins University Press, 1998), pp. 58–129.
[53]  Porter, *Crisis*, p. 12.   [54]  Dilthey, 'Imagination', p. 162.   [55]  *Ibid.*, p. 97.

# 29

# Theories of drama

## JOHN OSBORNE

Between 1830 and 1914 theorists of drama find themselves continually addressing the choice between investing characters and action with universal significance, and representing the particularity of the historical and social world. Much common ground is to be found in suspicion of drama and theatre as vehicles for this task, particularly following the explosion in popular forms such as melodrama and vaudeville. Saintsbury notes the 'divorce between drama and literature', and, while acknowledging that this would be inconceivable for any other period, allots fewer than twenty pages of his *History of Nineteenth Century Literature* (1901) to the drama.

The drama nevertheless continued to enjoy considerable esteem, though this bore fruit in aesthetics and criticism rather than in literary practice. Balzac, Flaubert, Zola and Tolstoy, Mallarmé, Villiers de l'Isle Adam and Rilke all wrote for the theatre; but for Realism the dominant form was the novel, exploited for its capacity to represent the world in extensive totality, while the major achievement of the Symbolists lies in their intensely conceptual poetry. Following Romanticism the drama was progressively opened up to socio-political material and its form came under the influence of the novel, but even as Naturalism seemed to have secured pre-eminence in the theatre it was being challenged by poetic forms focused on Being rather than the World.

Lukács (1916) notes that the Greek tragedians did not have to choose between extensive totality and intensive essence, because for them fullness and richness were not equated with proximity to life in particularized form.[1] Similarly for Bradley (1909) the characters in Greek tragedy are never merely types or personified abstractions, because no distinction is made between the ethical power they represent and their personality.[2] In this Idealist view the dramatic characters are exponents of the *Weltgeist* which has become fragmented and individualized on its entry into the

---

[1] Georg Lukács, *Die Theorie des Romans: Ein geschichtsphilosophischer Versuch über die Formen der großen Epik* (Neuwied and Berlin: Luchterhand, 1971), p. 33.
[2] A. C. Bradley, 'Hegel's Theory of Tragedy' in *Oxford Lectures on Poetry* (London: Macmillan, 1965), p. 77.

World; (ancient) tragedy, the supreme literary genre, thus reveals the world process as a whole, in concentrated essence.

Hegel recognized that the disregard for the individual, implicit in his reading of Sophocles' *Antigone*, presupposed a heroic objectivity that was alien to the modern, Christian, Romantic worldview with its focus on personal subjectivity. In his theory of genres the *Schauspiel* (drama), exemplified in the work of Shakespeare, is proposed as the characteristic modern form. Despite his privileging of classical tragedy for its direct concern with the world-historical process, Hegel therefore paved the way for the rejection of the abstraction of neo-classical drama by the Realists. Simultaneously the process of liberation from the formal constraints of the Aristotelian model was completed by the theories of the Romantics, culminating in Victor Hugo's Preface to *Cromwell* (1827), which resolved the *querelle des anciens et des modernes* in favour of the moderns.

Briefly, however, it looked as if dramatic theory might be entering a period of revisionism, when, overshadowing Hugo and *Les Burgraves* (1843), François Ponsard emerged, to be heralded with *Lucrèce* ('Lucretia', 1843) as the new Racine, and subsequently with *L'Honneur et l'argent* ('Honour and Money', 1853) as the new Molière. The acclaim that Ponsard enjoyed was based on the need for reorientation after the excesses of Romanticism; *Lucrèce* may lay claim to Classicism on the strength of its Roman theme, but not by virtue of any adherence to Aristotelian rules. In fact Ponsard sought compromise, seeing in the 'Romantic' performance of Racine by the actress Rachel a meeting of the classical and the modern; he remained dedicated to the 'correction' of Shakespeare by Racine and the 'completion' of Racine by Shakespeare. Rejecting the categories 'classic' and 'Romantic', he claimed to recognize only the distinctions 'true' and 'false', with 'bon sens' rather than Idealist philosophy as the supreme judge;[3] for others Ponsard's synthesis amounted to styleless heterogeneity.[4] At the end of the century, when his name was being cited as a synonym for convention and mediocrity,[5] two of his contemporaries would speak more directly to modern dramatists.

While acknowledging the liberating achievement of Romanticism and inclining to Shakespeare rather than Racine, Alfred de Musset remains resolutely individualist in his views. In the spirit of historical relativism, evident in his contemporary G. H. Lewes's criticism of the Romantic

---

[3] François Ponsard, 'A propos d'Agnès de Méranie' in *Œuvres complètes*, 3 vols. (Paris: Levy, 1865–76), vol. III, p. 352.

[4] Honoré de Balzac, *Lettres à Madame Hanska*, ed. Roger Pierrot, 2 vols. (Paris: Editions du Delta, 1968), vol. II, p. 213; Charles Baudelaire, 'Les Mystères galants des théâtres de Paris' in *Œuvres complètes*, ed. Claude Pichois, 2 vols. ([Paris]: Gallimard, 1976), vol. II, p. 1004.

[5] Pierre Quillard, 'Courrier des théâtres', *Le Figaro*, 24 June 1897.

August Wilhelm Schlegel,[6] Musset deplores any tendency to exclusivity. Rather than reopening the *querelle*, he calls for a renewed classical tragedy alongside Romantic drama, seeing no possibility of a synthesis. Setting aside traditional polarities, he distinguishes instead between Realists (Calderon and Mérimée), who show effects, and essentialists (Racine and Shakespeare), who show causes.[7] The qualities which he attributes to the essentialists, however, reveal the ambivalence of his position. By 'cause' Musset clearly understands timeless human qualities, yet in these same terms his Realist successors will justify a drama in which historical contingency is the major determinative force, and, echoing Musset, they will demand the renunciation of effect.[8]

Musset's practice confirms his aspiration to essentialism. After the failure of *La Nuit venétienne* ('The Venetian Night', 1830), he renounced the practical theatre and all elements of the Realist drama of circumstance. His Renaissance and eighteenth-century settings exclude the concrete problems of the bourgeois condition, while his minimalist plots and his indifference to local colour emphasize his primary concern with poetic expression.

Whereas Musset's 'proverbes' appealed to the lyrical dramatists of the *fin de siècle*, Büchner's uncompromising Realism would appeal to the Naturalists. In an apologia for *Dantons Tod* ('Danton's Death', 1835) Büchner declared that the Idealist dramatists produced nothing but 'marionettes with sky-blue noses and affected rhetoric'.[9] In Modernist manner he inserted his critique into his text, where Danton exposes Robespierre's virtuousness as theatrical effect, and where Camille uses the image of the marionette to denounce the abstraction of characterization, language and structure typical of Idealist drama, prompting the association between neo-Classicism and disregard for the individual.[10] In the narrative *Lenz* (1835) Büchner develops a parallel with the visual arts, when the eponymous hero states his preference for the contemplative absorption of Dutch interiors over the idealization of neo-Classicism.[11]

In Russia Vissarion Belinsky played a decisive role in the replacement of aesthetic by social values, although his progress in the direction of Realism was more gradual. His formative years were marked by the apolitical idealism which dominated Muscovite thought in the 1830s.

---

6   Rosemary Ashton, *G. H. Lewes: A Life* (Oxford: Clarendon Press, 1991), p. 29.
7   Alfred de Musset, 'De la tragédie, à propos des débuts de Mademoiselle Rachel' in
    *Œuvres complètes en prose*, ed. Maurice Allem, Bibliothèque de la Pléiade, 49 ([Paris]:
    Gallimard, 1951), p. 915; *La Coupe et ses lèvres* ('The Cup and its Lips') in *Poésies
    complètes*, ed. Maurice Allem ([Paris]: Gallimard, 1957), p. 159.
8   Musset, 'De la tragédie', p. 905.
9   Georg Büchner, *Sämtliche Werke, Briefe und Dokumente*, ed. Henri Poschmann, 2 vols.
    (Frankfurt: Deutscher Klassiker, 1992–9), vol. II, p. 411.
10  *Ibid.*, vol. I, pp. 44–5.   11   *Ibid.*, pp. 235–6.

Unlike Büchner, he argued that art should transform ordinary reality, and he rejected Naturalism as failing to reveal any rational idea or purpose. However, building on Hegel's distinction between the ancient and modern periods in the history of art, he began, in an article on Aleksandr Griboedov's *Woe from Wit* (1840), to argue for a reconciliation between the clarity of classical form and Romantic wealth of content, while insisting that the subject of art is the universal rather than the contingent. Only in his later writings did he begin to advocate the deployment of Realist techniques informed by social purpose, praising Gogol for his attention to ordinary people.[12]

Illustrating the erratic evolution of dramatic theory, the German Hebbel assumes a position that is more Hegelian than Hegel's. Underlying this is a pessimistic worldview which leads him to embrace the heroic form of tragedy regarded by Hegel as too harsh for modern subjectivity. For Hebbel the function of drama is to make visible the world process, in which the individual is pitted against the universal, his guilt consisting in his very individuality. Combining Hegel's philosophy of history with his theory of tragedy, Hebbel shifts the focus from Being to Becoming. Tragic guilt, in this scheme of things, has nothing to do with morality, but is incurred by the necessary assertion of individuality, or the will in Schopenhauer's sense. Where Schopenauer, however, sees the purpose of tragedy in revealing the futility of all things, and teaching extreme resignation,[13] Hebbel assents to an historical process that can be furthered only by the assertion of individual will. Authentic tragedy ends with reconciliation: the cathartic recognition of the existentially given duality of the world process and the subordinate role of the individual within it.

Hebbel differs from Büchner in remaining an Idealist. The broad circumstantial Realism and the individuality of characterization which the latter had admired in J. M. R. Lenz (1751–92) obscure for Hebbel any underlying idea.[14] He regarded historical drama as legitimate only when history is seen in terms of problems rather than presented as chronicle.[15] Hebbel therefore recommends locating the dramatic action at a turning point in world history, in which an individual confronts a world order that is resistant to his will. The proper subject of drama is the latent crisis, not any day-to-day detail.

[12] René Wellek, 'Social and Aesthetic Values in Russian Nineteenth-Century Literary Criticism' in *Continuity and Change in Russian and Soviet Thought*, ed. Ernest J. Simmons (New York: Russell & Russell, 1967), pp. 382–8.
[13] Arthur Schopenhauer, *Die Welt als Wille und Vorstellung* ('The World as Will and Idea', 1819), ed. Ludger Lütkehaus, 2 vols. (Zurich: Haffmann, 1988), vol. I, pp. 335–6.
[14] Friedrich Hebbel, Diaries in *Werke*, eds. Gerhard Fricke, Werner Keller and Karl Pörnbacher, 5 vols. (Munich: Hanser, 1963–7), vol. IV, pp. 268–71.
[15] Friedrich Hebbel, 'Vorwort zur "Maria Magdalene"' in *Werke*, vol. I, p. 312.

This privileging of deep structure gives to Hebbel's notion of drama a conceptual clarity absent from the work of his Austrian contemporary Franz Grillparzer. Coming from the tradition of the Catholic baroque, the latter maintained a preference for the allusiveness of intuition and symbol.[16] Moved by religious concerns, he is even less sympathetic than Hebbel to the imitation of history or nature. Whereas Hebbel's drama of ideas will find its successor in the work of Ibsen, Grillparzer contributed to the line of development exploited by Hofmannsthal.

From the disregard of social questions there follows a devaluation of the domestic drama as developed by Diderot and Lessing.[17] Hebbel's *Maria Magdalene* (1843) is nevertheless evidence of a synthesizing impulse, shared by his contemporary Otto Ludwig. The metaphysical symbolism of Hebbel's conflicts was, however, alien to Ludwig. In the concrete Realism of Shakespeare he recognized a source for the inductive learning of the techniques of the drama, and in Shakespearean cosmology an inspiration for an anti-tragic 'poetic Realism', which maintains the freedom and the representative status of the classical hero while grounding his actions in historical and social circumstance to reveal a congruity between causal and moral coherence.[18] Whereas the certainties of Hebbel bore fruit in a dramatic *œuvre* of substance, the unresolved tensions in Ludwig's theory are reflected in resigned reversion to the narrative, a form more suited to an age not convinced of the freedom of the will.

French and Russian writers are less inhibited about direct engagement with the realities of the contemporary world. Taking his point of departure in the aesthetics of Schiller, Gogol argued for the function of the stage as a moral institution, comic representation being a travesty of the ideal, transcending satire and leading through the exposure of shortcomings to a reconciliation with flawed human nature. Even before the religious turn evident in his later work, Gogol saw himself opposed to a *Zeitgeist* which favoured the trivial, exemplified for him in the French theatre, with its spirit of light amusement, flawed by striving for effect. However, anticipating the Symbolists' response to Ibsen's dramas, he came to insist on the allegorical character of *The Government Inspector*, its target being society in general. Against Gogol's views that change should be effected by a renewal of personal morality rather than the reform of institutions, the social-critical interpretation of Belinsky prevailed, and this play came to be seen as a model for the satire of public corruption in Tsarist Russia.

[16] Franz Grillparzer, Diaries in *Sämtliche Werke: Historisch-Kritische Ausgabe*, ed. August Sauer, 3 Abteilungen, 39 vols. (Vienna: Schroll, 1909–35), *Sämtliche Werke*, Abteilung II, vol. VIII, p. 177 and vol. XI, pp. 197–8.

[17] Hebbel, 'Vorwort zur "Maria Magdalene"', pp. 326–8.

[18] Otto Ludwig, *Shakespeare-Studien*, ed. Moritz Heydrich (Halle: Gesenius, 1901), p. 303.

The positivist materialists Nikolai Chernyshevsky, Nikolai Dobrolyubov and Dmitry Pisarev developed the social turn in Belinsky's late
criticism to a radically anti-aesthetic extreme, seeking from literature a
naturalistic reflection of life as a basis for the moral impact of the work of
art.[19] They were opposed by Apollon Grigoriev, who criticized Dobroli-
ubov for seeing only the social satire in Ostrovsky's dramas of the emergent Russian merchant class, and ignoring his significance as a national
poet. Nevertheless Grigoriev resembles the Realists in his continued belief
in the moral function of art, which he saw as a protest against narrow
conventions of behaviour.[20]

Underpinned by the social philosophy of Saint-Simon and the theories
of Auguste Comte, the Social Realist tendency enters French literary criticism through Sainte-Beuve and Taine, finding its first dramatists in Emile
Augier and Alexandre Dumas *fils*. Renewing the link with the domestic
drama of the eighteenth century, they take up the subjects of Diderot's
plays, claiming for the stage a moral function, and for themselves the role
of defenders of marriage and the family. Dumas argued that the dramatist should reveal the deeper causes underlying the problems of society,
so as to provoke discussion by the public and action by the lawgiver; this
aspiration to an extra-theatrical utility presupposes an implacably logical
causation and so a firm command of dramatic structure.[21]

A victim of censorship, and widely charged with sensationalism for his
predilection for subjects from the *demi-monde*, Dumas sought to distinguish his work and that of Augier from the more meretricious dramas
of contemporaries such as Eugène Scribe, whose concerns he saw as
restricted to dramatic situation and theatrical effect.[22] He lent his argument a turn reminiscent of Hebbel by identifying the contemporary age
as a crisis point in history, in which, as in Hebbel's and, later, Ibsen's
dramas, the position of woman has a defining significance. Dumas, too,
claims for the contemporary Realist drama a significance which transcends its historical and local particularity, relating specific problems to
universal causes, while nevertheless remaining social rather than existential in character.[23]

The most significant criticism of this form did not relate to subject
matter, but to the instrumentalization of art in the service of an ideology.
However, in Augier's drama Baudelaire did not recognize the language of
virtue, only the language of the counting house. For him the half-hearted

[19] Wellek, 'Social and Aesthetic Values', pp. 388–96.
[20] Robert T. Whittaker, *Russia's Last Romantic: Apollon Grigor'ev (1822–1864)* (Lewis-
ton, NY: Edwin Mellen Press, 1999), pp. 88–94, 287–9.
[21] Alexandre Dumas *fils*, Preface to *Un père prodigue* (1868) in *Théâtre complet*, 8 vols.
(Paris: Calman Lévy, 1896–9), vol. III, p. 211.
[22] *Ibid.*, pp. 218–19.
[23] Alexandre Dumas *fils*, Preface to *Diane de Lys* (1868) in *Théâtre complet*, vol. I, p. 199.

moralizing of the bourgeoisie was no better than the moralizing of the socialists; art is useful because it is art.[24]

Dumas's didacticism was also subjected to criticism from Francisque Sarcey, who shifted the debate decisively towards formal questions, insisting that the major impulse behind the work of the great dramatists of the past derived from their recognition of the nature of theatre as a public medium. Conscious of the historical as well as the psychological constitution of the public, he recognized the mutability of conventions of representation; on the one hand he rejected neo-classical dramaturgy as not corresponding to contemporary taste; on the other he rejected the generic impurity of Romantic dramaturgy, seeing its juxtaposition of the comic and the tragic as incompatible with the limited flexibility of the emotional capacities.[25] For Sarcey a play is not a reproduction of life, but an aggregate of conventions designed to produce in the spectator the illusion of life, and he insists that the audience is the necessary condition to which dramatic art must accommodate its means.[26] It is for this very 'accommodation' that he commended the contemporary *pièce bien faite*, praising Dumas for the skill with which he manipulates the audience into accepting the logic of his structures, rather than for the substantive content of the solutions he proposes. In this spirit he describes *La Dame aux camélias* as one of the truest and most moving works ever to have appeared in the theatre.[27] Sarcey therefore differs fundamentally from Baudelaire in assenting to the artifice that is an essential part of theatre. He does so, however, as its increasingly embattled defender in the face of an anti-theatricality that is characteristic of Modernist theatre in most of its forms.

In support of his audience-based aesthetic, Sarcey wrote: 'It is possible that a King may at some time or other indulge the fantasy of seating himself alone in a playhouse and having played for himself alone some piece commanded by him . . . The King represents the absent audience.'[28] Not for long did this remain a purely hypothetical case. Ludwig II of Bavaria was to do just this, and, rather than representing the absent audience, to create in the minds of his actors the disturbing sense that they were not performing before an audience at all.[29]

24 Charles Baudelaire, 'Les Drames et les romans honnêtes' in *Œuvres complètes*, vol. II, pp. 39–41.
25 Francisque Sarcey, 'Essai d'une esthétique de théâtre' (1876) in *Quarante ans de théâtre: feuilletons dramatiques*, 8 vols. (Paris: Bibliothèque des Annales politiques et littéraires, 1900–2), vol. I, pp. 152, 158.
26 *Ibid.*, p. 128.
27 Francisque Sarcey, 'La Dame aux camélias' (1884) in *Quarante ans de théâtre*, vol. V, p. 199.
28 Sarcey, 'Essai d'une esthétique', p. 128.
29 Kurt Hommel, *Die Separatvorstellungen vor König Ludwig II von Bayern: Schauspiel, Oper, Ballet* (Munich: Laokoon, 1963), pp. 33–4.

The paradox that Dumas, a consummate craftsman, should have regarded as subordinate precisely those technical qualities for which Sarcey admired him is an indication of the extent of anti-theatrical prejudice. Dumas's fastidious distancing of himself from his contemporaries was, however, far from being generally accepted. More often than not he was mentioned alongside Scribe and Victorien Sardou as an exponent of the characteristically French *pièce bien faite*,[30] which enjoyed remarkable success, even in Berlin after the Franco-Prussian War. This success is acknowledged in the emphasis on construction in practical dramaturgical guides, ranging from Percy Fitzgerald's *Principles of Composition and Dramatic Effect* (1870) and Frank Archer's *How to Write a Good Play* (1892) to Georges Polti's *Les Trente-six situations dramatiques* (1895). On the other hand, the reliance on formulas was held to be a contributory cause of the decline of the dramatic genre; the superficiality of the commercial theatre of French provenance becomes a topos in dramatic theory and criticism in the second half of the century.

The comedies of Eugène Labiche constitute a special case. He too drew his subjects from contemporary bourgeois society and his characters speak everyday language; for him too the plan of the drama is of primary importance.[31] Labiche, however, makes no claim to Realism; he derives dramatic interest not from the logically comprehensible development of characters and their feelings, but from the sequence of situations and events without regard to plausibility; the dynamics of his plots have the abstraction of a game of chequers.[32] In Labiche's automaton-like characters Bergson will find behaviour that illustrates his theory of comedy, by defying rational causality to reveal directly the 'pure' sentiments that lie behind the norms and conventions of society.[33]

Hermann Hettner's *Das moderne Drama* ('Modern Drama', 1852) and Gustav Freytag's *Die Technik des Dramas* ('Technique of the Drama', 1863) are responses to the gulf between the status accorded to the dramatic genre in criticism and the place of serious drama in the contemporary theatre. Hettner's work is the intervention of a literary theorist, arguing from Aristotelian principles, where the practising critic, Sarcey, defers to the audience. After the 'false idealism' of the Romantics, Hettner seeks to re-establish the relationship between literature and society by furthering the development of a contemporary dramatic form. He

[30] Henry James, *The Scenic Art: Notes on Acting and the Drama: 1872–1901*, ed. Allan Wade (New Brunswick, NJ: Rutgers University Press, 1948), pp. 8, 56, 101, 118, 137.
[31] Emmanuel Haymann, *Labiche ou l'esprit du Second Empire* (Paris: Orban, 1988), p. 100.
[32] Sarcey, 'Eugène Labiche' (1870) in *Quarante ans de théâtre*, vol. IV, p. 402.
[33] Henri Bergson, *Le Rire: essai sur la signification du comique*, 5th edn (Paris: Alcan, 1908), pp. 160–72.

notes the discrepancy between the revolutionary political programme of
the dramatists of Young Germany and the aesthetic conventionality of
their routine techniques of melodrama and intrigue. Underlying his work,
however, is a decline in the belief in the political function of a drama of
effective action, which had informed dramatic theory before the failed
revolution of 1848. Writing at a time of politically 'realist' compromise,
when Wagner, in Swiss exile, is developing the Symbolist and mythological at the expense of the social aspects of his theories, when Robert Prutz
resignedly accepts the provisional renunciation of the dramatic genre,
when Ferdinand Lassalle's *Franz von Sickingen* is criticized by Marx
and Engels as a (Schillerian) tragedy of an aristocratic individual, without the (Shakespearean) representation of the revolutionary forces active
among the masses, Hettner defines 'Fate' as the prevalent socio-political
situation.[34]

Freytag's work withdraws the drama even further from social engagement. Combining cultural and historical relativism with the search for
universal principles of composition, but basing his argument on a limited number of classic dramatists, Freytag argues for the maintenance of
the generically pure Aristotelian drama. Whereas narrative forms explore
characters and events alongside each other, the drama shows characters
and actions emerging from each other. Drama consists of the interpersonal conflict of strong-willed individuals, with no place for the problems
of contemporary life. For all the respect that his arguments enjoyed, they
were deployed in the service of a form without possibility of development.
In Germany Freytag's generation produced no drama of note; only with
the social drama of Hauptmann, which Freytag stubbornly rejected, was
it restored to life.[35]

Despite variations of national origin and ideology, there remains a
substantial amount of common ground in terms of poetics among the
mid-century Realists. The serious modern drama is analytical, addressing
the question of why people do what they do. The answers show both
a rejection of transcendental explanations and an increasing distrust of
formulaic plots and mechanistically theatrical intrigue. The emphasis on
social or psychological causation, however, continues to be mitigated by
an idealist and optimistic belief in individual freedom of the will. Good
sense and technical pragmatism outweigh revolutionary conviction and
aesthetic innovation. In mainstream Realist criticism there is no perceived
need to question the resources of the contemporary theatre, conventional

34  Hermann Hettner, *Das moderne Drama: Aesthetische Untersuchungen von Hermann Hettner* (1852), ed. Paul Alfred Merbach, Deutsche Literaturdenkmale des 18. und 19. Jahrhunderts 151 (Berlin and Leipzig: B. Behr, 1924), p. 84.
35  Gustav Freytag, *Briefe an Albrecht von Stosch*, ed. Hans F. Helmolt (Stuttgart: Deutsche Verlags-Anstalt, 1913), pp. 273, 275, 277.

styles of acting or the traditional structure of the drama. However, the ground was being prepared for radical reform. Increasingly sophisticated techniques of 'Realization',[36] exploited initially for their visual effect and legitimized by an appeal to historical authenticity, find their way into dramatic production, notably in Charles Kean's 'Revivals'. Criticized initially as merely decorative distraction, such elements had the potential to become an important instrument of interpretation.

The practical achievement of Wagner in Bayreuth, as his own director in his own theatre, marks the most complete implementation of this tendency, but Wagner's impact on the development of the drama depends more on the symbolic dimension to his work. The test case for attitudes to theatre reform was provided by the European tours of the Meiningen Court Theatre (1874–90). As the company passed through Berlin, Vienna, London, Brussels and Moscow, it encountered severe critics in Paul Lindau, Ludwig Speidel, Clement Scott, Francisque Sarcey, Jules Claretie and Aleksandr Ostrovsky, but qualified admirers in Otto Brahm, William Archer, André Antoine and Stanislavsky. The most influential established critics were thus lined up against three men who were to become the founders of Naturalist theatre, together with Archer, the leading English advocate of the new drama. Common to the former is the fear that if scenery, costumes, ensemble, crowd scenes and stage management were cultivated to excess, attention would be diverted from the words of the dramatist to details of production. For them 'spectacle' should remain firmly subordinate, the action being carried forward by articulate performers. In the contrasting preferences of the two major novelist-critics of the period, Henry James and Theodor Fontane, one finds an urbane echo of this controversy.

With the advent of Naturalism, the materialist and scientific tendencies stimulated by thinkers such as Taine, Marx, Darwin, Haeckel and Claude Bernard are given a radical turn: individuals do not have control over, or even understanding of, their own destiny; they are not free to exercise choice and incur guilt, but are seen as products of society and the laws of nature. Zola and his followers therefore propose a basis for literature in the impersonal observation of empirical reality, conducted in the manner of a scientific experiment, revealing the influence of heredity and environment. For Dumas, advocating a drama that affects society, the clarity of the message takes precedence over photographic accuracy,[37] whereas

---

[36] S. Martin Meisel, *Realizations: Narrative, Pictorial, and Theatrical Arts in Nineteenth-Century England* (Princeton University Press, 1983).

[37] Alexandre Dumas *fils*, Preface to *Le Fils naturel* (1868) in *Théâtre complet*, vol. III, p. 31.

the truth that Zola sought required that the details be shown. Subject matter which had hitherto been largely absent from the drama, including material from the lower reaches of society, is privileged, because it is here that the operation of the full range of deterministic factors is most immediately evident.

Zola's theories were initially concerned with the novel, but after the failure of the first naturalist dramas in the 1870s, his attention shifted to the theatre. In 'Le Naturalisme au théâtre' (1878) he expressly challenges the Aristotelian distinction between the narrative and dramatic genres, even when appearing to concede certain fundamental differences. He recognizes the primacy of action in drama, but only to criticize its structuring according to certain stereotypes, and to shift the focus to the study of man in his environment. He concedes that the theatre has its own laws, but sees them as derived from spectacle rather than dialogue or interpersonal conflict. At the same time Edmond de Goncourt, building on Diderot's distinction between *tableau* and *coup de théâtre*, replaces the closed dramatic with a looser, epic structure, to make from the novel *Germinie Lacerteux* a 'pièce en 10 tableaux' (1888).

The development of the drama in accordance with such theories required the application of newer techniques of dramatic production. For Antoine, following Zola, milieu acquires an active role, and so the stage set becomes an environment that determines the way the actors move and the action unfolds.[38] Similarly the firm location of individuals within society and their subjection to only barely comprehended biological and social forces require the development of a new style of acting. It therefore very soon became clear that the plays of Zola and Ibsen, Hauptmann and Chekhov, demanded new theatres. The Free Theatre movement, led by Antoine, followed by Brahm and Stanislavsky, met this demand.

One of its first functions was to secure the performance of the new drama by circumventing the censorship provoked by challenging subject matter, for in the first instance it was the content of these plays which attracted critical attention, corresponding as they did to the demand made by the Danish critic Georg Brandes that the theatre should submit contemporary problems to debate. Despite the differences between the social worlds of Ibsen and Zola, both writers were heralded for the courage with which they rejected notions of *bienséance*. *Ghosts* stood alongside *Thérèse Raquin* in the programme of Antoine's Théâtre Libre and Brahm's Freie Bühne, exemplifying the progress of art in absorbing

---

[38] Emile Zola, 'Le Naturalisme au théâtre' in *Les Annales du théâtre et de la musique*, eds. Edouard Noel and Edmond Stoullig, IV (1878), p. xl; André Antoine, 'Causerie sur la mise en scène', *La Revue de Paris*, 10 (1903), p. 603.

ever more nature;[39] in this respect Gerhart Hauptmann was heralded as the 'fulfilment of Ibsen'.[40]

Naturalist theory, however, continued to insist on the objectivity of the work of art, maintaining one important Aristotelian precept: the complete absence of the voice of the dramatist.[41] Consequently Ibsen refused to be pressed into the service of the women's movement on the basis of *A Doll's House*. From an early point in Ibsen criticism there is even a tendency to play down the social and historical particularity of the causation and to read the specific cases as symbols of universal issues. Otto Brahm, while acknowledging the social concerns of Ibsen's plays, sought to generalize their varied themes into the single conflict of the individual and society.[42] Ibsen is thus seen to parallel Hebbel, and in an essay by Leo Berg (1889) is pulled back from the Naturalist current.

Such qualifications affected the relationship between Naturalism and socialism, particularly in Germany, where Marxist criticism had, in Franz Mehring, an eloquent spokesman, schooled in the Sickingen debate. Less extreme than Chernyshevsky in his valorization of the practical, Mehring nevertheless subordinated the aesthetic dimension of literature, dismissing the formal experiments of the literary avant-garde as irrelevant at a time of political struggle. Contemptuous of claims for the non-political universality of the classics of German drama, he emphasized their basis in the historical situation of their age, seeing in them an expression of the aspirations of the emergent middle classes.[43] He followed Engels in condemning the accumulation of minor contingent detail in contemporary Naturalist drama, and, while praising the social-critical element in certain works of Hauptmann, he repeated the Marxist criticism of the failure to acknowledge the promise of social revolution held out by the rising working-class movement. Mehring was resistant to the attempt of Bruno Wille to extend the influence of the literary avant-garde to the working classes. Brought in by the (Marxist) Social Democrats to lead the Freie Volksbühne ('Free People's Theatre') in 1892, Mehring maintained an aesthetically conservative repertoire based on classical works and contemporary plays with explicit social content, but excluding Büchner's *Dantons Tod*.

---

[39] Otto Brahm, 'Der Naturalismus und das Theater' (1891), in *Theater, Dramatiker, Schauspieler*, ed. Hugo Fetting (Berlin: Henschelverlag, 1961) p. 404.

[40] Theodor Fontane, 'Hauptmann: Vor Sonnenaufgang' (1889) in *Sämtliche Werke*, eds. Edgar Groß *et al.*, 24 vols. (Munich: Nymphenburger Verlagshandlung, 1959–74), vol. xxii/ii, p. 713.

[41] S. Ibsen's letter to Sophus Schandorph, in Henrik Ibsen, *Samlede Verker: Hundreårsutgave*, eds. Francis Bull, Halvdon Koht and Didrik Arup Seip, 21 vols. (Oslo: Gyldendal, 1928–57), vol. xvii, p. 450.

[42] Otto Brahm, 'Henrik Ibsen' (1886) in *Kritische Schriften*, ed. Paul Schlenther, 2 vols. (Berlin: S. Fischer, 1913–15), vol. ii, p. 193.

[43] Franz Mehring, *Gesammelte Schriften*, eds. Thomas Höhle, Hans Koch and Josef Schleifstein, 12 vols. (Berlin: Dietz, 1960–3), vol. x, pp. 252–8.

Whereas Büchner's formal innovation deflected attention from the political content of his drama, the moral offence given by Nora's exit at the end of Ibsen's *A Doll's House* exactly parallelled the aesthetic offence to conservative critics. When Nora exits to take off her costume and return in her everyday clothes to sit (for the first time in the play) and talk seriously (for the first time in their marriage) to Helmer, not only is she renouncing the play-acting of her former life, but the dramatist is denouncing the 'well-made play' in which she has hitherto figured; in leaving the stage she is leaving the conventions of theatre. Recognizing this, Heinrich Laube, the director of the Burgtheater, objected that the conclusion of *A Doll's House* took the play out of its genre; Ibsen replied that formal categories should be adapted to the literature of the time, not vice versa.[44]

This self-reflexive mode of dramatic theorizing is also employed by Chekhov, where it can be seen as a development of the anti-aesthetic impulse of Chernyshevsky. In *The Seagull* (1896) Dorn observes of Treplev's play within the play: 'He produces an effect, that's all, and mere effects don't get you all that far.'[45] Nina, initially drawn to this inauthentic world, learns (like Nora) and changes; 'acting' is thus distinguished from play-acting and associated with conscious acts. By showing the failure of Treplev's play Chekhov ridicules the theatricalization of life.[46]

The dramaturgical programme implicit in these two plays corresponds to the aims of Arno Holz: to reduce to a minimum the constraints imposed by the technical resources available, and to replace traditional poses with an ever closer approximation to real life, in short: 'gradually to get rid of "theatre" from the theatre'.[47] Like Ibsen and Chekhov, Holz begins, in the prose sketch *Papa Hamlet* (1889), with satire of the theatrical mode, but, critical of the rhetorical diction of Ibsen's plays, he insists that the language of drama should be the language of real life.[48] With Johannes Schlaf he sought to put this into practice in *Die Familie Selicke* (1890), whose quasi-phonographical recording of speech and minimalist action were felt to point towards a drama that diverged totally from what had hitherto been customary, suggesting that the future might belong to plays that were no longer plays at all.[49]

44  Ibsen, *Samlede Verker*, vol. XVII, p. 388.
45  Anton Chekhov, *The Oxford Chekhov*, trans. and ed. Ronald Hingley, 9 vols. (London: Oxford University Press, 1967), vol. II, p. 276.
46  Stephen C. Hutchings, *Russian Modernism: The Transfiguration of the Everyday* (Cambridge University Press, 1997), p. 103.
47  Arno Holz, 'Evolution des Dramas' in *Das Werk*, ed. Hans W. Fischer, 10 vols. (Berlin: Dietz, 1924–5), vol. X, p. 214.
48  *Ibid.*, p. 213.
49  Theodor Fontane, 'Holz/Schlaf: Die Familie Selicke' in *Sämtliche Werke*, vol. XXII/ii, p. 734.

Chekhov too came to the drama from the prose sketch, but with less confidence in his challenge to generic purity. On completing *The Seagull* he wrote to Aleksei Suvorin: 'It's turned out like a story...reading my new-born play has convinced me again that I'm not a playwright at all.'[50] But Vladimir Nemirovich-Danchenko saw Chekhov's 'failure' in the same way as Zola and Antoine had seen the failure of the Naturalist drama in France: as a reflection on the limits of the existing theatre. Like Stanislavsky, he had been critical of the acting in the reformist Meiningen productions, but this very deficiency had revealed the potential of *mise-en-scène*. The lengthy texts in which dramatis personae are characterized, and set and costume described, are symptomatic of the Naturalist dramatist's leaning to the narrative mode; from the theatre they demand a wider range of resources, precision in their use and, if their functional integration in the dramatist's scheme is to be recognized, subjection to the unifying control of an interpreter-director. In the case of Chekhov this was provided by Stanislavsky and the Moscow Arts Theatre; in the case of Hauptmann by Brahm and the Deutsches Theater.

Likewise the extensive stage directions made increased demands on actors and actresses. In the earlier part of the century the organizational structure of the theatre, with members of a company allocated a particular 'line of business', had favoured stereotypical acting. The great virtuosi offered different styles, but always their own styles: Bernhardt and Ziegler the picturesque, Wolter the vocal, Ristori, Salvini and Rossi the psychological. Whether they toured as guest stars or, like Irving, performed with their own company, they stood out against the background provided. The denial of individual heroism and the thematization of man's place in society, evident in the increased number of characters in the plays of Hauptmann and Chekhov, also required actors to act for each other within an ensemble, rather than seeking directly to affect the audience: 'absorption' rather than 'theatricality'.

This is illustrated in Brahm's hypothetical casting of *Ghosts*: as Mrs Alving he proposed Anna Haverland, an actress who did not cultivate effect, but revealed the cause behind the effect.[51] The actress who was acknowledged to embody most fully the new style was Eleonora Duse, whose 'tattered translation, with few advantages, with meagre accessories' of the role of Marguerite Gautier, while providing a 'fine vindication' of *La Dame aux camélias*, may not, Henry James suspected, have been 'the very performance Dumas intended'.[52] Hofmannsthal relates her style explicitly to generic impurity: 'She performs the transitions, she fills

[50] Quoted from *The Oxford Chekhov*, vol. II, p. 334.
[51] Otto Brahm, 'Ibsens Gespenster' (1884) in *Kritische Schriften*, vol. I, pp. 73–4.
[52] James, *The Scenic Art*, pp. 263–4.

in the gaps in motivation, she reconstructs in the drama the psychological novel.'[53]

In his *Preface to Miss Julie* (1888) Strindberg provided the most succinct account of the implications of the new dramaturgy. Older techniques of illusion lack conviction for the modern scientific and secular age; men have tried to create a new drama by putting new ideas into the old forms rather than adapting the old form to the new content. In consequence Strindberg argues for the modernization of form, so that it corresponds to subject matter taken from real life and shown in all its complexity, in terms of both motivation and characterization. He does not believe in 'theatrical characters', based on a simplified view of the immutability of the soul, but wants people to appear as everyday human beings in the performance of their daily work. He demands dialogue which proceeds irregularly, as in real life, rather than the 'mathematically constructed' dialogue favoured by contemporary French dramatists. The modern drama must show causes rather than effects; not content with seeing something happen, inquisitive modern man must know why it happens. The drama should reconstruct the psychological novel, and so Strindberg acknowledges a greater debt to the work of the Goncourt brothers than to anything else in contemporary literature.

Strindberg concludes with a series of observations covering technical questions, from the interval and the interior design of the theatre to lighting, decor, mime and dumbshow, which confirm his commitment to the greatest possible illusion, and make theatre reform a condition of the success of the newer dramaturgy. While awaiting such a theatre, he concludes, dramatists must write to create a stock of plays in readiness for the repertoire that will be needed.

The apparent implication that this was to be a repertoire of plays showing the relationship between character and milieu was not to be borne out by Strindberg's own subsequent development; and in any case his Naturalism is already qualified when he attributes the complexity of *Miss Julie* to the fact that life is seen from more than one viewpoint. Commenting on the development of Holz's theory, Schlaf notes a similar shift from Zola's 'A work of art is a corner of nature seen through a temperament' to the perspectivist 'A work of art is a slice of life seen not through the temperament of the artist, but of all the people he wishes to present.'[54] At this time a number of writers were seeking access to more varied subjective perspectives, prompted by the perception of a

---

53  Hugo von Hofmannsthal, 'Eleonora Duse' in *Gesammelte Werke in Einzelausgaben*, ed. Herbert Steiner, 15 vols. (Stockholm and Frankfurt: S. Fischer, 1952–9), *Prosa* I, pp. 67–8.
54  Quoted in Holz, 'Die Kunst: ihr Wesen und ihre Gesetze' in *Das Werk*, vol. X, p. 336.

recrudescence of faith and contemporary neo-mysticism.[55] Hardly had Naturalism reached the theatre when key elements of its programme were called into question; with Hermann Bahr's *Die Überwindung des Naturalismus* ('The Overcoming of Naturalism', 1891) its demise was openly pronounced. The way was open for more radical experiments, conducted, however, alongside a stubbornly resistant Naturalism.

In 1887 Ferdinand Brunetière, who saw it as the function of the critic to foster those characteristics which point to the future, had already declared the 'bankruptcy of Naturalism'. In 1890 he published a comprehensive study of the evolution of the literary genres, combining aspects of Taine's determinism with a Hegelian view of history, and arguing that the hierarchy of the genres varies from epoch to epoch. Notwithstanding his relativism vis-à-vis Aristotelian poetics, he seeks to develop his own arguments from a single absolute principle. Taking issue with Zola, and provocatively undertaking the rehabilitation of Scribe,[56] he defines the law of the theatre in terms of the dynamics of dramatic action: 'what we ask the theatre, is the spectacle of a will striving towards a goal, and conscious of the means which it employs'. Despite denying any interest in metaphysical questions, he argues for renewal of the drama as an expression of the power of the will: 'the belief in determinism is more favourable to the progress of the novel, but the belief in free will is more favourable to the progress of dramatic art'.[57] He declares that the great error of the French Naturalists had been to confuse the two opposed genres – thereby at least acknowledging their consistency of purpose.

Brunetière's argument is as much moralistic as historical, echoing Nietzsche's view that the philosophy of determinism is a symptom of the decline of the will. Brunetière's call for a drama of free will reflects the voluntarist trends displacing determinism in the thought of the 1890s, but his poetics point back to a time when the theatre had not yet developed resources other than the spoken word, the expression of the will *par excellence*. He thus brings about a renewal of mid-century discussions about the fundamental nature of drama (as distinct from theatre) and prolongs more recent debates in a way which indicates how uneven the naturalist revolution had been in its effects. In his *Art of the Dramatist* (1903) the American critic Brander Matthews reasserts Brunetière's belief in the freedom of the will and follows him in his definition of the dramatic

[55] Jacques Robichez, *Le Symbolisme au théâtre: Lugné-Poe et les débuts de L'Œuvre* (Paris: L'Arche, 1957), pp. 217–22.

[56] Ferdinand Brunetière, 'La Réforme du théâtre', *Revue des deux mondes*, 98 (1890), pp. 697–9; see also René Doumic, *De Scribe à Ibsen: causeries sur le théâtre contemporain*, 5th edn (Paris: Perrin, 1901), pp. 1–11.

[57] Barrett H. Clark, *European Theories of the Drama* (New York and London: Appleton, 1929), pp. 407, 410.

as the unfolding of this will in a firmly constructed plot, with articulate dialogue as its principal means; like Freytag he sees a clear distinction between drama and novel. In *Play-Making* (1912) William Archer, on the other hand, develops the determinist position, showing that there are many classic and modern dramas that do not depend for their effect on any clash of wills. In replacing the criterion of conflict with the more comprehensive one of crisis, but denying the need for the depiction of any 'marked crisis', he preserves drama's access to 'the broad picture of a social phenomenon or environment', and he defends the convergence of the genres, reducing the distinction between drama and novel to a matter of degree: 'It is the slowness of its process which differentiates the typical novel from the typical play.'[58]

In *The Corner Stones of Modern Drama* (1906) Henry Arthur Jones sought to reconcile the views of Brunetière and Archer.[59] He notes the dominant influence of Ibsen, but, as a latecomer, he praises the Norwegian dramatist for the precision with which he traces the progress of the inner life rather than for any analysis of the origin of psychic conflicts. In his *Introduction to Brunetière's 'Law of the Drama'* (1914) he therefore admits to greater sympathy with Brunetière's voluntarism than Archer's determinism, but, in search of a general law which accommodates both the active and the passive hero, he avoids commitment to either position. Like Scribe's new apologists, Brunetière and René Doumic, Jones emphasizes the structure of the plot, dispensing with questions about its source: 'all the successful dramatists of the past have been . . . ignorant of modern psychology and sociology [they] were obliged to construct their plays on the vicious first principle of telling an interesting story in a well framed concrete scheme'. Jones's need to reject the dramaturgy of those 'others, who have discovered that it is the first business of the playwright not to have a story or a plot, but to have "ideas" and a "mission"',[60] is a further indication of the asymmetrical development of drama and dramatic theory around the turn of the century.

The most prominent contemporary advocate of the drama of ideas, George Bernard Shaw, shared Jones's admiration of Ibsen, while differing in emphasizing his social criticism. At the same time Shaw added his voice to the European critique of the dramatic and theatrical conventions of the nineteenth century. However, steeped in the traditions of the theatre of the grand school, exemplified by Sullivan, Ristori, Salvini and Coquelin, he maintains a belief in the continued viability of the older style, when deployed in the service of the philosophy of the present age.

[58]  *Ibid.*, pp. 480, 479.
[59]  See also Clayton Hamilton, *Studies in Stagecraft* (London: Grant Richards, 1914).
[60]  Clark, *European Theories*, pp. 468–9.

Unlike Strindberg's, his aim was indeed to put new wine into old bottles; while recognizing and exploiting recent modifications of technique, he minimizes their importance, regarding technique as subordinate to content.[61]

In Shakespeare's plays Shaw recognizes the product of unconscious vision, where he demands philosophical understanding. For him the true function of drama is to express and propagate the dramatist's view of life, and its form should be consciously shaped by the will of the dramatist to affect the public; that is to say, it must be rhetorical in its style. Shaw thus differs from Galsworthy, the impartial Naturalist, whose characters have feelings which they cannot express, and who aims 'to set before the public no cut and dried codes, but the phenomena of life and character, selected and combined, but not distorted by the dramatist's outlook,... leaving the public to draw such poor moral as nature may afford'.[62] Shaw is closer to the early German Expressionists who call for a moral theatre of ideas, and reject Hauptmann's drama of the inarticulate.[63]

Like the Expressionists, Shaw also insists that the deployment of the resources of the drama of passion in the drama of ideas does not imply the intellectualization of the passions, but a drama of impassioned argument, both among the dramatis personae and directly between dramatist and audience: 'emotion exists only to make thought live and move us'.[64] His impact depended, however, on his programmatic intellectualism; the respect in which Shaw was held as a man and critic was not matched by his influence on the development of drama or dramatic theory. Hofmannsthal points to a failure to meet certain contemporary demands: 'this intellectual mentality can stimulate only a slight, restless vibration in the deeper reaches of the human soul... it cannot provoke that true shock which precedes a violent transformation'.[65]

For Hofmannsthal, Shaw resembles Hebbel, the dramatist of problems, who practises an almost intrusive analysis of his characters, rather than Grillparzer, the dramatist who resolves the problem in an image.[66]

---

[61] George Bernard Shaw, Preface to *Three Plays for Puritans* in *The Bodley Head Bernard Shaw: Collected Plays with their Prefaces*, ed. Dan H. Laurence, 7 vols. (London: Reinhardt, 1970–4), vol. II, pp. 43–4.

[62] John Galsworthy, 'Some Platitudes Concerning Drama' in *The Works of John Galsworthy*, Manaton Edition, 29 vols. (London: Heinemann, 1923–35), vol. XVII, p. 196.

[63] Ferdinand Hardekopf, 'Das moralische Theater', *Die Schaubühne*, V (1909), p. 2; Hans Landsberg, *Los von Hauptmann!* (Berlin: Hermann Walter, 1900).

[64] George Bernard Shaw, 'Sardoodledom' (1895) in *The Drama Observed*, ed. Bernard F. Dukore, 4 vols. (University Park: Pennsylvania State University Press, 1993), vol. II, p. 357.

[65] Hugo von Hofmannsthal, 'Blick auf den geistigen Zustand Europas' in *Gesammelte Werke, Prosa* IV, pp. 76–7.

[66] Hugo von Hofmannsthal, 'Rede auf Grillparzer', in *Gesammelte Werke, Prosa* IV, pp. 121, 126.

Hofmannsthal also sees something of this abstraction in Ibsen, in whose self-analytical characters he does not recognize real people in a real environment, but variations of a single Modernist type, a symbolic projection of the soul of the dramatist in search of something to give meaning to an otherwise merely reflective life.[67] Hofmannsthal might be said to be appropriating Ibsen (and criticizing Shaw) in order to underpin the Symbolist aesthetic of his own early lyric dramas. However, standing somewhat aside from contemporary literary movements, he remained a wide-ranging critic and dramatist rather than a prescriptive theorist. Drawn to collaboration with Richard Strauss by the Symbolist analogy between dramatic and musical structure, he nevertheless moderated any tendency to abstraction by an insistence on the need to root the language of even operatic characters in time and place.[68]

The desire to penetrate to the 'deeper reaches of the soul' had taken second place to the pursuit of scientific objectivity during the period of high Naturalism, without ever being entirely suppressed. In his Zurich writings of the 1850s Wagner had developed a critique of the modern spoken drama, seeing it as derivative of epic forms and so related to the novel. Its prosaic rationality and empirical precision were for him a symptom of the alienation of the individual and the decline of the sense of religious and cultural community. Opera, on the other hand, has the capacity to renew the theatre, restoring emotive immediacy by developing the expressive (musical), as opposed to the significative and descriptive (linguistic) dimension, thereby re-establishing the basis of drama in myth rather than modern society. Such views were furthered by the renewed discussion of Aristotle's *Poetics*, notably in Jacob Bernays's *Grundzüge der verlorenen Abhandlung des Aristoteles über die Wirkung der Tragödie* ('Elements of Aristotle's Lost Essay on the Effect of Tragedy', 1857), where catharsis is interpreted as a medical term, shifting emphasis away from the moral-didactic effect on the audience, as favoured by the theorists of the eighteenth century.

In 'Richard Wagner et Tannhäuser à Paris' (1861), Baudelaire takes up the argument for drama as a total work of art, transcending rational intelligibility and giving direct access to emotion, myth and dream. The basis of authentic drama in myth, the privileging of the older tragedians over the 'Socratic' proto-Modernist Euripides, the origin of tragedy in music and its predicted revival in opera, and above all the relationship between the dream and free artistic creation were then given decisive

[67] Hugo von Hofmannsthal, 'Die Menschen in Ibsens Dramen' in *Gesammelte Werke, Prosa* I, p. 95.
[68] Hugo von Hofmannsthal, '*Der Rosenkavalier*: Zum Geleit' in *Gesammelte Werke, Prosa* IV, p. 429.

emphasis by Nietzsche in *The Birth of Tragedy* (1872). Despite its title, however, this is an essay in the psychology of art rather than the history of dramaturgy. Its impact on the development of theories of drama was important, but indirect.

In one respect Wagner remained a prisoner of the older tradition: for his decor he had been happy with the Realistic sets and costumes of Max Brückner. Adolphe Appia, however, saw such decor as a symptom of the decline of theatre from its cultic origins into purely illustrative spectacle, and thus a contradiction of the Wagnerian project. He proposed – vainly, in the face of the resistance of Wagner's widow, Cosima – a radically new approach to the staging of Wagner's operas, stripping away all reference to empirical reality and using space, light and movement to lead the imagination beyond the material world.

Baudelaire's response to the Wagnerian union of the arts was consolidated in Eduard Schuré's *Le Drame musical* (1875), but with a shift of emphasis from fusion at the level of execution to unity at the level of poetic creation. Unlike Appia, the Symbolists do not see theatre as a resource to be exploited; recalling Musset, Théodore Wyzewa asserts the superiority of the text to its performance.[69] In 'Richard Wagner, rêverie d'un poète français' (1885) Mallarmé concurs, arguing that Wagner's achievement was flawed by his continued recourse to the characters and plot of traditional drama, and the burden of the legend, which stifles the creative freedom of the imagination.

The reception of Ibsen's plays in France postdated the Symbolists' appropriation of Wagner, so that they were simultaneously claimed by the Naturalists and the Symbolists. Villiers de l'Isle Adam, less radical than his Symbolist admirers in his attitude to dramatic conventions, proposed a distinction between the play as a formal vehicle and its metaphysical content,[70] which provides the basis for Maeterlinck's devaluation of Ibsen's Realistic textures: 'Ibsen... gives his characters very detailed, clear and individual lives, and he seems to lay great store by these little signs of humanity. But... deep down he does not care! The apparent and conventional reality of these secondary beings is there only to make us accept, and to give substance to, the *third person... the Unknown*.'[71] Succeeding with Ibsen, where Appia had failed with Wagner, Aurélien

[69] Théodore de Wyzewa, 'Notes sur la peinture wagnérienne', *Revue wagnérienne*, 2 (1886–7), p. 104.
[70] Villiers de l'Isle Adam, 'Une littérature dramatique nouvelle' (1884) in *Œuvres complètes*, eds. Alan Raitt and P. -G. Castex, 2 vols. ([Paris]: Gallimard, 1986), vol. II, pp. 1532–6.
[71] Maurice Maeterlinck, *Introduction à une psychologie des songes*, quoted from Patrick McGuinness, *Maurice Maeterlinck and the Making of Modern Theatre* (Oxford University Press, 2000), p. 55.

Lugné-Poë completed the appropriation with his production of *The Lady from the Sea* (1892). Subsequently, as a mirror image of Brahm's Naturalist productions in Berlin, Ibsen came to occupy a central place in the repertoire of the Théâtre de l'Oeuvre.

Maeterlinck himself was likewise seen by Camille Mauclair as an exponent of such an ambiguous dramatic form, whose true value resides in the purely symbolic significance of the dramaturgy,[72] the Aristotelian 'representation of an action' being the most superficial element of the drama. The question that had informed most of nineteenth-century dramaturgy, 'Why are all these people behaving in this way?', recedes before the lyric contemplation of the transcendent irrationality of Being, accessible in the freedom of the imaginative life. In Maeterlinck's theory of drama, dialogue and setting are of no importance for themselves; the 'everyday' is not excluded, but it is reduced to a façade behind which unfolds a more solemn dialogue; action does not follow rationally comprehensible laws of causation; the characters move like sleepwalkers, guided by occult forces towards an enigmatic destiny.[73]

Unwilling to accommodate themselves to the conventions of representational *mise-en-scène*, the Symbolists questioned the utility of decorations, especially the material type, which in the work of their Naturalist contemporaries anchor the action in the causal nexus of the social world. Collaborating closely with contemporary artists including Vuillard, Bonnard and Toulouse-Lautrec, they reverted to the painted canvas as an expressive support of the poetic word. They regarded the actor as an intruder, preventing the spectator from communing directly with the poet, and therefore proposed the attenuation of gesture, the stylization of declamation and the reduction of the number of actors, even to the point of mono-drama. Ironically, just as Büchner's work was beginning to penetrate the theatre, the abstraction of the marionette came to exercise a special fascination, along with the Pierrot figure and dance, in which, as in Yeats's 'Among Schoolchildren', the work and its interpreter were felt to be totally one.

In theatrical practice the radical avant-garde had a number of exponents throughout Europe: Craig in England, Georg Fuchs in Germany, Meyerhold, Bryusov and (after 1905) Stanislavsky in Russia. Despite their ideological heterogeneity, their association with different contemporary dramatists and divergences in their approach to the resources of the theatre, they were united in their desire for the emancipation of these

72 Camille Mauclair in *L'Estafette*, 21 November 1891, quoted in Robichez, *Le Symbolisme*, p. 167.
73 Maurice Maeterlinck, *Le Trésor des humbles* (Paris: Mercure de France, 1895), pp. 179–201.

resources from the task of representation and their fusion in the service of poetic expression. The minimalism of dramaturgy was matched by a minimalism of *mise-en-scène*. Justifying the former in terms which paradoxically recall Büchner's defence of Realism in *Lenz*, Maeterlinck had declared: 'An old man, seated in his arm-chair . . . – submitting with bent head to the presence of his soul and his destiny – motionless as he is, does yet live in reality a deeper, more human, and more universal life than the lover who strangles his mistress, the captain who conquers in battle, or the husband who "avenges his honour".'

Even while questioning Brunetière's emphasis on the primacy of action, Archer stated:

The tendency of recent theory, and of some recent practice, has been to widen the meaning of the word [dramatic], until it bursts the bonds of all definition. Plays have been written . . . in which the endeavour of the dramatist has been to depict life not in moments of crisis, but in its most level and humdrum phases . . . 'Dramatic' in the eyes of writers of this school has become a term of reproach synonymous with 'theatrical'.[74]

The consequence of a full implementation of such theory would be for external action to be suppressed and language reduced to silence; indeed Maeterlinck, an apologist of silence, was resistant to performance of his plays.[75] The anti-theatrical prejudice in nineteenth-century dramatic theory, however, finds its *ne plus ultra*, on the one hand, in Alfred Jarry's proclamation of the uselessness of 'theatre' in the theatre, and, on the other, in Kandinsky's totally abstract deployment in *Der gelbe Klang* ('The Yellow Sound', 1912) of the theatrical resources of colour, sound and motion, where the play of light might be the sole action and the human voice be used without words.

Archer's caution is more typical of the situation at the beginning of the twentieth century. Galsworthy, considering his own work alongside that of Synge and Masefield, summed up the prospects for drama in England as follows:

our drama is renascent . . . because of a new spirit . . . in part the gradual outcome of the impact on our home-grown art, of Russian, French, and Scandinavian influences . . . What, then, are to be the main channels down which the renascent English drama will float . . . ? The one will be the broad and clear-cut channel of naturalism, down which will course a drama . . . faithful to the seething and multiple life around us . . . the other . . . a poetic prose-drama . . . whose province will be to disclose the elemental soul of man and the forces of Nature.[76]

---

[74] Clark, *European Theories*, p. 479.
[75] Cf. Maurice Maeterlinck, 'Le Silence' in *Le Trésor des humbles*, pp. 7–25.
[76] Galsworthy, 'Some Platitudes', pp. 205–7.

This pluralist response to the variety of options available has a parallel in the eclecticism of Hauptmann, Hofmannsthal and Wilde. It was, however, to be the great dualists, Ibsen, the early Strindberg and Chekhov, whose work is deeply informed by that tension between the extensive and the intensive which underlay the development of nineteenth-century dramaturgy, who would secure the firmest place in the literary canon and the repertoire of the theatre.

# *Literature and other disciplines*

# Literary criticism and models of science

## GREGORY MOORE

Reflecting on trends in literary theory, George Saintsbury spoke in 1890 with evident distaste of 'the notion, now warmly championed by some younger critics both at home and abroad, that criticism must be of all things "scientific"'.[1] Though this grand old man of Victorian letters had little time for such faddish notions, it ought really to have come as no surprise that practitioners of the perennially slippery discipline of literary criticism would eventually look to the natural sciences to anchor it more firmly. For one of the distinctive features of intellectual life in the latter half of the nineteenth century was the belief – organized by Auguste Comte into a comprehensive philosophy which he christened 'positivism' – that the scientific method could and should be applied beyond the precincts of the material world to every other sphere of thought and action. The effective alliance of dispassionate observation, inductive reasoning and experimentation had accomplished so much in so little time, transforming the planet and the way people understood it, that science seemed an unstoppably creative force that promised to enrich and expand knowledge forever. 'The *natural sciences*', wrote a starry-eyed Wilhelm Scherer, Professor of German Literature at the University of Vienna, in 1870, 'ride like a conquering hero in the triumphal chariot to which we are all bound.'[2]

If psychology and political economy had recently abandoned intuition and speculation in favour of empirical research; if Buckle's *History of Civilization in England* (1857–61) had revealed the unbending laws governing human behaviour past and present; if even socialism (at least according to Friedrich Engels) had become a science, thanks to Marx's demonstration of class conflict as the motor of history; then why should criticism not be similarly renewed? Those who would bring the habits of scientific inquiry to the study of literature might have had different opinions as to how it could be done and the extent to which it was

[1] George Saintsbury, 'The Kinds of Criticism' in *Essays in English Literature 1780–1860*, 3rd edn (London: Charles Scribner's Sons, 1896), p. xi.
[2] Wilhelm Scherer, 'Die neue Generation' in *Vorträge und Aufsätze zur Geschichte des geistigen Lebens in Deutschland und Oesterreich* (Berlin: Weidmann, 1874), p. 411.

even practicable, but they shared a concern with raising standards. They turned to science in the genuine hope that it would allay uncertainty, resolve disputes and consecrate those fundamental truths that for the moment lacked authority because, as William Whewell remarked of the humanities, they had 'not yet been fixed by means of distinct and permanent phraseology, and sanctioned by universal reception, and formed into a connected system, and traced through the steps of their gradual discovery and establishment'.[3] For some this meant eliminating the judicial dimension of criticism altogether in favour of a meticulously descriptive and analytical model, whilst others insisted that, at the very least, aesthetic judgements could no longer be derived from the arbitrary emotional responses of individual commentators or supported by ever more rickety metaphysical scaffolding; the value of a work of art had to be based on ascertainable facts drawn from an investigation of history, psychology, sociology, economics and other adjacent disciplines.

In some ways, the proposals for a scientific criticism were symptomatic of a crisis of confidence in the humanities that was first felt towards the end of the nineteenth century and has troubled them ever since. What purpose did the study of literature serve? If it could not aspire to the rank of science – and thus contribute to the advancement of knowledge – then for these critics it served no purpose at all. Regardless of whether we find this answer to the nagging doubts about the validity of their profession persuasive or not, their efforts – often independently of one another – to redefine their role mark the beginnings of modern literary theory.


## Pioneers: psychology

One of the earliest bids to use science – or at least make a rhetorical appeal to its prestige – in literary analysis was undertaken by G. H. Lewes (1817–78). In *Principles of Success in Literature*, a series of essays published in 1865, he argues that good writing is achieved not by accident but through the conscious mastery of a 'scientific Method', for all literature is 'founded upon psychological laws, and involves principles which are true for all peoples and for all times'. He adduces three such principles: Vision, Sincerity and Beauty. By 'Vision' Lewes is actually referring to the realm of the imagination and, in exploring the part it plays in literary creation, he draws heavily on his own theories of cognition, later elaborated in his five-volume *Problems of Life and Mind* (1874–9). The mind of the artist, he concludes, has an unusual capacity for turning sense

---

[3] William Whewell, *Philosophy of the Inductive Sciences*, 2 vols. (London: Parker, 1847), vol. I, p. 7.

impressions into concrete images, whereas the less gifted tend to assimilate these impressions as mere abstractions. The Principle of Sincerity
demands that literature be moral or intellectually honest. The Principle
of Beauty refers to style. Though style is an art and therefore incommunicable, it is nevertheless subordinated to certain laws which together
constitute 'the Philosophy of Criticism': Economy, Simplicity, Sequence,
Climax and Variety. But for all Lewes's invocation of psychology and his
promise to expound them 'scientifically', these unilluminating and largely
tautologous laws owe more to common sense than to empirical research
(for example, Economy 'rejects whatever is superfluous').[4] Ultimately,
Lewes delivers not so much a theoretical treatise on the psychology of
literary composition as a practical guide to writing well – which Herbert
Spencer had already done more succinctly in *The Philosophy of Style*
(1852), a dissertation on the rhetorical strategies that most efficiently
engage a reader's mental faculties.

Like his largely ignored *Poetics* (1852), Eneas Sweetland Dallas's
(1828–79) *The Gay Science* (1866) was 'an attempt to settle the first
principles of Criticism, and to show how alone it can be raised to the dignity of a science'. Starting from the premise that the immediate end of art
and literature is 'to give pleasure', he concludes that criticism must be the
'science of the laws and conditions under which pleasure is produced'; in
other words, criticism must be founded on psychology, a systematic study
of mental functions and in particular the operations of the imagination.
By 'imagination', or the 'hidden soul', Dallas understands the unconscious and automatic activity of the mind that is not only the source of
art, but also the explanation and measure of its worth: 'Art is poetical
in proportion as it has the power of appealing to what I may call the
absent mind, as distinct from the present mind, on which falls the great
glare of consciousness, and to which alone science appeals.'[5] For Dallas,
then, criticism ought to consist in making the contents of the absent mind
available for the scrutiny of the present mind.

The man often greeted by his peers as the first and most formidable
of critics to apply scientific methods to literature was Hippolyte Taine
(1828–93). Taine is discussed more fully elsewhere in this volume, but
because of his extraordinary influence on subsequent iterations of scientific literary criticism, a brief outline of his principal contributions to this
debate is unavoidable here.

Taine's approach – as famously set forth in the introduction to his *History of English Literature* (1863) – is to view works of art and literature

4   G. H. Lewes, *Principles of Success in Literature* (Boston: Allyn & Bacon, 1891), pp. 22,
    133.
5   E. S. Dallas, *The Gay Science*, 2 vols. (London: Chapman & Hall, 1866), vol. I, pp. 91,
    316.

not as the occasions for value judgements based on *a priori* definitions of beauty or on some deeply subjective response, but as positive facts, as products of law-bound and empirically observable processes whose characteristics must be described and causes explained. The literary historian à la Taine therefore treats the work not as an aesthetic object or end in itself, but merely as a 'document' that reveals information about its creator: 'while his eyes read the text, his soul and mind pursue the continuous development and the ever changing succession of the emotions and conceptions out of which the text has sprung: in short he works out its psychology'. This does not mean, however, that Taine takes a primarily biographical approach to literature, of the kind pioneered by Sainte-Beuve. He is concerned less with the individual author than with the national mentality of which a writer is an unwitting yet pre-eminent representative. There is, Taine argues, 'a system in human sentiments and ideas', a certain way of thinking shared by members of a society and expressed through its culture. This way of thinking is the result of the unceasing interplay of three historical forces: Taine's celebrated triad of *race*, *milieu* and *moment*, where *race* is the totality of hereditary dispositions and instincts, *milieu* the physical and social environment, and *moment* the temporal framework. Literary works are instructive precisely because they 'make sentiments visible' and are thus a record of the spiritual development of a given people: 'It is . . . chiefly by the study of literatures that one may construct a moral history, and advance toward the knowledge of psychological laws, from which events spring . . . I intend to write the history of a literature, and to seek in it for the psychology of a people.'[6]

Taine is scarcely interested in textual analysis or questions of literary merit. Indeed, the introduction to the *History of English Literature* is less a theory of literature than one of history and, for all the trappings of Naturalism, his ideas owe more to Hegel than to any properly scientific procedure. What is more, as some contemporaries were quick to point out, Taine's work is bedevilled by a notable lack of rigour and credible evidence, and, despite his claims to the contrary, he was conspicuously unable to prevent value judgements, dogma and personal taste from creeping back into his narrative. In this, too, he proved influential.

## Scherer and 'literary positivism' in Germany

Wilhelm Scherer (1841–86) liked to fancy himself the spokesman for a 'new generation' of sober, positivistically inclined scholars who would

[6] Hippolyte Taine, *History of English Literature*, 4 vols. (London: Chatto & Windus, 1877), vol. I, pp. 7, 13, 35.

abandon not only the dry antiquarianism of traditional textual criticism but also, just as their colleagues in the natural sciences had done, the legacy of Hegelianism and Romanticism. Inspired by his reading of Comte, Buckle and Taine, Scherer demanded in the 1860s a reorientation of literary history, aligning it not with metaphysical conjectures but with hard facts. Yet facts alone were insufficient. Like Buckle, Scherer saw it as the historian's responsibility not merely to enumerate events but to fathom their causes, to reveal the laws that govern historical progress, just as the scientist disclosed the laws operative in the cosmos at large. As he wrote in his *Geschichte der deutschen Sprache* ('History of the German Language', 1868): 'we believe with Buckle that determinism . . . is the cornerstone of all true comprehension of history. We believe with Buckle that the goals of historical science are essentially related to those of the natural sciences insofar as we seek knowledge of the spiritual powers in order to master them, just as physical forces are pressed into human service with the help of the natural sciences.'[7] Scherer's originality, then – at least in the field of German professional philology – lies largely in his affirmation of the historicity of literature and his attempt to go beyond predecessors such as Gervinus and Hettner by identifying the engine of literary change.

Scherer is perhaps best known for the so-called 'wave theory' that underpins his popular *Geschichte der deutschen Literatur* ('History of German Literature', 1883). Surveying the totality of literary evolution in the German-speaking lands, he claimed to be able to discern a pattern of peaks and troughs recurring at regular intervals. High points were reached in the years 600, 1200 and 1800 and corresponding nadirs resulted in 900 and 1500. In between, literary activity found itself on either an upward or a downward curve. Hence past and future developments could be plotted with some accuracy: the trend that had culminated with Weimar Classicism had begun around 1650 and would end about 1950. This periodicity was caused by a variety of external social, political and cultural factors: literature always flourishes in times of liberty and openness to foreign influences; its decadence is concurrent with wars and religious oppression.

Thanks to this unconvincing scheme, Scherer has been seen as a crudely reductive and unsophisticated thinker. In fairness, however, and notwithstanding his occasionally rather extreme programmatic assertions, he had no intention of subordinating history to the natural sciences. Like his friend Wilhelm Dilthey, Scherer desired a meaningful transfer of scientific methods that would preserve the distinctiveness of the humanities. As

---

7  Wilhelm Scherer, *Geschichte der deutschen Sprache*, 2nd edn (Berlin: Weidmann, 1878), p. xiii.

well as the merit of pursuing the train of causality linking seemingly disparate events, both men also emphasized the importance of careful observation, analytical investigation and above all the comparative approach,
the equivalent, in their eyes, of laboratory experiment. The cooperation
between those toiling in the exact sciences also impressed Scherer and
Dilthey. For too long the different branches of the humanities had worked
contiguously but not collaboratively; in an age of increasing specializa-
tion Scherer clearly recognized the potential for and the mutual benefits of
interdisciplinary research – which might issue in what he called a 'general
comparative science of history'. For the most important problems, he was
sure, 'lie at the borderlands of the sciences. The psychologist stands at
the dissecting table, the linguist learns from the physiologist, the political
historian goes to school with the economist, and the cultural historian
should be a man with ten heads, who sees through man's entire physical
and spiritual life in its causal connections.'[8] Literary studies thus had for
Scherer a place within the framework of a wider social and cultural history that would also encompass the historiography of economics, politics,
warfare, language and so on.

Perhaps the most coherent statement of Scherer's vision of empirically
orientated literary research is his posthumously published and largely
neglected *Poetik* ('Poetics', 1888). In it, he is concerned not with aesthetic judgement but with the properties of the poetic work and the various processes involved in its creation and reception. Of particular interest
here are a naturalistic account of the origin of poetry and his use of an
economic model to figure literary consumption. The former is a good
example of his method of 'reciprocal illumination' (*wechselseitige Erhel-
lung*), which he first used to assay linguistic phenomena in *Geschichte
der deutschen Sprache*. It is founded on the premise that certain modes
of human behaviour are more or less the same throughout all periods
of history. Therefore it ought to be possible to make inferences about
remote ages of which we have only fragmentary records by applying to
them data derived from modern experience. (Likewise, we might enhance
our understanding of more recent events by pondering those of an older
date.) Drawing on the findings of Darwin, Tylor and others, Scherer seeks
in *Poetik* to uncover the genesis of poetry in part by reference to the practices of existing 'primitive peoples' such as Australian Aborigines. The
evidence suggests to him that poetry arises from rudimentary expressions
of joy and feelings of pleasure, especially the erotic impulse, and satisfies
a basic need for amusement or play. Even later and more intricate poetic
forms whose purpose is to disseminate knowledge possess a tremendous

[8]  Scherer, 'Die neue Generation', p. 410.

power to move their listeners, precisely because the ideas they convey are associated with such primordially agreeable sensations.

These anthropological speculations are not as intriguing as Scherer's chapters on the economics and sociology of literature. In addition to its 'ideal' or moral value, literature has an exchange value: the 'poetic product' is 'today a commodity like any other',[9] whose worth has been determined by the law of supply and demand ever since the invention of the printing press and the rise of the book market. Hence a critic must consider how the means by which literature is transmitted between author and public have become more complex. Modern institutions such as journals, publishers, book retailers and lending libraries all have an influence on poetic production and price by competing for the public's favour. These help in turn to create new literary vehicles: the feuilleton, for example. Indeed, Scherer is especially interested in the surrogate role played by the newspaper in contemporary society: as a source of entertainment it fulfils the old community-building function of poetry (which he envisions, of course, as designed to articulate and stimulate feelings of pleasure). He even wonders whether the newspaper might be analysed in relation to different poetic genres: to didactic verse (because it seeks to inform) and to the lament (the obituaries).

Continuing in this vein, Scherer further identifies the 'factors of production' that allegedly conspire in the manufacture of poetry: nature, capital and labour. Nature furnishes the inexhaustible store of raw materials with which the poet works. Capital is the sum of traditions, canons and artefacts accumulated by earlier generations and available for the poet to exploit. Labour is the manner in which the poet appropriates, invests and increases the capital bequeathed to him. How this scheme explains (rather than merely redescribes) the creative process is unclear; once again, though, it is an expression of Scherer's unwavering conviction that literary texts are not the achievement of sovereign legislators but the effects of a chain of more or less visible causes. It was the task of the critic to pick out and evaluate these and other influences on style, structure and theme – which, in a phrase borrowed from Goethe, he elsewhere termed 'Ererbtes, Erlebtes, Erlerntes' ('the inherited, the experienced, the learned') – always with the aim of ascertaining what was unique to a writer and what shared: his class origins, his education, his temperament, his physical constitution, his relation to his public, whether he be professional or amateur, guided more by imagination or taste, and so on.

These aims were soon reiterated and multiplied by Scherer's protégé, Erich Schmidt (1853–1913), who sketched a dizzyingly ambitious map of

---

9  Wilhelm Scherer, *Poetik* (Berlin: Weidmann, 1888), p. 122.

the direction a future 'inductive poetics' ought to take. His credo was that 'literary history should be part of the evolutionary history of a people's spiritual life', investigating – 'like modern natural science' – the never-ending sequence of 'heredity and adaptation' in literary commerce.[10] To meet this goal he sees as necessary first of all an extensive collection of statistical data based on bibliographical surveys of book production throughout the centuries, from which could be deduced, among other things, reading habits and hence when and where particular genres flourished. This would be linked to an inquiry into the development of form that took account of the vicissitudes of metre, rhyme and classical influence; of shifts in poetic diction, the use of rhetorical figures and syntactical arrangements, not only in groups but in individual writers also; the impact of foreign languages and literatures; the relation of a writer to national or regional traditions and to his predecessors; the effect of geography, temperament and racial interbreeding; the divergent atmosphere of the various metropolitan centres; the political system, the class, the degree of prosperity into which the author was born; the role of religion, education, philosophy, women; and finally a work's legacy, its significance for succeeding generations.

This encyclopedic enterprise would seem unfeasible, even crazy: a descriptive mania that neglected not even the smallest detail. Yet some of Schmidt's hopes were realized (and his techniques utilized) in those areas in which the empirical method of the so-called 'Scherer School', the prevailing academic orthodoxy between 1870 and 1900, could reckon a number of lasting accomplishments to its credit: the historical-critical editions of Goethe, Schiller, Herder, Klopstock, Wieland, Kleist and others, and – especially – the authoritative biographies of Lessing (by Schmidt himself), Goethe (Goedeke, Meyer) and Herder (Haym). It was perhaps these latter contributions – still readable and useful today – that best exemplified Scherer's and Schmidt's desire to grasp both the totality of the writer and his complex relation to his world. Nevertheless, their approach had its limits and by 1910 was superseded by Dilthey's *Geistesgeschichte* ('intellectual history') in German universities. Although Dilthey was generous in his praise for Scherer's *Poetik*, he explicitly rejected the attempt to imitate the epistemic framework of the natural sciences. Where these seek to 'explain' (*erklären*) phenomena as the effect of impersonal forces, practitioners of the human and social sciences should aim to 'understand' (*verstehen*): to come into contact with the lived experience of a writer,

---

[10]   Erich Schmidt, 'Wege und Ziele der deutschen Literaturgeschichte' ('Ways and Goals of German Literary History') in *Charakteristiken* ('Character Studies') (Berlin: Weidmann, 1886), p. 491.

a hermeneutical recapturing of the past that requires imagination and empathy as well as reason.

## Evolution

If criticism was to assume the mantle of science, it was inevitable that it would turn to the most powerful and culturally significant theory in the second half of the nineteenth century: Darwinism. Already anthropologists and ethnologists had tried to elucidate the genesis of art and literature in evolutionary terms. Darwin himself suggested that the lyric poem might have its roots in the mating calls of primitive hominids, and similar theories were advanced by Karl Groos in *Die Spiele der Thiere* ('The Play of Animals', 1896) and its sequel *Die Spiele der Menschen* ('The Play of Man', 1899), Ernst Grosse in *Anfänge der Kunst* ('Beginnings of Art', 1894), Charles Letourneau in *L'Evolution littéraire dans les diverses races humaines* ('Literary Evolution Among the Various Human Races', 1894), and Konrad Lange in *Das Wesen der Kunst* ('The Nature of Art', 1901).

By far the most systematic and sustained application of evolutionism to literary criticism was undertaken by Ferdinand Brunetière (1849–1906), professor at the Ecole Normale and editor-in-chief of the *Revue des deux mondes*. In his *L'Evolution des genres dans l'histoire de la littérature* ('The Evolution of Genres in the History of Literature', 1890) and elsewhere, he applauded Taine's efforts to import the procedures of natural science into the study of literature. Yet that did not make criticism a science as such. Brunetière may have attacked the subjectivism and impressionism of commentators such as Anatole France, but he also reproached Taine – not without some justification – for going too far by treating a text as an 'archival document', an imprint of the culture and epoch in which it came into being, and not as a thing in its own right. Criticism, he declared, must be directed towards the work itself and not the author or his surroundings: otherwise it loses sight of its business of judging, classifying and explaining the work according to *aesthetic* as well as scientific principles and is reduced to little more than an annex of history or psychology. By enlisting the theory of evolution Brunetière believed that he would be better equipped not only to discern the causal mechanisms of literary growth and decline, but also to put criticism on a sounder footing *and* refocus its evaluative gaze on its proper object.

Brunetière's first step was to dispense with Taine's trinity of external forces, which he decided were superfluous, in favour of an impulse supposedly inherent in literature itself and part of the ubiquitous 'silent movement' that shapes the world around us. The 'evolutionary method', which follows the same principles no matter whether it is employed in biology or criticism, attempts to 'comprehend and determine the nature, direction, force and character of this movement'.[11] In truth, however, Brunetière's understanding of evolution relies more on Herbert Spencer than it does on Darwin. Unlike Darwin, Spencer alleged that biological evolution was just one instance of a 'law of progress' unfolding on a cosmic scale – visible 'in the development of the Earth, in the development of Life upon its surface, the development of Society, of Government, of Manufactures, of Commerce, of Language, Literature, Science, Art'[12] – and consisting in the expansion of all phenomena from simple and incoherent states to conditions of structural complexity; or, in Spencer's well-known formula, 'the transformation of the homogeneous into the heterogeneous'. Brunetière simply takes that definition and applies it exclusively and explicitly to criticism, concluding that literary genres are analogous to zoological species and subject to the same laws: 'Without doubt, the differentiation of genres operates in history like that of species in nature, progressively, by the transition of one into many, from the simple to the complex, from the homogeneous to the heterogeneous.'[13]

Importantly and controversially, Brunetière saw genres not as an arbitrary label attached to entities sharing a family resemblance, but as the building blocks of literary evolution, present in some elementary fashion even before the actual creation of the work. In the same way that Darwin had introduced a new genealogical system of classification to replace the older ones of Linnaeus and Cuvier (in Brunetière's assessment every advance in science is due to innovations in taxonomy), the new criticism, modelled on the theory of descent, adopts the 'genealogical point of view'. The critic examines not the writer or work in isolation, or in the context of his milieu, but his relations to his predecessors, contemporaries and successors in the lineage of a given genre.

The concept of evolution, Brunetière continues, explains not only how genres burgeon forth, but also how and why, after achieving maturity, they are eventually supplanted by others in a competitive 'struggle for existence', degenerate and become extinct or slowly metamorphose into new kinds. It explains, too, how 'formes *inférieures*' can persist because they are adapted to stable and less taxing conditions of existence (in primitive cultures, for example). Most crucially, it explains what Taine's doctrine – with its conjuring of impersonal and uniformly acting

---

[11]  Ferdinand Brunetière, 'La doctrine évolutive et l'histoire de la littérature' in *Etudes critiques sur l'histoire de la littérature française* (Paris: Hachette, 1905), p. 16.

[12]  Herbert Spencer, 'Progess: Its Law and Causes' (1857) in *Essays: Scientific, Political and Speculative*, 3 vols. (London: Williams & Norgate, 1891), vol. I, p. 10.

[13]  Ferdinand Brunetière, *L'Evolution des genres dans l'histoire de la littérature* (Paris: Hachette, 1922), p. 20.

forces – is unable to account for: the uniqueness of writers, a variable that, for Brunetière, holds the key to the patterning of literary history. Take the example of brothers Pierre and Thomas Corneille. They were born of the same race, at the same moment, in the same milieu – and yet they possessed vastly different talent and hence vastly different significance. Because it implies contingency and chance, natural selection (and here Brunetière reverts to more orthodox Darwinism) enables Brunetière, or so he surmises, to transcend Taine's more rigid determinism and to cast light on the emergence of men of genius. For the motor of both biological and literary evolution is the *'divergence of characters'*.[14] Just as Darwin resolved the question of the origin of species by observing that, for some mysterious reason, even when members of a population are exposed to the same environmental influences, random variations can occur in individual organisms that alter the development of the species, so Brunetière maintains that from time to time there appear individual figures who have the power to modify the course of literature and to inaugurate new literary genres. Genius is therefore what Darwin called a 'sport' – a conceit also entertained by John Matthews Manly, who, rejecting a gradualist approach, applied the mutation theory of Hugo de Vries to literary evolution to explain the sudden, unprecedented advent of novel forms.[15]

Brunetière thought his broad construal of 'Darwinism' also yielded objective criteria for literary judgement. If the burden of criticism was to classify a particular work in relation to the progress of its genre, then it was at the peak of that genre's maturity that it should be measured. The higher a work appeared on the upward trajectory of generic development, the greater its value. In this way, critical judgement supposedly no longer depended on personal taste, but followed ineluctably from evolutionary principles observable in the phylogeny of literature. Needless to say, Brunetière's system is deeply problematic. Who decides when a genre has reached its height – something that can be settled only retrospectively, and which must inevitably remain a subjective verdict? By what yardstick does one establish how far removed from this point a given work of art is? In what sense do genres exist autonomously?

Brunetière was by no means the only critic to claim the theory of evolution in the name of criticism. For John Addington Symonds (1840–93), art – like everything else belonging to human nature – is in a state of transition and 'exhibits qualities analogous to those of an organic complex undergoing successive phases of germination, expansion, efflorescence,

---

[14] *Ibid.*, p. 20.
[15] John Matthews Manly, 'Literary Forms and the New Theory of the Origin of Species', *Modern Philology*, 4 (1907), 577–95.

and decay'. Artistic evolution is the unfolding of a wholly necessary and predetermined process to which even the 'prime agents', the 'men of genius', are subordinated.[16] These cycles of growth and dissolution are structurally identical regardless of the mode of artistic expression: Italian painting (*Renaissance in Italy*, 1887) passes through the very same stages as Elizabethan drama (*Shakspere's Predecessors in the English Drama*, 1884), though Symonds does allow for the existence of 'hybrid' types such as Roman tragedy. Such a scheme, he is confident, promises to deliver criticism from 'the caprice of connoisseurship and the whims of dilettantism' by concentrating on 'tracing and explaining what Goethe and Oken termed the *morphology* of their subject'. Symonds's ideal critic is the 'scientific analyst', the 'natural historian of art and literature', who inspects 'each object in relation to its antecedents and its consequents'; who, rather like Taine, 'makes himself acquainted with the conditions under which the artist grew, the habits of his race, the opinions of his age, his physical and psychological peculiarities'. But this is only the beginning of his task. For even the rigorously scientific critic 'cannot abnegate the right to judge'. As such it is his 'supreme duty' to train his faculty of judgement and to temper the inevitable intrusion of subjectivity into his work not only by studying things in their historical connections, but also by reflecting deeply on the canons underlying his evaluations. 'To this extent, then, through the perception of what criticism ought to be, through the definition of its province, and through the recognition of what is inevitably imperfect in its instrument, the method tends to being in its own way scientific.' And by 'scientific' Symonds has in mind something rather like the German concept of *Wissenschaft*; criticism ultimately has less in common with geology or mathematics than with disciplines such as ethics or political economy, being 'a department of systematised and coordinated knowledge'.[17]

Hutcheson Macaulay Posnett trod a different path. In his *Comparative Literature* (1886), a book avowedly indebted to the thought of Spencer and the historian Henry Maine, he transfers to the history of literature their thesis of a passage from the homogeneous to the heterogeneous, from collective to individual life. He is thus principally concerned with the ways in which *social* evolution and environmental influences on culture affect the 'progress and decay' of literary expression, manifested in the 'deepening and widening of personality'. His focus is the relation of the solitary human being to the group: 'In the orderly changes through which this relation has passed, as revealed by the comparison of literatures belonging to different social states, we find our main reasons for

---

[16] John Addington Symonds, *Essays, Speculative and Suggestive*, 2 vols. (London: Chapman & Hall, 1890), vol. I, pp. 57–8.
[17] *Ibid.*, pp. 10, 12, 66, 98–9, 78, 70.

treating literature as capable of scientific explanation.' Though he concedes that there are other standpoints from which the art and criticism of literature may be considered – for example, the 'statical influences' comprising the climate, soil, animal and plant life of different countries – these are insufficient by themselves to grasp 'the secrets of literary workmanship'. It was therefore necessary to adopt 'the gradual expansion of social life, from clan to city, from city to nation, from both of these to cosmopolitan humanity, as the proper order of our studies of comparative literature'.[18]

As envisaged by Posnett, then, comparative literature was a quasi-scientific enterprise that saw itself as an adjunct to Victorian ethnology. This outlook was shared by two of Posnett's successors, Francis B. Gummere and A. S. Mackenzie. Gummere's *The Beginnings of Poetry* (1901) is similarly preoccupied with the differentiation of human societies throughout history and the way this movement is mirrored in their literature. His aim is to plot the 'evolutionary curves' of early 'communal' and modern 'artistic' poetry, and pinpoint the moment at which they diverge. Dissociating himself from Brunetière, Gummere claims to be interested not in the genealogy of specific poets and genres, but in poetry as such, or rather with the 'elements' of poetry. A ballad, for example, cannot be traced back to a primitive form; yet its component parts – such as choral singing, dancing, improvisation – certainly can. The same goes for the distinguishing characteristics of the later 'poetry of art' (e.g. variation): these elements must be confronted with 'ethnological and sociological facts' to determine the course and mechanisms of poetic evolution.[19]

For Mackenzie, author of *The Evolution of Literature* (1911), an 'objective criticism of literature' that would 'attain to the dignity or even a semblance of science' was possible only by broadening and deepening our conception of what constituted 'literary art' and by regarding its study as a 'subdivision of anthropology', which he called 'Literatology'. This research involves more than mere 'literary Darwinism' or the transposition of biological concepts such as the struggle for existence or natural selection, which he insists are wholly inadequate for explaining human activities. Instead Mackenzie investigates the different artefacts of the four stages of culture that he discriminates – Primitiveness, Barbarism, Autocracy, Democracy – in order to arrive at laws governing the origin and transformation of literature as a whole and the constant interplay between it and society. Thus, his inquiry is not confined to a single genre or culturally discrete type but seeks out the structural similarities

18   Hutcheson Macauley Posnett, *Comparative Literature* (London: Kegan Paul, 1886), pp. 72, 86, 20, 86.
19   Francis B. Gummere, *The Beginnings of Poetry* (Freeport, NY: Books for Libraries Press, 1970), pp. 27, 28.

underlying all forms of literary expression, irrespective of their historical, geographical or ethnic context. Indeed, he thought his scientific and
comparative method would pave the way for 'the ultimate brotherhood
of humanity' and enable men more readily to 'appreciate that cosmopolitan literature which is beginning to knit the peoples of the earth in a
spiritual unity'. He deduces three 'provisional' laws (provisional because,
like all scientific hypotheses, they can be falsified): the Law of Progress,
the Law of Initiative and the Law of Responsiveness, each of which can
be expressed as a mathematical formula. Thus, for example, the Law
of Progress states that $A = S + W$ (or 'the average literary advance in a
given community is directly proportional to the width and depth of man's
attainment of consciousness of self and of the world').[20]

## Sociology and early reception theory

In his 1888 book *La Critique scientifique* Emile Hennequin (1859–88)
signalled his break with traditional criticism by proposing a new mode
of research that he called 'aesthopsychology'. Defined as 'the science of
the work of art as sign', this line of investigation was, as Hennequin happily acknowledged, inspired by Taine; but, like Brunetière, Hennequin
offered a corrective to what he saw as the insufficiencies of his predecessor's theory, which he thought valid only for relatively simple cultures
and their products. Instead he emphasized the individuality of the author,
his public and the texture of the work itself – indeed, the purpose of criticism was to describe how the last is a reflection of the former two (but
not to evaluate this relationship). Hennequin's programme comprised
three separate levels of analysis, each guided by a different scientific
methodology – the aesthetic, the psychological, the sociological – and
each with its own object.

The first step in the *critique scientifique* is to determine the exact nature
of the 'aesthetic' emotions aroused by a literary work; that is to say, the
distinct and intensely personal psychical phenomena that, unlike 'real'
emotions, are not translated into actions and remain ends in themselves.
The analyst then proceeds to a careful appraisal of the formal properties
of a text with the aim of discovering the means by which the author, both
wittingly and unwittingly, provokes these states of consciousness in the
reader – his vocabulary, cadences, way of framing sentences and para-
graphs, punctuation, tone, choice of subjects, scenes, characters, themes,
metaphor and so on. Hennequin, then, is not interested in beauty for

---

[20] A. S. Mackenzie, *The Evolution of Literature* (New York: Crowell, 1911), pp. 2, 392,
6, 8, 396.

its own sake: aesthetic considerations are preliminary, much as 'pure physics uses the laws of mechanics'. The second stage requires the critic to infer the *faits mentaux*, the intellectual and moral characteristics of the author, from the *indices esthétiques*, the artistic particularities and strategies of his work – the presumption being that if certain conceptual or stylistic elements are present in a text the author must possess a corresponding ability, the 'requisite mental organization', bodied forth or signified by them. To achieve its goal, namely 'the complete knowledge of a mind' through its artefacts, the *critique scientifique* borrows from the resources of experimental psychology (Hennequin himself appeals to authorities such as Spencer, Taine and the alienist Henry Maudsley), with a promise to repay its debt by making its results available to future research, thus rendering to psychology 'the same services as human dissection to medicine'.[21]

The final 'sociological' part of Hennequin's project is the most arresting. He suggests that the critic should not probe the background of an artist but rather draw conclusions about his readers (of whom the work is also a 'sign'), for these must have a mindset analogous to his own: that is why his work appeals to them and why they respond in the way that they do. The artist creates his own audience, in other words, and it is by building up a profile of this audience that the spirit of a nation can be revealed: 'a literature expresses a nation, not because the latter produces it but because it adopts and admires it'.[22] Hennequin's own 'aesthopsychological' analysis of Victor Hugo, for example, purports to show that Hugo's devotees share the same traits displayed by both the author and the works he composed – verbalism, exaggeration, simple-mindedness, lack of ideas, impracticality, humanitarian optimism and socialism. We thus get a sense (a vague one, admittedly), through the case of Hugo and his public, of the intellectual peculiarities and defects of the French people in general, and of the literary classes in particular, from 1830 to 1886.

This concern with how works and their authors are received is shared by Gustave Lanson (1857–1934), one of the leading exponents of literary positivism in France. In an essay entitled 'L'esprit scientifique et la méthode de l'histoire littéraire' ('The Scientific Spirit and the Method of Literary History', 1909),[23] Lanson contended that criticism was irreducibly though legitimately impressionistic and that the 'scientific method of literary history' consisted in being able to distinguish between one's cognitive and emotional response to literature and to reduce the role of

[21] Emile Hennequin, *La Critique scientifique*, 2nd edn (Paris: Librairie académique Didier, 1890), pp. 22, 67, 88, 92.
[22] *Ibid.*, p. 162.
[23] Gustave Lanson, 'L'esprit scientifique et la méthode de l'histoire littéraire' in *Méthodes de l'histoire littéraire* (Paris: Les Belles Lettres, 1925), pp. 21–37.

the latter to a minimum. A few years earlier, however, he had gone much further in mapping out a scientific approach to literature.

In 'L'histoire littéraire et la sociologie' ('Literary History and Sociology', 1904), Lanson places the reception of literature at the centre of what he calls 'literary sociology'. The advantage of the 'sociological point of view', he contends, is that it 'helps to orient ourselves in factual research, to formulate problems, and to interpret results; it expands, elevates and above all specifies our studies'. More specifically, Lanson is thereby led to formulate six 'inductive, relative, approximate laws of limited scope' that describe the dynamic and shifting interrelations between society, texts and their readers.[24] For example, the 'law of correlation between literature and life' states that literature expresses not just, as Taine argued, the manners and mentality of a society, but also its desires and dreams. Literature compensates for the deficiencies and dreariness of everyday existence and, by giving voice to tomorrow's reality rather than today's only, it anticipates or creates the conditions for new readers. But if books affect their readers directly, by helping to establish unity in the intellectual or emotional life of social groups, by forging communities, by acting as conductors of public opinion, then the opposite is also true: literature is transformed, enriched, impoverished and distorted by subsequent generations, and the meaning of a work, along with the idiosyncrasies of its author, may dissolve into the changing image that posterity develops of them.

This process can be observed in the production of masterpieces. These are the result of a collaborative effort not only because they are the culmination and crystallization of numerous previous ventures tending in the same direction, but also because the public seeks and projects itself into a text (even if unconsciously), demanding its appearance. If a work is too innovative, however, it will be rejected and revived only when its potential readership is ready. In this way, literary history accommodates a large sociological dimension: the conditions under which a text is not only produced but also successively received reveal a complex network of social determinants and cultural presuppositions.

### Medical materialism

Few critics have enjoyed the spectacular (if short-lived) international success of Max Nordau (1849–1923). His *Entartung* (1892; translated into

---

[24] Gustave Lanson, 'L'histoire littéraire et la sociologie' (1904) in *Essais de méthode, de critique et d'histoire littéraire* (Paris: Hachette, 1965), pp. 61–80; a translation by Nicholas T. Rand and Roberta Hatcher appeared as 'Literary History and Sociology', *PMLA*, 110 (1995), 220–35 (p. 230).

English as *Degeneration* in 1895), one of Europe's ten best-selling books of the 1890s, was a cranky and cantankerous polemic against modern art and literature, one that seemed to channel perfectly the anxieties of *fin de siècle* cultural decadence. Yet although it was dismissed as sensational, philistine and downright wrongheaded by figures such as George Bernard Shaw, it is worthwhile noting that Nordau, who was a physician as well as a novelist and journalist, intended his jeremiad as 'an attempt at a really scientific criticism, which does not base its judgment of a book upon the purely accidental, capricious, and variable emotions it awakens – emotions depending on the temperament and mood of the individual reader – but upon the psycho-physiological elements from which it sprang'.[25] In other words, Nordau advocated a reductively medicalized version of literary criticism: texts were no longer – as with Taine and Hennequin – merely signs of an individual or collective mentality but actual symptoms of an author's underlying neurological disorder, which it was the job of the alienist-critic to diagnose. The value of a work of art did not lie in a reader's subjective and unquantifiable response but was, rather, a function of the measurable health of its creator.

Nordau's screed draws its title and authority from one of the most potent scientific discourses of the late nineteenth century. Degeneration was the flipside of evolution: the appalling human costs exacted by the rapid urbanization and industrialization of Western societies had cast doubt on the Victorian faith in progress. Europe – or so it seemed – was sliding inexorably towards biological and cultural ruin, the overpopulated slums of its major cities the breeding-ground for a new, atavistic subspecies and the hereditary social pathologies it carried. Nordau's originality was to extend the possibilities of who or what could be classed as 'degenerate'. 'Degenerates', he writes in his preface, 'are not always criminals, prostitutes, anarchists, and pronounced lunatics; they are often authors and artists.'[26] Accordingly, his aim is to prove, through individual case studies and a wealth of documentary evidence, that contemporary fashions in literature are at bottom merely 'manifestations of more or less pronounced moral insanity, imbecility, and dementia'.[27] Hence, Wagner and the Symbolists are examples of 'mysticism' ('the expression of the inaptitude for attention, for clear thought and control of the emotions, [which] has for its cause the weakness of the higher cerebral centres'); Nietzsche and Oscar Wilde (predictably enough) are revealed to be suffering from 'Ego-mania' ('an effect of the faulty transmission by the sensory nerves, of obtuseness in the centres of perception, of aberration of instincts from a craving for sufficiently strong impressions, and of the

---

[25] Max Nordau, *Degeneration* (Lincoln: University of Nebraska Press, 1993), p. vi.
[26] *Ibid.*, p. v.   [27] *Ibid.*, p. vi.

great predominance of organic sensations over representative consciousness'); and Zola is a typical specimen of 'false Realism' (characterized by
'pessimism and the irresistible tendency to licentious ideas, and the most
vulgar and unclean modes of expression').[28]

The depravity of these figures is exhibited not so much in their often
distasteful subject matter as in their shared commitment to formal experimentation. Nordau opposed the invention of new genres not only because
he believed that the ancient ones were flexible enough but because these
'had been given by the nature of human thought itself'.[29] Only once our
cognitive apparatus had evolved in a different direction would there be
any need for literary or artistic innovation – and this would arise quite
spontaneously. Degenerate writers are degenerate precisely because they
have deviated from the mainstream of literary and biological evolution.

'A pathological book on a pathological subject' was how William James
aptly described *Entartung*, and it is in Nordau that we see at its most striking the gap between a critic's avowed commitment to scientific objectivity and the moral prepossessions that inform his judgements. Nordau's
literal-mindedness and obliquity are often staggering, yet his overnight
notoriety led to a trend for 'pathographies' or retrospective diagnoses of
famous writers that sought to demonstrate how mental or physical illness
shaped their creative work. While these later critics (who were mostly psy-
chiatrists and doctors) did not – like Nordau – explicitly aim to discredit
a writer by dwelling on his medical history, there was nevertheless still a
tendency to 'explain' entirely with reference to his morbidity, as if that
were the only influence operative on his imagination. Perhaps the most
prominent pathographer in Germany (where this genre of criticism seems
to have been most at home) was Paul Julius Möbius (1853–1907), who
wrote seminal treatises on Goethe (1898), Nietzsche (1902), Schopenhauer (1904) and Schumann (1906).

Nordau's book is dedicated to Cesare Lombroso, whose much-
translated *Genio e follia* ('Genius and Madness', 1863) helped bring up
to date Dryden's dictum that 'Great wits are sure to madness near allied.'
Perhaps the foremost British critic to follow in Lombroso's footsteps,
and the man responsible for introducing his ideas to an English-speaking
public, was Havelock Ellis (1859–1939). As early as 1885 he described
criticism as 'a complex development of psychological science',[30] and speculation about the nature and heredity of genius remained almost his sole
preoccupation as a literary commentator. In his preface to *The New
Spirit* (1890) he describes the subsequent essays on representative writers

[28] *Ibid.*, p. 536.    [29] *Ibid.*, p. 545.
[30] Havelock Ellis, 'The Present Position of English Criticism' (1885) in *Views and Reviews*
(London: Harmsworth, 1932), p. 37.

of the age as so many 'sphygmographic tracings' (that is, records of the rate, strength and uniformity of the arterial pulse):[31] here he is interested in the personalities of men of genius as revealed by their works. The work is explained as the product of a particular temperament, and the temperament is in turn explained as the product of particular geographical and genealogical factors. Thus, Ibsen's disposition 'to philosophic abstraction and... strenuous earnestness, mingling with the more characteristically northern imaginative influences', are due to his combined Scottish and German ancestry.[32] Or the peculiarities of Addison's prose style are imputed to his Scandinavian forebears.

These assumptions about the 'etiology' of genius are elaborated in a later article, in which Ellis, oppugning the eugenicist Francis Galton, examines the 'racial' extraction of five poets generally acknowledged as geniuses by the Victorians (Tennyson, Browning, Swinburne, Rossetti and Morris) and of seven other living writers. The proportion of 'mixed and foreign blood' in these two groups, Ellis finds, is much greater than average and much greater than in scientific or political geniuses. Imaginative genius, he concludes, is at least partly the result of crossbreeding between two European races, the tall, fair Nordic race and the short, dark Celtic race.[33]

Ellis outlines another approach to the nature of literary genius in 'The Colour-Sense in Literature', providing statistical tables that set forth the frequency with which the names of basic colours occur in the works of a number of British poets from Chaucer onwards. This technique, he claims, 'enables us to take a definite step in the attainment of a scientific aesthetic, by furnishing a means of comparative study'. The subject of this comparative study, however, is not the tenor of the poems in which these colour-words appear, but rather the characters of the poets themselves. His statistics, according to Ellis, are 'an instrument for investigating a writer's personal psychology, by defining the nature of his aesthetic colour-vision'.[34]

## Inductive and judicial criticism

Most of the critics considered thus far have tended to view literature as a natural product shaped by certain historical, psychological, evolutionary, sociological forces and to understand it in the light of such external

---

[31] Havelock Ellis, *The New Spirit* (London: Bell, 1890), p. v.   [32] *Ibid.*, p. 137.
[33] Havelock Ellis, 'The Ancestry of Genius' (1893) in *Views and Reviews*, pp. 68–85.
[34] Havelock Ellis, 'The Colour-Sense in Literature', *Contemporary Review*, 69 (1896), p. 729.

agencies. A very different conception of scientific criticism is advanced by Richard Green Moulton (1849–1924), who prefaces his book *Shakespeare as a Dramatic Critic* (1885) with a 'plea for an inductive science of literary criticism' that would be distinct from and eventually supersede the older 'judicial criticism', given to prescriptive fault-finding and belletristic trifling, and would examine 'the phenomena of literature as they actually stand, enquiring into and endeavouring to systematise the laws and principles by which they are moulded and produce their effects'. Such a development would not only crown the gradual movement away from judgement and towards analysis which Moulton claims to detect in the annals of literary criticism, but indeed mark an advance for science itself, whose 'whole progress... consists in winning fresh fields of thought to the inductive methods'. Nevertheless, he does concede to judicial criticism a role in literary study, but one that is entirely without the realm of science: 'It finds its proper place on the creative side of literature, as a branch in which literature itself has come to be taken as a theme for literary writing; it thus belongs to the literature treated, not to the scientific treatment thereof.'[35] It is the failure to keep judicial and analytical criticism separate that has resulted in the muddled thinking and falsehoods associated with traditional reviews.

If an inductive science is, according to Moulton's rather perfunctory definition, a branch of knowledge occupied directly with facts, then, in the case of literature, these facts are to be 'observed' only in the text itself and not in the author's biography or milieu. Yet the aesthetic 'details' of a work are notoriously open to the most diverse interpretation: different readers are often left with conflicting impressions of a book or poem. This does not imply that the content of literature lacks positivity, because other sciences like astronomy and psychology routinely face the same uncertainty with respect to the observation of phenomena. The inductive critic must therefore attempt to reconcile the range of possible individual responses with the text's objective features, which represent 'the *limit* on the variability of the subjective impressions'. The interpretation of literature is then analogous to a 'scientific hypothesis, the truth of which is tested by the degree of completeness with which it explains the details of the literary work as they actually stand. That will be the true meaning of a passage, not which is the most worthy, but which most nearly explains the words as they are; that will be the true reading of a character which, however involved in expression or tame in effect, accounts for and reconciles all that is represented of the personage.' In this way, the critic should

---

[35] Richard G. Moulton, *Shakespeare as a Dramatic Critic: A Popular Illustration of the Principles of Scientific Criticism* (Oxford: Clarendon Press, 1885), pp. 22, 1, 21–2.

be able to arrive at 'a superstructure of exposition' which relies not on some given authority, but rather 'upon a basis of indisputable fact'.[36]

Moulton thus suggests that the chief office of inductive criticism is to distinguish 'literary species' and provide descriptions of authorial practice that will generate general propositions rather than disconnected details. For literature is a 'part of nature' and 'thing of development' that falls into varieties distinct in kind from one another. Only by freeing himself from historical prejudices and the interference of fixed standards of judgement, by according to 'the early forms of his art the same independence he accords to later forms', will the critic become a real scientific investigator and fully grasp the unique characteristics of each work and the variety to which it belongs.[37]

Far from insisting on a sharp division between scientific and judicial criticism, John MacKinnon Robertson recognized that, as 'a way of teaching, a means of propaganda, a method of trying to persuade other people to think as we do', all criticism is to a greater or lesser degree judicial. To overcome or compensate for its built-in partiality, criticism must not seek to parody the procedures or concepts of natural science – 'since neither microscope nor scalpel, neither re-agent nor hammer, can be applied to literary problems' – but rather to learn from its epistemology. Science for Robertson amounts to little more than 'ordered and concatenated explanation' or a habit of consistency. Hence criticism can only improve if its practitioners acquire this habit in their judgements: 'just as consistency in propositions is the test of truth, just as relatedness or harmony in things or aspects is the source and criterion of visible beauty, so a twofold consistency, logical and aesthetic, is the test of rightness in criticism; the starting-point in the one case as in the other being, not any absolute theory of truth or beauty, but just a certain measure of common opinion'.[38] Like science, criticism is not a solitary enterprise but a dialectical and collective process. It necessitates reasoning from a common ground to a new ground, on the basis of established facts, so that a certain amount of rational agreement among a certain number of educated people can be achieved; this agreement serves in turn as the point of departure for new criticism and even new literary production.

Robertson's 'critical science' not only depends on consistent argument; it is, furthermore, the 'science of consistency in appreciation, since the science of that would involve the systematic study of all the causes – in ourselves, in a book, and in an author – which go to determine our individual judgements'. In a sense Robertson's idea of scientific criticism is

[36] *Ibid.*, p. 25.    [37] *Ibid.*, pp. 32, 36, 37, 39.

[38] John MacKinnon Robertson, 'Theory and Practice of Criticism' in *New Essays Towards a Critical Method* (London: Fisher Unwin, 1897), pp. 43, 16–17.

psychological, because it embraces the study of mental characteristics. It is not, however, the mental characteristics of the author that are of primary importance, but those of the critic. His task is to examine his own trains of thought 'scientifically' to ensure that he does not, in his pronouncements, betray the discrepancies and one-sidedness that his initial, naïve response must inevitably contain. If he is unable to share the widespread applause for a particular author, it is his business as a scrupulous critic to weigh the praise of others, to ask himself whether he has missed something, to consider the cast of mind of 'those who bestow it, and then, if he thinks he can, to explain it in terms of the prejudice, or limitation, or deficient culture of the admirers; or, if he cannot, to seek *objectively* for the merits which delight them'.

Robertson thus demands a metacriticism, 'a criticism of criticism' that is ever alert to the necessarily provisional nature of literary judgement and to its complex determinants. The 'perfect scientific critic' would be watchful, self-aware and qualify 'his every judgment... with a confession of faith, bias, temperament, and training'. In this way, judgements come to be refined over time and to approach as closely as possible the goal, unattainable in practice, of value-neutrality. And while the status of literary truth is of a different order to that in the natural sciences (no critical proposition is verifiable in the same way as, say, the law of gravity), criticism has much to gain from channelling the 'spirit of science', in the same way as neighbouring disciplines such as jurisprudence have benefited from it: 'first, in the mere habit of exactitude, the avoidance of inconsistency, the sense of the importance of proofs; secondarily, in the probable stimulus to speculative or theorising thought; and ultimately in the probable widening of philosophic view in general, and of estimate of human capacity in particular'.[39]

Efforts to establish a scientific criticism met with little success in the nineteenth century and did not last long into the next one (although I. A. Richards's demand that criticism be 'a cooperative technique of enquiry that may become entitled to be named a science'[40] is a rare later example). This failure can in part be attributed to the fact that most of the writers we have considered erected theoretical edifices resting on rather shaky foundations. Their systems possessed endemic weaknesses; they borrowed concepts whose application beyond the domain for which they were originally designed is dubious, illicit or misleading, and exposed themselves to the same charges of subjectivism and caprice that they levelled at traditional commentators. Another reason for the failure of a scientific criticism is the sheer number and diversity of the schemes

[39] *Ibid.*, pp. 17, 24, 24–5, 43.
[40] I. A. Richards, *Coleridge on Imagination* (London: Kegan Paul, 1934), p. xii.

advanced. This meant that there was little or no agreement – beyond a shared desire for reform – about the definition or function of criticism. What is criticism? What are its objects? Its ambit? Its methodology? Is it an independent science? Or merely a branch of other, already established disciplines? What is the nature of aesthetic judgement? The inability of the writers discussed here to provide persuasive answers to these questions meant that, while a contemporary like Edward Dowden endorsed their wish that the practice of criticism stretch beyond mere dilettantish appreciation of beauty and 'be exact and thorough or it is of little worth', he also cautioned that critics should not lose sight of the bigger picture: 'that we do not forget the end of study in the means, that we somehow and at some time get beyond the apparatus'.[41] His warning, however, went unheeded.

[41] Edward Dowden, 'Hopes and Fears for Literature', Fortnightly Review, 45 (1889), pp. 182–3.

# 31

# Literature and the arts

BETH S. WRIGHT

## Introduction: the new audience and the breakdown of 'ut pictura poesis'

A dizzying variety of visual and literary styles developed between 1830 and 1914, including Romanticism, Realism and Pre-Raphaelitism, Naturalism and Impressionism, Symbolism, Cubism and Futurism. The many innovative relationships between literature and the arts encompassed a proliferation of illustrated texts and graphic works carrying captions; a more prominent role for art criticism; styles of writing which stressed visual descriptiveness; and connections between the visual, theatrical and musical arts. Underlying these developments was a challenge to the long-standing analogy 'ut pictura poesis' ('as is painting, so is poetry'), coined by Horace and taken up especially in the Renaissance.

Based on social and economic assumptions regarding scale, site, public and patron, this analogy had proposed a union between style, subject, content and audience in the so-called 'hierarchy of genres'.[1] In this aesthetic and thematic hierarchy, historical painting was presumed to embody eternally significant meaning – allegorical, religious and literary as well as historical – through idealized forms, smooth and regular contours, and areas of simplified colour. Genre painting, lower in the hierarchy, was viewed as representing the contingent aspects of the real world, including even grotesque forms, dappled light and scintillating colour patches. The elite, both secular and religious, were expected to commission large-scale works to enlighten and inspire the public. But from the eighteenth century onwards, small-scale genre works were sold after their production to bourgeois private viewers, whose realistic vision of the world would be reaffirmed instead of elevated or idealized. Hence, in 1890, when Aurier called for a modern art 'at once subjective, synthetic, symbolic and ideist' and thereby free from easel-painting's commercialism, he was arguing for a return to this social and aesthetic system

---

[1] See, for example, Rensselaer Lee, 'Ut pictura poesis': The Humanistic Theory of Painting (New York: Norton, 1967).

588

in which lucid and inspirational visual art – being commissioned – was produced intentionally.[2]

The modern viewpoint, however, was not that of an omniscient observer looking back with the wisdom of hindsight but that of the 'flâneur', described in 1858 as 'a mobile and impassioned daguerreotype'.[3] The intersection of declining official support for the arts with the aggrandizement of individual consciousness meant that more and more avant-garde approaches to art were exhibited in alternative sites. Embattled artists wrote manifestos and sought literary champions. In 1846 Baudelaire called for informed critics capable of interpreting the 'anarchic liberty' of individual artists' technically and conceptually sophisticated work for a mass audience.[4] The number of periodicals devoted solely to art increased more than tenfold in France between 1820 and 1885, from six to sixty-five.[5]

Literary support for the arts was facilitated by authors having direct knowledge of art themselves as well as close friendships with artists. At times artist, author, aesthetician and art critic were one and the same person. Delacroix wrote poetry, novels and art-historical essays. Rossetti's poetry was written to accompany his paintings or inspired them. Gautier, poet and art critic, trained to become a painter (as did Fromentin, Jules de Goncourt and Thackeray); he served as president of the Société Nationale des Beaux-Arts. A newly literate mass audience craved increasingly visual texts: illustrated periodicals (*Illustrated London News*, *L'Illustration*), texts with hundreds of vignettes or with typographic displays (Mallarmé's plastic prose-poem 'Un coup de dés' [1897] used eleven typefaces).[6] Thackeray's illustrations to his own *Vanity Fair* (1847–8) acted dialogically with (or against) his text. Some publishers claimed that illustrators' textual commentary made them full partners of the authors.[7] Flaubert and Mallarmé refused to have their works illustrated.

As these inventive approaches to illustration indicate, the tendency in aesthetics between 1830 and 1914 was towards the expressive and affective rather than the mimetic. We shall see a development from

2  G. Albert Aurier, 'Le Symbolisme en peinture: Paul Gauguin' in *Symbolist Art Theories. A Critical Anthology*, ed. Henri Dorra (Berkeley: University of California Press, 1994), pp. 200–1.
3  Victor Fournel, *Ce qu'on voit dans les rues* (Paris: Delahaye, 1858), p. 261.
4  Charles Baudelaire, 'Salon de 1846' in *Curiosités esthétiques: l'art romantique*, ed. H. Lemaître (Paris: Garnier, 1990), p. 194.
5  See Gustave Lebel, 'Bibliographie des revues et périodiques d'art parus en France de 1746 à 1914', *Gazette des beaux-arts*, 38 (1951), pp. 49, 57.
6  Michel Melot, 'Le texte et l'image' in *Histoire de l'édition française*, eds. Roger Chartier and Henri-Jean Martin, 4 vols. (Paris: Promodis, 1985), vol. III, p. 287.
7  Beth S. Wright, '"That Other Historian, the Illustrator": Voices and Vignettes in Mid-Nineteenth-Century France', *Oxford Art Journal*, 23 (2000), pp. 120, 134.

art and literature based on *sensation* (Romanticism) to one based on *form* (Realism, Pre-Raphaelitism and Victorian art), the analysis of *effect* (Naturalist literature and Impressionist art), *symbol* (Post-Impressionism and Symbolism), and finally the *dynamic fusion of space and time* (Cubism and Futurism). By 'prolonging the sensation', Romantic artists like Delacroix communicated an inspiring literary text's content in paintings or lithographs which retained the visual medium's full potency. Realist and Pre-Raphaelite artists rejected Romanticism's expression of the artist's subjectivity for a representation of material reality which could be read as an anecdotal narrative. The recognition that objective reality is seen according to subjective, differentiated responses (compare Zola's adage that a work of art was 'a corner of creation seen through a temperament') led to the next stage in Naturalist literature and Impressionist visual art: observation itself, the dynamic process of responding to the world, became the theme of the work as 'open air' melted form into effects of light and colour.[8] Then in Symbolism, truth was sought in a subjectivity more universal and eternal than would be possible for any individual in any transient instant: in the Idea, the dream, the mythic construction of the human condition, intuitively present in psychic consciousness. Finally in Cubism and Futurism consciousness was analysed metaphysically, to include time as well as space.

## Romanticism: 'prolong the sensation'

Delacroix believed that art should present forms as conduits to emotion and thought: 'like a solid bridge to support your imagination...amplifying where it is possible, and...prolonging the sensation by every means'. Each object in pre-existing reality needed to be transmuted before it could enter the artwork as an 'eloquent hieroglyph'.[9] In his works inspired by Shakespeare, Walter Scott or Goethe he went beyond representational figuration of a text's actions to visualize its content and expressive mood.[10] Goethe praised Delacroix's *Faust* (1827–8) for its lithographs: 'M. Delacroix has in some scenes surpassed my own vision.'[11]

[8]  Emile Zola, 'Les Réalistes au salon' in *Emile Zola: Salons*, ed. F. W. J. Hemmings and R. J. Niess (Geneva: Droz, 1959), p. 73.
[9]  Eugène Delacroix, *The Journal of Eugène Delacroix*, ed. Hubert Wellington, trans. Lucy Norton (London: Phaidon Press, 1995), pp. 213–14.
[10] See Beth S. Wright, 'Painting Thoughts: An Introduction to Delacroix' and Paul Joannides, 'Delacroix and Modern Literature' in *The Cambridge Companion to Delacroix*, ed. Beth S. Wright (Cambridge University Press, 2001), pp. 1–7, 130–53.
[11] J. W. von Goethe in *Conversations of Goethe with Johann Peter Eckermann*, ed. J. K. Moorhead (New York: Da Capo Press, 1998), p. 136.

Delacroix exemplified Romanticism for Baudelaire, who defined this style in his *Salon of 1846* as the pre-eminently modern mode of expression, seeking 'intimacy, spirituality, color, aspiration towards the infinite' in preference to representation. Baudelaire explained that Delacroix's 'melodious color' (as well as his facture and impasto), capable of stirring the spectator's emotions before the subject could be recognized, could amplify content because it was liberated from objective representation.[12] Such an art was diametrically opposed to the crisply representational pictorial narratives by Victorian and Pre-Raphaelite artists, which could be analysed and decoded with equal pleasure in graphic reproductions.

## Correspondences: Colour, Music and Literature

Analogies between colour and music recurred throughout the nineteenth century, from Delacroix's expression of mood and content to Whistler's abstracting harmonies from nature. Inspired by E. T. A. Hoffman's story of the musician Kreisler (1815), Baudelaire explored synaesthesia in his poetry, particularly in two poems published in *Les Fleurs du mal* (1857). In 'Correspondances' (1846) colours, scents and sounds corresponded with one another:

> Dans une ténébreuse et profonde unité,
> Vaste comme la nuit et comme la clarté,
> Les parfums, les couleurs et les sons se répondent.
>
> Into one deep and shadowy unison
> as limitless as darkness and as day,
> the sounds, the scents, the colors correspond.[13]

In 'Les Phares' (which he cited in his review of Delacroix's retrospective exhibition in the 1855 Exposition Universelle) Baudelaire compared Delacroix's colour harmonies of complementary red and green ('lake of blood darkened by the green shade of the firs') to the sound of fanfares in Weber's music (*FM*, p. 18).

Music itself was seeking such a union with the other arts. The revolutions of 1830 and 1848–9 and the Italian risorgimento in the 1860s, as well as Romanticism's yearning for a past age, stimulated an interest in themes relating to nationalist struggles. Experiments with local colour led to the inclusion of programmatic references to geography.

---

12  Michael Fried, 'Painting Memories: On the Containment of the Past in Baudelaire and Manet', *Critical Inquiry*, 10 (1984), p. 512.
13  Baudelaire, 'Correspondances' in *Les Fleurs du mal*, trans. Richard Howard (Boston: David R. Godine, 1982), p. 15. Hereafter cited as *FM*.

Folk references in the work of Chopin, Liszt, Grieg and Dvořák expanded harmonic, melodic, rhythmic, orchestral and instrumental vocabulary. Literary works by Shakespeare, Goethe, Walter Scott and Byron provided inspiration for works by Mendelssohn, Liszt, Tchaikovsky and other composers which 'told a story' in the succession of emotional moods. Berlioz, inspired by Shakespeare for his dramatic symphony *Roméo et Juliette* (1839), as well as by Goethe and Byron, also created a semi-confessional musical narrative of love and death, his *Symphonie fantastique* (1830).

The seeking of a more complete union of aural and narrative emotional expression stimulated opera's development into the pre-eminent musical form of the later nineteenth century. Verdi's and Wagner's enriched musical, thematic and visual presentations were simultaneously innovative and popular. Wagner had been impressed by Auber's 'Picturesque' in such 'music-paintings' of the 1820s and 1830s as his *La Muette de Portici* (1828), but he sought an even more powerful 'dramatic plasticity'. As he explained in *Das Kunstwerk der Zukunft* ('The Artwork of the Future', 1849) and *Oper und Drama* ('Opera and Drama', 1851), the *Gesamtkunstwerk* was to go beyond the Hegelian 'sensual appearance of the idea' to 'realize a poetic intent' capable of generating a 'communicative action'.[14] Instead of the rational sequencing and explicitness of narrative exposition, Wagner used the evocative power of myth and legend, expressed in 'a dream-state that quickly carries it on to perfect clairvoyance'.[15] When Wagner's works were performed in Paris in 1861, Baudelaire explained, citing Liszt, that Wagner's motifs were '*personifications of ideas*; their re-emergence is the signal for the renewed interplay of the feelings that the words spoken do not *explicitly indicate*'.[16] Wagner would stimulate the Symbolist authors and artists to promote an art based on subjectivism rather than the description of external action or appearance.


## Victorian and Pre-Raphaelite art: anecdote and significant form

While Romanticism's emphasis on subjectivity persisted throughout the nineteenth century, a new and opposed viewpoint arose which centred on material form. During the 1830s, artists (carrying recently invented tube paints) began to leave their studios and reproduce nature's light and

---

[14] Thomas S. Grey, *Wagner's Musical Prose: Texts and Contexts* (Cambridge University Press, 1995), pp. 96, 115, 155.
[15] Charles Baudelaire, 'Richard Wagner and *Tannhäuser* in Paris' in *Baudelaire: Selected Writings on Art and Artists*, trans. P. E. Charvet (Harmondsworth: Penguin, 1972), p. 339. Hereafter cited as *SW*.
[16] *Ibid.*, p. 350.

colour in *plein air* painting. Optical technological innovations included new media arts devoted to leisure entertainment (from the panorama and diorama at the beginning of the nineteenth century to the motion picture in 1895), scientific and medical inventions such as the X-ray, and above all the publication of the daguerreotype photographic process in 1839.

If artists were to provide an impassioned reproduction of the world's forms (one which new technologies were not yet capable of matching) it would be through narrative signification. Ruskin, who wished to maintain the power of the arts to educate and inspire, wrote that Victorian and Pre-Raphaelite painting was beginning 'to take its proper position beside literature' in offering the viewer an invented visual chronicle of the world pregnant with meaning.[17] For Ruskin each object in Holman Hunt's *The Awakening Conscience* required 'tragical' reading. It was not a replica of its real-world counterpart but a denotation of the female protagonist's anguish and resolution to turn away from sin: 'a mind...fevered by violent and distressful excitement' sees objects 'thrust themselves forward with a ghastly and unendurable distinctness'.[18]

Lessing's separation of the visual from the temporal arts in *Laokoon* (1766) was challenged. The hyper-illusionistic rendition of each significant object and figure dissolved compositional centrality and lucidity, a hallmark of historical painting. Frith's paintings were often compared to novels. The *Athenaeum*'s description of *The Derby Day* (1856–8) as a 'scene...as it were, in four volumes' acknowledged that its anecdotal prolixity required temporally extended spectatorship.[19] This succession of equalized visual anecdotes was antithetical to the 'visual instant' of neo-classical painting, with its centralized, eternal focal point. Rather than highlighting significant meaning, Frith's panoramic canvas appears to extend beyond the frame, uniting the multifarious experience of the spectator's reality with the feigned reality enclosed in the painting.

This concentration on significant form, whether in concrete reality or in artistic creations, meant subordinating such strictly pictorial aspects of facture, impasto and colouristic verve as Delacroix had employed to communicate content in his Romantic literary images. In contrast, Ruskin described art as 'nothing but a noble and expressive language, invaluable as the vehicle of thought, but by itself nothing'; the nobler and more numerous the ideas, the better the artwork.[20] Realist, Victorian

[17]  John Ruskin, *The Complete Works of John Ruskin*, eds. E. T. Cook and Alexander Wedderburn, 39 vols. (London: George Allen, 1903–12), vol. v, p. 126.
[18]  John Ruskin, *The Art Criticism of John Ruskin*, ed. Robert L. Herbert (1964; rpt New York: Da Capo Press, 1987), p. 399.
[19]  *Athenaeum*, 1 May 1858, p. 565; rpt in Martin Meisel, *Realizations: Narrative, Pictorial, and Theatrical Arts in Nineteenth-Century England* (Princeton University Press, 1983), p. 379.
[20]  Ruskin, *Complete Works*, vol. iii, p. 87.

and Pre-Raphaelite anecdotalism analysed through significant forms, as in Hogarth's 'problem pictures', could be decoded with as much pleasure in arranged photographs or graphic reproductions as in paintings. Hogarth's *Rake's Progress* (1733-4) and *Marriage à-la-Mode* (1743) (included in Great Britain's 1862 International Exhibition) inspired Frith's *Road to Ruin* (1878) and *The Race for Wealth* (1880) as well as Trollope's novel *The Way We Live Now* (1874-5). Critics like Ruskin accepted (even preferred) dismissal of the painter's visible address in colour, brushwork and impasto in order to gain a mass audience responsive to visually transparent communication of thematic (rather than sensual or emotive) content. Whistler realized that this very attractiveness constituted a menace to modern art, and asserted that art critics who sought 'a literary climax' were degrading art.[21]

In France, where Whistler had begun his career, the balance between solid representation of form (objective reality) and fluctuating representation of light and colour (the viewer's stance, the impact of space and time) tipped towards the latter. Naturalism in art and literature, and later Impressionist art, would concentrate on those aspects of observed reality which were transitory, subjectively realized, and directed towards the perception and rendition of *effect* rather than *object*.

## Naturalist literature and Impressionist art

Naturalist and Impressionist authors and artists, while maintaining an interest in observing the world, did so with increasing recognition of that world's dynamic play of light, colour and transmutation of substance. Castagnary defined Impressionism in 1874 as subjectively driven in that its representation *of* nature was in truth a representation of an individual response *to* nature: 'They are *impressionists* in the sense that they render not the landscape, but the sensation produced by the landscape.'[22] Specializing in transient exterior effects such as fog, sunrise or moving water, Impressionist artists like Monet became participants in the fluctuating and dynamic states which they were attempting to render. The challenge in Impressionism (and later Post-Impressionism and Symbolism) was how to render external reality in an individualized vision without overbalancing into either uninflected objectivity or indecipherable subjectivity.

[21] James McNeill Whistler, *The Gentle Art of Making Enemies* (London: Heinemann, 1892), p. 146.
[22] Richard Shiff, *Cézanne and the End of Impressionism: A Study of the Theory, Technique, and Critical Evaluation of Modern Art* (University of Chicago Press, 1984), p. 2.

Taine argued in *De l'intelligence* (1870) that reality was not binary (mind [subject] and matter [object]) but unified in an elementary unitary sense experience – the impression – which was simultaneously intellectual force and material substance.[23] In 1883 the poet Laforgue (who had attended Taine's course at the Ecole des Beaux-Arts, 1880–1) explained that Impressionist artists were able to intuit 'flashes of identity between subject and object' because the 'natural' ('impressionist') eye discovered the world through colour and light, not the 'dead language of linear contour', seeing reality in 'the living atmosphere in which forms are decomposed, refracted, and reflected in continually changing variations'.[24]

Zola affirmed: 'I did not merely support the Impressionists, I translated them into literature by the strokes, colour notes, the palette of many of my descriptions.'[25] Berthe Morisot (who knew Zola by 1868) agreed, noting a 'parallel between this literature and the painting of the new school'.[26] Zola was a member of the Café Guerbois group by 1867, which included the painters Manet, Degas, Bazille and Berthe Morisot and the critics Astruc and Duranty. Zola dedicated *Mon Salon* (May 1866) (his articles in *L'Evénement* on the Salon of 1866) to his childhood friend Cézanne and his novel *Madeleine Férat* (1868) to Manet. Fantin-Latour included Zola's portrait in *Un atelier aux Batignolles* (1870), depicting Manet at his easel, surrounded by his supporters in painting and in art criticism.

Zola's own literary fiction often referred to modern art's styles, subjects and personalities. *L'Œuvre* (1886) centres on the development of Impressionist and Post-Impressionist painting; the biographies and careers of Manet, Monet, Whistler, Cézanne and other artists are alluded to, and their paintings are described. The character Nana in Zola's *L'Assommoir* (1877) inspired Manet's painting (1877) of a half-dressed actress watched by a male admirer in her dressing room, which in turn inspired a scene in Zola's novel *Nana* (1880). Both Morisot's watercolour *On the Balcony, Meudon* (1874) and Zola's *Un page d'amour* (1878) present a woman and a female child contemplating a panoramic view of Paris from the balcony of a private house in Passy. Like Monet in *Boulevard des Capucines* (1873), Zola describes people hurrying down city streets as 'black dots' in *Un page d'amour* and *L'Œuvre*. But although Zola adopted Impressionist effects in his Naturalist literary works, his support for Impressionist art waned as their art gained wider recognition. Claude, the protagonist in

23  *Ibid.*, pp. 45–6.
24  Jules Laforgue, 'Critique d'art: l'Impressionisme' in *Œuvres complètes. Vol. 3: Mélanges posthumes* (Paris: Mercure de France, 1903), pp. 135–6.
25  Henri Hertz, 'Emile Zola, témoin de la vérité', *Europe*, 30 (952), pp. 32–3.
26  Denis Rouart, *The Correspondence of Berthe Morisot*, trans. Betty Hubbard (New York: Wittenborn, 1957), p. 89.

*L'Œuvre* (combining Monet, Manet and Cézanne), was unable to bring to fruition a solid work of genius.

For Zola, Manet's art and Naturalist literature were parallels to the scientific method. As he explained in 'Le Roman expérimental' (1880), Naturalist literature was not photography but the literary form of the modern drive towards scientific experimentation which put primary emphasis on the act of observation, not the inert matter observed: Claude Bernard's experimental method. The observer, having 'photographed phenomena', then analysed the observation which had been provoked. The author's imagination, which 'breathed life' into the novel, was grounded in observable reality, divined through 'induced observation'.[27]

While Zola was perturbed by Manet's sketchy brushwork rendering transient light effects, Mallarmé was delighted. Mallarmé was seeking an art (visual or textual) which would 'paint not the thing but the effect it produces'.[28] His essay on Manet and Impressionism (1876) praised the artist's successful 'fusion' or 'struggle' in *Le Linge* between solid forms and evanescent light and space. He had depicted air 'with its perpetual metamorphosis and its invisible action rendered visible', 'as if it held an enchanted life'.[29]

A truthful representation of *plein air* effects of light and colour challenged the academic approach, which was based on the logical and permanent rendering of solid form. Even some Impressionists worried that transient sensations were dissolving content as well as object. In 1886 Pissarro, influenced by Seurat, explained to his dealer that he had changed his style from 'romantic Impressionism' to 'scientific Impressionism'; Chevreul's and Rood's colour theories had shown him how to stabilize and heighten nature's luminosity through optical mixture, decomposing tones into their constituent elements.

While colour harmonies were being constructed as 'scientific' representations of actual site and time, they were also seen as statements of ideal beauty (analogous to pure harmonies of sound) and expressions of mood. In 1868 Swinburne described Gautier's poetry and paintings by Whistler and Moore as a 'melody of colour, symphony of form'.[30] 'All

---

[27] Emile Zola, 'Le Roman expérimental' in *Œuvres complètes*, ed. Maurice Le Blond, 50 vols. (Paris: Typographie François Bernouard, 1927–9), vol. XLI, pp. 12, 15, 18–19, 20.

[28] Stéphane Mallarmé, *Correspondance*, eds. H. Mondor, J. P. Richard and L. J. Austin, 11 vols. (Paris: Gallimard, 1959–85), vol. I, p. 137.

[29] Stéphane Mallarmé, 'The Impressionists and Edouard Manet' in Penny Florence, *Mallarmé, Manet and Redon: Visual and Aural Signs and the Generation of Meaning* (Cambridge University Press, 1986), p. 14.

[30] A. C. Swinburne in *Strangeness and Beauty: An Anthology of Aesthetic Criticism 1840–1910*, eds. Eric Warner and Graham Hough 2 vols. (Cambridge University Press, 1983), vol. I, p. 244. Hereafter cited as *SB*.

art constantly aspires towards the condition of music', Pater stated in 1877; visual, linguistic and aural arts addressed the 'imaginative reason' through the senses.[31] In 1877 Whistler's law-suit against Ruskin for libelling his *Nocturne in Black and Gold* (1875) as 'a pot of paint flung at the public's face' allowed Whistler to argue for liberating visual aspects from representational ends. He had chosen this title 'to indicate an artistic interest alone in the work . . . It is an arrangement of line, form and colour first.' He had not intended to *represent* fireworks at Cremorne gardens but to *create*, just as Beethoven wrote symphonies and sonatas rather than 'airs . . . interesting for their associations': 'As music is the poetry of sound so is painting the poetry of sight, and the subject-matter has nothing to do with harmony of sound or of colour.'[32] In 1888 Mallarmé translated Whistler's *Ten O'Clock Lecture* (1885) into French.

## Symbolism: to objectify the subjective

In the 1880s and 1890s Symbolist writers and theorists turned away from Impressionism's rendering of natural effects. The Goncourt brothers, trained as draughtsmen and sketchers, produced fiction, art criticism and art history written in what Verlaine and other admirers described as 'plastic prose'. Influenced by Schopenhauer's *Die Welt als Wille und Vorstellung* ('The World as Will and Idea', 1818), Symbolists believed that objective reality was constructed by the perceptive and contemplative subject. Symbolism was the antithesis of Impressionism, the poet Gustave Kahn stating in 1886: 'the essential goal of our art is to objectify the subjective (the exteriorization of the Idea) instead of subjectifying the objective (nature seen through a temperament)'.[33] The exteriorized Idea, liberated from responsibilities to subject matter, would be recognized by the 'imaginative reason' in a seamless union of form and content (as in music). Charles Henry constructed analogies between colour, linear direction and emotion in 'dynamogenic' (joyful) or 'inhibitory' (gloomy) expression. Henry's theories, which influenced the Neo-Impressionists Seurat and Signac, appeared in the periodical *La Vogue*, which also published Rimbaud, Verlaine, Huysmans and Jarry.

Gauguin maintained close ties to Mallarmé and other Symbolist writers after his departure for the South Seas. Proposing an approach parallel to Whistler's, Gauguin described his works as 'symphonies and harmonies that represent nothing *real* . . . express no idea directly, but

---

[31]  Walter Pater, 'The School of Giorgione' in *SB*, vol. II, pp. 25, 27.
[32]  Whistler, *Gentle Art*, p. 126.
[33]  Shiff, *Cézanne and the End of Impressionism*, p. 38.

they should make one think as music does without the aid of ideas or images'.[34] By insisting on communication without linear thought or photographic imagery, artists and writers were urging society, 'brutalized' by the positive sciences' insistence on the material, to return to mysticism and contemplation. Joris-Karl Huysmans, a novelist and art critic, and a friend of the Goncourt brothers and Zola as well as of the artists Redon and Moreau, became a contemplative who entered a Benedictine monastery and wrote on Christian symbolism in *La Cathédrale* (1898). Huysmans used vivid and concrete language to celebrate the visual as timeless icon rather than time-bound representation. In *Certains* (1889), a collection of his art reviews, Huysmans described his visit in 1886 to Goupil's exhibition of Moreau's watercolours, where he saw 'Salome holding in a cup the glowing head of the Precursor, macerated in phosphorus'. The impact of Moreau's works was even more clear after he left the gallery and found himself on the bleak streets of modern Paris where commerce and expediency had stifled beauty: the artist's work 'stands outside time, escapes into distant realms, glides over dreams, away from the excremental ideas oozing from a whole populace'.[35]

Moreau and Huysmans maintained theme and object in their contemplation of beauty. Gauguin extracted 'the dominant element' of form and colour from objects, urging artists to 'derive this abstraction from nature by dreaming before it'.[36] Building on Gauguin's recommendation, Aurier proposed an 'ideistic' art in which 'objects appear to the artist only as *signs*'.[37] For Aurier and the Symbolists the aim of art was to express an idea, a thought or a dream.

This idea was by no means necessarily 'literary'. Concerning his *Who Are We? Whence Come We? Whither are We Going?* (1899) Gauguin wrote to the Symbolist poet and art critic Fontainas 'my dream cannot be grasped. It embodies no allegory: a musical poem, it needs no libretto (as Mallarmé has said).'[38] Maeterlinck wished to replace human beings with 'a shadow, a reflection, a projection of symbolic forms' in his play *Pelléas et Mélisande* (1892), which communicated through nonverbal scenic image rather than reasoned discourse, and disengaged character from action. In 1886 Téodor de Wyzewa praised Wagner, whose *Gesamtkunstwerk* united plastic, emotive and intellectual elements, and advocated 'Wagnerian painting' in which the art of sensation (the visual,

[34] John Rewald, *The History of Impressionism*, 4th edn (New York: Museum of Modern Art; distributed by New York Graphic Society, Greenwich, CT, 1973), p. 574.
[35] Joris-Karl Huysmans, *Certains* (Paris: Stock, 1889), pp. 17–20.
[36] Cited in Herschel B. Chipp, *Theories of Modern Art* (Berkeley: University of California Press, 1984), p. 60.
[37] Aurier, 'Le Symbolisme en peinture', pp. 155–64.
[38] Cited in Dorra, *Symbolist Art Theories*, pp. 208–10.

plastic arts), the art of conception (literature) and the art of emotion (music) would come together to accomplish 'the renewal of art' in a 'sacred world of higher and better life'.[39]

Aspiration towards a higher world was also stimulated by dismay at contemporary humanity's capacity for irrational and instinctual behaviour. During the 1890s Freud developed the theory and method of treatment known as psychoanalysis, which gained the attention of a wider audience after publication of *The Interpretation of Dreams* (1900) and the First International Congress of Psychoanalysis in Salzburg (1908). Freud himself mined theatrical, fictional and visual works of art for psychological insights.[40] Munch's 'Saint-Cloud Manifesto' (1890) (for what would become the multi-canvas *Frieze of Life* project) proposed a representation of lovers not as individuals but as expressions of passions and biological drives (Freud's 'unconscious') 'in that moment when they are not themselves, but only one of the thousands of sexual links tying one generation to another generation'.[41] In an article titled 'Psychic Naturalism' (1894) Munch's friend the novelist Przybyszewski described the figures in his paintings as 'chemical preparations of the... animalistic, reason-less soul as it... screams in wild cramps of pain, and howls for hunger'.[42] Artists and authors, having rejected a static image of the material world seen from a unique viewpoint and transient personalized sensations and emotions, now probed the unconscious to reveal universal urges.

## Space, time and the participating spectator: Cubism and Futurism

For some Symbolist authors the plunge into subjective intuition was, paradoxically, directed towards a metaphysical consciousness of space and time in the external world. Henri Bergson's theories received an enthusiastic popular reception; he gave public lectures at the Collège de France after 1900 and undertook lecture tours in Italy (1911), England (1911) and America (1913). According to Bergson, consciousness was constructed dynamically and comprehensively; time was sensed as subjective 'duration' rather than as a succession of equal normative units;

39  Téodor de Wyzewa in *Art in Theory 1815–1900: An Anthology of Changing Ideas*, eds. Charles Harrison, Paul Wood and Jason Gaiger (Oxford: Blackwell, 1998), pp. 1004–5.
40  See Jack Spector, 'The State of Psychoanalytic Research in Art History', *Art Bulletin*, 70 (1988), 51–8.
41  Quoted in Reinhold Heller, *Munch: His Life and Work* (London: University of Chicago Press, 1984), pp. 63–4.
42  Stanislaw Przybyszewski, 'Psychischer Naturalismus' in *Das Werk des Edvard Munch: Vier Beiträge*, ed. Stanislaw Przybyszewski (Berlin: S. Fischer, 1894), pp. 16–17.

Bergson saw time and subjectivity as united in cognition of the 'profound self'.[43] The fluctuating sensations which had interested the Symbolists were now seen in an 'intuition of the duration', ascertained through the 'convergence of [the] action' of 'many different images'.[44] For Bergson, who exercised a formative impact on Symbolist poetry, 'The poet is he with whom feelings develop into images, and the images themselves into words.'[45]

Bergson had advocated successive and accumulated images rather than one fixed, photographic representation. The ideal medium for this was cinema, invented by the Lumière brothers in 1895, which Mallarmé, who decried illustration's constriction of text, thought capable of offering an effective translation of a text. Bergson's theories, Einstein's theory of relativity, and cinema encouraged artists to cease conceiving of three-dimensional space according to Albertian perspective (as if through a 'transparent window' onto a fixed, three-dimensional world of stable objects). As Metzinger explained, Cubist simultaneity permitted a static painting to offer ' a concrete representation of [the object], made up of several successive aspects. Formerly a picture took possession of space, now it reigns also in time.'[46] Time, intuited through consciousness, united form and observer. In their art manifesto *Du Cubisme* (1912), Gleizes and Metzinger proposed a new definition of pictorial space which involved the artist's and the spectator's 'tactile and motor sensations' so that 'our whole personality... contracting or expanding, transforms the plane of the picture'.[47]

Futurist artists and theorists accelerated Cubism's dynamic fusion of space and time. Each object's 'interior force' and its impact on neighbouring objects and context, rendered in dynamic 'force-lines', would encircle spectators and force them to 'participate in the action... struggle... with the persons in the picture'.[48] In his Futurist manifesto (1908) the poet Marinetti urged modern Italians to liberate themselves from the dead weight of heritage, to celebrate the new 'beauty of speed', to 'glorify war – the only true hygiene of the world'.[49] Only a few years later Futurists would attempt to glorify actual warfare, after the outbreak of the First World War.

[43] Henri Bergson, *Time and Free Will* (1889), trans. F. L. Pogson (1910; rpt New York: Macmillan, 1960), pp. 6–11, 28–39.
[44] See Mark Antliff, *Inventing Bergson: Cultural Politics and the Parisian Avant-Garde* (Princeton University Press, 1993), p. 50.
[45] Bergson, *Time and Free Will*, p. 15.
[46] See Stephen Kern, *The Culture of Time and Space 1880–1918* (Cambridge, MA: Harvard University Press, 1983), pp. 43–5.
[47] Albert Gleizes and Jean Metzinger in *Modern Artists on Art*, ed. Robert L. Herbert (Englewood Cliffs, NJ: Prentice Hall, 1964), p. 8.
[48] Chipp, *Theories of Modern Art*, p. 296.     [49] *Ibid.*, pp. 286–7.

The styles and unions of media employed during the period between 1830 and 1914 are still influential in the early twenty-first century, and they have stimulated new developments. The construction of an installation in which the spectator participates, the idea of art as event or 'happening' rather than object – which the Futurists and Dadaists explored at the beginning of the twentieth century – recur today in Christo's 'wrappings' and revelations of environments. Wagner would have appreciated the production in 2005 of *Tristan und Isolde* in Los Angeles and Paris, with video art by Bill Viola behind the singers, making the elements of fire and water a visible part of the scenic action. Media in video, graphic and computer technologies conjoin the visual, aural and textual in a multitude of complex and increasingly individualized ways. The consumer of pre-existing aesthetic products now may become a co-producer whose remixing combines music, internet clips, photographs and text. When we look back almost two hundred years we recognize that our predecessors identified aesthetic issues which still preoccupy us. Their theories, examples and insights are not only significant in their own context, but may also stimulate our own solutions to controversies which they could not foresee, employing technologies which they did not know.

# 32

# Biblical scholarship and literary criticism

## DAVID LYLE JEFFREY

Though easily overlooked by the student of nineteenth-century literary criticism, the Bible and biblical criticism are among its most important sources. To be sure, by this time much of the general influence of biblical literature and its study had been so thoroughly absorbed in the hermeneutics and reading practices of the well-educated English reader as to be almost invisible or indistinct from normative and ostensibly secular habit. To the broadly analytical mind of a reader alienated from religion, such as Karl Marx, the lineaments of Christian hermeneutic theory and practice remained nonetheless all too visible. Though he was speaking primarily of Germany, not England, and of social and political institutions rather than canonical texts, what he observed in 1844 applies well enough to nineteenth-century literary criticism in general: 'Criticism of religion', he asserts, 'is the premise of all criticism.'[1] But, though Marx was clearly an important new adversary of religion, biblical religion in particular, his point was in itself nothing new to religious discourse; indeed, it was one drawn from the mainstream of traditional biblical hermeneutics itself. To see this, to grasp the accumulated weight of the supposition he identified for the nineteenth century, requires a brief recapitulation.

In Western intellectual tradition the juxtaposition of religion and cultural criticism is foundational. In his seminal Christian treatise on method for reading scripture, St Augustine had insisted (decisively for Western tradition) that literary texts and literary training appropriate to the understanding of Holy Scriptures were to be found in useful measure among the secular writings of Roman and Greek culture. The idea of literary criticism as cultural criticism, now commonplace, gets much of its early momentum from Augustine's method. The biblical text, and approved ways of reading it, were believed by all parties in his time to have subverted the religious and political value structures of Roman culture.[2] Thus, though

---

[1] Karl Marx, *Selected Early Writings*, trans. Rodney Livingstone and Gregor Benton (New York: Vintage Books, 1975); cf. Erich Auerbach, *Mimesis: The Representation of Reality in Western Literature*, trans. Willard Trask (Princeton University Press, 1953), p. 451.

[2] This is the premise and thesis of his massive *De civitate dei*.

Augustine's *De doctrina Christiana* recommends the reading of specific classical texts (e.g. Virgil, Homer, Plato), the 'Egyptian gold' of classical literature, it is evident that he adopts much of pre-Christian literature into a canon of value in which the Bible orders literary understanding, and its ethical values undergird and transvalue broader aesthetic norms.[3] These assumptions persist well into the nineteenth century, and are evident even in Matthew Arnold's *Literature and Dogma*, which adduces Augustine if only to counteract his influence.

The pre-modern history of literary criticism knows no hermeneutic principle more fundamental than the interpretation of present texts in the light of a sometimes invisible but never entirely absent earlier text. The later Renaissance and eighteenth centuries, of course, feature something of an Augustan rather than Augustinian revival; accordingly, they return to the gold and silver of Latin literature and to the currency of its critical theory on what they take to be its own terms. In the eighteenth century, among Augustans both literary and ecclesiastical, Roman literature achieved for a time an apparently pre-eminent cultural authority in privileged quarters. Across the full social spectrum, however, it proved less attractive. With the demise of Enlightenment classicism under sharp social criticism from voices as diverse as Blake, Godwin, Wollstonecraft and Shelley on the secularist side, and the Wesleys, Smart, Wilberforce and the Clapham sect on the Christian side, it had become evident by the end of the eighteenth century that neo-classical rationalism, high culture and social elitism had worked together to create increasingly unsustainable social prejudices and conditions. Unavoidably, then, by 1830 (with the controversies surrounding enactment of the Roman Catholic Relief Act of 1829 at the forefront of public consciousness) perennial religious questions – and criticism of religion – were at the heart of all reflection on culture and meaning. Marx was on point.

## The Bible and the university

It is important to keep in mind that Matthew Arnold was appointed Professor of Poetry at Oxford only in 1857, and that he was the first in a long line of chair holders to practise primarily in the area of English literature, or great texts translated into English and held to be foundational. In European universities generally, from their beginnings in the thirteenth century until early in the nineteenth century, the relationship of all the arts (and even the study of law) to theology, at the heart of

---

3 See D. L. Jeffrey, *People of the Book: Christian Identity and Literary Culture* (Grand Rapids, MI, and Cambridge: Eerdmans, 1996), pp. 71–96.

the curriculum, was more or less organic and taken for granted. Even in the pursuit of classical languages and their attendant Greek and Roman literatures, while what we might take to be the epistemological object of study was self-evidently as advertised, there was at least tacit intellectual referral back to a curricular foundation in biblical studies. This is evident in much more than matters of common method or linguistic training; since the time of the monastic *studium,* with more or less predictable consequences, the object of all of the humanities disciplines had been the elaboration of humane learning as a kind of *ancilla* to the 'queen of the sciences'. Thus, for example, when the Italian humanist Francis Petrarch said 'we should study...so that the Gospel of Christ echoes in our hearts...to it the study of everything else should be referred', or when he defined theology as 'poetry about God', he was articulating a normative view of the relationship of scripture to the disciplines of humanistic inquiry.[4]

Much in this traditional perspective remained normative even as over time its strength weakened. Isaac Newton in the *Scholium generale* appended to his *Philosophiae naturalis principia mathematica* (1713) connected his mechanics and his views of absolute time and space to a conception of God which these presuppose, and his cosmogony and theories of number are reiterated rather matter-of-factly in his commentaries on the biblical books of Daniel and Revelation.[5] In not dissimilar fashion, though it is seldom noticed now, the interpretation of the Bible still played a formative role in the philosophical thinking of Hobbes, Locke and Spinoza, as well as in the literary theory expressed in John Dennis's *The Grounds of Criticism in Poetry* (1704), William Wordsworth's *Prelude* and, of course, Coleridge's *Biographia Literaria, Confessions of an Inquiring Spirit* and *The Statesman's Manual.*[6] But by the beginning of the nineteenth century, for a complex of reasons rehearsed by Henning Graf Reventlow and Hans Frei among others, the status of the Bible as a kind of epistemological norm in legal, political, philosophical and literary thinking was coming to an end along with confidence in its divine inspiration and inerrancy.[7] In *Literature and Dogma* it is quite precisely the normative authority of the Bible that Arnold wishes not merely to call into question, but now, at the religious level, finally to demolish. He was not so much the first to do so as among the first to see that it had,

---

[4] Francis Petrarch, *Rerum Familiarum libri,* ed. and trans. Aldo S. Bernardo (Baltimore, MD: Johns Hopkins University Press, 1984), 6.2.4; 10.4.
[5] See F. E. Manuel, *Isaac Newton: Historian* (Cambridge, MA: Harvard University Press, 1963), and *The Religion of Isaac Newton* (Oxford University Press, 1974).
[6] Anthony John Harding, *Coleridge and the Inspired Word* (Kingston and Montreal: McGill-Queens University Press, 1985), pp. 74–112.
[7] Isaac Newton, *Observations on the prophecies of Daniel and St. John* (London, 1733).

perhaps irrevocably, already happened – that biblical criticism itself had undermined the religious authority of the Bible such that it could not much longer function as a standard for cultural authority.

## Scripture among the disciplines

One of the most remarked-upon moments leading up to this point was a curricular decision taken by Baron Wilhelm von Humboldt, in establishing the University of Berlin in 1809. He decided formally to separate the study of theology from the study of the humanities, which then became a separate faculty. Humboldt's model subsequently became influential for English and eventually American universities. Though literary theory and critical practice alike had since Augustine been largely co-extensive with biblical hermeneutics and exegesis, a new 'wall of separation' was swiftly built and zealously guarded. A growing consensus among scholars in both religion and literature now regards this Germanic disciplinary prophylaxis as having been too extreme and, certainly in its later developments, unproductive. We may well agree with Stephen Prickett that 'the separation of traditional literary concepts from their biblical roots by the *Gletscherwall* of the Humboldtian university reforms of the early nineteenth century was in the long run as damaging to literary theory as it was to biblical studies'.[8]

For one thing, the split tended to result in academic anxieties, perhaps especially in theology and biblical studies, which sought increasingly to justify a place in the university through methodological redefinition of the discipline as a *Wissenschaft*, particularly a species of linguistic, anthropological and social science. German Higher Criticism was in this regard responding to the trends already established in the work of scholars such as Fr. Richard Simon (*Histoire critique du Vieux Testament* [1678, published in English translation in 1681], and *Critical History of the New Testament* [published in England in 1689]). Methodologically, Simon had pioneered the employment of methods drawn from linguistics, history and the social sciences, and was perhaps the first to argue forcefully that the Bible was a book like any other book and should be treated as such; for Simon, later to be expelled from his religious order, the idea of the Holy Spirit as general author of the Bible was no longer sustainable.[9]

By the time of Voltaire's *Dictionnaire philosophique* (1764) an effective methodological naturalism in study of the biblical text was common in

8  Stephen Prickett, *Words and the Word: Language, Poetics and Biblical Interpretation* (Cambridge University Press, 1986), pp. 37–94; cf. *Reading the Text: Biblical Criticism and Literary Theory*, ed. Stephen Prickett (Oxford: Blackwell, 1991), p. 201.
9  See Prickett, *Reading the Text*, pp. 136–47.

the approach of atheist, deist and even many pietist Christian theologians and biblical scholars alike. John Locke's *A Paraphrase and Notes on the Epistles of St. Paul* (1707) had articulated (in the essay on method which prefaces his commentary) an analysis of Paul as a human author, and argued that a coherent understanding of his letters requires that they be read in the same manner as any other literary text. In this respect echoing Simon, Locke also warned against underestimating the importance of a reader's individual presuppositions –'how at this day, everyone's Philosophy, regulates everyone's interpretation of the Word of God'.[10] Locke was able on these grounds to affirm the independent Bible reader as a kind of epistemological necessity and, as a consequence, necessarily to disaffirm the hitherto normative expectation that the biblical text would be read within, or at least in correspondence with, a traditional community of readers. Anthony Collins, Locke's disciple, in *A Discourse of the Grounds and Reasons of the Christian Religion* (1724), had presaged the split made explicit by Humboldt in his emphasis on reading the Bible for its literal sense only, by which he meant something quite narrowly literalistic, namely its correspondence to independent textual witness or archaeological verification of factual matter in the gospels and Old Testament narratives.[11]

Arnold knew Collins's work well, and though he cites Collins as among those who 'conduct their attacks on the current evidences for Christianity in such a manner as to give the notion that in their opinion Christianity itself... is a cheat and imposture', he thinks that Collins and those of his opinion now 'need greatly to be re-surveyed from the point of view of our own age',[12] by which he means to say of course that their attack on the religious authority of the Bible assists his own argument. The German supernaturalist Siegmund Jacob Baumgarten (1706–57), a believer in the Bible as divinely inspired, tried to counter arguments like that of Collins, but within a method likewise directed to demonstrating its factuality by rational analytical means.[13] The emphasis on proving or disproving the Bible's authority by a focus on prophecy and fulfilment, seeking correlation of narrative and independent archaeological or textual confirmation of historical fact, had by the early nineteenth century become common to

[10] John Locke, *A Paraphrase and Notes on the Epistles of St. Paul to the Galatians, 1 and 2 Corinthians, Romans, Ephesians* (1707), ed. Arthur W. Wainwright, 2 vols. (Oxford University Press, 1987), vol. I, p. 114.

[11] Henning Graf Reventlow, *The Authority of the Bible and the Rise of the Modern World* (London: SCM, 1984), pp. 354–6.

[12] Matthew Arnold, *Literature and Dogma: An Essay towards a Better Apprehension of the Bible* (London: Smith, Elder, 1873), pp. 84–5. Hereafter cited as *LD*.

[13] Hans Frei, *The Eclipse of Biblical Narrative: A Study in Eighteenth and Nineteenth Century Hermeneutics* (New Haven, CT, and London: Yale University Press, 1974), pp. 88–91.

fideist and sceptic alike, while the older way of reading the text with a high degree of attunement to its figurative discourse, to the prayed poetry of the psalms, wisdom books, moral law and parable, had become a habit of pietists almost exclusively. Thus, the age-old conversation between classical and biblical poetics, or between pagan and biblical literature, had effectively been silenced. By the 'literal level' of the text biblical scholars of all parties increasingly had come to mean 'that which can be authenticated as factual', rather than 'the primary literary construct'. In that respect, Humboldt's divorce of theology and the humanities in the new curriculum at Berlin only formalized a separation that had been in the making for some time, but it also presaged a further devaluation of the literary status of the Bible even as an object of literary criticism and poetics.

It is as one in whom the split has been thoroughly internalized that Arnold will attend to the literary rather than scientific character of biblical language. Much in the vein of Collins and his own predecessor Robert Lowth, he describes it as a 'language of poetry and emotion, approximative language, thrown out, as it were, at certain great objects which the human mind augurs and feels after, but not language accurately defining them' (*LD*, p. 93). Elsewhere he will resist firmly the kind of literary (poetic) criticism by which Augustine and the tradition derive a cognitive, creedal structure (*LD*, pp. 150–1). To be preserved as a literature of continuing cultural value it is essential, Arnold maintains, that the language of the Bible be regarded as inherently vague and ambiguous.

## The Oxford Chair of Poetry

It should be evident that, had the prevalent academic and religious *schola* been more or less the full story of which Arnold and his contemporaries sought an account, there would be little need for this chapter on 'Biblical scholarship and literary criticism'. But there was a secondary development already afoot, and in the end it let poetry mingle again with biblical study. Here the critical history had a local beginning. In England, as the incoming Professor of Poetry at Oxford back in 1741, Robert Lowth had given a series of lectures entitled *De sacra poesi Hebraeorum praelectiones academicae* ('Lectures on the Sacred Poetry of the Hebrews'). Lowth's lectures, published in 1753 and annotated by Johann David Michaelis in 1770, had a revolutionary effect both on German biblical critics and, through their translation into English in 1787, on English poets and novelists. Lowth not only showed the originary character of Hebrew parallelism to have produced a poetic different from and not reducible to European poetic forms and metric analysis, but also demonstrated that poetic or figural writing was the essential mode both of the Hebrew Bible and of the parables of Jesus in the New Testament. His insistence on cultural, linguistic and historical setting as basic to biblical poetics, and his suggestion that what Thomas Blackwell, in his *Life and Writings of Homer* (1785), had accomplished for Homer had comparable validity for biblical study, once again put biblical poetry on the same shelf as classical poetry. In the preface to his translation of *Isaiah* (1778) Lowth developed further a point he had made in his *Lectures*, namely that the Hebrew word for 'prophet' (*nabhî*) was used also of poets and musicians 'under the influence of divine inspiration'; in this way he linked the authority of prophecy to 'the language of poetry'. Suddenly the field focus had shifted quite dramatically away from preoccupation with verifiability and predictive accuracy, and in such a way as to bypass the narrow debates of the contesting sceptics and fideists.[14]

Thus Robert Lowth, in however apparently innocuous and obscure a fashion, in his series of Latin lectures as Professor of Poetry at Oxford, began a critical revolution of sorts to which not only poets such as Blake and Coleridge but successor critics such as Arnold were to be heir.[15] Though for a time much less visible to practitioners in biblical studies than to poets and literary critics, Lowth's work was to persist as a kind of avant-garde or underground stimulus for fresh literary approaches to the Bible in German as well as English precincts. Perhaps the German example of most moment for students of literary criticism is *Vom Geist der hebräischen Poesie* (1782–83) by Johann Gottfried von Herder, as much for its evident contrast with the response to the nineteenth-century English poets as for its apparent affirmations.[16]

Herder, like the English Romantic poets, was influenced both by pietism and by the subjective individualism championed by Jean-Jacques Rousseau, what his interpreter Friedrich Meinecke was later to term 'the inwardness and individuality of the human soul'.[17] Herder's views were approved in turn by Goethe and by Coleridge. But though his stated intention was 'to illustrate and make intelligible the beauties and sublimities of Hebrew poetry, by comparing it, in all its varieties, with the productions of Greek and Roman art'[18] and though he acknowledged Lowth and the annotations of Michaelis as his immediate inspiration, Herder's object had been to set the primal narratives of the Old Testament in the context of the history of mythology, and his method is not the academic discourse

[14] Prickett, *Words and the Word*, pp. 105–10.
[15] *Ibid.*, pp. 110–23.   [16] Frei, *Eclipse*, pp. 183–7.
[17] Friedrich Meinecke, *Die Entstehung des Historismus*, 2 vols. (Munich and Berlin: R. Oldenbourg, 1936), vol. III, p. 361.
[18] James Marsh, Translator's Preface to Johann Gottfriend Herder, *The Spirit of Hebrew Poetry* (Burlington, VT: Edward Smith, 1833), p. 4.

of biblical scholars but a rather quaint imitation of the dialogues of Plato. In this he recalls Shaftesbury, Diderot and Lessing.

The influence is here more than a matter of genre or style: 'In human fashion must one read the Bible; for it is a book written by men for men: Human is the language, human the external means with which it was written and preserved; human finally is the sense with which it may be grasped, every aid that illumines it, as well as the aim and use to which it is to be applied.'[19] As Hans Frei has shown, however, Herder here departs from Lowth's attempt to situate Hebrew poetry in the *classis* of Greek and Roman discourse and poesis, recalling the Bible rather to contemporary European literary discourse and literary approaches. Herder's emphasis is on the 'spirit' of the present age, the *Zeitgeist*, and his conviction is that in order to read responsively one must submit to an *Einfühlung*, an 'aesthetically uncritical' yet paradoxically aesthetic rather than theological 'empathy', almost a charismatic possession by the 'spirit' of the whole body of extant poetry. This rather nebulous, almost mystical desire to enter into 'the spirit of the culture' renders Herder oblivious to distinctions between factuality and fact-likeness, such that for him the whole category of historical consciousness need not be connected to 'any specific occurrence that had actually taken place'.[20] Thus, even as he was coming to the attention of Coleridge, Herder was becoming marginal to German Higher Criticism of the Bible in the universities, where an intensified preoccupation with archaeology and historical factuality was steadily to gather momentum through the nineteenth century. But Herder is nonetheless a herald of some central themes of Matthew Arnold and his contemporaries.

## Hegel and Hegelianism

A second current of Germanic influence was to depend on subsequent developments in the philosophical seminars of the University of Berlin. This phase may be said to begin with G. W. F. Hegel, who was appointed to the Chair of Philosophy at Berlin in 1818, just nine years after Humboldt's momentous academic separation of theology from the other humane disciplines. Hegel's 'Absolute Idealism' made natural his identification of what he called 'the Infinite' or 'the Absolute' with the God of the Bible. A strongly Platonist flavour is apparent throughout his philosophy of religion: it is sufficient here to note that in his *Lectures*, during a

---

[19] Johann Gottfried Herder, *Sämtliche Werke*, 33 vols. (Hildesheim: G. Olms, 1968), vol. x, p. 7.
[20] Frei, *Eclipse*, p. 187.

discussion of *Vorstellung*, or 'representation' in thinking where religion is concerned, he makes a direct comparison of the gospel and Plato's myths; just as the latter express higher (intelligible) truths allegorically, so does the Bible, and not merely in the parables of Jesus. These truths are embodied in narrated events and characters, but the intelligible truths themselves are the significant factors in human historical development, whether or not specific individuals whose lives are so shaped ever become conscious of the process. Hegel does not himself deny to the gospel accounts of Jesus their historical status; rather, he grants to them additionally the supervening status of myth, a 'representative' (*Vorstellung*) of 'internal' truths which are the more 'substantial' element, 'the very thing that is the proper object of reason'.[21]

Hegel is himself more important for the history of theology than for his own direct impact on biblical studies, yet despite his apparently orthodox contention that the incarnation is the most philosophically significant of Christian doctrines, he finds little to distinguish between Socrates and Jesus as 'representations' of the divine sent into the world. The resurrection and the ascension are not verifiable as historical events; Jesus is resurrected only in the sense that he 'lives' in the church. But Hegel is doubtful that the church can continue in existence in a time when biblical critics and philosophers have both 'moved beyond' the simple piety in which they were raised. Notably, part of the reason is his perception of an inadequacy of the national church in fulfilling its mission to imitate Christ, embodying and so representing the immutable truths of the gospel. 'The salt has lost its savour', Hegel says, nowhere more clearly than among the clergy; effectively, the level of *Vorstellung* on which ordinary people depend has vanished from the lives of those charged with teaching it.

When Marx asserted that 'the criticism of religion is the premise of all criticism', he went on to say that 'the foundation of irreligious criticism is this: man makes religion, religion does not make man'.[22] But these last words are a paraphrase of Ludwig Feuerbach's sardonic observation in *Das Wesen des Christentums* (*The Essence of Christianity*) that 'Man first unconsciously and involuntarily creates God in his own image, and after this God consciously and voluntarily creates man in his own image.'[23] Hegelian Platonist idealism has, in Hegel's disciple, taken on a neo-Aristotelian or Baconian colouration: 'What in the infinite being can I perceive to be a subject, a being? Only that which is a predicate, a quality of myself' (p. 401). The evident self-referentialism in such a passage

[21] G. W. F. Hegel, *Lectures on the Philosophy of Religion*, trans. E. B. Speirs and J. B. Sanderson, 3 vols. (London: Kegan Paul, Trench, Trubner, 1895), vol. 1, B.2.3.
[22] Marx, *Selected Early Writings*, p. 63.
[23] Ludwig Feuerbach, *The Essence of Christianity*, trans. George Eliot (New York: Harper, 1854), p. 118.

grew to be normative and struck some as elitist. Marx came to think a good deal less of Feuerbach, whom he had earlier admired as a bright light among the 'young Hegelians'. But shrewdly, he also recognized that the essential atheism of Feuerbach's statement was of a sort predicated upon an enervation of biblical Christianity achieved substantially by an extension of Hegel's own reasoning. Religious transcendence is affirmed by Feuerbach, but redefined as a kind of *reductio* of the collective intuition of the race to a representation in the religious consciousness of the individual. For Feuerbach, 'religion is man's earliest and also indirect form of self-knowledge' (p. 13), a kind of primitive intuition from the *Urdummheit* (or childhood of the race) which gradually obtains an illusory ontological status. The adumbration of Hegel's thought in Feuerbach on this point is, given its premises, now antithetical to biblical theology: as Merold Westphal summarizes it, 'the transition from (theistic) religion to (atheistic) philosophy is simply the developmental discovery of the projective character of religious knowledge, the realization that consciousness is self-consciousness, that God is humankind'.[24]

Along with Hegel's own Platonist idealism, any real place for the Bible has at this point vanished. George Eliot, in her fervent preface to her translation (*The Essence of Christianity*, 1854) of Feuerbach's *Das Wesen des Christentums* (1841), is transparent about this recognition: 'Having proceeded far beyond Hegel as well as Kant, Feuerbach belongs to the Berlin master's disciples who scented the theological residue in his teaching... and stripped it off... Feuerbach wants, in the end, to help man secure his due.'[25] Theology, as Eliot says, repeating her source, has become anthropology (p. xiv). This is regarded by Eliot as 'liberating knowledge' (p. xix), evidence of an ascent of human reasoning that recognizes the eclipse of biblical narrative, a growing consensus that, in Feuerbach's words, 'It is nothing more than a fixed idea [Hegel might have said, *Vorstellung*] that stands in most glaring contradiction to our fire and life insurance companies, our railroads and steam engines, our picture galleries, our military and industrial schools, our theatres and scientific museums' (as quoted by Eliot, p. xix). One may now perhaps smile at the examples, but the self-confident optimism, modern materialism and *Wissenschaft* expressed in this passage in Feuerbach were, of course, often to be repeated. Rudolf Bultmann's 'glaring contradiction' was to be the general use of electricity; Matthew Arnold's trump card, a little less electrifying perhaps, was to be the growing sophistication of literary criticism.

24  Merold Westphal, *Suspicion and Faith: The Religious Uses of Modern Atheism* (Grand Rapids, MI: Eerdmans, 1993), p. 127.
25  George Eliot, Translator's Preface to Feuerbach, *Essence of Christianity*, p. xii.

There was at first a tendency on the part of some to resist the 'higher' biblical criticism as foreign and obscurantist. Thomas Babington Macaulay, when he received as a gift a three-volume study (*The Evidences of the Genuineness of the Gospels*, 1837–44) by Andrews Norton, wrote Norton a letter to say, 'I have stolen a few minutes daily, while dressing and undressing, to make acquaintance with the theological writers of Germany.'[26] Macaulay was actually much more receptive to such matters than this disparaging letter suggests: he had read Schleiermacher in Thirwall's translation, as well as W. H. Mills's observations on the *Attempted Application of Pantheistic Principles to the Theory and Historic Criticism of the Gospels* (1840), itself a reply to David F. Strauss. But Macaulay relished rather than lamented the contestation and indeterminacy of biblical interpretations, perhaps indeed because, as William R. McKelvy has put it, he 'understood . . . that hermeneutic indeterminacy was the theoretical basis for the liberal state'.[27]

It is difficult to know how far to press such a thesis, or how to detect in literary texts the absorption of such influences upon literary minds. Confident attempts have been made where Victorian authors are concerned. In one such case, Terence Allan Hoagwood has argued that Elizabeth Barrett's *A Drama of Exile* (1844) and Jean Ingelow's *The Story of Doom* (1867) both imitate in their form 'the documentary arguments of the Higher Criticism'.[28] While any such individual argument may be debatable, there can be little doubt about the influence of such approaches to biblical literature upon the translators of the German critics themselves.

In large part because of George Eliot's translation (1847) of his *Leben Jesu* (1835, 1836), D. F. Strauss was one of the Hegelians who would come to have a large influence in England.[29] Strauss argued in this work that the historical events of the life and death of Christ gave rise to essentially mythic expressions in the early Christian church; these relegated the historical matter itself to a secondary interest. Strauss was not, like Hegel, given to mystical Idealism, but regarded the central elements of biblical narrative as needing to be spiritually interpreted so as to show that in their final significance it is really humanity writ large that dies, rises and ascends into heaven. As Eliot translates him, for Strauss, 'the history [of Jesus] is not enough; it is not the whole truth; it must be

[26] Thomas Babington Macaulay, *The Letters of Thomas Babington Macaulay*, 6 vols. (New York: Cambridge University Press, 1974–81), vol. III, p. 338.

[27] William R. McKelvy, 'Primitive Ballads, Modern Criticism, Ancient Skepticism: Macaulay's *Lays of Ancient Rome*', *Victorian Literature and Culture*, 28 (2000), p. 303.

[28] Terence Allan Hoagwood, 'Biblical Criticism and Secular Sex: Elizabeth Barrett's *A Drama of Exile* and Jean Ingelow's *A Story of Doom*', *Victorian Poetry*, 42 (2004), p. 176.

[29] U. C. Knoepflmacher, *Religious Humanism and the Victorian Novel: George Eliot, Walter Pater, and Samuel Butler* (Princeton University Press, 1965), pp. 44, 48–9.

transmuted from a past fact into a present one; from an event external to you, it must become your own intimate experience'.[30] Something of this order of personal experience seems – especially in novellas such as those in *Scenes of Clerical Life* (1857–8) – to allow Eliot to hallow nostalgically the biblical religion of her youth as a kind of memory of pastoral innocence.

Towards the end of her life, Barry Qualls has argued, she turned more directly to its personal sources, 'because she found there a narrative of survival through history that suggested the power of language and literature'.[31] In this respect she may have been more Hegelian than those she translated, Strauss in particular. There is, moreover, a certain class condescension mixed with the charity in Eliot's nostalgia, as may be seen in her defence of the portrayal she affords in *Adam Bede* of the piety of Rector Irwine: 'These fellow-mortals, everyone, must be accepted as they are: you can neither straighten their noses nor brighten their wit, nor rectify their dispositions; and it is these people – amongst whom your life is passed – that it is needful you should tolerate, pity and love.'[32] The note struck here is to become both familiar and dominant, as much a matter of tone as an inflection of argument in the public campaign of Matthew Arnold for a new 'national religion'.

## Literary criticism and criticism of religion

A book by which Matthew Arnold and most English readers in the later nineteenth century came to know Hegel's thought more proximately was the Scottish Hegelian J. H. Stirling's two-volume *The Secret of Hegel* (1865). For Stirling, Feuerbach and Strauss are 'atheistic materialists', while Hegel himself is still to be regarded as a species of Christian. But in his summary of Hegel's religious thought Stirling expresses a certain hauteur and self-congratulatory tone regarding the 'Higher Criticism' that would seem to have become particularly attractive to Arnold: 'since Christ, God is inward to man: he is our conscience. We no longer ask the will of God from external oracles, but from our own selves; that is, we are now a law unto ourselves, we are to our own selves in the place of God, we are ourselves God, God and man are identified.'[33] It is clear enough that Stirling's 'Englished' Hegel is in fact one from whom the 'theological

---

[30] David F. Strauss, *Leben Jesu* (Tubingen: C. F. Osiander, 1835), p. 784; trans. George Eliot as *The Life of Jesus Critically Examined* (London: Swan Sonnenschein, 1847).

[31] Barry Qualls, in *The Cambridge Companion to George Eliot*, ed. George Levine (Cambridge University Press, 2001), p. 136.

[32] George Eliot, *Adam Bede* (New York: Harper, 1859), ch. 17, p. 267. See also the helpful commentary of Knoepflmacher, *Religious Humanism*, pp. 54–5.

[33] James Hutchinson Stirling, *The Secret of Hegel*, 2 vols. (London: Longman, Green, Longman, Roberts, & Green, 1865), vol. I, p. 149.

residue' has indeed been 'stripped off', but in whom theology has become not so much anthropology as, incipiently, psychology.

Whereas George Eliot had in 1854 identified herself completely with Feuerbach she was by the late 1860s expressing some sense of distance from the Germanic Higher Criticism. U. C. Knoepflmacher has convincingly connected Eliot to Arnold with respect to a growing desire for a specific identification of 'the highest results of past and present influences' with culture, perhaps specifically cultural authority of the sort once held by the Bible.[34] In *Literature and Dogma* (1873) Arnold argues that Strauss, for example, simply lacked the 'larger, richer, deeper, more imaginative mind' to realize the full potential of his conclusions in *Leben Jesu* for finally transcending the exhausted narrowness of 'historic method' (*LD*, pp. xxv–xxviii). It would be, as Knoepflmacher puts it, the 'imaginative mind... of Arnold himself' that he believed could realize the potential of higher criticism, now clearly an antithesis to Christian doctrine, to cancel out archaic thinking and make way for a new and higher development.[35] The emerging new synthesis would be built upon the English predilection for using the Bible as a handbook for forming ethical consciousness. Arnold and Eliot may have been somewhat alike in looking for continuance of 'a moral tradition that could embody an authoritative 'power not ourselves'.[36] For Arnold, however, who had commenced his polemical career as a political essayist, the goal was a secular religion that might preserve the erstwhile political authority of a weakening and fracturing national church (*LD*, p. xviii).

In the English context, in which as in no other Western European country the English Bible had long been a foundational literature with cultural authority not entirely dependent on the state church, it was political prudence as well as cultural self-understanding that led Arnold to the development of his grand project. It appears chiefly in four volumes: *St. Paul and Protestantism* (1870), *Literature and Dogma* (1873), *God and the Bible* (1875) and *Last Essays on Church and Religion* (1877), though early formulations are to be found in his chapter on 'Spinoza and the Bible' inserted into the 1869 edition of *Essays in Criticism*. His argument concerning St Paul is essentially that the metaphorical language of intense spiritual experience in St Paul has been distorted and made at once forensic and polemical by Calvinism in particular, a tradition that has forged from it a reductive and yet prolix 'machinery of covenants, conditions, bargains and parties-contractors, such as could have proceeded from no one but the born Anglo-Saxon man of business'.[37] To his disdain of the class of Dissenters and Low

[34] Knoepflmacher, *Religious Humanism*, pp. 53, 62–71.
[35] *Ibid.*, p. 64.    [36] *Ibid.*
[37] Matthew Arnold, *St. Paul and Protestantism* (London: Smith, Elder, 1870), p. 12.

Church Anglicans (a nation of petty shopkeepers, one assumes) Arnold adds a denigration of the wishful thinking of the Methodists, whom he sees as too much concerned with hope and heaven to note that Paul's own chief concern is with temporal righteousness; on Arnold's account the Apostle's chief theme and argument demonstrates the abiding importance for human well-being of attention to the universal moral law.

*Literature and Dogma*, as this chapter has been suggesting, becomes the centre piece of Arnold's new theology, and here it becomes clearest that he is appealing directly to readers whose religious sensibilities are essentially Broad Church Anglican. Authentic religion, he argues, must have an 'authentic' Bible. To have such a Bible one must be cognizant, as a first step, 'that the language of the Bible is fluid, passing and literary, not rigid, fixed, and scientific... After all, the Bible is *not* a talisman, to be taken and used literally.'[38] This position, which many would have identified with Low Church Protestants and even Catholics, might in itself have seemed well calculated to obtain ready agreement from his target audience. But almost immediately he shocks his readers with the revelation that he regards *all* churches as suspect in their use of biblical literature: 'neither is any existing Church a talisman, whatever pretensions of the sort it may make, for giving the right interpretation of the Bible. But only true culture can give us this interpretation' (*LD*, p. xx).

That 'true culture', he goes on to make clear, informed by a rich and comparative literary education, has as its goal 'to know the best that has been thought or said in the world'. If the Bible is to be saved as a moral authority for a modern 'true culture', it must be saved from *all* the churches by effective secularization. Dogmatic theology of every sort must go (*LD*, p. 3). Miracles have likewise to go, as symbolic accretions on the promulgations of deeper values that have taken on poetic expression. Also to be expunged, as Arnold argues in the fourth and fifth chapters, are dogmatic interpretations of biblical prophecy. The idea of God as a personal Being or First Cause of creation is similarly untenable (*LD*, pp. xvii, 15–16). God is simply 'the power not ourselves that makes for righteousness' (*LD*, pp. 125, 190). All of these other historic components of Christian teaching are *Aberglaube*, superfluous belief no more valuable than 'Jewish exegesis, based on a mere unintelligent catching at the letter of the Old Testament, isolated from its context and real meaning' (*LD*, p. 113; cf. p. 117). The true, essential meaning of religion is 'conduct', which for Arnold is 'not simply morality, but morality touched by emotion' (*LD*, p. 16). This is accordingly where the true value of the Bible is to be

---

[38]  Later Arnold says: 'The language of the Bible, then, is literary, not scientific language; language *thrown out* at an object of consciousness not fully grasped, which inspired emotion' (*LD*, pp. 30–1).

recognized, for it is in poetry, in great works of the literary imagination, that our emotions are aroused and given high purpose.

In an early anticipation of the American 'Jesus Seminar' of the late twentieth century, Arnold observes that 'to extract even from his reporters the true Jesus entire, is . . . impossible; to extract him in considerable part is one of the highest conceivable tasks of criticism'. Arnold's redacted Jesus has value as a luminous moral exemplar, possessed of evident tranquillity, a method and a secret knowledge. This special *gnosis*, Arnold adds, 'produced a total impression of his *epieikeia* or sweet reasonableness' (*LD*, pp. 120, 126, 139). Arnold characterizes the uneducated disciples as having failed to interpret these finer qualities sufficiently. His rhetoric on this point takes the form of a condescension to the unenlightened, distinctly reminiscent of some of the Hegelians: 'As the Jews were always talking about the Messiah, so they were always talking, we know, about God. And they believed in God's Messiah after their notion of him, because they believed in God after their notion of *him*; – but both notions were wrong.' The creeds of the church, however, are much worse, being metaphysical abstractions peculiar to the 'Aryan genius' to which even Semitic simplicity is in such matters to be preferred. Rather than creeds or theological doctrine, then, we still need the Bible itself, but *simpliciter*, 'for the right inculcation of righteousness', even as 'for the right inculcation of the method and secret of Jesus, we need the *epieikeia*, the sweet reasonableness of Jesus' (*LD*, pp. 141, 150–3, 225).

Restricting Bible reading to reading *it* as imaginative literature preserves this value unencumbered by theological accretions; this conception of the Bible alone is to constitute the socially acceptable, 'true' Bible for English culture. Some measure of Arnold's success in this regard is surely the enormous secular attention to the Bible 'as literature' that, indebted to him, has arisen especially since the work of Northrop Frye.[39]

But Arnold has not finished his criticism of the Bible of the Christian churches. Because 'the *Aberglaube* has sprung out of a false criticism of the literary records in which the doctrine is conveyed', then 'orthodox divinity' or conventional biblical theology 'is, in fact, an immense literary misapprehension' (*LD*, p. 121). Arnold regards the literary criticism now required for a right reading of the Bible to be 'extremely difficult', and he asserts that only those who have the highest order of literary training and cultural formation can conduct such criticism. The Bible, so far from being, as the Reformation proclaimed it, a book for the masses is properly a book suited to the care of a secular clerisy. People of lesser

---

[39] Northrop Frye, *Anatomy of Criticism* (Princeton University Press, 1957), *Secular Scripture: A Study of the Structure of Romance* (Cambridge, MA: Harvard University Press, 1973), and *The Great Code: The Bible and Literature* (New York: HBJ, 1982).

attainment 'who take short cuts and tell themselves fairy-tales' do so because 'bringing in everlasting righteousness is too much for their narrow minds... They are like people who have fed their minds on novels or their stomachs on opium; the reality of things is flat and insipid to them' (*LD*, p. 195). Karl Marx, had he read this far in *Literature and Dogma*, would surely have smiled to see such language from a spokesman for British upper-class culture.

*God and the Bible* is a defence of *Literature and Dogma*, occasioned by a large outpouring of hostile criticism. Some of this criticism was prompted by Arnold's disparaging remarks about individual defenders of more orthodox readings of the Bible, such as the famous dissenting preacher Charles Haddon Spurgeon and the bishops of Winchester (Samuel Wilberforce) and Gloucester (Charles John Ellicott). Some letters came from readers incensed by the dismissive tone of his 'demythologizing' of more conventional understandings of the Bible; still other critics of Arnold were repelled by what they, with T. S. Eliot later on, saw as Arnold's attempt 'to set up Culture in the place of Religion'.[40] Arnold's riposte was to reiterate his argument, but to gain advantage from strawman opponents with whom he thought few among his critics would be willing to identify.

From 1873 to 1875 the American evangelist Dwight L. Moody and his music leader, Ira Sankey, had been on an evangelistic tour in Britain. Arnold went to hear them, and made a caricature of the sermon and its audiences. The large audiences of Moody he characterized as bourgeois, 'the last people who will come to perceive all this... chiefly made up from the main body of lovers of our popular religion – the serious and steady middle class'.[41] But the basic argument of *Literature and Dogma* is not significantly advanced either here or in his *Essays on Church and Religion* (1877). In fact, ironically enough, as David De Laura has argued, despite his 'avowed agnosticism, his pose of empiricism, and his resistance to the transcendental and metaphysical, Arnold persistently appeals to a covert supernaturalism in the religious writings and in the literary writings of the final decade'.[42]

## Evangelical tradition

In however backhanded a fashion, Arnold's attention to the evangelist Dwight Moody paid compliment to a strain of Christianity certainly to

[40] T. S. Eliot, *Selected Essays: 1917–32* (New York: Harcourt, Brace, 1934), pp. 434, 436.
[41] Matthew Arnold, *God and the Bible* (London: Smith, Elder, 1887), p. xv.
[42] David J. DeLaura, *Hebrew and Hellene in Victorian England: Newman, Arnold, and Pater* (Austin: University of Texas Press, 1969), p. xvii.

be distinguished from the one with which he was most familiar, and yet which contributed profoundly to the absorption of the biblical tradition into literary and art criticism in the nineteenth century. We may see this quite clearly in the luminous and prolific career of John Ruskin.

Ruskin was raised in a pious, evangelical home and under the preaching ministry of a forceful exponent of Calvinist biblical typology, Henry Melville.[43] As a boy might in such circumstances, he memorized large tracts of the King James Bible, particularly from the Psalms, Proverbs of Solomon and the Sermon on the Mount,[44] and by the age of twelve had composed eighteen sermons of his own on the Pentateuch in a typically Scottish-Calvinist typological mode.[45] Although decades later, in *Praeterita* (1886), he would claim that by fourteen he no longer held to his mother's view that the Bible was to be read literally, it has been evident to critics that his lifelong method of close reading, attention to minute details in poetics and paintings, along with an instinct for seeing typology in painterly iconography, stems from the evangelical training in Bible reading of his early years.[46] Moreover, in his mid-thirties he was still systematically memorizing parts of the Bible and studying it daily.[47] Yet Ruskin came (partly under the influence of F. D. Maurice) to lay aside the Calvinist doctrine of salvation only for the 'elect', and shortly after that to move beyond the anti-Catholicism of his upbringing.[48]

By 1858 he famously abandoned evangelicalism altogether, even rejecting fundamental tenets of Christianity of any stripe a few years later.[49] But his commitment to 'the language of Types... a better one than Greek or Latin', exhibiting the 'life-giving, purifying and sanctifying influences of the Deity upon his creatures', remained as firm as ever, even if altered in application, undiminished in authority to set forth God's 'eternity and His TRUTH'.[50] It is the highly developed instinct for typology in his criticism that has led Harold Bloom to regard Ruskin as 'one of the first, if not indeed the first, "myth" or "archetypal" critic... the linking or transitional figure between allegorical critics of the elder Renaissance kind, and those of the newer variety, like Northrop Frye, or like W. B. Yeats in his criticism'.[51] Ruskin's art criticism, likewise, has been seen as powerfully

[43] Michael Wheeler, *Ruskin's God* (Cambridge University Press, 1999), pp. 14–17.
[44] *Ibid.*, pp. 12, 24.
[45] Van Aken Burd, 'Ruskin's Testament of his Boyhood Faith: *Sermons on the Pentateuch*' in *New Approaches to Ruskin*, ed. Robert Hewison (London: Routledge & Kegan Paul, 1981), p. 1.
[46] George Landow, *Aesthetic and Critical Theories of John Ruskin* (Princeton University Press, 1971), pp. 250, 265.
[47] Burd, 'Ruskin's Testament', p. 10.     [48] Wheeler, *Ruskin's God*, p. 17.
[49] Jeffrey L. Spear, 'Ruskin as a Prejudiced Reader', *English Literary History*, 49 (1982), pp. 73–98, 76–80.
[50] John Ruskin, *The Stones of Venice* (London: Smith, Elder, 1851), pp. 11–41.
[51] Harold Bloom, 'Introduction' in John Ruskin, *The Literary Criticism of John Ruskin* (Garden City, NY: Doubleday, 1965), p. xvi.

shaped by biblical typology and exegesis, notably in *Modern Painters,
Seven Lamps of Architecture* and *The Stones of Venice*.[52]

This same Calvinistic tradition of typology seems to have helped
Thomas Carlyle to form his own ideas about symbolism. According to
George Landow, evidence of this appears in Carlyle's statement in *Heroes
and Hero-Worship* that 'this so-solid-looking material world is, at bottom, in very deed, Nothing: is a visual, factual Manifestation of God's
power and presence – a shadow hung out by Him on the bosom of the void
Infinite; nothing more'.[53] Ruskin, meanwhile, wrestling with the evangelical shibboleth concerning idolatry where painting was concerned (especially representation of the deity), was perhaps thinking of the legendary
regard for St Luke as the patron saint of his favourite art when, in a Christmas sermon of 1836 (on Luke 2:13–14), he remarked on the ordering of
physical and spiritual sight in terms commensurate with those of Carlyle:
'Man can only realize – or try to realize the Unseen by his experience of
the Seen.'[54] Both of these passages dimly echo St Paul in Romans 1:20;
neither requires more theological reflection than to accept the Pauline
remark in a *sola scriptura* context as a typological guide. For critics
raised in an evangelical context the reflex was evidently persistent.[55]

At Oxford, the great Plato scholar Benjamin Jowett was tutor both
to Walter Pater and to Gerard Manley Hopkins. Jowett's work on *The
Epistles of St. Paul* (1855) is effectively pre-critical, but his essay 'On the
Interpretation of Sacred Scripture' (1861), if not quite so dramatically
as Bishop John Colenso's *The Pentateuch and Book of Joshua Critically
Examined* of a year later, was a much discussed and highly controversial
attempt to introduce Germanic historical criticism to England. Yet
it would seem that Jowett exercised little influence regarding biblical
criticism on his notable students.[56] Pater was far more influenced by
Ruskin,[57] and in his extension of images traditionally symbolic for
Christ – as well as theological attributes – and transferring them to the
Greek myths, he did so in a way that echoes the typological method and
theory of Ruskin.[58] This, despite his well-known jibes at Christianity,
particularly Anglican evangelicalism,[59] is in some respects more reliable
an indicator of the perdurability of evangelical biblical exegesis in its

[52]  *Ibid.*, pp. 26–30.
[53]  V. Landow, *Aesthetic and Critical Theories*, p. 370; Thomas Carlyle, *Heroes, Hero-
      Worship and the Heroic in History* (London: John Wiley, 1840), pp. 81–2.
[54]  Quoted in Wheeler, *Ruskin's God*, p. 22.
[55]  Spear, 'Ruskin as a Prejudiced Reader', pp. 73–98.
[56]  Prickett, *Reading the Text*, pp. 199–200.
[57]  A. C. Benson, *Walter Pater* (New York: Macmillan, 1906), pp. 7–9.
[58]  Gerald Cornelius Monsman, *Pater's Portraits* (Baltimore, MD: Johns Hopkins Univer-
      sity Press, 1967), pp. 201–8.
[59]  Lawrence Evans, 'Introduction' in Walter Pater, *Letters of Walter Pater* (Oxford:
      Clarendon Press, 1970), p. xxi.

vestigial form than the much more explicit biblical allusion in the poetry and critical reflections of Hopkins. Despite having been raised in the same tradition, Hopkins came to be thoroughly infused with a love for liturgical beauty and recast his biblical knowledge in the light of a medieval Catholic sacramental synthesis.

It should not be imagined on this account that Germanic Higher Criticism had entirely driven out evangelical influences from either the university or the world of literary and art criticism. Ruskin, haunted, found it necessary especially during his spiritual crisis of 1858 to debate with the immensely popular and gifted orator of the Baptists, Charles Haddon Spurgeon (1834–92). Yet despite Spurgeon's lack of success in making a convert, Ruskin seems to have admired the eloquent Spurgeon in a way that Arnold could not. Ruskin attended Spurgeon's sermons, corresponded with Robert and Elizabeth Browning about him, and defended him in print.[60] This in turn brought public opprobrium; Ruskin was satirized as a shoe-shine boy in a *Punch* cartoon entitled 'Ruskin at the Feet of Spurgeon'.[61] But undeniably, both in Britain and in the Commonwealth, a new generation of working-class as well as middle-class readers of literature (and eventually journalists and critics) were being to a considerable degree shaped in their views of the Bible by popular evangelical preaching and the wide dissemination of cheap editions of the Bible, perhaps principally by the British and Foreign Bible Society.[62] These Bibles were widely available, side by side with novels, from railway station booksellers, and many read them like novels.

In the meantime, it became increasingly common, even among the literati, to sympathize with Samuel Butler's irritated witticism that 'The Bible is like the poor; we have it always with us, but we know very little about it.'[63] Butler knew some of the Higher Criticism, and employed it in his anonymous pamphlet 'The Evidence of the Resurrection of Jesus Christ as Contained in the Four Evangelists' (1865). But this was Straussian rehash, like his pamphlet 'The Fair Haven' (1873), little more than an excuse for yet another assault upon a few of his father figures. The argument aims for higher ground, even if it does not attain it; as Knoepflmacher has observed, 'Butler could not give his assent to a mere "essence" of Christianity', and in the last chapter of his *Erewhon Revisited* (1901) he firmly rejects any Hegelian transmutation of the 'Christ Ideal', whether that of 'Arnold, George Eliot or Pater'.[64] In some

---

[60]  Wheeler, *Ruskin's God*, pp. 127–31.      [61]  *Punch*, March 1857, p. 129.

[62]  Sue Zemka, *Victorian Testaments: The Bible, Christology, and Literary Authority in Early-Nineteenth-Century British Culture* (Stanford University Press, 1997), pp. 190–223.

[63]  Samuel Butler, *The Notebooks of Samuel Butler. Vol. 1: 1874–1883*, ed. Hans-Peter Breuer (New York: Doubleday, 1967), p. 649.

[64]  Knoepflmacher, *Religious Humanism*, p. 247.

ways Butler's marked lack of interest in protagonists on either side of the long debate made him a harbinger of twentieth-century responses among literary critics to the Victorian obsession with Higher Criticism: it had become largely uninteresting.

Criticism of religion had moved to another front. John Henry Newman, himself of evangelical upbringing, continued to think that Bible reading in churches, homes and privately, had been 'of service', but he came to lament 'indiscriminate' and 'promiscuous' Bible reading as in itself insufficient for consistent doctrine.[65] In his *Apologia pro vita sua* (1864) and *Grammar of Assent* (1870) he was formally engaged in an apologetic for the Roman Catholic Church, and this required of him no sustained addressing of the question of scriptural authority precisely because his task was to supersede all arguments about the authority of the Bible with an argument for the authority of the church. On this view 'the matter of revelation is not a mere collection of truths, not a philosophical view, not a special morality ... but an authoritative teaching' (*Grammar*, p. 302). One takes the package entire or not at all, and it is the essence of Newman's argument that the content of the package is most emphatically dogma and not literature; it is clear that he has Arnold in mind when he characterizes the insufficiency of 'our national form' which 'professes to be little more than thus reading the Bible and living a correct life' (*Grammar*, p. 63). Newman's Bible is a text one ought to read meditatively and liturgically in the context of a formal profession of creedal, dogmatic faith – hence, as a sacramental sustenance for the inner life rather than as 'history' (*Grammar*, p. 79).

It may surprise us that, to different ends, Protestants were also leaving the Higher Criticism behind in favour of a kind of apologetic which foregrounded the poetic imagination as having more value for an apprehension of the divine than any 'academic' approach to the biblical text. The Church of Scotland cleric George MacDonald, in his essay on 'The Imagination', suggests that in the mythopoeic discovery of the imagination in ourselves we have primary evidence of the *imago dei*. In his stories and literary essays alike he argues for an innate apprehension of the divine (which he claims to find anticipated in Ruskin) and develops a theory of reading for story rather than, more narrowly, theology, for 'the reality of Christ's nature is not to be proved by argument. He must be beheld.'[66] To any person who 'believes in the Son of God' in this way, he asserts, 'poetry returns in a mighty wave; history unrolls itself in harmony; science shows crowned with its own aureole of holiness. There is no enlivener of

---

[65] John Henry (Cardinal) Newman, *An Essay in Aid of a Grammar of Assent* (1870; rpt University of Notre Dame Press, 1979), p. 63. Hereafter cited as *Grammar*.
[66] George MacDonald, *A Dish of Orts* (London: Sampson, Low, Marston, 1893), pp. 2–3, 254; cf. p. 206.

the judgment, no strength of the intellect, to compare with the belief in a live Ideal, at the heart of all personality, as of every law.'[67] This is a very long way indeed from the Higher Criticism, and though MacDonald was aware of it, and indeed made good use of such distillations as the sermons of F. D. Maurice (in his incorporation of Isaiah's poetry into his fiction), mythopoesis certainly supersedes both biblical criticism and dogmatic apologetics in his work.[68]

MacDonald was a universalist, though he remained uneasily within the Scottish kirk; he did not become, as Newman thought a person with his convictions must, a Unitarian (*Grammar*, p. 198). In an obverse case, G. K. Chesterton began 'among people who were Unitarians and Universalists but who were well aware that a great many people around them were becoming agnostics or even atheists'. He describes, in his own version of Newman's taxonomy, 'two tendencies in what was called the emancipation of faith from the creeds and dogmas of the past'. The optimistic strain, says Chesterton, 'led to the glorious fairy-land of George MacDonald, the other led into the stark and hollowed hills of Thomas Hardy'.[69] Chesterton's own 'Ethics of Elfland' chapter in *Orthodoxy* (1908) shows that whatever his early temptation to darkness may have been, he emerged from it as something of a Newmanized MacDonald. Even in his literary criticism of *Robert Browning* (1903), where there was certainly occasion for comment, he bypassed the Higher Criticism for deeper issues. What in Matthew Arnold had been a preoccupation – the intellectual rehabilitation of the Bible as imaginative literature rather than a source for religious doctrine – in part because of the prestige of Arnold's Chair of Poetry at Oxford, had by the time of the Great War been comfortably institutionalized in intellectual high culture, there certified by the resources of Hegelian philosophy and the German Higher Criticism. But beyond the university walls the Higher Criticism was of little interest. 'Criticism of religion', as Marx would have it, was now far more vigorous at the margins of high culture, outside the establishment, and there, among the followers of Spurgeon, Newman, MacDonald and the blustery Chesterton, as well as with George Bernard Shaw and the Fabian Socialists, it had taken root as a quest for a new authority no longer to be identified either with state religion or, it must be acknowledged, with the settled orthodoxies of academic literary criticism.

---

[67] *Ibid.*, pp. 75.
[68] Kirstin Jeffrey Johnson, 'Curdie's Intertextual Dialogue: Engaging Maurice, Arnold, and Isaiah' in *George MacDonald: Literary Heritage and Heirs*, ed. Roderick McGillis (Wayne, PA: Zossima Press, 2008), pp. 153–82.
[69] Gilbert Keith Chesterton, *Autobiography* (London: Hutchinson, 1937), p. 171.

# Select bibliography and further reading

## Contexts and conditions of criticism 1830–1914

### Primary sources

Allen, Grant, 'The Decay of Criticism', *Fortnightly Review*, 31 (1882), 339–51.

Bagehot, Walter, 'The First Edinburgh Reviewers' in *Literary Studies*, ed. R. H. Hutton, 2 vols., London: Longmans, Green, 1884, vol. I, pp. 1–40.

Lewes, G. H., 'The Condition of Authors in England, Germany and France', *Fraser's Magazine*, 35 (1847), 285–95.

Morley, John, 'Memorials of a Man of Letters', *Fortnightly Review*, 23 (1878), 596–610; rpt in *Nineteenth-Century Essays*, ed. Peter Stansky, University of Chicago Press, 1970, pp. 261–80.

Oakley, Frederick, 'Periodical Literature', *Dublin Review*, 34 (1853), 541–66.

Saintsbury, George, *History of Nineteenth Century Literature*, London: Macmillan, 1896.

Stephen, Leslie, 'The First Edinburgh Reviewers', *Cornhill Magazine*, 38 (1878); rpt in *Hours in a Library*, new edn, 3 vols., London: Smith, Elder, 1899, vol. III, pp. 241–69.

### Secondary sources

Brake, Laurel, *Subjugated Knowledges*, Basingstoke: Macmillan, 1994.

Chielens, Edward (ed.), *American Literary Magazines: The Eighteenth and Nineteenth Centuries*, New York: Greenwood Press, 1986.

Demata, M. and Duncan Wu (eds.), *British Romanticism and the Edinburgh Review*, London: Palgrave, 2002.

Demoor, Marysa, *Their Fair Share: Women, Power and Criticism in the Athenaeum, from Millicent Garrett Fawcett to Katherine Mansfield 1870–1920*, Aldershot: Ashgate, 2000.

Easley, Alexis, *First Person Anonymous: Women Writers and Victorian Print Media, 1830–1870*, Aldershot: Ashgate, 2004.

Klancher, Jon, *The Making of English Reading Audiences 1790–1832*, Madison: University of Wisconsin Press, 1987.

Maurer, Oscar, 'Anonymity vs Signature in Victorian Reviewing', *Texas Studies in English*, 27 (1948), 1–28.

Parker, Mark, *Literary Magazines and British Romanticism*, Cambridge University Press, 2000.

Roper, Derek, *Reviewing before the Edinburgh 1788–1802*, Newark: University of Delaware Press, 1978.

Shattock, Joanne, 'Spreading it Thinly: Some Victorian Reviewers at Work', *Victorian Periodicals Newsletter*, **9** (1976), 84–7.

    *Politics and Reviewers: The Edinburgh and the Quarterly in the Early Victorian Age*, Leicester University Press, 1989.

Treglown, Jeremy and Bridget Bennett (eds.), *Grub Street and the Ivory Tower*, Oxford: Clarendon Press, 1998.

## Literary studies and the academy

### Primary sources

Arnold, Matthew, 'Schools in the Reign of Queen Victoria' in *The Last Word: The Complete Prose Works of Matthew Arnold*, ed. R. H. Super, vol. XI, Ann Arbor: University of Michigan Press, 1977.

Bradley, A. C., *The Teaching of English Literature*, Glasgow: James MacLehose & Sons, 1891.

Bremner, C. S., *Education of Girls and Women in Great Britain*, London: Swan Sonnenschein, 1897.

Chambers, R. W., *The Teaching of English in the Universities of England*, English Association Pamphlets, 53, [London]: English Association, 1922.

Collins, John Churton, *The Study of English Literature: A Plea for Its Recognition and Organization at the Universities*, London: Macmillan, 1891.

M'Cormick, William S., 'English Literature and University Education' in *Three Lectures on English Literature*, Paisley and London: Alexander Gardner, 1889.

Masson, David, *British Novelists and their Styles: Being a Critical Sketch of the History of British Prose Fiction*, Cambridge: Macmillan, 1859.

Morley, Henry, *English Writers: An Attempt Towards a History of English Literature*, 11 vols., London: Cassell, 1887.

Quiller-Couch, Arthur, *On the Art of Writing*, new edn, Cambridge University Press, 1923.

Raleigh, Walter, *Style*, London: Edward Arnold, 1897.

    *The Study of English Literature: Being the Inaugural Lecture Delivered at the University of Glasgow on Thursday, October 18th, 1900*, Glasgow: James MacLehose & Sons, 1900.

Saintsbury, George, *A Short History of English Literature*, London: Macmillan, 1898.

Shaw, Thomas B., *A History of English Literature*, London: John Murray, 1864.

### Secondary sources

Altick, Richard D., *The English Common Reader: A Social History of the Mass Reading Public 1800–1900*, University of Chicago Press, 1957.

Baldick, Chris, *The Social Mission of English Criticism 1848–1932*, Oxford: Clarendon Press, 1987.

Collini, Stefan, *Public Moralists: Political Thought and Intellectual Life in Britain 1850–1930*, Oxford: Clarendon Press, 1991.

Doyle, Brian, *English and Englishness*, London and New York: Routledge, 2003.

Engel, A. J., *From Clergyman to Don: The Rise of the Academic Professional in Nineteenth-Century Oxford*, Oxford: Clarendon Press, 1983.

Golby, J. M. and A. W. Purdue, *The Civilisation of the Crowd: Popular Culture in England 1750–1900*, Stroud: Sutton, 1999.

Marriott, Stuart, *Extramural Empires: Service and Self-Interest in English University Adult Education 1873–1983*, University of Nottingham, 1984.

McMurtry, Jo, *English Language, English Literature: The Creation of an Academic Discipline*, London: Mansell, 1985.

Palmer, D. J., *The Rise of English Studies: An Account of the Study of English Language and Literature from its Origins to the Making of the Oxford English School*, London: University of Hull, 1965.

Potter, Stephen, *The Muse in Chains: A Study in Education*, London: Jonathan Cape, 1937.

Purvis, June, *A History of Women's Education in England*, Milton Keynes: Open University Press, 1991.

Tillyard, E. M. W., *The Muse Unchained: An Intimate Account of the Revolution in English Studies at Cambridge*, London: Bowes & Bowes, 1958.

## Women and literary criticism

### Primary sources

Eliot, George, *Adam Bede* (1859); rpt Harmondsworth: Penguin, 1980.
  *The George Eliot Letters*, ed. Gordon Haight, 9 vols., New Haven, CT: Yale University Press, 1954–78.

Flaubert, Gustave and George Sand, *Flaubert–Sand: The Correspondence*, trans. Francis Steegmuller and Barbara Bray, New York: Knopf, 1993.

Fuller, Margaret, *Papers on Literature and Art* (1846); rpt New York: AMS Press, 1972.
  *The Letters of Margaret Fuller*, ed. Robert Hudspeth, 6 vols., Ithaca, NY: Cornell University Press, 1983–94.
  *Woman in the Nineteenth Century* (1845) in *The Essential Margaret Fuller*, ed. Jeffrey Steele, New Brunswick, NJ: Rutgers University Press, 1992, pp. 245–378.

Jameson, Anna, *Winter Studies and Summer Rambles in Canada* (1838), 2 vols., New York: Wiley and Putnam, 1839.
  *Legends of the Madonna* (1852), 4th edn, London: Longmans, Green, 1867.
  *Sacred and Legendary Art* (1848), 2 vols; rpt New York: AMS Press, 1970.
  *Shakespeare's Heroines* (1832), ed. and intro. Cheri Hoeckley, Peterborough, Ontario: Broadview Editions, 2005.

Martineau, Harriet, *Biographical Sketches, 1852–1868*, 3rd edn, London: Macmillan, 1870.

*Society in America* (1837), 3 vols., rpt New York: AMS Press, 1966.
*Autobiography* (1877), ed. Gaby Weiner, 2 vols., London: Virago Press, 1983.
Staël, Germaine de, *Corinne, or Italy*, intro. and trans. Avriel Goldberger, New Brunswick, NJ: Rutgers University Press, 1991.

### Secondary sources

Adams, Kimberly VanEsveld, *Our Lady of Victorian Feminism: The Madonna in the Work of Anna Jameson, Margaret Fuller, and George Eliot*, Athens: Ohio University Press, 2001.
Ashton, Rosemary, *George Eliot: A Life*, New York: Penguin, 1996.
Auerbach, Nina, *Woman and the Demon*, Cambridge, MA: Harvard University Press, 1982.
Beer, Gillian, *George Eliot*, Bloomington: Indiana University Press, 1986.
Besser, Gretchen Rous, *Germaine de Staël Revisited*, New York: Twayne, 1994.
Chevigny, Bell Gale, *The Woman and the Myth: Margaret Fuller's Life and Writings*, rev. edn, Boston: Northeastern University Press, 1994.
David, Deirdre, *Intellectual Women and Victorian Patriarchy: Harriet Martineau, Elizabeth Barrett Browning, and George Eliot*, Ithaca, NY: Cornell University Press, 1987.
Easley, Alexis, *First-Person Anonymous: Women Writers and Victorian Print Media, 1830–70*, Aldershot: Ashgate, 2004.
Johnston, Judith, *Anna Jameson: Victorian, Feminist, Woman of Letters*, Aldershot: Scolar Press, 1997.
Lootens, Tricia, *Lost Saints: Silence, Gender, and Victorian Literary Canonization*, Charlottesville: University of Virginia Press, 1996.
Moers, Ellen, *Literary Women*, New York: Oxford University Press, 1985.
Sanders, Valerie, *Reason over Passion: Harriet Martineau and the Victorian Novel*, New York: St. Martin's Press, 1986.
Thomson, Patricia, *George Sand and the Victorians*, New York: Columbia University Press, 1977.

## Literature and nationalism

### Primary sources

Channing, William Ellery, *The Importance and Means of a National Literature*, London: Edward Rainford, 1830.
Debreczeny, Paul and Jesse Zeldin (eds.), *Literature and National Identity: Nineteenth-Century Russian Critical Essays*, Lincoln: University of Nebraska Press, 1970.
Du Ponceau, Peter S., *A Discourse on the Necessity and Means of Making Our National Literature Independent of that of Great Britain*, Philadelphia: E. G. Dorsey, 1834.
Fox, William Johnson, *Lectures Addressed Chiefly to the Working Classes*, 4 vols., London: Charles Fox, 1846.

Hallam, Arthur Henry, 'On Some of the Characteristics of Modern Poetry' (1831) in *The Broadview Anthology of Victorian Poetry and Poetic Theory*, ed. Thomas J. Collins and Vivienne Rundle, Peterborough: Broadview Press, 2000, pp. 540–55.

Home, Henry (Lord Kames), *Sketches of the History of Man* (1774); rpt Hildesheim: Georg Olms, 1968.

Mazzini, Giuseppe, 'Europe: Its Condition and Prospects', *Westminster Review*, 112 (1852), 236–50.

O'Brien, William, *The Influence of the Irish Language on Irish National Literature and Character*, Cork: Guy, 1892.

Renan, Ernest, *Poetry of the Celtic Races and Other Studies*, trans. William G. Hutchison (1896); rpt London: Kennikat Press, 1970.


### Secondary sources

Anderson, Benedict, *Imagined Communities: Reflections on the Origin and Spread of Nationalism*, rev. edn, New York: Verso, 1991.

Chatterjee, Partha, *Nationalist Thought and the Colonial World: A Derivative Discourse*, Minneapolis: University of Minnesota Press, 1986.

Gellner, Ernest, *Nations and Nationalism*, Ithaca, NY: Cornell University Press, 1983.

Lloyd, David, *Nationalism and Minor Literature: James Clarence Mangan and the Emergence of Irish Cultural Nationalism*, Berkeley: University of California Press, 1987.

Resnick, David, 'John Locke and Liberal Nationalism', *History of European Ideas*, 15 (1992), 511–17.

Smith, Anthony D., 'Neo-Classicist and Romantic Elements in the Emergence of Nationalist Conceptions' in *Nationalist Movements*, ed. Anthony D. Smith, London: Macmillan, 1976, pp. 74–87.

   *The Nation in History: Historiographical Debates about Ethnicity and Nationalism*, Hanover: University Press of New England, 2000.

   *Nationalism: Theory, Ideology, History*, Cambridge: Polity, 2001.

Trumpener, Katie, *Bardic Nationalism: The Romantic Novel and the British Empire*, Princeton University Press, 1997.


## Germany: from restoration to consolidation: Classical and Romantic legacies

### Primary sources

Börne, Ludwig, *Sämtliche Schriften*, eds. Inge and Peter Rippmann, Düsseldorf: Melzer, 1964–8.

Gutzkow, Karl, *Gutzkows Werke. Zehnter Teil: Aufsätze zur Literaturgeschichte*, ed. Reinhold Gensel (1912); rpt Hildesheim and New York: G. Olms, 1974.

   *Liberale Energie: Eine Sammlung seiner kritischen Schriften*, ed. Peter Demetz, Frankfurt, Berlin and Vienna: Ullstein, 1974.

Heine, Heinrich, *Works*, trans. Charles Godfrey Leland, London: Heinemann; New York: D. Appleton, 1892–1906.

*Sämtliche Schriften*, ed. Klaus Briegleb, 6 vols., Munich: Carl Hanser, 1968–75; rpt Munich: Deutscher Taschenbuchverlag, 1997.

Herwegh, Georg, *Frühe Publizistik 1837–1841*, ed. Bruno Kaiser, Glashütten im Taunus: Detlev Auvermann KG, 1971.

Menzel, Wolfgang, *German Literature*, trans. Thomas Gordon, 4 vols., Oxford: D. A. Talboys, 1840.

Wienbarg, Ludolf, *Ästhetische Feldzüge*, Hamburg: Hoffman & Campe, 1834.

*Zur neusten Literatur*, 2nd edn, Hamburg: Hoffmann & Campe, 1838.

## Secondary sources

Berman, Russell A., *Between Fontane and Tucholsky: Literary Criticism and the Public Sphere in Imperial Germany*, New York, Bern and Frankfurt: Peter Lang, 1983.

Bucher, Max, Werner Hahl, Georg Jäger and Reinhold Wittmann (eds.), *Realismus und Gründerzeit: Manifeste und Dokumente zur deutschen Literatur 1848–1880*, Stuttgart: Metzler, 1976.

Eisele, Ulf, *Realismus und Ideologie: Zur Kritik der literarischen Theorie nach 1848 am Beispiel des 'Deutschen Museums'*, Stuttgart: Metzler, 1976.

Hohendahl, Peter Uwe (ed.), *Literaturkritik: Eine Textdokumentation zur Geschichte einer literarischen Gattung. Vol. IV: 1848–1870*, Vaduz: Topos, 1984.

(ed.), *Geschichte der deutschen Literaturkritik*, Stuttgart: Metzler, 1985.

Höhn, Gerhard, *Heine-Handbuch: Zeit – Person – Werk*, Stuttgart and Weimar: Metzler, 2004.

Kuttenkeuler, Wolfgang, *Heinrich Heine: Theorie und Kritik der Literatur*, Stuttgart: Kohlhammer, 1972.

Steinecke, Hartmut, *Literaturkritik des Jungen Deutschland: Entwicklungen – Tendenzen – Texte*, Berlin: E. Schmidt, 1982.

Thormann, Michael, 'Der programmatische Realismus der *Grenzboten* im Kontext von liberaler Politik, Philosophie und Geschichtsschreibung', *Internationales Archiv für Sozialgeschichte der deutschen Literatur*, 18 (1993), 37–68.

## France: the continuing debate over Classicism

### Primary sources

Baudelaire, Charles, *Œuvres complètes*, ed. Claude Pichois, 2 vols., Paris: Gallimard, 1974–5.

Chateaubriand, François-René de, *Mémoires d'outre-tombe*, ed. Maurice Levaillant, 2 vols., Paris: Flammarion, 1949.

Hugo, Victor, *Œuvres complètes: édition chronologique*, vol. III, ed. Jean Massin, 18 vols., Paris: Club Français du Livre, 1967.

Laharpe, Jean de, *Lycée, ou cours de littérature ancienne et moderne*, vol. I, Paris: Fermin Didot, 1821.

Restif de La Bretonne, Nicolas-Edme, *Les gynographes ou idées de deux honnêtes femmes sur un projet de règlement proposé à toute l'Europe, pour mettre les femmes à leur place & opérer le bonheur des deux sexes: avec des notes historiques et justificatives, suivies des noms des femmes*, 2 vols., The Hague: Gosse & Ruet, 1777.

Staël, Germaine de, *De la littérature considérée dans ses rapports avec les institutions sociales* (1800) in *Œuvres complètes*, 3 vols., vol. I, Paris: Firmin Didot frères, 1836.

'Essai sur les fictions' (1795) in *Œuvres complètes*, 3 vols., vol. I, Paris: Firmin Didot frères, 1836.

*De l'Allemagne*, ed. Simone Balayel, Paris: Garnier-Flammarion, 1968.

Stendhal, *De l'amour*, ed. Henri Martineau, Paris: Garnier, 1959.

*Racine et Shakespeare* in *Œuvres complètes*, ed. Victor del Litto and Ernest Abravanel, 50 vols., vol. XXXVII, Geneva and Paris: Slatkine, 1986.

### Secondary sources

Boulard, Gilles, 'Ferdinand Brunetière et le Classicisme, ou la conjonction des nationalismes', *Revue d'histoire littéraire de la France*, 100 (2000), 217–35.

Bray, René, *Chronologie du Romantisme (1804–1830)*, Paris: Nizet, 1963.

Brunetière, Ferdinand, *L'évolution des genres dans l'histoire de la littérature. Vol. I: L'évolution de la critique*, Paris: Hachette, 1906.

Desmarais, Cyprien, *Essai sur les classiques et les romantiques* (1824); rpt Geneva: Slatkine, 1973.

Hamrick, L. Cassandra, 'Artistic Production and the Art Critic in a Bourgeois Era: The Case of Théophile Gautier', *Il confronto letterario: quaderni del Dipartimento di Lingue et Letterature Straniere Moderne dell'Universita di Pavia*, 17 (2000), 241–63.

'Borel, Gautier et Baudelaire: de la "périphérie" du romantique au centre du "moderne"' in *Poésie et poétique en France, 1830–1890: hommage à Eileen Souffrin-Le Breton*, ed. Peter J. Edwards, New York: Peter Lang, 2001, pp. 77–108.

Lanson, Gustave, *Histoire de la littérature française*, ed. Paul Tuffrau, Paris: Hachette, 1967.

Lanyi, Gabriel, 'Debates on the Definition of Romanticism in Literary France (1820–30)', *Journal of the History of Ideas*, 41 (1980), 141–50.

Pasco, Allan H., *Sick Heroes: French Society and Literature in the Romantic Age, 1750–1850*, University of Exeter Press, 1997.

Pocock, Gordon, *Boileau and the Nature of Neo-Classicism*, Cambridge University Press, 1980.

## England: Romantic legacies

### Primary sources

Carlyle, Thomas, *Critical and Miscellaneous Essays*, 7 vols., London: Chapman & Hall, 1879.

Coleridge, Samuel Taylor, *The Friend* (1818), ed. Barbara E. Rooke, Bollingen Series LXXV, London and Princeton: Routledge/Princeton University Press, 1969.

Dallas, E. S., *The Gay Science*, 2 vols., London: Chapman & Hall, 1866.

De Quincey, Thomas, 'Letters to a Young Man whose Education has been Neglected' in *Collected Writings of Thomas De Quincey. Vol. x: Literary Theory and Criticism*, ed. David Masson, London and Edinburgh: A. & C. Black, 1896.

Keble, John, *Occasional Papers and Reviews*, Oxford University Press, 1877.
*Keble's Lectures on Poetry*, trans. E. K. Francis, 2 vols., Oxford University Press, 1912.

MacDonald, George, *England's Antiphon*, London: Macmillan, 1878.
*A Dish of Orts*, London: S. L. Marston, 1882; published in the USA as *The Imagination and Other Essays*, Boston: Lothrop, 1883.

Newman, J. H., *Essays Critical and Historical*, 2 vols., London: Longman, 1871.

Schlegel, Friedrich, *Philosophical Fragments*, trans. Peter Firchow, Minneapolis: University of Minnesota Press, 1991.

### Secondary sources

Abrams, M. H., *The Mirror and the Lamp*, New York: Oxford University Press, 1953.

Ashton, Rosemary, *G. H. Lewes: A Life*, Oxford: Clarendon Press, 1991.
*The German Idea: Four English Writers and the Reception of German Thought 1800–1860*, London: Libris, 1994.

Bowie, Andrew, *Aesthetics and Subjectivity*, Manchester University Press, 1990.
*From Romanticism to Critical Theory*, London: Routledge, 1997.

Hilton, Tim, *John Ruskin: The Early Years; The Later Years*, New Haven, CT: Yale University Press, 2000.

Isbell, John Claiborne, *The Birth of European Romanticism: Truth and Propaganda in Staël's 'De l'Allemagne' 1810–1813*, Cambridge University Press, 1994.

Perkins, David, *Is Literary History Possible?*, Baltimore, MD: Johns Hopkins University Press, 1992.

Prickett, Stephen, *Coleridge and Wordsworth: The Poetry of Growth*, Cambridge University Press, 1970.
*Words and the Word: Language, Poetics and Biblical Interpretation*, Cambridge University Press, 1986.

Wellek, René, 'Carlyle and the Philosophy of History' in *Confrontations: Studies in the Intellectual Relations between Germany, England, and the United States during the Nineteenth Century*, Princeton University Press, 1965.

### England: literature and culture

#### Primary sources

Carlyle, Thomas, *Collected Works*, 30 vols., London: Chapman & Hall, 1869.

Pater, Walter, *Appreciations, with an Essay on Style*, London: Macmillan, 1889.

*The Renaissance: Studies in Art and Poetry: The 1893 Text*, ed. Donald L. Hill, Berkeley and Los Angeles: University of California Press, 1980.

Ruskin, John, *The Works of John Ruskin*, ed. E. T. Cook and Alexander Wedderburn, 39 vols., London: George Allen, 1903–12.

Shaw, George Bernard, *Major Critical Essays*, London: Constable, 1932.

*The Complete Plays with Prefaces*, 6 vols., New York: Dodd, Mead, 1963.

### Secondary sources

Austin, Linda M., *The Practical Ruskin: Economics and Audience in the Late Work*, Baltimore, MD, and London: Johns Hopkins University Press, 1991.

Buckler, William E., *Walter Pater: The Critic as Artist of Ideas*, New York and London: New York University Press, 1987.

Daley, Kenneth, *The Rescue of Romanticism: Walter Pater and John Ruskin*, Athens: Ohio University Press, 2001.

Erikson, Lee, *The Economy of Literary Form: English Literature and the Industrialization of Publishing 1800–1850*, Baltimore, MD, and London: Johns Hopkins University Press, 1996.

Iser, Wolfgang, *Walter Pater: The Aesthetic Moment*, trans. David Henry Wilson, Cambridge University Press, 1987.

Loesberg, Jonathan, *Aestheticism and Deconstruction: Pater, Derrida and De Man*, Princeton University Press, 1991.

McKelvy, William R., *The English Cult of Literature*, Charlottesville: University of Virginia Press, 2006.

Riede, David G., *Oracles and Hierophants: Constructions of Romantic Authority*, Ithaca, NY, and London: Cornell University Press, 1991.

Roe, Frederick William, *Thomas Carlyle as a Critic of Literature*, New York: Columbia University Press, 1910.

St. Clair, William, *The Reading Nation in the Romantic Period*, Cambridge University Press, 2004.

Shuter, William, *Re-Reading Walter Pater*, Cambridge University Press, 1999.

Vanden Bossche, Chris, *Carlyle and the Search for Authority*, Columbus: Ohio State University Press, 1991.

## Literary nationalism and US Romantic aesthetics

### Primary sources

Barlow, Joel, *The Connecticut Wits*, ed. Vernon Louis Parrington, New York: Harcourt, Brace, 1926.

Bradford, William, *Of Plymouth Plantation, 1620–1647*, ed. Samuel Eliot Morrison, New York: Modern Library, 1967.

Dickens, Charles, *American Notes for General Circulation*, New York: Penguin, 2000.

Emerson, Ralph Waldo, *Journal and Miscellaneous Notebooks*, eds. Alfred R. Ferguson *et al.*, Cambridge, MA: Harvard University Press, 1960–82.

Jacobs, Harriet, *Incidents in the Life of a Slave Girl*, ed. Valerie A. Smith, New York: Oxford University Press, 1990.

632 Select bibliography and further reading

Poe, Edgar Allan, *The Complete Works of Edgar Allan Poe*, ed. James A. Harrison, 16 vols., New York: Thomas Y. Crowell, 1902.

Sewall, Samuel, *The American Puritans: Their Prose and Poetry*, ed. Perry Miller, New York: Columbia University Press, 1982.

Trollope, Frances, *Domestic Manners of the Americans*, New York: Knopf, 1949.

### Secondary sources

Cavell, Stanley, *Emerson's Transcendental Etudes*, ed. David Hodge, Palo Alto, CA: Stanford University Press, 2003.

Hutchison, William R., *The Transcendentalist Ministers: Church Reform in the New England Renaissance*, New Haven, CT: Yale University Press, 1959.

Matthiessen, F. O., *American Renaissance: Art and Expression in the Age of Emerson and Whitman*, New York: Oxford University Press, 1941.

Menand, Louis, *The Metaphysical Club: A Story of Ideas in America*, New York: Farrar, Straus & Giroux, 2001.

Miller, Perry, *The Raven and the Whale: The War of Words and Wits in the Era of Poe and Melville*, New York: Harcourt, Brace & World, 1956.

(ed.), *The Transcendentalists: An Anthology*, new edn, Cambridge, MA: Harvard University Press, 1971.

Rose, Anne C., *Transcendentalism as a Social Movement, 1830–1850*, New Haven, CT: Yale University Press, 1981.

Van Leer, David, *Emerson's Epistemology: The Argument of the Essays*, Cambridge University Press, 1986.

Vendler, Helen, *Part of Nature, Part of Us: Modern American Poets*, Cambridge, MA: Harvard University Press, 1980.

## Russia: literature and society

### Primary sources in English

Grigoriev, A. A., *My Literary and Moral Wanderings*, trans. R. Matlaw, New York: Dutton, 1962.

Gumilev, Nikolai, *On Russian Poetry*, ed. and trans. D. Lapeza, Ann Arbor: Ardis, 1977.

Ivanov, Vyacheslav, *Selected Essays*, ed. M. Wachtel, trans. R. Bird, Evanston, IL: Northwestern University Press, 2001.

Mandelstam, Osip, *The Complete Critical Prose and Letters*, ed. J. G. Harris, trans. J. G. Harris and C. Link, Ann Arbor: Ardis, 1979.

Matlaw, R. E. (ed.), *Belinsky, Chernyshevsky, and Dobrolyubov: Selected Criticism*, New York: E. P. Dutton, 1962.

Proffer, C. R. (ed.), *Modern Russian Poets on Poetry*, Ann Arbor: Ardis, 1976.

Rosenthal, B. G. and M. Bohachevsky-Chomiak, *A Revolution of the Spirit: Crisis of Value in Russia, 1890–1924*, trans. M. Schwartz, Newtonville, MA: Oriental Research Partners, 1982.

## Secondary sources

Berlin, Isaiah, *Russian Thinkers*, London: Hogarth Press, 1978.
Clowes, Edith W., *The Revolution of Moral Consciousness: Nietzsche in Russian Literature, 1892–1914*, DeKalb: Northern Illinois University Press, 1988.
  *Fiction's Overcoat: Russian Literary Culture and the Question of Philosophy*, Ithaca, NY: Cornell University Press, 2004.
Dowler, Wayne, *Dostoevsky, Grigor'ev, and Native Soil Conservatism*, University of Toronto Press, 1982.
Kuleshov, V. I., *Istoriia russkoi kritiki: 18.-19. vv*, 2nd edn, Moscow: Prosveshchenie, 1978.
Moser, Charles, *Esthetics as Nightmare: Russian Literary Theory, 1855–1870*, Princeton University Press, 1989.
Pachmuss, Temira, *Zinaida Hippius: An Intellectual Profile*, Carbondale: Southern Illinois University Press, 1971.
Randall, Francis B., *Vissarion Belinskii*, Newtonville: Oriental Research Partners, 1987.
Rosenthal, Bernice Glatzer, *Dmitri Sergeevich Merezhkovsky: The Development of the Revolutionary Mentality*, The Hague: M. Nijhoff, 1975.
Scanlan, James P., *Dostoevsky the Thinker*, Ithaca, NY: Cornell University Press, 2002.
Schapiro, Leonard, *Turgenev: His Life and Times*, Cambridge, MA: Harvard University Press, 1978.
Terras, Victor, *Belinskij and Russian Literary Criticism: The Heritage of Organic Aesthetics*, Madison: University of Wisconsin Press, 1974.
  (ed.), *Handbook of Russian Literature*, New Haven, CT: Yale University Press, 1986.
Tikhonova, E. Iu. V. G., *Belinskii v spore so slavianofilami*, Moscow: URSS, 1999.

## Literary autonomy: the growth of a modern concept

### Primary sources

Buckler, William E. (ed.), *Walter Pater: Three Major Texts*, New York University Press, 1986.
Coleridge, Samuel Taylor, *The Collected Works of Samuel Taylor Coleridge*, ed. Kathleen Coburn, 16 vols., London and Princeton: Routledge & Kegan Paul/Princeton University Press, 1969–2001.
Gautier, Théophile, *The Works of Théophile Gautier*, trans. and ed. F. C. de Sumichrast, 24 vols., New York: George D. Sproul, 1900.
Heine, Heinrich, *Heinrich Heine: Schriften zur Literatur*, ed. Karl Kraus, Stuttgart: P. Reclam, 1986.
Kant, Immanuel, *Critique of Judgment*, trans. Werner S. Pluhar, Indianapolis: Hackett, 1987.
Mallarmé, Stéphane, *Selected Prose, Poems, Essays, and Letters*, trans. Bradford Cook, Baltimore, MD: Johns Hopkins University Press, 1956.

Schiller, Friedrich, *On the Aesthetic Education of Man*, trans. Elizabeth M. Wilkinson and L. A. Willoughby, Oxford: Clarendon Press, 1967.
Weintraub, Stanley (ed.), *Literary Criticism of Oscar Wilde*, Lincoln: University of Nebraska Press, 1968.

## Secondary sources

Adorno, Theodor, *Ästhetische Theorie*, Frankfurt: Suhrkamp, 1973.
Bowie, Andrew, *Aesthetics and Subjectivity: From Kant to Nietzsche*, New York: St. Martin's Press, 1990.
Eagleton, Terry, *The Ideology of the Aesthetic*, Oxford: Blackwell, 1990.
Gadamer, Hans Georg, *Wahrheit und Methode: Grundzüge einer philosophischen Hermeneutik*, Tübingen: J. C. B. Mohr, 1986.
Habib, M. A. R., *A History of Literary Criticism: From Plato to the Present*, Malden: Blackwell, 2005.
Hammermeister, Kai, *The German Aesthetic Tradition*, Cambridge University Press, 2002.
Isbell, John Claiborne, *The Birth of European Romanticism: Truth and Propaganda in Staël's 'De l'Allemagne'*, Cambridge University Press, 1994.
Loesberg, Jonathan, *A Return to Aesthetics: Autonomy, Indifference, and Postmodernism*, Stanford University Press, 2005.
Seel, Martin, *Aesthetics of Appearing*, trans. John Farrell, Stanford University Press, 2005.
Wimsatt, William K. and Cleanth Brooks, *Literary Criticism: A Short History*, 2 vols., University of Chicago Press, 1983.

## Hegel's aesthetics and their influence

### Primary sources

Hegel, G.W. F., *Hegel's Lectures on the History of Philosophy*, vol. III, trans. E. S. Haldane and Frances H. Simson, London and New York: Routledge & Kegan Paul/Humanities Press, 1963.
*Aesthetics: Lectures on Fine Art*, vol. I, trans. T. M. Knox, Oxford University Press, 1975.
*Aesthetics: Lectures on Fine Art*, vol. II, trans. T. M. Knox, Oxford University Press, 1975.
*Hegel's Science of Logic*, trans. A. V. Miller, London and New York: George Allen & Unwin/Humanities Press, 1976.
*Hegel's Phenomenology of Spirit*, trans. A. V. Miller, Oxford: Clarendon Press, 1979.
*Hegel's Logic: Being Part One of the Encyclopaedia of the Philosophical Sciences (1830)*, trans. William Wallace, Oxford University Press, 1982.
*Hegel: On the Arts*, trans. Henry Paolucci, Smyrna, DE: Griffon House, 2001.
*Hegel on Tragedy*, ed. and intro. Anne and Henry Paolucci, 1982; rpt Smyrna, DE: Griffon House, 2001.

## Secondary sources

Bosanquet, Bernard, *A History of Aesthetic* (1892); rpt London and New York: George Allen & Unwin/Humanities Press, 1966.

Bradley, A. C., 'Hegel's Theory of Tragedy' in *Oxford Lectures on Poetry* (1909); rpt New York and London: St. Martin's Press/Macmillan, 1965.

Bungay, Stephen, *Beauty and Truth: A Study of Hegel's Aesthetic*, Oxford University Press, 1984.

Etter, Brian K., *Between Transcendence and Historicism: The Ethical Nature of the Arts in Hegelian Aesthetics*, SUNY Press, 2006.

Jameson, Fredric, 'Towards Dialectical Criticism' in *Marxism and Form: Twentieth-Century Dialectical Theories of Literature*, Princeton University Press, 1971.

Maker, William (ed.), *Hegel and Aesthetics*, SUNY Press, 2000.

Moss, Leonard, 'The Unrecognized Influence of Hegel's Theory of Tragedy', *Journal of Aesthetics and Art Criticism*, 28 (1969), 91–7.

Pillow, Kirk, *Sublime Understanding: Aesthetic Reflection in Kant and Hegel*, London and Cambridge, MA: MIT Press, 2000.

Pinkard, Terry, *Hegel: A Biography*, Cambridge University Press, 2001.

Roche, Mark William, *Tragedy and Comedy: A Systematic Study and a Critique of Hegel*, SUNY Press, 1998.

Taylor, Charles, *Hegel*, Cambridge University Press, 2008.

## Marx, Engels and early Marxist criticism

### Primary sources

Ball, A. H. R. (ed.), *Selections from the Prose Works of William Morris*, Cambridge University Press, 1931.

Baxandall, Lee and Stefan Morawski (eds.), *Karl Marx and Frederick Engels on Literature and Art*, New York: International General, 1973.

Labriola, Antonio, *Essays in the Materialistic Conception of History*, trans. Charles H. Kerr, Chicago: Charles H. Kerr, 1908.

Lamire, Eugene D. (ed.), *The Unpublished Lectures of William Morris*, Detroit: Wayne State University Press, 1969.

Marx, Karl and Frederick Engels, *On Literature and Art*, Moscow: Progress, 1976.

Mehring, Franz, *The Lessing Legend*, trans. A. S. Grogan, New York: Critics Group Press, 1938.

Morton, A. L. (ed.), *Political Writings of William Morris*, London: Lawrence & Wishart, 1979.

Plekhanov, Georgi, *Art and Social Life*, ed. Andrew Rothstein, London: Lawrence & Wishart, 1953.

*Art and Society and Other Papers in Historical Materialism*, New York: Oriole Editions, 1974.

Raddatz, Fritz J. (ed.), *Marxismus und Literatur: eine Dokumentation in drei Bänden*, 3 vols., Hamburg: Rowohlt, 1969.

Solomon, Maynard (ed.), *Marxism and Art: Essays Classic and Contemporary*, Detroit: Wayne State University Press, 1979.


## Realism, Naturalism and Symbolism in France

### Primary sources

Balzac, Honoré de, *Ecrits sur le roman*, Paris: Librairie générale française, 2000.
Baudelaire, Charles, *Œuvres complètes*, ed. Claude Pichois, 2 vols., Paris: Gallimard, Bibliothèque de la Pléiade, 1976.
Becque, Henry, *Œuvres complètes*, vol. VII, Paris: G. Crès, 1926.
Brunetière, Ferdinand, *Questions de critique*, Paris: Calmann Lévy, 1890.
  *Nouvelles questions de critique*, Paris: Calmann Lévy, 1890.
Champfleury (Jules-François-Félix Husson), *Le Réalisme*, Paris: Michel Lévy, 1857.
Courbet, Gustave, *Letters of Gustave Courbet*, ed. and trans. Petra ten-Doesschate Chu, University of Chicago Press, 1992.
Duranty, Edmond, *La Nouvelle peinture*, Paris: Dentu, 1876.
Flaubert, Gustave, *Correspondance*, vol. I, ed. Jean Bruneau, Paris: Gallimard, Bibliothèque de la Pléiade, 1973.
France, Anatole, *La Vie littéraire*, Paris: Calmann Lévy, 1926.
Gourmont, Remy de, *Decadence and Other Essays on the Culture of Ideas*, trans. William Bradley, 1922; rpt London: George Allen & Unwin, 1930.
Hennequin, Emile, *Quelques écrivains français*, Paris: Perrin, 1890.
Huysmans, Joris-Karl, *L'Art moderne/Certains*, Paris: Editions 10/18, 1975.
Lemaître, Jules, *Les Contemporains: études et portraits littéraires*, Paris: H. Lecène & H. Oudin, 1886.
Maupassant, Guy de, *Pierre et Jean*, Paris: Albin Michel, 1984.
Renan, Ernest, *L'Avenir de la science*, Paris: Calmann Lévy, 1890.
Sarcey, Francisque, *Quarante ans de théâtre*, Paris: Bibliothèque des annales politiques et littéraires, 1900.
Scherer, Edmond, *Etudes sur la littérature contemporaine*, vol. II, Paris: Calmann Lévy, 1891.
Zola, Emile, *Le Roman expérimental*, Paris: Garnier-Flammarion, 1971.


### Secondary sources

Antoniu, Annette, *Anatole France, critique littéraire*, Paris: Boivin, 1929.
Bonnet, Gilles, *Champfleury, écrivain chercheur*, Paris: Champion, 2006.
Chauvin, Charles, *Renan: 1823–1892*, Paris: Desclée de Brouwer, 2000.
Compagnon, Antoine, *Connaissez-vous Brunetière? Enquête sur un antidreyfusard et ses amis*, Paris: Seuil, 1997.
Crouzet, Marcel, *Un méconnu du réalisme: Duranty (1833–1880). L'homme, le critique, le romancier*, Paris: Librairie Nizet, 1964.
LeGouis, Catherine, *Positivism and Imagination: Scientism and its Limits in Emile Hennequin, Wilhelm Scherer, and Dmitrii Pisarev*, Lewisburg, PA: Bucknell University Press, 1997.

Lloyd, Rosemary, *Baudelaire's Literary Criticism*, Cambridge University Press, 1981.

Nordmann, Jean-Thomas, *Taine et la critique scientifique*, Paris: Presses Universitaires de France, 1992.

Pichois, Claude, *Philarète Chasles et la vie littéraire au temps du romantisme*, 2 vols., Paris: J. Corti, 1965.

Seys, Pascale, *Hippolyte Taine et l'avènement du naturalisme: un intellectuel sous le Second Empire*, Paris: L'Harmattan, 1999.

Vircondelet, Alain, *Joris-Karl Huysmans*, Paris: Plon, 1990.

Ziegler, Robert, *The Mirror of Divinity: The World and Creation in J.-K. Huysmans*, Newark: University of Delaware Press, 2004.

## Symbolism and Realism in Germany

### Primary sources

Hegel, G. W. F., *Vorlesungen über die Äesthetik* [Lectures on Aesthetics], Berlin: Aufbau, 1955.

Keller, Gottfried, *Der grüne Heinrich* [Green Henry], Munich: Winkler, 1978.

Lukács, Georg, *Die Theorie des Romans* [The Theory of the Novel], Darmstadt and Neuwied: Luchterhand, 1971.

Vischer, F. T., *Aesthetik oder Wissenschaft des Schönen* [Aesthetics or the Science of the Beautiful], Stuttgart: Macken, 1857.

### Secondary sources

Albrecht Bernd, Clifford, *Poetic Realism in Scandinavia and Central Europe 1820–1895*, Columbia, SC: Camden House, 1995.

Kohl, Stefan, *Realismus: Theorie und Geschichte* [Realism: Theory and History], Munich: Fink, 1977.

Plumpe, Gerhard (ed.), *Theorie des bürgerlichen Realismus: eine Textsammlung* [The Theory of Bourgeois Realism: A Collection of Texts], Stuttgart: Reclam, 1985.

Steinecke, Hartmut (ed.), *Romanpoetik in Deutschland: von Hegel bis Fontane* [The Poetics of the Novel in Germany], Tübingen: Narr, 1984.

  *Romanpoetik von Goethe bis Thomas Mann: Entwicklungen und Probleme der 'demokratischen Kunstform' in Deutschland* [The Poetics of the Novel from Goethe to Thomas Mann: Developments and Problems of the 'Democratic Art Form' in Germany], Munich: Fink, 1987.

Swales, Martin, *Epochenbuch Realismus: Romane und Erzählungen* [Epoch Book on Realism: Novels and Novellas], Berlin: Schmidt, 1997.

## Nineteenth-century British critics of Realism

### Primary sources

Eigner, Edwin M. and George J. Worth (eds.), *Victorian Criticism of the Novel*, Cambridge University Press, 1985.

Kaminsky, Alice (ed.), *Literary Criticism of George Henry Lewes*, Lincoln: University of Nebraska Press, 1964.

Lee, Vernon, *Art and Life*, New York: Routledge, 1896.

Olmsted, John Charles, *A Victorian Art of Fiction: Essays on the Novel in British Periodicals*, 3 vols., New York: Garland, 1979.

Pinney, Thomas (ed.), *Essays of George Eliot*, New York: Columbia University Press, 1963.

### Secondary sources

Arata, Stephen, 'Realism' in *Cambridge Companion to the Fin de Siècle*, ed. Gail Marshall, Cambridge University Press, 2007, pp. 169–88.

Armstrong, Nancy, *Fiction in the Age of Photography: The Legacy of British Realism*, Cambridge, MA: Harvard University Press, 1999.

Becker, George J. (ed.), *Documents of Modern Literary Realism*, Princeton University Press, 1963.

Levine, Caroline, *The Serious Pleasures of Suspense: Victorian Realism and Narrative Doubt*, Charlottesville: University of Virginia Press, 2003.

Levine, George, *The Realistic Imagination: English Fiction from Frankenstein to Lady Chatterley*, University of Chicago Press, 1981.

Menke, Richard, *Telegraphic Realism: Victorian Fiction and Other Information Systems*, Stanford University Press, 2008.

Novak, Daniel A., *Realism, Photography and Nineteenth-Century Fiction*, Cambridge University Press, 2008.

Ortiz-Robles, Mario, *The Novel as Event*, Ann Arbor: University of Michigan Press, 2010.

Stang, Richard, *The Theory of the Novel in England, 1850–1870*, New York: Columbia University Press, 1959.

## American literary Realism

### Primary sources

Chesnutt, Charles W., *Stories, Novels and Essays*, New York: Library of America, 2002.

Chopin, Kate, *Complete Novels and Stories: At Fault, Bayou Folk, A Night in Acadie, The Awakening, Uncollected Stories*, New York: Library of America, 2002.

Crane, Stephen, *Prose and Poetry: Maggie, a Girl of the Streets; The Red Badge of Courage; Stories, Sketches, Journalism; The Black Riders; War is Kind*, New York: Library of America, 1984.

Dreiser, Theodore, *Sister Carrie, Jennie Gerhardt, Twelve Men*, New York: Library of America, 1987.

Howells, William Dean, *Novels, 1875–1886: A Foregone Conclusion, A Modern Instance, Indian Summer, The Rise of Silas Lapham*, New York: Library of America, 1982.

James, Henry, *Novels 1881–1886: Washington Square, The Portrait of a Lady, The Bostonians*, New York: Library of America, 1985.

Twain, Mark, *Mississippi Writings: Tom Sawyer, Life on The Mississippi, Huckleberry Finn, Pudd'nhead Wilson*, New York: Library of America, 1982.

Wharton, Edith, *Novels: The House of Mirth, The Reef, The Custom of the Country, The Age of Innocence*, New York: Library of America, 1986.


## Secondary sources

Bell, Michael Davitt, *The Problem of American Realism: Studies in the Cultural History of a Literary Idea*, University of Chicago Press, 1993.

Kaplan, Amy, *The Social Construction of American Realism*, University of Chicago Press, 1988.

Pizer, Donald, *Realism and Naturalism in Nineteenth-Century American Literature*, rev. edn, Carbondale: Southern Illinois University Press, 1984.

  (ed.), *Documents of American Realism and Naturalism*, Carbondale: Southern Illinois University Press, 1998.

Shi, David, *Facing Facts: Realism in American Thought and Culture, 1850–1920*, New York: Oxford University Press, 1995.

Sundquist, Eric J., 'Realism and Regionalism' in *Columbia Literary History of the United States*, ed. Emory Elliott, New York: Columbia University Press, 1988, pp. 501–24.

# Decadence and *fin de siècle*

## Primary sources

Baudelaire, Charles, *Œuvres complètes*, ed. Yves-Gérard Le Dantec, Paris: Gallimard, 1951.

D'Annunzio, Gabriele, *Prose di romanzi*, ed. Ezio Raimondi, 2 vols., Milan: Arnoldo Mondadori, 1988.

Gautier, Théophile, *Mademoiselle de Maupin*, ed. Eugène Fasquelle, Paris: Bibliothèque- Charpentier, 1922.

Huysmans, Joris-Karl, *Œuvres complètes*, 18 vols. (1928–34); rpt Geneva: Slatkine, 1972.

Mann, Thomas, *Gesammelte Werke*, 13 vols., Frankfurt: Fischer, 1990.

Nietzsche, Friedrich, *Werke*, ed. Karl Schlechta, 3 vols., Munich: Hanser, 1954–66.

Nordau, Max, *Entartung*, 2 vols., Berlin: Carl Duncker, 1892.

Pater, Walter, *The Library Edition of the Works of Walter Pater*, 10 vols., London: Macmillan, 1910.

Verlaine, Paul, *Œuvres complètes*, Paris: Albert Messein, 1927.

Wagner, Richard, *Gesammelte Schriften*, ed. Julius Kapp, 14 vols., Leipzig: Hesse & Becker, 1914.

Wilde, Oscar, *The First Collected Edition of the Works of Oscar Wilde, 1908–1922*, ed. Robert Ross, 15 vols., London: Dawsons of Pall Mall, 1969.


## Secondary sources

Bahr, Hermann, *Studien zur Kritik der Moderne*, Frankfurt: Rütten & Loening, 1894.

Baldick, Robert, *The Life of J-K Huysmans*, Oxford: Clarendon Press, 1955.

Buckley, Jerome Hamilton, *The Triumph of Time: A Study of the Victorian Concepts of Time, History, Progress and Decadence*, Cambridge, MA, and Oxford: Harvard University Press/Oxford University Press, 1966.

Ellmann, Richard, *Oscar Wilde*, London: Hamish Hamilton, 1987.

Furness, Raymond (ed.), *The Dedalus Book of German Decadence: Voices of the Abyss*, Sawtry and New York: Dedalus/Hippocrene, 1994.

Ledger, Sally and Roger Luckhurst (eds.), *The Fin de Siècle: A Reader in Cultural History*, Oxford University Press, 2000.

Norton, Robert E., *Secret Germany: Stefan George and his Circle*, Ithaca, NY, and London: Cornell University Press, 2002.

Praz, Mario, *The Romantic Agony*, trans. Angus Davidson, 2nd edn, Oxford University Press, 1951.

Sutton, Emma, *Aubrey Beardsley and British Wagnerism in the 1890s*, Oxford University Press, 2002.

Thornton, R. K. (ed.), *Poetry of the Nineties*, London: Penguin, 1970.

Weintraub, Stanley, *Beardsley*, London: Penguin, 1972.

Woodhouse, John, *Gabriele D'Annunzio: Defiant Archangel*, Oxford University Press, 1998.

## The avant-garde in early twentieth-century Europe

### Primary sources

Ades, Dawn (ed.), *The Dada Reader: A Critical Anthology*, London: Tate, 2006.

Apollonio, Umbro (ed.), *Futurist Manifestos*, London: Thames & Hudson, 1973.

Benson, Timothy O. and Éva Forgács (eds.), *Between Worlds: A Sourcebook of Central European Avant-Gardes, 1910–1930*, Cambridge, MA, and London: MIT Press, 2002.

Caws, Mary Ann (ed.), *Manifesto: A Century of Isms*, Lincoln and London: University of Nebraska Press, 2001.

(ed.), *Surrealism*, London: Phaidon, 2004.

Lankheit, Klaus (ed.), *Der Blaue Reiter: Dokumentarische Neuausgabe*, Munich and Zurich: Piper, 1984.

Lewis, Percy Wyndham (ed.), *Blast: Review of the Great English Vortex*, Santa Barbara: Black Sparrow Press, 1982.

Motherwell, Robert (ed.), *The Dada Painters and Poets: An Anthology* (1951); rpt Boston: G. K. Hall, 1981.

Proffer, Ellendea and Carl R. Proffer (eds.), *The Ardis Anthology of Russian Futurism*, Ann Arbor: Ardis, 1980.

## Secondary sources

Berghaus, Günter (ed.), *International Futurism in Arts and Literature*, Berlin: Walter de Gruyter, 2000.

Black, Jonathan, Christopher Adams, Michael J. K. Walsh and Jonathan Wood, *Blasting the Future! Vorticism in Britain 1910–1920*, London: Philip Wilson, 2004.

Breton, André, *Conversations: The Autobiography of Surrealism*, New York: Paragon House, 1993.

Bury, Stephen (ed.), *Breaking the Rules: The Printed Face of the European Avant Garde 1900–1937*, London: British Library, 2007.

Cardinal, Roger, *Expressionism*, London: Granada, 1984.

Cox, Neil, *Cubism*, London: Phaidon Press, 2000.

Dachy, Marc, *Dada: The Revolt of Art*, London: Thames & Hudson, 2006.

Durozoi, Gérard, *History of the Surrealist Movement*, London: University of Chicago Press, 2002.

Kuenzli, Rudolf, *Dada*, London: Phaidon Press, 2006.

Markov, Vladimir, *Russian Futurism: A History*, Berkeley and Los Angeles: University of California Press, 1968.

Nadeau, Maurice, *History of Surrealism*, Cambridge, MA: Harvard University Press, 1965.

Perloff, Marjorie, *The Futurist Moment: Avant-Garde, Avant-Guerre, and the Language of Rupture*, Chicago and London: Chicago University Press, 1986.

Poggioli, Renato, *The Theory of the Avant-Garde*, Cambridge, MA, and London: Belknap Press, 1968.

Richter, Hans, *Dada: Art and Anti-Art*, London: Thames & Hudson, 1965.

Russell, Charles, *Poets, Prophets and Revolutionaries: The Literary Avant-Garde from Rimbaud through Postmodernism*, Oxford University Press, 1985.

Švestka, Vlček, *Czech Cubism 1909–1925*, Prague: Modernista, 2007.

Wees, William C., *Vorticism and the English Avant-Garde*, University of Toronto Press, 1972.

# Charles-Augustin Sainte-Beuve

## Primary sources

Sainte-Beuve, Charles-Augustin, *Causeries du lundi*, 16 vols., Paris: Garnier, 1850–60.

*Nouveaux lundis*, 13 vols., Paris: Calmann Lévy, 1862–64.

*Portraits littéraires*, rev. edn, 3 vols., Paris: Garnier, 1868–84.

*Les cahiers de Sainte-Beuve, suivis de quelques pages de littérature antique*, ed. Jules Troubat, Paris: Alphonse Lemerre, 1876.

*Chateaubriand et son groupe littéraire sous l'empire: Cours professé à Liège en 1848–1849*, rev. edn, vol. I, Paris: Calmann Lévy, 1878.
*Portraits contemporains* (1845), rev. edn, 5 vols., Paris: Calmann Lévy, 1881–2.
*Port-Royal*, 7th/8th edn, 7 vols., Paris: Hachette, 1908–10.

### Secondary sources

Bellessort, André, *Sainte-Beuve et le XIXe siècle*, Paris: Perrin, 1927.
Bénichou, Paul, *L'Ecole du désenchantement: Sainte-Beuve, Nodier, Musset, Nerval, Gautier*, Paris: Gallimard, 1992.
Casanova, Nicole, *Sainte-Beuve*, Paris: Mercure de France, 1995.
Fumaroli, Marc, *Littérature et conversation: la querelle Sainte-Beuve–Proust*, Cassal Lecture, University of London, 1991.
Leroy, Maxime, *La Politique de Sainte-Beuve*, Paris: Gallimard, 1941.
*Vie de Sainte-Beuve*, Paris: J. B. Janin, 1947.
Michaut, Gustave, *Sainte-Beuve*, Paris: Librairie Hachette, 1921.
Molho, Raphaël, *L'Ordre et les ténèbres ou la naissance d'un mythe du XVIIe siècle chez Sainte-Beuve*, Paris: Librairie Armand Collin, 1972.
Troubat, Jules, *Souvenirs du dernier secrétaire de Sainte-Beuve*, Paris: Calmann-Lévy, 1890.

## Hippolyte Taine

### Primary sources

Taine, Hippolyte, *Essai sur les fables de La Fontaine*, Paris: Joubert, 1853.
*Histoire de la littérature anglaise*, 2nd edn, 5 vols., Paris: Hachette, 1866.
*Les Philosophes classiques du XIXe siècle en France* (originally published as *Les Philosophes français du XIXe siècle*, 1857); rpt Paris: Hachette, 1876.
*Philosophie de l'art*, 7th edn, 2 vols., Paris: Hachette, 1895.
*Essai sur Tite-Live* (1856); rpt Paris: Hachette, 1896.
*Nouveaux essais de critique et d'histoire* (1865); rpt Paris: Hachette, 1896.
*De l'intelligence*, 2 vols. (1870); rpt Paris: Hachette, 1903.
*H. Taine: sa vie et sa correspondance*, 4 vols., Paris: Hachette, 1905–8.
*Essais de critique et d'histoire*, 14th edn, Paris: Hachette, 1923.
*Les Origines de la France contemporaine*, 5 vols. (1875–93); rpt Paris: Robert Lafont, 1986.

### Secondary sources

Bergson, Henri, *Essai sur les données immédiates de la conscience*, Paris: Presses Universitaires de France, 1927.
Khan, Shalom, *Science and Aesthetic Judgement*, London: Routledge & Kegan Paul, 1953.
Nias, Hilary, *The Artificial Self: The Psychology of Hippolyte Taine*, Oxford: Legenda, 1999.

'Hippolyte Taine' in *Key Writers on Art: From Antiquity to the Nineteenth Century*, ed. Chris Murray, London: Routledge, 2003, pp. 212–18.

Nordmann, Jean-Thomas, *Taine et la critique scientifique*, Paris: Presses Universitaires de France, 1992.

Zola, Emile, *Mes haines*, Paris: Faure, 1866.

## Francesco De Sanctis

### Primary sources

De Sanctis, Francesco, *Opere di Francesco De Sanctis*, ed. Carlo Muscetta, Turin: Einaudi, 1958. This twenty-three-volume edition of De Sanctis's work remains the most complete compilation and is organized as follows:

Vol. I: *La giovinezza. Memorie postume seguite da testimonianze biographiche di amici e discepoli*, ed. Gennaro Savarese, 1972.

Vols. II and III: *Purismo illuminismo storicismo*, ed. Attilio Marinari, 1975.

Vol. IV: *La crisi del Romanticismo*, 1973.

Vol. V: *Lezioni e saggi su Dante*, ed. Sergio Romagnoli, 1967.

Vol. VI: *Saggio critico sul Petrarca*, ed. Nicollo Gallo, 1983.

Vol. VII: *Verso il realismo. Prolusioni e lezioni zurighesi sulla poesia cavalleresca, frammenti di estetica, saggi di metodo critico*, ed. Nino Borsellino, 1965.

Vol. VIII: *Storia della letteratura italiana*, ed. Nicollò Gallo, 1971.

Vol. IX: *Storia della letteratura italiana*, ed. Nicollò Gallo, 1971.

Vol. X: *Scelta di scritti critici*, ed. Gianfranco Contini, 1949.

Vol. XI: *Manzoni e la Scuola Cattolico-Liberale e il Romanticismo a Napoli*, eds. Carlo Muscetta, Giorgio Candeloro and Dario Puccini, 1983.

Vol. XII: *Mazzini e la scuola democratica*, eds. Carlo Muscetta and Giorgio Candeloro, 1961.

Vol. XIV: *L'arte, la scienza e la vita*, ed. Maria Teresa Lanza, 1972.

Vol. XV: *Il Mezzogiorno e lo stato unitario*, ed. Franco Ferri, 1972.

Vol. XVI: *I partiti e l'educazione della nuova Italia*, ed. Nino Cortese, 1970.

Vol. XVII: *Un viaggio elettorale*, ed. Nino Cortese, 1968.

Vols. XVIII–XXIII *Epistolario*, eds. Muzio Mazzocchi Alemanni, Giovanni Ferretti *et al.*, 1956.

### Secondary sources

Apweiler, Arnold, *Begründer der italienischen Komparatistik: Francesco De Sanctis und Arturo Graf*, Aachen: Shaker, 1997.

Barbuto, Gennaro Maria, *Ambivalenze del moderno: De Sanctis e le tradizioni politiche italiane*, Naples: Liguori, 2000.

Beales, Derek and Eugenio F. Biagini, *Il Risorgimento e l'unificazione dell'Italia*, Bologna: Il Mulino, 2002.

Bruno, Francesco, *De Sanctis e il realismo*, Naples: Edizioni scientifiche italiane, 2000.

Caratozzolo, Vittorio, *Francesco De Sanctis: parastoria della letteratura italiana. La fantasaggistica e l'impero del verosimile*, Naples: Guida, 2006.

Davis, John A., *Italy in the Nineteenth Century 1796–1900*, Oxford University Press, 2000.

Holub, Renate, *Antonio Gramsci: Beyond Marxism and Postmodernism*, London: Routledge, 1992.

Piccone, Paul, *Italian Marxism*, Berkeley: University of California Press, 1983.

## Matthew Arnold

### Primary sources

Matthew Arnold, *The Complete Prose Works of Matthew Arnold*, ed. R. H. Super, 11 vols., Ann Arbor: University of Michigan Press, 1960–77.

*The Poems of Matthew Arnold*, ed. Kenneth Allott, 2nd edn, rev. Marian Allott, London: Longman, 1979.

*The Letters of Matthew Arnold*, ed. Cecil Y. Lang, 6 vols., Charlottesville: University of Virginia Press, 1996–2001.

Arnold, Thomas, *Introductory Lectures on Modern History*, Oxford University Press, 1842.

### Secondary sources

Anderson, Warren D., *Matthew Arnold and the Classical Tradition*, Ann Arbor: University of Michigan Press, 1965.

apRoberts, Ruth, *Arnold and God*, Berkeley: University of California Press, 1983.

Collini, Stefan, *Arnold*, Oxford University Press, 1988.

DeLaura, David J., *Hebrew and Hellene in Victorian England: Newman, Arnold, and Pater*, Austin: University of Texas Press, 1969.

Honan, Park, *Matthew Arnold: A Life*, Cambridge, MA: Harvard University Press, 1983.

Livingston, James C., *Matthew Arnold and Christianity: His Religious Prose Writings*, Columbia: University of South Carolina Press, 1986.

Machann, Clinton, *The Essential Matthew Arnold: An Annotated Bibliography of Major Modern Studies*, New York: G. K. Hall, 1993.

*Matthew Arnold: A Literary Life*, New York: St. Martin's Press, 1998.

Mazzeno, Laurence W., *Matthew Arnold: The Critical Legacy*, Rochester, NY: Camden House, 1999.

Murray, Nicholas, *A Life of Matthew Arnold*, London: Hodder & Stoughton, 1996.

Pratt, Linda Ray, *Matthew Arnold Revisited*, New York: Twayne, 2000.

Schneider, Mary W., *Poetry in the Age of Democracy: The Literary Criticism of Matthew Arnold*, Lawrence: University Press of Kansas, 1989.

Sterner, Douglas W., *Priests of Culture: A Study of Matthew Arnold and Henry James*, New York: Peter Lang, 1999.

Stone, Donald, *Communications with the Future: Matthew Arnold in Dialogue*,
   Ann Arbor: University of Michigan Press, 1997.
Trilling, Lionel, *Matthew Arnold*, rev. edn, New York: Columbia University Press,
   1958.

# Henry James

## Primary sources

James, Henry, *Notes on Novelists*, New York: Charles Scribner's Sons, 1914.
   *The American Essays*, ed. Leon Edel, New York: Vintage, 1956.
   *Autobiography*, ed. F. W. Dupee, New York: Criterion, 1956.
   *The Painter's Eye*, ed. John L. Sweeney, London: Rupert Hart-Davis, 1956.
   *The Scenic Art*, ed. Allan Wade, New York: Hill and Wang, 1957.
   *Notebooks*, eds. F. O. Matthiessen and Kenneth Murdock, New York: Oxford
      University Press, 1961.
   *French Poets and Novelists* (1878); rpt New York: Grosset & Dunlap, 1964.
   *Partial Portraits* (1888); rpt Ann Arbor: University of Michigan Press, 1970.
   *Letters*, ed. Leon Edel, 4 vols., Cambridge, MA: Harvard University Press,
      1974–84.
   *Literary Criticism*, ed. Leon Edel and Mark Wilson, 2 vols., New York: Library
      of America, 1984.

## Secondary sources

Daugherty, Sarah B. *The Literary Criticism of Henry James*, Athens: Ohio Uni-
   versity Press, 1981.
Edel, Leon, *Henry James: The Master, 1901–1916*, Philadelphia: Lippincott,
   1972.
Freedman, Jonathan, *Professions of Taste: Henry James, British Aestheticism,
   and Commodity Culture*, Stanford University Press, 1990.
Gard, Roger (ed.), *Henry James: The Critical Heritage*, London: Routledge &
   Kegan Paul, 1968.
Jones, Vivien, *James the Critic*, New York: St. Martin's Press, 1985.
Kaplan, Fred, *Henry James: The Imagination of Genius*, New York: Morrow,
   1992.
Lodge, David, *Author, Author*, New York: Viking, 2004.
Lubbock, Percy, *The Craft of Fiction* (1921); rpt New York: Viking, 1957.
Pearson, John H., *The Prefaces of Henry James: Framing the Modern Reader*,
   University Park: Pennsylvania University Press, 1997.
Rawlings, Peter (ed.), *Critical Essays on Henry James*, Aldershot: Scolar Press,
   1993.
Roberts, Morris, *Henry James's Criticism*, Cambridge, MA: Harvard University
   Press, 1929.
Tanner, Tony, *Henry James and the Art of Nonfiction*, Athens: University of
   Georgia Press, 1995.

Veeder, William and Susan M. Griffiths (eds.), *The Art of Criticism: Henry James on the Theory and Practice of Fiction*, University of Chicago Press, 1986.

## Georg Brandes

### Primary sources

#### In Danish

Brandes, Georg, *Dualismen i vor nyeste philosophie*, Copenhagen: Gyldendal, 1866.
*Æsthetiske studier*, Copenhagen: Gyldendal, 1868.
*Den franske æstetik i vore dage*, Copenhagen: Gyldendal, 1870.
*Kritiker og portraiter*, Copenhagen: Gyldendal, 1870.
*Forklaring og forsvar: en antikritik*, Copenhagen: Gyldendal, 1872.
*Hovedstrømninger i det nittende arhundredes litteratur*, vols. I–VI, Copenhagen: Gyldendal, 1872–90.

#### In English translation

Brandes, Georg, *Lord Beaconsfield: A Study*, New York: Harper, 1878.
*William Shakespeare*, New York: Macmillan, 1898.
*Hellas: Travels in Greece*, New York: Macmillan, 1899.
*Main Currents in Nineteenth Century Literature*, vols. I–VI, New York: Macmillan, 1901–5.
*Reminiscences of My Childhood and Youth*, New York: Duffield, 1906.
*Friedrich Nietzsche*, New York: Macmillan, 1909.
*Ferdinand Lassalle*, New York: Macmillan, 1911.
*Wolfgang Goethe*, New York: N. L. Brown, 1924.
*Voltaire*, New York: A. & C. Boni, 1930.
*Michelangelo: His Life, His Times, His Era*, New York: Ungar, 1963.

### Secondary sources

Asmundsson, Doris R., *Georg Brandes: Aristocratic Radical*, New York University Press, 1981.
Bay, Carl Erik, *Kulturradikale kapitler fra Georg Brandes til Otto Gelsted*, Copenhagen: C.A. Reitzel, 2003.
Bourguignon, Annie, Konrad Harrer and Jørgen Stender Clausen (eds.), *Grands courants d'échanges intellectuels: Georg Brandes et la France, l'Allemagne, l'Angleterre*, Bern: Peter Lang, 2009.
Harsløf, Olaf (ed.), *Georg Brandes og Europa*, Copenhagen: Det kongelige Bibliotek/Museum Tusculanums Forlag, 2004.
Hertel, Hans (ed.), *Det stadig moderne gennembrud: Georg Brandes og hans tid set fra det 21. århundrede*, Copenhagen: Gyldendal, 2004.
Hertel, Hans and Sven Møller Kristensen (eds.), *The Activist Critic: A Symposium on the Political Ideas, Literary Methods and International Reception of Georg Brandes*, Copenhagen: Munksgaard, 1980.

Houe, Poul, 'Georg Brandes' begreb om det 18. århundrede' in *Opplysning i Norden*, ed. Heiko Uecker, Frankfurt: Peter Lang, 1998, pp. 265–72.

Nolin, Bertil, *Georg Brandes*, Boston: Twayne, 1976.

Rømhild, Lars Peter, *Georg Brandes og Goethe*, Copenhagen: Museum Tusculanums Forlag, 1996.

Sæther, Astrid, Jørgen Dines Johansen and Atle Kittang (eds.), *Ibsen og Brandes: Studier i et forhold*, Oslo: Gyldendal, 2006.

## Theories of genre

### Primary sources

Bagehot, Walter, *Literary Studies, Essays and Belles-Lettres*, vol. ii, New York: E. P. Dutton, 1864.

Brunetière, Ferdinand, *Etudes critiques sur l'histoire de la littérature française*, vol. vi, Paris: Librairie Hachette, 1925.

Croce, Benedetto, *Brevario di estetica*, trans. Patrick Romanell, Indianapolis: Hackett, 1965.

*Poetry and Literature: An Introduction to its Criticism and History* [*La Poesia*], trans. Giovanni Gullace, Carbondale: Southern Illinois University Press, 1981.

*The Aesthetic as the Science of Expression and of the Linguistic in General* [part of the *Estetica*], trans. Colin Lyas, Cambridge University Press, 1992.

Dallas, E. S., *Poetics*, London: Smith, Elder, 1852.

*The Gay Science*, 2 vols., London: Chapman & Hall, 1866.

Dilthey, Wilhelm, *Selected Works. Vol. v: Poetry and Experience*, ed. Rudolf A. Makkreel and Frithjof Rodi, Princeton University Press, 1985.

Gasset, Ortega y, *Meditations on Quixote*, trans. Evelyn Rugg and Diego Marín, New York: Norton, 1961.

Gervinus, Georg Gottfried, *Geschichte der Deutschen Dichtung*, vol. v, Leipzig: Wilhelm Engelmann, 1853.

Hebbel, Friedrich, 'My Word Concerning the Drama' in *Three Plays by Hebbel*, trans. Marion W. Sonnenfeld, Lewisburg, PA: Bucknell University Press, 1971.

Hunt, Leigh, *Imagination and Fancy*, New York: George P. Putnam, 1851.

Mill, John Stuart, *Essays on Poetry*, ed. F. Parvin Sharpless, Columbia: University of South Carolina Press, 1976.

Very, Jones, *Essays and Poems*, ed. R. W. Emerson, Boston: Charles C. Little and James Brown, 1839.

Vischer, Friedrich Theodor, *Aesthetik oder Wissenschaft des Schönen. Vol. v: Die Dichtkunst*, Stuttgart: Karl Mäckten, 1857.

### Secondary sources

Fishelov, David, *Metaphors of Genre*, University Park: Pennsylvania State University Press, 1993.

Fowler, Alastair, *Kinds of Literature: An Introduction to the Theory of Genres and Modes*, Cambridge, MA: Harvard University Press, 1982.

Guillén, Claudio, *Literature as System: Essays Toward the Theory of Literary History*, Princeton University Press, 1971.

Rajan, Tilottama, 'Theories of Genre' in *The Cambridge History of Literary Criticism. Vol. V: Romanticism*, ed. Marshall Brown, Cambridge University Press, 2000, pp. 226–49.

## Theories of the novel

### Primary sources

Bain, Alexander, *The Emotions and the Will*, 2nd edn, London: Longmans, Green, 1865.

Brunetière, Ferdinand, *L'Evolution des genres dans l'histoire de la littérature: leçons professées à l'Ecole normale supérieure*, Paris: Hachette, 1898.

Flaubert, Gustave, *The Letters of Gustave Flaubert, 1830–1857*, trans. Francis Steegmuller, Cambridge, MA: Harvard University Press, 1980.

*The Letters of Gustave Flaubert, 1857–1880*, trans. Francis Steegmuller, Cambridge, MA: Harvard University Press, 1982.

Hennequin, Emile, *La Critique scientifique*, Paris: Perrin, 1888.

Masson, David, *British Novelists and Their Styles: Being a Critical Sketch of the History of British Prose Fiction*, Cambridge and London: Macmillan, 1859.

Spielhagen, Friedrich, *Beiträge zur Theorie und Technik des Romans*, Göttingen: Vandenhoeck & Ruprecht, 1967.

Zola, Emile, *The Experimental Novel and Other Essays*, trans. Belle Sherman, New York: Cassell, 1893.

### Secondary sources

Cohen, Margaret, *The Sentimental Education of the Novel*, Princeton University Press, 1999.

Graham, Kenneth, *English Criticism of the Novel, 1865–1900*, Oxford: Clarendon Press, 1963.

Hale, Dorothy, *Social Formalism: The Novel in Theory from Henry James to the Present*, Stanford University Press, 1998.

McKeon, Michael (ed.), *Theory of the Novel: A Historical Approach*, Baltimore, MD: Johns Hopkins University Press, 2000.

Olmsted, John Charles, *A Victorian Art of Fiction: Essays on the Novel in British Periodicals*, 3 vols., New York: Garland, 1979.

Stang, Richard, *The Theory of the Novel in England, 1850–1870*, New York: Columbia University Press, 1959.

Wellek, René, *A History of Modern Criticism: 1750–1950*, New Haven, CT: Yale University Press, 1965.

# Theories of poetry

## Primary sources

Buchanan, Robert, *The Fleshly School of Poetry*, London: Strahan, 1872.

Cousin, Victor, *Lectures on the True, the Beautiful, and the Good*, trans. O. W. Wight, New York: D. Appleton, 1854.

Lanier, Sidney, *The Science of English Verse*, New York: C. Scribner's Sons, 1880.

Mill, John Stuart, *Collected Works of John Stuart Mill. Vol. I: Autobiography and Literary Essays*, eds. John M. Robson and Jack Stillinger, University of Toronto Press, 1981.

Patmore, Coventry, *Essay on English Metrical Law*, ed. Mary Augustine Roth, Washington: Catholic University of America Press, 1961.

Poe, Edgar Allan, 'The Rationale of Verse' in *Complete Tales and Poems of Edgar Allan Poe*, New York: Random House, 1975, pp. 908–42.

Saintsbury, George, *A History of English Prosody from the Twelfth Century to the Present Day*, 3 vols., London: Macmillan, 1923.

Swinburne, Algernon Charles, *William Blake: A Critical Essay*, New York: Benjamin Blom, 1868.

Twain, Mark, 'The Walt Whitman Controversy', *Virginia Quarterly Review*, 83 (2007), 128–38.

## Secondary sources

Armstrong, Isobel, *Victorian Poetry: Poetry, Poetics and Politics*, New York: Routledge, 1993.

Ashton, Jennifer, *From Modernism to Postmodernism: American Poetry and Theory in the Twentieth Century*, New York: Cambridge University Press, 2007.

Ferguson, Frances, *Solitude and the Sublime: Romanticism and the Aesthetics of Individuation*, New York: Routledge, 1992.

Grossman, Allen, *The Long Schoolroom: Essays in the Bitter Logic of the Poetic Principle*, Baltimore, MD: Johns Hopkins University Press, 1998.

Hammermeister, Kai, *The German Aesthetic Tradition*, Cambridge University Press, 2002.

Hönnighausen, Lothar, *The Symbolist Tradition in English Literature: A Study of Pre-Raphaelitism and Fin de Siècle*, trans. Gisela Hönnighausen, New York: Cambridge University Press, 1988.

Kivy, Peter, *Philosophies of Arts: An Essay in Differences*, Cambridge University Press, 1997.

Knapp, Steven, *Literary Interest: The Limits of Anti-Formalism*, Cambridge, MA: Harvard University Press, 1993.

Lentricchia, Frank, 'Four Types of Nineteenth-Century Poetic', *Journal of Aesthetics and Art Criticism*, 26 (1968), 351–66.

Loesberg, Jonathan, *Aestheticism and Deconstruction: Pater, Derrida, and de Man*, Princeton University Press, 1991.

Porter, Laurence M., *The Crisis of French Symbolism*, Ithaca, NY: Cornell University Press, 1990.

## Theories of drama

### Primary sources

Archer, William, *Play-Making: A Manual of Craftsmanship*, Boston: Small, Maynard, 1912.

Brunetière, Ferdinand, *The Law of the Drama*, trans. Philip M. Hayden, New York: Columbia University, 1914.

Clark, Barret H., *European Theories of the Drama*, New York and London: Appleton, 1925.

Freytag, Gustav, *Die Technik des Dramas*, Leipzig: S. Hirzel, 1876.

Marx, Karl and Friedrich Engels, *Über Kunst und Literatur*, Berlin: Henschel, 1950.

Schumacher, Claude (ed.), *Naturalism and Symbolism in European Theatre: 1850–1918*, Cambridge University Press, 1996.

Shaw, George Bernard, *The Drama Observed*, ed. Bernard F. Dukore, 4 vols., University Park: Pennsylvania State University Press, 1993.

Sidnell, Michael J. (ed.), *Sources of Dramatic Theory. vol II: Voltaire to Hugo*, Cambridge University Press, 1994.

Symons, Arthur, *Plays, Acting and Music: A Book of Theory*, London: Duckworth, 1903.

Wagner, Richard, *Opera and Drama*, trans. William Ashton Ellis (1893); rpt Lincoln and London: University of Nebraska Press, 1995.

### Secondary sources

Bentley, Eric, *The Theory of the Modern Stage*, Harmondsworth: Penguin, 1976.

Hamilton, Clayton, *The Theory of the Theatre*, New York: H. Holt, 1910.

Matthews, Brander, *A Study of the Drama*, Boston: Longmans, Green, 1910.

Meisel, Martin, *Shaw and the Nineteenth-Century Theater*, Princeton University Press, 1963.

Rowell, George (ed.), *The Victorian Theatre: A Survey*, London: Oxford University Press, 1956.

Rydel, Christine A. (ed.), *Russian Literature in the Age of Pushkin and Gogol: Poetry and Drama*, Detroit: Gale, 1999.

## Literary criticism and models of science

### Primary sources

Brunetière, Ferdinand, 'La doctrine évolutive et l'histoire de la littérature' in *Etudes critiques sur l'histoire de la littérature française*, Paris: Hachette, 1905.

Ellis, Havelock, *The New Spirit*, London: Bell, 1890.

   'The Colour-Sense in Literature', *Contemporary Review*, **69** (1896), 714–29.

   *Views and Reviews*, London: Harmsworth, 1932.

Gummere, Francis B., *The Beginnings of Poetry* (1901); rpt Freeport, NY: Books for Libraries Press, 1970.

Hennequin, Emile, *La Critique scientifique*, 2nd edn, Paris: Librairie académique Didier, 1890.

Lanson, Gustave, 'L'esprit scientifique et la méthode de l'histoire littéraire' in *Méthodes de l'histoire littéraire*, Paris: Les Belles Lettres, 1925, pp. 21–37.

'L'histoire littéraire et la sociologie' (1904) in *Essais de méthode, de critique et d'histoire littéraire*, Paris: Hachette, 1965, pp. 61–80.

Lewes, G. H., *Principles of Success in Literature*, Boston: Allyn & Bacon, 1891.

Mackenzie, A. S., *The Evolution of Literature*, New York: Crowell, 1911.

Manly, John Matthews, 'Literary Forms and the New Theory of the Origin of Species', *Modern Philology*, 4 (1907), 577–95.

Moulton, Richard G., *Shakespeare as a Dramatic Critic: A Popular Illustration of the Principles of Scientific Criticism*, Oxford: Clarendon Press, 1885.

Nordau, Max, *Degeneration*, Lincoln: University of Nebraska Press, 1993.

Robertson, John MacKinnon, 'Theory and Practice of Criticism' in *New Essays towards a Critical Method*, London: Fisher Unwin, 1897, pp. 1–53.

Scherer, Wilhelm, *Vorträge und Aufsätze zur Geschichte des geistigen Lebens in Deutschland und Oesterreich*, Berlin: Weidmann, 1874.

*Geschichte der deutschen Sprache*, 2nd edn, Berlin: Weidmann, 1878.

Schmidt, Erich, *Charakteristiken*, Berlin: Weidmann, 1886.

Symonds, John Addington, *Essays, Speculative and Suggestive*, 2 vols., London: Chapman & Hall, 1890.

## Secondary sources

Babbitt, Irving, *The Masters of Modern French Criticism*, London: Constable, 1913.

Caramaschi, Enzo, *Critiques scientistes et critiques impressionistes: Taine, Brunetière, Gourmont*, Pisa: Goliardica, 1963.

Dekkers, Odin, *J. M. Robertson: Rationalist and Literary Critic*, Aldershot: Ashgate, 1998.

Hocking, Elton, *Ferdinand Brunetière: The Evolution of a Critic*, Madison: University of Wisconsin Studies in Language and Literature, 1936.

Kindt, Tom and Hans-Harald Müller, 'Dilthey gegen Scherer: Geistesgeschichte contra Positivismus. Zur Revision eines wissenschaftshistorischen Stereotyps', *Deutsche Vierteljahrsschrift für Literaturwissenschaft und Geistesgeschichte*, 74 (2000), 685–709.

Kolk, Rainer, 'Wahrheit – Methode – Charakter: Zur wissenschaftlichen Ethik der Germanistik im 19. Jahrhundert', *Internationales Archiv für Sozialgeschichte der deutschen Literatur*, 14 (1998), 50–73.

LeGouis, Catherine, *Positivism and Imagination: Scientism and its Limits in Emile Hennequin, Wilhelm Scherer, and Dmitrii Piasrev*, Lewisburg, PA: Bucknell University Press, 1997.

Salm, Peter, *Three Modes of Criticism: The Literary Theories of Scherer, Walzel, and Staiger*, Cleveland, OH: Case Western Reserve University Press, 1968.

Weimar, Klaus, *Geschichte der deutschen Literaturwissenschaft*, Paderborn: Fink, 2003.
Wellek, René, *Concepts of Criticism*, Newhaven, CT: Yale University Press, 1963.


## Literature and the arts

### Primary sources

Delacroix, Eugène, *Journal 1822–1863*, ed. Régis Labourdette, Paris: Plon, 1996.
  *Journal*, ed. Michèle Hannoosh, 2 vols., Paris: José Corti, 2009.
Laforgue, Jules, *Œuvres complètes*, ed. Michèle Hannoosh, 3 vols., Lausanne: L'Age d'Homme, 1986–2000.
Ruskin, John, *The Complete Works of John Ruskin*, eds. E. T. Cook and Alexander Wedderburn, 39 vols., London: George Allen, 1903–12.
  *The Art Criticism of John Ruskin*, ed. Robert L. Herbert (1964); rpt New York: Da Capo Press, 1987.
Wagner, Richard, *Prose Works of Richard Wagner*, trans. William Ashton Ellis, 8 vols., London: K. Paul, Trench, Trübner, 1892–9.
Whistler, James McNeill, *The Gentle Art of Making Enemies*, 2nd edn, London: Heinemann, 1892.
Zola, Emile, *Salons*, ed. F. W. J. Hemmings and R. J. Niess, Geneva: Droz, 1959.


### Secondary sources

Berg, William J., *The Visual Novel: Emile Zola and the Art of His Time*, University Park: Pennsylvania State University Press, 1992.
Collier, Peter and Robert Lethbridge (eds.), *Artistic Relations: Literature and the Visual Arts in Nineteenth-Century France*, New Haven, CT, and London: Yale University Press, 1992.
Flint, Kate, *The Victorians and the Visual Imagination*, Cambridge University Press, 2000.
Florence, Penny, *Mallarmé, Manet and Redon: Visual and Aural Signs and the Generation of Meaning*, Cambridge University Press, 1986.
Grey, Thomas S., *Wagner's Musical Prose: Texts and Contexts*, Cambridge University Press, 1995.
Kern, Stephen, *The Culture of Time and Space 1880–1918*, Cambridge, MA: Harvard University Press, 1983.
Meisel, Martin, *Realizations: Narrative, Pictorial, and Theatrical Arts in Nineteenth-Century England*, Princeton University Press, 1983.
Wettlaufer, Alexandra K., *In the Mind's Eye: The Visual Impulse in Diderot, Baudelaire and Ruskin*, Amsterdam and New York: Rodopi, 2003.
Wright, Beth S., *The Cambridge Companion to Delacroix*, New York and Cambridge: Cambridge University Press, 2001.

## Biblical scholarship and literary criticism

### Primary sources

Arnold, Matthew, *St. Paul and Protestantism*, London: Smith, Elder, 1870.
 *Literature and Dogma: An Essay towards a Better Apprehension of the Bible*,
 London: Smith, Elder, 1873.
 *God and the Bible*, London: Smith, Elder, 1887.
Butler, Samuel, *The Notebooks of Samuel Butler. Vol. I (1874–1883)*, ed. Hans-
 Peter Breuer (1967); rpt New York: Doubleday, 1984.
Carlyle, Thomas, *Heroes, Hero-Worship and the Heroic in History*, London: John
 Wiley, 1840.
Herder, Johann Gottfried, *The Spirit of Hebrew Poetry* (1783), trans. J. Marsh,
 2 vols., Burlington, VT: Edward Smith, 1833.
Locke, John, *A Paraphrase and Notes on the Epistles of St. Paul to the Galatians,
 1 and 2 Corinthians, Romans, Ephesians* (1707), ed. Arthur W. Wainwright,
 2 vols., Oxford University Press, 1987.
Newman, John Henry (Cardinal), *An Essay in Aid of a Grammar of Assent*
 (1870), Notre Dame and London: University of Notre Dame Press, 1979.
Ruskin, John, *Praeterita*, 2 vols., New York: John Wiley, 1886–7.
Schleiermacher, Friedrich, 'Introduction to General Hermeneutics' in *The
 Hermeneutics Reader*, ed. Kurt Mueller-Vollmer, New York: Continuum,
 2006.

### Secondary sources

Boyle, Nicholas, *Sacred and Secular Scriptures: A Catholic Approach to Litera-
 ture*, University of Notre Dame Press, 2005.
DeLaura, David J., *Hebrew and Hellene in Victorian England: Newman, Arnold,
 and Pater*, Austin: University of Texas Press, 1969.
Frei, Hans, *The Eclipse of Biblical Narrative: A Study in Eighteenth and Nine-
 teenth Century Hermeneutics*, New Haven, CT, and London: Yale University
 Press, 1974.
Jeffrey, David Lyle, *People of the Book: Christian Identity and Literary Culture*,
 Grand Rapids, MI, and Cambridge: Eerdmans, 1996.
Knoepflmacher, U. C., *Religious Humanism and the Victorian Novel: George
 Eliot, Walter Pater, and Samuel Butler*, Princeton University Press, 1965.
Krueger, Christine L., *The Reader's Repentance: Women Preachers, Women Writ-
 ers, and Nineteenth-Century Social Discourse*, University of Chicago Press,
 1992.
Landow, George, *Aesthetic and Critical Theories of John Ruskin*, Princeton Uni-
 versity Press, 1971.
McKelvy, William R., 'Primitive Ballads, Modern Criticism, Ancient Skepticism:
 Macaulay's *Lays of Ancient Rome*', *Victorian Literature and Culture*, **28**
 (2000), 287–309.
Prickett, Stephen, *Words and the Word: Language, Poetics and Biblical Interpretation*, Cambridge University Press, 1986.

(ed.), *Reading the Text: Biblical Criticism and Literary Theory*, Oxford: Blackwell, 1991.

Wheeler, Michael, *Ruskin's God*, Cambridge University Press, 1999.

Zemka, Sue, *Victorian Testaments: The Bible, Christology, and Literary Authority in Early-Nineteenth-Century British Culture*, Stanford University Press, 1997.

# Index

Herbert, George 168
Herder, Johann Gottfried von 52, 100,
112, 127, 218, 469, 482, 572
influence in English-speaking world
164–6
influence in Russia 207, 208–9
*The Spirit of Hebrew Poetry* 165,
608–9
Hérédia, José Maria de 146, 148, 151
Herschel, J. F.W. 28
Hertel, Hans 476
Herwegh, Georg 133
Herzen, Aleksandr 206, 209, 211
Hettner, Hermann 569
*Das moderne Drama* 546–7
hexameters (verse form) 97–8
hierarchy of genres 588–9
Hill, George Birkbeck 69
historicism 495–6, 505
problems of 499–500
psychology of 493–4
resurgence 502
histories, literary 169–71
Hoagwood, Terrence Allan 612
Hobbes, Thomas 604
*Leviathan* 492
Hobsbawm, E. J. 100
Hodson, Frodsham 104
Hoffman, Charles Fenno 188
Hoffmann, E. T. A. 191, 591
Hofmannsthal, Hugo von 15, 352,
543, 552–3, 556–7, 561
*Das Märchen der 672 Nacht* 352
*Der Tor und der Tod* 352
Hogarth, William 593–4
Holberg, Ludvig 472
Hölderlin, Friedrich 251
Holitscher, Arthur, *Der vergiftete
Brunnen* 353–4
Holloway, John 423
Holmes, Oliver Wendell, Jr 204
Holy Roman Empire 313, 319
dissolution 115, 116
Holz, Arno 551, 553
*Die Familie Selicke* 551
*Papa Hamlet* 551

*Home and Foreign* 24
Homer 140, 146, 222, 436, 505, 608
*Iliad* 263–4, 490
*Odyssey* 490
Hönninghausen, Lothar 527, 532
Hood, Thomas 26
Hook, Sidney 271
Hopkins, Gerard Manley 180, 527,
619–20
Hopkins, Pauline Elizabeth 337
Horace (Q. Horatius Flaccus) 588
*Household Words* 154
Howard, June 335
Howells, William Dean 10, 43–4, 331,
332, 333–4, 338–9, 440, 450,
451, 453, 456, 457, 459
*Criticism and Fiction* 333, 338, 520
*The Hazard of New Fortunes* 334
'Novel-Writing and Novel-Reading'
490
*The Rise of Silas Lapham* 334
Hubner, Karl, 'The Silesian Weavers'
281
Huelsenbeck, Richard 364, 374
'Dadaistic Manifesto' 369
Hughes, Thomas 57
Hugo, Victor 14, 142–3, 148, 298,
379, 390, 446, 492, 579
*Les Burgraves* 144, 145
*Hernani* 139–40, 144
*Odes et ballades* 139
Preface to *Cromwell* 142, 304–5,
484, 540
Huidobro, Vicente 359, 363
Humboldt, Wilhelm von 52–3, 219,
605, 606, 607, 609
influence 238
Hume, David 4, 107, 113, 273
'Of National Characters' 103–6
Hunt, Leigh 26, 158
'What is Poetry?' 488–9
Hunt, Thornton 29
Hunt, William Holman, *The
Awakening Conscience* 593
Huret, Jules 342
Hutcheson, Francis 50, 232

poetic realism 135–6, 318–19, 543
poetic theory 524–38
  correspondence theory 526–8, 536
  and the divine 525–6
  focus on reading experience 534–6
  *see also* poetry
poetry 15, 258–9, 260
  appropriate themes 532–3
  autonomy 262–3
  censorship debate 533
  definition of 167–8
  distinguished from prose 261–2
  essential characteristics 261–3
  etymology 525
  figurative language 262
  fusion with prose 318–19
  genres 261, 263–7
  in Hegelian theory 261–7
  Hegelian theory of 262
  *see also* drama; epic poetry; poetic theory
  highest realization of romantic art 260–1
  historical utility 529–30
  mass readership 532, 533
  new genres 533–4
  practical role in life 530–1
  primary/secondary poets 167
  psychological theory of 166–8
  *see also* poetic theory
political events, impact on literary criticism 2
Polti, Georges, *Les trente-six situations dramatiques* 546
Ponsard, François 540
  *L'Honneur et l'argent* 540
  *Lucrèce* 144–5, 540
Pope, Alexander 436
Porter, Charles A. 149, 538
Porter, Laurence 536–7
positivism 394, 565
  literary 579–80
Posnett, Hutcheson Macauley
  *Comparative Literature* 576–7
postmodernism 270–1, 476

poststructuralism 270–1
Potebnya, Aleksandr 6, 219
  *Thought and Language* 219
Potter, Stephen 57
Pound, Ezra 49, 363
Praz, Mario 343, 354
Pre-Raphaelite 590, 593–4
Prévost-Paradol, Lucien-Anatole 393
Prickett, Stephen 605
Prince, John Critchley 83
Protestantism 172
Proust, Marcel 148, 241, 309, 385
  *Contre Sainte-Beuve* 387–8
Prussia, education in 52–3
Prussian-Austrian alliance 116–17
Prutz, Robert 9, 130, 317–18, 547
  *Deutches Museum* 134
Pryse, Marjorie 337
Przybyszewski, Stanislaw 599
psychology 585–6
  historicism 493–4
Public Libraries Movement 55–6
Pugin, Augustus Welby
  *Contrasts* (1836) 156
Puoto, Masilio 407
Puritanism, criticism of 429, 431–2, 450
purposiveness 262–3
  concept of 234
Pusey, Edward Bouverie 163, 420
Pushkin, Aleksandr 207, 212, 222
  criticisms 213, 215, 362
  praised by Gogol 207
  *The Captain's Daughter* 217
  *Evgeny Onegin* 211, 213
  *The Tales of Belkin* 218
*Putnam's Monthly Magazine* 44

Qualls, Barry 613
quarterlies *see* periodicals
*The Quarterly* 2, 23, 28–9, 35
  readership 25
  style of criticism 24
Quillard, Pierre 151
Quiller-Couch, Sir Arthur 3, 49, 69–70, 71

Made in the USA
Middletown, DE
22 August 2023

37145925R00395